Aug 2020.

CELEBR
TH
SAINTS

New Revised Edition

20/08. Bernard. Love for and from God.
04/09. A rdg from a sermon by St Aug.
01/12. Charles de Foucauld.
07/12 Ambrose of Milan.
01/01. William St Thierry - God's love forms our purpose.
02/01. Basil the Gt. - Steadiness, gaze on God.
02/01 Gregory of Nazianzus - fellowship.
02/01. Serapheum of Sarov - joy.
07/12 Ambrose of Milan.

ROBERT ATWELL is Bishop of Exeter and Chair of the Liturgical Commission of the Church of England.

CELEBRATING THE SAINTS

New Revised Edition

Daily spiritual readings
to accompany the Calendars
of
The Church of England
The Church of Ireland
The Scottish Episcopal Church
and
The Church in Wales

compiled and introduced by

Robert Atwell

CANTERBURY
PRESS
Norwich

revised edition 1999
enlarged edition 2004
new revised edition 2016

First published in 1998 by the Canterbury Press Norwich
Editorial office
3rd Floor, Invicta House
108–114 Golden Lane
London EC1Y 0TG, UK

Canterbury Press is an imprint of Hymns Ancient & Modern Ltd
(a registered charity)
13A Hellesdon Park Road, Norwich,
Norfolk NR6 5DR, UK

www.canterburypress.co.uk

British Library Cataloguing in Publication data

A catalogue record for this book is available
from the British Library

978 1 84825 882 2

Typeset by Regent Typesetting
Printed and bound in Great Britain by
Ashford Colour Press Ltd

Contents

Introduction

What would you go to the stake for? An eminent theologian once told me that there were only two doctrines for which he would be prepared to die: original sin and the communion of saints. It was an eccentric choice, but over the years I have had cause to ponder his wisdom.

To some both doctrines are outmoded, theological whales marooned on Dover beach in the roar of the retreating tide of faith. Certainly neither doctrine dovetails with ideas of progress or with the values of contemporary society. Original sin speaks of an inherent disposition to put self at the centre, often with disastrous and destructive results. It exposes the shadow-side of humanity: the trenches of the First World War, Auschwitz, Hiroshima, the Soviet death camps, the rape of the Amazonian rain-forests – things we would rather forget. It pulls humanity back from the indulgence of illusion, forcing us to a more realistic appraisal of ourselves. It points to our clay feet.

We could caricature such talk as depressing and defeatist. In reality it is full of hope because it refuses to pander to self-deception. It demands we take responsibility for our actions, but it sets limits on culpability: it's not all our fault. None of us begins life with a clean slate. We are the inheritors not only of genes but of family baggage. Our early years instil in us patterns of behaviour. As we grow up we are shaped by our communities and the history of our nations. Our capacity to act freely is impaired. This is something Augustine grasped with total clarity.

It would indeed be depressing if this were all, but the picture the Scriptures paint is not of a graceless world. The gospel insists that we do not have to be the victims of our genes, our mistakes, or the failings of earlier generations. The way of the cross invites movement and transformation, but it is a journey into truth, not in spite of it. It is at this point that the doctrine of the communion of saints emerges from the ashes of human failure as a testament of glory. It is the theological counterpoise to the doctrine of original sin because it points to the triumph of grace in a fallen world.

In the Apostles' Creed we confess our belief in the communion of saints, our participation in the company of those who will that their lives should be shaped and transformed by the life, death and resurrection of Jesus Christ. We are, in Gregory Dix's immortal phrase:[1] the *plebs sancta Dei* – the holy common people of God. Over the centuries the Church has come to recognize particular individuals within this company in whom God's purposes of love, mercy, peace and justice have been specially revealed. In its Calendar the Church designates some of them to be named companions on our journey, holding them up as models of faithful discipleship.

The custom of remembering these 'friends of God' has been one of the delights of Christian people down the centuries. William Law, the Anglican Divine and non-Juror, writing in 1729 in his treatise *A Serious Call to a Devout and Holy Life*, identified praise and thanksgiving to God as the common thread which runs through their lives:

> Would you know him who is the greatest saint in the world? It is not he who prays most or fasts most; it is not he who gives most alms; but it is he who is always thankful to God, who receives everything as an instance of God's goodness and has a heart always ready to praise God for it. If anyone would tell you the shortest, surest way to all happiness and perfection, he must tell you to make a rule to thank and praise God for everything that happens to you. Whatever seeming calamity happens to you, if you thank and praise God for it, it turns into a blessing. Could you therefore work miracles, you could not do more for yourself than by this thankful spirit; it turns all that it touches into happiness.

In the lives of the saints it is as if the intense white light of the gospel has passed through a prism and been refracted into its constituent colours, making visible the spectrum of God's call to holiness. In the outcome of their lives we glimpse little by little the face of the Christ who is coming to gather up all things in himself. The saints celebrate the vocation of the whole people of God to share in his very being. But this summons to life is challenging as well as comforting because the saints also confront us with the realities of judgement and mortality. They challenge us to resurrection *now*, to abundant living *now*, but define the way as via the cross, a dying and rising with Christ. The martyrs in particular question our priorities, particularly if we see staying alive as an end in itself. The martyrs redefine life and death by placing both within the eternal purposes of God. In the words of Athanasius of Alexandria, writing in the fourth century:

> Death is a pilgrimage, a lifetime's pilgrimage which none of us must shirk. It is a pilgrimage from decay to imperishable life, from mortality to immortality, from anxiety to tranquillity of mind. Do not be afraid of the word death: rather rejoice in the blessings which follow a happy death. After all, what is death but the burial of sin and the harvest of goodness? [2]

Historical Background

This perspective first became evident during the persecutions in the way that Christians commemorated the martyrs on the anniversary not of their births, but of their deaths – their *dies natalis* or *natalicia* – literally their birthday to eternal life. From the outset, Christians remembered before God their contemporaries who had died for the faith, recorded and circulated the stories of their witness and the circumstances of their deaths.[3] With such commemorations the liturgical year of the Church began to take shape. Our forebears had a strong sense of the mutual and reciprocal nature of prayer between the living and the departed. The account of the martyrdom of Polycarp in around 155 is a case in point. It is probably the oldest authentic narrative of a Christian martyrdom outside the New Testament. The Christians of Smyrna wrote to other churches sharing the news of his courageous death, and how:

> When it was all over we gathered up his bones, more precious to us than jewels, finer than pure gold, and we laid them to rest in a place we had already set aside. There, the Lord permitting, we shall gather and celebrate with great gladness and joy the day of his martyrdom as a birthday. It will serve as a commemoration of all who have gone before us, and training and preparing those of us for whom a crown may be in store.[4]

Accounts such as these formed the mind and memory of the Church. As Tertullian observed in his *Apologeticum* at the beginning of the third century: 'the blood of the martyrs is the seed-bed of the Church' – *sanguis Christianorum semen.* It became customary for their *passions*, as they were called, to be read aloud during the celebration of the Eucharist on the anniversary of their deaths either in church or at the place of their burial. To eat and drink the Eucharist was to share in the same heavenly banquet which the martyrs now enjoyed in glory. Their annual commemoration must have been a moving event in the life of a Christian community. It distilled within the consciousness of the Church a powerful sense of solidarity, of a belonging in Christ which transcended death.

With the toleration of Christianity at the beginning of the fourth century, the concept of martyrdom shifts and broadens. Preaching to the people of Milan, Ambrose says:

> Just as there are many kinds of persecution, so there are many forms of martyrdom. You are a witness to Christ every day of your life. ... A witness is one who testifies to the precepts of the Lord Jesus and supports his deposition by deeds. Many are martyrs of Christ and confess the Lord Jesus each day in secret. This kind of martyrdom and faithful witnessing to Christ was known to the apostle Paul, who said: 'Our boast is this, the testimony of our conscience.'[5]

It was not long before it became customary for certain outstanding Christians who had not been martyred to be also commemorated liturgically. Martin of Tours (d.397) seems to have been the first person so commemorated. Here was a man whose life and example pointed people to Christ in such a profound way that he was considered worthy of veneration. In time, bishops, confessors and teachers of the faith, monks, nuns and missionaries all came to be honoured alongside the martyrs. As Augustine comments in one of his sermons:

> The holy martyrs imitated Christ even to the point of shedding their blood in emulation of his passion. But it was not only the martyrs who imitated him. When they passed into eternity, the bridge was not broken down, nor did the fountain dry up after they drank from it. Indeed, the garden of the Lord contains not only the roses of martyrdom but also the lilies of virginity, the ivy of marriage, and the violets of widowhood. So no one, my dear friends, need despair of his or her vocation.[6]

Ambrose, Augustine and their fellow bishops were always careful to distinguish between the worship offered to God and the veneration due to his saints. Augustine states unequivocally that:

> We, the Christian community, assemble to celebrate the memory of the martyrs with ritual solemnity because we want to be inspired to follow their example, share in their merits, and be helped by their prayers. Yet we erect no altars to any of the martyrs, even in the martyrs' burial chapels themselves. ... What is offered is offered always to God who crowned the martyrs. ... We venerate them with the same veneration of love and fellowship that we give to the saints of God still with us. But the veneration strictly called 'worship' or *latria,* that is, the special homage belonging only to the divinity, is something we give and teach others to give to God alone.[7]

If such a distinction was clear to Augustine, it became less clear to others in the centuries that followed. There was a blurring of theological subtleties. Increasingly saints were being venerated chiefly as workers of miracles. People judged holiness by a person's reputation for working miracles because the ability to perform miracles was a sure sign that the person was a 'friend of God'. Furthermore their earthly remains were believed to effect their presence,[8] their very physicality providing powerful access to the courts of heaven. The medieval Church (at least in the West) began to divide up the faithful departed into those *for* whom it was appropriate to pray, and those *to* whom it was appropriate to turn for aid,[9] a practice known as the 'invocation of saints'. It was inevitable that the popular veneration of images, pilgrimages, and the extravagant cult of individual saints, together with certain 'abuses' associated with the doctrine of purgatory, should end up provoking a cry for reform.

Like their continental counterparts (and indeed the Catholic reformers at the Council of Trent) the English Reformers (and here we may include their Irish, Scottish and Welsh counterparts) were concerned to eliminate abuses, and above all to restore Christ to his pre-eminent position as sole mediator between God and man. 'There is one mediator between God and humankind, Christ Jesus, himself human' (1 Timothy 2.5). The saints were to be commemorated not for their intercession or miracles, but solely for the holiness of their lives and for the example they offer the living. This emphasis is evident in the first English Prayer Book of 1549:

> And here we do give unto thee most high praise, and hearty thanks, for the wonderful grace and virtue, declared in all thy saints, from the beginning of the world: and chiefly in the glorious and most Blessed Virgin Mary, mother of thy Son Jesus Christ our Lord and God, and in the holy Patriarchs, Prophets, Apostles and Martyrs, whose examples, O Lord, and steadfastness in thy faith, and keeping thy holy commandments, grant us to follow. We commend unto thy mercy, O Lord, all other of thy servants which are departed hence from us, with the sign of faith, and now do rest in the sleep of peace: Grant unto them, we beseech thee, thy mercy, and everlasting peace, and that, at the day of the general resurrection, we and all they which be of the mystical body of thy Son, may altogether be set on his right hand.

This was the theological position of the Church of England as it emerged from the controversies of the sixteenth century. Uniquely among the reformed churches, the Church of England (initially under the influence of Thomas Cranmer, and later under Archbishop Matthew Parker during the reign of Elizabeth I) retained a Calendar of Saints, and required that some of them be commemorated by a special collect and readings.[10] This liturgical framework shaped definitively the worship of Anglicanism. Among some of the reformers, notably Hugh Latimer, Bishop of Worcester, there also emerged a return to the idea of prayer uniting the mystical body of Christ. Writing in 1533 he says:

> As touching the saints in heaven, they be not our mediators by way of redemption; for so Christ alone is our mediator and their both: so that the blood of martyrs hath nothing to do by way of redemption; the blood of Christ is enough for a thousand worlds. But by way of intercession, so saints in heaven may be mediators, and pray for us: as I think they do when we call not upon them; for they be charitable, and need no spurs … They be members of the mystical body of Christ as we be, and in more surety than we be. They

> love us charitably. Charity is not idle; if it be, it worketh and sheweth itself: and therefore I say, they wish us well, and pray for us.[11]

This was not the universal opinion of the English Reformers, but it was certainly the view of the Caroline Divines that succeeded them. Thomas Traherne (1636–74) writes movingly of the communion of saints, calling the saints 'storehouses of God's holy word' and 'living conduit-pipes of the Holy Ghost'.[12] This more generous vision appealed to many nineteenth-century Anglicans, and not just the Tractarians. Bishop Westcott writing of the communion of saints says:

> If the outward were the measure of the Church of Christ, we might well despair. But side by side with us, when we fondly think like Elijah or Elijah's servant that we stand alone, are countless multitudes whom we know not, angels whom we have no power to discern, children of God whom we have not learnt to recognize. We have come to the kingdom of God, peopled with armies of angels and men working for us and with us because they are working for God. And though we cannot grasp the fullness of the truth, and free ourselves from the fetters of sense, yet we can, in the light of the Incarnation, feel the fact of this unseen fellowship; we can feel that heaven has been re-opened to us by Christ.[13]

Rediscovering the Saints

Today the controversies which exercised the minds of our sixteenth-century forebears seem remote. Most people are agnostic about what specialized knowledge (if any) individual saints have of the living. And yet, perhaps because of the fragmentation of society, people are increasingly aware of the need to give concrete expression to their sense of solidarity in Christ. Christians across a wide spectrum of theological opinion once again talk of the saints not simply in terms of fellowship, but of *communion.* There is renewed emphasis on the Christian life as a participation in the life of the Trinity: a communion with God and one another in Christ, empowered by the Holy Spirit. And the currency of this participation is prayer in which the whole Church shares, living and departed.

In parallel with this theological *rapprochement*, the cult of celebrity in society has had the unexpected side-effect of rekindling interest in the saints as *persons*. As a cultural phenomenon, it received additional stimulus through the policy of Pope John Paul II who canonized more saints than any of his predecessors put together. His policy has been interpreted as an instrument of evangelization. It was a concerted attempt to place before a new generation a raft of contemporary role-models of Christian discipleship in order to excite holiness.

Unlike the Roman Catholic Church, the Anglican Communion has no formal process of canonization. Nevertheless, the most recent revisions of the Calendars of the Church of England, the Church of Ireland, the Scottish Episcopal Church, and of the Church in Wales reflect aspirations similar to those of Pope John Paul II. The compass of their national Calendars is more inclusive and more contemporary in feel than anything that has gone before. Until comparatively recently, one could have been forgiven for thinking that there were no more saints after 1500!

Celebrating the Saints Today

In the final chorus of T. S. Eliot's *Murder in the Cathedral,* written to commemorate the martyrdom of Thomas of Canterbury, the women cry out to God:

> We thank thee for thy mercies of blood,
>   for thy redemption by blood.
> For the blood of thy martyrs and saints
> Shall enrich the earth, shall create the holy places.
> For wherever a saint has dwelt, wherever a martyr has given
>   his blood for the blood of Christ,
> There is holy ground, and the sanctity shall not depart from it
> Though armies trample over it, though sightseers come with
>   guide-books looking over it;
> From where the western seas gnaw at the coast of Iona,
> To the death in the desert, the prayer in forgotten places by the
>   broken imperial column,
> From such ground springs that which forever renews the earth
> Though it is forever denied.

Holy places, the tombs of the saints and the places of pilgrimage still shape our landscape and our memory of the story of Christianity in Britain and Ireland. They have a certain sacramental quality. The saints point us to God, reminding us of lives transfigured and given meaning by the impress of the spirit of God. After the apostles and martyrs it is good to honour the great heroes of the faith who laid the foundations of Christianity in these isles: Aidan, Alban, Bede, David, Patrick, Columba, and Augustine of Canterbury. In addition to these pioneers of the faith, the new Anglican Calendars also include a significant representation of early Celtic saints which is thoroughly welcome. Taken together, they constitute an insight into the rich spiritual heritage of this corner of Western Europe.

The revised Calendars are also more *catholic* in the sense that they include women and men from a variety of countries and cultures; people like Oscar Romero, Elizabeth of Russia, Janani Luwum, Manche Masemola, and Dietrich Bonhoeffer, all of whom gave their lives for Christ. At a time when nationalistic and sectarian movements are the ascendance across the world, greater international representation can foster a vision of the Church that transcends national boundaries. In our schools, particularly those serving multi-cultural communities, the religious and social education of children of different faiths can be greatly helped through learning about the lives of one another's heroes and saints. We often learn more through stories than through concepts. To this end, I hope that this anthology with its biographical sketches and readings will be a valuable resource.

The new Calendars are also much more *ecumenical.* The inclusion of great Christian figures from other communions, including those who died for their convictions, provides not only opportunities for exploring the richness of other traditions, but also opportunities for penitence. Their stories challenge us to fresh examination of our perceptions about the past. All churches are rooted in history, but also distorted by history. We need to learn how fellow Christians from whom we have been historically and theologically separated for generations understand the tragedy as well as the glory of Christian history. As Mark Santer has written:

> There is a connection between our self-identification as members of particular communities and the stories we tell about the past. It is by the things we remember, and the way we remember them, and by the things we fail to remember, that we identify ourselves as belonging to this or that group. What we remember, or do not remember, moulds our reactions and our behaviour towards others at a level deeper than that of conscious reflection.[14]

I hope this anthology will enable the ecumenical encounter to deepen and heal the corporate memory of the Church.

About this anthology and edition

The literature included in this anthology spans over two thousand years. It contains extracts from the lives of saints and the accounts of martyrdoms. There are extracts from sermons, hymns, theological treatises, letters, journals, prayers and poems. It forms a rich treasury for reflection. As Bishop Jeremy Taylor, writing in the seventeenth century, advised: 'To distinguish festival days from common, let it not be lessening the devotion of ordinary days, but enlarge upon the holy day.'[15] This book is designed to assist in the process of 'enlargement'. Together with its companion volume, *Celebrating the Seasons*, it seeks to recover our Christian roots.

In this latest edition the additions and changes to the national Calendars of the Anglican Church in Ireland, Scotland and Wales, have been incorporated alongside those of the Church of England. As one would expect, there is a strong family likeness between our Calendars. Major Feast Days and Festivals are, by and large, identical though there are occasional differences in date, title and solemnity of lesser feasts and commemorations which reflect the different histories of the Church in Britain and Ireland. Where there is a clash of date, an attempt has been made to follow the majority view. Changes are noted in the index of commemorations at the back of the book.

Some saints' days are supplied with a choice of readings. In the case of Major Feast Days the readings have been chosen to reflect a spectrum of Patristic, Medieval, Reformation (and occasionally contemporary) spirituality. Sources of extracts, translations and notes are listed at the end of the book, together with biographical sketches of writers not already covered by their inclusion in the various calendars. To keep extracts within reasonable limits whilst maintaining their sense, sentences or paragraphs have sometimes been omitted or transposed. Occasionally these omissions are noted by dots, but normally the text has been left free of marks so as not to distract the reader. Any abridgement, paraphrase or alteration of a text is recorded in the notes. The vast majority of extracts do not exceed 500 words. Where a longer extract is reproduced, square brackets indicate sections which may be omitted if desired.

The saints offer exciting and contrasting models of how to follow Christ. They constitute individual stars in the galaxy of faith. Their variety and vitality affirms the worthwhileness of the Christian endeavour. Thomas Merton writes of the call to holiness in these words:

> Unlike the animals and the trees, it is not enough for us to be what our nature intends. It is not enough for us to be individuals. For us, holiness is more than humanity. If we are never anything but men and women, never anything but people, we will not be saints and we will not be able to offer to God the worship of our imitation, which is sanctity. It is true

> to say that for me sanctity consists in being *myself* and for you sanctity consists in being *yourself* and that, in the last analysis, your sanctity will never be mine and mine will never be yours, except in the communism of charity and grace. For me to be a saint means to be myself. Therefore the problem of sanctity and salvation is in fact the problem of finding out who I am and of discovering my true self.[16]

The saints teach us something profound about being a Christian in the world today, about being a human being. Though diverse, they are united in their witness to the crucified and risen Christ. Like John the Baptist, they point consistently away from themselves to Jesus Christ: 'He must grow greater, and I must grow smaller.' In making their lives and writings more accessible, may our generation be inspired in our discipleship and renewed in our participation in the body of Christ that transcends continents and centuries.

Robert Atwell

Notes

1 Gregory Dix, *The Shape of the Liturgy*, London, 1945, p.744.
2 Athanasius, *On the Blessing of Death*, 4, 15.
3 In all probability, the custom of commemorating martyrs was something that Christians inherited from Judaism. Since at least the time of the Maccabean Revolt, martyrs were very important in the life and thought of Jewish communities.
4 *Martyrdom of Polycarp*, 9.
5 Ambrose, *Commentary on Psalm 118*, 20, 47–9.
6 Augustine, *Sermon* 304.
7 Augustine, *Against Faustus*, 20, 21.
8 The inscription on the tomb of St Martin of Tours is a good example: 'Here lies Martin the bishop, of holy memory, whose soul is in the hand of God; but he is fully here, present and made plain in miracles of every kind.' See Peter Brown, The Cult of the Saints, London, 1981, pp.4ff.
9 This tendency was emerging even in the time of Augustine. He wrote: 'At the table of the Lord we do not commemorate the martyrs in the same way as we commemorate others who rest in peace, in order to pray for them also. We commemorate them rather so that they may pray for us, that we may follow closely in their footsteps; for they have reached the fullness of that love of which our Lord spoke when he said: "Greater love has no one than to lay down his life for his friends." *Homilies on St John's Gospel*, 84, 2.
10 The *1549 Prayer Book* drastically pruned the number of Saints' Days to those with scriptural warrant. The *1552 Prayer Book* relaxed this rule somewhat, adding commemorations of George, Laurence, Clement of Rome and Lammas Day. In 1561 Elizabeth I issued a royal decree which added a further fifty-eight Feasts to the Calendar, and yet more were added in the revisions of 1604 and 1662. None of these additional Saints' Days, however, were provided with propers to enable their liturgical observance.
11 Hugh Latimer, 'Articles Untruly, Falsely, Uncharitably Imputed to me by Dr Powell of Salisbury', *Sermons and Remains of Bishop Hugh Latimer*, Cambridge, 1844, pp.234 & 236.
12 Thomas Traherne, *Poems, Centuries and Three Thanksgivings*, ed. Anne Ridler, Oxford, 1966.
13 B. F. Westcott, *Christus Consummator*, London, 1886, p.58.
14 Mark Santer, 'The Reconciliation of Memories', *Their Lord and Ours*, ed. Mark Santer, London, 1982, p.160.
15 Jeremy Taylor, *The Rule and Exercises of Holy Living,* VI.
16 Thomas Merton, *Seeds of Contemplation,* London, 1961, pp.24–5.

JANUARY

1 January

The Naming and Circumcision of Jesus

The celebration of this scriptural festival marks three events: first, the naming of the infant Jesus; secondly, the performance of the rite of circumcision as a sign of the covenant between God and Abraham 'and his children for ever' – thus Christ's keeping of the Law; thirdly and traditionally, it is honoured as the first shedding of the Christ's blood. The name Jesus means literally 'Yahweh saves'. Theologically, it may be linked to the question asked by Moses of God: 'What is your name?' 'I am who I am' was the reply; hence the significance of Jesus' own words: 'Before Abraham was, I am.' The feast has been observed in the Church since at least the sixth century.

A Reading from the treatise *On Contemplating God*
by William of St Thierry

O God, you alone are the Lord. To be ruled by you is for us salvation. For us to serve you is nothing else but to be saved by you! But how is it that we are saved by you, O Lord, from whom salvation comes and whose blessing is upon your people, if it is not in receiving from you the gift of loving you and being loved by you? That, Lord, is why you willed that the Son of your right hand, the 'man whom you made so strong for yourself', should be called Jesus, that is to say, Saviour, 'for he will save his people from their sins'. There is no other in whom is salvation except him who taught us to love himself when he first loved us, even to death on the cross. By loving us and holding us so dear he stirred us up to love himself, who first had loved us to the end.

You who first loved us did this, precisely this. You first loved us so that we might love you. And that was not because you needed to be loved by us, but because we could not be what you created us to be, except by loving you. Having then 'in many ways and on various occasions spoken to our fathers by the prophets, now in these last days you have spoken to us in the Son', your Word, by whom the heavens were established, and all the power of them by the breath of his mouth. For you to speak thus in your Son was an open declaration, a 'setting in the sun' as it were, of how much and in what sort of way you loved us, in that you spared not your own Son, but delivered him up for us all. Yes, and he himself loved us and gave himself for us.

This, Lord, is your word to us; this is your all-powerful message: he who, 'while all things kept silence' (that is, were in the depths of error), 'came from the royal throne', the stern opponent of error and the gentle apostle of love. And everything he did and everything he said on earth, even the insults, the spitting, the buffeting, the cross and the grave, all that was nothing but yourself speaking to us in the Son, appealing to us by your love, and stirring up our love for you.

alternative reading

A Reading from a sermon of Mark Frank

This name 'which is above every name' has all things in it, and brings all things with it. It speaks more in five letters than we can do in five thousand words. It speaks more in it than we can speak today; and yet we intend today to speak of nothing else, nothing but Jesus, nothing but Jesus.

Before his birth the angel announced that this child, born of Mary, would be great: 'he shall be called Son of the Highest, and the Lord God shall give him the throne of his father David'. The angel thus intimates that this was a name of the highest majesty and glory. And what can we say upon it, less than burst out with the psalmist into a holy exclamation, 'O Lord our Governor, O Lord our Jesus, how excellent is thy name in all the world!' It is all 'clothed with majesty and honour'; it is 'decked with light'; it comes riding to us 'upon the wings of the wind'; the Holy Spirit breathes it full upon us, covering heaven and earth with its glory.

But it is a name of grace and mercy, as well as majesty and glory. For 'there is no other name under heaven given by which we can be saved', but the name of Jesus. In his name we live, and in that name we die. As Saint Ambrose has written: 'Jesus is all things to us if we will.' Therefore I will have nothing else but him; and I have all if I have him.

The 'looking unto Jesus' which the apostle advises, will keep us from being weary or fainting under our crosses; for this name was set upon the cross over our Saviour's head. This same Jesus at the end fixes and fastens all. The love of God in Jesus will never leave us, never forsake us; come what can, it sweetens all.

Is there any one sad? – let him take Jesus into his heart, and he will take heart presently, and his joy will return upon him. Is any one fallen into a sin? – let him call heartily upon this name, and it will raise him up. Is any one troubled with hardness of heart, or dullness of spirit, or dejection of mind, or drowsiness in doing well? – in the meditation of this name, Jesus, all vanish and fly away. Our days would look dark and heavy, which were not lightened with the name of the 'Sun of Righteousness'; our nights but sad and dolesome, which we entered not with this sweet name, when we lay down without commending ourselves to God in it.

So then let us remember to begin and end all in Jesus. The New Testament, the covenant of our salvation, begins so, 'the generation of Jesus'; and 'Come Lord Jesus', so it ends. May we all end so too, and when we are going hence, commend our spirits into his hands; and when he comes, may he receive them to sing praises and alleluias to his blessed name amidst the saints and angels in his glorious kingdom for ever.

2 January

Basil the Great and Gregory of Nazianzus

Bishops and Teachers of the Faith, 379 & 389

Note: In Wales, the saints are observed separately: Gregory of Nazianzus on 9 May, and Basil the Great on 14 June.
In Scotland, Basil the Great, Gregory of Nazianzus and Gregory of Nyssa are celebrated jointly on 14 June.

Gregory and Basil were two friends bound together by their desire to promote and defend the divinity of Christ as proclaimed in the Nicene Creed. This was against the seemingly overwhelming pressure from both Church and State for the establishment of Arianism, which denied Christ's divinity and thus the whole Christian doctrine of the Trinity. Basil was renowned for being headstrong and forceful in comparison to his friend Gregory, who would rather spend his days in prayer and living the simple, ascetic life. Gregory's brilliance in oratory and theological debate meant that a hidden life was virtually impossible and Basil drew him into the forefront of the controversy. Their joint persuasive eloquence convinced the first Council of Constantinople, meeting in 381, that their teaching was the truly orthodox one and the Council ratified the text of the Nicene Creed in the form it is used in the East to this day. Basil died in the year 379 and Gregory ten years later.

A Reading from a letter of Basil the Great to Gregory of Nazianzus, written in about 358 following Basil's move to Pontus in Cappadocia

What I do, day and night, in this remote spot, I am ashamed to write to you about. I have abandoned my career in the city because I am convinced that it will only make me further depressed. Within myself, I am still largely unresolved: I am like a traveller on the ocean who has never been on a voyage before and becomes ill and seasick. Such folk moan because the ship is large and has such an enormous swell, and yet the moment they transfer to a smaller boat or dinghy, they are tossed about even more and become violently ill. Wherever they go, they cannot escape from their nausea and depression. My internal state is something like this. I carry my own problems with me wherever I go and there is no escape.

So in the end, I have got very little out of my solitude. What I ought to have done, what would have helped me to walk securely in the footsteps of Jesus who has led me on the path of salvation, would have been to have come here long ago. Has not our Lord said: 'If any would come after me, let them deny themselves, take up their cross and follow me'?

We must strive for a quiet mind. The eye cannot appreciate an object set before it if it is perpetually restless, glancing here, there and everywhere. No more can our mind's eye apprehend the truth with any clarity if it is distracted by a thousand worldly concerns. For just as it is impossible to write upon a wax tablet without first having erased the marks on it, so it is impossible to receive the impress of divine doctrine without unlearning our inherited preconceptions and habitual prejudices. Solitude offers an excellent opportunity in this process because it calms our passions, and creates space for our reason to remove their influence.

Let there be, therefore, places such as this, where we may pursue such spiritual training without interruption, nourishing our souls with thoughts of God. After all, what can be better than to imitate the choirs of angels, to begin a day with prayer, honouring our Creator with hymns and songs? And as the day brightens, to pursue our daily tasks to the accompaniment of prayers, seasoning our labour with hymns as if they were salt? Such soothing melodies compose the mind and establish it in tranquillity.

Our one concern is to flourish in self-control and courage, justice and wisdom, and all those other virtues in their various categories which guide the good person in the proper conduct of life.

alternative reading

A Reading from the eulogy preached in 379 by Gregory of Nazianzus following the death of his life-long friend, Basil the Great

Basil and I were at Athens at the time. Like streams of a river, we originated from a common source in our native land, but in going abroad to pursue our studies we had become separated; but now, as if it were planned, as if God had wanted it this way, we found ourselves reunited.

I was not alone during this time in holding my friend, the great Basil, in high regard. I needed no convincing of his seriousness of purpose, his mature and wise conversation, but I sought to persuade others unacquainted with him, to share my regard for him. He was already well respected by many since his reputation had gone before him, with the result that he was accorded the special distinction of being almost the only new student in Athens to escape the treatment generally doled out to newcomers.

This was the prelude to our friendship. This was the kindling of that flame that was to bind us together. We recognised a bond of mutual love. Gradually we were able to admit our affection for one another and to recognise our common ambition to dedicate ourselves to lives of true wisdom. From then on we became inseparable friends, sharing the same lodgings, the same table, the same sentiments, our eyes fixed on the same goal. Our mutual affection grew ever warmer and stronger.

We were driven on by the same hope: the pursuit of learning. This is an area of life notoriously open to jealousy; but between us there was none. Indeed, in some sense rivalry intensified our zeal. For there was indeed a contest between us. But it was not about who should have first place, but about how one could yield it to the other. For each of us regarded the achievement of the other as his own.

We seemed to have a single soul animating two bodies. And, while we could not believe those who claim that 'everything is contained in everything', yet in our experience, we were certainly intimately bound up in one another's lives. Our sole object and ambition was virtue and a life so oriented in hope to the blessings that await us, that we severed our attachment to this life before we had to depart it. With this in view we ordered our life and actions, following the guidance of God's law, and at the same time spurred each other on to virtue. And, if it is not too much to say, we were for each other a rule and a pair of scales for discerning good from evil.

Different men have different names, either derived from their ancestors or to do with their jobs and achievements. But our great ambition, the great name we relished, was to be Christian, and to be called Christians.

A Reading from a poem by John McGuckin

Saint Gregory Nazianzen

Of all the ancients,
You I think I could live with,
        (some of the time)
comfortable in you
like an old coat
sagged and fraying at the back,
(its pockets drooping with important
nothings
like string, and manuscripts of poems)
perfect for watching you off your guard,
rambling round your country garden,
planting roses, not turnips,
contrary to the manual
for a sensible monk;
master of the maybe;
anxious they might take you up all wrong;
shaking your fist at an Emperor,
        (once he had turned the corner
        out of sight);
every foray into speech
a costed regret.

Your heart was like a spider's silk
swinging wildly at the slightest breeze,
too tender for this tumbling world
of mountebacks, and quacks and gobs,
but tuned to hear the distant voices
of the singing stars

        and marvel at the mercy of it all.

2 January

Munchin

Abbot, seventh century

Munchin, a seventh-century monk, affectionately known as 'The Wise', is honoured in Limerick and known as patron of the city. The 'little monk' inaugurated a tradition of prayer and study in a golden period of Irish Christianity and Celtic monastic life.

A Reading from *The Rule of Carthage*,
a Celtic monastic Rule dating from the seventh century,
concerning the duties of an abbot of a community

It is a wonderful distinction if you are the leader of a church, but it would be better by far that you assume in a worthy manner the patrimony of the King.

Sublime is the undertaking you bear if you are the leader of a church; you must protect the rights, whether small or great, of the monastery.

Preach diligently what Christ, the holy one, commands; what you ask of others should be what you yourself do.

You should love the souls of all, just as you love your own. It is your duty to exalt every good and to root out all evil.

Your learning should be visible to all, and not hidden like a candle under a bushel. Your business is to heal all your monks, whether they be strong or weak.

It is your responsibility to judge each one according to his rank and according to his deeds, so that they may present themselves with you at the judgement in the presence of the King.

It is your responsibility to encourage the seniors who are weighed down by sorrow and sickness, that they may frequently invoke the King with floods of tears.

Yours is the duty of instructing the young, that they fall not into sin and the devil not drag them away to his house reeking of death.

You are to return thanks for each and every one who carries out his function in the one pure Church.

Yours is to reprimand the wayward, to correct all, to bring to order the disorderly, the stubborn, the wilful, and the wretched.

Patience, humility, prayers, beloved charity, steadiness, generosity, calmness are to be expected of you.

It is no light task to teach all people in truth, and to foster unity, forgiveness, sincerity, and uprightness in all things.

Be faithful to the constant preaching of the gospel for the instruction of all, and to the offering of the Body of the great Lord on the holy altar.

2 January

Seraphim of Sarov

Monk and Spiritual Guide, 1833

Born in 1759 at Kursk in Russia, Seraphim entered the Monastery of our Lady at Sarov near Moscow when he was twenty years old. He lived as a Solitary for over thirty years but his gifts as a staretz, or spiritual guide, became more widely known until he found himself sharing his gift of healing spirit, soul and body with the thousands who made the pilgrimage to his monastery. The 'Jesus Prayer' formed the heart of his own devotional life and he stressed the need for all Christians to have an unceasing communion with the person of Jesus. He died on this day in the year 1833 and is revered in the Russian Orthodox Church as 'an icon of Orthodox Spirituality'.

A Reading from a conversation of Seraphim of Sarov with Nicholas Motovilov concerning aims of the Christian life

It was Thursday. The day was gloomy. Snow lay deep on the ground and snowflakes were falling thickly from the sky when Father Seraphim began his conversation with me in the plot near his hermitage over against the river Sarovka, on the hill which slopes down to the river-bank. He sat me on the stump of a tree which he had just felled, and himself squatted before me.

'Prayer, fasting, watching,' he said, 'and all other Christian acts, however good they may be, do not alone constitute the aim of our Christian life, although they serve as the indispensable means of reaching this aim. The true aim of our Christian life is to acquire the Holy Spirit of God.

'We must begin by a right faith in our Lord Jesus Christ, the Son of God, who came into the world to save sinners, and by winning for ourselves the grace of the Holy Spirit who brings into our hearts the kingdom of God and lays for us the path to win the blessings of the future life.

'Every virtuous act done for Christ's sake gives us the grace of the Holy Spirit, but most of all is this given through prayer; for prayer is somehow always in our hands as an instrument for acquiring the grace of the Spirit. You wish, for instance, to go to church and there is no church near or the service is over; or you wish to give to the poor and there is none by you or you have nothing to give; you wish to perform some other virtuous act for Christ's sake and the strength or the opportunity is lacking. But this in no way affects prayer; prayer is always possible for everyone, rich and poor, noble and simple, strong and weak, healthy and suffering, righteous and sinful. Great is the power of prayer; most of all does it bring the Spirit of God and easiest of all is it to exercise.

'Prayer is given to us in order to converse with our good and life-giving God and Saviour; but even here we must pray only until the Holy Spirit descends on us in measures of his heavenly grace known to him. When he comes to visit us, we must cease to pray. How can we pray to God "Come and abide in us, cleanse us from all evil, and save our souls, O gracious Lord," when he has already come to us to save us who trust in him and call on his holy name in truth, that humbly and with love we may receive him, the Comforter, in the chamber of our souls, hungering and thirsting for his coming?

'Acquire therefore, my son, the grace of the Holy Spirit by all the virtues in Christ; trade in those that are most profitable to you. Thus, if prayer and watching give you more of God's grace, pray and watch; if fasting gives much of God's Spirit, then fast; if almsgiving gives more, give alms. Be always as a candle, burning with earthly fire, lighting other candles for the illumination of darkened places, but without its own light ever being diminished.

For if this is the reality of earthly fire, what shall we say of the fire of the grace of God's Holy Spirit?'

alternative reading

A Reading from a conversation of Seraphim of Sarov with Nicholas Motovilov concerning 'The Acquisition of the Holy Spirit'

'How', I asked Father Seraphim, 'can I know that I am in the grace of the Holy Spirit? How can I discern for myself his true manifestation in me?'

After these words I glanced at his face and there came over me an even greater reverent awe. Imagine in the centre of the sun, in the dazzling light of its midday rays, the face of a man talking to you. You see the movement of his lips and the changing expression of his eyes, you hear his voice, you feel someone holding your shoulders; yet you do not see his hands, you do not even see yourself or his figure, but only a blinding light spreading far around for several yards and illuminating with its glaring sheen both the snow blanket which covered the forest glade and the snowflakes which besprinkled me and the great Elder. You can imagine the state I was in!

'How do you feel now?' Father Seraphim asked me.

'Extraordinarily well,' I said.

'But in what way? How exactly do you feel?'

I answered, 'I feel such calmness and peace in my soul that no words can express it.'

'What else do you feel?' he inquired.

'An extraordinary joy in my heart.'

Father Seraphim continued, 'When the Spirit of God comes down to us and overshadows us with the fullness of his inspiration, then the human soul overflows with unspeakable joy, for the Spirit of God fills with joy whatever he touches. This is the joy of which the Lord speaks in the Gospel.

'Foretastes of joy are given to us now, and if they fill our souls with such sweetness, well-being and happiness, what shall we say of that joy which has been prepared in heaven for those who weep here on earth? And you, my dear, have wept enough in your life on earth; yet see with what joy the Lord consoles you even in this life? Now it is up to us, my dear, to add labours to labours in order to go from strength to strength, and to come "to the measure of the stature of the fullness of Christ", so that the words of the Lord may be fulfilled in us.'

2 January

Vedanayagam Samuel Azariah

Bishop in South India and Evangelist, 1945

Samuel Azariah was born in 1874 in a small village in South India, his father, Thomas Vedanayagam, being a simple village priest, and his mother, Ellen, having a deep love and understanding of the Scriptures. Samuel became a YMCA evangelist whilst still only nineteen, and secretary of the organization throughout South India a few years later. He saw that, for the Church in India to grow and attract ordinary Indians to the Christian faith, it had to have an indigenous leadership and reduce the strong western influences and almost totally white leadership that pervaded it. He was ordained priest at the age of thirty-five and bishop just three years later, his work moving from primary evangelism to forwarding his desire for more Indian clergy and the need to raise their educational standards. He was an avid ecumenist and was one of the first to see the importance to mission of a united Church. He died on 1 January 1945, just two years before the creation of a united Church of South India.

A Reading from An Ecumenical Venture: *The History of Nandyal Diocese in Andhra Pradesh* by Constance Millington

Azariah had two great priorities in his work: evangelism and the desire for Christian unity.

He understood evangelism to be the acid test of Christianity. When asked what he would preach about in a village that had never heard of Christ, Azariah answered without hesitation: 'The resurrection.' From a convert he demanded the full acceptance of Christianity which would include baptism and which could therefore include separation from family and caste. He claimed that Christianity took its origin in the death and resurrection of Jesus Christ and the outburst of supernatural power that this society manifested in the world.

Azariah recognised that because four-fifths of Indian people live in villages, for the Church to be an indigenous one it must be a rural Church. He was constantly in the villages, inspiring and guiding the teachers, clergy and congregations. He blamed the missionaries for not training people in evangelism, and thought their teaching had been mission centred instead of Church centred, and he pleaded with missionaries to build up the Indian Church. Much of the Christian outreach in his area was among the outcast people. Gradually as Christianity spread amongst the villages, the social situation began to change, the Christian outcasts gaining a new self-respect as they realised their worth in the eyes of God.

Azariah considered that one of the factors that hampered evangelism, and possibly the deepening of the spiritual life of the convert, was the western appearance of the Church in both its buildings and its services. As early as 1912 he had visions of a cathedral for the diocese to be built in the eastern style, where all Christians could feel spiritually at home regardless of their religious background and race. Building was delayed because of the Great War in Europe, but finally his dream was realised when the cathedral of The Most Glorious Epiphany was consecrated on 6 January 1936. The building is a beautiful structure embodying ideas from Christian, Hindu and Moslem architecture. Its dignity and spaciousness create a very different effect from that of the nineteenth and twentieth century Gothic churches and furnishings scattered elsewhere in India.

If evangelisation of India was Azariah's first priority, the second was that of Church unity. He saw the two as inter-related. He believed that a united Church was in accordance with the will of God, 'that we may all be one', and he also believed that a United Church would be more effective for evangelism. Addressing the Lambeth Conference in 1930 he pleaded:

> In India we wonder if you have sufficiently contemplated the grievous sin of perpetuating your divisions and denominational bitterness in these your daughter churches. We want you to take us seriously when we say that the problem of union is one of life and death to us. Do not, we plead with you, do not give us your aid to keep us separate, but lead us to union so that you and we may go forward together and fulfil the prayer, 'That we may all be one'.

3 January

Morris Williams

Priest and Poet, 1874

Morris Williams (usually known as 'Nicander', his bardic name) was born at Caernarfon in 1809. He was apprenticed to a carpenter. Once his literary and academic gifts became clear, Nicander was helped to enter King's School, Chester, and Jesus College, Oxford, where he graduated in 1835. He was ordained in the same year, serving his first curacy at Holywell. In 1847 he was appointed perpetual curate of Amlwch, becoming rector of Llanrhuddlad in 1859. Nicander assisted with the revision of the Welsh version of the Book of Common Prayer and edited the 1847 edition of Llyfr yr Homiliau (The Book of Homilies). He was a pioneer of the Tractarian movement in the Diocese of Bangor and used his considerable poetic gifts to promote its ideals. Some of the poems from his collection Y Flwyddyn Eglwysig (The Church Year), published in 1843, were adapted into hymns which had a profound impact on the spiritual lives of Welsh-speaking Anglicans. He died in the year 1874.

A Reading from a post-communion hymn
of Morris Williams (Nicander)

Gyda'r saint anturiais nesu,
Dan fy maich, at Allor Duw;
Bwrdd i borthi'r tlawd newynog,
Bwrdd i nerthu'r egwan yw;
Cefais yno, megis, gyffwrdd
Corff drylliedig Iesu glân,
Yn y fan fe doddai 'nghalon
Fel y cwyr o flaen y tân.

O fy Iesu bendigedig,
Golwg iawn ar Waed dy Groes
Sydd yn toddi'r mawr galedwch

Fu'n diffrwytho dyddiau f 'oes;
Gad, O gad im, dirion
Arglwydd,
Fyw a marw yn dy hedd;
Bydd di'r cyfan oll i'm henaid,
Yma a thu draw i'r bedd.

(With the saints I ventured to approach,
Under my burden, the altar of God:
A table to feed the hungry poor,
It is a table to strengthen the weak;
I was able, as it were, to touch
The broken body of holy Jesus,
At once my heart melted
Like the wax before the fire.

O my blessed Jesu,
A true sight of the blood of thy cross
Melteth the great hardness
Which destroyed the days of my life.
Let, O let me, gentle Lord
Live and die in thy peace:
May thou be all in all to my soul
Here and beyond the grave.)

6 January

The Epiphany

The subtitle in The Book of Common Prayer of this, one of the principal feasts of the Church, is 'The Manifestation of Christ to the Gentiles'. This emphasizes that, from the moment of the Incarnation, the good news of Jesus Christ is for all: Jew and Gentile, the wise and the simple, male and female. Nothing in the Greek text of the Gospels indicates that the Magi were all male or even three in number, and the idea that they were kings is a much later, non-scriptural tradition. The date chosen to celebrate this feast is related to the choice of the Winter Solstice for the celebration of the Nativity of Christ: the northern European pre-Christian tradition celebrated the birth of the Sun on 25 December whereas the Mediterranean and East customarily observed 6 January as the Solstice. As often happens, the two dates merged into a beginning and an end of the same celebration. The Western Church adopted 'the twelve days of Christmas' climaxing on the eve of Epiphany, or 'Twelfth Night'. The implication by the fifth century was that this was the night on which the Magi arrived. The complications of dating became even more confused with the changing in the West from the Julian to the Gregorian Calendar, the Eastern Church refusing to play any part in such a radical change. So this day remains the chief day of celebrating the Incarnation in Orthodox Churches.

A Reading from a sermon of Peter Chrysologos

In the mystery of our Lord's incarnation there were clear indications of his eternal Godhead. Yet the great events we celebrate today disclose and reveal in different ways the fact that God himself took a human body. Mortals, enshrouded always in darkness, must not be left in ignorance, and so be deprived of what they can understand and retain only by grace.

In choosing to be born for us, God chose to be known by us. He therefore reveals himself in this way, in order that this great sacrament of his love may not be an occasion for us of great misunderstanding.

Today the Magi find, crying in a manger, the one they have followed as he shone in the sky. Today the Magi see clearly, in swaddling clothes, the one they have long awaited as he lay hidden among the stars. Today the Magi gaze in deep wonder at what they see: heaven on earth, earth in heaven, humankind in God, God in human flesh, one whom the whole universe cannot contain now enclosed in a tiny body. As they look, they believe and do not question, as their symbolic gifts bear witness: incense for God, gold for a king, myrrh for one who is to die.

So the Gentiles, who were the last, become the first: the faith of the Magi is the first fruits of the belief of the Gentiles.

Today Christ enters the Jordan to wash away the sins of the world. John himself testifies that this is why he has come: 'Behold the Lamb of God, behold him who takes away the sins of the world.' Today a servant lays his hand on the Lord, a man lays his hand on God. John lays his hand on Christ, not to forgive but to receive forgiveness.

Today, as the psalmist prophesied: 'The voice of the Lord is heard above the waters.' What does the voice say? 'This is my beloved Son, in whom I am well pleased.'

Today the Holy Spirit hovers over the waters in the likeness of a dove. A dove announced to Noah that the flood had disappeared from the earth; so now a dove is to reveal that the world's shipwreck is at an end for ever. The sign is no longer an olive-shoot of the old stock: instead, the Spirit pours out on Christ's head the full richness of a new anointing by the Father, to fulfil what the psalmist had prophesied: 'Therefore God, your God, has anointed you with the oil of gladness above your fellows.'

Today Christ works the first of his signs from heaven by turning water into wine. But water has still to be changed into the sacrament of his blood, so that Christ may offer spiritual drink from the chalice of his body, to fulfil the psalmist's prophecy: 'How excellent is my chalice, warming my spirit.'

alternative reading

A Reading from a hymn of Ephrem of Syria

Who, being a mortal, can tell about the Reviver of all,
Who left the height of his majesty and came down to smallness?
You, who magnify all by being born, magnify my weak mind
  that I may tell about your birth,
  not to investigate your majesty,
  but to proclaim your grace.
Blessed is he who is both hidden and revealed in his actions!

It is a great wonder that the Son, who dwelt entirely in a body,
    inhabited it entirely, and it sufficed for him.
Although limitless, he dwelt in it.
His will was entirely in him; but his totality was not in him.
Who is sufficient to proclaim that
    although he dwelt entirely in a body,
    still he dwelt entirely in the universe?
Blessed is the Unlimited who was limited!

Your majesty is hidden from us; your grace is revealed before us.
    I will be silent, my Lord, about your majesty,
    but I will speak about your grace.
Your grace made you a babe;
    your grace made you a human being.
Your majesty contracted and stretched out.
Blessed is the power that became small and became great!

The Magi rejoiced from afar; the scribes proclaimed from nearby.
The prophet showed his erudition, and Herod his fury.
The scribes showed interpretations; the Magi showed offerings.
It is a wonder that to one babe the kinspeople
    rushed with their swords,
    but strangers with their offerings.
Blessed is your birth that stirred up the universe!

alternative reading

A Reading from a sermon of Lancelot Andrewes preached before King James I at Whitehall in 1620

What place more proper for him who is 'the living bread that came down from heaven', to give life to the world, than Bethlehem, the least and lowest of all the houses of Judah. This natural birthplace of his sheweth his spiritual nature. Christ's birth fell in the sharpest season, in the deep of winter. As humility his place, so affliction his time. The time and place fit well.

And there came from the East wise men, Gentiles; and that concerns us, for so are we. Christ's birth is made manifest to them by the star of heaven. It is the Gentiles' star, and so ours too. We may set our course by it, to seek and find, and worship him as well as they. So we come in, for 'God hath also to the Gentiles set open a door of faith,' and that he would do this, and call us in, there was some small star-light from the beginning. This he promised by the Patriarchs, shadowed forth in the figures of the Law and the Temple and the Tabernacle, and foresung in the Psalms, and it is this day fulfilled.

These wise men are come and we with them. Not only in their own names, but in ours did they make their entry; came and sought after, and found and worshipped, their Saviour and ours, the Saviour of the whole world. A little wicket there was left open, whereat divers Gentiles did come in, but only one or two. But now the great gate set wide opens this day for all – for these here with their camels and dromedaries to enter, and all their carriage. Christ is not only for russet cloaks, shepherds and such; but even grandees, great states such as these came too; and when they came were welcome to him. For they were sent for and invited by this star, their star properly.

They came a long journey, and they came an uneasy journey. They came now, at the worst season of the year. And all but to do worship at Christ's birth. They stayed not their coming till the opening of the year, till they might have better weather and way, and have longer days, and so more seasonable and fit to travel in. So desirous were they to come with the first, and to be there as soon as possibly they might; broke through all these difficulties, and behold, they did come.

And we, what excuse shall we have if we come not? If so short and easy a way we come not, as from our chambers hither? And these wise men were never a whit less wise for so coming; nay, to come to Christ is one of the wisest parts that ever these wise men did. And if we believe this, that this was their wisdom, if they and we be wise in one Spirit, by the same principles, we will follow the same star, tread the same way, and so come at last whither they are happily gone before us.

[In the old ritual of the Church we find that on the cover of the canister wherein was the sacrament of his body, there was a star engraven, to shew us that now the star leads us thither, to his body there. So what shall I say now, but according as Saint John saith, and the star, and the wise men say 'Come'. And he whose star it is, and to whom the wise men came, saith 'Come'. And let them that are disposed 'Come'. And let whosoever will, take of the 'Bread of Life which came down from heaven' this day into Bethlehem, the house of bread. Of which bread the Church is this day the house, the true Bethlehem, and all the Bethlehem we have now left to come to for the Bread of Life – of that life which we hope for in heaven. And this our nearest coming that here we can come, till we shall by another coming 'Come' unto him in his heavenly kingdom.]

alternative reading

A Reading from a poem by William Blake

The Divine Image

To Mercy, Pity, Peace, and Love
All pray in their distress;
And to these virtues of delight
Return their thankfulness.

For Mercy, Pity, Peace, and Love
Is God, our father dear,
And Mercy, Pity, Peace, and Love
Is Man, his child and care.

For Mercy has a human heart,
Pity a human face,
And Love, the human form divine,
And Peace, the human dress.

the very brinks of it, an argument, I hope, that God is bringing me to the Land of Promise, for that was the way by which of old he led his people; but before they came to the sea, he instituted a Passover for them, a lamb it was, but it was to be eaten with very sour herbs, as in the twelfth of Exodus.

I shall obey, and labour to digest the sour herbs, as well as the lamb, and I shall remember that it is the Lord's Passover; I shall not think of the herbs, nor be angry with the hands which gathered them, but look up only to him who instituted the one, and governeth the other. For men can have no more power over me, than that which is given them from above. I am not in love with this passage through the Red Sea, for I have the weakness and infirmity of flesh and blood in me, and I have prayed as my Saviour taught me, and exampled me, that this cup of red wine might pass away from me. But since it is not that my will may, his will be done; and I shall most willingly drink of this cup as deep as he pleases, and enter into this sea, ay and pass through it in the way that he shall be pleased to lead me.

And I pray God bless all this people, and open their eyes, that they may see the right way; for if it fall out that the blind lead the blind, doubtless they will both into the ditch. For myself, I am (and I acknowledge it in all humility) a most grievous sinner in many ways, by thought, word and deed, and therefore I cannot doubt but that God hath mercy in store for me a poor penitent, as well as for other sinners. I have, upon this sad occasion, ransacked every corner of my heart, and yet I thank God, I have not found any of my sins that are there, any sins now deserving death by any known law of this kingdom. And yet thereby I charge nothing upon my judges.

And though I am not only the first archbishop, but the first man that ever died in this way, yet some of my predecessors have gone this way, though not by this means. Many examples great and good, and they teach me patience, for I hope my cause in heaven will look of another dye than the colour that is put upon it here upon earth.

I will not enlarge myself any further. I have done. I forgive all the world, all and every of those bitter enemies, or others whatsoever they have been which have any ways prosecuted me in this kind, and I humbly desire to be forgiven first of God, and then of every man, whether I have offended him or no, if he do but conceive that I have. Lord, do thou forgive me, and I beg forgiveness of him, and so I heartily desire you to join with me in prayer.

11 January

David of Scotland

King of Scots, 1153

The fourth son of Queen Margaret of Scotland, David succeeded his brothers as king, and continued their policy of bringing Scotland closer to Norman England in its secular and religious institutions. In place of decaying Culdee foundations such as those in St Andrews, Melrose and Jedburgh, he introduced monastic communities of Roman observance, favouring reforming orders. These exercised a powerful, civilizing influence and became centres of education, care for the sick and relief of the poor. He founded royal burghs and promoted a feudal system in the Norman style. He died in the year 1153.

A Reading from the treatise *Pastoral Care* by Gregory the Great

Christian leaders are enemies to our Redeemer if on the strength of the good works they perform, they desire to be loved by the Church more than by Christ; indeed, such servants are guilty of adulterous thinking. Although in truth it is the bridegroom who sends gifts through his servants to his bride the Church, the servants are busy trying to secure the eyes of the bride for themselves. When such self-love captures the mind, it propels a person either into inordinate laxity or into brutal irascibility. From love of self, the leader's mind becomes lax. He sees people sinning, but dares not correct them because he is frightened their love for him will be weakened; or even worse, rather than reprove them, he will actually go so far as to gloss over their faults with adulation.

Leaders tend to display such an attitude to those of whom they are frightened, those whom they think can wreck their pursuit of temporal glory. By contrast, folk who (in their estimation) cannot harm them, they constantly hound with bitter and harsh words. Incapable of admonishing such people gently, they abandon any pretence of pastoral sensitivity, and terrify them into submission by insisting on their right to govern. The divine word rebukes such leaders when the prophet says: 'You ruled over the people with force and with a high hand.' Such leaders love themselves more than their Creator, and brag of the qualities of their leadership. They have no real idea about what they should be doing, and are infatuated by power. They have no fear of the judgement that is to come. They glory arrogantly in their temporal power; it gives them a thrill to do what is wrong with no one to restrain them, made confident by the lack of opposition.

Those who act in such ways, and expect others to be silent, witness against themselves, for they want to be loved more than the truth, and expect no criticism. Of course, no one in a position of leadership can go through life without sinning; but we should always want truth to be loved rather than ourselves, and should not seek to protect others from the truth. We learn from Scripture that Peter willingly accepted the rebuke of Paul, and that David willingly accepted the reprimand of his servant Nathan. Good leaders, who are not trapped by self-love, welcome free and sincere criticism as an opportunity to grow in humility. It is important, therefore, that the gift of leadership should be exercised with the great art of moderation, in order that those in their care should have freedom of speech and not feel intimidated from expressing an opinion. Good leaders will want to please their people, but always in order to draw them to the love of truth.

11 January

Rhys Prichard, William Williams, Isaac Williams

Clergy, Spiritual Writers and Poets

Rhys Prichard (known as 'Yr Hen Ficer' – 'The Old Vicar') was probably born near Llandovery in 1579. He graduated from Jesus College, Oxford, in 1603, a year after his ordination to the priesthood, and was appointed vicar of Llandovery. In 1626 he became Chancellor of St Davids Cathedral. Prichard was one of the most effective communicators of the Christian message in Welsh history. His teachings were contained in easily remembered verses in colloquial Carmarthenshire Welsh. After Prichard's death his poems were collected by Stephen Hughes in Canwyll y Cymro (The Welshman's Candle). The impact of this often-reprinted volume on Welsh Christianity has been compared with that of Bunyan's Pilgrim's Progress. He died in the year 1644 and was buried in the churchyard of the cathedral.

William Williams was born at Llanfair-ar-y-bryn, Carmarthenshire, in the year 1717. He underwent a conversion while listening to Howell Harris preach, was ordained deacon and served as curate of Llanwrtyd. His Methodist leanings became clear and the Bishop of St Davids refused to ordain him priest. Between 1744 and 1787 he published collections of hymns which played a major part in guiding and strengthening the development of the Methodist revival. They provided a communal expression of intensely personal experience, and established him as the greatest Welsh hymn-writer. He also wrote two long religious poems and several prose works, including a guide to Christian marriage. He died in the year 1791.

Isaac Williams was born at Cwmcynfelyn, near Aberystwyth, in 1802, and educated at Trinity College, Oxford. He was ordained in 1829, and was curate to John Henry Newman. He became a leading figure in the Oxford Movement, contributing to the Tracts for the Times, and helping build the first Tractarian church in Wales, at Llangorwen. In 1841 he left Oxford and became a country curate at Bisley and then Stinchcombe, where he died in the year 1865. He was the author of a considerable amount of devotional poetry, including The Cathedral, The Baptistery and The Altar, and some of his hymns are still sung. He was a gentle, quiet, reserved man, committed to prayer and to the pastoral care of his parishes.

A Reading from the poetry of Rhys Prichard

The Life and Death of Christ

Let ev'ry Christian who desires to know,
What to his Saviour happen'd here below,
Draw near – whilst I his incarnation tell,
And what, 'till death, unto our Lord befell.

The word was God (e'er heav'n and earth were made,
Or the foundations of the world were laid.)
The Second Person of the sacred Three,
And the creator of all things that be.

When to fair Bethl'em Mary arriv'd,
(Where David and his ancestors erst liv'd)
To be enroll'd, and Caesar's tax to pay,
Her reck'ning was fulfil'd that very day.

At twelve years old, a wonder to relate!
He with the rabbis enter'd to debate,
Until those sages wonder'd how a child
Cou'd be with such prodigious knowledge fill'd.

Thus on the cross the blessed Jesus die'd –
Who, his heart's blood, forth gushing from his side,
With love unutterable, freely gave,
The souls of his true votaries to save!

alternative reading

A Reading from a poem by William Williams

Love for God

I look across the distant hills,
  Hour upon hour I wait;
The sun is almost set, my dear –
  Come, for it groweth late!

Now all my loves abscond from me
  And faithless prove at length;
There's a sweet sickness holds me, though,
  A love of mightier strength.

The children of the world can know
  Nothing of such grace
As sucks my liking and intent
  Off each created face.

Let me be faithful whilst I live,
  Aimed level at thy praise,
No pleasure under the firmament
  Steal my distracted gaze!

Pull my heart's fondness, all compact,
  From fickle things away
Unto the One whose faith is sure
  For ever and for aye!

Under the blue sky nothing is
  That love of life affords,
But satisfaction stays within
  The house that is my Lord's.

Zest and desire have died to me,
  For the world's flowers fall;
Only an ebbless vanity
  Is running through it all.

A Reading from a hymn of Isaac Williams

Disposer supreme, and judge of the earth,
Who choosest for thine the weak and the poor,
To frail earthen vessels, and things of no worth,
Entrusting thy riches which aye shall endure;

Throughout the wide world their message is heard,
And swift as the wind it circles the earth;
It echoes the voice of the heavenly Word,
And brings unto mortals the hope of new birth.

Their cry thunders forth, 'Christ Jesus is Lord',
Then Satan doth fear, his citadels fall:
As when those shrill trumpets were raised at thy word,
And one long blast shattered proud Jericho's wall.

O loud be the call, and stirring the sound,
To rouse us, O Lord, from sin's deadly sleep;
May lights which thou kindlest in darkness around,
The dull soul awaken, her vigil to keep.

All honour and praise, dominion and might,
To thee, Three in One, eternally be,
Who pouring around us thy glorious light,
Dost call us from darkness thy glory to see.

11 January

Mary Slessor

Missionary in West Africa, 1915

Mary Slessor was born into a working-class, Presbyterian family in Aberdeen in 1848. As a child in Dundee, she was enthralled by stories of missions in Africa. For years, she read diligently as she worked in the mills, and eventually, in 1875, she was accepted as a teacher for the mission in Calabar, Nigeria. Her fluency in the local language, physical resilience and lack of pretension endeared her to those to whom she ministered. She adopted unwanted children, particularly twins who would otherwise, according to local superstition, have been put to death. She was influential in organizing trade and in settling disputes, contributing much to the development of the Okoyong people with whom she later settled. She died, still in Africa, on this day in the year 1915.

A Reading from *Far Above Rubies* by Richard Symonds

Partly as a result of her lack of formal education, particularly in Presbyterian theology, Mary Slessor took a broad-minded view of local beliefs and customs when she arrived in Calabar, and as a result acquired an unusual understanding of them. The local people, she was often to insist, were not irreligious; they believed in God but were troubled by their belief in evil spirits.

She rapidly acquired a remarkable fluency in the Efik language. In the afternoons, when teaching was finished, it was her duty to visit women in the town, dosing ailments, instructing in housecraft and needle-work, vaccinating against smallpox, and counselling. She was also sent to visit the Mission Stations, travelling by river and on foot through the forest, and found the rural people more congenial than the more sophisticated population of the town.

The European lifestyle of her fellow missionaries irked her, and she longed to work among 'the untouched multitudes'. Accordingly she asked to be posted further inland among the Okoyong, a Bantu tribe who had no direct contact with Europeans. Now commenced her practice of living entirely on local food, at first because this enabled her to send part of her salary home to Scotland, and later because it brought her closer to Africans. From there she supervised schools, dispensed medicines, trained teachers and visited villages to preach. She became an intrepid traveller. It was here that she began to adopt the children who were later to accompany her everywhere, even to Scotland when she went on leave. Most of them were twins, who were always considered as offspring of evil spirits and abandoned, if not murdered. Others were orphans of slave mothers who had died.

Refreshed by home leave in 1907, Mary returned with two European helpers who took over her station and enabled her to move once more in order to set up a women's industrial training centre. Long experience had convinced her that the problems of the women were economic. They had no status except as dependants, and were exploited by men as labourers. If they were not attached to some man, they could be insulted or injured with impunity. She saw the solution as the establishment of centres where unattached women could support themselves by farming and industrial work.

Mary Slessor's religion is quite as interesting as the work which it inspired. Although she recollected that as a girl 'hell fire' had driven her into the kingdom, she found it a kingdom of love and tenderness and mercy, and never sought to bring anyone into it by shock. 'Fear is not worship,' she said, 'nor does it honour God.'

In her own lifetime she became something of a legend. In spite of terrible illness and pain, her radiance and thankfulness for the privilege of her work remained until the end. She died in 1915, surrounded by adopted children. Her last words were in Efik as she prayed: 'O God, release me soon.'

12 January

Aelred

Abbot of Rievaulx, 1167

Aelred was born at Hexham in 1109. His father was a priest and he entered the Cistercian Order at Rievaulx in about 1133, after spending some years in the court of King David of

Scotland. He became Abbot of Revesby in 1143 and returned to Rievaulx four years later to become abbot and there to spend the remainder of his life. He was profoundly influential through his spiritual writings, which he began at the request of Bernard of Clairvaux, the two having a similar approach to the spiritual life. Because of this, Aelred was often called 'The Bernard of the North'. He died on this day at Rievaulx in the year 1167.

A Reading from the *Pastoral Prayers* of Aelred of Rievaulx

A Special Prayer for Wisdom

These things, my Hope,
I need for my own sake.
But there are others that I need
not only for myself, but for the sake of those
to whom you bid me be a power for good,
rather than merely a superior.

There was a wise king once, who asked
that wisdom might be given him to rule your people.
His prayer found favour in your eyes,
you did hearken thereto;
and at that time you had not met the cross,
nor shown your people that amazing love.
But now, sweet Lord, behold before your face
your own peculiar people,
whose eyes are ever on your cross,
and who themselves are signed with it.

You have entrusted to your sinful servant
the task of ruling them.
My God, you know what a fool I am,
my weakness is not hidden from your sight.
Therefore, sweet Lord, I ask you not for gold,
I ask you not for silver, nor for jewels,
but only that you would give me wisdom,
that I may know to rule your people well.

O fount of wisdom, send her from your throne of might,
to be with me, to work with me,
to act in me, to speak in me,
to order all my thoughts and words and deeds and plans
according to your will,
and to the glory of your name,
to further their advance and my salvation.

alternative reading

A Reading from the treatise *On Spiritual Friendship* by Aelred of Rievaulx

What happiness, what security, what joy to have someone to whom you dare to speak on terms of equality as to another self; one to whom you need have no fear to confess your failings; one to whom you can unblushingly make known progress you have made in the spiritual life; one to whom you can entrust all the secrets of your heart and before whom you can place all your plans! What, therefore, is more pleasant than so to unite to oneself the spirit of another and of two to form one, that no boasting is thereafter to be feared, no suspicion to be dreaded, no correction of one by the other to cause pain, no praise on the part of one to bring a charge of adulation from the other.

'A friend,' says the Wise Man, 'is the medicine of life.' Excellent, indeed, is that saying. For medicine is not more powerful or more efficacious for our wounds in all our temporal needs than the possession of a friend who meets every misfortune joyfully, so that, as the Apostle says, shoulder to shoulder, they 'bear one another's burdens'. Even more – each one carries his own injuries even more lightly than that of his friend. Friendship, therefore, heightens the joys of prosperity and mitigates the sorrows of adversity by dividing and sharing them. Hence, the best medicine in life is a friend.

Even the philosophers took pleasure in the thought: not even water, nor the sun, nor fire do we use in more instances than a friend. In every action, in every pursuit, in certainty, in doubt, in every event and fortune of whatever sort, in private and in public, in every deliberation, at home and abroad, everywhere friendship is found to be appreciated, a friend a necessity, a friend's service a thing of utility.

Friendship is a stage bordering upon that perfection which consists in the love and knowledge of God, so that from being a friend of our neighbours, we become the friend of God, according to the words of the Saviour in the gospel: 'I will not now call you servants, but my friends.'

12 January

Benedict Biscop

Abbot of Wearmouth, Scholar, 689

Born a Northumbrian nobleman in 628, Benedict Biscop served at the court of King Oswy of Northumbria until he joined Wilfrid of York on his pilgrimage to Rome to the tombs of the apostles. He made a second trip accompanied by the King's son and on his way home was clothed a monk at the Benedictine house of Lérins. It was on his third trip to Rome that he met and returned to England with Theodore, the newly-appointed Archbishop of Canterbury, who made him Abbot of Saint Augustine's in 669. Five years later, he was permitted to make his own foundation at Wearmouth, which he had built in the Roman style and endowed with a huge library. He encouraged the development of the Uncial script which also acted as a vehicle for the propagation of the Roman Rite. His own scholarship, and that promoted through the religious houses he founded, played a large part in the acceptance of the primacy of Roman over Celtic practice throughout the north of England. Benedict Biscop died on this day in the year 689.

A Reading from *The Lives of the Abbots* by the Venerable Bede

Christ's devoted servant Biscop, called Benedict, built by the grace of God, a monastery in honour of Peter, the most blessed chief of the Apostles, near the mouth of the river Wear, on its north bank. Ecgfrith, the most revered and devout king of that people, supported him and gave him a grant of land. In spite of innumerable hardships from frequent journeys and illness, for sixteen years Biscop carefully ruled this monastery with the same piety with which he had built it. If I may cite the words of blessed Pope Gregory in which he glorifies the life of an abbot of the same name, 'Benedict was a man revered for the holiness of his life, blessed both in grace and in name.' He certainly had the judgement of an old man even from his earliest years, for his behaviour displayed a maturity well beyond his age, never surrendering his heart to dissipation. He was descended from a noble line of Angles, and by a corresponding nobility of mind was exalted to the everlasting company of the angels.

In conclusion, when he was a member of the court of King Oswy, he received at his hands an estate appropriate to his rank (he was then about twenty-five years old). But he turned his back on such worldly possessions so that he might secure for himself that which is eternal. In order that he might serve under the true King and earn an eternal kingdom in the heavenly city, he made light of temporal warfare and of a gift that would decay. He left his home, his family, and country for the sake of Christ and the Gospel, that he might receive a hundredfold and have eternal life. He turned his back on all sexual relations because he wanted to follow the Lamb radiant with the glory of chastity in the heavenly kingdoms. He refused to father mortal children, being foreordained of Christ to raise up for him immortal children, mature in all that belongs to the spirit, fit for the life of heaven.

13 January

Hilary

Bishop of Poitiers, Teacher of the Faith, 367

Note: In Scotland, Hilary is commemorated on 14 January.

Hilary was born at Poitiers in about the year 315; his family, though pagan, gave him an excellent education and he was proficient in Latin and Greek. After extensive personal study, he tells us that he was baptized at the age of thirty. He was elected bishop of the city in the year 350 and immediately became caught up in the Arian controversy, himself asserting that mortals of this world were created to practise moral virtues, thus reflecting the One in whose image they are made, the eternal and creative first cause, God; and that Jesus Christ, the incarnate Son of God, is of one substance with the Father. His learning and oratory led to his title of 'Athanasius of the West'. He was known as a gentle, kind friend to all, even though his writings seemed severe at times. He died in the year 367.

A Reading from the treatise *On the Trinity* by Hilary of Poitiers

When I began to search for the meaning of life, I was at first attracted by the pursuit of wealth and leisure. As most people discover there is little satisfaction in such things, and a life oriented to the gratification of greed or killing time is unworthy of our humanity. We have been given life in order to achieve something worthwhile, to make good use of our talents, for life itself points us to eternity. How otherwise could one regard as a gift from God this life which is painful, fraught with anxiety, and which starts in infancy with a blank mind and ends in the rambling conversations of the old? It is my belief that human beings, prompted by our very nature, have always sought to raise our sights through the teaching and practice of the virtues such as patience, chastity and forgiveness, in the conviction that a good life is secured only through good deeds and good thoughts. Could the immortal God have given us life with no other horizon but death? Could the Giver of good inspire us with a sense of life only to have it overshadowed by the fear of death?

Thus I sought to know the God and Father who has given us this great gift of life, to whom I felt I owed my existence, in whose service was honour, and on whom my hopes were fixed. I was inflamed by a passionate desire to apprehend or know this God.

Some religions teach that there are a variety of deities, with male gods and female gods, and people trace an entire lineage of them one from another. Other religions teach that there are powerful deities and less powerful ones, each with different characteristics. Yet others claim that there is no God at all and worship nature instead, which they say came into being purely by chance vibrations and collisions. Most people, however, admit that God exists, but feel that he is ignorant or indifferent to the lot of humanity.

I was reflecting on these various ideas when I chanced upon the books that, according to Jewish tradition, were written by Moses and the prophets. In them I discovered that God the creator bears witness to himself in these words: 'I am who I am.' I was amazed by the perfection of this insight which puts into intelligent language the incomprehensible knowledge of God. Nothing better suggests God as Being. 'The God who is' can have neither end nor beginning.

I came to see that there is no space without God: space does not exist apart from God. God is in heaven, in hell, and beyond the seas. God lives in everything and enfolds everything. God embraces all that is, and is embraced by the universe: confined to no part within it, he encompasses all that exists.

My soul drew joy from contemplating the mystery of God's wisdom, his sheer majesty, and I worshipped the eternity and immeasurable greatness of my Father and creator. But I longed also to behold his beauty. And here my mind was baffled, overcome by its own limitations, but I discovered in these words of the prophet a magnificent statement about God: 'From the greatness and beauty of created things comes a corresponding perception of their creator.'

I then went on to learn the truths taught by the apostle in the fourth Gospel. I learned more about God than I had expected. I understood that my creator was God born of God. I learned that the Word was God and was with God from the beginning. I came to know the light of the world. I understood that the Word was made flesh and dwelt among us and that those who welcomed him became children of God – not by a birth in flesh but in faith.

In all this my soul had discovered a hope bigger than I had ever imagined possible. It is a gift of God offered to everyone. My soul joyfully received the revelation of this mystery because by means of my flesh I was drawing near to God; by means of my faith I was called to a new birth. I was given freedom and empowered to receive a new birth from on high.

13 January

Kentigern (Mungo)

Missionary Bishop in Strathclyde & Cumbria, 603

Note: In Wales, Kentigern is commemorated on 14 January.

Kentigern, also known affectionately as Mungo, which means 'darling', is reputed to have been the grandson of a British prince in southern Scotland and to have attended a monastic school at Culross. According to tradition, he became a missionary to the Britons living in Strathclyde and was elected their bishop. Following the persecution of Christians, he fled to Wales, but eventually returned to Strathclyde where he continued his work of evangelism. He died in the year 603 and his tomb is in Saint Mungo's Cathedral in Glasgow.

A Reading from *The Life of Saint Kentigern* by Jocelyn of Furness

Blessed Kentigern began to realise from his frequent falls and increasing frailty that the end of the earthly tent which housed his poor body was near at hand. The foundation of his faith had always been built upon a rock, and this continued to be the source of his inner strength. By this faith he was confident that he had 'a dwelling place, not made by hands, prepared for him in heaven' once his earthly home was dissolved.

Beloved by God and mortals alike, and aware that the hour for his departure from this world to the Father of lights was near, he was anointed, receiving forgiveness for his sins, and took strength from receiving the life-giving sacrament of the Lord's body and blood. So armoured, the ancient serpent, lying in wait at his heel, would be unable to sink in his poisoned fangs and inflict a lethal wound, but would rather flee vanquished, his head crushed.

Indeed, as a result of the Lord's action in quickly crushing Satan under his feet lest his soul be ensnared in its journey from Egypt, trapped by its 'enemies at the gate', this most excellent watchman was able to wait in patience upon the Lord who had saved him from the stormwind. In his life he had had to endure many perils and dangers on the open sea; and now, with the 'haven that he longed for' in sight he was grateful for the peaceful navigation of this final journey. In the inner region of his desires he had already cast the anchor of hope, an anchor which reached out within the veil to where the pioneer, the Lord Jesus, had gone before him.

In all this Jesus was preparing for Kentigern the only means of leaving the tents of Kedar and entering the land of the living, so that, as it were, this most excellent athlete might receive at the hands of the supernal king in that city of hosts, the heavenly Jerusalem, a crown of glory, a diadem of the kingdom which does not wither but which is eternal.

13 January

George Fox

Founder of the Society of Friends (Quakers), 1691

George Fox was born at Fenny Drayton in Leicestershire in 1624. The son of a weaver, he was himself apprenticed to a shoe-maker. He became something of a wayfarer from 1643 for about three years, loosening all ties with his family and friends. The 'Inner Light of the Living Christ' became his watchword in 1646 and he began to preach that the truth could only be found through the Inner Voice speaking directly to each soul. His society of 'The Friends of Truth' was formed at about this time, clearly as a protest against the authoritarianism of the Presbyterian system, and many believers joined. Because they welcomed God into the soul, often whilst in a state of trance, which caused much body movement, Gervase Bennet nicknamed them the Quakers in 1650; although meant as a term of abuse, it quickly became a name they themselves adopted. Fox spent several spells in gaol because of his determination to preach where he would and what he willed; he also made many missionary journeys around England, on the Continent and to North America and the West Indies. He had a charismatic personality combined with excellent organizational abilities, which proved a solid foundation for ensuring the continuance of his beliefs and practices. He died on this day in 1691.

A Reading from the Journal of George Fox for 1661

Our principle is, and our practices have always been, to seek peace and ensue it, and to follow after righteousness and the knowledge of God, seeking the good and welfare, and doing that which tends to the peace of all. We know that wars and fightings proceed from the lusts of men, out of which lusts the Lord hath redeemed us, and so out of the occasion of war. The occasion of which war, and war itself (wherein envious men, who are lovers of themselves more than lovers of God, lust, kill, and desire to have men's lives and estates) ariseth from the lust. All bloody principles and practices, we, as to our own particulars, do utterly deny, with all outward wars and strife and fightings with outward weapons, for any end or under any pretence whatsoever. And this is our testimony to the whole world.

That the spirit of Christ, by which we are guided, is not changeable, so as once to command us from a thing as evil and again to move unto it; and we do certainly know, and so testify to the world, that the spirit of Christ, which leads us into all Truth, will never move us to fight and war against any man with outward weapons, neither for the kingdom of Christ, nor for the kingdoms of this world.

And this is both our principle and practice, and hath been from the beginning, so that if we suffer, as suspected to take up arms or make war against any, it is without any ground from us; for it neither is nor ever was in our hearts, since we owned the Truth of God; neither shall we ever do it, because it is contrary to the spirit of Christ, his doctrine, and the practice of his apostles, even contrary to him for whom we suffer all things, and endure all things.

And whereas men come against us with clubs, staves, drawn swords, pistols cocked, and do beat, cut and abuse us, yet we never resisted them, but to them our hair, backs, and cheeks have been ready. It is not an honour to manhood nor to nobility to run upon harmless people who lift not up a hand against them, with arms and weapons.

15 January

Maurus and Placid

Disciples of Benedict, *c.*580

According to the Dialogues of Gregory the Great, written shortly after the death of Saint Benedict, Maurus and Placid were two boys entrusted to the care of Benedict at his monastery in Subiaco. The custom of giving children to monasteries in this way was already established by the sixth century: that they were children of the nobility indicates the level of the acceptance and influence of monasticism in the Christian West. Pope Gregory tells us that on one occasion Maurus saved the young Placid from drowning. Maurus later gave his name to the French Benedictine Congregation of Saint Maur (1621–1818) which became famous for its learning and scholarship.

A Reading from the *Dialogues* of Gregory the Great

As Benedict's influence spread over the surrounding countryside because of his signs and wonders, a great number of men gathered around him to devote themselves to the service of God. Christ blessed Benedict's work and before long he had established twelve monasteries in the locality, each with an abbot and twelve monks. There were some monks whom Benedict kept with him because he felt they needed his personal guidance.

It was about this time that pious noblemen from Rome first came to visit the saint and left their sons with him to be schooled in the service of God. Thus Euthicius brought his son Maurus, and a senator called Tertullus brought his son Placid, both of them very promising boys. Maurus was in fact a little older than Placid, and had already acquired solid virtue, and was soon to prove very helpful to his saintly master. But Placid was still only a child.

Once while blessed Benedict was in his room, one of his monks, the boy Placid, went down to the lake to get some water. But in letting the bucket fill too rapidly, the boy lost his balance, fell into the lake and the current seized him in no time at all and carried him about a stone's throw from the shore. Though inside the monastery at the time, the man of God suddenly became aware of what was happening and shouted to Maurus: 'Hurry, Brother Maurus. The boy Placid who just went down for water has fallen into the lake and the current is carrying him off.'

What followed was remarkable and unheard of since the time of Peter the apostle. Maurus asked for a blessing and on receiving it hurried out to fulfil his abbot's command. He kept on running even over the surface of the water till he reached the place where Placid was drifting helplessly. Pulling him up by the hair, Maurus dragged him to the shore, still under the impression that he was on dry land. It was only when he set foot on the ground that he looked over his shoulder and realised that he had walked across the surface of the water. He was suddenly overcome with fear and amazement at what had happened, and returned to his abbot and told him all about it.

The holy man refused to take any credit for the deed and attributed it to the obedience of his disciple. Maurus, on the other hand, claimed that it was due to the wisdom of his abbot's command. He could not have been responsible for the miracle himself, he said, since he was not even aware that he was performing it. While they were carrying on this friendly banter of humility, the question was settled by the boy who had been rescued. 'When I was being dragged out of the water,' Placid said, 'I sensed the abbot's cloak over my head; it was he whom I thought was rescuing me and bringing me to the shore.'

17 January

Antony of Egypt

Hermit and Abbot, 356

Born in about the year 251, Antony heard the gospel message: 'If you would be perfect, go, sell your possessions, and give the money to the poor, and you will have treasure in heaven; then come, follow me.' He was twenty years old and rich, following the death of his parents, but he did as the gospel instructed and went to live in the desert, living an austere life of manual work, charity and prayer. His many spiritual struggles left him both wise and sensible and he became a spiritual guide for many who flocked to him. His simple rule of personal discipline and prayer was taken up and spread throughout Christendom. He died peacefully in the desert in the year 356 at the great age of 105, asking that he be buried secretly, so that his person might be hidden in death as in life.

A Reading from *The Life of Antony* by Athanasius of Alexandria

Antony was an Egyptian by race. His parents were well born and prosperous, and since they were Christians, he also was reared in Christian manner. Following their death he was left alone with one young sister. He was about eighteen or even twenty years old, and he was responsible both for the home and his sister. Six months had not passed since the death of his parents when, going to the Lord's house as usual and gathering his thoughts, he considered while he walked how the apostles, forsaking everything, followed their Saviour, and how in the Acts of Apostles some sold what they possessed and took the proceeds and placed them at the feet of the apostles for distribution among those in need, and what great hope is stored up for such people in heaven.

He went into the church pondering these things, and just then it happened that the gospel was being read, and he heard the Lord saying to the rich young man: 'If you would be perfect, go sell what you possess and give to the poor, and you will have treasure in heaven.' It was as if by God's design he held the saints in his recollection, and as if the passage were read on his account. Immediately Antony went out from the Lord's house and gave to the townspeople the possessions he had from his forebears (three hundred very beautiful *arourae* of land) so that they would not disturb him or his sister in the least. And selling all the rest that was portable, when he had collected sufficient money, he donated it to the poor, keeping back a few things for his sister.

But when, entering the Lord's house once more, he heard in the gospel the Lord saying: 'Do not be anxious about tomorrow', he could not remain any longer, but going out he gave those remaining possessions also to the needy. Placing his sister in the charge of respected and trusted virgins, and giving her over to the convent for rearing, he devoted himself from then on to the discipline rather than to the household, giving heed to himself and patiently training himself. There were not yet many monasteries in Egypt, and no monk knew at all the great desert, but each of those wishing to give attention to his life disciplined himself in isolation, not far from his own village. At first Antony also began by remaining in places proximate to his village. And going forth from there, if he heard of some zealous person anywhere, he searched him out like the wise bee.

He worked with his hands, having heard that 'he who is idle, let him not eat'. He spent what he made partly on bread, and partly on those in need. He prayed constantly, since he learned also that it is necessary to pray unceasingly in private. For he paid such close attention to what was read that nothing from Scripture did he fail to take in – rather he grasped everything, and in him the memory took the place of books.

Living his life in this way, Antony was loved by all. People used to call him 'God-loved', and some hailed him as 'son', and others as 'brother'.

17 January

Charles Gore

Bishop and Founder of the Community of the Resurrection, 1932

Born in 1853, Gore became one of the most influential of Anglican theologians. He helped reconcile the Church to some aspects of Biblical criticism and scientific discovery, yet was catholic in his interpretation of the faith and sacraments. He was also concerned to bring catholic principles to bear on social problems. As an Oxford don and then as a Canon of Westminster, he was renowned for his preaching. In the 1890s, he was the founder – and first leader – of the Community of the Resurrection, which in later years settled at Mirfield in Yorkshire. From 1902, he was successively Bishop of Worcester, Birmingham and Oxford. He was much mourned at his death on this day in the year 1932.

A Reading from *Belief in God* by Charles Gore

The world in which we live today can only be described as chaotic in the matter of religious beliefs. Of course, there are very many persons whom lack of seriousness or lack of education render indifferent to religious problems. And there are some intelligent and serious people who more or less deliberately and successfully seclude themselves from the strife of tongues and live unmoved in the light of their own religious traditions; and others again who, in despair of attaining the religious peace which they need by any other means, take refuge under the shelter of some religious authority which admits of no questioning, whether it be the Roman Catholic Church or Christian Science. But wherever men and women are to be found who care about religion and feel its value, and who at the same time feel bound, as they say, 'to think for themselves', there we are apt to discover the prevailing note to be that of uncertainty and even bewilderment, coupled very often with a feeling of resentment against the Church or against organised religion on account of what is called its 'failure'.

It is my belief that a great deal of scepticism is due, not really to the absence of adequate grounds for conviction, but to confusion of mind, to an excessive deference to current intellectual fashions, and to the fact that a person has never thoroughly and systematically faced the problems. It seems to me that the right course for anyone who cannot accept the mere voice of authority, but feels the imperative obligation to 'face the arguments' and to think freely, is to begin at the beginning and to see how far he can reconstruct his religious beliefs, stage by stage on a secure foundation, as far as possible without any preliminary assumptions. This at least is the only course which the present writer has found himself able either to adopt in his own case or to recommend to others. It means an equally frank cross-questioning of traditional religious beliefs and of the current dogmas of the contemporary intellectual world. This is too often forgotten. There is a very large number of people who reject traditional religious authority with contempt, and go on even naively to accept, without any serious questioning, the oracles of the day.

Deliberately to enter upon this process of reconstruction from the beginning does not, of course, require the abandonment of the religious beliefs and practices which someone holds already. Quite the contrary. He will make the most of the precious gift of faith, even while he is enquiring into its basics. It is part of the experience he is to interpret. It gives him his understanding of the questions at issue.

Moreover, though the process of reconstruction will be different in the case of each person, according as the intellectual equipment and opportunity of individuals are different, yet it ought to be possible for all who have to face life for themselves and use their powers of thought. All that is really essential is sincerity and the readiness to make the necessary effort of mind. It is the aim of my writing to help especially the ordinary educated man and woman in this process.

alternative reading

A Reading from an essay entitled *The Holy Spirit and Inspiration* by Charles Gore

It is because of the gradualness of the Spirit's method that it lays so great a strain on human patience. The spiritually-minded of all ages have tended to find the visible Church a very troubled and imperfect home. Most startling disclosures of the actual state of ecclesiastical disorder and moral collapse, may be gathered out of the Christian Fathers. Thus to found a 'pure Church' has been the instinct of impatient zeal since Tertullian's day. But the instinct has to be restrained, the visible Church has to be borne with, because it is the Spirit's purpose to provide a home for the training and improvement of the imperfect. 'Let both grow together unto the harvest.' 'A bruised reed will he not break, and smoking flax will he not quench.' The Church must have her terms of communion, moral and intellectual: this is essential to keep her fundamental principles intact, and to prevent her betraying her secret springs of strength and recovery. But short of this necessity she is tolerant. It is her note to be tolerant, morally and theologically. She is the mother, not the magistrate.

No doubt her balanced duty is one difficult to fulfil. At times she has been puritanical, at others morally lax; at times doctrinally lax, at others rigid. But, however well or ill she has fulfilled the obligations laid on her, this is her ideal. She is the guardian, the depository of a great gift, a mighty presence, which in its essence is unchanging and perfect, but is realised very imperfectly in her experience and manifested life.

This is what Saint Thomas Aquinas means when he says 'that to believe in the Church is only possible if we mean by it to believe in the Spirit vivifying the Church'. The true self of the Church is the Holy Spirit, but a great deal in the Church at any date does not belong to her true self, and is obscuring the Spirit's mind. Thus the treasure is in earthen vessels, it is sometimes a light hid under a bushel; and the Church is the probation of faith, as well as its encouragement.

18 January

The Confession of Peter

The beginning of the ministry of the Apostle Peter at Rome has been commemorated in that city from ancient times. The feast, known as the 'Chair of Peter', is a reminder of the chair or cathedra on which a bishop sits and teaches. The traditional readings for the day include Peter's acclamation of Jesus, 'You are the Messiah, the Son of the living God', a confession which has given its name to this commemoration. Since 29 June may be observed as the feast of both Peter and Paul, today's feast allows Peter to be commemorated alone, and mirrors the remembrance of Paul a week later. These two days, the Confession of Peter and the Conversion of Paul, bracket the Week of Prayer for Christian Unity. As Paul's conversion reminds us that we are united in a call to proclaim Jesus among the nations, so Peter's confession reminds us that we are united in proclaiming the divine revelation of Jesus Christ, 'the Son of the living God'.

A Reading from a sermon by Leo the Great

The Lord once asked the apostles what people thought of him. As long as they related the uncertainties of the foolish about him, they all said the same. But when Jesus asked the disciples what they themselves actually thought, it was the man who held first place among the apostles who was first to confess the Lord.

Peter declared, 'You are the Christ, the son of the living God.' To this Jesus replied, 'Blessed are you, Simon Bar-Jonah, for flesh and blood has not revealed this to you, but my Father who is heaven.' In other words, you are blessed because my Father has taught you this. You have not been deceived by the opinions of the world, but informed by heavenly inspiration; it was not flesh and blood, but the One whose Son I am who has revealed this to you.

Jesus continued, 'And I tell you', meaning, that as my Father has revealed to you my divinity, so I will now make known to you your high position: 'that you are Peter.' What Jesus means is that I am the secure rock, the cornerstone which unites, that foundation which no one else can ever lay. But you Peter also are a rock because by my strength you are made firm, with the result that you and I share together those things which are my special prerogative by right.

'And on this rock I shall build my church, and the gates of hell shall not prevail against it.' On this strong foundation, Jesus says, I will build an everlasting temple and my church will rise high to heaven upon the strength of this faith. The gates of hell will not imprison this confession, nor the chains of death bind it. Your voice is the voice of life: as it lifts up to heaven those who confess it, so it plunges into hell those who deny it. That is why Jesus said to blessed Peter, 'I will give you the keys of the kingdom of heaven. Whatever you bind on earth shall be bound in heaven, and whatever you loose on earth shall be loosed in heaven.'

The right to this power was handed on to the other apostles and the provisions of this decree have been passed on to all the leaders of the church. But it was not an idle gesture to put into one person's keeping what was to be communicated to all. This commission was given to Peter in particular because the example of Peter is placed before all the leaders of the church.

alternative reading

A Reading from a homily by John Chrysostom

Peter was to be entrusted with the keys of the church, or rather, he was entrusted with the keys of heaven; to him would be committed the whole people of God. The Lord said to him, 'Whatever you bind on earth shall be bound in heaven, and whatever you loose on earth shall be loosed in heaven.' Peter was inclined to be severe, so if he had also been impeccable, what forbearance would he have displayed towards those in his charge? His falling into sin was a providential grace to teach him from experience to be kind in his dealing with others.

Just reflect who it was whom God was permitting to fall into sin – Peter, the head of the apostles, the firm foundation, the unshakeable rock, the most important member of the church, the safe harbour, the strong tower; Peter, the one who had said to Christ, 'Even if I have to die with you I shall never deny you'; Peter, who by divine revelation confessed the truth saying, 'You are the Christ, the Son of the living God.'

The gospel relates that on the night that Christ was betrayed Peter went indoors and was standing beside the charcoal fire warming himself when a serving girl accosted him and said, 'You too were with him yesterday.' But Peter answered, 'I do not know him.' And yet, just now Peter, you said, 'Even if I have to die with you.' And yet here you are denying him and saying that you do not know him. O Peter, is this the content of your promise? You were never tortured or beaten; but at the words of a girl you take refuge in denial.

Once again the girl said to him, 'You too were with that man yesterday.' And again he said, 'I have no idea what you are talking about.' Who was it that spoke to you that prompted you to make such a denial? It was not some important person, but a woman, a doorkeeper, an outcast, a servant, someone of no account. She spoke to you and you answered with a flat denial. What a strange thing, here is a girl, a prostitute, accosting Peter and he is immediately shaken in his faith! Peter, the pillar, the rampart, could not bear the threat of a girl! She had but to speak and the pillar swayed, the rampart moved!

A third time she repeated, 'You too were with that man yesterday.' And a third time he denied it. Finally, Jesus looked at him, reminding him of his declaration of loyalty. Peter understood, repented of his sin, and wept. Mercifully, however, Jesus forgave him his sin because he knew that Peter, being human, was weak.

Now, as I have suggested already, the reason why God's plan permitted Peter to sin was because he was to be entrusted with the whole people of God, and sinlessness would have compounded his severity and might have made him intolerant towards his brothers and sisters. He fell into sin so that remembering his own sin and the Lord's forgiveness, he might also forgive others out of love for them. This was God's providential ordering. The one to whom the church was to be entrusted, the pillar of the churches, the harbour of faith, was allowed to sin. Peter, the teacher of the world, was permitted to sin in order that having been forgiven himself, he might be merciful to others.

18 January

Amy Carmichael

Founder of the Dohnavur Fellowship, spiritual writer, 1951

Amy Carmichael was born in 1867 at Millisle, County Down, to a Presbyterian family. In 1892 she felt called to be a missionary and went first to Japan, before going to India. She finally settled at Dohnavur and began her work with children. Eventually this work led to the founding of the Dohnavur Fellowship in 1926 'to save children in mortal danger'. An accident in 1931 left her an invalid, but she lived on in India, where she exercised a valued ministry as a spiritual teacher and writer. She remained at Dohnavur for the rest of her life, dying on this day in 1951.

A Reading from *Things as they are: mission work in southern India* by Amy Carmichael

Success – what is it worth? So transparent a thing is the glamour of success to clear-seeing poet-eyes, and should it dazzle the Christian to whom nothing is of any worth but the thing that endures? Should arguments based upon comparisons between the apparent success of work at home as distinguished from work abroad influence us in any way? Is it not very solemn, this calm, clear setting forth of a truth which touches each of us? 'Every man's work shall be made manifest, for the Day shall declare it, because it shall be revealed by fire, and the fire shall try every man's work of what sort it is.' And as we realise the perishableness of all work, however apparently successful, except the one work done in the one way God means, oh, does it not stir us up to seek with an intensity of purpose which will not be denied, to find out what that one work is?

The same thought comes out in the verse which tells us that the very things we are to do are prepared before, and we are 'created in Christ Jesus' to do them. If this is so, then will the doing of anything else seem worthwhile when we look back and see life as God sees it?

19 January

Wulfstan

Bishop of Worcester, 1095

Born in about the year 1009, Wulfstan's first twenty-five years after his ordination were spent in the monastery at Worcester. Against his will, he was elected Bishop of Worcester in 1062, but went on to prove an able administrator and pastor. He carefully and gently nurtured both

Church and State through the transition from Saxon to Norman rule. He died at Worcester on this day in the year 1095.

A Reading from *The Life of Saint Wulfstan* by William of Malmesbury

Having been consecrated a bishop, Wulfstan immediately turned his mind to works of piety; indeed, the very next day he dedicated a church to Blessed Bede. It was fitting that he should have begun his episcopal ministry by dedicating a church to one whose name stands first in English scholarship. That day Wulfstan watered the people with so flowing a sermon that no one doubted that he was inspired by the Holy Spirit with the same powerful eloquence that had once moved the tongue of Bede. And not only on this occasion but throughout his life, the fame of Wulfstan's preaching meant that wherever he was to dedicate a church, large crowds of people gathered to hear him.

He loved preaching, and always spoke about Christ, resolutely setting Christ before his hearers so that even the most reluctant might hear his name. In his personal discipline, in vigils and in fasting, he was no less rigorous. His prayers assaulted heaven, so that of him and others like him, the Lord rightly said: 'The kingdom of heaven has suffered violence, and the violent take it by force.'

Wulfstan maintained a balanced life, never relinquishing his two-fold calling. Although bishop, he remained obedient to the discipline of the monastic life: as a monk, his way of life revealed the authority of a bishop. His integrity singled him out from his contemporaries. To any who came to him for counsel, he was full of wisdom and accessible. If a discernment had to be made, he was impartial in his assessments and swift to give his decision. When he was put in the role of judge, he would always err on the side of mercy. He would never seek the patronage of the rich or reject the poor for their poverty. He was unmoved by flattery and disliked the flatterer. He would never distort the claims of justice out of fear of the powerful, nor pay them any honour they did not merit. When he was praised for a good deed, Wulfstan praised the grace of God that had made it possible; and thus he never succumbed to pride.

If ever Wulfstan was ridiculed, he forgave those who ridiculed him, secure in a good conscience, but this occurred seldom since he cherished each person in his care as if his own child, with the result that all loved him as their father. His heart was always glad and his face bright because even in this life he was already tasting in hope of the waters of the wells of heaven; indeed, now he is drinking long draughts.

Although he never neglected the interior life of his soul, he was never slack or lazy in dealing with the exterior duties that required his attention. He built many churches in the diocese, beginning each project with zeal, and completing each nobly. Foremost among these was the cathedral church of Worcester which Wulfstan erected from its foundation to its final stone. The number of monks in the cathedral monastery increased and he brought them under the *Rule* of the Order.

Yours, O Lord, are the graces that we praise in Wulfstan, seeing that all our life is yours.

20 January

Richard Rolle of Hampole

Spiritual Writer, 1349

Richard Rolle was born in about the year 1300 in Thornton in Yorkshire, where he first began to live the hermit life at the age of eighteen, after breaking off his education at the University of Oxford. After moving his hermitage to several other sites, he finally settled close to the Cistercian nuns at Hampole, also in Yorkshire, where he undertook much of his prolific writing on mysticism and asceticism. He wrote in Latin but also produced many texts directly in English and even in the Northumbrian dialect. His writings were widely influential and he was venerated for at least three hundred years after his death on this day in the year 1349.

A Reading from *The Form of Living* by Richard Rolle

Three degrees of love I wish to describe to you, because I would like you to reach the highest. The first degree is insuperable when nothing which is contrary to the love of God can overcome it, but it is robust in the face of all temptations, and constant, whether you are in easy circumstances or in anxiety, in good health or in sickness, so that it seems to you that for the sake of retaining it perpetually you would not anger God one single time, not for all the world. In this mode your love shall be insuperable, which nothing can pull down – rather it goes darting upward. Blessed is he or she who is in this degree, yet even so those are more blessed who, having obtained this degree, might attain to the second, which is inseparable.

Inseparable is your love when all your heart and your thought and your strength are so wholly, so entirely and so perfectly fastened, fixed and confirmed in Jesus Christ that your thought never slips away from him, never being parted from him except for sleeping; and as soon as you wake up, your heart is with him.

The third degree of love is the highest and most wonderful to attain; that is called singular because it has no equal. Singular love is the state where all comfort and consolation are excluded from your heart except those of Jesus Christ alone. Other delight and other joy it does not desire, for in this degree the sweetness of him is so invigorating and enduring, his love so burning and cheering that he or she who is in this degree can as easily feel the fire of love burning in their soul as you can feel your finger burn if you put it in the fire.

That fire, provided it is hot, is so delightful and so wonderful that I cannot describe it. Then your soul is loving Jesus, thinking Jesus, desiring Jesus, breathing only in its desire for him, singing to him, catching fire from him, resting in him. Then the song of praising and of love has arrived. Then your thought turns into song and into harmony. Then you feel compelled to sing the psalms which previously you recited; then you have to spend a long time over just a few psalms. Then death will seem to you sweeter than honey, because then you are most certain to see him whom you love. Then you can boldly declare: 'I am languishing with love'; and you can say: 'I am sleeping but my heart is awake.'

The soul which has attained this third degree of love, then, is like burning fire and like the nightingale which loves song and harmony and exhausts itself in its great love; for in this way the soul is only comforted by its praising and loving of God, and until death comes is singing spiritually to Jesus and in Jesus.

21 January

Agnes

Child-Martyr at Rome, 304

The reason Agnes is one of the most well-known and widely-venerated of the early Roman martyrs is perhaps because of the expression of mature resilience and sheer bravery in a twelve-year-old girl. Agnes is reputed to have refused an arranged marriage because of her total dedication to Christ and stated that she preferred even death of the body to the death of her consecrated virginity. The growing veneration for the state of consecrated virginity at this time, combined with the last, major Roman persecution under the emperor Diocletian, climaxing in the shedding of an innocent child's blood, placed her at the forefront of veneration almost from the moment the persecution ended. She is believed to have died in the year 304 and her feast has ever since been celebrated on this day.

A Reading from the treatise *On Virginity* by Ambrose, Bishop of Milan

Today is the birthday of Saint Agnes. She is said to have suffered martyrdom at the age of twelve. The cruelty which did not spare even so young a child serves only to demonstrate more clearly the power of faith which found witness in one so young.

There was not even room in her little body for a wound. Though she could barely receive the sword's point, she could overcome it. Girls of her age tend to wilt under the slightest frown from a parent. Pricked by a needle, they cry as if given a mortal wound. But Agnes showed no fear of the blood-stained hands of her executioners. She was undaunted by the weight of clanging chains. She offered her whole body to the sword of the raging soldiers. Too young to have any acquaintanceship with death, she nevertheless stood ready before it. Dragged against her will to the altar of sacrifice, she was ready to stretch out her hands to Christ in the midst of the flames, making the triumphant sign of Christ the victor on the altars of sacrilege. She was even prepared to put her neck and hands into iron bands – though none of them was small enough to enclose her tiny limbs.

Is this a new kind of martyrdom? The girl was too young to be punished, yet old enough to wear a martyr's crown; too young for the contest, but mature enough to gain victory. Her tender years put her at a disadvantage, but she won the trial of virtue. If she had been a bride, she could not have hastened to her wedding night as much as she, a virgin, went with joyful steps to the place of her execution, her head adorned with Christ himself rather than plaits, with a garland woven of virtues instead of flowers.

Everyone was weeping, but she herself shed no tears. The crowds marvelled at her spendthrift attitude to life, discarding it untasted, but as if she had lived it to the full. All were astonished that one not yet of legal age, could give testimony to God. It was her final achievement that people believed that she must have received the inner resource for such testimony from God, for humanly speaking it was impossible. They reasoned that what is beyond the power of nature can only come from its creator.

You can imagine with what threats the executioner tried to frighten her; what promises were made to seduce her; indeed, how many people there were who would have been prepared to marry her! But she answered, 'It would insult my Spouse if I were to give myself to another. I will be his who first chose me for himself. Executioner, why do you delay? If eyes that I do not want, desire this body, then let it perish.'

She stood still, praying, and offered her neck. You could see the executioner trembling as though he were himself condemned. His right hand began to shake, and his face drained of colour aware of her danger, though the child herself showed no fear. In one victim then, we are given a twofold witness in martyrdom, to modesty and to religion. Agnes preserved her virginity and gained a martyr's crown.

22 January

Vincent of Saragossa

Deacon, first Martyr of Spain, 304

Vincent was born in Saragossa in Aragon in the latter part of the third century and was ordained to the diaconate by Valerian, his bishop in that city. When the Diocletian persecutions began, both men were brought before the Roman governor but, because Valerian stammered badly, he relied on Vincent to speak for them both. Vincent spoke eloquently for both his bishop and his church, proclaiming the good news of Jesus Christ and condemning paganism. He so angered the governor that he was immediately condemned to a painful death, reputedly on the gridiron. Thus he lived and gave his life in the tradition of Stephen, the first martyr and also a deacon; he died in the year 304 and his feast has been celebrated on this day since the persecutions ended in the year 312.

A Reading from a sermon of Augustine

With the eyes of faith we have just beheld an amazing sight, the sight of Vincent conquering far and wide. He conquered through the words he spoke and the punishment he received; he conquered in his confession of faith and in the sufferings he endured; he conquered when they burnt his flesh in the fire and threatened him with drowning; finally, he conquered even as he was being tortured and in death itself.

Who ever gave such endurance to one of his soldiers, if not the one who first shed his own blood for them? Of such it is said in the psalms: 'You, O Lord, are my hope, my trust, from my youth.'

A great struggle procures great glory: not human or worldly glory, but that which is divine and eternal. It is faith which contends, and when faith contends no one can overcome the flesh. For although our flesh may be torn and mutilated, who can ever perish when we have been redeemed by the blood of Christ? A wealthy person cannot bear to part with his wealth, so how can Christ ever be made to let go of those whom he has bought with his own blood? Vincent's death stands as a tribute not to the glory of man but to the glory of God.

From God comes all endurance. True endurance is holy, religious and upright. Christian endurance is a gift of God. There are thieves who bear torture with great endurance, not yielding, and overcoming their torturer; but afterwards they will be punished by eternal fire. It is the reason for death which distinguishes the endurance of the martyr from that of the hardened criminal. The punishment may be the same, but the reasons are different.

Vincent would have used in his prayers the very words from the psalms we have just sung: 'Judge me, O God, defend my cause against an ungodly people.' There was no doubt about his cause because he struggled for truth, for justice, for God, for Christ, for the faith, for the unity of the Church, for undivided love.

24 January

Cadoc

Abbot, 577

Cadoc was born of royal parentage about the year 497, and was educated at the monastic school of Tathan at Caerwent (Monmouthshire). He established a monastery at Llancarfan, in the Vale of Glamorgan, which soon became famous. The twelfth-century Life of Saint Cadoc tells us: 'There eagerly flowed together, from various districts of the whole of Britannia, very many clerics to Saint Cadoc, like rivers to the sea, that they might attain to imitate his wisdom and practice; for he always welcomed eagerly all, who steadily toiled in the service of God and paid heed to the divine scriptures.' Cadoc made visits to Ireland to study in the monastery of Lismore, and there was a frequent interchange between Llancarfan and Irish monasteries. With the coming of the Yellow Plague in the year 547, Cadoc fled to Brittany and established churches there. He returned to Llancarfan to rule as abbot-king of Glamorgan; and in his old age retired to Beneventum, probably near Brecon. There in the year 577 he was murdered by a soldier as he entered the church.

A Reading from *The Life of Saint Cadog*

There eagerly flowed together from various districts of the whole of Britannia very many clerics to Saint Cadog like rivers to the sea, that they might attain to imitate his wisdom and practice; for he always welcomed eagerly all who steadily toiled in the service of God and paid heed to the divine Scriptures. Hence the venerable man began to raise up a huge heap of earth, and to make in the same a very beautiful cemetery dedicated to the honour of God, wherein the bodies of the faithful might be buried round about the temple. Then, when the heap was completed, and the cemetery in the same prepared, he made four large foot-paths across four slopes of the mountains surrounding his monastery, making passable what had been impassable before, following literally and spiritually the teaching of the Gospel which states, 'Prepare a way for the Lord: make his paths straight.' Similarly, this man of God not only by labouring bodily with his hands converted crooked, uneven, and rough ways into smooth, but also turned the hearts of many, rough and perverse with diverse errors, into the straight way of the Lord.

Cadog also chose another place for himself, and caused to be thrown up in it from the soil of the earth another round tumulus like a fort, and on the tumulus to be erected what in the speech of the Britons is called Cadog's Kastil. For Cadog deemed it right to spend his life in the labours of his own hands, fearing to consume in idleness the labours of another, hoping by the stress of present endeavour to pass over to the glory of eternal rest, according to that saying of the Psalmist, 'You shall eat the labour of your hands', and that of the Apostle Paul,

'Let every one of you labour, working with your own hands, that you may have something to contribute to those in need'. And again, 'Let none of you eat the bread of idleness.' And again, 'He who refuses to work, let him not eat.'

24 January

Francis de Sales

Bishop of Geneva, Teacher of the Faith, 1622

Note: In Wales, Francis de Sales is commemorated on 23 January.

Francis de Sales was born in 1567 in the castle at Sales in Savoy. He was educated in Paris and Padua, first as a legal advocate, and then as a priest. His preaching against Calvinism began in 1593 to win back the Chablais to Roman Catholicism. In 1599 he was appointed Bishop-Coadjutor of Geneva, and moved to Annecy from where he administered the diocese when he became the Diocesan in 1602. It was not until 1799 that Roman Catholic worship was officially permitted again in Geneva. In his preaching and writings, particularly his book Introduction to the Devout Life, Francis concentrated on putting prayer and meditation within the reach of all Christians. He died at Lyons on 28 December 1622 and his body was translated to Annecy on this day in the year 1623.

A Reading from *Introduction to the Devout Life* by Francis de Sales

The world ridicules devotion in life, caricaturing devout people as peevish, gloomy and sullen, and insinuating that religion makes a person melancholy and unsociable. But the Holy Spirit, speaking through the mouths of the saints, and indeed through our Saviour himself, assures us that a devout life is wholesome, pleasant and happy.

The world observes how devout people fast, pray and suffer reproach; how they nurse the sick, give alms to the poor, restrain their temper and do similar deeds which in themselves and viewed in isolation, are hard and painful. But the world fails to discern the interior devotion which renders these actions agreeable, sweet and pleasant.

Look at the bees: they suck the bitter juice from thyme and convert it into honey because that is their nature. Devout souls, it is true, do experience bitterness in works of self-discipline, but they are engaged in a process that converts such bitterness into a delicious sweetness. Sour green fruits are sweetened by sugar, bringing a ripeness to what had been unwholesome to the palate. In the same way, true devotion is a spiritual sugar which takes away the bitterness of self-discipline. It counteracts the poor person's discontent and the rich person's smugness; the loneliness of the oppressed and the conceit of the successful; the sadness of one who lives alone and the dissipation of the one who is at the centre of society. In a word its gift is an equanimity and balance which refreshes the soul.

In creation God has commanded the plants to bring forth fruit, each according to its kind. Similarly, he commands all Christians, who are the living plants of his Church, to bring forth the fruits of devotion according to each person's ability and vocation. The practice of devotion will need to be adapted to the capabilities, jobs and duties of each individual. For example, it is not appropriate for a bishop to be leading the solitary life of a Carthusian; or for the father of a family to be refusing to put aside money as if he were a Franciscan; or for a tradesman to spend the entire day in church as if he were a religious; or for someone in religious vows to be endlessly interrupted by the needs of his neighbour as a bishop must be. Such a pattern of life and devotion is incompatible and ridiculous.

True devotion, however, harms no one; on the contrary, it brings a person to wholeness. If our devotional life is not compatible with our lawful vocation then it is manifestly false. Aristotle says that the bee extracts honey from flowers without ever injuring them, leaving them as fresh and as whole as it finds them. True devotion does better still; it not only does no harm to our vocation and employment, it adorns and beautifies them.

25 January

The Conversion of Paul

The conversion of the anti-Christian zealot, Saul, to the Apostle Paul is clearly related in the Acts of the Apostles, but it has to be remembered that this was a beginning of a process. Saul took some time to become Paul and to begin to understand the dimensions of his call to preach – to Jew and to Gentile – the saving power of Jesus, the Son of God. It was a whole life's journey for him. In his Letter to the Church in Galatia, Paul writes: 'God set me apart before I was born and called me through his grace. Three years after [the Damascus Road conversion], I went up to Jerusalem.' The preparation for this moment of his conversion was his whole life. This feast has been celebrated in the Church since the sixth century but became universal in the twelfth century.

A Reading from a homily *'In Praise of Saint Paul'* by John Chrysostom

Paul, more than anyone else, shows us what humanity really is, in what our nobility consists, and of what virtue this particular animal is capable. Each day Paul aimed ever higher; each day he rose up with greater ardour and faced with new eagerness the dangers that threatened him. He summed up his attitude in the words: 'I forget what is behind me and push on to what lies ahead.' When he saw death imminent, he bade others share his joy: 'Rejoice and be glad with me.' And when danger, injustice and abuse threatened, he said: 'I am content with weakness, mistreatment and persecution.'

These he called the weapons of righteousness, thus telling us that he derived immense profit from them.

Thus, amid the traps set for him by his enemies, with exultant heart he turned their every attack into a victory for himself; constantly beaten, abused and cursed, he boasted of it as though he were celebrating a triumphal procession and taking trophies home, and offered thanks to God for it all: 'Thanks be to God who is always victorious in us!' This is why he was far more eager for the shameful abuse that his zeal in preaching brought upon him than we are for the most pleasing honours, more eager for death than we are for life, for poverty than we are for wealth; he yearned for toil far more than others yearn for rest after toil. The one thing he feared, indeed dreaded, was to offend God; nothing else could sway him. Therefore, the only thing he really wanted was always to please God.

The most important thing of all to Paul, however, was that he knew himself to be loved by Christ. Enjoying this love, he considered himself happier than anyone else; were he without it, it would be no satisfaction to be the friend of principalities and powers. He preferred to be loved and be the least of all, or even to be among the damned, than be without that love and be among the great and honoured.

To be separated from that love was, in his eyes, the greatest and most extraordinary of torments; the pain of that loss would alone have been hell, and endless, unbearable torture. So too, in being loved by Christ he thought of himself as possessing life, the world, the angels, present and future, the kingdom, the promise and countless blessings. Apart from that love nothing saddened or delighted him; for nothing earthly did he regard as bitter or sweet.

Paul set no store by the things that fill our visible world, any more than one sets value on the withered grass of the field. As for tyrannical rulers or the people enraged against him, he paid them no more heed than gnats. Death itself and pain and whatever torments might come were but child's play to Paul, provided that thereby he might bear some burden for the sake of Christ.

I urge you, therefore, not only to admire, but also to follow his example of virtue. For in this way we will be able to share in the same crown of glory.

alternative reading

A Reading from a sermon of Augustine

Today we heard in our reading from the Acts of the Apostles how the apostle Paul from being a persecutor of Christians, became the great preacher of Christ. The encouragement we draw from his conversion, to which he himself testifies in his letters – indeed, he says, it was for this reason that he was pardoned by God for his sins, for the rage and violence with which he had dragged Christians to their death, for the way he became an agent of the fury of the Jews, not only in the stoning of the holy martyr Stephen but in delivering up and bringing many for punishment – is that none of us should ever despair of ourselves. Even if, like Paul, we have committed terrible sins, become ensnared in great crimes, we should never think ourselves beyond the reach of Christ's pardon who, hanging on the cross, prayed for his persecutors, saying: 'Father, forgive them, for they know not what they do.'

From a persecutor Paul was changed into a preacher and teacher of the nations. As he says when writing to Timothy, 'I was a blasphemer, a persecutor, and a man of violence: but I received mercy so that in me, as the foremost, Jesus Christ might display the utmost patience, making me an example to those who would come to believe in him for eternal life.' For by the grace of God we are healed of our sins in which we lay languishing. The medicine which heals our souls is God's alone because though the soul can wound itself, it is unable to heal itself.

With regard to our bodies, though it lies within our power to let ourselves become ill, it is not equally within our power to recover. If we push ourselves too hard or live self-indulgently, if we pursue a lifestyle incompatible with good health and abuse our bodies, one day we will fall ill and not be able to recover our health. In such circumstances we call for the help of a doctor. So also with the soul. That we should fall into sin that leads to death, exchanging mortality for immortality, allowing ourselves to be seduced by the devil, was all within our power. But healing is the prerogative of God alone.

It is to the afflicted and troubled that Christ the doctor comes, saying: 'The healthy have no need of the doctor, but those who are sick. I have not come to call the righteous, but sinners.' Christ is calling sinners to peace, he is calling the sick to health.

26 January

Timothy and Titus

Companions of Paul

On the day following the Conversion of Saint Paul, the Church remembers his two companions, Timothy and Titus, whom he describes as 'partners and fellow-workers in God's service', and to whom the so-called 'Pastoral Epistles' are dedicated. Timothy, we are told, was a native of Lystra in Asia Minor, who had a Jewish mother and a Greek father, whilst Titus was wholly Greek. It was because of Titus that Paul stood out against compulsory circumcision but, to avoid suspicion from other Jews, Paul insisted that Timothy be circumcised. Christian Tradition associates Timothy with the Christian community at Ephesus, and Titus with the care of the Christian community in Crete where he is honoured as the first bishop of Gortyna. Both men are honoured in the Church for their devotion and faithfulness to the gospel.

A Reading from a homily of John Chrysostom

Why did Paul write a second letter to Timothy? In his previous letter he had said that 'I hope to come to see you shortly,' but it is clear that this meeting did not take place. So instead of visiting him in person, Paul now consoles Timothy by letter – perhaps Timothy was grieving for Paul's absence, oppressed by the responsibilities of government which had been committed to him? For we should remember that even great people, when placed at the helm and charged with steering the course of the Church, can be overwhelmed, as it were, by the waves of duties that confront them. This was certainly the case when the gospel began first to be preached, when the ground was unploughed, and people were unresponsive and hostile. There were also many false teachings emanating from Jewish teachers which needed to be confronted.

Paul addresses Timothy not merely as his son, but as his 'beloved son'. Paul had called the Galatians his children, at the same time adding how he found himself once again 'in labour over them'. But here he bears particular witness to the virtue of Timothy by calling him beloved. Where love does not arise spontaneously with nature, it must come from an appreciation of worth. Our natural children are loved by us both on account of their worth and from the sheer force of nature; but when the children of faith are so loved, it can be for no other reason than their intrinsic worth. And this was especially the case with Paul who never acted from partiality.

Paul reminds Timothy 'to rekindle the gift of God that is within you through the laying on of my hands'. One can guess from these words how dispirited and dejected Paul must have believed Timothy to be at this time. Paul's words remind us that much zeal is required to stir up the gift of God in us. Just as a fire requires fuel, so grace requires our glad and willing consent if it is to be fervent. For it lies within our power to kindle or extinguish the grace of God within each of us. That is why Paul admonishes us: 'Do not quench the Spirit.' The Spirit is quenched by sloth and carelessness, but kept alive by being watchful and diligent.

As Paul goes on to say: 'God did not give us a spirit of fear, but rather a spirit of power and of love and of self-discipline.' In other words, we have not received the Spirit that we should not need to make any effort in life, but rather that we may speak with boldness. Many people are dominated by a spirit of fear, as is evident from the countless histories of wars. But to us God has given a spirit of power and of love for himself.

This is the work of grace, and yet not only of grace: we too have a part to play. For the same Spirit that makes us cry out 'Abba, Father!' inspires us with love both for God and for our neighbour that we may love one another. Love arises from this power, and from not being afraid; for nothing is so sure to dissolve love as fear and the suspicion of betrayal.

alternative reading

A Reading from the *Ecclesiastical History* of Eusebius of Caesarea

By his preaching to the Gentiles, Paul laid the foundations of the churches from Jerusalem by a circuitous route as far as Illyricum. This is obvious both from his own words and from those of Luke recorded in the Acts of the Apostles. From Peter's words we can gather the names of the provinces in which he preached the Gospel of Christ to the circumcised, proclaiming the message of the new Covenant. This is clearly stated in the letter which, as I have said, is accepted as his and in which he writes to the Hebrews of the Dispersion in Pontus and Galatia, Cappadocia, Asia and Bithynia. Of course, how many of them and which ones became genuine enthusiasts, and were judged fit to shepherd the churches founded by the apostles, is not easy to determine, except those whose names can be extracted from Paul's statements. For he had innumerable fellow-workers or, as he called them, 'fellow-soldiers'. Most of them he has honoured with an imperishable memory, paying them constant tribute in his various letters. Again, Luke in the Acts, in listing Paul's disciples, mentions them by name. We may instance Timothy, stated to have been the first bishop appointed to the see of Ephesus, as was Titus to the churches of Crete.

28 January

Thomas Aquinas

Priest, Philosopher and Teacher of the Faith, 1274

Thomas Aquinas has been described as the greatest thinker and teacher of the medieval Church. Born at Rocca Secca, near Aquino, in Italy, Thomas was educated first by the Benedictines at Monte Cassino, and then at the University of Naples. Against his family's wishes, he joined the mendicant Dominican Order of Preachers. His profound, theological wisdom and capacity to impart this, as well in homilies as in hymns, along with his gentleness of spirit in dealing with all, earned him the title 'the Angelic Doctor'. He died on 7 March

1274, en route to the Council of Lyons, and his feast has been celebrated on this day since 1970.

A Reading from the foreword and beginning of the *Summa Theologiae* of Thomas Aquinas

Since it is the duty of a teacher of Catholic truth not only to build up those who are mature in their faith, but also to shape those who are just beginning – as the apostle Paul himself records, 'As infants in Christ, I fed you with milk, not solid food, because you were not ready for it' – so the declared purpose of this work is to convey the things that pertain to the Christian religion in a way that is readily accessible to beginners.

We have noticed that newcomers are invariably put off reflecting more deeply upon their faith by various writings, intimidated partly by the swarm of pointless questions, articles, and arguments, but also because essential information is being communicated under the constraints of textual commentary or academic debate rather than sound educational methods, and because repetition breeds boredom and muddled thinking.

Eager, therefore, to avoid these and similar pitfalls, and trusting in the help of God, we shall try in this work to examine the claims of Christian teaching, and to be precise and clear in our language, as far as the matter under discussion allows.

It is clear that Christian teaching employs human reason, not so as to prove anything because that would undermine the merit of believing, but rather in order to elucidate the implications of its thought. We should note that just as grace never scraps our human nature, but instead brings it to perfection, so in the same way our natural ability to reason should assist faith as the natural loving inclination of our will yields to charity.

30 January

Charles

King and Martyr, 1649

Born in 1600, the second son of King James I, Charles became heir apparent when he was twelve on the death of his elder brother. He succeeded to the throne in 1625, where he came up against the increasing power of an antagonistic Parliament. Combined with the religious puritanism which was prevalent, this made Charles staunch in his resistance of the power of either force in the land. He frequently dismissed sittings of Parliament and tried to enforce high-church Anglican practice throughout both kingdoms of England and Scotland. Opposition resulted in civil war. After Charles' imprisonment and trial, he was put to death on this day in 1649. Although some see him as a victim of his own pride, his faith and willingness to die for what he believed in are not in doubt.

A Reading from a letter of Charles I to his son, the Prince of Wales, and delivered into the hands of his chaplain, the Bishop of London, just before his execution on 30 January 1649

With God, I would have you begin and end, who is King of Kings, the sovereign disposer of the kingdoms of the world, who pulleth down one and setteth up another. The best government and highest sovereignty you can attain to is to be subject to him, that the sceptre of his word and spirit may rule in your heart. The true glory of princes consists in advancing God's glory, in the maintenance of true religion and the Church's good; also in the dispensation of civil power, with justice and honour to the public peace.

Piety will make you prosperous, at least it will keep you from becoming miserable; nor is he much a loser that loseth all, yet saveth his own soul at last. To which centre of true happiness, God (I trust) hath and will graciously direct all these black lines of affliction which he hath been pleased to draw on me, and by which he hath (I hope) drawn me nearer to himself. You have already tasted of that cup whereof I have liberally drunk; which I look upon as God's physic, having that in healthfulness which it wants in pleasure.

Above all, I would have you, as I hope you are already, well grounded and settled in your religion, the best profession of which I have ever esteemed that of the Church of England, in which you have been educated; yet I would have your own judgement and reason now sealed to that sacred bond which education hath written, that it may be judiciously your own religion, and not other men's custom or tradition which you profess.

Let nothing seem little or despicable to you in matters which concern religion and the Church's peace, so as to neglect a speedy reforming and effectually suppressing errors and schisms. What may seem at first but as a hand-breadth, by seditious spirits, as by strong winds, are soon made a cover and darken the whole heaven.

Never charge your head with such a crown as shall, by its heaviness, oppress the whole body, the weakness of whose parts cannot return anything of strength, honour, or safety to the head, but a necessary debilitation and ruin. Your prerogative is best showed and exercised in remitting rather than exacting the rigour of the laws; there being nothing worse than legal tyranny.

In these two points of preservation of established religion and laws, I may (without vanity) turn the reproach of my sufferings, as to the world's censure, into the honour of a kind of martyrdom, as to the testimony of my conscience – the troublers of my kingdoms having nothing else to object against me but this, that I prefer religion and laws established before those alterations they propounded. And so indeed I do, and ever shall, till I am convinced by better arguments than what hitherto have been chiefly used against me – tumults, armies, and prisons.

I know God can – I hope he will – restore me to my rights. I cannot despair, either of his mercy, or my people's love and pity. At worst, I trust I shall but go before you to a better kingdom, which God hath prepared for me, and me for it, through my Saviour Jesus Christ, to whose mercy I commend you, and all mine.

Farewell, till we meet, if not on earth, yet in heaven.

31 January

Edan

Bishop of Ferns, 632

This bishop, the founder of Ferns diocese in County Wexford, is variously named Edan or Aedan, or M'Aed oc (Mogue). From early years the diocese has had a close link with the Church in Wales, and there was a traditional, though not chronological, spiritual relationship between David of Wales and Mogue of Ferns. He died on this day in the year 632.

A Reading from a homily of Gregory the Great

Our Lord said to his disciples: 'See, I am sending you out like lambs among wolves.' There are many people, when put in positions of authority, who become hard and severe, relishing the chance to tear their subordinates to pieces, and using their power to terrify and hurt those whom they are called to serve. There is no love in their hearts because they always need to be in control: they forget that they are called to nurture their people as a parent. They exchange humility for pride in the positions they occupy, and though outwardly they may sometimes appear indulgent, inwardly they are full of anger. It is of them that in another place in the Gospels our Lord says: 'They come to you in sheep's clothing, but inwardly they are ravenous wolves.'

My friends, we should remember that we are sent as lambs among wolves, and must therefore guard our innocence lest malice overtake us. Those who undertake any pastoral office should never be the cause of evil, and should actually be prepared to have to endure it. By gentleness they must soften the anger of the violent: wounded ourselves by ill treatment, we can bring healing to other sinners. If on a particular occasion a zeal for justice requires a display of severity, then let severity have its source in love and not brutality. In this way, authority is demonstrated outwardly, and inwardly we experience a true parental love for those in our care. This is what our blessed Master was teaching us when he himself demonstrated that his was no selfish love, being unconcerned with worldly honour or ambition.

31 January

Charles Mackenzie of Central Africa

Bishop and Missionary, 1862

The Universities Mission to Central Africa was formed in response to an appeal by David Livingstone. Charles Mackenzie was consecrated bishop in Cape Town in 1861 to lead this mission from South Africa up the Zambesi towards Lake Nyassa. The missionaries' preaching of the gospel and their efforts to secure the release of slaves provoked opposition from native leaders and Portuguese colonists. Charles succumbed to illness and died only a year after his consecration, a man of transparent and humble Christian devotion.

A Reading from *Mackenzie's Grave* by Owen Chadwick

Mackenzie was the simplest of men, if the epithet *simple* is used in its complimentary sense. Though an able mathematician, he was in a manner an unlearned man. He was content with a simple, practical faith. He barely felt the need of philosophizing about faith, of studying Christian history or Christian thought, he was uninterested in theological argument and believed himself incompetent, he took no pleasures in metaphysics. His was the logic of the heart, not of the head. Do we need oratory, or eloquence, or erudition? Like several of the mid-Victorian leaders of religion, he could not find the sparks to kindle truth in the volumes of systematic thinking which burdened the shelves of libraries in English vicarages. Dogmatic theology was necessary but arid. It was poetry and sermons which guided his mind in the apprehension of Scripture; not the intellectual, but the evocative which watered the channels of a living faith without which dogmas and articles were but a cheerless and infertile desert of prose.

He was simple in not romanticizing himself or his mission. No thought crossed his mind that the venture was heroic. The African needed christianizing and civilizing – few people would or could go out to do it – he had better offer himself in default of better men. It was impossible for him to dramatize himself. It was therefore impossible for him to be eloquent, rhetorical, imaginative.

He was simple in not possessing tact; or, if tact be admitted to be a complex quality of diverse components, in not being able to be diplomatic. He had no guile, and no capacity for compromise. He said what he thought when he thought it. He could not say what would please, if he did not think it to be true. His mind was limpid to the beholder as a deep pool in the mountains. He was so little conscious of himself that he could not ask himself the question, what will others think of you if you do or say this? In consequence, he was able to speak for others on religious subjects, and the deepest matters of the heart, without embarrassing them and without being himself embarrassed. It was as natural for him to speak about God as about the next meal, and his hearers accepted it as naturally. It was natural for him to speak about God because he lived in a world where God was real as the capstan on the ship. But if he had no tact, he had grace. In another man it might have been called charm; but the word charm has a ring of veneer, of polish, of cultivation. In Mackenzie, it was an open-hearted friendliness which seemed to issue from the inmost sanctuary of the soul. Men disagreed with what he said; they did not resent the way he said it. He possessed that rare faculty of being outspoken without being aggressive.

31 January

John Bosco

Priest, Founder of the Salesian Teaching Order, 1888

Born in 1815 to a peasant family, John Bosco spent most of his life in the Turin area of Italy. He had a particular call to help young men and pioneered new educational methods, for example, in rejecting corporal punishment. His work with homeless youth received the admiration even of anticlerical politicians and his promotion of vocational training, including evening classes and industrial schools, became a pattern for others to follow. To extend the work, he founded in 1859 a religious community, the Pious Society of Saint Francis de Sales, usually known as the Salesians. It grew rapidly and was well-established in several countries by the time of his death on this day in the year 1888.

A Reading from a letter of John Bosco

If we want to be thought of as those who have the real happiness of our pupils at heart, and who help each to fulfil his role in life, you must never forget that you are taking the place of parents who love their children. I have always worked, studied, and exercised my priesthood out of love for them. And not I alone, but the whole Salesian Order.

How often in my long career has this great truth come home to me! It is so much easier to get angry than to be patient, to threaten a boy rather than to persuade him. I would even say that usually it is so much more convenient for our own impatience and pride to punish them rather than to correct them patiently with firmness and gentleness.

I recommend to you the love Saint Paul had for his new converts. When he found them inattentive and unresponsive to his love, that same love led him to tears and prayers.

Be careful not to give anyone reason to think that you act under the impulse of anger. It is difficult to keep calm when administering punishment. But it is very necessary if you are not to give the impression that you are simply asserting your authority or giving vent to your anger. Let us look on those over whom we have a certain authority, as sons. Let us be determined to be at their service, even as Jesus came to obey and not to command. We should be ashamed to give the least impression of domineering. We should only exercise authority in order the better to serve the boys.

That was how Jesus treated his apostles. He put up with their ignorance and dullness and their lack of faith. His attitude towards sinners was full of kindness and loving friendship. This astonished some and scandalised others, but to others it gave enough hope to ask forgiveness from God.

Given that the boys in our charge are to be seen as our sons, we must put aside all anger when we correct their faults, or at least restrain it so much that it is almost completely suppressed. There must be no angry outburst, no look of contempt, no hurtful words. Instead, like true parents, really intent on their children's welfare and growth, show them compassion now, and always hold out hope for the future.

FEBRUARY

1 February

Brigid

Abbess of Kildare, *c.*525

Brigid (also known as Bride) was born in the latter part of the fifth century, of humble origin just five miles from Kildare. She was to become first a nun in the monastery there and then its abbess. She is believed to have been baptized by Saint Patrick and the stories of her portray a woman of great compassion who, like many Celtic saints, had a particular affinity with animals and the natural world. Her life was written in the middle of the seventh century and is the earliest life of an Irish saint. She is said to have been consecrated a bishop by Bishop Ibor, because of her resemblance to the Virgin Mary, but this may have been put abroad to support the claim of the primacy of the Abbey of Kildare. By her prayers and miracles, she is reputed to have strongly influenced the formation of the Church throughout Ireland, where she is, with Patrick, the patron saint. She died in about the year 525.

A Reading from *The Life of Saint Brigid* by Cogitosus

Holy Brigid, whom God had chosen beforehand to be conformed and predestined to his image, was born of noble Christian parents. As the chosen of God, she was indeed a girl of great modesty, who as she grew in years grew also in serenity.

Once a wild boar which was being hunted charged out of the forest, and in the course of its panicked flight careered into a herd of pigs that belonged to the most blessed Brigid. She noticed its presence and she blessed it. Immediately the creature lost its sense of fear and settled down quietly amongst the herd of pigs. See, my friends, how even the wild beasts and animals could not resist either her bidding or her will, but served her docilely and humbly.

On another occasion the blessed Brigid felt a tenderness for some ducks that she saw swimming on the water and occasionally taking wing. She bid them fly to her, and a great flock of them flew towards her, without any fear, as if they were humans under obedience to her. She touched them with her hand and embraced them tenderly. She then released them and they flew into the sky. And as they did so she praised God the Creator of all living things, to whom all life is subject, and for the service of whom all life is gift.

From these and many other episodes which demonstrated her power, it is certain that blessed Brigid could command the affections of wild animals, cattle and the birds of the air.

alternative reading

A Reading from an Old Irish hymn to Saint Brigid

Ultán's Hymn

Brigid, woman ever excellent, golden, radiant flame,
Lead us to the eternal kingdom, the brilliant, dazzling sun.

May Brigid guide us past crowds of devils,
May she break before us the attack of every plague.

May she destroy within us the taxes of our flesh,
The branch with blossoms, the mother of Jesus.

The true virgin, easy to love, with great honour,
I shall be forever safe with my saint of Leinster.

One of the columns of the land with Patrick pre-eminent,
The adornment above, the royal queen.

May our bodies when we are old be in sackcloth,
From her grace may Brigid rain on us.

We pray to Brigid by the praise of Christ
That we may be worthy of the heavenly kingdom.

2 February

The Presentation of Christ in the Temple

This day marks the completion of forty days since the birth of Jesus, when Mary and Joseph took the child to the Temple in Jerusalem. The requirement in Levitical law was for Mary to be 'cleansed', the completion of her purification following the birth of a male child. Until that day, she could touch no holy thing nor enter the sanctuary. Yet on seeing the Holy Family, Simeon praised God and acclaimed the infant as 'the light to enlighten the nations', and the prophet Anna gave thanks and proclaimed him her Redeemer. The image of Christ as the Light has led to the celebration of light countering darkness, with candles often taking a central place in the observance of this festival.

A Reading from a sermon of Sophronius of Jerusalem

Let us all hasten to meet Christ, we who honour and venerate the divine mystery we celebrate today. Everyone should be eager to join the procession to share in this meeting. Let no one refuse to carry a light. Our bright shining candles are a sign of the divine splendour of the one who comes to expel the dark shadows of evil and to make the whole universe radiant with the brilliance of his eternal light. Our candles also show how bright our souls should be when we go to meet Christ.

The God-bearer, the most pure Virgin, carried the true Light in her arms and brought him to help those who lay in darkness. In the same way, we too should carry a light for all to see and reflect the radiance of the true light as we hasten to meet him.

Indeed, this is the mystery we celebrate today, that the Light has come and has shone upon a world enveloped in shadow; the Dayspring from on high has visited us and given light to those who were sitting in darkness. This is our feast, and we join in procession with lighted candles to show both that the light has shone upon us and to signify the glory that is yet to come to us through him. So let us hasten all together to meet our God.

The true light has come, 'the light that enlightens every person who is born into this world'. Let all of us, beloved, be enlightened and be radiant with its light. Let none of us remain a stranger to this brightness; let no one who is filled remain in the darkness. Let us be shining ourselves as we go together to meet and to receive with the aged Simeon the light whose brilliance is eternal. Rejoicing with Simeon, let us sing a hymn of thanksgiving to God, the Origin and Father of the Light, who sent the true Light to dispel the darkness and to give us all a share in his splendour.

Through Simeon's eyes we too have seen the salvation of God which he has prepared for all the nations, and has revealed the glory of us who are the new Israel. As Simeon was released from the bonds of this life when he had seen Christ, so we too were at once freed from our old state of sinfulness. By faith we too embraced Christ, the salvation of God the Father, as he came to us from Bethlehem. Gentiles before, we have now become the people of God. Our eyes have seen God made flesh, and because we have seen him present among us and have cradled him in our minds, we are called the new Israel. Never let us forget this presence; every year let us keep this feast in his honour.

alternative reading

A Reading from a hymn of Ephrem of Syria

Praise to you, Son of the Most High, who has put on our body.

Into the holy temple Simeon carried the Christ-child
and sang a lullaby to him:
    'You have come, Compassionate One,
    having pity on my old age, making my bones enter
    into Sheol in peace.
    By you I will be raised
    out of the grave into paradise.'

Anna embraced the child; she placed her mouth
upon his lips, and then the Spirit rested upon her lips,like Isaiah
whose mouth was silent until a coal drew near
to his lips and opened his mouth.
Anna was aglow with the spirit of his mouth.

She sang him a lullaby:
'Royal Son,
despised son, being silent, you hear;
hidden, you see; concealed, you know;
God-man, glory to your name.'

Even the barren heard and came running with their provisions.
The Magi are coming with their treasures.
The barren are coming with their provisions.
Provisions and treasures were heaped up suddenly among the poor.

The barren woman Elizabeth cried out as she was accustomed,
'Who has granted to me, blessed woman,
to see your Babe by whom heaven and earth are filled?
Blessed is your fruit
that brought forth the cluster on a barren vine.'

Praise to you, Son of the Most High, who has put on our body.

alternative reading

A Reading from a sermon of Guerric of Igny

Today as we bear in our hands lighted candles, how can we not fail to remember that venerable old man Simeon who on this day held the child Jesus in his arms – the Word who was latent in a body, as light is latent in a wax candle – and declared him to be 'the light to enlighten the nations'? Indeed, Simeon was himself a bright and shining lamp bearing witness to the Light. Under the guidance of the Spirit which filled him, he came into the temple precisely in order that, 'receiving your loving kindness, O God, in the midst of your temple', he might proclaim Jesus to be that loving kindness and the light of your people.

Behold then, the candle alight in Simeon's hands. You must light your own candles by enkindling them at his, those lamps which the Lord commanded you to bear in your hands. So come to him and be enlightened that you do not so much bear lamps as become them, shining within yourselves and radiating light to your neighbours. May there be a lamp in your heart, in your hand and in your mouth: let the lamp in your heart shine for yourself, the lamp in your hand and mouth shine for your neighbours. The lamp in your heart is a reverence for God inspired by faith; the lamp in your hand is the example of a good life; and the lamp in your mouth are the words of consolation you speak.

We have to shine not only before others by our good works and by what we say, but also before the angels in our prayer, and before God by the intentions of our hearts. In the presence of the angels our lamps will shine with unsullied reverence when we sing the psalms attentively in their sight or pray fervently; before God our lamp is single-minded resolve to please him alone to whom we have entrusted ourselves.

My friends, in order to light all these lamps for yourselves, I beg you to approach the source of light and become enlightened – I mean Jesus himself who shines in Simeon's hands to enlighten your faith, who shines on your works, who inspires your speech, who makes your prayer fervent and purifies the intentions of your heart. Then, when the lamp of this mortal life is extinguished, there will appear for you who had so many lamps shining within you the light of unquenchable life, and it will shine for you at the evening of your life like the brightness of the noonday sun. And though you may think your light is quenched in death, you will rise like the daystar and your darkness be made bright as noon. As Scripture says, 'No longer will you need the light of sun to shine upon you by day, or the light of the moon by night; but the Lord will be an everlasting light for you.' For the light of the new Jerusalem is the Lamb. To him be glory and praise for ever.

3 February

Seiriol

Abbot, sixth century

Seiriol (often known as Seiriol Wyn – 'Seiriol the Fair') was the son of Owain Danwyn ab Einion Yrth ap Cunedda Wledig. During the first half of the sixth century he became the founder and first abbot of Penmon in Anglesey. He also gave his name to Ynys Seiriol, to which he used to retire for periods of prayer and meditation. Another of Seiriol's retreats was at Penmaenmawr. Sir John Wynn of Gwydir wrote that 'this Seiriol had an hermitage at Penmaenmawr, and there had a chapel where he did bestow much of his time in prayers, the place being then an uncouth desert and unfrequented rock'. An Anglesey tradition says that Seiriol's soul friend was Cybi, and that the two holy men would meet at midday at the wells of Clorach, halfway between Penmon and Holyhead (Caergybi), to talk and pray together.

A Reading from the *Conferences* of John Cassian

The activity of our heart may be compared, not inappropriately, to that of a mill which is activated by the circular motion of water. The mill cannot cease operations so long as it is driven round by the pressure of the water, and then it becomes quite feasible for the person in charge to decide whether he prefers wheat or barley or darnel to be ground. And one thing is clear: only that will be ground which is fed in by the person who is in charge.

In a similar fashion, the mind is under constant pressure in this life. From all sides temptation comes in torrents to drive it along and in no way will it be free of turbulent thoughts. But the workings of zeal and diligence will decide which of these thoughts may be allowed in and cultivated. And, as I have said already, if we turn to the constant meditation on Scripture, if we lift up our memory to the things of the spirit, to the longing for perfection and to the hope of future blessedness, then the thoughts deriving from all this will of necessity be spiritual and they will hold the mind where thoughts have been.

However, if we are overcome by sloth or by carelessness, if we give ourselves over to dangerous and useless chattering, if we are caught up in worldly cares and in profitless worries, then there will follow in effect from this a harvest of tares to serve as a ministry of death to our hearts. As the Lord and Saviour of us all proclaimed, where treasure lies for our works and for our hopes, our hearts will of necessity abide there too.

3 February

Anskar

Archbishop of Hamburg Missionary in Denmark and Sweden, 865

Anskar was a native of Picardy. At the age of four, following his mother's death, he was entrusted to the care of the monastery of Corbie near Amiens where, at the age of thirteen, he was professed as a monk. Following the conversion of King Harold of Denmark to Christianity in 826, Anskar was sent to Schleswig and attempted to start a Christian school there. His first attempt to Christianize the Danes failed and he went on to Sweden, where he is reputed to have built the first Christian church. In 832 he was consecrated Archbishop of Hamburg, but in 845 the town was sacked by Vikings and he transferred the see to Bremen. He continued to work amongst the Danes, preaching widely throughout Scandinavia. He was much-loved for his work with the poor and in mitigating the slave trade. Praised for his good deeds, he is said to have replied: 'If I were counted worthy to stand before God, I would ask him one single thing, that of by grace becoming a good human being.' Anskar is the patron saint of Denmark. He died at Candlemastide in the year 865.

A Reading from *The Life of Saint Anskar* by his disciple Rimbert

When the emperor wanted to send back Harold to his native land and regain the crown with his help, he looked for a holy and pious man who would accompany the king, and teach both him and his people the doctrine of salvation in order to be converted and made steadfast in faith. The Abbot of Corbie informed him that he knew of a monk in his monastery who was ablaze for the holy faith and wanted to suffer much for the name of God.

Later, a delegation from Sweden arrived with a message for the emperor Louis. They said that among their people there were many who wanted to embrace the Christian faith; even the king himself was favourable to the thought of receiving Christian priests if the emperor would most graciously send some wise preachers. Again the name of Anskar was mentioned. The man of God clearly understood the task entrusted to him. He became ablaze with the love of God, and saw it as a great joy to be allowed to work for the salvation of souls.

How blessed, how worthy of all praise and commendation, was Anskar! He imitated the greatest of the saints and was endowed with unnumbered virtues. He was holy in thought and chaste in body and, like the virgins, followed the Lamb wherever he went. As a confessor of Christ he remains for ever, and shall occupy a glorious place among those who have confessed Christ. In the new creation he will sit with the apostles on their lofty seat of judgement, judging the world which he had turned his back on. He will receive with the martyrs the crown of justice and the divinely promised palm of martyrdom.

For it is clear that there are two kinds of martyrdom: one occurs when the Church is at peace and is hidden from sight; the other occurs during times of persecution and is visible to all. Anskar desired both kinds of martyrdom, but in the end only attained one. For day after day, with tears, vigils, fasts, disciplining the flesh and mortifying his bodily desires, he offered up to God a sacrifice on the altar of his heart, and in so doing attained a martyrdom as far as is possible in a time of peace.

He was indeed a martyr because, as the apostle Paul says, the world was crucified to him and he to the world. He was a martyr because, amid the temptations of the evil one, the enticements of the flesh, the persecutions of the heathen, and the opposition of Christians, he persevered to the end of his life unperturbed, immovable, and unconquerable as a confessor of Christ. He was indeed a martyr because the word 'martyr' means 'witness', and he was a witness of God's word and of the name of Christ.

Therefore, just as Anskar was in all things an imitator of Christ, so we should strive to be imitators of him. In so doing Anskar will live with us on earth to the end of the world, and we will be worthy to live with him in heaven when our present life is over. He will live with us on earth if the holiness of his life and the remembrance of his teaching recall him to us. We too shall live with him in heaven if we follow his example, if with all our strength and desire we long for him to whom Anskar has gone before us, Jesus Christ our Lord.

3 February

Saints and Martyrs of Europe

In the Acts of the Apostles it is related how Paul, accompanied by Barnabas and Luke, crossed the Dardanelles from Asia, and first brought the good news of Jesus Christ into Europe. Paul's extensive journeys, to which his letters bear witness, laid the foundations of the Church in Greece. He and others, including Peter, preached the gospel in Rome before the first persecutions began under Nero. In the following centuries many martyrs and missionaries spread the gospel message over the Roman Empire, and after the fall of Rome to the barbarians who occupied its lands. In turn they took their new-found faith to their pagan kin in northern and eastern Europe. Since then, the Church in Europe has not lacked faithful people in every age who have continued to proclaim the kingdom of God to all who have eyes to see and ears to hear.

A Reading from the treatise *On the Unity of the Church* by Cyprian of Carthage

The Church is one, and by her fertility has extended by degrees into many lands. In the same way the sun has many rays, but its light is one; a tree has many branches but a single trunk drawing nourishment from a deep root; many streams can issue from a single source. In each case, multiplicity is fed from a single source and unity is preserved in the source itself. You cannot separate a ray from the sun any more than you can divide its light. Break off a branch from a tree, and once broken it will bud no more. Dam a stream from its source and the water will dry up. In the same way, the Church, flooded with the light of the Lord, puts forth her rays throughout the world, but it is an identical light that is being diffused, and the unity of the body is not impaired. She extends her branches over the whole world in rich abundance. She pours out her generous rivers but there is one source, one Mother, abundant in the fruit of her own creativity. We are born in the womb of the Church; we are nourished by her milk; and we are animated by her Spirit.

4 February

Gilbert of Sempringham

Founder of the Gilbertine Order, 1189

Born in 1083 in Sempringham, Lincolnshire, the son of the squire, Gilbert became the parish priest in 1131. He encouraged the vocation of seven women of the village and formed them into a company of lay sisters. A group of lay brothers also came into being and they all kept the Benedictine Rule. Gilbert was unsuccessful in his bid to obtain pastoral guidance from Cîteaux for the incipient communities and they came under the ambit of Augustinian canons, Gilbert himself becoming the Master. At his death in 1189, aged 106, there were nine double monasteries in England and four of male canons only. It was the only purely English monastic foundation before the Dissolution of the Monasteries in the sixteenth century.

A Reading from *The Book of Saint Gilbert*

When all these arrangements had been made and Gilbert had called them all, both men and women, into the unity of fellowship and the bond of peace, that through and in the One he might lead them all to the One, then he made from the multitude one heart and one soul in God; before each individual, varying according to sex, age, and rank, he set a certain way of life and a goal 'which right living cannot fall short of or exceed'. In order, however, to rely upon an authority, so that he might not be judged arrogant or presumptuous if he was shameless in rejecting other men's ways and imposing his own, even though he was under the control of the Holy Spirit, and to ensure that those under him kept carefully to the way which had been shown them, he imposed upon his followers a double discipline of religious life. Before the nuns he set for observation the *Rule of Saint Benedict,* before the clerks the *Rule of Saint Augustine*, and to all he preached the examples of Christ and his saints and the teaching of the Gospels and the apostles. Thus while he upheld the righteousness of monks and of clerks for those under his authority, in himself he strayed not at all from the monastic standard of perfection.

alternative reading

A Reading from a letter of Gilbert of Sempringham
to his canons of Malton

Gilbert of Sempringham, by God's mercy whatever he is, or rather was, to his dear sons the canons and brethren of Malton, everlasting salvation in the Lord together with God's blessing and his own.

While it was allowed and while in his mercy God furnished me with the ability, I used occasionally to pay personal visits to you as to my dearest sons; and with such teaching as matched my knowledge and my powers, I would summon and draw you towards the love of God. Oh that success had crowned my efforts! But now I am entirely bereft of bodily strength, so that by passing beyond the veil of flesh I must depart from this life which has been bitter and wearisome to me for a long while. And because from now on I shall not be able to speak with you face to face, I do not hesitate in this written form to urge you as strongly as I can: for God's sake and for the salvation of your souls pay more careful attention to divine love than you have up till now, by repressing vice, exalting truth and justice, and keeping the rules and traditions of your Order.

And you can do this the more carefully and strictly because you are free from the concerns which occupy others in the Order, and because you have the opportunity to exercise discipline within the Order in such a way that the unruliness of others may be prevented. For this is why I have particularly brought you together, that our Order may be protected and exalted through the strictness of your religious observance. If you think that my care has helped you in any way, do not refuse to grant me a reward for my labours: with devout prayers earnestly beg that God in his mercy will not enter into judgement upon me but of his great kindness may instead see fit to obliterate my sins and grant me everlasting rest.

To you whom I leave behind, I give and bequeath the peace and mercy of God, together with God's blessing and my own. By the authority entrusted me by God, as far as I may, I also absolve all those who shall in future love our Order and defend the unity of our congregation, from all the offences which, through ignorance, weakness, negligence, or contempt, they committed against the rules of our Order. But those who scheme to bring about dissension and discord in our community must know that my absolution can be of no use to them, for, unless they are penitent and arrive at a suitable penance, it is clear that they remain guilty in the sight of God. However, I do not suspect any of you of this fault, but am confident in the Lord concerning you all, that from now on you will be more diligent than hitherto in performing all your duties which relate to the soul's salvation, helped as you are by our Saviour's grace; and thus my joy in your fellowship will be increased in God's presence. May he see fit to provide such joy, whose kingdom and power endure unto everlasting. Amen.

4 February

Manche Masemola

Martyr, 1928

Manche Masemola was born in 1913 and lived her short life in Marishane, a small town near Pietersburg, South Africa, and was declared a martyr by the South African Church less than a decade after her death in 1928. Manche's journey to martyrdom began when she and her cousin joined baptism preparation classes in 1927. Every time she returned, Manche was beaten by her parents. Once her mother tried to stab her with a spear. Eventually her mother stole Manche's clothes, but she ran away naked and hid. When her mother found her, she beat Manche until she died. Manche was killed before she was baptized; however, she had predicted to her priest that she would be 'baptized in her own blood'. A statue of her now stands on the west front of Westminster Abbey.

A Reading from *Imperialism, mission and conversion: Manche Masemola of Sekhukhuneland* by Mandy Goedhals

Manche Masemola spent her short life in Sekhukhuneland. She died as a martyr in 1928, fifty years after the British defeat of the Pedi paramount Sekhukhune swung the balance of power in the Transvaal decisively in favour of colonial society. But the Pedi did not easily submit to the colonial order, and any understanding of Manche's life and death is rooted in the struggle for political, economic and cultural autonomy in the northern Transvaal.

Manche Masemola is perhaps appropriately representative of the great masses of South Africa and even the numberless people of Africa itself because like them, she has been hidden from history. It is difficult to imagine a more marginalized person. A member of an oppressed race, as a young woman within her own society, she owed respect and obedience to all except younger children. Living out her life in a poverty-stricken reserve, she knew only a rural existence and a domestic economy dependent on subsistence agriculture. Her labour was controlled by her parents, and she could not read or write. To this day Sekhukhuneland falls into one of the most impoverished regions in South Africa, with low levels of literacy, income and life expectancy and where about three-quarters of the children live in poverty. On some grounds, there may be questions about whether Manche is an appropriate figure to commemorate as a Christian martyr, particularly in her attitude to the standards imposed by mission Christianity with regard to Pedi custom and contemporary gender roles, but it is possible to argue that she pointed beyond the conventions of her own time in both areas. In entering the initiation school, in her attitude to the wearing of traditional dress, even to her desire to be a good daughter, Manche accepted the vales and customs of the Pedi, but she was resolved to be a Christian. Her recorded words tend to universalise and stereotype her life and death, but in the very confined sphere in which she lived she submitted to both Christian and Pedi expectations that women's work should be confined to domestic duties and performed with unquestioning obedience. At the same time, to confess Christ in her own time and place was an act of rebellion, a serious challenge to constituted authority.

Manche Masemola lived her life in the context of the Pedi struggle to restrict the intrusion of colonial power, represented by white officials, farmers and missionaries, and enforced through the imposition of taxes, individual tenure and migrant labour. The effort to preserve their rural existence and autonomy meant the assertion of other power relations within Sekhukhuneland, including emphasis on chiefly rule, traditional family and gender relationships and maintenance of the initiation school. It is important to understand these social, political and economic processes. Manche Masemola's life was deeply rooted in Pedi society, yet the good news for which she is a witness is not only for Sekhukhuneland, nor is she simply a representative of an oppressed and needy people: she offers the world her hope, perseverance and fortitude.

6 February

The Martyrs of Japan

Almost fifty years after Francis Xavier had arrived in Japan as its first Christian apostle, the presence of several thousand baptized Christians in the land became a subject of suspicion to the ruler Hideyoshi, who soon began a period of persecution. Twenty-six men and women, Religious and lay, were first mutilated and then crucified near Nagasaki in 1597, the most famous of whom was Paul Miki. After their martyrdom, their bloodstained clothes were kept and held in reverence by their fellow Christians. The period of persecution continued for another thirty-five years, many new witness-martyrs being added to their number.

A Reading from a contemporary account of the martyrdom of Paul Miki and his companions in Japan during February 1597

The crosses were set in place. Father Pasio and Father Rodriguez took turns encouraging the victims. Their steadfast behaviour was wonderful to see. The Father Bursar stood motionless, his eyes turned heavenward. Brother Martin gave thanks to God's goodness by singing psalms. Again and again he repeated, 'Into your hands, Lord, I entrust my life.' Brother Francisco Blanco also thanked God in a loud voice. Brother Gonsalvo in a very loud voice kept saying the Our Father and the Hail Mary.

Our brother Paul Miki saw himself standing now in the noblest pulpit he had ever filled. To this congregation he began by proclaiming that he was a Japanese and a Jesuit, and that he was dying for preaching the gospel. He gave thanks to God for this wonderful blessing, and he ended with these words:

> As I come to this supreme moment of my life, I am sure none of you would suppose I want to deceive you. And so I tell you plainly: there is no route to salvation except the one that Christians follow. My religion teaches me to pardon my enemies and all who have offended me. I do gladly pardon the emperor and all who have brought about my death, and I beg them to seek Christian baptism.

Then he looked at his comrades and began to encourage them in their final struggle. Joy glowed in all their faces, and in that of Luis most of all. When a Christian in the crowd called out to him that he would soon be in heaven, his hands and his whole body strained upward with such joy that every eye was fixed upon him.

Antonio, hanging at Luis' side, looked toward heaven and called upon the holy names of Jesus and Mary. He began to sing a psalm, 'O Praise the Lord, all you children!' He had learned this at the catechetical school in Nagasaki, for among the tasks given to the children there had been included the learning of some psalms such as these.

The others kept repeating, 'Jesus, Mary!' Their faces were serene. Some of them even took to urging the people standing by to live worthy Christian lives. In these and other ways they showed their readiness to die.

Then, according to Japanese custom, four executioners began to unsheathe their spears. At this dreadful sight, all the Christians cried out, 'Jesus, Mary!' And a storm of anguished weeping then arose to batter the very skies. The executioners killed them one by one – one thrust of the spear, then a second blow. It was over in a very short time.

A Reading from *The Epitome of the Divine Institutes* by Lactantius

Things may be said with justice in this world. But who will hear them when those who exercise authority get angry and feel threatened by the exercise of personal liberty? In religion alone has liberty placed her dwelling. Here is an area of life which above all others should be a matter of free will: none should be put under compulsion to worship that which they do not wish to.

Thus, if some through fear of threats, or overwhelmed by pain when under torture, agree to offer detestable sacrifices, you should know that they are not doing so of their own free will. They will not do voluntarily what they are made to do under compulsion. As soon as the opportunity arises and their liberty is restored, they will flee to God, and with prayers and tears beseech his mercy for what they have had to endure; and pardon is never denied them. What then do those who mutilate the body but who cannot change the will, hope to accomplish by their actions?

If others, terrified neither by threats nor by torture, are prepared to maintain their faith and forfeit their life, against such people cruelty exerts all its strength, contriving unspeakable tortures, unbearable pain, just because it is known that death for the sake of God is deemed glorious, and that victory consists in rising above torment and in laying down one's life for faith and religion. Against such people the torturers go into competition: they will not risk allowing their victims to die; instead they devise new and subtle cruelties to compel the human spirit to submit to bodily pain. Should they fail, they pause, applying to the wounds they have inflicted every care, knowing that pain from repeated torture is worse when wounds are raw. In these ways they ply their trade against the innocent. They consider themselves pious, just and even religious (for with such rites they believe their gods will be pleased) and denigrate the martyrs as impious and wild people. What perversity this is, to call an innocent and tortured victim a desperate and impious creature, while the torturer is called just and pious!

It is said that those who revile the religious observances of the State which have been handed down by their ancestors, are rightly and deservedly punished. But what if those ancestors were fools in adopting empty religious rites? Are we Christians to be prohibited from pursuing a true and better course? Why should we abandon our liberty and become enslaved and addicted to what is false? Allow us to be wise and to seek after truth. If it suits the authorities to defend the practice of ancestral religion, then why, for example, are the Egyptians exempt who worship cattle and creatures of every kind as gods? Why are actors in the theatre allowed to ridicule the gods? Why is someone honoured because he has mocked the gods with a display of wit? Why are philosophers listened to when they argue that there are no gods, or that if they do exist, that they have no care or interest in human affairs, or that there is no providential ordering to the world?

Of all the human race it would seem that the only ones who are judged irreligious are Christians who follow after the truth of God. Since this truth is both justice and wisdom, these people brand it as a crime, counting it irreligion or folly; they obviously do not understand the nature of what is deceiving them, when they call evil good, and good evil.

9 February

Teilo

Bishop, sixth century

Teilo was born at Penally, near Tenby, and studied along with David at Paulinus' school at Llanddeusant, near Llandovery. Legend has it that Teilo, along with David and Padarn, went on pilgrimage to Jerusalem where, it is said, all three were consecrated bishops. What is more certain is that Teilo had episcopal oversight of a number of monasteries in west Wales, the chief being Llandeilo Fawr. With the coming of the Yellow Plague in 547, Teilo fled to Brittany, staying with Samson at Dol for seven years, and founding a number of churches. Soon after his return to Llandeilo Fawr, Teilo died. Three churches – Penally, Llandeilo Fawr and Llandaff – each claimed to have his body. The twelfth-century Book of Llandaff says that 'miracles proved that Teilo's body was undoubtedly brought to Llandaff', and his shrine on the south side of the high altar in the cathedral became a place of pilgrimage. Teilo is one of the patron saints of Llandaff.

A Reading from *The Life of Saint David* by Rhigyfarch the Wise

One night an angel appeared to Dewi and said, 'Prepare yourself tomorrow, put on your sandals and leave for Jerusalem. Set off on the journey you have longed to make. I shall call two others to be your travelling companions, namely Eliud' (now known as Teilo, since he was once a monk in his monastery) 'and also Paternus' (now known as Padarn and whose manner of life and virtues are contained in his own story). But the holy father, amazed at the authoritative command said, 'But how shall this be? For those whom you promise as companions are three or more days distant from us and from each other. It is impossible for us to gather here tomorrow.' The angel replied, 'Tonight I shall go to each of them, and they shall come to the meeting place that I shall now show you.'

Without delay the saint disposed of the contents of his cell and set out early in the morning with his brothers' blessing. He arrived at the meeting place where he found his promised companions, and they all set out together. As fellow travellers they were equals and no one considered himself superior to another; each of them was servant and each of them was master. They were diligent in prayer, and watered their way with tears; their merits increased with each step they took. They were one in mind, in joy, and in sorrow. They sailed across the Channel and came to Gaul.

Finally, they approached the city of Jerusalem, the goal of their desire. But in the night before their arrival an angel appeared to the Patriarch in a dream saying, 'Three Christian men from the lands of the West are approaching whom you will receive with joy and hospitality. Bless them and consecrate them as bishops for me.' The Patriarch then prepared three thrones of greatest distinction, and when the holy men reached the city, he greatly rejoiced and warmly welcomed them to the thrones prepared for them. Refreshed by spiritual conversation, they gave thanks to God.

Having completed everything, they decided to return to their own land. They said farewell to the Patriarch and returned home. Each of them awaited the promise of the Patriarch and received the gifts conveyed by angels, Dewi in the monastery called Llangyvelech, Paternus

(Padarn) and Eliud (Teilo) in their own monasteries. Therefore the common people say that they came down from heaven.

10 February

Scholastica

Sister of Benedict, Abbess of Plombariola, *c.*543

Scholastica is a more shadowy figure than her famous brother, Benedict. She too was born at Nursia, central Italy, around the year 480. At an early age she chose to consecrate herself to God, but probably continued to live at home. Only after Benedict moved to Monte Cassino did she settle at Plombariola nearby, joining or maybe founding a nunnery under his direction. As abbess she sought to follow his Rule, and met him each year at a house near his monastery where they would praise God together and discuss spiritual matters. She died in about the year 543. Benedict had a vision of her soul rising up to heaven and, collecting her body, he had her buried in the tomb prepared for himself. Scholastica soon became a figure for veneration by all nuns who followed Benedict's Rule.

A Reading from the *Dialogues* of Gregory the Great

Saint Benedict's sister, Scholastica, who had been consecrated to almighty God in early childhood, used to visit her brother once a year. On these occasions he would go down to meet her in a house belonging to the monastery, a short distance from the entrance.

For this particular visit he joined her there with a few of his disciples and they spent the whole day singing God's praises and conversing about the spiritual life. When darkness was setting in, they took their meal together and continued their conversation at table until it was quite late. Then the holy nun said to him 'Please do not leave me tonight; let us keep on talking about the joys of heaven till morning.'

'What are you saying, sister?' he replied. 'You know I cannot stay away from the monastery.' At her brother's refusal, Scholastica folded her hands on the table and rested her head upon them in earnest prayer. When she looked up again, there was a sudden burst of lightning and thunder, accompanied by such a downpour that Benedict and his companions were unable to set foot outside the door.

Realising that he could not return to the monastery in this terrible storm, Benedict complained bitterly. 'God forgive you, sister,' he said, 'What have you done?' Scholastica simply answered, 'When I appealed to you, you would not listen to me. So I turned to my God and he heard my prayer. Leave now if you can. Leave me here and go back to your monastery.'

This, of course, he could not do. He had no choice now but to stay, in spite of his unwillingness. They spent the entire night together and both of them derived great profit from the holy converse they had about the interior life. We need not be surprised that in this instance the woman proved mightier than her brother. Do we not read in Saint John that God is love? Surely it is no more than right that her influence was greater than his, since hers was the greater love.

Three days later as he stood in his room looking up toward the sky, the man of God beheld his sister's soul leaving her body and entering the court of heaven in the form of a dove. Overjoyed at her eternal glory, he gave thanks to almighty God in hymns of praise. Then Benedict sent some of his brethren to bring her body to the monastery and bury it in the tomb he had prepared for himself. The bodies of these two were now to share a common resting place just as in life their souls had always been one in God.

14 February

Cyril and Methodius

Apostles to the Slavs, Patrons of Europe, 869 & 885

Constantine (his later monastic name was Cyril) and his older brother Methodius were born in Salonika and educated in Constantinople. At the invitation of its Prince, and with the authority of the Patriarch of Constantinople, the brothers went in 863 to Moravia (the modern Czech Republic and Slovakia) to reform the Church on Byzantine lines. They conceived their mandate in broad terms because they had no desire to impose on the people foreign usages as earlier Frankish clergy had imposed Latin usages. Instead they sought to promote a truly indigenous Christianity. To this end Cyril, who was an outstanding scholar and linguist, created an alphabet for the Slavic language which still bears his name (Cyrillic) and set about translating the Scriptures and other liturgical texts into the language (now known as Old Slavonic). In the course of their work they negotiated controversy and opposition with tact and pastoral skill. Cyril died on this day in the year 869, whilst the brothers were in Rome, there to obtain papal support for their evangelistic work. Methodius returned to Moravia as bishop where he completed the translation of the Bible and continued his missionary work. He died in what is now Hungary in the year 885.

Today Cyril and Methodius are honoured not only as the 'Apostles to the Slavs', and along with Benedict as 'Patrons of Europe', but also as forerunners of an authentic ecumenism between the two great branches of Christendom.

A Reading from the *Old Slavonic Life of Constantine (Cyril)*

Constantine, already burdened by many hardships, became ill. At one point during his extended illness, he experienced a vision of God and began to sing this verse from the psalms: 'My spirit rejoices and my heart exults for we shall go into the house of the Lord.' Afterwards he remained dressed in the vestments that were to be venerated later, and he rejoiced for an entire day, saying: 'From now on, I am not the servant of the emperor or of any man on earth, but of almighty God alone. Before, I was dead, but now I am alive, and I shall live for ever. Amen.' The following day he assumed the monastic habit and took the religious name Cyril. He lived the life of a monk for fifty days.

When the time came for him to set out from this world to the peace of the heavenly homeland, he prayed to God with his hands outstretched and his eyes filled with tears: 'O Lord, my God, you have created the choirs of angels and spiritual powers; you have stretched forth the heavens and established the earth, creating all that exists from nothing.

You hear those who obey your will and keep your commands in holy fear. Hear my prayer now and protect your faithful people, for you have established me as their unsuitable and unworthy servant.

'Keep them free from harm and all the worldly cunning of those who blaspheme you. Build up your Church and gather all into unity. Make your people known for the unity and profession of their faith. Inspire the hearts of your people with your Word and your teaching. You called us to preach the gospel of your Christ and to encourage them to lives and works pleasing to you.

'I now return to you your people, your gift to me. Direct them with your powerful right hand and protect them under the shadow of your wings. May all praise and glorify your name, the Father, Son, and Holy Spirit. Amen.'

Once he had exchanged the gift of peace with everyone, he said: 'Blessed be God, who did not hand us over to our invisible enemy, but freed us from his snare and delivered us from perdition.' He then fell asleep in the Lord at the age of forty-two.

14 February

Valentine

Martyr at Rome, *c.*269

Valentine was a priest or a bishop of Terni who was martyred at Rome under the Emperor Claudius. The association of his commemoration with lovers seems to have originated either from the traditional day in medieval belief when birds mated, or more likely, from a link with the pagan Lupercalia festival in Rome, which occurred on the Ides of February. For Christians, the day marks an acknowledgement of an all-loving God who blesses those who love one another, as Jesus implored his own disciples to do.

A Reading from a letter of Cyprian of Carthage

God is watching us as we go into battle and engage in the combat of faith. His angels are watching us, and so is Christ himself. How great is the dignity of that glory, how great the happiness of fighting knowing that we have God as our protector, and Christ as our judge when he crowns us with the wreath of victory!

Let us be ready for battle then, my friends, engaging with all our strength, our minds prepared, our faith sound, armed with true determination. Let the army of God march to where the battle sounds. The apostle Paul has described to us the armour of God; so let us take up these arms, confident in the spiritual and heavenly protection they offer, that on the evil day we may be able to withstand the assaults of the devil and beat them back.

Let us put on the breastplate of righteousness, that our hearts may be fortified and safe against the darts of the enemy. As for shoes, let our feet be wearing the teaching of the gospel, so that when we start trampling on the head of the serpent, crushing his head, he will be unable to bite back and overpower us.

Bravely let us carry the great shield of faith into battle, so that with its protection we can parry whatever the enemy may hurl at us.

Let us also protect our head with the helmet of salvation, that our ears may be closed to delusive commands that would only lead us to destruction, our eyes shielded from the sight of graven images, our foreheads fortified to protect the sign of God we bear, and our mouths emboldened that in victory we may confess Christ is Lord.

Finally, let us take up in our right hand the sword of the Spirit, that it may repudiate false sacrifices. It is the same right hand that in the Eucharist receives the body of the Lord that will one day also embrace the Lord himself, receiving from him a heavenly crown.

My beloved friends, let these things take hold of our hearts. Let this be our daily preparation for battle, our nightly meditation, so that if the day of persecution overtake us, as soldiers of Christ we will be ready, well-equipped in his precepts, and unafraid of the battle, but prepared for a crown.

alternative reading

A Reading from the poetry of George Herbert

Love

Love bade me welcome: yet my soul drew back,
Guilty of dust and sin.
But quick-ey'd Love, observing me grow slack
From my first entrance in,
Drew nearer to me, sweetly questioning,
If I lack'd any thing.

A guest, I answer'd, worthy to be here:
Love said, You shall be he.
I the unkind, ungrateful? Ah my dear,
I cannot look on thee.
Love took my hand, and smiling did reply,
Who made the eyes but I?

Truth Lord, but I have marr'd them: let my shame
Go where it doth deserve.
And know you not, says Love, who bore the blame?
My dear, then I will serve.
You must sit down, says Love, and taste my meat:
So I did sit and eat.

15 February

Sigfrid

Bishop, Apostle of Sweden, *c.*1045

The name of Sigfrid is connected with at least three different places in Sweden, all of which are associated with its first Christian king Olof Skötkonung: Husaby in the west, where the king is supposed to have been baptized; Sigtuna where the king founded a Christian town and royal Mint; and Växjö (pronounced Vek-sha) where Sigfrid built a church and was consecrated bishop. Sigfrid was most probably an Englishman sent by King Ethelred to assist in the evangelization of Norway and Sweden in the eleventh century. Two chronologies are possible. He may have arrived in Sweden before the year 1000, in which case he could have been the royal baptizer; or he may have sailed from England later in 1016 in the company of the Norwegian king Olaf. He is known to have taken with him two fellow missionaries, both of whom were eventually consecrated bishops. Sigfrid died in Växjö in around 1045 (though a date as late as 1069 is also possible), and is much revered throughout Scandinavia.

A Reading from *The Life of Saint Sigfrid* by an unknown author

At that time there was in Sweden a king by the name of Olaf, righteous, wise and also pious – although he was a heathen. When God touched his heart, the king sent a message to his friend and liegeman, the English king Ethelred, asking him to commission a person able to teach the Christian religion.

The English king called together many clerics and priests to take part in a general synod, but among them no one was found willing to submit to such a dangerous venture for God's sake, because everyone knew the ferocious nature of this people, and fear had seized their hearts. When the synod had been in session for three days, Saint Sigfrid stood up in the middle of the assembly. He was Bishop of York and a man of great reputation, a pious and learned man. He offered to go himself.

At last he arrived at Varend in the southern part of Sweden, a very fertile country with rivers plentiful with fish, with bees and honey, with meadows and rich cornfields, with deep and vast forests, rich in game. It was to this part that the holy bishop first arrived, and he was led by the Lord to the place called Vaxjo, where a church now exists built in his honour and that of Saint John the Baptist, and where the seat of the bishop still is.

15 February

Thomas Bray

Priest, Founder of the SPCK and the SPG, 1730

Born at Marton in Shropshire in 1656, Thomas Bray was educated at Oxford and subsequently ordained. He was chosen by the Bishop of London to assist with the work of organizing the Church in Maryland in the USA. During an extended delay in his setting out

due to legal complications, he managed to organize a system of free parochial libraries, initially for use in America but later also instituted in England. This led to his founding the 'Society for the Promotion of Christian Knowledge' (SPCK) in 1698. He finally set sail for Maryland in 1699. Though well received by the governor, Bray found that he could better promote his purposes from England. On his return to Europe, he also founded the 'Society for the Propagation of the Gospel' (SPG). He died on this day in 1730.

A Reading from a sermon preached by Thomas Bray at St Paul's Cathedral, 19 December 1697

Proportionately as the assistances given 'to many to righteousness' shall be extensive and lasting, in the same measure we must suppose the degrees of glory will be allotted to such piety. It will, therefore, follow that those pious persons will most effectually consult their future happiness and provide best for an exalted glory, who shall expend most in fixing libraries of necessary and useful books in Divinity, in order to the instruction both of minister and people.

Such indeed cannot be said, by so doing, to hazard their persons in the converting of mankind, and may not be entitled thereby to the reward of martyrs and confessors. But however, they may be much more instrumental in 'turning many to righteousness' even than those who actually labour in the work itself, because that, in effect, it will be they who preach, catechise, and instruct those parts of the world as well in future as in the present age. It is they who will be the fountain; we shall be only the conduit-pipes through which the waters of life will be conveyed to the people. And therefore, except we shall bestir ourselves very much, they will far outstrip us in the pursuit of eternal glory.

In short, those who shall make such a lasting provision for the instruction and conversion of any considerable part of mankind may, in so doing, be very well looked upon as a sort of apostle to those parts of the world. And if so, we may conclude a great deal concerning the degrees of glory wherewith such shall be recompensed, from that promise of our Saviour to his apostles: 'Verily, I say unto you, when the Son of Man shall sit on the throne of his glory, ye also shall sit upon the twelve thrones, judging the twelve tribes of Israel.' For though we are not to conclude from these words that any besides the Twelve shall be exalted to the highest degrees of happiness, yet from hence we may clearly gather that, proportionately as persons shall approach nearest to the apostles in evangelising mankind, they shall be placed nearer and nearer to them upon the several ascents to the highest stations in the kingdom of heaven.

17 February

Finan of Lindisfarne

Bishop, 661

Finan, an Irish monk of Iona, succeeded Aidan as Bishop of Lindisfarne, and carried his missionary work south of the Humber. Peada, King of the Middle Angles, and Sigbert, King of the East Saxons, were among his converts. He built the monastery at Whitby and vigorously upheld the Celtic ecclesiastical traditions against those coming from the south who followed Roman usage. He died in the year 661.

A Reading from *A History of the English Church and People* by the Venerable Bede

Finan, who had come from the Scottish island and monastery of Iona, succeeded Aidan as bishop and held the office for a considerable time.

About this time the Middle Angles, ruled by their king Peada, son of Penda, accepted the true Faith and its sacraments. Accordingly, Peada was baptized by Bishop Finan, together with his companions and thanes and all their servants, at a well-known village belonging to the king known as Walbottle. Then, taking with him four priests, chosen for their learning and holy life, to instruct and baptize his people, the king returned home full of joy. The four priests were Cedd, Adda, Betti, and Diuma.

Finan built a church on the Island of Lindisfarne suitable for an episcopal see, constructing it, however, not of stone, but of hewn oak thatched with reeds after the Celtic manner. The church was later dedicated by the most reverend Archbishop Theodore in honour of the blessed apostle Peter. But Eadbert, a later Bishop of Lindisfarne, removed the thatch, and covered both roof and walls with sheets of lead.

At about this time there arose a great and recurrent controversy in the church concerning the correct observance of Easter. Those trained in Kent and Gaul maintained that the Celtic observance was contrary to that of the universal Church. The most zealous champion of the true Easter was in fact a Scot named Ronan, who had been instructed in Gaul and Italy concerning the authentic practice of the Church. But he utterly failed to move Finan who was a hot-tempered man whom reproof made only more obstinate and openly hostile to the truth. When Finan died, he was succeeded by another Irishman called Colman, under whom the controversy became even more acrimonious.

17 February

Janani Luwum

Archbishop of Uganda, Martyr, 1977

Note: In Scotland, Janani Luwum is commemorated on 3 June.

Janani Luwum was born in 1922 at Acholi in Uganda. His childhood and youth were spent as a goatherd but he quickly showed an ability to learnand absorb knowledge when given the opportunity. Soon after he became a teacher, he was converted to Christianity and was eventually ordained in 1956, becoming Bishop of Northern Uganda in 1969 and Archbishop of Uganda in 1974. Idi Amin had come to power in Uganda in 1971 as the result of a military coup and his undemocratic and harsh rule was the subject of much criticism by the Church and others. After Amin received a letter from the bishops protesting at the virtual institution of state murder, Janani and two of Amin's own government ministers were stated as having been found dead following a car accident. It emerged quickly that they had in fact died on the implicit instructions of the President. Janani's enthusiasm for the good news of Jesus, combined with his willingness to sacrifice even his own life for what he believed in, led him to his martyrdom on this day in the year 1977.

A Reading from *Janani* by Margaret Ford

During 1976 the preaching of both Churches, Anglican and Roman Catholic, became more direct. 'Uganda is killing Uganda,' Janani told the men at the police barracks at Nsambya during an official visit at the end of August. 'We look to you to uphold the laws of our land. Do not abuse this privilege.' Afterwards some thanked the archbishop for speaking so openly, and showing them so clearly their responsibility. But others were afraid his words would annoy the President, whose anger might fall on them.

Janani continued to attend government functions. 'Even the President needs friends,'he would say. 'We must love the President. We must pray for him. He is a child of God.' He feared no one but God who was the centre of his life. But his wish that the Church of Uganda should have a guiding influence upon the government misled some people, who complained that he lived a comfortable life and was on the government side. When the Archbishop met one of his critics in December, he made clear the truth. In words that proved prophetic, he told him: 'I do not know for how long I shall be occupying this chair. I live as though there will be no tomorrow. I face daily being picked up by the soldiers. While the opportunity is there, I preach the gospel with all my might, and my conscience is clear before God that I have not sided with the present government, which is utterly self-seeking. I have been threatened many times. Whenever I have the opportunity, I have told the President the things the Churches disapprove of. God is my witness.'

18 February

Colman of Lindisfarne

Bishop, 676

Colman was a monk of Iona, like Aidan and Finan, whom he succeeded as Bishop of Lindisfarne. At a critical time in the disagreement between the Celtic and Roman traditions about the date of Easter and other usages, which led to the Synod of Whitby, Colman led the Celtic party. However, at the Synod the Northumbrian king was persuaded by Wilfrid's arguments in favour of the Roman usage. Colman resigned his see and retired initially to Iona, and then to Ireland, where he died in the year 676. Bede gives a glowing account of his person and ministry.

A Reading from *A History of the English Church and People*
by the Venerable Bede

King Oswy opened the council at Whitby by observing that all who served the one God should observe one rule of life, and furthermore since they all hoped for a share in the one kingdom of heaven, they should not differ in celebrating the sacraments of heaven. The synod, therefore, had the task of determining which party observed the truer tradition, and he decreed that this should be loyally accepted by all. The king then directed his own bishop Colman to speak first, and to explain his own rite and custom.

Colman said, 'The Easter customs which I observe were taught me by my superiors who sent me here as a bishop. All my ancestors, men and women beloved of God, are known to have observed these same customs. And lest any condemn or reject them as being false, it is recorded that they owe their origin to the blessed evangelist Saint John, the disciple especially loved by our Lord, and indeed by all the churches over which he presided.'

When judgement was eventually given, the company began to disperse. Colman, seeing that his teachings had been rejected and his observance discounted, resolved to withdraw and to take with him all who still wished to follow him, that is all who still dissented from the Catholic observance of Easter and the form of monastic tonsure.

He took with him all the Irish monks he had collected at Lindisfarne, together with about thirty English monks whom he had also formed in monastic life. Leaving some of the brothers to tend his own church, he first visited the island of Iona from which he had originally been sent to preach the word to the English. Subsequently, however, he retired to a small island at some distance from the west coast of Ireland, known as Inishboffin, meaning the Isle of the White Heifer. On his arrival, he founded a monastery, and established there the monks of both races whom he had gathered.

18 February

John of Fiesole (Fra Angelico)

Priest and Painter, 1455

and

Andrei Rublev

Religious and Painter, *c.*1430

John of Fiesole was born near the end of the fourteenth century in Tuscany. In 1407 he became a Dominican friar, taking the name John, and was ordained. After decorating the walls of the friary at Fiesole, his ministry became one of visual preaching through his great skills as a painter of human figures. He was nicknamed Fra Angelico (Brother Angel) because of the beauty of the faces, human and angelic, that he painted. He died at Rome in 1455.

Andrei Rublev was born in Russia, probably in the 1360s, and was a monk at the monastery of Saint Sergius. He became a painter of frescoes and icons, and his name is associated with the painting of several great churches in the region around Moscow. He developed a new style, infusing his work with a gentleness and harmony at one with his spirituality, a style hugely influential in the Russian Church. He died around the year 1430 and was canonized by the Russian Orthodox Church in 1988.

In honouring them, the Church in Wales remembers today all those whose ministry is exercised through their creativity and artistic skills.

A Reading from a treatise *On the Incarnation and the Holy Icons* by John of Damascus

In former times God, who is without form or body, could never be depicted. But now that God has appeared in the flesh and dwelt among us, I make an image of God in so far as he has become visible. I do not venerate matter; but I venerate the creator of matter who became matter for my sake, who willed to make his dwelling in matter; who worked out my salvation through matter. I shall never cease, therefore, to venerate the matter which wrought my salvation. Do not insult matter, for it is honourable. Nothing is without honour that God has made.

How could God be born out of material things which have no existence in themselves? God's body is God because he joined it to his person by a union which shall never pass away. The divine nature remains the same; the flesh created in time is henceforth quickened by reason-endowed soul. Because of this I salute all matter with reverence because God has filled it with his grace and power. Through it my salvation has come to me. Was not the thrice-happy and thrice-blessed wood of the cross matter? Was not the holy and exalted mount of Calvary matter? Was not the life-bearing rock, the holy and life-giving tomb, the fountain of our resurrection, was it not matter? Is not the ink in the most holy book of the Gospels matter? Is not the life-giving altar matter? Do we not receive from it the bread of life? Are not gold and silver matter? From them we make crosses, patens, chalices! And over and above all these things, is not the Body and Blood of our Lord matter?

Thus either do away with the honour and veneration all these material things deserve, or accept the tradition of the Church and the veneration of icons. Learn to reverence God and his friends; follow the inspiration of the Holy Spirit. Never despise matter, for matter is not despicable. God has made nothing despicable. Rather, contemplate the glory of the Lord, for his face has been unveiled.

alternative reading

A Reading from *Ponder these things* by Rowan Williams

One of the most significant features of icons is the direction in which the eyes are drawn by gestures and lines. Thus, in the great Trinity icon of Andrei Rublev, the inclination of the heads and the (very muted) gestures of the hands tell us a great deal about what Rublev is saying – what he is 'writing', since Orthodox Christians speak of the 'writing', not the painting, of an icon – about the relations of the divine persons. In that sense, all icons 'show a way'; they invite us to follow a line, a kind of little journey, in the picture. It is not, of course, a peculiarity of icons: there are plenty of great Western images that require something similar, most powerfully, perhaps, the Isenheim altar piece of Grünewald, with John the Baptist's immensely elongated forefinger pointing towards the crucified. But in the icon, we are not talking about dramatic gestures that underline a point, but rather about the journey the eye has to take *around* the entire complex image: wherever you start, you are guided by a flow of lines, and the path travelled itself makes the 'point' – though 'point' is quite the wrong word, suggesting as it does that the icon has one simple message to get across, rather than being an invitation to a continuing action of contemplating.

19 February

Thomas Burgess

Bishop, Teacher of the Faith, 1837

Thomas Burgess was born at Odiham in Hampshire in 1756. Ordained in 1784, he became a prebendary of Durham Cathedral ten years later. After his appointment as Bishop of St Davids in 1803, he began to reform his diocese, concentrating on improving the education and preparation for ministry of the clergy. His efforts culminated in the foundation of St David's College, Lampeter, in 1822. Although he never fully mastered the Welsh language, he encouraged the work of the literary and cultural movement led by 'yr hen bersoniaid llengar' ('the old literary parsons'), who were busy rescuing and reviving the Eisteddfod. Burgess was translated to Salisbury in 1825 and died there in the year 1837. Rowland Williams described him as 'the best English prelate the Principality ever saw'.

A Reading from *Bishop Burgess and Lampeter College* by D. T. W. Price

Thomas Burgess appears to have been much more accessible to his clergy than some of his predecessors had been. He was a gentle and unassuming man, much more of a pastor than a prelate, although no one knew 'better how to assume that dignity of manner which effectually represses undue familiarity'. As time went on, and as the number ordained by him gradually increased, he came to know more and more of his clergy personally. He examined his ordinands himself, setting aside a week before ordination services for that purpose. He looked for academic competence – knowledge of the Bible, a good grasp of Greek, and ability to write clear English – and also for evidence of personal faith and vocation. He believed that 'personal religion' was 'no less essential to a clergyman than professional learning … they should never be disunited'. He wrote several pamphlets on the solemn duties of the sacred ministry.

His admirers write enthusiastically of his insistence that any clergyman who was to serve in a parish in which church services were conducted in Welsh had to be examined for fluency in Welsh, although there is some doubt as to how strictly this was enforced, especially about what knowledge of Welsh could be regarded as adequate. The incompetence of many clergymen in Welsh, especially in preaching in Welsh, was undoubtedly a major reason for the growth of Nonconformity, as Burgess realized: 'the Welsh language is with the sectaries a powerful means of seduction from the Church'.

Most of Burgess's activities were those of a typically conscientious scholarly and devout *English* bishop, but in two of his ventures he took especial note of his Welsh surroundings. One of these was the College at Lampeter, and the other was his part in shaping the development of the Eisteddfod movement.

Some of the clergy of the Church of England in Wales, as it then was, had for centuries shown a great concern for Welsh literature and culture. Others had, of course, been unconcerned, or even hostile. Burgess hoped that the Cambrian Society [of which he was a founding member in Dyfed] would improve the educational standards of the clergy. He also hoped that the Church would make more positive use of the Welsh language in its services, to check Nonconformity. Researchers were sent to different parts of Wales to record folk-tunes and the words of songs and poems, and to locate printed books in Welsh and the repositories of manuscripts. It was a formidable programme.

Before long there were Cambrian Societies in Gwynedd, Powys, and Gwent as well as Dyfed. Not all the clergy were in favour, but Burgess was not deflected from his intentions. The real hope of the 'literary parsons' was to engage the interest of the gentry in Welsh traditions and to show them that Welsh was a respectable language to speak. The support of the Lord Bishop of St Davids was obviously most valuable in this endeavour.

20 February

Saints, Martyrs and Missionaries of Africa

Today we remember all those who have witnessed to the good news of Jesus Christ throughout Africa. History records many martyrs and other saints from Africa. Amongst them we number: the early saints and martyrs of North Africa such as Perpetua and her companions, Augustine of Hippo, and Monica his mother; the great missionaries of the nineteenth century in Central and Southern Africa, including James Hannington and Mary Slessor, and martyrs like Charles Mackenzie, Bernard Mizeki, and Charles Lwanga and his companions in Uganda; and twentieth-century heroes such as Charles de Foucauld and Janani Luwum and other great figures in our own time. We think of these people, together with all those who have proclaimed the Gospel in Africa, and who continue to proclaim it by word and deed.

Note: For readings on the above mentioned saints and other African saints, see their individual entries as follows:

Manche Masemola	4 February
Perpetua	7 March
Augustine of Hippo	28 August
Mary Slessor	11 January
Charles Mackenzie	31 January
Bernard Mizeki	18 June
Charles Lwanga	3 June
Charles de Foucauld	1 December
Janani Luwum	17 February

A Reading from a homily of Pope Paul VI on the occasion of the canonization of the Ugandan Martyrs, 18 October 1964

Every time we utter the word 'martyr' in the sense it has acquired in Christian hagiography, we should bring to our mind's eye a drama evoking horror and wonder. Horror, because of the injustice which unlooses such a drama with the instruments of power and cruelty; horror, again, because of the blood which is shed and of the death so unfeelingly inflicted; wonder, then, because of the simple strength which submits without struggle or physical resistance to torment, happy and proud to witness to the unconquerable truth of a faith which has fused itself with life.

Life, however, dies, faith lives on. We see brute as opposed to moral force; the first knowing in its very success defeat; the second, triumph in failure! Martyrdom, then, is a drama: an appalling drama, let it be said, but one rich in teaching. The unjust and evil violence which it brings about tends almost to be forgotten, while in the memory of centuries the gentleness which makes the offering of self a sacrifice, a holocaust, remains with all its lustre and attractiveness; a supreme act of love and faithfulness with regard to Christ; an example and a witnessing, and enduring message to contemporary and future generations alike. Such is martyrdom: such has been the glory of the Church through the centuries, and which we commemorate today.

These African martyrs add a new page to that list of victorious men and women that we call the martyrology, in which we find the most magnificent as well as the most tragic stories. The page that they add is worthy to take its place alongside those wonderful stories of ancient Africa, which we who live today, being of little faith, thought we should never see repeated.

We are familiar with the lives of the great saints, martyrs and confessors, of Africa, such as Cyprian, Felicity and Perpetua, and the great Augustine. Who would have imagined that one day we should be adding to that list those names of Charles Lwanga, Matthias Molumba Kalemba and their twenty companions? Nor should we forget those others of the Anglican Communion who died for the sake of Christ.

These martyrs of Africa have indeed laid the foundation of a new age. We should not dwell on the religious persecutions and conflicts, but rather on the rebirth of Christian and civil life that has begun.

For from the Africa that was sprinkled with the blood of these martyrs, the first of this new age (and, God willing, the last, so sublime, so precious was their sacrifice), there is emerging a free and independent Africa.

23 February

Polycarp

Bishop of Smyrna, Martyr, c.155

Honoured as one of the first Christian martyrs, Polycarp had been Bishop of Smyrna on the Adriatic coast of Asia Minor for over forty years when the persecution of Christians began. He was arrested and given the option to renounce his faith and so save his life. His response was: 'I have served him for eighty-six years, and he has done me no wrong. How can I blaspheme my king who saved me?' He was burnt at the stake. His remains were gathered together and buried outside the city; thus began the practice of celebrating the Eucharist over his burial place on the anniversary of his death. This custom also developed at the martyrs' tombs in the Roman catacombs. Polycarp died in about the year 155.

A Reading from a contemporary account of the martyrdom of Polycarp, Bishop of Smyrna

Polycarp was led before the proconsul. He questioned him saying, 'Take the oath, and I will let you go. Curse your Christ!' Polycarp replied, 'I have served him for eighty-six years, and he has done me no wrong. How can I blaspheme my king who saved me?' But the proconsul persisted, saying: 'Swear by the spirit of Caesar!' But Polycarp answered, 'If you are really so foolish as to think that I would do such a thing, and if you pretend that you do not know who I am, then hear this plainly: I am a Christian.'

When the fire was ready, Polycarp took off his outer garments, loosened his belt, and even removed his sandals. The irons with which the fire was equipped were fastened around him; but when they tried to nail him to the stake as well, he said, 'Let me be. The One who gives me the strength to endure the flames will give me the strength to stay in them without you making sure of it with nails.' So they did not nail him, but only tied him up. Bound like that, his arms behind his back, he looked like a noble ram, selected from some great flock, a burnt offering, acceptable and made ready for God. Looking up to heaven, he said:

> O Lord God almighty, Father of your beloved and blessed child Jesus Christ, through whom we have received knowledge of you, the God of angels and powers, and of all creation, of all the generations of righteous who live in your sight, I bless you for counting me worthy of this day and of this hour, so that I might be numbered among your martyrs and share the cup of your Christ, and so rise again to eternal life in body and soul in the immortality of the Holy Spirit. May I be received today into the company of your martyrs as a rich and acceptable sacrifice, in the way you have prepared and revealed, and have now brought to completion, for you are a God of truth in whom no falsehood can exist. So I praise you for all that you have done. I bless you through our eternal high priest in heaven, your beloved child, Jesus Christ, through whom be glory to you, together with him and the Holy Spirit, now and for ever. Amen.

As soon as he said 'Amen' and completed his prayer, the officers in charge lit the fire. A huge sheet of flame burst out, but those of us privileged to witness it, and who have been spared to tell the tale, saw an amazing sight. For the fire took on the shape of a great vault, like a ship's sail unfurling and billowing out in the wind, the flames forming a wall around the body of the martyr. Indeed, the body did not look like burning flesh, but like bread that is baking, or like gold and silver being refined in a furnace. There was also a pervasive sweet smell in the air as of incense or some precious spice.

Finally, when they realised that his body was slow to be destroyed by the fire, they ordered an executioner to reach in and stab Polycarp to death. And as he did so, a dove flew out, and much blood poured out, dousing the flames.

When it was all over we gathered up his bones, more precious to us than jewels, finer than pure gold, and we laid them to rest in a place we had already set aside. There, the Lord permitting, we shall gather and celebrate with great gladness and joy the day of his martyrdom as a birthday. It will serve as a commemoration of all who have gone before us, and training and preparing those of us for whom a crown may be in store.

27 February

George Herbert

Priest, Poet, 1633

Born in 1593 into the aristocratic Pembroke family, George Herbert went up to Cambridge in 1614, eventually becoming a Fellow of Trinity College. At the age of twenty-five, he became Public Orator in the University and then a Member of Parliament, apparently destined for a life at court. To everyone's surprise, he decided to be ordained and, after spending a time with his friend Nicholas Ferrar at Little Gidding, he was made deacon in 1626. He married in 1629, was priested in 1630 and given the care of souls of the parish of Bemerton, near Salisbury, where he spent the rest of his short life. He wrote prolifically, his hymns still being popular throughout the English-speaking world. His treatise The Country Parson on the priestly life, and his poetry, especially The Temple, earned Herbert a leading place in English literature. He never neglected the care of the souls of Bemerton, however, and encouraged attendance at the weekday recitation of the daily office, calling to mind the words of his hymn, 'Seven whole days, not one in seven, I will praise thee.' He died on this day in 1633.

A Reading from *The Country Parson* by George Herbert

The Country Parson, when he is to read divine services, composeth himself to all possible reverence; lifting up his heart and hands and eyes, and using all other gestures which may express a hearty and unfeigned devotion. This he doth, first, as being truly touched and amazed with the majesty of God before whom he then presents himself; yet not as himself alone, but as presenting with himself the whole congregation whose sins he then bears, and brings with his own to the heavenly altar to be bathed and washed in the sacred laver of Christ's blood.

Secondly, as this is the true reason of his inward fear, so he is content to express this outwardly to the utmost of his power; that being first affected himself, he may affect also his people, knowing that no sermon moves them so much to a reverence, which they forget again, when they come to pray, as a devout behaviour in the very act of praying. Accordingly his voice is humble, his words treatable, and slow; yet not so slow neither as to let the fervency of the supplicant hang and die between speaking, but with a grave liveliness between fear and zeal, pausing yet pressing, he performs his duty.

Besides his example, he having often instructed his people how to carry themselves in divine service, exacts of them all possible reverence, by no means enduring either talking, or sleeping, or gazing, or leaning, or half-kneeling, or any undutiful behaviour in them, but causing them, when they sit or stand or kneel, to do all in a straight and steady posture as attending to what is done in the church, and everyone, man and child, answering aloud both *Amen*, and all other answers which are on the Clerk's and people's part to answer; which were also to be done not in a huddling or slobbering fashion, gaping, or scratching the head, or spitting even in the midst of their answer, but gently and pausably, thinking what they say; so that while they answer, *As it was in the beginning, is now, and ever shall be etc.* they meditate as they speak, that God hath ever had his people that have glorified him as well as now, and that he shall have so for ever. And the like in other answers. This is what the apostle calls 'a reasonable service' when we speak not as parrots without reason, or offer up such sacrifices as they did of old which was of beasts devoid of reason; but when we use our reason, and apply our powers to the service of him that gives them.

If there be any of the gentry or nobility of the parish who sometimes make it a piece of state not to come at the beginning of the service with their poor neighbours, but at mid-prayers, both to their own loss and of theirs also who gaze upon them when they come in, and neglect the present service of God, he by no means suffers it, but after divers gentle admonitions, if they persevere, he causes them to be presented: or if the poor churchwardens be affrighted with their greatness, notwithstanding his instruction that they ought not to be so, but even to let the world sink, so they do their duty; he presents them himself, only protesting to them that not any ill will draws him to it, but the debt and obligation of his calling being to obey God rather than men.

alternative reading

Aaron

Holiness on the head,
Light and perfections on the breast,
Harmonious bells below, raising the dead
To lead them unto life and rest:
Thus are true Aarons drest.

Profaneness in my head,
Defects and darkness in my breast,
A noise of passions ringing me for dead
Unto a place where is no rest:
Poor priest thus am I drest.

Only another head
I have, another heart and breast,
Another music, making live not dead,
Without whom I could have no rest:
In him I am well drest.

Christ is my only head,
My alone only heart and breast,
My only music, striking me ev'n dead;
That to the old man I may rest:
And be in him new drest.

So holy in my head,
Perfect and light in my dear breast,
My doctrine tuned by Christ, (who is not dead,
But lives in me while I do rest):
Come, people; Aaron's drest.

March

1 March

David

Bishop of Menevia, Patron of Wales, *c.*601

David, or Dewi, was a monk and a bishop in the sixth century. He was reputed to be an exemplar of the ascetic, spiritual life but was also highly regarded for his kindness and compassion to others, particularly the poor and the sick. He is believed to have founded the monastery at Menevia, now St Davids, and also at least a dozen other monasteries. He is said to have based his Rule for his monasteries on that of the Egyptian desert monks, with a strong emphasis on hard work, abstinence from alcohol and a refraining from unnecessary speech. He died in about the year 601 and has been regarded as the patron saint of Wales since at least the twelfth century.

A Reading from *The Life of Saint David* by Rhigyfarch the Wise

Although our Lord loved and knew his own before creating the world, still there are some whom he makes known with many signs and revelations. And so that saint who was baptized David, but who is known as Dewi by the common people, was not only foretold by the true prophecies of angels thirty years before he was born, first to his father and then to Saint Patrick, but was also proclaimed as one who was endowed with secret gifts and blessings.

During his life, throughout the whole land, the brothers built monasteries: everywhere the sounds of churches were in evidence, everywhere voices were raised to heaven in prayer; everywhere the virtues were unweariedly brought back to the bosom of the Church; everywhere the offerings of charity were distributed to the needy with an open hand. The holy bishop Dewi was the supreme overseer, the supreme protector, the supreme preacher, from whom all received the content and structure of virtuous living. For all people he was the order, the dedication, the benediction, the absolution, the correction. He was instruction to the studious, life to the needy, an upbringing to orphans, support to widows, a leader to fathers, a Rule to monks, a way of life to secular clergy; he was all things to all people. He was brought to a ripe old age and was praised as the leader of the whole British race and the ornament of his country.

When the day was approaching of his departure, an angel spoke with him, saying: 'Make ready, and gird yourself; for on the first day of March our Lord Jesus Christ, in the company of a great host of angels, shall come to meet you.' From that hour onward until the day of his death, he remained in the church to preach.

When the third day of the week arrived, at cock-crow, the monastery was filled with choirs of angels, and was melodious with heavenly singing, and filled with the most delightful fragrance. At the hour of matins, whilst the monks were singing hymns, psalms and canticles, our Lord Jesus Christ deigned to bestow his presence for the consolation of the father, as he had promised by the angel. On seeing him, and entirely rejoicing in spirit, he said: 'Take me with you.' With these words, and with Christ as his companion, David gave up his life to God; and attended by the escort of angels, he sought the gates of heaven.

His body, borne on the arms of holy brethren, and accompanied by a great crowd, was with all honour committed to the earth, and buried in the grounds of his own monastery: but his soul, set free from the bounds of this transitory life, is crowned throughout endless ages.

alternative reading

A Reading from a medieval Latin sequence

David, star of heavenly splendour,
latter covenant's defender,
glitters o'er Britannia;
by his holy conversation,
by the true faith's conservation,
he adorns Menevia.

As the harbinger was naméd
by the angel, so proclaiméd
was he e'er his natal day;
hart and honey, water flowing,
mystic signs of fame foreshowing,
Christ's devoted thrall portray.

He, the Britons' champion fearless,
of the Welsh the teacher peerless,
takes the heavenly freeman's part;
now the Sage, the city quitting,
seeks the vale's retreat befitting
men of humbleness of heart.

Dewi Sant his sons acclaim him!
From his birth the people name him
Dewi Ddyfrwr – 'Waterman';
halt and maimed and blind he healeth,
Satan in confusion reeleth
at the Christian psalmist's ban.

Whilst a treatise he was writing,
God, this man of law requiting,
gilds the letters of the tome;
Holy David, be our pleader,
as thy namesake, be our leader,
our Goliath overcome!

2 March

Chad

Bishop of Lichfield, Missionary, 672

Note: Chad may be commemorated with Cedd on 26 October. In Wales, Chad is commemorated on 20 May.

Chad was born in Northumbria, the youngest of four sons, all of whom became both priests and monks. They entered the monastery on the isle of Lindisfarne and were taught by Saint Aidan. Chad's brother Cedd had founded the abbey at Lastingham and, on his brother's death, Chad was elected abbot. During the confusion in ecclesiastical discipline between the Celtic-oriented Anglo-Saxon hierarchy and the pressure from Rome for conformity, Chad became Bishop of York for a time. He graciously stepped back with the arrival in Britain of Theodore, who doubted the validity of indigenous consecrations. This was eventually rectified and Chad became Bishop of Mercia, a huge diocese the centre of which he moved from Repton to Lichfield. Chad travelled extensively and became much loved for his wisdom and gentleness in otherwise difficult situations. The plague was prevalent at this time and Chad died on this day in the year 672.

A Reading from *A History of the English Church and People* by the Venerable Bede

King Alhfrith sent the priest Wilfrid to the king of the Gauls to be consecrated bishop for himself and his people. He was detained overseas for a considerable time on account of his consecration, and King Oswy sent to Canterbury to be consecrated Bishop of York, a holy man, modest in his ways, learned in the Scriptures, and zealous in carrying out their teaching. This was a priest named Chad, a brother of the most reverend Bishop Cedd, who at that time was Abbot of the monastery of Lastingham.

On arriving in Canterbury, they found that Archbishop Deusdedit had died and that no successor had as yet been appointed in his place. They therefore went to the province of the West Saxons where Wine was bishop. He consecrated Chad with the assistance of two bishops of the British.

When he became bishop, Chad immediately devoted himself to maintaining the truth and purity of the Church, and set himself to practise humility and temperance, and to study. After the example of the apostles, he travelled on foot and not on horseback when he went to preach the gospel, whether in cities or country districts, in towns, villages, or strongholds; for he was one of Aidan's disciples and always sought to instruct his people in the ways and customs of his master Aidan and his own brother Cedd.

Later, however, when Theodore of Tarsus was consecrated Archbishop of Canterbury, he was asked to judge between Wilfrid and Chad. When he informed Bishop Chad that his consecration was irregular, the latter replied with the greatest humility: 'If you believe that my consecration as bishop was irregular, I willingly resign the office; for I have never thought myself worthy of it. Although unworthy, I accepted it solely under obedience.' At this humble reply, Theodore assured him that there was no need for him to give up his office, and himself completed his consecration according to Catholic rites.

At that time King Wulfere of Mercia desired Archbishop Theodore to supply him and his people with a bishop. Theodore therefore suggested to King Oswy that Chad might become their bishop. Chad was by this time living in retirement at his monastery at Lastingham, Wilfrid ruling the bishopric of York. Theodore ordered Chad to ride a horse when he was faced with a long journey; but Chad was hesitant, having long been accustomed to ministering on foot. The archbishop knew Chad to be a man of great holiness, and as if to persuade him to take his advice, helped Chad into the saddle with his own hands.

Thus it was that Chad received the bishopric of the Mercians. He established his episcopal seat in the town of Lichfield where he also died and was buried, and where the succeeding bishops of the province have their see to this day.

4 March

Adrian of May Island

Abbot, and his Companions, Martyrs, 875

Adrian, who according to tradition was of Hungarian descent, settled with many companions in Fife to evangelize the Picts. During the Viking raids he is said to have softened the raiders' fury and to have converted some. A fierce raid in 875 obliged him to retire with his companions to the island of May in the Firth of Forth. There they were killed by the Danes. The island, with a monastery founded by King David I, became an important centre of pilgrimage.

A Reading from *The Epitome of the Divine Institutes* by Lactantius

Faith is a large part of justice. We, who bear the name of Christian, must cling to this perception, especially when matters touch religion because God is prior and superior to the claims of this world. It is indeed a glorious thing to lay down one's life for friends, parents and children; and they who do so win for themselves lasting remembrance and praise. But it is much more glorious to do so for the sake of God who will bestow on us eternal life in place of death. When we are forced to shun God and return to pagan practices, no threat, no intimidation, should undermine our resolve to guard the faith delivered to us.

Let God be ever before our eyes and in our hearts, by whose inner help we can conquer bodily pain and any torture inflicted upon us. Let us think of nothing except the prize of immortality. Even if our limbs are hacked off or we be burnt, we shall endure whatever suffering is inflicted upon us by those made insane by their tyrannical cruelty.

Lastly, let us strive to bear death itself, not grudgingly or with faint hearts, but freely and without fear, knowing what glory shall be ours in the presence of God as we triumph over the world and attain his promises. What good things, what blessedness, shall be ours in exchange for our brief afflictions and the loss of this present life! And even if we be denied the chance to witness to God in this way, be assured that faith will have its reward in the day of peace.

5 March

Non

Mother of David of Wales, sixth century

According to Rhigyfarch's Life of Saint David, Non (whom he assumes was a nun) was raped by Sant, King of Ceredigion. She gave birth to a son: Dewi Sant or Saint David. The Welsh version of her story says that he was her only child, but Irish tradition also makes her the mother of two daughters, Mor and Magna. She is said to have moved to Brittany where her cult is centred on Dirinon. Her tomb can be seen there and her life was the subject of a Breton mystery play performed at Dirinon in her honour. In Brittany her protection during childbirth has long been invoked by pregnant women. Non's holy well and the ruins of her chapel are just outside St Davids. She is also connected with Llannon (Ceredigion), Llannon (Carmarthenshire), and traditionally with Altarnon in Cornwall.

A Reading from *The Life of Saint David* by Rhigyfarch the Wise

Sant, king of the people of Ceredigion, departed for Dyfed and, while passing through it, chanced on a girl called Non, who was exceedingly beautiful and modest. The king, who was filled with desire, violated her. She for her part knew no man either before or after, but continuing in chastity of mind and body, led a most faithful life, for from the time of her conceiving she lived on bread and water alone. There, in that very place where she was violated, and where she conceived, was a small meadow, pleasing to the eye and, by grace, covered with heavenly dew. In that meadow there also appeared two large stones, one at her head and one at her foot, which had not been seen before, for the earth, rejoicing at the conception, opened its bosom in order both to preserve the girl's modesty and as a sign of the importance of her child.

The mother, as her womb grew, followed the usual custom and entered a church in order to offer alms and oblations for the child's birth; and here a certain teacher was preaching the Word to the people. As the mother entered, he was suddenly struck dumb, as if by an obstruction in his throat. When he was asked by the people why he had interrupted his sermon and fallen silent, he replied, 'I can talk to you in ordinary conversation, but cannot preach to you. Go outside, and I shall remain here alone to see if I shall then be able to preach.'

The people went outside while the mother concealed herself and hid in a corner. She did not disobey the command but remained on account of the great thirst she felt for the commandments of life and to prove the privilege of so great a child. Then although he strove with all his heart, he could again do nothing, as if he were prevented by heaven. Terrified by this, he cried out with a loud voice, 'I beg anyone who may be hiding from me to reveal themselves and to make themselves known.' Then she answered, 'Here I am, hiding.'

Under divine guidance he said, 'Go out and let the people come back into the church.' As soon as this was done, he preached as usual with a fluent tongue. The mother confessed, when she was asked, that she was pregnant. It was quite clear to all that she was about to bring into the world a child who would excel all the learned men of Britain with the privilege of his honour, the splendour of his wisdom, and the eloquence of his speech. This was borne out by the subsequent merits of Dewi's life.

5 March

Kieran of Seirkeiran

Bishop and Monk, *c.*545

Kieran or Ciaran was both bishop and monk. Born in west Cork, but from an Ossory family, he appears to have travelled to Europe where he was ordained. On his return to Ireland, he settled at Seir (Saighir) near Birr, first as a hermit and then as abbot of a large monastery there. He also had a hermitage on the island of Cape Clear, off west Cork. Fascinating tales of his life surrounded by the animals of his neighbouring woods have often been re-told. He died on this day in about the year 545.

A Reading from *The Rule of Carthage*,
a Celtic monastic rule dating from the seventh century,
concerning the duties of a spiritual director

If you are a spiritual director to someone, do not barter his soul; be not as the blind leading the blind; do not leave him in neglect.

Let penitents confess to you with candour and integrity, and do not accept their alms if they refuse to be guided by you.

Even though you accept offerings from your penitents, do not allow these people a great part in your affections; rather let them be as fire on your body, a danger to your strength.

Pay their dues of fasting and prayer; if not, you will have to pay for the sins of all.

Instruct the unlearned that they may bend to your will. Do not allow them to fall into the path of sin by your example.

Do not be miserly with others for the sake of wealth; your soul is of more value to you than riches.

You shall share these treasures with strangers, whether they are powerful or not. You shall share them with the poor from whom you can expect to receive no reward.

You shall share them with the elderly and widows. I am telling you no lie, but do not give them to sinners who have already sufficient wealth.

You shall give to each in turn, and with the greatest secrecy, but without pomp and without boasting, for in this lies its virtue.

When you go to communion you should do so with great fear, confessing your sins, and in peace with all your neighbours.

The love of God is to be the only real and lasting love of your heart; as the Body you approach is pure, so must you be holy when you receive it.

He who is faithful in all of this, which is to be found in the Scriptures, is privileged if he is a priest, but let him not be privileged and unworthy.

6 March

Baldred

Hermit and Bishop, 608

Baldred, thought to have been a devoted disciple of Kentigern, whom he may have succeeded as Bishop of Glasgow, lived as a hermit on the Bass Rock, off the coast of East Lothian. However, he engaged in missionary work on the mainland and became known as the apostle of East Lothian. He died on this day in the year 608.

A Reading from an ancient Gaelic invocation

Rune before Prayer

I am bending my knee
In the eye of the Father who created me,
In the eye of the Son who purchased me,
In the eye of the Spirit who cleansed me,
        In friendship and affection.
Through thine own Anointed One, O God,
Bestow upon us fullness in our need,
        Love towards God,
        The affection of God,
        The smile of God,
        The wisdom of God,
        The grace of God,
        The fear of God,
        And the will of God
To do on the world of the Three,
As angels and saints
Do in heaven;
        Each shade and light,
        Each day and night,
        Each time in kindness,
        Give thou us thy Spirit.

7 March

Perpetua, Felicity and their Companions

Martyrs at Carthage, 203

The moving, contemporary account of these early third-century, African martyrs proved to be of great significance in the life of the early Church. Vibia Perpetua was a young, married noblewoman of Carthage, and Felicity was her personal slave. Saturas was possibly a priest and there were two other men, Saturninus and Revocatus, the latter also a slave. Felicity was pregnant and gave birth to her child while in prison. It seems most of them were catechumens when arrested and only baptized later in prison. They were condemned as Christians by the Roman authorities and dispatched to the public arena, there to be mauled by wild animals. The contemporary account of their deaths was much circulated secretly throughout the Christian congregations and brought renown to their courage and encouragement to their fellow Christians in the face of adversity. They were martyred for their faith on this day in the year 203.

A Reading from a contemporary account of the martyrdom of Perpetua, Felicity and their companions at Carthage in the year 203

If ancient examples of faith, which testify to the grace of God and give us encouragement, are honoured and recorded for posterity in writing, so that by reading them the deeds of God are glorified and others are strengthened, why should we not in our generation also set down new witnesses which serve these ends. One day their example will also be ancient and important to our children, if at this present time, because of the reverence we accord to antiquity, they seem less weighty to us.

When the day of their victory dawned, the martyrs marched from the prison to the amphitheatre, their faces joyful yet dignified, as if they were on their way to heaven. If they trembled at all, it was for joy, not fear. Perpetua took up the rear of the procession. She looked noble, a true wife of Christ and beloved of God, her piercing gaze causing spectators to avert their eyes. With them also went Felicity, rejoicing that her baby had been born safely that she might now fight with beasts, one flow of blood to be succeeded by another, ready to exchange her midwife for a gladiator that she might undergo the labour of a second baptism.

The women were stripped naked, placed in nets and were brought into the arena to face a mad heifer. Even the crowd was horrified seeing in one net a delicate young girl, and in the other a woman, fresh from childbirth, her full breasts still dripping with milk. So the women were recalled and dressed in loose clothing. Perpetua was thrown to the animal first, falling on her back. She stood up and saw that Felicity had been crushed to the ground. She went and gave her her hand to help her up; and so they stood, side by side.

Now that the cruelty of the mob had been appeased, they were recalled to the Gate of Life. There Perpetua was supported by a certain Rusticus, a catechumen at the time, who was keeping close to her. She called her brother to her and the catechumen, and spoke to them both saying: 'Stand firm in your faith, and love one another. Do not let our suffering be a stumbling-block to you.'

As the show was ending, her brother was thrown to a leopard, and with one bite was so drenched with blood that as he came back the crowd shouted out (in witness to his second baptism) 'Well washed! Well washed!' Indeed he was saved who had been washed in this way. Then he became unconscious, and was thrown with the rest into the place where they have their throats cut.

But the mob demanded that the Christians be brought back into the open so that they could watch the sword being plunged into their bodies, and so be party to the spectacle of their murder. The martyrs rose unbidden to where the mob wanted them, after first kissing one another, that they might seal their martyrdom with the kiss of peace. Each received the sword without resistance and in silence. Perpetua, however, had yet to taste more pain. She screamed as she was struck on the bone; then she herself had to guide the fumbling hand of the novice gladiator to her throat. Perhaps so great a woman who was feared by the unclean spirit, could not otherwise be killed, unless she herself gave her consent.

O most courageous and blessed martyrs! Truly are you called and chosen for the glory of Jesus Christ our Lord! All you who seek to magnify, honour and adore the glory of Christ, should read the story of these new witnesses, who no less than the ancient witnesses, have been raised up for the Church's edification; for these new manifestations of virtue testify that the same Holy Spirit is working among us now.

8 March

Felix

Bishop, Apostle to the East Angles, 647

Born in Burgundy at the beginning of the seventh century, Felix reputedly converted the exiled King Sigbert of the East Angles and, after the king's return to Britain, was consecrated bishop and then persuaded by the king to follow him to effect the conversion of his subjects. He was commissioned by Honorius, Archbishop of Canterbury, to this work and made Dunwich the centre of his new See. He established schools and monasteries and ministered in his diocese for seventeen years. He died in the year 647.

A Reading from *A History of the English Church and People* by the Venerable Bede

Not long after King Eorpwold's acceptance of Christianity, he was killed by a pagan named Ricbert, and for three years the province of the East Angles relapsed into heathen ways, until Eorpwold's brother Sigbert came to the throne. Sigbert was a devout Christian and a man of learning. He had been an exile in Gaul during his brother's lifetime, and it was there that he was converted to the Christian faith. As soon as he began his reign, he laboured to bring about the conversion of the entire kingdom.

In this enterprise he was nobly assisted by Bishop Felix, who came to Archbishop Honorius from the Burgundian region, where he had been born and ordained. By his own wish, he was sent by the archbishop to preach the word of life to this nation of the Angles. Nor did he fail in his purpose; for, like a good farmer, he reaped an abundant harvest of believers in this spiritual field. He delivered the entire province from its long-lasting wicked ways and unhappiness, brought it to the Christian faith and works of righteousness, and in full accord with the significance of his own name, guided it towards eternal felicity.

He established his episcopal see at Dunwich; and after ruling the province as its bishop for seventeen years, he ended his days there in peace.

8 March

Duthac

Bishop of Ross, 1068

Duthac was born in Scotland, studied in Ireland, and on his return to Scotland became Bishop of Ross in the eleventh century. He was renowned for his missionary zeal, his compassion, his ready espousal of poverty and the austerity of his life. He was described as the 'saint reckoned to be the most venerated in the land of Ross'. His relics, kept at Tain, were an object of pilgrimage throughout the Middle Ages. He died in the year 1068.

A Reading from a sermon of Caesarius of Arles

When our Lord tells us in the Gospel that those who wish to become his followers must renounce themselves, his words seem harsh. We imagine that he is imposing a heavy burden on us. But an order is no burden when it is issued by someone who helps in carrying it out.

To what place are we to follow Christ if not where he has already gone? We know that he has risen and ascended into heaven: there, we must follow him. We should not despair, although by ourselves we can do nothing, because we have Christ's promise. Heaven was indeed beyond our reach before our Head ascended there; but now, if we are his members, why should we despair of arriving there ourselves? Is there any reason? True, many fears and afflictions confront us in this world; but if we follow Christ, we shall reach a place of perfect happiness, perfect peace, and everlasting freedom from fear.

Yet let me issue this warning from the lips of the apostle Paul: those who claim to abide in Christ should walk as he walked. Would you follow Christ? Then be humble as he was humble; do not scorn his lowliness if you wish to reach his exaltation. Human sin made the road rough, but Christ's resurrection has levelled it. By walking the road himself, he has transformed the narrowest of tracks into a royal highway.

Two feet are needed to run along this highway: humility and charity. Everyone wants to reach the goal; and the first step along the route is humility. Why take strides that are too big for you? Do you want to be perpetually falling down rather than ascending? Begin then, with the first step of humility, and you will already be climbing.

In addition to telling us to renounce ourselves, our Lord and Saviour also said that we should take up our cross and follow him. What does this mean? Bearing every irritation with patience. This is part of following Christ. When you begin to follow Christ's way of life and commandments, you can anticipate resistance from every quarter. You will be opposed, mocked, and even persecuted. This will happen at the hands not only of unbelievers, but also of those who appear to belong to the Body of Christ, but who are in reality excluded from it by virtue of their evil ways. People who are Christians only in name never stop persecuting those who are genuine.

So if you want to follow Christ, take up his cross without delay. Endure hardship, and do not be overcome by it.

8 March

Edward King

Bishop of Lincoln, 1910

Born in London in 1829, Edward King, both as a priest and then as a bishop, was revered for the holiness of his life and the wisdom of his counsel. He was Chaplain, then Principal, of Cuddesdon Theological College, followed by a dozen years as a professor of theology in Oxford, during which time he exercised a great influence on a generation of ordinands. In 1885, he was consecrated Bishop of Lincoln, a position he held until his death. His advocacy of Catholic principles in ritual as well as theology involved him in controversy, but his significant gift to the Church was his example as a pastoral and caring bishop to both clergy and laity.

A Reading from a sermon of Edward King preached in 1893

'Thy gentleness hath made me great.' Such was the reflection of the author of this psalm as he looked back over the course of his life. It was not his own natural gifts, not his great valour, not his own cleverness, much less his own goodness, but simply the gentleness of God, by which he would account for his having reached that position in life which had raised him above so many of his fellow-men, and which had been truly great because by it he had been a help and blessing to many.

In the Prayer Book the words of this psalm run: 'Thy loving correction hath made me great.' This suggests the possibility of improvement, the need of discipline, and a high standard to be reached. The effect of the gentleness or loving correction of God was to raise the natural character of the Psalmist to a higher level than he could otherwise have reached. It should be the same in the application which I have ventured to give to these words this morning.

With the resolve to stand firm and true in the defence of God's truth, remember that the lesson of gentleness implies patience and long-suffering, and waiting for God's good time and for one another. The progress (thank God) of the Church of England has been wonderful in the last fifty years. There is indeed much yet to be done, many prejudices to be put aside, much ignorance to be enlightened, much indifference to be awakened. But we need to remember the words of our text, 'Thy gentleness hath made me great'. God has waited patiently for us and brought us up to where we are. Let us try to do to others as God has done to us, and by gentleness to lead them on and make them great. While there is life, there is hope: the penitent thief was accepted at the eleventh hour. The grace of God is as strong today as then. Even the end of a wasted life God will not reject if it be offered with a contrite heart, with true faith in the power of the Saviour's blood.

Let all impatience, then, all harsh judgements of others, all self-seeking, be put aside, and all love of power and the desire to be first. Rather let us strive to take the lower place, 'in honour preferring one another'. Then, when all is over, and we are set down at the Supper of the Lamb, and the Bridegroom comes in to see the guests, and the great reversal of human judgements shall take place, and the first shall be last and the last first, may we hope to hear his voice saying to us: 'Friend, come up higher.' Meanwhile, 'let patience have her perfect work', and let gentleness be the characteristic of your strength.

8 March

Geoffrey Studdert Kennedy

Priest, Poet, 1929

Born in 1883, Studdert Kennedy was a young vicar in Worcester who became an army chaplain during the First World War. His warm personality soon earned the respect of soldiers, who nicknamed him 'Woodbine Willie', after the brand of cigarettes he shared with them. After the First World War, he became a writer and regular preacher, drawing large crowds, who were attracted by his combination of traditional sacramental theology with more unconventional theological views. He worked tirelessly for the Christian Industrial Fellowship, but his frail health gave way and he died (still a young man) on this day in the year 1929.

A Reading from *The Hardest Part* by Geoffrey Studdert Kennedy

This is not a theological essay. It is rather a fairly faithful and accurate account of the inner ruminations of an incurably religious man under battle conditions. Battles do not make for carefully balanced thought. There is one main idea in what I have written, but I believe that it is a true idea. We must make clear to ourselves and to the world what we mean when we say: 'I believe in God the Father Almighty.'

Good people have told me that my writing is crude and brutal. I would remind you that it is not, and it could not be as crude as war, or as brutal as a battle. The brutality of war is literally unutterable. There are no words foul and filthy enough to describe it. Yet I would remind you that this indescribably filthy thing is the commonest thing in history, and that if we believe in a God of love at all, then we must believe in the face of war and all it means. The supreme strength of the Christian faith is that it faces the foulest and filthiest of life's facts in the crude brutality of the cross, and through them sees the glory of God in the face of Jesus Christ.

Thousands of men who have fought out here, and thousands of their womenkind who have waited or mourned for them at home, have dimly felt that the reason and explanation of all this horror was somehow to be found in a crucifix – witness the frequent reproductions of wayside Calvaries in our picture papers and the continual mention of them in our soldiers' letters home. Yet when you talk to soldiers you find that the Calvary appeals to them rather as the summary of their problems than their solution.

The vision of the suffering God revealed in Jesus Christ, and the necessary truth of it, first began to dawn on me in the narrow streets and shadowed homes of an English slum. All that war has done is to batter the essential truth of it deeper in, and cast a fiercer light upon the cross. A battlefield is more striking, but scarcely more really crude and brutal than a slum. Only we have all been suddenly forced to realise war more or less, while it has taken God centuries to make some of us recognise the existence of slums.

In Christ I meet the real God. In him I find no metaphysical abstraction, but God speaking to me in the only language I can understand, which is the human language; God revealed in the only terms I can begin to comprehend which are the terms of perfect human personality. In him I find the truth that human sin and sorrow matter to God, indeed, are matters of life and death to God, as they must be to me. In him I find the truth that the moral struggle of man is a real struggle because God is in it, in it and beyond it too, for in the risen Christ who conquered death and rose again I find the promise and the guarantee that the moral struggle of our race will issue in victory.

10 March

Kessog

Missionary Bishop and Martyr, *c.*700

The memory of many of the missionaries who brought the Christian faith to Scotland during the so-called Dark Ages is preserved mainly in the dedications of churches in their honour. The name of Kessog (or Mackessock) is thus preserved as a missionary bishop who laboured in the lands of Lennox among the Picts towards the end of the seventh century. He lived in a cell on Monk's Island, Loch Lomond. According to tradition, he was born of Irish royal descent in Cashel, capital of Munster, and is said to have been martyred near Luss on Loch Lomondside around the year 700.

A Reading of verses from an Old Irish poem,
from the eighth or ninth century

All alone in my little cell

All alone in my little cell, without the company of anyone; precious has been the pilgrimage before going to meet death.

A hidden secluded little hut, for the forgiveness of my sins: an upright, untroubled conscience toward holy heaven.

Sanctifying the body by good habits, trampling like a man upon it: with weak and tearful eyes for the forgiveness of my passions.

Passions weak and withered, renouncing this wretched world; pure and eager thoughts; let this be a prayer to God.

Heartfelt lament toward cloudy heaven, sincere and truly devout confessions, swift showers of tears.

A cold and anxious bed, like the lying down of a doomed man: a brief, apprehensive sleep as in danger, invocations frequent and early.

Treading the paths of the Gospel; singing psalms at every hour; an end of talking and long stories; constant bending of the knees.

May my creator visit me, my Lord, my King; may my spirit seek him in the everlasting kingdom where he dwells.

All alone in my little cell, all alone thus; alone I came into the world, alone I shall go from it.

If by myself I have sinned through pride of this world, hear me lament for it all alone, O God!

16 March

Boniface of Ross

Bishop, eighth century

The name of Cuiritan, or Boniface, is linked with two important Christian sites in Scotland: Restenneth in Angus, where he baptized the Pictish king Nechtan in 710, and founded a monastery; and Rosemarkie on the Black Isle, where in 716 he re-founded a monastery at a place originally associated with Saint Moluag. He is said to have come from Italy, even perhaps from Rome. He was certainly of the Roman, rather than the Celtic, tradition – all his foundations were dedicated to Saint Peter – so Nechtan's Christianity sought its inspiration from the south rather than from the Celtic West. He was famous for founding churches. The date of his death is not known.

A Reading from the treatise *Pastoral Care* by Gregory the Great

No one ventures to teach any art unless it has first been learned through deep reflection. It would be rash indeed, therefore, if someone untrained should aspire to the pastoral office, seeing that the government of souls is the art of arts! For who does not realise that the wounds of the mind are more hidden than the internal wounds of the body? And yet, whereas people who have no knowledge of the effect of drugs would hesitate to put themselves forward as physicians of the body, there are some who although utterly ignorant of spiritual teaching profess themselves to be physicians of the heart. In the providence of God, those in high office in our society now tend to have a regard for religion, but there are some in the Church who aspire to glory and honour by an outward show of authority. They crave to appear as teachers and enjoy pontificating over others. As the truth [of the Gospel] attests, 'They seek first the greetings of those in the market place, the places of honour at feasts, and the seats of honour in the synagogues.'

Such people are less able to administer the office of pastoral care that they have undertaken worthily because they aspire to the tutorship of humility by the path of vanity. In such a tutorship, the tongue becomes merely a purveyor of jargon because there is a gap between what is learned and what is taught. Certainly, no one does more harm in the Church than one who has the name and rank of sanctity, but who acts perversely.

The conduct of a pastor should so far surpass the conduct of the people as the life of a shepherd sets a person apart from his flock. For a person who is so regarded that the people are deemed his flock, is bound to consider what is necessary to maintain uprightness of life. It is vital, therefore, that such a person be pure in thought, exemplary in conduct, discreet in keeping confidences, a good speaker, a person of wide sympathies, mature in the practice of contemplation, a humble companion to those who lead good lives, unflagging in zeal for righteousness in opposition to the vice of evil-doers. Such a person must not be distracted from the care of the inner life by preoccupation with what is external.

Pastors should be exemplary in conduct, so that by their manner of living they demonstrate a way of life to those in their care with the result that the flock, following the teaching and conduct of their shepherd, advances through example rather than mere words. For one who is obliged to speak of high ideals by virtue of position, by the same token should display them through their lives. The voice of such a leader will penetrate the hearts of hearers more readily if the leader's way of life is proclaiming the same message.

17 March

Patrick

Bishop, Missionary, Patron of Ireland, *c.*460

Patrick was born somewhere on the west coast of Britain around the year 390, and was captured by Irish raiders when he was sixteen years old and taken to Ireland as a slave. After six years, he escaped and seems to have gone to the Continent. He eventually found his way back to his own family, where his previously nominal Christian faith grew and matured. He returned to Gaul and was there trained as a priest and much influenced by the form of monasticism evolving under Martin of Tours. When he was in his early forties, he returned to Ireland as a bishop, and made his base at Armagh, which became the centre of his See. He evangelized the people of the land by walking all over the island, gently bringing men and women to a knowledge of Christ. Although he faced fierce opposition and possible persecution, he continued his missionary journeys. Despite being unsuccessful in his attempts to establish the diocesan system he had experienced in Gaul, his monastic foundations proved to be the infrastructure required to maintain the faith after his death, which occurred on this day in the year 460.

A Reading from the *Confession* of Patrick

I was taken captive to Ireland when I was about sixteen years old, together with many thousands of others. At that time I did not know the true God. There I sought him and there I found him. I am convinced that God protected me from all evil through his Spirit who lives and works in me to this very day.

Therefore I give thanks to my God unceasingly who has kept me faithful in times of trial, so that today I offer sacrifice to him confidently, the living sacrifice of my life to Christ my Lord, who has sustained me in all my difficulties. And so I say, 'Who am I, Lord, and what is my calling that you should co-operate with me with such a display of divine power? Today, in the midst of heathen peoples, I exalt and magnify your name in all places, not only when things are going well, but also when I am under pressure.'

Whether I receive good or ill I always render thanks to God who taught me to trust him unreservedly. His answer to my prayer inspired me in these latter days to undertake this holy and admirable work – in spite of my ignorance – and to imitate those who, as the Lord had foretold, would preach the gospel to all the nations before the end of the world. We have seen it; it has happened. We are indeed witnesses that the gospel has been preached in remote areas, in places beyond which no one has ventured.

How did I come by this wisdom which was not my own, I who knew neither how my life would unfold nor the wisdom of God? What was the source of the gift I was to receive later in my life, the wonderful and rewarding gift of knowing and loving God, even though it meant leaving my homeland and family?

It was the over-powering grace of God at work in me, and no virtue of my own, which enabled all these things. I came to the Irish heathen to preach the gospel. I have had to endure insults from unbelievers; I have heard my mission ridiculed; I have experienced persecution to the point of imprisonment; I have given up my freeborn status for the good of others. Should I be worthy, I am even ready to surrender my life, promptly and gladly, for his name; and it is here in Ireland that I wish to spend my remaining days, if the Lord permits me.

In all this I am in debt to God who has given me an abundance of grace with the result that through me many people have been born again in God, and later confirmed, and that clergy have been ordained everywhere. All this was for a people newly come to faith whom the Lord has called from the ends of the earth as he foretold through his prophets: 'To you the nations will come from the ends of the earth and will say, "How false are our idols which our ancestors made for themselves, and how useless they are."' And again: 'I have made you a light for the nations so that you will bring salvation to the ends of the earth.'

18 March

Cyril of Jerusalem

Bishop, Teacher of the Faith, 386

Born in about the year 315, probably in Caesarea, Cyril became Bishop of Jerusalem when he was about thirty-four years old. There he nurtured both the resident Christian population and the many pilgrims, following the end of the era of persecution, who were beginning to make their way from all over Christendom to the places associated with Christ. Cyril taught the faith in line with the orthodoxy of the Council of Nicaea and the credal statement that became associated with it. Though he found difficulty with the word in that creed which described Jesus as being 'of one substance with the Father', nevertheless he took the side of the Nicene Party against the Arians, who denied the divinity of Christ. His teaching through his Catechetical Lectures, intended for those preparing for baptism, show him to have been a man profoundly orthodox and sound. His liturgical innovations to celebrate the observance of Holy Week and Easter are the foundation of Christian practices to this day. He died in the year 386.

A Reading from the *Catechetical Lectures* of Cyril of Jerusalem

The Church is called catholic because it is spread throughout the whole world, from one end of the earth to the other, and because it teaches in its totality and without any omission every doctrine which ought to be brought to the knowledge of humankind, concerning things both that are seen and unseen, in heaven and on earth. It is called catholic also because it brings into religious obedience every sort of person, rulers and ruled, learned and simple. It also makes available a universal remedy and cure to every kind of sin, whether of soul or body, and possesses within itself every kind of virtue that is named, whether it is expressed in deeds or words or in spiritual graces of every sort.

The Church is well named because it literally calls everyone out, and assembles them together, as the Book of Leviticus records, 'Assemble the congregation before the doors of the tabernacle of witness.' We should note that this is the first time that the word occurs in Scripture, and it does so in the context where Aaron is appointed high priest. In Deuteronomy also, God says to Moses, 'Assemble to me the people, and I will make them hear my words, that they may learn to fear me.' But since then the Jews have fallen out of favour because of their plotting against the Lord, so the Saviour has built up from among the gentiles a second assembly or Church, our holy Christian Church, and spoke of it to Peter saying: 'And upon this rock I will build my Church, and the gates of hell shall not prevail against it.'

This is the holy Church which is the mother of us all. She is the bride of our Lord Jesus Christ, the only-begotten Son of God. She is the form and image of the heavenly Jerusalem which is free and the mother of us all. Once she was barren, but now she has many children.

19 March

Joseph of Nazareth

In the Gospel according to Matthew, Joseph is depicted as a good man, a working carpenter, who trusted in God. He received God's messenger who shared with him God's will for him and for Mary, to whom he was engaged to be married. Luke's Gospel describes how Joseph took the new-born child as if he were his own. He was with Mary when, on the fortieth day after the birth, Jesus was presented in the Temple, 'where every first-born male is designated as holy to the Lord'. The adoption of Jesus by Joseph also established Jesus in the descent of David, to accord with the prophecy that Israel's deliverer would be 'of the house and lineage of David'.

A Reading from a sermon of Bernardine of Siena

There is a general rule concerning all special graces given to any human being. Whenever divine grace chooses someone to receive a special grace, or to accept a high vocation, God adorns that person with all the gifts of the Spirit needed to fulfil the task.

This general rule is especially true of that holy man Joseph. He was chosen by the eternal Father to be the faithful guardian and protector of the most precious of all his treasures, namely, his divine Son; and of Mary, who became his wife. This was the task laid upon him which he carried out faithfully right to the end, when he heard the Lord say to him, 'Good and faithful servant, enter into the joy of your Lord.'

A comparison may be made between Joseph and the whole Church of Christ. Joseph was the specially chosen man through whom and under whom Christ entered the world fittingly and appropriately. Thus, if the whole Church stands in the debt of the Virgin Mary, since it was through her child-bearing that it was able to receive Christ, surely after her, it owes special thanks and honour to Joseph.

For in him the Old Testament finds its fitting close. In him the noble line of patriarchs and prophets comes to its promised fulfilment. What God in his goodness had offered to them as a promise, Joseph held in his arms. Clearly, Christ cannot now deny to him the same intimacy, respect and high dignity which he gave him on earth, as a son to his father. We should rejoice that in heaven Christ completes and perfects all that he gave to Joseph in Nazareth.

Thus we can understand how the summoning words of the Lord, 'Enter into the joy of your Lord', apply so well to this man. In fact, although the joy of eternal happiness enters into our souls, the Lord preferred to say to Joseph, 'Enter into joy.' In using these words his intention was to alert us to their hidden meaning. They convey not only that this holy man now possesses an inner joy, but also that it surrounds him and enfolds him like the fathomless deep.

20 March

Cuthbert

Bishop of Lindisfarne, Missionary, 687

Note: In Wales, Cuthbert is commemorated on 4 September.

Cuthbert was probably born in the Scottish lowlands around the year 640. At the age of eight a prophetic remark from a playmate turned his mind to sober and godly thoughts, and his upbringing as a shepherd gave him ample time for prayer. One night he saw in the sky a dazzling light and angels carrying a soul up to heaven, and resolved to dedicate his life to God. Some years later Cuthbert came to Melrose Abbey asking to be admitted as a monk. It was from here that he began his missionary work, which he continued from Lindisfarne when he became abbot there. Consecrated bishop in 685 he remained an indefatigable traveller and preacher, walking all over his diocese, and spending time as a hermit on Farne Island in between. After only a year however, he felt his end coming and resigned his office, dying on Farne in the company of a few of his monks.

A Reading from *The Life of Cuthbert* by the Venerable Bede

When Cuthbert came to the church and monastery of Lindisfarne he handed on the monastic rule by teaching and example; moreover, he continued his custom of frequent visits to the common people in the neighbourhood, in order to rouse them up to seek and to merit the rewards of heaven.

Some of the monks preferred their old way of life to the rule. He overcame these by patience and forbearance, bringing them round little by little through daily example to a better frame of mind. At chapter meetings he was often worn down by bitter insults, but would put an end to the arguments simply by rising and walking out, calm and unruffled. Next day he would give the same people exactly the same admonitions, as though there had been no unpleasantness the previous day. In this way he gradually won their obedience. He was wonderfully patient and unsurpassed for courage in enduring physical or mental hardship. Though overwhelmed by sorrow at these monks' recalcitrance, he managed to keep a cheerful face. It was clear to everyone that it was the Holy Spirit within giving him strength to smile at attacks from without.

Such was his zeal for prayer that sometimes he would keep vigil for three or four nights at a stretch. Whether he was praying alone in some secret place or saying psalms, he always did manual work to drive away the heaviness of sleep, or else he would do the rounds of the island, kindly inquiring how everything was getting on, relieving the tedium of his long vigils and psalm-singing by walking about.

After many years in the monastery he finally entered with great joy and with the goodwill of the abbot and monks into the remoter solitude he had so long sought, thirsted after, and prayed for. To learn the first steps of the hermit's life he retired to a more secluded place in the outer precincts of the monastery. Not till he had first gained victory over our invisible enemy by solitary prayer and fasting did he take it on himself to seek out a remote battlefield farther away from his fellows. The Inner Farne is an island far out to sea, unlike Lindisfarne which is an island in the strict sense of the word only twice a day, when cut off by the tide. The Inner Farne lies a few miles to the south-east of Lindisfarne, cut off on the landward side by very deep water and facing, on the other side, out towards the limitless ocean. Cuthbert was the first man brave enough to live there alone.

Towards the end of his life this venerable man of God was elected Bishop of Lindisfarne. Following the teaching and practice of the apostles, he adorned his office with good works. He protected the flock committed to him by constant prayer on their behalf, by wholesome admonition and – which is the real way to teach – by example first and precept later.

21 March

Passing of Benedict of Nursia

Abbot of Monte Cassino, Father of Western Monasticism, Patron of Europe, *c.*550

Note: See also the Feast of Benedict on 11 July.

Benedict was born in Nursia, central Italy, around the year 480. As a young man he was sent to study in Rome, but was soon appalled by the corruption in society and withdrew to live as a hermit at Subiaco. He quickly attracted disciples and began to establish small monasteries in the neighbourhood. Around the year 525, a disaffected faction tried to poison him, so Benedict moved to a deserted pagan temple at Monte Cassino with a band of loyal monks. According to Gregory the Great, who recorded his life in the second book of his Dialogues some forty years after Benedict's death, it was there that he wrote his Rule. Benedict had a fundamentally incarnational view of life, and as this extract from Gregory reveals, saw the whole world in God, permeated with light. He died on this day at Monte Cassino in about the year 550.

A Reading from the *Dialogues* of Gregory the Great

Long before the night office began, Benedict, the man of God, was standing at his window where he watched and prayed while the rest of the community were still asleep. In the dead of night he suddenly beheld a flood of light shining down from above more brilliant than the sun, and with it every trace of darkness cleared away. Another remarkable sight followed. According to his own description, the whole world was gathered up before his eyes in what appeared to be a single ray of light.

How is it possible for anyone to see the whole universe at a glance? All creation is bound to appear small to a soul that sees the creator. Once it beholds a little of God's light, it finds all creatures small indeed. The light of holy contemplation enlarges the mind in God until it transcends the world. In fact, the soul that sees God rises even above itself, and as it is drawn upward in God's light, all its inner powers unfold. Then, when it looks down from above, it understands how limited everything really is that before had seemed beyond its grasp. Why should it surprise us, then, that Benedict should have seen the whole world gathered up before him after this inner light had transported him so far above this world? Of course, in saying that the world was gathered up before his eyes, I do not mean that heaven and earth contracted, but rather that his spirit was enlarged. Absorbed as he was in God, it was now easy for him to see all that lay beneath God.

Six days before he died Benedict gave orders for his tomb to be opened. Almost immediately, he was seized with a violent fever that rapidly wasted his remaining energy. Each day his condition grew worse until finally, on the sixth day, he had his disciples carry him into the chapel where he received the body and blood of our Lord to gain strength for his approaching end. Then, supporting his weakened body on the arms of his brethren, he stood with his hands raised to heaven, and as he prayed he breathed his last.

That day two monks, one of them at the monastery, the other some distance away, received the very same revelation. They both saw a magnificent road covered with rich carpeting and glittering with thousands of lights. From his monastery it stretched eastward in a straight line until it reached up into heaven. And there in the brightness stood a man of majestic appearance who asked them, 'Do you know who passed this way?' 'No,' they replied. 'This,' he told them, 'is the road taken by blessed Benedict, the Lord's beloved, when he went to heaven.' His body was laid to rest in the Chapel of Saint John the Baptist, which he had built to replace the altar of Apollo.

21 March

Thomas Cranmer

Archbishop of Canterbury, Reformation Martyr, 1556

Note: In Wales, Thomas Cranmer is commemorated jointly with Hugh Latimer, Nicholas Ridley and Robert Ferrar (see below).

Born in Aslockton in Nottinghamshire in 1489, Thomas Cranmer, from an unspectacular Cambridge academic career, was recruited for diplomatic service in 1527. Two years later he joined the team working to annul Henry VIII's marriage to Catherine of Aragon. He was made Archbishop of Canterbury in 1533 and duly pronounced the Aragon marriage annulled. By now a convinced Church reformer, he married in 1532 while clerical marriage was still illegal in England. He worked closely with Thomas Cromwell to further reformation, but survived Henry's final, unpredictable years to become a chief architect of Edwardian religious change, constructing two editions of The Book of Common Prayer in 1549 and 1552, the Ordinal in 1550, and the original version of the later Thirty-Nine Articles. Cranmer acquiesced in the unsuccessful attempt to make Lady Jane Grey Queen of England. Queen Mary's regime convicted him of treason in 1553 and of heresy in 1554. Demoralized by imprisonment, he signed six recantations, but was still condemned to the stake at Oxford. Struggling with his conscience, he made a final, bold statement of Protestant faith. Perhaps too fair-minded and cautious to be a ready-made hero in Reformation disputes, he was an impressively learned scholar, and his genius for formal prose has left a lasting mark on Anglican liturgy. He was burnt at the stake on this day in the year 1556.

A Reading from the Preface to *The First Prayer Book of King Edward VI* published in 1549

There was never anything by the wit of man so well devised, or so surely established, which in continuance of time hath not been corrupted, as (among other things) it may plainly appear by the common prayers in the Church, commonly called divine service: the first and original ground whereof, if a man would search out by the ancient fathers, he shall find that the same was not ordained, but of good purpose, and for a great advancement of godliness. For they so ordered the matter that the whole Bible (or the greatest part thereof) should be read over once in the year, intending thereby, that the clergy (and specially such as were ministers of the congregation) should by often reading and meditation of God's word be stirred up to godliness themselves, and be more able to exhort others by wholesome doctrine, and to confute them that were adversaries to the truth. And further, that the people by daily hearing of holy Scripture read in the Church should continually profit more and more in the knowledge of God, and be the more inflamed with the love of his true religion.

But these many years past, this godly and decent order of the ancient fathers hath been so altered, broken, and neglected, by planting in uncertain stories, legends, responds, verses, vain repetitions, commemorations, and synodals, that commonly when any book of the Bible was begun, before three or four chapters were read out, all the rest were unread. And in this sort the Book of Isaiah was begun in Advent, and the book of Genesis in Septuagesima;

but they were only begun and never read through. After a like sort were other books of holy Scripture used.

And moreover, whereas Saint Paul would have such language spoken to the people in the church as they might understand and have profit by hearing the same, the service in this Church of England (these many years) hath been read in Latin to the people, which they understand not; so that they have heard with their ears only; and their hearts, spirit and mind have not been edified thereby. Moreover the number and hardness of the rules, the manifold changings of the service, was the cause that to turn to the book was so hard and intricate a matter, that many times there was more business to find out what should be read, than to read it when it was found out.

These inconveniences therefore considered: here is set such an order, whereby the same shall be redressed. Furthermore by this order, the curates shall need none other books for their public service but this book and the Bible: by the means whereof the people shall not be at so great charge for books as in time past they have been.

And where heretofore, there hath been great diversity in saying and singing in churches within this realm, some following Salisbury use, some Hereford use, some the use of Bangor, some of York, and some of Lincoln: now from henceforth, all the whole realm shall have but one use.

alternative reading

A Reading from *A Defence of the True and Catholic Doctrine of the Sacrament of the Body and Blood of our Saviour Christ* by Thomas Cranmer

As meat and drink do comfort the hungry body, so doth the death of Christ's body and the shedding of his blood comfort the soul, when she is after her sort hungry. There is no kind of meat that is comfortable to the soul, but only the death of Christ's blessed body; nor no kind of drink can quench her thirst, but only the blood-shedding of our Saviour Christ, which was shed for her offences.

For as there is a carnal generation and a carnal feeding and nourishment, so is there also a spiritual generation and a spiritual feeding. And as every man, by carnal generation of father and mother, is carnally begotten and born into this mortal life, so is every good Christian spiritually born by Christ unto eternal life. And as every man is carnally fed and nourished in his body by meat and drink, even so is every good Christian man spiritually fed and nourished in his soul by the flesh and blood of our Saviour Christ.

And although our carnal generation and our carnal nourishment be known to all men by daily experience and by our common senses; yet this our spiritual generation and our spiritual nutrition be so obscure and hid unto us, that we cannot attain to the true and perfect knowledge and feeling of them but only by faith, which must be grounded upon God's most holy word and sacraments.

And for this consideration our Saviour Christ hath not only set forth these things most plainly in his holy word, that we may hear them with our ears; but he hath also ordained one visible sacrament of spiritual regeneration in water, and another visible sacrament of spiritual nourishment in bread and wine, to the intent that, as much as is possible for man, we may see Christ with our eyes, smell him at our noses, taste him with our mouths, grope him with our hands, and perceive him with all our senses. For as the word of God preached putteth Christ into our ears, so likewise these elements of water, bread, and wine, joined to God's word, do after a sacramental manner put Christ into our eyes, mouths, hands, and all our senses.

21 March

Thomas Cranmer, Hugh Latimer, Nicholas Ridley and Robert Ferrar

Bishops, Teachers of the Faith and Martyrs

Note: For biographies and readings:

Thomas Cranmer	see above
Hugh Latimer	see 16 October
Nicholas Ridley	see 16 October
Robert Ferrar	see below

Robert Ferrar was born around the year 1500 in Halifax in Yorkshire. An Augustinian Canon, he was Prior of Nostell, near Pontefract, and surrendered it peacefully at the Dissolution of the Monasteries. He subsequently married, and was perhaps chaplain to Thomas Cranmer, and later to the Duke of Somerset. On the accession of Edward VI, Somerset became Protector, and in 1548 Ferrar was made Bishop of St Davids. He worked to further the reform of the Church in Wales, but was obstructed by his cathedral chapter, and after the fall of Somerset, was imprisoned. When Mary I acceded to the throne, he was deprived of his see, condemned as a heretic, and burned at Carmarthen on 30 March 1555, one of only three burnings to take place in Wales under Queen Mary. He remarked that if he were seen to stir from the pain of burning, then the doctrines for which he died need not be believed; but he stood in the flames holding out his hands till they were burned to stumps, and he was then struck on the head, ending his suffering.

A Reading from *The Welsh and their Religion* by Glanmor Williams

Coming to the Diocese of St Davids early in 1549, Robert Ferrar spent only three troubled and unhappy years there. He resided at Abergwili and spent much of his time in Carmarthen, where he became a familiar but highly controversial figure. A sincere and well-intentioned Reformer, he ran into serious conflict from the outset. He quarrelled bitterly with a powerful group among his own cathedral clergy – most of them men with reforming sympathies, ironically enough. They found allies among influential gentry and merchants who had good reason for disliking Ferrar's attempts to recover a measure of control over ecclesiastical properties which had passed into the control of these laymen.

By 1552 his enemies were too strong for him, and he was ordered to be imprisoned. In prison he remained for the rest of Edward VI's reign. After Mary (1553–8) came to the throne he was kept in close confinement with a number of other leading Protestant clergy opposed to the Marian regime, all of whom were to be among the first martyrs of Mary's reign. It seems very likely that these first executions were planned by Bishop Gardiner as an awful example intended to deter and dishearten Protestants. To intensify the impact of the burnings and widen the range of their effects, most of the first victims were burnt either in their own home towns or at the scene of some of their most recent labours.

On 14 February 1555 Ferrar, having already appeared before Gardiner, was sent down to Carmarthen to face examination by his Marian successor, Bishop Henry Morgan. Morgan was slow to condemn Ferrar. Possibly he hoped that he would recant and that a spectacular apostasy by a Protestant bishop might be as a salutary a lesson to others as his execution. Or perhaps it was that Morgan had enough humanity not to want to see his predecessor condemned to a cruel death. Whatever the reason Morgan summoned him to his presence on six separate occasions between 26 February and 13 March. All in vain! Ferrar refused to retract any of what his judges denounced as his 'heresies, schisms, and errors'.

So, on 30 March 1555, the townspeople of Carmarthen were to witness one of the earliest of the Marian Protestant martyrdoms and the only burning for religion's sake to take place in the town during the sixteenth century. Brought to Carmarthen's most public open site, Ferrar died bravely. Beforehand, according to Foxe the martyrologist, he had said to Richard Jones, second son of Sir Thomas Jones of Abermarlais, 'that if he saw him once to stir in the pains of his burning he should then give no credit to his doctrine'.

24 March

Macartan

Bishop, *c.*505

Tradition names Macartan as the 'strong man' of Saint Patrick, who established the Church in Clogher and spread the Gospel in Tyrone and Fermanagh. An eighth-century manuscript of the gospels, associated with a silver shrine, Domnach Airgid, in the Royal Irish Academy, is linked with the early Christian life of Clogher diocese. Macartan is thought to have died in about the year 505.

A Reading from an Old Irish homily

We shall avoid the punishments of hell by hard work and study, by fasting and prayer, by righteousness and mercy, by faith and love. For whoever fulfils these commandments, God shall call them to himself on the Day of Judgement, saying to them, 'Come, you blessed of my Father, possess the kingdom which has been prepared for you from the beginning of the world.'

We should strive, therefore, for the kingdom of heaven which is unlike the human dominion of this present world which earthly kings love. It blinds like mist, it slays like sleep, it wounds like a point, it destroys like a blade, it burns like fire, it drowns like a sea, it swallows like a pit, it devours like a monster. But not like that is the kingdom which the saints and the righteous strive for. It is a bright flower in its great purity, it is an open sea in its great beauty, it is a haven full of candles in its true brilliance, it is the eye's delight in its great loveliness and pleasantness, it is a flame in its fairness, it is a harp in its melodiousness, it is a feast in its abundance of wine.

Blessed are they who shall come into the kingdom where God himself is, a King, great, fair, powerful, strong, holy, pure, just, knowing, wise, merciful, loving, beneficent, old, young, wise, noble, glorious, without beginning, without end, without age, without decay. May we enter the kingdom of that King, may we merit it and may we dwell there unto the ages of ages. Amen.

24 March

Walter Hilton of Thurgarton

Augustinian Canon, Mystic, 1396

Born in 1343, Walter Hilton studied Canon Law at Cambridge, but after a period as a hermit, he joined the community of Augustinian Canons at Thurgarton in Nottinghamshire in about 1386. Highly regarded in his lifetime as a spiritual guide, he wrote in both Latin and English and translated several Latin devotional works. Controversy with Enthusiasts and with the Lollard movement gave a sharper definition to his exposition of the aims, methods and disciplines of traditional spirituality. Amongst his major works, The Scale of Perfection *(Book Two) declares that contemplation, understood in a profoundly Trinitarian context as awareness of grace and sensitivity to the Spirit, may and should be sought by all serious Christians. He died on this day in the year 1396.*

A Reading from *The Scale of Perfection* by Walter Hilton

Love works in a soul, opening the spiritual eye to gaze upon Jesus by the inspiration of special grace, and making it pure, subtle and fit for the work of contemplation. The greatest scholar on earth cannot with all his wit imagine what this opening of the spiritual eye is, or fully declare it with his tongue, for it cannot be acquired by study or through human toil alone, but principally by the grace of the Holy Spirit, together with the work of the person concerned. I am afraid to speak of it at all, for I feel myself to be ignorant; it goes beyond my experience, and my lips are unclean. Nevertheless, because I think Love asks and Love commands, I shall for that reason say a little more of it, as I suppose Love to teach.

This opening of the spiritual eye is that luminous darkness and rich nourishing that I have spoken of before, and it may be called purity of spirit and spiritual rest, inward stillness and peace of conscience, highness of thought and solitude of soul, a lively feeling of grace and secrecy of heart, the waking sleep of the spouse and tasting of heavenly savour, burning in love and shining in light, entrance to contemplation and reforming in feeling. All these terms are given by various persons in holy writing, for each of them have spoken of it as he felt in grace, and although they all show it in diverse words, nevertheless all are united in the truth they affirm.

For a soul that through the visitation of grace has one has all, because when a soul sighing to see the face of Jesus is touched through the special grace of the Holy Spirit, it is suddenly changed and turned from the plight that it was in to another way of feeling. It is wonderfully separated from the love and pleasure of all earthly things and drawn first into itself, so much so that it has lost the savour of the bodily life and of everything that is, save only Jesus.

And then it is clean from all the filth of sin, so far that the memory of it and all inordinate affection for any creature is suddenly washed and wiped away, so that there is no obstacle in the middle between Jesus and the soul, but only the life of the body.

And then it is in spiritual rest, because all painful doubts and fears and all other temptations of spiritual enemies are driven out of the heart, so that they do not trouble it or sink into it for the time. It is at rest from the annoyance of worldly business and the painful vexation of wicked stirrings, but it is very busy in the free spiritual work of love, and the more it labours, the more rest it feels.

This restful labour is very far from idleness of the flesh and from false confidence. It is full of spiritual work, yet it is called rest, because grace loosens the heavy yoke of carnal love from the soul, making it strong and free through the gift of the spiritual love, in order to work gladly, gently and with delight in everything where it is stirred to work by grace. Therefore it is called a holy idleness and a most busy rest, and so it is in stillness from the great shouting and bestial din of fleshly desires and unclean thoughts.

This stillness is made by the inspiration of the Holy Spirit through the beholding of Jesus, because his voice is so sweet and so strong that it puts silence in a soul instead of the chattering of all other speakers, for it is a voice of virtue.

24 March

Paul Couturier

Priest, Ecumenist, 1953

Born in 1881 in Lyons, France, Paul Couturier was destined from early years for the priesthood. His concern for Christian unity began as a result of his work with Russian refugees in Lyons, and was fostered through his profession at the Benedictine Priory of Amay in Belgium, a community devoted to the growth of understanding between Eastern and Western Churches. He commended the observance of a Week of Prayer for Unity and, in the 1930s, widened his contacts to incorporate people of the Anglican, Lutheran and Reformed traditions. Celebrating the eucharist each day brought into focus his whole life of work and prayer for unity within the Church. The growing circle of friends and followers became an 'invisible monastery', praying for 'the visible unity of the Kingdom of God, such as Christ willed and by means which he wills'. He died on this day in the year 1953.

A Reading from *Ecumenical Testament* by Paul Couturier

At the altar of the holy sacrifice at which I celebrate the holy mysteries, there is present on its way Godward, finding completion there if needs be – so my Catholic faith affirms – every sacrificial element in what my Christian brethren have retained of the eucharistic *agape* of the first Maundy Thursday.

At the choir office, at the breviary prayed alone, in silent prayer, my Protestant, Anglican or Orthodox brothers and sisters pray with me and in me in my prayer. And likewise, I am present and have my part in the loyal and sincere prayer which is lifted up to God through the splendours of the divine liturgy and offices of the convinced Orthodox. I am present and have my part in the public prayers of Anglicans – those lovely canticles – matins and evensong, which have never since the sixteenth century ceased to rise to God in every English cathedral – those masterpieces of the faith of our medieval ancestors – and in the private prayers of fervent Anglicans, and still more in the service of Holy Communion; I am present and have my part in the worship, the prayers, measured and full of faith, and in the profound hymns of Protestantism, and particularly in the fervent commemoration of the Last Supper held by my Protestant brethren.

O God, how can I be unaware that pleasing you depends on the generosity of my reply 'Yes' to your known will, following the example of the Virgin of Nazareth, who remains the Gospel model of all human acquiescence to the divine will: 'Let be done unto me according to your Word.' You allow it to be so – every creature must seek you from its own place on earth, wherever that may be; 'You that enlightens everyone coming into the world', O Word of God become Christ! We are all, every one, advancing towards the truth which is yourself, for ever pursued, as we all are, by your love, by your Spirit. We set out upon this journey, always without ceasing. We never arrive. In the words of Paul, 'Brethren, I do not reckon myself to have apprehended it yet. But forgetting those things that are behind, and reaching out to that which lies ahead, I press on towards the goal.' Christ is the Way by which we go, the Truth to which we make our way, on and on, the range is infinite – the Life in which we dwell here below, through the darkness of faith, despite our sin, provided we repent of it; later – yet always soon – in 'the Father's bosom' – the home where there is no more sin, and where the spirit walks or rather runs from glory to glory.

24 March

Oscar Romero

Archbishop of San Salvador, Martyr, 1980

Oscar Arnulfo Romero y Galdamez was born in a small village in El Salvador in 1917. Ordained priest, he was known as a quiet and unassuming pastor. By 1977, amidst the political and social turmoil suffered by his country, he was therefore seen as a neutral choice to be its Archbishop. Courageously, however, he began to speak out against violence and his homilies supported the demands of the poor for economic and social justice. He refused to be silenced and continued to preach even under threat of assassination. On this day in 1980, whilst presiding at Mass, Archbishop Romero was assassinated by a gunman. He has since been widely regarded as a martyr for the faith.

A Reading from an address by Oscar Romero delivered on 2 February 1980, some six weeks before his assassination as he presided at the Eucharist

I shall not try to talk, and you cannot expect me to talk, as would an expert in politics. Nor will I even speculate, as someone might who was an expert, on the theoretical relationship between faith and politics. No, I am going to speak to you simply as a pastor, as one who, together with his people, has been learning the beautiful but harsh truth that the Christian faith does not cut us off from the world but immerses us in it, that the Church is not a fortress set apart from the city. The Church follows Jesus who lived, worked, battled and died in the midst of a city, in the *polis*. It is in this sense that I should like to talk about the political dimension of the Christian faith: in the precise sense of the repercussions of the faith on the world, and also of the repercussions that being in the world has on the faith.

We ought to be clear from the start that the Christian faith and the activity of the Church have always had socio-political repercussions. By commission or omission, by associating themselves with one or another social group, Christians have always had an influence upon the socio-political makeup of the world in which they live. The problem is about the 'how' of this influence in the socio-political world, whether or not it is in accordance with the faith.

The essence of the Church lies in its mission of service to the world, in its mission to save the world in its totality, and of saving it in history, here and now. The Church exists to act in solidarity with the hopes and joys, the anxieties and sorrows, of men and women. Like Jesus, the Church was sent 'to bring good news to the poor, to heal the contrite of heart, to seek and save what was lost'. To put it in one word – in a word that sums it all up and makes it concrete – the world that the Church ought to serve is, for us, the world of the poor.

Our Salvadoran world is no abstraction. It is not another example of what is understood by 'world' in developed countries. It is a world made up mostly of people who are poor and oppressed. What we say of that world of the poor is that it is the key to understanding the Christian faith, to understanding the activity of the Church, and the political dimension of that faith and that ecclesial activity. It is the poor who tell us what the *polis* is, what the city is, and what it means for the Church really to live in that world.

25 March

The Annunciation of our Lord to the Blessed Virgin Mary

The story of the announcement of the coming of God made flesh in the person of his Son, Jesus the Christ, the Anointed One, is heard in today's proclamation of the good news from the Gospel of Luke. The feast marks the conception of Christ in the womb of Mary and has been celebrated in the Church at least since the late fourth century. The perfect humanity and the complete divinity of Jesus are affirmed, following the controversies around those orthodox assertions, which themselves led to the acknowledgement of Mary as Theotokos, 'the God-bearer', which in the West became translated as 'Mother of God'. The celebration thus took on strong associations with the person of Mary, and became known in England as 'Lady Day'. In recent years, the Church has re-affirmed the day as a Feast of our Lord, on which his virgin-mother still has a unique place of honour and veneration.

A Reading from a sermon of Cyril of Alexandria, preached at the Council of Ephesus in 431, in which he celebrates the special dignity accorded to Mary, the bearer of the Incarnate Word of God

We hail you, O mysterious and Holy Trinity who has gathered us together in council in this church of Holy Mary, the God-bearer.

We hail you, Mary, the God-bearer, sacred treasure of all the universe, the star which never sets, the crown of virginity, the sceptre of true law, a temple which cannot be destroyed, the dwelling place of one who cannot be contained.

O Mother and Virgin, we hail you for the sake of the one whom the holy Gospels call 'blessed', the one who 'comes in the name of the Lord'.

We hail you Mary, for in your virginal womb you held the one whom the heavens themselves cannot contain, one through whom the Trinity is glorified and worshipped throughout the world; through whom the heavens exult; through whom angels and archangels rejoice; through whom demons are put to flight; through whom the tempter was thrown out of heaven; through whom fallen creation is raised up to the heavens; through whom the whole world, held captive by idolatry, has now come to know the truth; through whom holy baptism is given to those who believe, anointing them with the 'oil of gladness'; through whom churches have been founded throughout the world; through whom the nations have been converted.

What more can I say? It is through you, Mary, that the light of the only-begotten Son of God has shone upon those 'who dwell in darkness and the shadow of death'. It is through you that prophets have spoken of the future, that the apostles have preached salvation to the nations, that the dead have been raised, that monarchs are reigning in the name of the Trinity.

Is there a single person who can sufficiently set forth the praises of Mary? She is both Mother and Virgin. What a wondrous thing! In fact it is so wonderful that I am overwhelmed by it. Has anyone ever heard of a builder who was stopped from dwelling in the temple he himself had built? Has anyone the right to speak ill of the one who bestowed upon his own servant the title of 'mother'? This is why today everyone is rejoicing.

Today, therefore, may we the Church worship and adore the unity, may we worship and honour the undivided Trinity, by singing the praises of Mary ever Virgin, and the praises of her Son and immaculate Spouse, to whom be glory for ever and ever.

alternative reading

A Reading from a sermon of Mark Frank

'Dominus tecum', the Lord Christ's being with Mary, is the chief business the Church commemorates in this day. Her being 'blessed', and all our being 'blessed', 'highly favoured', or favoured at all, either men or women being so, all our hail, all our health, and peace and joy, all the angels' visits to us, or kind words, all our conferences with heaven, all our titles and honours in heaven and earth, that are worth the naming, come only from it.

For *Dominus tecum* cannot come without them; he cannot come to us but we must be so, must be highly favoured in it, and blessed by it. So the incarnation of Christ, and the annunciation of the blessed Virgin, his being incarnate of her, and her blessedness in him with her, make it as well our Lord's as our Lady's day. More his, because his being Lord made her a Lady, else a poor carpenter's wife, God knows; all her worthiness and honour, as all ours, is from him; and we too take heed today, or any day, of parting them; or so remembering her as to forget him; or so blessing her, as to take away any of our blessing him; any of his worship, to give to her.

Let her blessedness, the respect we give her, be among women still; such as is fit and proportionate to weak creatures, not due and proper only to the creator, that *Dominus tecum*,

Christ in her be the business: that we take pattern by the angel, to give her no more than is her due, yet to be sure to give her that, and particularly upon this day.

[And yet the day being a day of Lent, seems somewhat strange. It is surely no fasting work, no business or occasion of sadness this. What does it then, or how shall we do it then, in Lent this time of fast and sorrow? Fast and feast too, how can we do it? A feast it is today – a great one, Christ's incarnation – a day of joy, if ever any; and Lent a time of sorrow and repentance, the greatest fast of any. How shall we reconcile them?

Why thus: the news of joy never comes so seasonable as in the midst of sorrow; news of one coming to save us from our sins, can never come more welcome to us than when we are sighing and groaning under them; never can an angel come more acceptably than at such time with such a message. It is the very time to be filled when we are empty; the only time for *Dominus tecum*, for our Lord's being with us when we have most room to entertain him. *Dominus tecum*, Christ is the main business, both of our fasts and feasts; and it is the greatest order to attend his business in the day and way we meet it, be it what it will.]

For from Christ's being with Mary and with us it is that we are blessed. From his incarnation begins the date of all our happiness. If God be not with us all the world cannot make us happy, much less blessed. For God hath exalted the humble and meek, the humble handmaid better than the proudest lady. Blessed the devout affection that is always watching for her Lord in prayer and meditations; none so happy, so blessed, as she; the Lord comes to none so soon as such.

Note: The fourth and fifth paragraphs may be omitted from the above reading if the feast has had to be transferred out of Lent.

alternative reading

A Reading from a poem by Margaret Saunders

Madonna

Black Madonna,
Let me climb on your lap.
Feel my heart
  beating with yours.
Hear your voice
  call me child.
Tell me of the blessing
  of the wise wound
  and the falling blood.
Tell me of the richness
  of my womanhood
  and of the travail
  to bring its darkness to birth.

Tell me of the pain
  and emptiness and loss
  when the sword pierced through your soul also.
Mary
Empty vessel
God-bearer
    and bearer of God's sorrow.

26 March

Harriet Monsell

Founder of the Community of St John the Baptist, Clewer, 1883

Of Irish parentage, Harriet Monsell (née O'Brien) was born in 1811. After the death of her clergyman husband, she went to work in a penitentiary at Clewer near Windsor. Here, under the guidance of the local Vicar, T. T. Carter, she was professed as a Religious in 1852 and subsequently became the first Superior of the Community of St John the Baptist. Under her care, the community grew rapidly and undertook a range of social work in a variety of locations, with foundations in India and America by the 1880s. The sisters cared for orphans, ran schools and hospitals, and opened mission houses in parishes. In 1875 Mother Harriet retired as Superior through ill health, moving to a small hermitage in Folkestone, where she died on Easter Day 1883.

A Reading from *A Joyous Service* by Valerie Bonham

The Community of Saint John the Baptist has the unique distinction of being founded *after* the work for which it became well known. Like many another great philanthropic endeavour the rescue work amongst 'fallen women' was not planned, but began because the need was there, and it seemed expedient to answer it.

During the 1840s it had become a point of scandal that while there were a number of secular Penitentiaries for rescuing fallen women, the Established Church was doing nothing. The problem of prostitution was one which stirred the conscience of some nineteenth-century churchmen particularly deeply. Its very intractability was a challenge to action, and suggested the necessity for new methods and a new approach. Thus was born the idea for a safe refuge for women, a 'House of Mercy'. The project was in part the brainchild of a clergyman, T. T. Carter, but it only became a reality through the involvement of a recently widowed woman, Harriet Monsell.

Born in Ireland in 1811, Harriet had married Charles Monsell in 1839 who, not long after his ordination, contracted tuberculosis. She kept a journal during the last weeks of her husband's life in which she graphically describes his final hours, and how he died in her arms, her companions in the room having fallen asleep. 'I was alone with God,' she wrote. 'After resting for a while I returned to the room and knelt beside him. And as I prayed I felt God's call to work for Him.' Carter was later to describe Harriet's experience as 'self-consecration in sorrow'.

She offered to help Carter in his project, but at first, simply on a daily basis. Gradually it seemed that this was the work to which God had called her; and accordingly, on Ascension Day, 29 May 1851, she was admitted and clothed by Carter as a Sister of Mercy. Harriet Monsell had not joined a Religious Community because at this stage there was no community, no convent, no Rule: just Harriet clothed as a Sister of Mercy, alone with a growing conviction that this was the call she had awaited. But in parallel there was Carter's growing conviction that *only* if the workers lived as Sisters of Mercy under a Rule would the rescue work grow and prosper.

During 1852 two other women came to the House of Mercy to seek admission as sisters. And so it was that on Saint Andrew's Day, 30 November 1852, Harriet Monsell was professed in the presence of Samuel Wilberforce, Bishop of Oxford, and installed as the first Superior of the Community of St John the Baptist.

Over the succeeding years, Harriet Monsell gained a reputation for her wisdom and understanding which manifested itself in a ministry of counselling to all and sundry, so that people came from far and wide to consult her. All whom she encountered were left with the impression of a dynamic personality of great spiritual force, yet wholly sensible and down to earth. She could be forceful and sometimes had to be, but she remained an immensely likeable person, full of warmth and with a sense of humour which manifested itself at unlikely times. There can be little doubt that the very special personality of Harriet Monsell attracted women to Clewer, for though by the early 1850s sisterhoods were springing up like mushrooms in the Church of England, yet none grew so rapidly as Clewer.

28 March

Patrick Forbes and the Aberdeen Doctors

Bishop, and Teachers of the Faith

Patrick Forbes was Bishop of Aberdeen from 1618 to his death in 1635, a time of upheaval for the Church in Scotland. He was widely recognized as a man 'guid, godly and kynd'. His background was Presbyterian, but he applied himself diligently to his episcopal duties. He was also Chancellor of the University of Aberdeen and, through his work there, his name is associated with several colleagues: Robert Baron, first Professor of Theology in Marischal College; William Leslie, Principal of King's College; James Sibbald, Minister of St Nicholas, Aberdeen; Alexander Scroggie, Minister of Old Aberdeen; Alexander Ross, Minister of New Aberdeen; and John Forbes, second son of the bishop and Professor of Divinity in King's College. They encouraged sound learning and personal godliness, and in the partisan atmosphere of the time found a way to transcend the confessional limits of theological thinking and to work for harmony, tolerance and mutual understanding. They strenuously opposed the National Covenant which abolished episcopacy in Scotland. For refusing to subscribe to it, John Forbes was deprived of his chair in 1639, and went into exile.

A Reading from a Funeral Speech, delivered by Dr Alexander Scroggie on the occasion of the death of Bishop Patrick Forbes

As he was largely honoured by God, in blood, in name, and descent of an honourable stock; so he honoured it with all the true ornaments of virtue and wisdom: in his private life by his piety and religion; and constant profession of the truth in the strictest sort, by diligent and profitable hearing thereof, and living accordingly; and as a godly Christian, teaching others by his example, he might have said as Gideon 'as I do, so do ye'.

Thereafter received to be a pastor and churchman, he was not an idle shepherd, but diligent and pains-taking from his entry in ministry, and feeding of the people with sound doctrine powerfully delivered; always resident, and never a deserter of the flock, and in that time ever vigilant by all means to procure the peace of the Church and the staff of the binders unbroken, but to be still knit together in God and the spirit of concord and unity.

Thereafter his calling to the episcopal dignity was rare and exemplary, without his knowledge or seeking, directly or indirectly, without ambition or usurpation, hunting after places and preferment as many do through ambition and love of gain and glory, not awaiting on the Lord's calling.

He being preferred to be a bishop, overseer, and president of others in the Church, and to be employed in matters of weightiest importance, and having put on that sacred honour, yet was he never less in his own apprehension whatever he seemed to others; not stately, but gentle, courteous, and affable to all.

His first and foremost care was for the House of God, and especially of the Cathedral Church where he did reside, edifying and repairing the ruins thereof, and furnishing it with ornaments convenient, and which had lain waste and desolate since the Reformation, wanting a preacher, because they who sacrilegiously had impropriated the tithes wanted conscience to provide a minister and maintenance for him. And that there might always be an able and godly ministry, he caused found a profession of divinity, and a rent for the entertainment thereof in all times coming. The benefit whereof the country hath already with great contentment beholden.

And in his frequent visitations of the churches in his diocese, he removed from many places lubbards, and purged out all unclean and unprofitable ministers – planted churches where there were none, and caused endow them with land and living, that there might be maintenance in the House of God for the prophets and their sons after them.

29 March

Woolos

King, sixth century

Woolos or Gwynllyw was the son of Glywys, whose kingdom of Glywysing stretched from eastern Carmarthenshire to Monmouthshire. His early military exploits led him to be known as Gwynllyw Filwr ('Gwynllyw the Warrior'). He married Gwladys, the daughter of Brychan Brycheiniog (having first abducted her, according to the earliest version of his life). Their son was Cadoc, one of the greatest of the Welsh saints. Woolos built a church on the site in Newport where the cathedral bearing his name now stands.

Legend has it that he chose that particular place because he found a white ox with a black spot on its forehead there. Woolos and Gwladys are said to have settled in a nearby hill-fort, where they spent the rest of their days devoutly 'enjoying the fruits of their labour, and taking nothing which belonged to other persons'.

A Reading from *The Life of Saint Cadog*

After a long interval of time, King Gwynllyw (Woolos) desired with ardent affection on account of the excessive sweetness of her fame that a certain girl should be joined to him in lawful wedlock. Born of most noble lineage, of elegant appearance, very beautiful moreover in form, and clad in silk raiment, the girl's name was Gwladys, the daughter of a certain chieftain called Brychan. Accordingly he sent very many messengers to the virgin's father to the end that they might more resolutely demand that she be given to him in marriage. It was to them that blessed Cadog was born.

The aforesaid Gwynllyw was, however, given to carnal allurements, and used to instigate with his servants various plunderings and robberies, living entirely contrary to God's law and right. In such ways he befouled his life with many blemishes. By contrast, his son the blessed Cadog assuredly built his church on four foundations: justice, prudence, fortitude, and temperance. His monastery was full of monks singing, reading, and praying, whom Saint Cadog continually encouraged with divine exhortation, the Holy Spirit co-operating with him, to the worship of the Deity, to the duty of mutual love, and rendering the service of mercy to the poor.

Then the man of God, Cadog, deeply sighing at the wicked acts of his father and grieving on his account, sent faithful messengers from among his disciples, namely Finnian, Gnawan, and Elli, that they might convert him from every error and from the malice of wickedness, and transfer him to the service of the Godhead. They carefully made a point of meeting him and unanimously admonished him together with his chief men for their behaviour, saying that he should renounce the devil and his pomp and crimes, and recover his reason by doing penance and entrust himself to the counsel of his son, Cadog, and also should confess to God and his son his faults.

On hearing this, his wife Gwladys, prompted by the spirit of Godhead, said, 'Let us believe in our son, and he will be a father to us in heaven.' And Gwynllyw answering says, 'Whatever he tells me to do I will do, and wherever he wills I will go.'

After an interval of some time Gwynllyw and his wife went forth by a vow to Theluch, and a messenger came from God to Cadog, saying that he should go to his parents with sacred admonitions. And so Gwladys, his mother, built for herself a church in Pencarnou, and King Gwynllyw soon erected another monastery, and in the same place he established those serving God. Then each parent invited Cadog, whose coming they devoutly received, and gave him the aforesaid churches, which they had built for themselves, and they handed over to his authority all that they had.

31 March

John Donne

Priest, Poet, 1631

Note: In Wales, John Donne is commemorated on 25 November.

John Donne was born in about the year 1571 and brought up as a Roman Catholic. He was a great-great nephew of Thomas More, although this seems to have had little influence on him because, as a youth, he was sceptical about all religion. He went up to Oxford when he was fourteen, studied further at Cambridge and perhaps on the Continent, and eventually discovered his Christian faith in the Church of England. After much heart-searching, he accepted ordination and later the post of Dean of St Paul's Cathedral. Much of his cynicism dissolved and he became a strong advocate for the discerning of Christian vocation, and in particular affirming his own vocation as a priest, loving and loved by the crucified Christ. The people of London flocked to his sermons. He died on this day in the year 1631.

A Reading from a sermon of John Donne, preached at Lincoln's Inn during the Easter Term 1620

I am body and soul, soul and faculties; and as Scripture says, 'I shall see God.' I, the same man, shall receive the crown of glory which shall not fade. I shall see; but I have had no looking-glass in my grave to see how my body looks in the dissolution; thus I know not how I shall see. I have had no hour-glass in my grave to see how my time passes; thus I know not when I shall see. For when my eyelids are closed in my death-bed, till I see eternity, the Ancient of Days, I shall see no more; but then I shall. Our sensitive faculties have more relation to the soul than to the body; but yet to some purpose, and in some measure, all the senses shall be in our glorified bodies.

'No man ever saw God and lived.' And yet, I shall not live till I see God; and when I have seen him I shall never die. What have I ever seen in this world, that hath been truly the same thing that it seemed to me? I have seen marble buildings, and a chip, a crust, a plaster, a face of marble hath pulled off, and I see brick-bowels within. I have seen beauty, and a strong breath from another tells me that that complexion is from without, not from a sound constitution within. I have seen the state of Princes, and all that is but ceremony. As he that fears God, fears nothing else, so he that sees God, sees everything else: when we shall see God, we shall see all things as they are. We shall be no more deluded with outward appearances: for, when this sight, which we intend here comes, there will be no delusory thing to be seen. All that we have made as though we saw in this world, will be vanished, and I shall see nothing but God, and what is in him; and him I shall see in the flesh.

Our flesh, even in the resurrection, cannot be a spectacle, a mere perspective glass to our soul. We shall see the humanity of Christ with our bodily eyes, then glorified; but, that flesh, though glorified, cannot make us see God better, nor clearer than the soul alone hath done all the time from our death to our resurrection. But as an indulgent father, or as a tender mother, when they go to see the king in any solemnity, or any other thing of observation and curiosity, delights to carry their child, which is flesh of their flesh, and bone of their bone, with them, and though the child cannot comprehend it as well as they, they are as glad that the child sees it as that they see it themselves; such a gladness shall my soul have that this flesh, (which she will no longer call her prison, nor her tempter, but her friend, her companion, her wife) that this flesh, that is, I, in the re-union, and re-integration of both parts, shall see God; for then, one principal clause in her rejoicing, and acclamation, shall be, that this flesh is her flesh; 'In my flesh I shall see God.'

alternative reading

Holy Sonnet

Batter my heart, three person'd God; for you
As yet but knock, breathe, shine, and seek to mend;
That I may rise, and stand, o'erthrow me, and bend
Your force, to break, blow, burn and make me new.
I, like an usurpt town, to another due,
Labour to admit you, but Oh, to no end,
Reason your viceroy in me, me should defend,
But is captiv'd, and proves weak or untrue.
Yet dearly I love you, and would be lov'd fain,
But am betroth'd unto your enemy.
Divorce me, untie, or break that knot again,
Take me to you, imprison me; for I
Except you enthrall me, never shall be free,
Nor ever chaste, except you ravish me.

A Hymn to God the Father

Wilt thou forgive that sin where I begun,
Which is my sin, though it were done before?
Wilt thou forgive those sins through which I run,
And do them still: though still I do deplore?
When thou hast done, thou hast not done,
For, I have more.

Wilt thou forgive that sin by which I won
Others to sin? and, made my sin their door?
Wilt thou forgive that sin which I did shun
A year, or two: but wallowed in, a score?
When thou hast done, thou hast not done,
For, I have more.

I have a sin of fear, that when I have spun
My last thread, I shall perish on the shore;
Swear by thy self, that at my death thy Sun
Shall shine as it shines now, and heretofore;
And, having done that, Thou hast done,
I have no more.

April

1 April

Gilbert of Caithness

Bishop, 1245

Gilbert de Moravia appears to have been a member of the family of the Lords of Duffus in Moray. He was for many years Archdeacon of Moray, and in 1223 was elected Bishop of Caithness. A devout churchman and an able statesman, his great work was the erection of a new cathedral at Dornoch, but his long episcopate was beneficial to his diocese in every way. He died in the year 1245.

A Reading from a letter of Ambrose of Milan

The Church's foundation is unshakeable and firm against the assaults of the raging sea. Waves lash at the Church, but they do not shatter it. Although the elements of this world constantly beat upon the Church with crashing sounds, the Church possesses the safest harbour of salvation for all in distress. Although it is tossed about on the sea, it rides easily on the rivers, especially those rivers of which Scripture speaks when it says, 'The rivers have lifted up their voice'. These are the rivers which flow from the heart of one who is given drink by Christ and who has received from the Spirit of God. When these rivers overflow with the grace of the Spirit, they lift up their voice.

There is also a stream which flows down on God's saints like a torrent. There is a rushing river which brings joy to the heart that is at peace and which makes for peace. Whoever has received from the fullness of this river, like John the Evangelist, like Peter and Paul, lifts up their voice. Just as the apostles lifted up their voices and preached the Gospel throughout the world, so those who drink these waters begin to preach the good news of the Lord Jesus.

Drink, then, from Christ, so that your voice may also be heard. Store up in your mind the water that is Christ, the water that praises the Lord. Store up water from many sources, the water that rains down from the clouds of prophecy.

Whoever gathers water from the mountains or draws it from springs, is personally a source of dew like the clouds. Fill your soul, then, with this water, so that your land may not be dry, but watered by your own springs. Whoever reads much and understands much, receives fullness, and whoever is full will refresh others.

Therefore, let your words be rivers, clean and limpid. Solomon says, 'The weapons of the understanding are the lips of the wise;' and in another place he says, 'Let your lips be bound with wisdom.' In other words, let the meaning of the words you utter shine forth, let understanding blaze out. Ensure that your addresses and expositions do not need to invoke the authority of others for support, but let your words be their own defence. Let no word escape your lips in vain or be uttered without depth of meaning.

1 April

Frederick Denison Maurice

Priest, Teacher of the Faith, 1872

Born into a Unitarian family in 1805, Frederick Maurice became an Anglican in his twenties and was then ordained. He was one of the founders of the Christian Socialist Movement, in which his particular concern was providing education for working men. As a theologian, Maurice's ideas on Anglican comprehensiveness have remained influential. His best-remembered book, The Kingdom of Christ, demonstrated his philosophical approach to theology. His radicalism was revealed in his attack on traditional concepts of hell in Theological Essays, which cost him his Professorship at King's College, London, in 1853. In 1866, however, he was given a chair in Cambridge, which he held until his death on this day in 1872.

A Reading from a sermon of F. D. Maurice 'On the Lord's Prayer', preached at Lincoln's Inn, 13 February 1848

The revelation that the God whom we call upon is 'Our Father' is grounded upon an act done on behalf of humanity – an act in which all men have a like interest; for if Christ did not take the nature of every rebel and outcast, he did not take the nature of Paul and John. Therefore the first sign that the Church was established upon earth in the name of the Father, and the Son, and the Spirit, was one which showed that it was to consist of men of every tongue and nation; the baptized community was literally to represent mankind. If it be so, the name 'Father' loses its significance for us individually, when we will not use it as the members of a family.

God has owned us as spiritual creatures, has claimed us in that character to be his own, to feel that the universe would be a horrible blank without him; that his absence would be infinitely more to us than to all creatures beside; that if he is not, or we cannot find him, consciousness, memory, expectation, existence, must be curses unbearable; but that when the burden of the world and of self is most crushing, we may take refuge from both in him – if at any time such convictions have dawned upon us, let us not hope to keep the blessing of them by our own skill and watchfulness. Let us say: 'Our Father, when we least remember thee, fix the thought of thy being deeper than all other thoughts within us; and may we, thy children, dwell in it, and find our home and rest in it, now and for ever.'

In the phrase 'Our Father' there lies the expression of that fixed eternal relation which Christ's birth and death have established between the littleness of the creature and the majesty of the creator; the one great practical answer to the philosopher who would make heaven clear by making it cold; would assert the dignity of the divine essence, by emptying it of its love, and reducing it into nothingness. 'Our Father which art in heaven' – there lies the answer to all the miserable substitutes for faith, by which the invisible has been lowered to the visible; which have insulted the understanding and cheated the heart; which have made united worship impossible, because that can only be when there is one Being, eternal, immortal, invisible, to whom all may look up together, into whose presence a way is opened for all, whose presence is a refuge from the confusions, perplexities and divisions of this world; that home which the spirits of men were ever seeking and could not find till he who had borne their sorrows and died their death, entered within the veil, having obtained eternal redemption for them, till he bade them sit with him in heavenly places.

7 April

Brynach

Abbot

A hermit who settled in Pembrokeshire, Brynach was apparently of Irish origin. He was said to have visited Rome and Brittany before landing in Wales at Milford Haven. From there he travelled to Llanboidy, Cilmaenllwyd and Llanfrynach (all places with churches dedicated to him), eventually settling at Nevern. There he lived a life of extreme asceticism, spending hours in prayer on Carn Ingli, the mountain above his cell. Local traditions about Brynach also mention his close relationship with the natural world, befriending and taming wild animals, and being able to converse with the birds. He represents a strand of early Welsh Christianity that reflects similar ideas and ideals to those of Francis of Assisi.

A Reading from a tenth-century Middle Welsh poem

Glorious Lord

Hail to you, glorious Lord!
May church and chancel praise you,
May chancel and church praise you,
May plain and hillside praise you,
May the three springs praise you,
Two higher than the wind and one above the earth,
May darkness and light praise you,
The cedar and the sweet fruit tree.
Abraham praised you, the founder of faith,
May life everlasting praise you,
May the birds and the bees praise you,
May the re-growth and the grass praise you.
Aaron and Moses praised you,
May male and female praise you,
May the seven days and the stars praise you,
May the lower and upper air praise you,
May books and letters praise you,
May the fish in the river praise you,
May thought and action praise you,
May the sand and the earth praise you,
May all the good things created praise you,
And I too shall praise you, Lord of glory,
Hail to you, glorious Lord!

8 April

Griffith Jones

Priest, Teacher of the Faith, 1761

A native of Pen-boyr in Carmarthenshire, Griffith Jones was born in 1683. He was a shepherd and, after attending the grammar school in Carmarthen, he was ordained in 1708. In 1711 he became Rector of Llandeilo Abercywyn, and five years later Rector of Llanddowror. His reputation as a preacher drew large numbers of people from all over South Wales to hear him. An increasing awareness of widespread illiteracy in Wales led him to set up a system of circulating schools, held for three months at a time in churches, barns or private houses. People of all ages were taught to read with the Welsh Prayer Book and Bible as their textbooks. By the time of Griffith Jones' death in 1761, 158,000 people had been taught to read in 3,495 of his schools. This astonishing achievement played a major part in the Welsh spiritual awakening of the eighteenth century.

A Reading from a letter of Griffith Jones

An uncharitable Christian is a down-right contradiction. Of all the enjoyments of this world, of all endowments of the human mind, and of all the heaven-born graces which adorn a pious soul, the most amiable and excellent charity is the greatest.

It is a charity that crowns and consummates the Christian character; which every genuine Christian aspires after, and can never be a Christian indeed without it. In brief, it is the substance of every virtue, of every duty, and of all obedience: without it, faith itself can avail no more to salvation, than infidelity. It unites the spirits of all good men in the bond of peace, and smothers all contention; softens all severe censure, and covereth a multitude of sins. It is indeed the sum of present and future bliss; and its nature, reward and joy never fail, but remain for ever, durable as eternity! In a word, it is the divine nature, and the offspring of God; and, if I may presume to advance one step farther, charity is so essential to goodness, perfection and felicity, that the want of it, if that was possible, (with awful reverence I write it) would divest the great Jehovah of his divinity; for God is love. And can we then be Christian, good or happy, without it?

9 April

Dietrich Bonhoeffer

Lutheran Pastor, Martyr, 1945

Dietrich Bonhoeffer was born in 1906 into an academic family. Ordained in the Lutheran Church, his theology was influenced by Karl Barth and he became a lecturer: in Spain, the USA and in 1931 back in Berlin. Opposed to the philosophy of Nazism, he was one of the leaders of the Confessing Church, a movement which broke away from the Nazi-dominated

Lutherans in 1934. Banned from teaching, and harassed by Hitler's regime, he bravely returned to Germany at the outbreak of war in 1939, despite being on a lecture tour in the United States at the time. His defiant opposition to the Nazis led to his arrest in 1943. His experiences led him to propose a more radical theology in his later works, which have been influential among post-war theologians. He was murdered by the Nazi police in Flossenburg concentration camp on this day in 1945.

A Reading from a letter of Dietrich Bonhoeffer to his friend Eberhard Bethge, written from Tegel Prison, dated 21 July 1944

During the last year or so I've come to know and understand more and more the profound this-worldliness of Christianity. The Christian is not a *homo religiosus*, but simply a human being, as Jesus was human – in contrast, shall we say, to John the Baptist. I don't mean the shallow and banal this-worldliness of the enlightened, the busy, the comfortable, or the lascivious, but the profound this-worldliness, characterised by discipline and the constant knowledge of death and resurrection.

I remember a conversation that I had in America thirteen years ago with a young French pastor. We were asking ourselves quite simply what we wanted to do with our lives. He said he would like to become a saint (and I think it's quite likely that he did become one). At the time I was very impressed, but I disagreed with him, and said, in effect, that I should like to learn to have faith. For a long time I didn't realise the depth of the contrast. I thought I could acquire faith by trying to live a holy life, or something like it. I suppose I wrote *The Cost of Discipleship* as the end of that path. Today I can see the dangers of that book, though I still stand by what I wrote.

I discovered later, and I'm still discovering right up to this moment, that it is only by living completely in this world that one learns to have faith. One must completely abandon any attempt to make something of oneself, whether it be a saint, or a converted sinner, or a churchman (a so-called priestly type!), a righteous person or an unrighteous one, a sick or a healthy one. By this-worldliness I mean living unreservedly in life's duties, problems, successes and failures, experiences and perplexities. In so doing we throw ourselves completely into the arms of God, taking seriously, not our own sufferings, but those of God in the world – watching with Christ in Gethsemane. That, I think, is faith; that is *metanoia*; and that is how one becomes a human being and a Christian. How can success make us arrogant, or failure lead us astray, when we share in God's sufferings through a life of this kind?

I am glad to have been able to learn this, and I know I've been able to do so only along the road that I've travelled. So I'm grateful for the past and present, and content with them. You may be surprised at such a personal letter; but for once I want to say this kind of thing, to whom should I say it?

May God in his mercy lead us through these times; but above all, may he lead us to himself.

alternative reading

A Poem by Dietrich Bonhoeffer, written in Tegel Prison, and dated 9 July 1944

Who am I?

Who am I? They often tell me
I would step from my cell's confinement
calmly, cheerfully, firmly,
like a squire from his country-house.

Who am I? They often tell me
I would talk to my warders
freely and friendly and clearly,
as though it were mine to command.

Who am I? They also tell me
I would bear the days of misfortune
equably, smilingly, proudly,
like one accustomed to win.

Am I then really all that which others tell of ?
Or am I only what I know of myself,
restless and longing and sick, like a bird in a cage,
struggling for breath,
as though hands were compressing my throat,
yearning for colours, for flowers, for the voices of birds,
thirsting for words of kindness, for neighbourliness,
trembling with anger at despotisms and petty humiliation,
tossing in expectation of great events,
powerlessly trembling for friends at an infinite distance,
weary and empty at praying, at thinking, at making,
faint, and ready to say farewell to it all?

Who am I? This or the other?
Am I one person today, and tomorrow another?
Am I both at once? A hypocrite before others,
and before myself a contemptibly woebegone weakling?
Or is something within me still like a beaten army,
fleeing in disorder from victory already achieved?

Who am I? They mock me, these lonely questions of mine.
Whoever I am, thou knowest, O God, I am thine.

9 April

Saints, Martyrs and Missionaries of South America

The Gospel was first brought to South America by the Spanish and Portuguese in the years after Columbus' landfall. Today we recall those who have worthily proclaimed the Gospel of Christ in South America: people like Bartolomé de las Casas and Martin de Porres who challenged the injustices inflicted on the native people, Allen Gardiner who died at the southernmost tip of the continent, and Oscar Romero, the Archbishop of San Salvador murdered in his cathedral for preaching economic and social justice. We give thanks for their witness and that of all the saints of God in South America.

Note: For readings on the above mentioned saints, see their individual entries as follows:

Bartolomé de las Casas	20 July
Martin de Porres	3 November
Allen Gardiner	6 September
Oscar Romero	24 March

A Reading from *The Cost of Discipleship* by Dietrich Bonhoeffer

The body of Christ takes up space on earth. That is a consequence of the incarnation. Christ came into his own. But at his birth they gave him a manger, for 'there was no room in the inn'. At his death they thrust him out, and his body hung between earth and heaven on the gallows. But despite all this, the incarnation does involve a claim to a space of its own on earth. Anything which claims space is visible. Hence the body of Christ can only be a visible body, or else it is not a body at all. The physical body of the man Jesus is visible to all, his divine sonship only to the eye of faith, just as that body as the body of God incarnate is visible only to faith. That Jesus was in the flesh was visible fact, but that he bore our flesh is a matter of faith.

A truth, a doctrine, or a religion need no space for themselves. They are disembodied entities. They are heard, learnt and apprehended, and that is all. But the incarnate Son of God needs not only ears or hearts, but living men and women who will follow him. That is why he called his disciples into a literal, bodily following, and thus made his fellowship with them a visible reality. That fellowship was founded and sustained by Jesus Christ, the incarnate Lord himself. It was the Word made flesh which had called them and created their bodily fellowship with him. Having been called, they could no longer remain in obscurity, for they were the light that must shine, the city set on the hill which must be seen. Their fellowship with him was visibly overshadowed by the cross and passion of Jesus Christ. In order that they might enjoy that fellowship with him, the disciples must leave everything else behind, and submit to suffering and persecution. Yet even in the midst of their persecutions they receive back all they had lost in visible form – brothers, sisters, fields and houses in his fellowship. The Church consisting of Christ's followers manifest to the whole world a visible community. Here were bodies which acted, worked and suffered in fellowship with Jesus.

10 April

William Law

Priest, Spiritual Writer, 1761

Born at King's Cliffe in Northamptonshire in 1686, William Law was educated at Emmanuel College Cambridge and, after ordination as a deacon, became a Fellow of the College in 1711. When George I came to the throne in 1714, William declined to take the Oath of Allegiance, being a member of the Non-Juror party who believed the anointed, but deposed, monarch James II and his heirs should occupy the throne. He lost his fellowship but in 1728 he was made a priest, and in the same year published A Serious Call to a Devout and Holy Life, which much influenced such people as Samuel Johnson and John and Charles Wesley. In it he stresses the moral virtues, a personal prayer life and asceticism. He returned to King's Cliffe in 1740, where he led a life of devotion, simplicity and caring for the poor. He remained there the rest of his life and died on this day in the year 1761.

A Reading from *A Serious Call to a Devout and Holy Life*
by William Law

Devotion signifies a life given or devoted to God. He therefore is the devout man who lives no longer to his own will, or the way and spirit of the world, but to the sole will of God, who considers God in everything, who serves God in everything, who makes all the parts of his common life parts of piety by doing everything in the name of God and under such rules as are conformable to his glory.

We readily acknowledge that God alone is to be the rule and measure of our prayers, that in them we are to look wholly unto him and act wholly for him, that we are only to pray in such a manner for such things and such ends as are suitable to his glory.

Now let anyone but find out the reason why he is to be thus strictly pious in his prayers and he will find the same as strong a reason to be as strictly pious in all the other parts of his life. For there is not the least shadow of a reason why we should make God the rule and measure of our prayers, why we should then look wholly unto him and pray according to his will, but what equally proves it necessary for us to look wholly unto God, and make him rule and measure of all the other actions of our life. For any of life, any employment of our talents, whether of our parts, our time, or money, that is not strictly according to the will of God, is not for such ends as are suitable to his glory, and are as great absurdities and failings as prayers that are not according to the will of God.

For there is no other reason why our prayers should be according to the will of God, why they should have nothing in them but what is wise, and holy, and heavenly, there is no other reason for this but that our lives may be of the same nature, full of the same wisdom, holiness, and heavenly tempers that we may live unto God in the same spirit that we pray unto him. Were it not our strict duty to live by reason, to devote all the actions of our lives to God, were it not absolutely necessary to walk before him in wisdom and holiness and all heavenly conversation, doing everything in his name and for his glory, there would be no excellency or wisdom in the most heavenly prayers. Nay, such prayers would be absurdities: they would be like prayers for wings when it was no part of our duty to fly.

As sure, therefore, as there is any wisdom in praying for the Spirit of God, so sure is it that we are to make that Spirit the rule of all our actions; as sure as it is our duty to look wholly unto God in our prayers, so sure is it that it is our duty to live wholly unto God in our lives. But we can no more be said to live unto God unless we live unto him in all the ordinary actions of our life, unless he be the rule and measure of all our ways, than we can be said to pray unto God unless our prayer look wholly unto him. So that unreasonable and absurd ways of life, whether in labour or diversion, whether they consume our time or our money, are like unreasonable and absurd prayers, and are as truly an offence unto God.

alternative reading

A Reading from *The Spirit of Love* by William Law

God always was and always will be the same immutable will to all goodness. So that as certainly as he is the creator, so certainly is he the blesser of every created thing, and can give nothing but blessing, goodness, and happiness from himself because he has in himself nothing else to give. It is much more possible for the sun to give forth darkness than for God to do, or be, or give forth anything but blessing and goodness. Now this is the ground and origin of the spirit of love in the creature; it is and must be a will to all goodness, and you have not the spirit of love till you have this will to all goodness at all times and on all occasions. You may indeed do many works of love and delight in them, especially at such times as they are not inconvenient to you, or contradictory to your state or temper or occurrences in life. But the spirit of love is not in you till it is the spirit of your life, till you live freely, willingly, and universally according to it.

For every spirit acts with freedom and universality according to what it is. It needs no command to live its own life, or be what it is, no more than need bid wrath be wrathful. And therefore when love is the spirit of your life, it will have the freedom and universality of a spirit; it will always live and work in love, not because of this or here or there, but because the spirit of love can only love, wherever it is or goes or whatever is done to it. As the sparks know no motion but that of flying upwards, whether it be in the dark of the night or in the light of the day, so the spirit of love is always in the same course; it knows no difference of time, or persons, but whether it gives or forgives, bears or forbears, it is equally doing its own delightful work, equally blessed from itself. For the spirit of love, wherever it is, is its own blessing and happiness because it is the truth and reality of God in the soul, and therefore is in the same joy of life and is the same good to itself, everywhere and on every occasion.

10 April

William of Ockham

Friar, Philosopher, Teacher of the Faith, 1347

Born at Ockham in Surrey in about the year 1285, William entered the Franciscan Order and, as a friar, he first studied and then taught at Oxford. His writings were ever the subject of close scrutiny, this being a time when heresy was suspected everywhere, it seemed, but he never received any formal condemnation. Later in life, he entered the controversy between the rival popes and had to flee for his life. His much-used principle of economy, often referred to as 'Ockham's Razor', stated that only individual things exist and that they are directly understood by the thinking mind and that this intuitive knowledge is caused naturally. His doctrine of God led him to destroy the thirteenth-century concept of the relationship between theology and philosophy, and he took the study of the philosophy of religion onto a new level. He died on this day in the year 1347.

A Reading from *John Wyclif and his English Precursors* by Gerhard Lecher

The ablest and most strongly-marked representative of theological and philosophical thinking in the first half of the fourteenth century was a man who was born in England, and trained under the influence of the English spirit, but who spent the later portion of his life on the Continent, partly at the University of Paris, and partly at the court of the Emperor Louis of Bavaria. His name was William of Ockham (Occam), a man who as a scholar, as a writer, as a Franciscan friar, and finally as a strenuous leader of the opposition against the absolutism of the papacy, took a position of great prominence in his day. His philosophical nominalism had a prophetic and national significance, inasmuch as it prepared the way for that inductive method of philosophising which was put forward several centuries later by his own countrymen, Francis Bacon, Thomas Hobbes and John Locke.

His protest against papal absolutism, against the assertion of an unlimited *plenitudo potestatis* of the pope, was the result of clear, self-conscious, profound reflection. He declared it to be totally erroneous, heretical, and dangerous to souls, to maintain that the pope, by the ordinance of Christ, possesses unlimited power, both spiritual and temporal. If this were so, he argues, he might depose princes at his pleasure, and likewise the possessions and goods of ordinary people. We should all be the pope's slaves; and in spiritual things the position would be the same. In that case the law of Christ would bring with it intolerable slavery, much worse than the Old Testament ever knew; whereas the gospel of Christ, in comparison with the old covenant, is a law of liberty.

In this connection Ockham opposes, in the most emphatic manner, the assertion of some flatterers of the Roman Court, that the pope has power to make new articles of faith; that he is infallible; that into no error, no sin of simony, can he possibly fall. He starts from the general principle, that the whole hierarchy, including the papal primacy, is not an immediately divine, but only a human order. In one place he even gives expression to the bold thought, that it would, to the general body of believers, be of more advantage to have several primates or chief priests (*summi pontifices*) than to have one only. The unity of the Church does not depend upon there being only one *summus pontifex;* the danger of moral corruption of the whole body is much greater with only one head than with several.

It was not Ockham's meaning to advise a leap from the ground of the absolute and sole domination of the papacy to that of an unconditioned parochial principle, as if this latter contained in it all the safeguards of truth and weal. No; only to the Church itself as a whole, but not to any part of it is the promise given that it can never fall into any error contradictory to the faith. Thus although all the members of a General Council should fall into error, the hope would not need on that account to be surrendered, that God would reveal his truth to babes, or would inspire those who already know the truth to stand up in its defence.

High above the pope, and high above the Church itself, in William of Ockham's view stands Christ the Lord. In his own words: 'The Head of the Church and its foundation is one – Christ alone.'

11 April

George Augustus Selwyn

First Bishop of New Zealand, 1878

George Augustus Selwyn was born in 1809, educated at Cambridge and upon ordination became curate of Windsor. In 1841 he was made the first Bishop of New Zealand and remained there for twenty-seven years, during the first years travelling when few roads or bridges existed. In the wars between colonists and Maoris he stood out heroically for Maori rights, at the cost of fierce attacks from both sides and grave personal danger in his efforts to part the warriors, until later he was revered as one of the founders of New Zealand as well as of its Church. He taught himself to navigate and gathered congregations in the Melanesian Islands. His Constitution for the New Zealand Church influenced the churches of the Anglican Communion and he was a chief founder of the Lambeth Conference of bishops. In 1868 he was persuaded to become the Bishop of Lichfield in England and died there on this day in the year 1878.

A Reading from a sermon of George Augustus Selwyn delivered before the University of Cambridge in 1854

In the mission-field, schism is an acknowledged evil. We make a rule, therefore, never to introduce controversy among a native people. If the ground has been preoccupied by any other religious body, we forbear to enter. And I can speak from observation, ranging over nearly half the Southern Pacific Ocean, that wherever this law of religious unity is adopted, there the gospel has its full and unchecked power. Missionaries must be ready at a moment to put their lives in their hands and go out to preach the Gospel to others, with no weapon but prayer, and with no refuge but in God.

I have visited many of the islands in their days of darkness, and therefore I can rejoice in the light that now bursts upon them, from whatever quarter it may come. I feel that there is an episcopate of love as well as of authority, and that these simple teachers, scattered over the wide ocean, are objects of the same interest to me as Apollos was to Aquila. If in anything they lack knowledge, it seems to be our duty to 'expound to them the way of God more perfectly', and to do this as their friend and brother, 'not as having dominion over their faith, but as helpers of their joy'.

Above all other things, it is our duty to guard against inflicting upon them the curses of our disunion, lest we make every little island in the ocean a counterpart of our own divided and contentious Church. And, further, I would point to the mission-field as the great outlet for the excited and sensitive spirit of the Church at home. There are minds which have placed before them an ideal perfection which can never be realised on earth. They burn with a zeal for God which cannot bear to be confined. Such men would be the very salt of the earth if they would but go out into the mission-field. There are five hundred millions of heathen still waiting for the gospel.

But how, you will ask, shall truth of doctrine be maintained if we tolerate in the mission-field every form of error, and provide no safeguard for the purity of the faith? I answer that, as running water purifies itself, so Christian work is seen to correct its own mistakes. Is it, then, a hope too unreasonable to be entertained, that the power which will heal the divisions of the Church at home may come from her distant fields of missionary work?

And now, my dear friends, I commend you to the grace of God's Holy Spirit. I go from hence if it be the will of God, to the most distant of all countries. There God has planted a standard of the cross, as a signal to his Church to fill up the intervening spaces. Fill up the void. The Spirit of God is ready to be poured out upon all flesh, and some of you are his chosen vessels. Again, I say, offer yourselves to the Primate of our Church. The voice of the Lord is asking, 'Whom shall I send, and who will go for us?' May many of you who intend, by God's grace, to dedicate yourselves to the ministry, answer at once: "Here am I: send me."

12 April

William Forbes

Bishop, 1634

Born in Aberdeen in 1585, William Forbes was for a time Professor of Logic in the university there. He ministered in Alford and Monymusk, then at St Nicholas' Church, Aberdeen. A theologian of European rank, his strongly patristic, eucharistic theology led him into controversy. His work has been used in international talks between Anglicans and Roman Catholics in modern times. He was nominated by Charles I in 1633 to be the first Bishop of Edinburgh, but he died within two months of his consecration.

A Reading from *Considerationes modestae*,
a treatise on justification, by William Forbes

Justifying faith (to speak accurately and theologically) is nothing else than a firm and sure assent of the mind, produced by the Holy Ghost from the word, by which we acknowledge all things revealed by God in the Scriptures, and especially those concerning the mystery of our redemption and salvation wrought by Christ to be most true, by reason of the authority of God who has revealed them.

Therefore, considered in itself and in its essence, it is nothing else than Catholic faith, which itself doubtless justifies a man, if all the other things which are necessary to justification accompany it.

And its subject is the intellect, and not the will, although belief is ruled by the will; for 'faith is a willing assent of the soul'; 'other things a man can do though unwilling; but he can believe only when he is willing'; and when the act of belief is in Scripture attributed to the heart, we must thereby understand the mind; since to believe, properly speaking, is nothing else than to assent to what is said, and to account it true; for thus far we have shown by many proofs that assurance is no part of faith, nor indeed does it properly belong to hope either; for assurance is an assurance not only of what is future, but also of what is present, as when any one confides in his strength when carrying a burden, or in his swiftness when he runs; yet it approaches nearer to the nature of hope than to that of faith, whence it is said to be 'hope strengthened'.

16 April

Padarn

Bishop, sixth century

The Welsh Triads describe Padarn as one of the 'three blessed visitors of the Island of Britain', along with David and Teilo. There is a tradition that the three saints travelled together on pilgrimage to Jerusalem. It is said that Padarn was presented with a choral cope there and the saint thus became regarded as a singer and musician. Padarn founded a major ecclesiastical centre at Llanbadarn Fawr in Ceredigion, of which he may have been the first bishop. Padarn's churches may be linked to the network of Roman roads and this might suggest that this connects the saint with residual Romano-British Christianity in mid-Wales (Padarn being the Welsh version of the common Latin name Paternus). This could imply that his missionary work preceded that of his two fellow 'blessed visitors'.

A Reading from *The Life of Saint David* by Rhigyfarch the Wise

One night an angel appeared to Dewi and said, 'Prepare yourself tomorrow, put on your sandals and leave for Jerusalem. Set off on the journey you have longed to make. I shall call two others to be your travelling companions, namely Eliud' (now known as Teilo, since he was once a monk in his monastery) 'and also Paternus' (now known as Padarn and whose manner of life and virtues are contained in his own story). But the holy father, amazed at the authoritative command said, 'But how shall this be? For those whom you promise as companions are three or more days distant from us and from each other. It is impossible for us to gather here tomorrow.' The angel replied, 'Tonight I shall go to each of them, and they shall come to the meeting place that I shall now show you.'

Without delay the saint disposed of the contents of his cell and set out early in the morning with his brothers' blessing. He arrived at the meeting place where he found his promised companions, and they all set out together. As fellow travellers they were equals and no one considered himself superior to another; each of them was servant and each of them was master. They were diligent in prayer, and watered their way with tears; their merits increased with each step they took. They were one in mind, in joy, and in sorrow. They sailed across the Channel and came to Gaul.

Finally, they approached the city of Jerusalem, the goal of their desire. But in the night before their arrival an angel appeared to the Patriarch in a dream saying, 'Three Christian men from the lands of the West are approaching whom you will receive with joy and hospitality. Bless them and consecrate them as bishops for me.' The Patriarch then prepared three thrones of greatest distinction, and when the holy men reached the city, he greatly rejoiced and warmly welcomed them to the thrones prepared for them. Refreshed by spiritual conversation, they gave thanks to God.

Having completed everything, they decided to return to their own land. They said farewell to the Patriarch and returned home. Each of them awaited the promise of the Patriarch and received the gifts conveyed by angels, Dewi in the monastery called Llangyvelech, Paternus (Padarn) and Eliud (Teilo) in their own monasteries. Therefore the common people say that they came down from heaven.

16 April

Magnus of Orkney

Martyr, *c.*1116

At the end of the eleventh century, the Earldom of Orkney was divided between cousins Haakon Paulson and Magnus Erlingsson, one a war-like Viking chief, the other a man of peace. They ruled jointly but uneasily for some years, but eventually Haakon claimed sole sovereignty. In the year 1116, a council was summoned for Easter, but Haakon arrived with a large force and refused to allow Magnus the option either of flight or of exile. Magnus faced his death heroically and with faith. The shrine for his remains, Kirkwall cathedral, was erected only twenty years after his murder.

A Reading from *The Life of Saint Magnus*

During the course of his life the holy Earl Magnus was transformed from Saul into Paul, from a slayer of men into a preacher. For all his past evil ways, he disciplined himself, daily acknowledging in sighs and acts of steadfast repentance his many sins. He emerged from this process a new person, as one inclined to honour God, as one whose nature God had changed from evil to good, from sinful to wholesome, from defiled into holy, from polluted into pure and blessed. Magnus was the conversion of your right hand, O almighty God! O God, you who are strong to save, gracious in your help, glad to raise up, and mighty to preserve us!

So it was that Magnus became a holy person. He began to cultivate the soil of his heart with the strong ploughshare of confession. He killed within himself the man of misfortune and hid him in the sand. He buried the idols of Laban under the roots of the trees. He tore out by the roots his sins and failings, and adorned himself with the virtues of good deeds in a godly manner and with manly steadfastness. He began to flourish like an olive tree, to be honoured for his good life and gracious works. Just as a cypress grows taller than other tress, so did Saint Magnus grow tall until he was truly *magnus*, a man as ‘great’ in divine things as he was in name.

Earl Magnus was renowned in his rule and exercise of authority. He was dignified and upright, a loyal friend and brave, both skilled and victorious in battle, yet gentle in peace. He was a strong ruler, gracious in his speech, merciful, and prudent in his counsel. He enjoyed everyone’s praise. He was generous with his money and to his chieftains. Every day he gave help to the poor for the love of God. He punished crime and theft, and had all

Vikings and violent men, rich and poor alike, slain. In his judgements he was no respecter of persons; he respected God's law more than the differences of birth. Magnus observed God's commandments with diligence in everything, and was unsparing of himself. His many and excellent virtues were visible to God but he was careful to hide from the eyes of men.

alternative reading

A Reading from *The Life of Saint Magnus*

The holy Earl Magnus came, as arranged, to Egilsey with his men to meet his cousin, Haakon. But when they saw Haakon's eight warships, Magnus knew instinctively that treachery was abroad. His men too saw the vast numbers of armed soldiers and realised that this was to be no peaceful meeting.

When he saw the treachery of Haakon, Magnus withdrew to a church on the island in order to pray, and was there throughout the night, not out of fear or dread, but rather to commit all to God. His men offered to fight and defend him, but Magnus answered, 'I will not have you place your lives in danger for me. If peace cannot be made between two kinsmen, then let it be as God wills. For I would rather suffer evil and treachery, than inflict it on others.'

In the morning, Earl Haakon dispatched four of his most fiercest warriors to seize Earl Magnus wherever he was. These four, who from their ferocity resembled more wild wolves than rational men, always thirsting for bloodshed, burst into the church just as mass was ending.

When Earl Magnus was brought before Earl Haakon, he said to Haakon with great calmness, 'You have not acted well, cousin, in breaking your oath, but perhaps you did so from the malice and with the egging on of others, rather than of your own free will. I will make you three offers.' Earl Haakon said, 'I will hear what you have to say.'

Holy Magnus said, 'My first offer is to quit this land for Rome or Jerusalem, to seek in pilgrimage the holy places of God where I might make atonement for both of us. I will take two ships with my men and such equipment as I need, and I swear that I will never set foot on Orkney again.'

This offer was quickly refused by Haakon and his men. Then said Earl Magnus, 'Since our lives are in your power, and since I know that I have offended God in many things and have need to make amends, send me to Scotland to friends of us both. Only allow me two men for company, and I vow never to return without your permission.'

This too they at once rejected, offering various reasons. 'Then,' said the brave knight, 'my options are limited. I have but one choice left which I offer you, for God knows I am more concerned for my salvation than for my human body. Let me be maimed in my limbs, or let my eyes be put out, and put me in so dark a dungeon that I never come out.' Then said Earl Haakon, 'This offer I accept, and demand no more.' But his men became angry and refused.

Then Earl Magnus begged leave to pray, and it was granted. He fell to the ground and gave himself to the power of God, offering himself in sacrifice. Not for himself alone did he pray, but for his enemies and murderers as well. He forgave them with his whole heart.'

When the noble martyr had ended his prayer and crossed himself, Lifolf struck him on the head a heavy blow with an axe. Earl Magnus fell to his knees, and in martyrdom forsook the miseries of this world for the everlasting joys of heaven. He whom the murderer dispatched from earth, God allowed to reign in heaven. His body fell to the earth, but his spirit was wonderfully taken up into the glory of heaven by the angels.

16 April

Isabella Gilmore

Deaconess, 1923

Born in 1842, Isabella Gilmore, the sister of William Morris, was a nurse at Guy's Hospital in London and in 1886, was asked by Bishop Thorold of Rochester to pioneer deaconess work in his diocese. The bishop overcame her initial reluctance and together they planned for an Order of Deaconesses along the same lines as the ordained ministry. She was made a deaconess in 1887 and a training house developed on North Side, Clapham Common, later to be called Gilmore House in her memory. Isabella herself retired in 1906. During her nineteen years of service, she trained head deaconesses for at least seven other dioceses. At her memorial service, Dr Randall Davidson predicted that 'Some day, those who know best will be able to trace much of the origin and root of the revival of the Deaconess Order to the life, work, example and words of Isabella Gilmore.' She died on this day in 1923.

A Reading from the writings of Isabella Gilmore

God has placed us in the world and we are to work for it and in it. We can make our secular work full of his Spirit, and we can make what we call our spiritual work full of the spirit of the world if we will; if Christ is not in us we are nothing, and can do nothing; if he is, then we can go on in peace and quietness, not troubling, rejoicing that the work was given us, full and running over, more than we could ever do, and that he blessed us in it, gave us love and gratitude beyond our deserts.

We must teach, but not argue against people's beliefs. Let them talk; if they abuse the Church as they often do at a first acquaintance, silence will stop them far more quickly than words. Get them to talk of something they do love; then talk to them of Jesus.

I think myself, the secret of all true work is knowledge of those for whom we work, and this takes so long to get, and means such single-hearted diligence; to go visiting with your heart up in the clouds or elsewhere is useless, you had better stay away; to go thinking you are going to teach is just as useless, but to go as a friend. Who can tell where your influence shall cease?

17 April

Donnan and his Companions

Martyrs, *c.*617

Donnan (or Dounan) was an Irish missionary, roughly contemporary with Columba, who worked in Galloway, Argyll and the islands of the Inner Hebrides. He established a monastery on the island of Eigg where he and fifty-two companions were massacred by Viking pirates in around the year 617.

A Reading from a sermon of Augustine

The Lord Jesus Christ not only instructed his martyrs through his teaching, he strengthened them through his own example. In order that those who would suffer for him might have an example to follow, he first suffered for them. He showed the way and became the way.

When we talk of death, we speak in terms of the body and the soul. In one sense, the soul cannot die, but in another it can. It cannot die inasmuch as the awareness of itself endures; yet it can die if it loses God. For just as the soul is the life of the body, so God is the life of the soul. The body perishes when the soul that is its life departs: the soul perishes when God casts it away. So lest God cast our souls away, let us always live in faith. Only so will we not fear to die for God, and not die abandoned by God.

The death of the body will always remain a fear. And yet Christ the Lord has made his martyrs a counter-balance to our fear. Why worry about the safety of limbs when we have been reassured that the hairs on our head are secure? Does not Scripture say that 'the very hairs on your head are numbered'? Why should our human frailty cause us to be so frightened when the truth has spoken thus?

Blessed indeed then, are the saints whose memory we commemorate on the day of their passion. In surrendering their security in this world, they received an eternal crown and immortality without end. As we gather to remember them in prayer, their example sends us messages of encouragement. When we hear how the martyrs suffered, we rejoice and glorify God in them. We do not grieve because they died. If they had not died, do you think they would still be alive today? Their confession of faith served to consummate what sickness would one day also have brought about.

Therefore, my dear friends, let us rejoice in their commemoration. Let us pray to God that we may follow in the steps of his martyrs. They were mortal like you: their manner of birth no different from yours. They had bodies no different from your own. We are all descended from Adam: we should all seek to return to Christ.

Honour the martyrs; praise, love, preach and honour them. But remember, worship only the God of the martyrs.

17 April

Stephen Harding

Abbot of Cîteaux, 1134

Robert of Molesme, Alberic and Stephen Harding, along with their companions, are honoured as the founders of the New Monastery in 1098 which in a short while came to be called the Abbey of Cîteaux. If the title of 'founder' of the Cistercian Order can be ascribed to any one man that person would be Stephen Harding, elected abbot in 1101 until his death in 1134. Today, however, the charism of the founder of the Order is more usually located in the group of twenty abbots who assembled for the General Chapter of 1123, among whom most significantly was Bernard of Clairvaux. It was from Abbot Stephen that Bernard received his monastic formation, and if nothing else, Stephen Harding is honoured for discernment in recognizing and fostering the outstanding gifts of this young monk. The desire of the Cistercians was to live the Rule of Saint Benedict more integrally, to rediscover the meaning of the monastic life and to translate their discovery into structures adapted to their age. The white monks were not satisfied with compromises or accommodations. It was essential values that concerned them, not an archaeological reconstruction of a past monastic age.

A Reading from the *Little Exordium*, one of the foundation documents of the Cistercian Order

The man of God, Alberic, after he had practised faithfully the regular discipline in the school of Christ for nine and a half years, went home to the Lord, glorious in faith and virtues and deservedly rewarded by God in eternal life.

His successor was a brother by the name of Stephen, an Englishman by nationality, who had also come there with the others from Molesme, a lover of the *Rule* and of the new place. During his time the brethren, together with the abbot, forbade the duke of the country or any other lord to keep court at any time in that monastery as they used to do before at the big festivals.

In order that in the house of God, in which it was their desire to serve God directly day and night, nothing should remain that savoured of pride and superfluity or that might eventually corrupt poverty, that safeguard of virtues, which they had chosen of their own free will, they resolved not to keep gold or silver crosses but only painted wooden ones; candelabra only of iron; thuribles only of copper or iron; chasubles only of wool or linen, without silk, gold or silver weave; albs or amices of linen only, also without silk or gold or silver. They eliminated the use of all kinds of elaborate coverings, copes, dalmatics and tunicles. But they retained silver chalices, not golden – though when it could be done, gold plated, as well as the communion tube of silver, gold plated if possible; stoles and maniples were of silk only, without gold or silver. They also ordered that the altar cloths be made of linen and without embroidery, and that the cruets should have nothing in gold or silver on them.

In those days the monastery increased in its possessions of land, vineyards, meadows and farmhouses; they did not decrease, however, in monastic discipline and therefore God visited that place at this time in pouring out his widest mercy over them; for they prayed, cried and wept before him day and night, groaning long and deep, and had almost come to the brink of despair because they had no successors.

But God's mercy sent to that community many learned clerks as well as laymen who were both powerful and distinguished in the world. Thirty all at once entered with joy into the cells of the noviciate and by bravely combating their own vices and the temptation of evil spirits completed their course. Through their example old and young of every walk of life and from various parts of the world were encouraged when they saw through them that what they had feared impossible, that is the observance of the *Rule*, was in fact possible. So they began to flock together there in order to bow their proud necks under the sweet yoke of Christ, and to love fervently the rigorous and burdensome precepts of the *Rule*, and they began to make the community wonderfully happy and strong.

18 April

Laserian

Abbot of Leighlin, 639

Laserian, often called affectionately 'Mo-laise', was Abbot of Old Leighlin. The cathedral, sheltering among the hills of County Carlow in Ireland, is a place of peace and beauty. It is said that Laserian may have received his training in Iona. His name is honoured in Scotland (Arran) as well as in other parts of Ireland (Inishmurray, off the coast of County Sligo). He died on this day in the year 639.

A Reading from *The Rule of Carthage*,
a Celtic monastic Rule dating from the seventh century,
concerning the duties of a monk

If you are a monk, living under discipline, then abandon all evil and live within the laws of the Church without laxity, without fault.

Let there be no carelessness in your lifestyle, no dissent, no hatred for anyone, no theft, no deceit, no gluttony, but always a perseverance that is good.

Have no private property, no bad habits, no valuables; do not grumble, do not insult anyone, be not jealous or proud.

Be not contentious or self-willed, do not emulate another, do

not be angry, do not persecute another, have no particular dislikes, be not aggressive or forceful.

Be not a weakling, do not despair, be not deceitful, not talkative, not a company seeker.

Do not be covetous or over-active; be not a slave to gluttony which destroys all good, be not a wine-bibber or over-jolly, let not silly talk be your constant companion.

Carry out everything with permission, and without hesitation or delay; never repay evil for evil while you live in this decaying body of clay.

Show humility and joy towards friend and stranger alike, and homage, obedience, and fealty towards every person.

Live in absolute poverty, being neither niggardly nor unjust, waiting for your reward by the graves of the saints.

You should be gentle, modest, and calm while carrying out your duties, performing each act, even if distasteful, with zeal and perseverance.

Be patient, sincere, and gentle towards all, making supplications and prayers to Christ at all times.

Always proclaim the truth and proscribe evil of all kinds, making frequent and honest confession under the guidance of a holy abbot.

The King above is worthy of having every action done with restraint of hands and feet, eyes and ears, mouth and heart.

Let us keep in mind the day of death, something common to all, and let us fear the pains of eternity that may be our lot after death.

It is a commendable practice joyfully to accept tribulation and to be patient with them at all times, mindful of the folk in heaven.

Let us reverence the seniors and be submissive to them, let us instruct the juniors with profit and diligence.

Let us pray for our contemporaries who have the greatest love of us, that they exchange not their Creator for the damned and obdurate demon.

Let us forgive all who have wronged us by voice, word, or deed, for such is the testament of the King of the stars.

It is the command of God that we love those who hate us in the world and that we return good for evil.

19 April

Alphege

Archbishop of Canterbury, Martyr, 1012

Alphege became a monk at Deerhurst near Gloucester and withdrew in later life to be a hermit in Somerset. The Archbishop of Canterbury, Dunstan, drew him back to be Abbot of Bath and, in 984, Bishop of Winchester. In 1005 he was made Archbishop of Canterbury, where his austere life and lavish almsgiving made him a revered and much-loved man. In the year 1011, the Danes overran south-east England, taking Alphege prisoner. They put the enormous ransom of £3000 on his head, but Alphege refused to pay it and forbade anyone from doing so, knowing that it would impoverish the ordinary people even more. He was brutally murdered by his captors at Greenwich on this day in the year 1012.

A Reading from the Anglo-Saxon Chronicle

In the year 1011 the king and his councillors sent to the Danish army and asked for peace, and promised them tribute and provisions on condition that they should cease their ravaging. They had already overrun much of the country. The disasters befell us through bad policy, in that they were never offered tribute in time nor fought against; but when they had done most to our injury, peace and truce were with them; and for all this truce and tribute they journeyed nonetheless in bands everywhere, and harried our wretched people, and plundered and killed them.

Then the Danes besieged the city of Canterbury between the Nativity of Saint Mary and Michaelmas Day, and eventually they got inside the city by treachery, for Aelfmaer, whose life Archbishop Alphege had saved, betrayed it. They captured the archbishop, and the king's reeve Aelfweard, and Abbess Leofrun of Minster-in-Thanet, and Bishop Godwine of Rochester; but they let Abbot Aelfmaer of Saint Augustine's monastery escape. So they took captive there all the ecclesiastics, men and women – it was impossible for any one to tell how many people that was – and they stayed afterwards in that burgh as long as they pleased.

After they had ransacked the whole burgh, they went to their ships, and took the archbishop with them.

Alphege became a captive, he who had been head of the English people and of Christendom. There could misery be seen where happiness was often seen before, in that wretched city from which first came to us Christianity and happiness in divine and secular things. The Danes kept the archbishop with them till the time when they martyred him.

Next year the Witan assembled at London for Easter, and stayed until the tribute had been paid. Then on the Saturday, the army became greatly incensed against the bishop because he would not promise them any money, and forbade that anything should be paid for him by way of ransom. They were also very drunk, for wine from the south had been brought there. They seized the bishop and brought him to their assembly on nineteenth of April, the eve of Low Sunday, and shamefully put him to death there. They pelted him with bones and ox-heads, until one of them struck him on the head with the back of an axe. He sank down with the blow, his holy blood falling on the ground, and he sent his holy soul to God's kingdom.

In the morning, his body was carried from Greenwich to London, and the bishops and citizens received it with all reverence and buried it in Saint Paul's Minster where God now reveals the powers of that holy martyr.

20 April

Beuno

Abbot, *c.*640

Beuno was probably born at Llanymynech and educated at the monastic school at Caerwent. He returned home and established a monastery there, later moving to Berriew. When the English invaded Wales Beuno left, calling with Tysilio at Meifod, and travelling on to Gwyddelwern near Corwen where he made another foundation. He then went to Holywell and finally to Gwynedd. There he settled at Clynnog in Arfon which was to become the centre of his cult. He was the greatest of the missionary saints of North Wales and he and his followers built many churches. Beuno died on the Sunday after Easter in about the year 640, and it is said that on his deathbed he had a vision of heaven. He was buried at Clynnog.

A Reading from *The Life of Saint Beuno*

Beuno lived on the land he had inherited from his father and built a church there, consecrating it in the name of Christ the Lord. He planted an acorn by the side of his father's grave, which grew into an oak tree of great height and thickness. From the crown of this tree there grew a branch right down to the ground and from the ground back up to the top of the tree so that the bend in the branch was touching the ground.

No one knows what God did for Beuno except God himself. And God shall come to the aid of whoever is known to do good. Beuno performed all the commandments of God. He gave food and drink to anyone he saw who was hungry and thirsty. Clothing for the naked, lodging for the stranger. He visited the sick and those in prison. He performed every good thing that holy Scripture tells us to do.

As Beuno's life was drawing to an end and his day approaching, on the seventh day after Easter he saw the heavens opening and the angels descending and ascending. Then Beuno said, 'I saw the Trinity, the Father, the Son, and the Holy Spirit, Peter and Paul and pure David, Deiniol, the saints and the prophets, the apostles and the martyrs, appearing to me. And in the midst there I see seven angels standing before the throne of the highest Father and all the fathers of heaven, singing, 'Blessed is the one you have chosen and have received and who shall dwell with you always.' I hear the cry of the horn of the highest Father summoning me and saying to me, 'My son, cast off your burden of flesh. The time is coming and you are invited to share the feast that shall not end with your brothers. May your body remain in the earth while the armies of heaven and the angels bear your soul to the kingdom of heaven, which you have merited here through your works.'

Let us then beseech the mercy of the all-powerful God by the help of Saint Beuno so that we may receive with him everlasting life in all eternity. Amen.

20 April

Maelrubha of Applecross

Abbot and Missionary, 722

Born near Derry in the year 642, Maelrubha joined Congall's community in Bangor. Around the year 671, however, he followed the Irish practice of 'wandering for Christ'. After two years of missionary work in the northeast of Scotland, he settled in the remote peninsula of Applecross, whence he founded many churches. He died at the age of eighty in the year 722.

A Reading from an ancient Irish prayer, often ascribed to Columcille

The Path I walk

The path I walk, Christ walks it. May the land in which I am be without sorrow.

May the Trinity protect me wherever I stay, Father, Son, and Holy Spirit.

Bright angels walk with me – dear presence – in every dealing.

In every dealing I pray them that no one's poison may reach me.

The ninefold people of heaven of holy cloud, the tenth force of the stout earth.

Favourable company, they come with me, so that the Lord may not be angry with me.

May I arrive at every place, may I return home; may the way in which I spend be a way without loss.

May every path before me be smooth, man, woman, and child welcome me.

A truly good journey! Well does the fair Lord show us a course, a path.

21 April

Anselm

Abbot of Le Bec, Archbishop of Canterbury, Teacher of the Faith, 1109

Anselm was born in Aosta, northern Italy, in 1033. As a young man, he left home and travelled north, visiting many monasteries and other centres of learning. One such visit was to the abbey of Bec, where he met Lanfranc who advised him to embrace monastic life. Anselm had a powerful and original mind and, during his thirty-four years at Bec (as monk, prior and finally abbot), he taught many others and wrote theological, philosophical and devotional works. When Lanfranc died Anselm was made Archbishop of Canterbury and had to subordinate his scholarly work to the needs of the diocese and nation. Twice he endured exile for championing the rights of the Church against the authority of the king but, despite his stubbornness, intellectual rigour, and personal austerity, he was admired by the Norman nobility as well as loved by his monks. He died in the year 1109.

A Reading from the *Proslogion* of Anselm

[O my soul, have you found what you were looking for?
I was seeking God,
    and I have found that he is above all things,
    and that than which nothing greater can be thought.
I have found him to be
    life and light, wisdom and goodness,
    eternal blessedness and the bliss of eternity,
    existing everywhere and at all times.

If I have not found my God,
    what is it that I have found and understood
    so truly and certainly?
But if I have found him,
    why do I not experience what I have found?
Lord God, if my soul has found you,
    why has it no experience of you?]

O Lord my God,
    my creator and my re-creator,
    my soul longs for you.
Tell me what you are, beyond what I have seen,
    so that I may see clearly what I desire.
I strive to see more,
    but I see nothing beyond what I have seen,
    except darkness.

Or rather I do not see darkness
which is no part of you,
but I see that I cannot see further
because of my own darkness.

Why is this, Lord?
Are my eyes darkened by my weakness,
or dazzled by your glory?
The truth is, I am darkened by myself
and also dazzled by you.
I am clouded by my own smallness
and overwhelmed by your immensity;
I am restricted by my own narrowness
and mastered by your wideness.
It is indeed more than a creature can understand!

In truth, Lord,
this is the light inaccessible in which you dwell.
Nothing can pierce through it to see you there.
I cannot look directly into it,
it is too great for me.
But whatever I see, I see through it,
like a weak eye
that sees what it does by the light of the sun,
though it cannot look at the sun itself.
My understanding cannot take it in,
it is too bright, I cannot receive it;
the eye of my soul
cannot bear to turn towards it for too long.
It is dazzled by its glory,
mastered by its fullness,
crushed by its immensity,
confounded by its extent.

O Light, entire and inaccessible!
Truth, whole and blessed!
How far you are from me who have come so close to you.
How remote you are from my sight,
while I am thus present in your sight.
Everywhere you are entirely present,
and I cannot see you.
In you I move and have my being,
and I cannot come to you.
You are within me and around me,
and I have no experience of you.

My God,
I pray that I may so know you and love you
    that I may rejoice in you.
And if I may not do so fully in this life,
    let me go steadily on
    to the day when I come to that fullness.
Let the knowledge of you increase in me here,
    and there let it come to its fullness.
Let your love grow in me here,
    and there let it be fulfilled,
    so that here my joy may be in great hope,
    and there in full reality.

Lord, you have commanded, or rather advised us,
    to ask by your Son,
    and you have promised that we shall receive,
    'that our joy may be full'.
That which you counsel
    through our 'wonderful counsellor'
    is what I am asking for, Lord.
    Let me receive
    that which you promised through your truth,
    'that my joy may be full'.

God of truth,
I ask that I may receive
    so that my joy may be full.
Meanwhile let my mind meditate on it,
    let my tongue speak of it,
    let my heart love it,
    let my mouth preach it,
    let my soul hunger for it,
    my flesh thirst for it,
    and my whole being desire it,
    until I enter into the joy of my Lord,
    who is God one and triune, blessed for ever. Amen.

23 April

George

Martyr, Patron of England, *c.*304

Saint George was probably a soldier living in Palestine at the beginning of the fourth century. He was martyred at Lydda in about the year 304, the beginning of the Diocletian persecution, and became known throughout the East as 'The Great Martyr'. There were churches in England dedicated to Saint George before the Norman conquest. The story of his slaying the dragon is probably due to his being mistaken in iconography for Saint Michael, himself usually depicted wearing armour; or it may again be a mistaken identity representing Perseus's slaying of the sea monster, a myth also associated with the area of Lydda. George replaced Edward the Confessor as Patron Saint of England following the Crusades, when returning soldiers brought back with them a renewed cult of Saint George. Edward III made Saint George patron of the Order of the Garter, which seems finally to have confirmed his position.

A Reading from a sermon of Peter Damian

My dear people, today's feast increases our joy in the glory of Eastertide like a precious jewel whose shining beauty adds to the splendour of the gold in which it is set.

Saint George, whom we commemorate today, moved from one kind of military service to another, exchanging the earthly office of tribune for the ranks of the army of Christ. Like a well disciplined soldier he first jettisoned the burden of his earthly possessions by giving all he had to the poor. Once free and unencumbered, and wearing the breastplate of faith, he was able to advance into the thick of the battle like a valiant soldier of Christ. From this we learn a clear lesson, that we cannot fight properly and boldly for the faith if we are frightened of losing our earthly possessions.

We are told that not only did Saint George fight against an evil king, but burning with the fire of the Holy Spirit and invincibly defended by the banner of the cross, he also defeated the Prince of this evil world in the person of his minion, encouraging the soldiers of Christ to bear themselves valiantly. Clearly, he had at his side the supreme and invisible Judge, who by his free choice allowed the hands of the evil to wreak their violence on Saint George. God gave the body of his martyr over to murderers, whilst guarding and protecting his soul unceasingly, defended as it was by the unconquerable fortress of faith.

So my dear people, let us not merely admire this soldier of the heavenly army: let us also imitate him. Let us lift our minds to the contemplation of that heavenly reward, fixing our hearts on it, never flinching whether the world smiles on us with its blandishments or menaces us with threats. And following the advice of Saint Paul, let us purify ourselves from every stain whether of body or soul, so that we too may in time be found worthy to enter that temple of blessedness on which our minds are fixed.

For all who wish to sacrifice themselves to God in the tabernacle of Christ, which is the Church, must first be cleansed by washing in the sacred font of baptism, and then be clothed in various garments, by which is meant virtues; as it is written in Scripture: 'Let your priests be clothed with righteousness.' For those who in baptism are reborn as a new creation in Christ must not put on again the signs of mortality; they have discarded their old humanity and put on the new, and now live in Christ, and will be continually renewed as they strive to live a pure life.

And so, purged of the stain of our old sin and radiant with the brightness of our new way of life, let us celebrate the paschal mystery by truly imitating the example of the blessed martyrs.

A Reading from a commentary on the Psalms by Ambrose of Milan

Just as there are many kinds of persecution, so there are many forms of martyrdom. You are a witness to Christ every day of your lives.

For example, you are a martyr for Christ when, mindful of the coming judgement of Christ, you maintain a chastity of body and mind in the face of the enticements of sexual promiscuity. You are a witness for Christ when, in the light of God's commandments, you resist the greed that would seize the possessions of a minor or violate the rights of a defenceless widow, and instead of inflicting injury offer them help. Christ wants such witnesses at his side. As Scripture declares: 'Defend the orphan, plead for the widow, and come let us reason together, says the Lord.' You are a witness for Christ when you resist pride, when on seeing the poor and needy, you tenderly take pity on them, preferring humility to arrogance. In all this you give your testimony not merely with your lips but with your deeds.

Who is a more reliable witness than one who, by observing the precepts of the gospel, 'confesses that Jesus Christ has come in the flesh'? For those who hear but who do not act are denying Christ, even though they may confess outwardly with their lips, their deeds repudiate their words. To the many who cry out 'Lord, Lord, did we not prophesy in your name, cast out demons and do many mighty deeds?' Christ will reply on that day: 'Depart from me, all you workers of evil.' A witness is one who testifies to the precepts of the Lord Jesus and supports his deposition by deeds.

Many are martyrs of Christ and confess the Lord Jesus each day in secret. This kind of martyrdom and faithful witnessing to Christ was known to the apostle Paul, who said: 'Our boast is this, the testimony of our conscience.' How many people have confessed outwardly but denied inwardly? It is said: 'Do not trust every spirit, but by their fruits you shall know which ones you should believe.'

Therefore my people, in interior persecutions be faithful and strong, so that you may be found worthy in any public persecutions. Even in interior persecutions we encounter kings and governors, judges whose power over us is frightening. You have an example in the temptations which assailed the Lord.

Elsewhere in Scripture we read: 'Let not sin reign in your mortal bodies.' If a sense of guilt controls you, you will feel as if you are constantly being accused by various kings, governors who are set over sinners. There are as many such kings as there are sins and vices; before these we are brought and before these we stand. These figures have their judgement-seats in our mind. But those who confess Christ, immediately depose them from their throne in the soul, and take them prisoner. For the judgement-seat of the devil cannot remain in place within us when Christ is enthroned.

24 April

Mellitus

Bishop of London, first Bishop at St Paul's, 624

Mellitus was a Roman abbot who was sent to England by Pope Gregory the Great to undergird the work of Augustine, who consecrated him Bishop of the East Saxons, with his see at London and his first church dedicated to Saint Paul. After some local setbacks and having to reside in northern France, he and his fellow bishops were recalled to England, but Mellitus was unable to return to London. He was made Archbishop of Canterbury in 619 and died on this day in the year 624. He was buried close to Augustine in the church of Saint Peter & Saint Paul in Canterbury.

A Reading *from A History of the English Church and People* by the Venerable Bede

In the year of our Lord 604, Augustine, Archbishop of Britain, consecrated two bishops, Mellitus and Justus. Mellitus was appointed to preach in the province of the East Saxons, which is separated from Kent by the river Thames, and bounded on the east by the sea. Its capital is the city of London, which stands on the banks of the Thames, and is a trading centre for many nations who visit it by land and sea.

At this time Sabert, Ethelbert's nephew through his sister Ricula, ruled the province under the dominion of Ethelbert, who, as already stated, governed all the English peoples as far as the Humber. When this province too had received the faith through the preaching of Mellitus, King Ethelbert built a church dedicated to the Holy Apostle Paul in the city of London, which he appointed as the episcopal See of Mellitus and his successors.

alternative reading

A Reading from a letter of Pope Gregory the Great to Mellitus following his departure for Britain in the year 601

To our well loved son Abbot Mellitus: Gregory, servant of the servants of God.

Since the departure of those of our fellowship who are accompanying you, we have become incredibly anxious, because so far we have received no news of the success of your journey. Therefore, when by God's help you reach our most reverend brother, Bishop Augustine, we wish you to inform him that we have been giving careful thought to the affairs of the English.

We have come to the conclusion that the temples of the idols that are erected among that people should on no account be destroyed. The idols should be destroyed, but the temples themselves should be aspersed with holy water, altars set up within, and relics deposited there. If these temples are well-built, they must be purified from the worship of demons and dedicated to the service of the true God. In this way, we hope that the people, seeing that their temples are not destroyed, may abandon their error and, flocking more readily to their temples as usual, may come to know and adore the true God.

And since they have a custom of sacrificing many oxen to demons, let some other solemnity be substituted in its place, such as a day of Dedication or the Festivals of the holy martyrs whose relics are enshrined there. On such occasions they may well construct shelters of boughs for themselves around the churches that were once temples, and celebrate the solemnity with devout feasting. They are no longer to sacrifice animals to the devil, but they may kill them for food to the praise of God, and give thanks to the Giver of all gifts for the plenty they enjoy. If the people are allowed some worldly pleasures in this way, they will more readily come to desire the joys of the spirit. For in my view it is impossible to eradicate all errors from obstinate minds at one stroke, and whoever wishes to climb a mountain does so gradually one step at a time, and not in one gigantic leap.

24 April

The Seven Martyrs of the Melanesian Brotherhood Solomon Islands

2003

During a period of civil unrest in the Solomon Islands which lasted from 2000 to 2003 the Melanesian Brotherhood and the other Anglican religious communities bravely worked for peace and reconciliation between the opposing factions and for the disarmament of the militant groups. In 2003 a group of guerrilla rebels kidnapped, tortured and killed Nathaniel Sado, a Melanesian Brother. His death was reported by an eyewitness on Easter Day. Knowing what the outcome might be, the Assistant Head Brother of the Melanesian Brotherhood, Robin Lindsay, went with five other brothers – Francis Tofi, Alfred Hill, Ini Paratabatu, Patteson Gatu and Tony Sirihi – aiming to find Brother Nathaniel, and if he was indeed dead, to bring his body home for burial. Three were killed when they arrived (on 24 April), the others a day later, after being tortured. The bodies of the seven martyrs were buried at the motherhouse of the Melanesian Brotherhood in the autumn. Their funerals, attended by crowds in the tens of thousands, saw an extraordinary outpouring of popular grief and affection, and their example of costly love has done much to heal the community divisions within the islands.

A Reading from a sermon preached in commemoration of the Seven Martyrs of the Melanesian Brotherhood by Richard Anthony Carter

Our Community has always been a place of joy and laughter very much as I imagine the first community of Christ's disciples would have been. Did not Christ call them to celebrate the wedding feast while the groom was still with them? It was the religious leaders who saw their work as that of condemnation and judgement, and in contrast Christ condemned hardness of heart and invited all to his wedding feast. It is right then that the Community should be a place of pan-pipes, song, dance and laughter, even in the face of struggle. The gospel transforms mourning into dancing. It is our pleasure to give and to go on being able to give. Even the tragedy of the death of our Brothers cannot extinguish our hope and spiritual joy. Thus, like a magnet, the Community continues to welcome all in the name of Christ: children and young people, parents and the elderly, the sick and the needy, the mentally disturbed, the traumatized, the lost and the sinful. For here is a place of acceptance and new life.

This is a blessing of simplicity that is so at odds with the message of our world whose unremitting message is that 'to be is to have'. Rather we proclaim that to be is to be in relationship with God and one another. We believe that obsessive materialism is a sin that keeps us prisoners. God's gifts free us to trust his love and to travel lightly. Like David we set aside the armour which would weigh us down and imprison us. God will be our protection. God will be our guide. The gentle shepherd boy can defeat the giants of fear even when the odds seem to be against him.

And you are blessed with the spirit of sacrifice. Sacrifice may seem more like pain or a curse, but it is your sacrifice to God which is at the heart of your calling, for God will not turn away from a heart that is broken and crushed. Sacrifice is essential to love; ask a mother and she will know as she struggles to feed her children. This vocation is about letting go of selfishness because of a greater love for one another. In that place of offering we discover a unity with God, where in fact we have nothing to fear. Our martyred Brothers teach us that. They went to the edge of life, a place where we all fear to go, and there they held to Christ. As St Francis said, 'Blessed are those who are found doing God's holy will at the hour of their deaths, for death will do them no harm.' Brother Francis Tofi's last words to me were these: 'I would be frightened to die if I was doing wrong, but I am not frightened to die if I am doing good.'

This then is our blessing: we have been called to be sons and daughters of the New Testament. It is not the old theology of personal gain and selfish power. It is not a religion of cargo cult waiting for material wealth to fall from the sky. It is not self-seeking, it is God-seeking, and yet in finding God we also find ourselves. This is the miracle of our faith, that in seeming vulnerability and powerlessness we too can enter into the mystery of salvation. At the bottom of the fall God takes over. In offering and in service we find the only power great enough to transform the world.

25 April

Mark

Evangelist

John Mark was a Jew and, according to Paul's Letter to the Colossians, was cousin to Barnabas. He accompanied Barnabas and Paul on their first missionary journey. Afterwards, he went to Cyprus with Barnabas and to Rome with first Paul and then Peter. The Gospel which bears his name is generally regarded as the earliest and was most likely written whilst he was in Rome. It was probably based as much on Peter's preaching of the good news as on Mark's own memory. Mark's Gospel has a sharpness and an immediacy about it, and he does not spare the disciples in noting their weaknesses and lack of understanding that Jesus the Christ would suffer for the world's redemption. Sharing in the glory of the resurrection means sharing in the giving of self, both in body and spirit, even to death; sharing the gospel was for all, in essence both excessively generous and ultimately sacrificial.

A Reading from the treatise *Against the Heresies*
by Irenaeus

Although the Church is spread throughout the world, even to the ends of the earth, it has received from the apostles and their followers the faith it professes.

It believes in one God, the Father Almighty, the creator of heaven and earth, the sea, and all that is in them; and in one Jesus Christ, the Son of God, who became incarnate for our salvation; and in the Holy Spirit, who announced through the prophets the purposes of God, the advent of our Lord Jesus Christ, his birth from the Virgin, his passion, his resurrection from the dead, and his bodily ascension into heaven, and his future manifestation from heaven in the glory of the Father 'to gather up all things in one', and to raise to life all human flesh, in order that in accordance with the will of the invisible Father, 'every knee in heaven and earth and under the earth shall bow' before Christ Jesus, our Lord and God, our Saviour and our King, and every tongue acknowledge him, and the whole creation be brought to his just judgement. Those who have sinned, be they angels, be they mortals who have renounced their faith, who have behaved profanely or who are unrighteous, shall be condemned to the eternal fire; whereas those who are righteous and holy, who have kept God's commandments faithfully, who have persevered in love whether from the outset of their lives, or by repenting of their evil actions, through the exercise of his grace shall be received into eternal glory.

As I have observed, this is the preaching and the faith which the Church although scattered throughout the world, continues to maintain carefully as if it lived together in one house. The church believes these truths as if it had but one soul, one heart, proclaiming them and teaching them and handing them on to others as if it spoke with one mouth. Although there are many different languages in the world, the content of the tradition is one and the same.

The beliefs of the Church planted in Germany are in accord with those of the Church in Spain and Gaul, the Church in the East, Egypt, Libya and Jerusalem, the centre of the world. Just as the sun, that creature of God, is identical wherever it shines throughout the whole world, so too the preaching of the truth shines everywhere, and enlightens all who wish to know the truth.

Someone who is an eloquent speaker among the leaders of the churches will teach nothing different from what I have outlined, for no one is greater than his master; nor will someone less gifted in eloquence be able to diminish the tradition. Our Christian faith is one and the same, and no matter how much you preach, you will never add to it; and no matter how little you say, the tradition will always be bigger than you.

26 April

Albert Ernest Laurie

Priest, 1937

Born in Edinburgh in 1866, Albert Laurie became a lay reader at Old St Paul's Church to finance his theological studies. He was ordained in 1890, and continued to serve there under Canon Mitchell Innes. When Canon Innes left, Laurie was unanimously elected rector of Old St Paul's. His entire ministry was spent in that one church. It was marked by personal holiness, faithful teaching and devoted pastoral ministry, especially to the poor of the Old Town. He died in the year 1937.

A Reading from *The Vision of God* by Albert Laurie

The General Thanksgiving suggests that we are to serve God not only with our lips but with our lives. Well, the Lord's Prayer is our Lord's life. His words and life are the same thing. You will find more and more that it will repay you to think and think deeper about the logical sequence of the phrases in the 'Our Father,' their association one to another, their place, and of course their meaning. I do not suppose Our Lord was giving a form [of prayer] at all. He may have meant it as a form as well, but it is the only form of prayer that is likely to be without danger to us. It grew out of his love for God because he sought God above all – sought God's glory and did not do it as an effort, but did it naturally because he realised what the true end of human life was, so this prayer grew naturally out of that and it is safe.

But I am not at all clear that it is very safe for us to be always using the same forms of prayer unless we can say it grows out of a living, growing fellowship with God and love of God. Everybody should be a little afraid of forms of prayer. Your own private prayers should be varied. You never know when a form has grown to be a form. You may be able to keep the same form all your life if it is an expression of reality. But the one form that we can always use without fear is the 'Our Father.' It is absolutely crucial. The word itself strikes at the very centre of human existence. Father and all the Father's ties, all that that word implies of relationship between child and Father. Our Lord did what he did and was what he was because of this sense of sonship. It was not just a doctrine he professed, not just a creed he subscribed to, but a living perception of truth.

27 April

Assicus (Tassach)

Bishop of Raholp, 470

Tassach was a close friend of Patrick, and as bishop of Raholp in Ireland, near Saul, attended Patrick on his death-bed. Tradition ascribes to him the skills of a brass-worker and coppersmith. He died on this day in the year 470.

A Reading from *The Life of Saint Patrick* by Muirchú

When the hour of his death was drawing near, Patrick received the sacrifice from Bishop Tassach – as the angel Victor had told him that he would – as food for his journey to the blessed life.

Angels kept vigil over Patrick's holy body with prayers and psalms during the first night of his funeral, while all those who came for this vigil slept that night. But on the other nights men watched over the body praying and singing psalms. When the angels departed to heaven they left behind in that place the sweetest of smells: it was like honey and the sweet smell that comes from wine. Thus it was fulfilled what was said in the blessing of the patriarch Jacob, 'Behold, the smell of my son is like the scent of a fruitful field blessed by the Lord.'

27 April

Christina Rossetti

Poet, 1894

Christina Rossetti was born in 1830 and was associated with the Pre-Raphaelite Brotherhood, of which her older brother, Dante, was a prominent member. Her elder sister became an Anglican Religious. Christina's own fame rests upon her poetry, which dealt mainly with religious subjects but also the sadness of unrequited or disappointed love. Her first recorded verses, addressed to her mother on the latter's birthday, were written on 27 April 1842. She was the author of the carol 'In the bleak mid-winter'. She died on 29 December 1894.

A Reading from the poetry of Christina Rossetti

Passing Away

Passing away, saith the World, passing away:
Chances, beauty and youth sapped day by day:
Thy life never continueth in one stay.
Is the eye waxen dim, is the dark hair changing grey
That has won neither laurel nor bay?
I shall clothe myself in spring and bud in May:
Thou, rootstricken, shall not rebuild thy decay
On my bosom for aye.
Then I answered: Yea.

Passing away, saith my soul, passing away:
With its burden of fear and hope, and labour and play,
Hearken what the past doth witness and say:
Rust in thy gold, a moth in thine array,
A canker is in thy bud, thy leaf must decay.

At midnight, at cockrow, at morning one certain day
Lo, the bridegroom shall come and shall not delay;
Watch thou and pray.
Then I answered: Yea

Passing away, saith my God, passing away:
Winter passeth after the long delay:
New grapes on the vine, new figs on the tender spray,
Turtle calleth to turtle in Heaven's May.
Though I tarry, wait for Me, trust Me, watch and pray:
Arise, come away, night is past, and lo it is day
My love, My sister, My spouse, thou shalt hear me say.
Then I answered: Yea.

Uphill

Does the road wind uphill all the way?
  Yes, to the very end.
Will the day's journey take the whole long day?
  From morn to night, my friend.

But is there for the night a resting-place?
  A roof for when the slow, dark hours begin.
May not the darkness hide it from my face?
  You cannot miss that inn.

Shall I meet other wayfarers at night?
  Those who have gone before.
Then must I knock, or call when just in sight?
  They will not keep you standing at that door.

Shall I find comfort, travel-sore and weak?
  Of labour you shall find the sum.
Will there be beds for me and all who seek?
  Yea, beds for all who come.

28 April

Peter Chanel

Missionary in the South Pacific, Martyr, 1841

Peter Chanel was born at Cras in France in 1803 and, after ordination, joined the Marist missionary congregation in 1831. In 1836 he was sent to the islands of the South Pacific to preach the faith. Peter and his companions brought healing medicines as well as the gospel and were much loved and respected. On the island of Futuna in the Fiji group, where Peter was living, the chief's son asked for baptism, which so infuriated his father that he dispatched a group of warriors with explicit orders to murder Peter. They attacked him with clubs, axes and knives and he died on this day in the year 1841. Within a year, the whole island was Christian, and Peter became revered throughout the Pacific Islands and Australasia as its protomartyr.

A Reading from *A History of Christian Missions* by Stephen Neill

The island of New Caledonia in the South Pacific, twice as large as Corsica, was first surveyed by the missionary Society of Mary (Marists) as a mission field in 1843. Four years later the murder of a lay brother led them to withdraw, but in 1851 the work was resumed.

An unexpected set of problems arose when France annexed the island and decided to convert it into a penal settlement. The discovery of the valuable minerals cobalt, chromium, and nickel led to an influx of prospectors and to the commercial exploitation of the islands; the indigenous population tended increasingly to be driven away into the mountainous and less fertile regions. Here was the classic case of the clash between an unsympathetic Western civilisation and a primitive and helpless people. Christian missions, Protestant as well as Roman Catholic, were the only hope of the New Caledonian people. The struggle was long and arduous, but the ordination of the first New Caledonian priest, a little more than a century after the arrival of the first missionaries, is evidence of the stirring of new life in a people that had been threatened with extinction.

The attempt of the Marists to enter Tonga was for a long time prevented by the solid opposition of the Protestants, headed by the redoubtable King George. Foiled in their first attempt, the Fathers wisely concentrated on two islands in the Fiji group which were still untouched by Protestantism, Wallis and Futuna. Both became wholly Roman Catholic islands.

Peter Chanel was born in France in 1803. As a young priest he worked for three years with good effect in a run-down country parish when in 1831 he was accepted as a member by the Marists. In 1836 he was one of a group of missionaries who arrived on the islands. He and two lay brothers were stationed on Futuna, an island where cannibalism had only recently been forbidden by the local ruler, Niuliki. They were at first well received; but, when Peter had learned something of the language and gained the people's confidence, jealousy and fear were aroused in Niuliki. This was aggravated by the conversion and baptism of his son and other young men.

Three years after his arrival, Peter Chanel was set upon by the local ruler's men and clubbed to death on 28 April 1841. When called on to justify his conversion to Christianity, one of Peter's catechumens spoke of him, 'He loves us; he does what he teaches; he forgives his enemies. His teaching is good.'

Today Peter Chanel is honoured as the first martyr of the Pacific Islands, and the patron saint not only of the islands, but of Australasia.

29 April

Catherine of Siena

Teacher of the Faith, 1380

Catherine Benincasa was born in 1347, the second youngest of twenty-five children. Pious from her earliest years, she overcame family opposition to her vocation and became a Dominican tertiary at the age of eighteen. Nourished by a life of contemplative prayer and mystical experience she devoted herself to active care for the poor and sick. She became increasingly sought after as an adviser on political as well as religious matters and, in 1376, she journeyed to Avignon as an ambassador to the Pope and influenced his decision to return to Rome. She wrote a Dialogue on the spiritual life as well as numerous letters of counsel and direction, which stressed her devotion to the Precious Blood of Jesus. She suffered a stroke on 21 April and died eight days later, on this day in the year 1380.

A Reading from *The Dialogue* by Catherine of Siena

Thanks be to you, eternal Father, that you have not despised me, your handiwork, nor turned your face from me, nor made light of my desires. In your light you have given me light. In your wisdom I have come to know the truth; in your mercy I have found your charity and affection for my neighbours. What has compelled you? Not my virtues, but only your charity.

Let this same love compel you to enlighten the eye of my understanding with the light of faith, so that I may know your truth, which you have revealed to me. Let my memory be great enough to hold your favours, and set my will ablaze in your charity's fire. Let that fire burst the seed of my body and bring forth blood; then with that blood, given for love of your blood, and with the key of obedience, let me unlock heaven's gate.

O eternal Trinity! O Godhead! That Godhead, your divine nature, gave the price of your Son's blood its value. You, eternal Trinity, are a deep sea. The more I enter you, the more I discover, and the more I discover, the more I seek you. You are insatiable, you in whose depth the soul is sated yet remains always hungry for you, thirsty for you, eternal Trinity, longing to see you with the light in your light. Just as the deer longs for the fountain of living water, so does my soul long to escape from the prison of my darksome body and see you in truth. O how long will you hide your face from my eyes?

O eternal Trinity, fire and abyss of charity, dissolve this very day the cloud of my body! I am driven to desire, in the knowledge of yourself that you have given me in your truth, to leave behind the weight of this body of mine and give my life for the glory and praise of your name. For by the light of understanding within your light I have tasted and seen your depth, eternal Trinity, and the beauty of your creation. Then, when I considered myself in you, I saw that I am your image. You have gifted me with power from yourself, eternal Father, and my understanding with your wisdom – such wisdom as is proper to your only-begotten Son; and the Holy Spirit, who proceeds from you and from your Son, has given me a will, and so I am able to love.

You, eternal Trinity, are the craftsman; and I your handiwork have come to know that you are in love with the beauty of what you have made, since you made of me a new creation in the blood of your Son.

O abyss! O eternal Godhead! O deep sea! What more could you have given me than the gift of your very self ?

30 April

Pandita Mary Ramabai

Translator of the Scriptures, 1922

Mary Ramabai was born in 1858, the daughter of a Sanskrit scholar who believed in educating women. Converting to Christianity, she nevertheless remained loyal to many aspects of her Hindu background, pioneering an Indian vision of the faith. She became well-known as a lecturer on social questions, becoming the first woman to be awarded the title 'Pandita'. She spent many years working for the education of women and orphans, founding schools and homes. Personally, she lived in great simplicity and was a prominent opponent of the caste system and child marriage. She died on this day in the year 1922.

A Reading from *Far Above Rubies* by Richard Symonds

Pandita Ramabai was pre-eminent among Indian women of her time as a social and educational reformer, Sanskrit scholar and translator of the Bible. She was devout in her faith and saved thousands of women and girls from lives of misery.

Her early life was an extraordinary and tragic adventure. Her father, Anant Shastri, was a Sanskrit scholar of the caste of the Chittapana Brahmins, many of whom occupied positions of distinction in Western India; he was a follower of the Bhakti faith, which focused on personal union with God. His main eccentricity was to believe in the education of women, with the result that from the age of eight Ramabai was instructed in Sanskrit literature.

Tragically, her father, mother and sister all died of starvation within months of one another, leaving only herself and her brother. They moved to Calcutta, then the capital city of India. It was here for the first time they came in contact with Christianity. They also met learned pundits who asked her to lecture to women on their duties according to the Shastras.

In studying books of Hindu law whilst preparing her lectures, Ramabai was struck by the fact that although the sacred books were inconsistent on many things, they were unanimous in holding that women as a class were bad, worse indeed than demons. Their only hope of liberation from millions of rebirths and suffering was through worship of a husband, with no other pleasure in life than the most degraded slavery to him. Women had no right to study the Vedas, and without knowing them no one could know the Brahma; without knowing Brahma no one could obtain liberation. Therefore no one could obtain liberation whilst incarnate as a woman.

Her disgust with these doctrines led her to associate with a reformist group, and eventually to embrace Christianity. Yet the Anglo-Catholic sisters of the Community of St Mary the Virgin (Wantage), who were responsible for Ramabai's conversion, were to watch her remarkable career unfold with as much dismay as gratification: for on becoming a member of the Church of England she continued to regard herself culturally as a Hindu, and she welcomed Ministers of all Christian denominations to conduct worship in the great church which she was to build for widows and orphans.

Writing to one of the sisters, she said:

> I am not bound to accept every word that falls down from the lips of priests and bishops; I have just freed myself from the yoke of the Indian priestly tribe. … I must be allowed to think for myself. God has given me an independent conscience. … You are all too learned and too spiritual, too wise, too faithful to your faith which you profess from your childhood, to understand my difficulties in accepting wholly the religion taught by you. You have never had the experience of choosing another religion which was foreign to you as I have.

As an educationalist Ramabai was a pioneer in India of methods which combined brainwork and handwork. As a social reformer, her work aroused an increasing sentiment against child marriage and in favour of Hindu remarriage and female education. Her example inspired the establishment of widows' homes elsewhere in India, often with her help. In persuading her high caste girls to sweep floors, and in emphasising the dignity of labour she set an example similar to that of Mahatma Gandhi. Her manner of living, like that of Gandhi, was one of extreme simplicity; she owned nothing but her clothes and books. It was observed how in her Christian life there was a continuation of all that was best in her Hindu life.

May

1 May

Philip and James

Apostles

Philip and James appear in the list of the twelve apostles in the first three Gospels, but are frequently confused with other early saints who share their names. In John's Gospel, Philip has a more prominent rôle, being the third of the apostles to be called by Jesus and then himself bringing his friend Nathanael to the Lord. Philip is presented as the spokesman for the other apostles who are questioning the capacity for feeding the five thousand and, at the Last Supper, enters into a dialogue with Jesus which leads to the 'Farewell Discourses' of our Lord. James is said to be the son of Alphæus and is often known as 'James the Less' to distinguish him from James the brother of John. He may also be the 'James the Younger' whose mother, in Mark's Gospel, is a witness at the Crucifixion. Both apostles are commemorated on the same day because the church in Rome where their relics rest was dedicated on this day in the year 560.

A Reading from a homily of John Chrysostom

The cross brought conviction to the world and drew the whole world to itself through the work of uneducated people. They succeeded not by preaching trivia, but by speaking of God, of true religion, of a way of living the gospel, and of the coming judgement. It turned peasants and illiterate folk alike into philosophers. See how the foolishness of God is wiser than human wisdom, and his weakness stronger! In what way was it stronger? It was stronger because it turned the world upside down; it gripped people, although countless individuals were busy trying to suppress the name of the Crucified, they only succeeded in promoting its cause. It flourished and grew; by contrast, they perished and withered away. The living who were fighting him who had died proved powerless.

And so, when the Greek tells me that I am a fool, all that he is doing is revealing his own foolishness. He thinks me a fool, but in reality I am wiser than the wise. When he ridicules me as being weak, he only demonstrates his own greater weakness. For by the grace of God, tax collectors and fishermen had the strength to achieve noble things, such things as neither monarchs nor orators nor philosophers, in a word, not the entire world searching in every direction, could even imagine.

Reflecting on this, Paul said: 'The weakness of God is stronger than human strength.' It is clear from this as well that the gospel is divine. For how else could twelve illiterate men have been inspired to attempt such enormous feats, men who lived on the banks of lakes or rivers, or in deserts? How else could it have occurred to these men, men who had scarcely ventured into a city or the forum, to take on the entire world? It is apparent from the gospel narratives that they were cowardly and timid. The scriptures never attempt to make excuses for them or to cover up their failings. In itself this is compelling evidence of the truth. What then does the gospel say about them? That after the innumerable miracles they had seen Christ perform, when he was arrested, some of them fled, and the one disciple who stayed behind denied him, and he was chief among them!

So then, here we have people who failed to stand up to the Jews when Christ was alive; and yet no sooner was Christ dead and buried, than they take on the whole world. How can this be unless Christ rose from the dead, talked with them and put fresh heart into them? If it were not so, would they have not have said to themselves: 'What is all this? If Christ did not have the strength to save himself, how can he protect us? He did not defend himself when he was alive, so will he reach out his hand to defend us now that he is dead? When he was alive he did not conquer a single nation, so how shall we convince the entire world by speaking his name?'

Would it not have been foolish to conceive of such an enterprise, let alone actually to do it? Surely it is obvious that if the disciples had not seen Jesus risen from the dead and received clear evidence of his power, they would never have risked such a gamble.

2 May

Athanasius

Bishop of Alexandria, Teacher of the Faith, 373

Athanasius was born in about the year 296 of Christian parents and educated at the Catechetical School in Alexandria. He was present at the Council of Nicæa as a deacon, accompanying his bishop Alexander, whom he succeeded as Patriarch of Alexandria in 328. Athanasius held firmly to the doctrines of the Church as defined by that Council, and became the leader of those opposed to the teachings of Arianism which denied the divinity of Christ. He was deposed from and restored to his see several times because of his uncompromising faith. In or out of exile, Athanasius continued to write. Ever the proponent of orthodoxy over heterodoxy, he expounded the need for the Church to teach the true doctrines of the faith rather than watered-down versions of it. He was a strong believer in asceticism as a means of restoring the divine image in humanity and thus a supporter of monasticism, which was in its nascent state at that time. He was a friend of Pachomius and wrote the Life of Antony of Egypt, which portrayed the monastic life as holding a balance between things earthly and heavenly. He died on this day in the year 373.

A Reading from the treatise *On the Incarnation of the Word*
by Athanasius of Alexandria

The Word of God, incorporeal, incorruptible, and immaterial, entered our world. Yet it was not as if the Word had ever been remote from it. Indeed, there is no part of creation deprived of his presence; together with his Father, he fills everything, everywhere, at all times.

In the loving-kindness of God the Word came to us, and was revealed among us openly. He took pity on the human race and on our weakness; he was moved by our corruption and our impotence to help ourselves; he saw our evil ways, and how little by little we were increasing in evil to an intolerable pitch of self-destruction; and lastly, he realised that he could no longer allow death to rule over us. Had death prevailed, creation would have perished, and the Father's work in fashioning us would have been in vain.

The Word, therefore, took to himself a body no different from our own, for he did not wish to be in just any body or simply to be seen. If he had wanted simply to be seen, he would have chosen another and nobler body. But he took our human body in all its particularity for his own, a body born of a pure and spotless virgin, who had had no sexual relations and who was therefore undefiled. The mighty creator built himself a temple within the Virgin's body, making it an instrument in which to dwell and to reveal himself.

In this way the Word received from human nature a body like our own; and since all are subject to the corruption of death, he surrendered his body to death for us all, and with supreme love offered it to the Father. His purpose in so doing was to destroy the law of corruption which was operating against us, since all humankind may be held to have died in him. This law, which spent its force on the Lord's body, could no longer have any power over those who share his humanity. Furthermore, this was the way in which the Word was able to restore the human race to immortality after it had fallen into corruption, and summon it back to life. As fire consumes straw, so he utterly destroyed the power that death had over us by means of the body he assumed and by the grace of the resurrection.

This was the reason why the Word assumed a mortal body, so that this body, sharing in the Word who is above all, might satisfy death's requirement in place of all. Through the indwelling Word, it would remain incorruptible, and by the grace of the resurrection, it would be freed for ever from corruption. In death the Word made a spotless sacrifice, an oblation of the body he had assumed. By dying for others, he immediately banished death for all humankind.

In this way the Word of God, who is above all, dedicated and offered his temple, the instrument that was his body, for us all, thus paying the debt that was owed. The immortal Son of God, united with all human beings by likeness of nature, fulfilled the requirements of justice, restoring humankind to immortality by the promise of the resurrection. The corruption of death no longer holds any power over men and women because of the Word who has come to dwell among us in his one body.

3 May

Henry Vaughan

Poet, 1695

Henry Vaughan was born in 1622 at Scethrog in Breconshire and studied medicine in London before returning home to practise. When the Civil War broke out, he joined the Royalist army, seeing action in Cheshire and being captured. In the following few years his younger brother, William, was killed, the king was executed, the Church Henry knew and loved was suppressed, and his beloved young wife, Catherine, died. In 1650 he published his first volume of religious verse, setting himself to work in the style of John Donne and, especially, George Herbert. His poetry analyses his experiences and shows an intense awareness of the divine meanings in ordinary things. In his troubles, Henry Vaughan found the crucified Saviour and, finding him, he found also light and hope and peace. He died at Scethrog on 23 April 1695, and was buried in the churchyard of Llansantffraed.

A Reading from the poetry of Henry Vaughan

The Night

Dear night! This world's defeat;
The stop to busy fools; cares check and curb;
The day of spirits; my soul's calm retreat
Which none disturb!
Christ's progress, and his prayer time;
The hours to which high heaven doth chime.

God's silent, searching flight:
When my Lord's head is fill'd with dew, and all
His locks are wet with the clear drops of night;
His still, soft call;
His knocking time; the soul's dumb watch,
When spirits their fair kindred catch.

Were all my loud, evil days
Calm and unhaunted as is thy dark tent,
Whose peace but by some angel's wing or voice
Is seldom rent;
Then I in heaven all the long year
Would keep, and never wander here.

But living where the sun
Doth all things wake, and where all mix and tire
Themselves and others, I consent and run
To ev'ry mire,
And by this world's ill-guiding light,
Err more than I can do by night.

There is in God (some say)
A deep, but dazzling darkness; As men here
Say it is late and dusky, because they
See not all clear.
O for that night! Where I in him
Might live invisible and dim.

Peace

My soul, there is a country
  Far beyond the stars,
Where stands a winged sentry
  All skilful in the wars,
There above noise, and danger
  Sweet peace sits crown'd with smiles,
And one born in a manger
  Commands the beauteous files,
He is thy gracious friend,
  And (O my soul awake!)
Did in pure love descend
  To die here for thy sake,
If thou canst get but thither,
  There grows the flower of peace,
The rose that cannot wither,
  Thy fortress, and thy ease;
Leave then thy foolish ranges;
  For none can thee secure,
But one, who never changes,
  Thy God, thy life, thy cure.

4 May

English Saints and Martyrs of the Reformation Era

Note: In Wales, Catholic and Protestant Saints and Martyrs of the Reformation Era are commemorated on 31 October.

This day is set aside to remember all who witnessed to their Christian faith during the conflicts in Church and State, which lasted from the fourteenth to the seventeenth centuries, but which were at their most intense in the sixteenth century. Though the reform movement was aimed chiefly at the papacy, many Christian men and women of holiness suffered for their allegiance to what they believed to be the truth of the gospel. As the movement grew in strength, it suffered its own internecine struggles, with one group determined that they were the keepers of truth and that all others were therefore at best in a state of ignorance and at worst heretical. In the twentieth century, ecumenical links drew the Churches closer to each other in faith and worship, and all now recognize both the good and evil that evolved from the Reformation Era.

A Reading from *Their Lord and Ours* by Mark Santer

Of the Elizabethan and Stuart martyrs, Edmund Campion is probably the best known outside the Catholic community. But in the community at large the names of the earlier martyrs, John

Fisher and Thomas More, are much better known, as are the Protestant martyrs, Cranmer, Latimer and Ridley. The difference is significant. Fisher and More died in the reign of Henry VIII. They were central figures in a Christian commonwealth which was not yet fragmented. They are remembered as public figures who belong to all England: Fisher, among other things, as Chancellor and great benefactor of the University of Cambridge, and More as Lord Chancellor of England. Forty-five years later, when Campion returned to England as a Jesuit missionary, he did so as a man who had deliberately rejected the Church of England to serve the cause of a persecuted minority. That is the community which has continued to remember him. To put the point differently: Anglicans do not naturally think of Fisher and More as 'Roman Catholics'. They do think of Campion, if they think about him at all, as a 'Roman Catholic'. He figures in the history of the Anglican community only as an outsider.

Most informed Anglicans are scarcely aware of the Roman Catholic martyrs who died in England between 1570 and 1680. Yet any Anglican who comes into close contact with English Catholicism will soon discover the vital importance to that community of the tradition of the martyrs. He will find a community which keeps the memory of those martyrs alive by liturgical observance and for whom it is natural to ascribe the cause of their deaths to the Church of England.

There is a connection between our self-identification as members of particular communities and the stories we tell about the past. It is by the things we remember, and the way we remember them, and by the things we fail to remember, that we identify ourselves as belonging to this or that group. What we remember, or do not remember, moulds our reactions and our behaviour towards others at a level deeper than that of conscious reflection.

In itself it is quite natural and proper that the various groups and societies we belong to should be characterised by particular myths and stories. Sin comes in when difference is turned into division, and when our different stories, with their distinctive emphases, distortions and omissions, are put to use for the maintenance of grievance, for self-justification and for keeping other people in the wrong. Sin borders on blasphemy when Christians justify their fear, loathing and persecution of each other in the name of Christ of whom we read in the gospel that he died to gather into one the scattered children of God.

No theological agreements between Churches will be sufficient for the restoration of communion unless they form part of a much profounder social reconciliation in which we can learn no longer to see each other as strangers, but rather to trust one another as friends. This means, among other things, that we must learn to tell new stories about ourselves and about one another. In other words, we need to re-educate our memories. We need to look at the past afresh. We must find out how far our prejudices conform to the facts, and what the same events look like to those who are heirs to another story. We must find out why we remember some things and others remember other things. Only in this way can we get free of our fantasies.

As we do this, we learn to see that those who suffered and died, though deeply estranged from each other in this life, died for the one faith. Though their differences ran so deep that they felt constrained to die for them, all died for the one Christ whom all tried to serve and to follow. That indeed is what makes a martyr: a martyr calls us to the imitation of Christ. The martyrs transcend our causes, our partial perceptions of the truth. They belong to us all, because they witness to the Christ who is Lord of us all.

5 May

Asaph

Bishop, seventh century

The biographer of Saint Kentigern (Cyndeyrn) states that when he founded a monastic settlement on the banks of the river Elwy, one of his favourite pupils was a nobly born boy named Asaph. The biography includes a story which underlines Asaph's obedience to his spiritual master. When Kentigern was recalled to Strathclyde to become Bishop of Glasgow, Asaph was unanimously appointed Bishop of Llanelwy (which later became known as St Asaph in English). He remained there for the rest of his life and was buried there. The cluster of names connected with Asaph in northern Flintshire (Llanasa, Pantasa and Ffynnon Asa) suggests that this may have been his native area.

A Reading from *The Life of Saint Kentigern*
by Jocelyn of Furness

When the day dawned, Kentigern summoned his disciples together, and addressed them in these words: 'Beloved, I speak to you as a man, conscious as I am of my age and infirmity. After much longing and deliberation I had wanted you to be the ones who closed my eyes in death, and for my bones to be buried in the womb of mother earth here in your midst. But it does not belong to us to be able to direct our course, and it has been enjoined on me by the Lord to return to my own church of Glasgow. We should not, and indeed dare not, go against the words of the Holy One, as Job says, or in any way go against it, but rather in all things obey God's commands to the end of our lives. You must stand fast in your faith, then dearly beloved: be strong, and always perform your duties with love.'

Kentigern said this and many other things in their presence, and lifting up his hand, he blessed them. Then, with the unanimous consent of all, he appointed Saint Asaph to the government of the monastery, and by petition of the people and the canonical election of the clergy, successor to his bishopric. Once again, he delivered a profound and lengthy sermon concerning faith, hope and love, on mercy, justice, humility and obedience, on holy peace and mutual patience, on the avoidance of vice and the acquisition of virtue, on the importance of observing the customs of the Holy Roman Church, on the maintenance and observance of discipline, and on constancy and perseverance in good works. When the sermon was over he enthroned Saint Asaph in the cathedral seat, and again blessing and bidding them all farewell, he left the church via the north door because he was going to face the northern enemy.

From that monastery a large number of the brethren, some six hundred and sixty-five in all, being unable and unwilling to live without Kentigern's leadership, went with him. Only three hundred brothers remained with Asaph.

8 May

Julian of Norwich

Spiritual Writer, *c.*1417

On this day in the year 1373, when she was thirty years old and suffering from what was considered to be a terminal illness, a woman of Norwich, whose own name is unrecorded, experienced a series of sixteen visions, which revealed aspects of the love of God. Following her recovery, she spent the next twenty years of her life pondering their meaning, eventually recording her conclusions in what became the first book written by a woman in English, Revelations of Divine Love. At an unknown point in her life, she became an anchoress attached to the Church of Saint Julian in Norwich, and it was by this name of Julian that she came to be known to later generations. She died around the year 1417.

A Reading from the conclusion to the *Revelations of Divine Love*
by Julian of Norwich

This book was begun by the gift and grace of God. I do not think it is done yet. We all need to pray God for charity. God is working in us, helping us to thank and trust and enjoy him. Thus does our good Lord will that we should pray. This is what I understood his meaning to be throughout, and in particular when he uttered those sweet, cheering words, 'I am the foundation of your praying.' I knew truly that the reason why our Lord showed it was that he wants it to be better known than it is. It is by our knowing this that he gives us grace to love and to hold to him. He regards his heavenly treasure on earth with so much love that he wants us to have all the greater light and consolation in the joys of heaven. So he draws our hearts away from the sorry murk in which they live.

From the time these things were first revealed I had often wanted to know what was our Lord's meaning. It was more than fifteen years after that I was answered in my spirit's understanding. 'You would know our Lord's meaning in this thing! Know it well. Love was his meaning. Who showed it you? Love. What did he show you? Love. Why did he show you? Love. Why did he show it? For love. Hold on to this and you will know and understand love more and more. But you will not know or learn anything else – ever!'

So it was that I learned that love was our Lord's meaning. And I saw for certain, both here and elsewhere, that before ever he made us, God loved us; and that his love has never slackened, nor ever shall. In this love all his works have been done, and in this love he has made everything serve us; and in this love our life is everlasting. Our beginning was when we were made, but the love in which he made us never had beginning. In it we have our beginning.

All this we shall see in God for ever. May Jesus grant this. Amen.

10 May

Comgall

Abbot of Bangor, 602

Comgall was the founder and first abbot of Bangor Abbey. It is said to have been the largest monastery in Ireland with as many as three thousand monks in the community at one time. Comgall visited Columba in Iona and worked closely with him in spreading the Gospel. Columbanus was trained at Bangor before setting out on his missionary journeys to Europe. There was a strong family-spirit in the community life at Bangor. Counselling, as well as instruction, was an important part of the training. To Comgall is attributed the saying, 'A man without a soul-friend is a body without a head.' He died on this day in the year 602.

A Reading from *The Rule of Comgall*

Be faithful to the rule of the gentle Lord, because therein lies your salvation. Far better that you not violate it while in this present life.

In this lies the heart of the rule: to love Christ, to shun wealth, to remain close to the heavenly king, and to be gentle towards all people.

What a wonderful road it is to remain faithful to self-denial, and to be eager for it. Let the monk daily bear in mind that he will die, and let him be zealous in his concern for every person.

The monk should make one hundred genuflections while chanting the psalm 'Blessed are those whose way is blameless', morning and evening. If this is done his reward will be great in the kingdom of heaven.

Let him, each morning, at the proper time, and with alacrity, completely prostrate himself three times, and let him make the sign of the cross over breast and face.

Do not practise long drawn-out devotions, but rather give yourself to prayer at intervals, as you would to food. Pious humbug is an invention of the devil.

A fire built of fern soon dies out. Do not be like flotsam, going with every current, if you wish to persevere in devotion.

When faced with innumerable battles against many vices, against the devil, or against the body, it is essential that you be resolute.

These three following counsels should be your guide, and nothing should be allowed to separate you from them: namely, have forbearance, humility, and the love of God in your heart.

Through fear comes the love of the king who heals every ill; for love of him we carry out his will and cherish his commandments.

The love of God embraces the whole world and powerfully restrains wandering thoughts. Fear is the master of repentance. The love of God determines the fervour of our piety.

Let us pray, then, to Christ in times of fear and hurt, that we may be granted relief. Our spiritual father will determine what penance we are to undertake.

The service of the Lord is light, wonderful and pleasant. It is an excellent thing to place oneself in the hands of a holy mentor, that he may direct one's path through life.

The advice of a devout sage is a great asset if one wishes to avoid the punishment [of hell]. No matter how much you esteem your strength of will, place yourself under the direction of another.

11 May

Odo, Maieul, Odilo, Hugh the Great and Peter the Venerable

Abbots of Cluny, 927–1157

The Abbey of Cluny was founded near Dijon in Burgundy in 909. To protect it from lay or episcopal usurpation its founder subjected it to the Church of St Peter in Rome, i.e. the papacy. In a climate of general decadence when the papacy itself was passing through a degrading and impotent phase, this meant little; but it did leave the new foundation free to grow and evolve. In due time its link with a reformed papacy became the axis of its greatness. Cluny stood for the supreme development of the liturgical life; a sense of adoration and intercession for the whole of society. It became the mother-house of a vast network of dependent monasteries, and its church was the largest in Europe until the sixteenth century. It had begun as simply a new and fervent monastery, but it had the good fortune to be ruled by a succession of exceptionally able, holy and long-lived abbots: Odo (927–42), Maieul (943–94), Odilo (994–1049), Hugh the Great (1049–1109), and Peter the Venerable (1122–57). Between them they led their community for over two centuries. They were saints and administrators, wise monks and prudent leaders, the friends and advisers of kings and popes. Between them they shaped not only the destiny of Cluny, but that of Europe itself.

A Reading from *The Life of Saint Odo of Cluny* by John of Salerno

Abbot Odo used to say that his means always sufficed both to feed the brethren and to give alms to the poor. Never did a poor man turn away empty from the bosom of his mercy. Whenever I went out with him from the monastery, he was always careful to ask if we had something for the poor; and if we had all that was necessary, he went on his way happily and without hesitation. And because he gave to all who asked him, by the power of God all things were supplied to him. He always had in mind that precept of Tobit: 'See that you turn not your face away from anyone who is poor, and give to all who ask of you.' If anyone had brought him a gift and seemed from his dress to be poor, Odo immediately estimated the value of his gift on an accurate balance and ordered the person to be given double.

When his ardent zeal for peace between kings and princes, and for the reform of monasteries, caused him to travel much about the country, robbers often lay in ambush for him. One day, no less than forty of them set upon him, and when their leader, by the name of Aymo, saw Odo and the brethren who accompanied him continually singing psalms as they went along the road, he was struck with compunction, and said to his companions, 'I never remember having seen such men, nor do I think their like has been seen elsewhere; let us leave them alone. There is an armed and vigorous man with them, and we cannot do them any harm without endangering ourselves.'

To this they replied, 'Then let us lift up this armed man on the points of our spears, and the others we will let go when we have first robbed them.' 'Turn your weapons against me first,' he replied, 'otherwise you will have nothing to do with them while I am alive.' So divided amongst themselves, the robbers disbanded. But their leader went after our father and did penance for his crimes, and afterwards gave up his evil life of robbery. But I do not think this happened immediately.

Such graciousness of spirit filled those with whom Odo consorted. His good spirits not only enlivened the cheerful, but restored those who were sad to true joy, and gave them lasting happiness. His tongue, as Scripture says, was a tree of life, a peaceable tongue; and his lips the sweetness of honey, honey that drips from the honeycomb; and the law of prudence was in his words.

It was at this time that our father's name, like a bright star, began to shine far and wide. He became known to kings, was familiar to bishops, beloved of the secular lords. For any monasteries that were built in their territories they handed over to his rule that he might reform and regulate them according to our customs.

alternative reading

A Reading from *Monastic Reform and Cluniac Spirituality* by Raffaelo Morghen

The spiritual movement which began with Cluny at the beginning of the tenth century not only promoted new forms of religious life within the monasteries of Europe and contributed to the vigorous affirmation of the religious ideals of the church of Pope Gregory VII, it also inspired new expressions of art in architecture and liturgical singing. Indirectly it assisted the revival of economic life by bringing about cultivation of waste land, causing houses, churches and villages to rise where previously there stretched forests and swamps as far as the eye could see, increasing the number of monasteries, free settlements, artisans and merchants, so that Cluniac houses often became centres of intense social life whose influence spread beyond the confines of the monastery.

This monastic reform reflected the spiritual needs of the common people, eager at the beginning of the second millennium for a freer life and a more personal religion. At the same time, monasticism raised within itself an aristocracy of great spirits who, to a large extent, influenced and dominated the whole of religious life and, directly and indirectly, social and political life in the tenth and eleventh centuries. Such men were Berno and Odo of Cluny, Odilo, Hugh and Peter the Venerable, the great abbots of Cluny.

Scarcely a century after the abbacy of Odo, Cluny attained its apogee in the time of Abbot Hugh. The huge Cluniac family was gathered into a single congregation of all the monasteries united in the community dependent on the mother house. The abbots of Cluny became among the most powerful seigneurs in Europe. The Cluniac monks, freed from manual work and giving themselves mainly to the liturgical office and prayer, seemed to be the representatives of a new spiritual aristocracy, whose sense of propriety and dignity, characteristic of the Cluniac spirit, showed, even in external forms, the interior impulse from which the monastic revival of the tenth century had started.

12 May

Thomas Rattray

Bishop, 1743

Thomas Rattray came of a long-established Perthshire family. He was distinguished while still a layman for his theological writings. As a liturgical and patristic scholar, and drawing on early Eastern liturgies, he exerted a decisive influence on the Scottish Communion Office of 1764, and thus on the eucharistic worship of the Episcopal Church in Scotland and in the United States of America. He was a leader among those who contended that the appointment of a bishop belonged properly to the clergy of the diocese, with the approbation of the laity. His election as Bishop of Brechin in 1727 was declared void by the College of Bishops. He was later elected Bishop of Dunkeld, and became Primus in 1739. An example of piety and strictness of life, he was one of the most learned bishops of his time. He died in the year 1743.

A Reading from *The Ancient Liturgy of the Church of Jerusalem*
by Thomas Rattray

From the [ancient] liturgies of Saint Mark, Saint Chrysostom, and Saint Basil, may be seen the wonderful harmony and agreement that is among them all in the following particulars, *viz.* (after the peoples bringing their oblations to the priest, and his presenting them on the altar) in the Sursum Corda, *Lift up your hearts*, with the people's response Habemus ad Dominum, *We lift them up unto the Lord*; in the thanksgiving introductory to the Words of Institution, and the people's joining with the priest in the *Seraphic Hymn* (as the Greeks call it), Holy, Holy, Holy etc. which always made a part of it; in rehearsing the history of the institution; in the prayer of oblation, or solemn offering of the bread and cup as the antitypes of the body and blood of Christ, in commemoration of his death and passion; in the invocation of the descent of the Holy Ghost upon them, to make them that very body and blood (as the instituted representatives of which they had been just before offered up) to make them, I say, by a mysterious change, though not in their substance, yet at least in their qualities, that very body and blood in energy and life-giving power, by which their consecration is fully completed: in the intercession in virtue of this commemorative sacrifice, in which there was always a commemoration of and prayer for the dead: in the *commendatio*, beseeching God to sanctify their souls and bodies, and make them worthy to communicate in these sacred mysteries.

12 May

Gregory Dix

Priest, Monk, Scholar, 1952

Born in 1901, George Dix was educated at Westminster School and Merton College, Oxford. After ordination to a Fellowship at Keble College, Oxford, he taught history before entering the novitiate of the Benedictine community at Pershore, taking the name Gregory. Shortly afterwards the community moved to Nashdom in Buckinghamshire, where Dix eventually made his life profession and was appointed Prior. Dix was one of the most influential figures of a generation of Anglo-Catholics who worked enthusiastically towards reunion with Rome. A gifted and popular preacher and spiritual director, Dix is best remembered as a liturgical scholar whose monumental work, The Shape of the Liturgy, has had an unparalleled influence over liturgical study and revision since it was first published in 1945. He died on this day in 1952.

A Reading from *The Shape of the Liturgy*
by Gregory Dix

Was ever another command so obeyed? For century after century, spreading slowly to every continent and country and among every race on earth, this action has been done, in every conceivable human circumstance, for every conceivable human need from infancy and before it to extreme old age and after it, from the pinnacles of earthly greatness to the refuge of fugitives in the caves and dens of the earth. Men have found no better thing than this to do for kings at their crowning and for criminals going to the scaffold; for armies in triumph or for a bride and bridegroom in a little country church; for the proclamation of a dogma or for a good crop of wheat; for the wisdom of the Parliament of a mighty nation or for a sick old woman afraid to die; for a schoolboy sitting an examination or for Columbus setting out to discover America; for the famine of whole provinces or for the soul of a dead lover; – one could fill many pages with the reasons why men have done this, and not tell a hundredth part of them. And best of all, week by week and month by month, on a hundred thousand successive Sundays, faithfully, unfailingly, across all the parishes of Christendom, the pastors have done this just to make the *plebs sancta Dei* – the holy common people of God.

14 May

Matthias

Apostle

After the betrayal of Jesus by Judas Iscariot, the apostles brought their number back to twelve by choosing Matthias to replace him. He was chosen by lot from amongst the disciples. According to Luke, the author of the Acts of the Apostles, the number of apostles had to be restored so that they might 'sit on thrones judging the twelve tribes of Israel'. It was conditional that they had to have been with Jesus during his earthly ministry and witnesses to the resurrection. The point of being chosen by lot, rather than by some democratic method, indicated the election or choosing by God, rather than by mortals.

A Reading from a homily of John Chrysostom

Peter was an impetuous man, and yet it was to him that Christ entrusted his flock; and therefore, as the first of the apostles, it was he who enjoyed the privilege of speaking first.

‘Friends, the Scripture must be fulfilled, which the Holy Spirit through David foretold concerning Judas, who became a guide to those who arrested Jesus.’ Observe how Peter never acts imperiously, but always seeks a common mind. He is seeking to console the disciples about what has just happened; because let there be no mistake, the action of Judas had devastated the disciples. And yet note the moderation of Peter’s language. He does not ridicule Judas, or label him ‘wretch’ or ‘criminal’; he simply states the facts.

‘We must choose someone from among those who accompanied us to take his place.’ Peter allowed the whole body of believers to choose, and so secured honour for the person elected, as well as avoiding any ill-feeling that might have arisen against himself. For occasions such as these invariably have evil repercussions. Did Peter himself then not have the right to choose? What was his motive in acting as he did? I think it is because he did not want to be charged with favouritism. Besides which, he still had not received the Spirit.

‘They put forward two names, Joseph called Barsabbas, who was surnamed Justus, and Matthias.’ Note that Peter did not himself select either of the two candidates who were put forward; and although it was he who had made the suggestion, he points out that it was not his own idea, but rather in fulfilment of an ancient prophecy. In other words, Peter is concerned to interpret, not to give orders.

He was also anxious that they should be eyewitnesses. Even though the Spirit was about to come, Peter was very particular on this point: ‘from among those who accompanied us during all the time that the Lord Jesus went in and out among us’. What was important for Peter was that they had lived with the Lord, rather than simply being one of the crowds who followed him. And then he said, ‘One of these must become with us a witness to his resurrection.’ This is important. Peter did not say, ‘a witness to his other acts’, but specifically, ‘a witness to his resurrection’. A witness would be more credible if he could say that this man with whom I ate and drank, and who was crucified, has risen again’.

‘All prayed together and said, “Lord, you know everyone’s heart: show us which of the two you have chosen.”’ You, not we. It was right for them to say that God knew the hearts of all, for the choice indeed was to be made by God and no one else. They spoke confidently in the assurance that one would be chosen. They did not even say ‘choose’, but ‘show’, show whom you have chosen, since they knew that all things had been preordained by God. ‘And they cast lots, and the lot fell upon Matthias.’

My friends, let us imitate the apostles. And here I wish to speak to those among you who are ambitious for preferment. If you believe that an episcopal election is in the hands of God, do not be displeased at its outcome. If you are, it is with God that you are displeased: it is with God you are exasperated. For God has made his choice, and God knows how to dispose things for the best. Quite often you will feel yourself more qualified than another candidate; but perhaps you were not the right person. Or again, you may be irreproachable in your life, your behaviour may be exemplary; but in the church, something more is wanted. One person is suitable for this post, another for that.

Finally, let me say why such events in the life of the church have become the subject of competition. It is because those of us who are called to the episcopate are more concerned with our own status in which we then take our repose, than in devoting ourselves to the care and leadership of our brothers and sisters.

14 May

Carthagh of Lismore

Religious, 637

The cathedral dedicated to Carthagh, or Macodi, continues worship first begun in the ancient monastery by the river Blackwater in the west of County Waterford. The graceful spire was highly praised by Thackeray on his Irish visit as 'the prettiest I have seen in, or I think, out of Ireland'. Carthagh died on this day in the year 637.

A Reading from an Old Irish poem

The Saints' Calendar of Adamnán

The saints of the four seasons,
I long to pray to them,
May they save me from torments,
The saints of the whole year!

The saints of the glorious springtime,
May they be with me
By the will
Of God's fosterling.

The saints of the dry summer,
About them is my poetic frenzy,
That I may come from this land
To Jesus, son of Mary.

The saints of the beautiful autumn,
I call upon a company not inharmonious,
That they may draw near to me,
With Mary and Michael.

The saints of the winter I pray to,
May they be with me against the throng of demons,
Around Jesus of the mansions,
The Spirit holy, heavenly.

The other calendar,
Which noble saints will have,
Though it has more verses,
It does not have more saints.

I beseech the saints of the earth,
I beseech all the angels,
I beseech God himself, both when rising and lying down,
Whatever I do or say, that I may dwell in the heavenly land.

15 May

Pachomius

Founder of cenobitic monasticism, 346

Pachomius is honoured as the first Christian monk who not simply tried to bring hermits together in groups, but actually organized them with a written Rule and structures of a communal life (cenobium). He is said to have been born in Upper Egypt, of pagan parents, and to have been a conscript in the imperial army. Upon discharge he was converted and baptized. He became a disciple of a hermit, and then in about 320, founded a monastery at Tabennisi near the Nile. He used his military experience to organize his growing number of followers, and by the time of his death in 346 he was ruling as abbot-general over nine monasteries for men and two for women. He is honoured, therefore, as the founder of cenobitic monasticism.

A Reading from the *Sarum Lectures* of David Knowles

Monasticism, as its etymology suggests, began with an individual's retirement from the world. Saint Antony the Great, usually known as the first monk, was in fact an anchorite and not the first of that family; but unlike the 'pure' hermits, such as Saint Paul of Egypt, he ultimately became the leader of a numerous family to whom he gave instructions and permanent help even when he had retired finally into the desert land near the Red Sea. But in the story of cenobitic monasticism the first name is Pachomius, the father of monks of the common life, who, like Saint Benedict, began as an anchorite but became in 315, as he thought under divine inspiration, the founder of a family of monks living and working together. Recruits came in floods, and when he died he was the father of a large group of monasteries containing possibly five thousand inmates.

Besides writing a *Rule*, Pachomius also organised every detail of a great institution. When he died, we might almost say that a perfect monastic order was in existence. Not only was all the material framework there – church, refectory, assembly room, cells, enclosure wall – not only was the daily life of prayer and work in all its parts arranged, not only was the spiritual discipline of chastity, poverty and obedience wisely established, but the whole complex was knit together by firm strands of control.

Within each monastery were numerous houses, each containing thirty or forty monks practising a particular craft. These houses themselves might be thirty or forty in number, making up a settlement of between one and a half and two thousand souls.

Within the houses were parties of ten or so under a foreman. Each house was governed by a master, and each monastery by a father or abbot. Pachomius himself remained at the head and lived in the head house of the whole institute.

At every level the superior could direct and transfer his monks and at every level there were regular reunions for spiritual conference and advice. In the monasteries there was, alongside the abbot, a minister who dealt with all economic matters – supplies of food and raw materials, distribution and sale of necessaries and products. Pachomius himself visited all the houses repeatedly, and twice a year there was a general gathering in his monastery. At Easter all came up to celebrate the Pasch and to baptize any catechumens, and at mid-August all the procurators or ministers came up to render an account of the year's workings. It was a remarkable achievement of planning and discipline.

15 May

Edmwnd Prys and John Davies

Priests and Translators, 1623 & 1644

Edmwnd Prys was born in Llanrwst in 1544 and educated at St John's College, Cambridge. In 1576 he was appointed Rector of Ludlow and Archdeacon of Merioneth, and settled in Tyddyn-du, Maentwrog, which was his home until his death in the year 1623. He was a close friend of William Morgan, whom he assisted with his translation of the Bible. Prys was a gifted Welsh poet, representing a Protestant humanism that wove together the strands of the Renaissance, the Reformation and the skills of the traditional Welsh poetic art. His Salmau Cân (1621), a collection of metrical psalms, combines careful translation and high poetic quality. It was reprinted over a hundred times and was used for congregational singing for many generations. He died in the year 1623.

John Davies was born in around the year 1567 in Llanferres, Denbighshire, and is renowned as one of the greatest scholars in Welsh history. He graduated from Jesus College, Oxford, and in 1604 became Rector of Mallwyd in Merionethshire where he lived for the remaining forty years of his life. He was responsible for revising the language of the Welsh Bible of 1620, establishing a text that would remain unaltered for over three centuries, and may also have revised the language of the 1621 Welsh Prayer Book. His concern for spiritual well-being led him to translate Llyfr y Resolusion from a work by Robert Parsons and to produce a new edition of Y Llyfr Plygain, the shortened prayer book intended for use by the laity in their homes. He died in the year 1644.

A Reading from Edmwnd Prys' metrical version of Psalm 23

Yr Arglwydd yw fy Mugail clau,
Ni ad byth eisiau arnaf;
Gorwedd a gaf mewn porfa fras,
Ar lan dwfr gloywlas araf.

Fe goledd f 'enaid, ac a'm dwg
'R hyd llwybrau diddrwg, cyfion;
Er mwyn ei Enw mawr di-lys,
Fe'm tywys ar yr union.

Pe rhodiwn, mi nid ofnwn hyn,
Yn nyffryn cysgod angau;
Wyt gyda mi, â'th nerth a'th ffon;
On'd tirion ydyw'r arfau?

Gosodaist Di fy mwrdd yn fras,
Lle'r oedd fy nghas yn gweled;
Olew i'm pen, a chwpan llawn,
Daionus iawn fu'r weithred.

O'th nawdd y daw y doniau hyn
I'm canlyn byth yn hylwydd;
A minnau a breswyliaf byth,
Â'm nyth yn nhŷ Arglwydd.

alternative reading

A Reading from *The Welsh and their Religion* by Glanmor Williams

Publishing the Bible in Welsh took three-quarters of a century to complete, from 1551 to 1620. In the process a series of formidable hurdles had to be surmounted. Intelligent use of contemporary editions of original texts of the Bible necessitated a high degree of scholarship and judgement in Latin, Greek, and Hebrew. There also had to be a sensitive deployment of the Welsh language itself. The little group of translators deserved well of their countrymen. The rapturous chorus of gratitude which first greeted their labours has fittingly echoed down the centuries. The services they rendered in laying the modern foundations of religion, language, literature, and national awareness in Wales were epoch-making.

The other prose works tended to mesh in with successive Biblical translations. Each new version of the Bible – that of Davies and Salesbury (1567), William Morgan (1588), and Parry and Davies (1620) – was followed or accompanied, as might be expected, by a new edition of the Prayer Book. In literary and scholarly terms the translation of the order of service was nearly as notable a feat as that of the Bible. The regular reading of it in Welsh parish churches, week in and week out, over the years engendered a real affection for it and contributed substantially to the anger felt by many when its use was prohibited by the Puritans in the mid seventeenth century.

There is no external evidence to indicate who undertook the translation of the Prayer Book of 1599; but the text itself makes it certain that it was prepared under the direction of William Morgan. His main helper was the youthful John Davies, who seems to have come to Llandaff to act as Morgan's assistant and secretary soon after graduating from Jesus College, Oxford, in 1594. Many years later, in 1621, Davies recalled how, for thirty years or so, he helped translate the Scriptures into Welsh, first as Morgan's assistant in the 1590s and later as Bishop Richard Parry's collaborator in preparing the Bible of 1620. The unmistakable similarities which exist between the translation of 1599 and that of 1620 suggest that Davies might have had quite a hand in the work in the course of his apprenticeship with Morgan. He may also have taken on much of the hack work involved in seeing the Prayer Book through the press.

16 May

Brendan the Navigator

Abbot of Clonfert, 577

Born in Tralee in the Diocese of Ardfert and Aghadoe, Brendan founded his monastic school in Clonfert where the present cathedral, with its outstandingly beautiful west door, recalls a great tradition. Brendan's travels, not only to Aghadown in Galway, but also among many islands round the coasts of Ireland and Scotland, and further still to Iceland, have stirred the imagination of many. Inspired by his adventures they have imitated his courage. Was it a companion of Brendan that founded the monastery on the summit of Skellig Michael? Did Brendan sail even further towards the sunset? He died on this day in the year 577.

A Reading from *The Voyage of Brendan*

Saint Brendan, son of Findlug, descendant of Alta of the line of Eogan, was born in the marshy region of Munster. He was a very ascetical man, famed for his miracles and was spiritual father to almost three thousand monks.

Saint Brendan selected seven monks from his community, shut himself in an oratory with them, and said to them, 'My most beloved fellow-warriors, I look to you for advice and help, for my heart and all my thoughts are united in a single desire. I have resolved in my heart, if only it be God's will, to seek that Promised Land of the Saints, of which Saint Barinthus has spoken. How does this seem to you, and what advice do you wish to give me?'

As soon as they knew their holy father's intention, they said with one voice, 'Father, your will is our will. Have we not left our families, have we not set aside our inheritance and put ourselves in your hands? And so we are ready to follow you to either death or life. We seek one thing only: the will of God.' And so Saint Brendan and those who were with him completed a forty-day fast, in three-day periods, before they set out.

One day they were sailing close to an island, covered with grass and filled with flowers and groves of trees. Saint Brendan said to them, 'See, our Lord Jesus Christ has given us a place in which to stay and celebrate his resurrection.'

As the hour for vespers approached, all the birds in the trees began to sing as if with a single voice, beating their wings against their sides: 'Praise is due to you, O God, in Zion, and to you shall vows be performed.' They continued to sing this verse antiphonally for a whole hour. To the man of God and his companions, this singing and rhythmic beating of wings seemed as sweet as a song of lamentation.

Then Saint Brendan said to his brothers, 'Take nourishment for your bodies, for today our souls have already been filled with divine food.' When supper was over they sang the Divine Office, and then slept till the third hour of the night. But Saint Brendan stayed awake and summoned his brothers to the vigil of the Holy Night with the verse, 'O Lord, open my lips'. When the holy man had finished praying, all the birds started to flap their wings and sing, 'Praise the Lord, all his angels, praise him, all his host'. They continued to sing for an hour, just as they had at vespers.

As the sun rose, they began to sing, 'And may the splendour of the Lord come upon us' with the same rhythm and chant that they had used at lauds. And then at terce, the same verse, 'Sing psalms to our God, sing psalms; sing psalms to our king, sing psalms with understanding.' At sext, 'Let thy face, O Lord, shine upon us and take pity on us'. At none they sang, 'Behold, how good and pleasant it is when brothers dwell in unity'. And so, day and night, the birds praised the Lord. Saint Brendan nourished his brothers on the feast of Easter until the octave day.

16 May

Caroline Chisholm

Social Reformer, 1877

Caroline Jones was born in 1808. On her marriage to Archibald Chisholm, she took her husband's Roman Catholic faith. They emigrated to Madras in 1831 where she set up a school for soldiers' daughters. In 1838, the family moved to Australia and, almost immediately, Caroline began to work for the vulnerable immigrants arriving at Sydney. She was especially concerned for the women, who were often lured and bullied into brothels. She set up a free Registry Office to help them obtain legitimate work and a shelter. She campaigned rigorously for improved conditions. She returned to Britain in 1846 to press for emigration reform and founded the Family Colonisation Loan Society. Her Christian ministry and action led to the ending of what had virtually been the institutionalization of the abuse of poor women.

A Reading from *Far Above Rubies* by Richard Symonds

When Caroline Chisholm and her husband arrived in Sydney, the transportation of convicts from Britain was about to end. Immigration of free colonists was now being financed from the sale of lands. Under the convict system about ten times as many males as females had been brought to New South Wales. To redress the balance large numbers of young women were being shipped out. They were often abused by the ships' officers. On arrival impostors would board the ships, pretending to employ servants, but in fact taking the women to brothels.

The needs of these women and girls provided Caroline's first cause in Australia. The work would take her from her family and involve expenses which she could barely afford. She would have to reclaim prostitutes and argue with pimps and procuresses, and when she sought help there would be a prejudice against her in influential circles because she was a Roman Catholic. Yet when she tried to persuade herself that this was not her responsibility, 'the delay pressed on my mind like a sin. I was impressed with the idea that God had in a peculiar manner fitted me for this work … On Easter Sunday I was enabled at the altar of our Lord to make an offering of my talents to the God who gave them. I promised to know neither country nor creed, but to serve all justly and impartially.'

Her achievements during her seven years in New South Wales were remarkable. With no official authority she settled 11,000 people and reunited six hundred families. She greatly raised the status of immigrant women and brought about hundreds of happy marriages. She caused higher standards to be expected among doctors and captains of immigrant ships. She came to be regarded as something of an institution in Sydney and was the only woman to be invited to give evidence before Government Committees on Immigration and on Unemployment. Her influence with the colony's leaders and the press, carefully and sparsely used, was usually highly effective in exposing scandals and in raising money for causes.

In all this Caroline successfully overcame prejudice against the intervention of women in public affairs and, by her evident fairness and lack of sectarian bias, to make a nonsense of allegations that she discriminated in favour of Roman Catholics. Even the Governor apologised publicly for having at first poured cold water on her various schemes and, when he returned to England, gave her valuable support in her struggle for a new immigration policy.

Politically, Caroline became more radical as she grew older. As time went on she found it less necessary to be restrained in expressing her opposition to the export of the English class system to Australia. She was singularly fortunate in her husband who recognised her inspiration and served loyally in a subordinate position under her leadership. Their children likewise enjoyed assisting in their mother's work from quite an early age.

It was for her shrewdness as much as her charity that people used to seek her help and advice. Though she was a formidable critic, she was generous in encouragement. In the words of one of her contemporaries, Caroline exhibited much goodness and generous pity, but even more 'an admirable obstinacy in doing good, a sublime stubbornness'.

19 May

Dunstan

Archbishop of Canterbury, Restorer of Monastic Life, 988

Dunstan was born near Glastonbury around 910 into a noble family. He received a good education and spent time at the court of the King of Wessex. A saintly uncle urged him to enter the monastic life; he delayed, but followed the advice on recovering from an illness. Returning to Glastonbury, Dunstan lived as a monk, devoting his work time to creative pursuits: illuminating, music, and metalwork. In 943 the new king made him abbot, and this launched a great revival of monastic life in England. Starting with Glastonbury, Dunstan restored discipline to several monasteries and promoted study and teaching. Under two later kings, he rose to political and ecclesiastical eminence, being chief minister and Archbishop of Canterbury under King Edgar. This enabled him and his followers to extend his reforms to the whole English Church. He is reputed to be the author of the coronation oath. In 970 Dunstan fell from political favour but continued as Archbishop of Canterbury, preaching and teaching. He died in the year 988.

A Reading from the earliest *Life of Saint Dunstan* by an unknown author

Dunstan diligently studied the books of the Irish pilgrims to Glastonbury, meditating on the path of the true faith, and always explored with critical scrutiny the books of other wise men which he perceived from the deep vision of his heart to be confirmed by the assertions of the holy fathers. Thus he controlled his way of life so that, as often as he examined the books of the divine scriptures, God spoke with him. Indeed, as often as he was released from secular cares and delighted with leisure for prayer, he seemed himself to speak with God.

Among his sacred studies of literature he also diligently cultivated the art of writing, that he might be sufficient in all things; and the art of harp-playing, and also skill in painting. He was, so to speak, a skilled investigator of all useful things.

At length when King Athelstan was dead, and the condition of the kingdom changed, the authority of the succeeding king, namely Edmund, ordered the blessed Dunstan, who was of approved way of life and erudite conversation, to appear before him, that he might be chosen and numbered among the royal courtiers and chief men of the palace. Not rashly resisting these orders, but rather remembering the Lord's command, he hastened to render to the king the things that were the king's, and to God the things that were God's.

Throughout his life it was his chief care to occupy himself constantly and frequently in sacred prayers and in the ten-stringed psalmody of David; or to pass the night in vigils, overcoming sweet sleep; or to sweat and labour in the concerns of the Church; or also, when he could see the first light of daybreak, to correct faulty books, erasing the errors of the scribes; or, giving judgement with a keen intelligence between individuals, to distinguish the true from the false; or by calm words to bring to harmony and peace all who were at enmity or quarrelling; or to benefit with his kind support widows, orphans, pilgrims and strangers in their necessities; or to dissolve by just separation foolish or wrongful marriages; or to strengthen by the word of life or by example the whole human order, triply divided in its proper and stable design; or with serene probity to support and enrich the churches of God by just contribution of his own procuring or from other sources; or to season with the celestial salt, that is, with the teaching of wholesome knowledge, the ignorant of both sexes, men and women, whoever he could, by day and night.

Thus it was that the English land was filled with Dunstan's holy teaching, shining before God and mortals alike as the sun and moon. When he resolved to render to Christ the Lord the due hours of his service and celebrations of masses, he so performed and recited them with his whole soul that he seemed to speak face to face with the Lord himself, even though beforehand he may have been much vexed by the agitated disputes of people. And as often as he fitly and splendidly discharged any other duties of his episcopal office, he always did so with a great flow of tears which the invisible indweller, the Holy Spirit, who constantly dwelt in him, mightily drew forth from the rivers of his eyes.

20 May

Alcuin

Deacon, Abbot of Tours, 804

Alcuin was descended from a noble Northumbrian family. Although the date and place of his birth are not known, he was probably born in the year 735 in or near York. He entered the cathedral school there as a child, continued as a scholar and became the Master. In 781, he went to Aachen as adviser to Charlemagne on religious and educational matters, and as Master of the Palace School, where he established an important library. Although not a monk and in deacon's orders, in 796 he became Abbot of Tours, where he died in 804. Alcuin wrote poetry, revised the lectionary, compiled a sacramentary and was involved in other significant liturgical work.

A Reading from a letter of Alcuin to Higbald, Bishop of Lindisfarne and his monks, condoling with them for the sack of Lindisfarne by the Danes on 8 June 793

The intimacy of your love used to rejoice me greatly when I was with you; but conversely, the calamity of your tribulation saddens me greatly every day, though I am absent; when the pagans desecrated the sanctuaries of God, and poured out the blood of saints around the altar, laid waste the house of our hope, trampled on the bodies of saints in the temple of God like dung in the street. What can we say except lament in our soul with you before Christ's altar, and say: 'Spare, O Lord, spare your people, and do not give your inheritance to Gentiles, lest the pagan say, "Where is the God of the Christians?"'

What assurance is there for the churches of Britain, if Saint Cuthbert, with so great a number of saints, defends not his own? Either this is the beginning of greater tribulation, or else the sins of the inhabitants have called it upon them. Truly it has not happened by chance, but is a sign that it was well merited by someone. But now, you who are left, stand manfully, fight bravely, defend the camp of God.

Yet do not be dismayed at this calamity. God chastises every son whom he receives; and thus perhaps he chastised you more harshly because he loved you more. Jerusalem, the city loved by God, perished with the temple of God in the flames of the Chaldeans. Rome, encircled by a crown of holy apostles and innumerable martyrs, was shattered by the ravages of pagans, but by the pity of God soon recovered. Almost the whole of Europe was laid desolated by the fire and sword of the Goths and Huns; but now, by God's mercy, it shines adorned with churches, as the sky with stars, and in them the offices of the Christian religion flourish and increase. Exhort yourselves in turn, saying: 'Let us return to the Lord our God, for he is bountiful to forgive, and never deserts them that hope in him.'

My brothers, let us love what is eternal, and not what is perishable. Let us esteem true riches, not fleeting ones, eternal, not transitory. Let us acquire praise from God, and not from mortals. Let us do what the saints did whom we praise. Let us follow their footsteps on earth, that we may deserve to be partakers of their glory in the heavens.

May the protection of the divine pity guard you from all adversity, and set you with your fathers in the glory of the celestial kingdom, O dearest brothers.

21 May

Helena

Protector of the Holy Places, 330

The Empress Helena came to power in the Roman Empire when her son Constantine became emperor, in the year 306. Although she had previously been abandoned by her husband, her son raised her to a position of great honour. As Helena was a Christian she gave her support to their cause, and in 326 she made a pilgrimage to the Holy Land. There she provided the wherewithal to found the building of a basilica on the Mount of Olives and another at Bethlehem. According to fourth-century historians, she discovered the cross on which Christ was crucified. In the Eastern Church, she is commemorated on this day, together with her son Constantine.

A Reading from the *Ecclesiastical History* of Socrates Scholasticus

Helena, the mother of the emperor Constantine, being divinely directed by dreams, went to Jerusalem. She sought carefully the sepulchre of Christ, from which he arose after his burial; and after much difficulty, by God's help she discovered it. What the cause of the difficulty was I will explain in a few words.

Those who embraced the Christian faith, after the period of his passion, greatly venerated this tomb; but those who hated Christianity, having covered the spot with a mound of earth, erected on it a temple to Venus, and set up her image there, not caring for the memory of the place. This succeeded for a long time; and it became known to Helena. Accordingly, having caused the statue to be thrown down, the earth to be removed, and the ground entirely cleared, she found three crosses in the sepulchre: one of these was that blessed cross on which Christ had hung, the other two were those on which the two thieves that were crucified with him had died. With these was also found the tablet of Pilate, on which he had inscribed in various characters, that the Christ who was crucified was King of the Jews.

Since, however, it was doubtful which cross they were in search of, the emperor's mother was not a little distressed; but from this trouble the bishop of Jerusalem, Macarius, shortly relieved her. And he solved the doubt by faith, for he sought a sign from God and obtained it. The sign was this: a certain woman of the neighbourhood, who had been long afflicted with disease, was now just at the point of death; the bishop therefore arranged it so that each of the crosses should be brought to the dying woman, believing that she would be healed on touching the precious cross. Nor was he disappointed in his expectation: for the two crosses having been applied which were not the Lord's, the woman still continued in a dying state; but when the third, which was the true cross, touched her, she was immediately healed, and recovered her former strength. In this manner then was the genuine cross discovered.

23 May

William of Perth (or Rochester)

1201

Tradition has it that William was a baker from Perth. Renowned for his acts of charity, he is said to have given every tenth loaf he baked to the poor. He adopted an abandoned boy and brought him up. On pilgrimage to Jerusalem in the year 1201, however, this youth murdered William on the road between Rochester and Canterbury. Though venerated as William of Rochester, he was never canonized.

A Reading from *The Mirror of Charity* by Aelred of Rievaulx

It was pride that distorted the image of God in us and led us away from God, not by means of our feet but by the desires of our hearts. Thus we return to God by following the same path, but in the opposite direction, by the exercise of these same desires; and humility renews us in the same image in which God created us. This is why Saint Paul calls on us to be mentally and spiritually remade, and to be clothed in the new self made in God's image. This renewal can only come about by fulfilling the new commandment of charity given us by our Saviour, and if the mind clothes itself in charity, our distorted memory and knowledge will be given new life and new form.

How simple it is to state the new commandment, but how much they imply – the stopping of our old habits, the renewal of our inner life, the reshaping of the divine image within us. Our power to love was poisoned by the selfishness of our desires, and stifled by lust, so that it has tended always to seek the very depths of deviousness. But when charity floods the soul and warms away the numbness, love strives towards higher and more worthy objects. It puts aside the old ways and takes up a new life, and on flashing wings it dies to the highest and purest goodness which is the source of its being.

This is what Saint Paul was trying to show the Athenians when he established from the books of their philosophers the existence of one God, in whom we live and move and have our being. Paul then quoted one of their own poets who said that we are God's offspring, and in the next sentence went on to enlarge on this saying. The Apostle was not using this quotation to prove that we are of the same nature or substance as God, and therefore unchangeable, incorruptible and eternally blessed like God the Son who was born of the Father from all eternity and is equal to the Father in all things. No, Saint Paul uses this passage from the poet Aratus to assert that we are the offspring of God because the human soul, created in the image of God, can share in his wisdom and blessedness. It is charity which raises our soul towards its destiny, but it is self-centred desire which drags it down to the things towards which, without God's help, it would not certainly be drawn.

24 May

John and Charles Wesley

Evangelists, Hymn Writers, 1791 & 1788

Note: In Scotland, John and Charles Wesley are commemorated on 3 March.

Born at Epworth Rectory in Lincolnshire, John Wesley was the son of an Anglican clergyman and a Puritan mother. He entered Holy Orders and, following a religious experience on this day in 1738, began an itinerant ministry which recognized no parish boundaries. This resulted, after his death, in the development of a world-wide Methodist Church. His spirituality involved an Arminian affirmation of grace, frequent communion and a disciplined corporate search for holiness. His open-air preaching, concern for education and for the poor, liturgical revision, organization of local societies and training of preachers provided a firm basis for Christian growth and mission in England. John died on 2 March 1791.

Charles shared with his brother John the building up of early Methodist societies, as they travelled the country. His special concern was that early Methodists should remain loyal to Anglicanism. He married and settled first in Bristol and later in London, concentrating his work on the local Christian communities. His thousands of hymns established a resource of lyrical piety which has enabled generations of Christians to re-discover the refining power of God's love. They celebrate God's work of grace from birth to death, the great events of

God's work of salvation and the rich themes of eucharistic worship, anticipating the taking up of humanity into the divine life. Charles died on 29 March 1788.

A Reading from the *Journal of John Wesley* for Wednesday 24 May 1738

I think it was about five this morning that I opened my Testament on those words: 'There are given unto us exceeding great and precious promises, even that you should be partakers of the divine nature.' Just as I went out, I opened it again on those words, 'You are not far from the kingdom of God.' In the afternoon I was asked to go to Saint Paul's. The anthem was 'Out of the deep have I called unto you, O Lord: Lord, hear my voice.'

In the evening I went very unwillingly to a society in Aldersgate Street, where one was reading Luther's preface to the Epistle to the Romans. About a quarter before nine, while he was describing the change which God works in the heart through faith in Christ, I felt my heart strangely warmed. I felt I did trust in Christ, Christ alone, for salvation: and an assurance was given me that he had taken away my sins, even mine, and saved me from the law of sin and death.

I began to pray with all my might for those who had in a more especial manner despitefully used me and persecuted me. I then testified openly to all there, what I now first felt in my heart. But it was not long before the enemy suggested, 'This cannot be faith; for where is thy joy?' Then was I taught, that peace and victory over sin are essential to faith in the Captain of our salvation; but that, as to the transports of joy that usually attend the beginning of it, especially in those who have mourned deeply, God sometimes giveth, sometimes withholdeth them, according to the counsels of his own will.

After my return home, I was much buffeted with temptations; but cried out, and they fled away. They returned again and again. I as often lifted up my eyes, and 'he sent me help from his holy place'. And herein I found [in what] the difference between this and my former state chiefly consisted. I was striving, yea, fighting with all my might under the law, as well as under grace. But then I was sometimes, if not often, conquered; now, I was always conqueror.

alternative reading

A Reading from a hymn of Charles Wesley based on Jacob's wrestling with the angel in the Book of Genesis

Wrestling Jacob

Come, O thou Traveller unknown
Whom still I hold, but cannot see,
My company before is gone,
And I am left alone with thee,
With thee all night I mean to stay,
And wrestle till the break of day.

I need not tell thee who I am,
My misery, or sin declare,
Thyself hast called me by my name,
Look on thy hands, and read it there.
But who, I ask thee, who art thou?
Tell me thy name, and tell me now.

In vain thou strugglest to get free,
I never will unloose my hold:
Art thou the Man that died for me?
The secret of thy love unfold.
Wrestling I will not let thee go,
Till I thy name, thy nature know.

Yield to me now – for I am weak;
But confident in self-despair:
Speak to my heart, in blessings speak,
Be conquered by my instant prayer,
Speak, or thou never hence shalt move,
And tell me, if thy name is Love.

'Tis Love, 'tis Love! Thou diedst for me,
I hear thy whisper in my heart.
The morning breaks, the shadows flee:
Pure Universal Love thou art;
To me, to all, thy bowels move,
Thy nature, and thy name, is Love.

25 May

The Venerable Bede

Monk of Jarrow, Scholar, Historian, 735

Bede was born in Northumbria around the year 670. When he was seven years old, his family gave him to the monastery of St Peter and St Paul at Wearmouth. He then moved to Jarrow, where he lived as a monk for the rest of his life. Although it seems he never travelled further than York, his monastery (first under Abbot Benedict Biscop and then Abbot Ceolfrith) was a centre of learning, and Bede studied extensively. He used all the resources available to write the most complete history of Christian England up to the year 729, as well as commentaries on books of the Bible. He was renowned for his monastic fidelity and his love of teaching, and was fondly remembered by his pupils, including his biographer. He died peacefully in 735 and is buried in Durham Cathedral.

A Reading from the conclusion to *A History of the English Church and People* by the Venerable Bede

I, Bede, servant of Christ and priest of the monastery of the blessed apostles Peter and Paul at Wearmouth and Jarrow, have, with the help of God and to the best of my ability, assembled these facts about the history of the Church in Britain, and of the Church of the English in particular, so far as I have been able to ascertain them from ancient documents, from the traditions of our forebears, and from my own personal knowledge.

I was born on the lands of this monastery, and on reaching seven years of age, I was entrusted by my family first to the most reverend Abbot Benedict and later to Abbot Ceolfrid for my education. I have spent all the remainder of my life in this monastery and devoted myself entirely to the study of the Scriptures. Amid the observance of the Rule and the daily task of singing the office in church, my chief delight has always been in study, teaching, and writing.

I was ordained deacon in my nineteenth year, and priest in my thirtieth, receiving both these orders at the hands of the most reverend Bishop John at the direction of Abbot Ceolfrid. From the time of my receiving the priesthood until my fifty-ninth year, I have made it my business, both for my own benefit and that of my brethren, to compile short extracts from the works of the venerable Fathers on the holy Scriptures, and to comment on their meaning and interpretation.

I pray you, merciful Jesu,
that as you have graciously granted me
joyfully to imbibe the words of your knowledge,
so you will also, of your goodness,
grant that I may come at length to you,
the fount of all wisdom,
and stand before your face for ever.

alternative reading

A Reading from a letter to Cuthwin describing the death of Bede, written by Bede's pupil Cuthbert the Deacon

On the Tuesday before the feast of the Ascension, his breathing became very much worse, and his feet began to swell. Even so, he spent the whole of that day teaching us, and dictated cheerfully, and among other things said several times: 'Be sure to learn your lessons quickly now; for I do not know how much longer I will be with you, or whether my Maker will take me from you very soon now.' It seemed clear to us that he knew very well when his end would be.

He spent all that night in thanksgiving, without sleep. When dawn broke that Wednesday, he gave further dictation on the work which we had begun. We were still working at nine o'clock when we went in procession with the relics of the saints, as the custom of that day required. One of us stayed with him, and said to him: 'Dear master, there is still one chapter left to be done of that book you were dictating; is it too much trouble if I question you about it?' But he replied 'It is not hard at all. Take up your pen and sharpen it, and then write quickly.' And so he did.

At three o'clock he said to me: 'I have a few valuables in my chest, some pepper, and napkins, and some incense. Run quickly and fetch the priests of our monastery, so that I may share among them these little presents God has given me.' I did so in great agitation; and when they were all present, he spoke to all and to each personally, encouraging and pleading with them to offer masses and prayers on his behalf; and they promised they would do this.

But they were very sad, and they all wept, especially when he said that he did not think they would see his face much longer in this world. Yet they rejoiced at one thing that he said: 'If it so pleases my Maker, the time has come for me to be released from this body, and to return to the One who formed me out of nothing. I have lived a long time, and the righteous Judge has provided for me well throughout my life. The time for my departure is near, and I long to be dissolved and be with Christ. My soul longs to see Christ my King in all his beauty.'

Having said this, and indeed several other things to our great profit, he spent his last day in gladness until the evening. Then Wilberht, the boy whom I mentioned earlier, said once again: 'Dear master, there is still one sentence that we have not yet written down.' And Bede said: 'Then write it quickly.' After a little while the boy said: 'There, it is written.' And he replied: 'Good! It is finished; you have spoken the truth. Hold my head in your hands. It would please me much if I could sit opposite the holy place where I used to pray, so that I may call upon my Father sitting up.'

And so it happened that as Bede sat upon the floor of his cell, singing 'Glory be to the Father and to the Son and to the Holy Spirit' he breathed his last. And we can believe without hesitation that, inasmuch as he always laboured in this life to the praise of God, so his soul journeyed to the joys of heaven for which he longed.

25 May

Aldhelm

Abbot of Malmesbury, Bishop of Sherborne, 709

Born in the year 639, Aldhelm became a monk at Malmesbury, and later was elected its abbot. When the growing Wessex diocese was divided in 705, he became the first Bishop of Sherborne, founding the abbey church. Aldhelm was a great scholar, teacher and singer who, according to Bede, completed the conquest of Wessex by his preaching. Tradition has it that he would attract listeners by his singing and then preach the gospel to them. It seems he may have also been responsible for introducing the Rule of St Benedict to the area. He built churches all over Dorset, and the headland commonly called Saint Alban's Head is in reality Saint Aldhelm's Head, where there is an ancient chapel. His old English verse, sung to harp accompaniment, was praised by King Alfred. Aldhelm died on this day in the year 709 at Doulting in Somerset, on his way to Malmesbury.

A Reading from *A History of the English Church and People* by the Venerable Bede

At the death of Bishop Haeddi, the bishopric of the province of the West Saxons was divided into two dioceses, one of which was assigned to Daniel, who rules it to this day, and the other to Aldhelm, who administered it with great energy for four years. Both bishops were well acquainted with ecclesiastical matters and learned in the study of the Scriptures.

While Aldhelm was still a priest, and abbot of the monastery known as Malmesbury, he was directed by a synod of his own people to write a notable treatise against the errors of the Britons who celebrate Easter at the wrong time and do other things contrary to the good practices and peace of the Church. By means of this treatise he persuaded many of the Britons who were subject to the West Saxons to conform to the Catholic celebration of our Lord's resurrection. He also wrote an excellent book *On Virginity*, which he composed in a double form in hexameter verse and prose on the model of Sedulius. He also wrote several other books; for he was a man of wide learning, with a polished style and, as I have said, extremely well-read both in ecclesiastical and general literature.

At his death, Forthere, who is also a man of great learning in the Scriptures, was appointed to the bishopric in his place and is still living today.

26 May

Augustine of Canterbury

First Archbishop of Canterbury, 605

Augustine was prior of the monastery of St Andrew in Rome. In 596, at the instigation of Pope Gregory the Great, he was dispatched as the leader of a group of forty monks to re-evangelize the English Church. Augustine appears to have been not a particularly confident person, and in Gaul he wanted to turn back, but Pope Gregory's firm resolution held the group to their mission. The monks finally landed in Kent in the summer of 597 where they were well received by King Ethelbert whose wife, Bertha, was a Christian. Once established, Augustine returned temporarily to Gaul to receive ordination as a bishop. Pope Gregory would have preferred London to have become the primatial see, but in the event Canterbury was chosen, and thus Augustine became the first Archbishop of Canterbury. He died in either the year 604 or 605.

A Reading from *A History of the English Church and People* by the Venerable Bede

King Ethelbert granted Augustine and his companions a dwelling in the city of Canterbury, which was the chief city of his kingdom, and in accordance with his promise he allowed them provisions and did not inhibit their freedom to preach. As soon as they had occupied the house given to them they began to emulate the life of the apostles and the primitive Church. They were constantly at prayer; they fasted and kept vigils; and they preached the word of life to whomsoever they could. They regarded worldly things as of little importance, and accepted only the necessities of life from those they taught. They practised what they preached, and were willing to endure any hardship, and even to the point of dying for the truths they proclaimed. Before long a number of people, admiring the simplicity of their holy lives and the comfort of their heavenly message, believed and were baptized. On the east side of the city stood an old church, built in honour of Saint Martin during the Roman occupation of Britain, where the queen, who was a Christian, used to pray. Here the monks first assembled to sing psalms, to pray, to celebrate the Eucharist, to preach, and to baptize, until the king's own conversion to the Faith gave them even greater freedom to preach and to build and restore churches everywhere.

At last the king himself, among others, attracted by the pure lives of these holy men and their joyous promises, the truth of which they confirmed by many miracles, believed and was baptized. Thenceforward great numbers gathered each day to hear the word of God, forsaking their heathen worship and entering the unity of Christ's holy Church. While the king was pleased at their faith and conversion, it is said that he would not compel anyone to accept Christianity; for he had learned from his instructors and guides to salvation that the service of Christ must be accepted freely and not under compulsion.

Meanwhile God's servant Augustine visited Arles and, in accordance with the command of the holy father Gregory, was consecrated archbishop of the English nation by Etherius, archbishop of that city.

26 May

John Calvin

Reformer, 1564

The French reformer John Calvin was born at Noyon in Picardy in 1509 and, since he was intended for an ecclesiastical career, he received the tonsure and his first benefice at the age of twelve, not untypical at this time. It proved to be the only order he ever received. Two years later he began studying theology at Paris but for some reason changed to law and moved to Orléans where he came under his first Protestant influences. He broke with the Roman Church in 1533, having had a religious experience which he believed commissioned him to purify and restore the Church of Christ. The first edition of his Institutes appeared in 1536, being a justification of Reformation principles. Calvin accepted a position in Geneva which involved organizing the Reformation in that city and, with a few absences, spent most of the rest of his life there, becoming the undisputed master of the moral and ecclesial lives of the citizenry. His pre-eminence could be seen in that he wrote to the Protector Somerset in England indicating to him what changes he felt should be made and corresponded similarly with other nations' leaders. During all this, his literary output never wavered. His immense reputation and influence have continued in the churches of the Reform to the present day. He died on this day in the year 1564.

A Reading from *The Institutes of the Christian Religion* by John Calvin

The covenant of life is not preached equally among all, and among those to whom it is preached, it does not gain the same acceptance either constantly or in equal degree. In this diversity the wonderful depth of God's judgement is made known. For there is no doubt that this variety also serves the decision of God's eternal election. If it is plain that it comes to pass by God's bidding that salvation is freely offered to some while others are barred from access to it, at once great and difficult questions spring up, explicable only when reverent minds regard as settled what they may suitably hold concerning election and predestination. A baffling question this seems to many. For they think nothing more inconsistent than that out of the common multitude of men and women some should be predestined to salvation, others to destruction.

How much the ignorance of this principle detracts from God's glory, how much it takes away from true humility, is well known. Yet Paul denies that this which needs so much to be known can be known unless God, utterly disregarding works, chooses those whom he has decreed within himself. 'At the present time,' he says, 'a remnant has been saved according to the election of grace. But if it is by grace, it is no more of works; otherwise grace would not be grace.'

If – to make it clear that our salvation comes about solely from God's mere generosity – we must be called back to the course of election, those who wish to get rid of all this are obscuring as maliciously as they can what ought to have been gloriously and vociferously proclaimed, and they tear humility up by the very roots. Paul clearly testifies that, when the salvation of a remnant of the people is ascribed to the election of grace, then only is it acknowledged that God of his mere good pleasure preserves whom he will, and moreover that he pays no reward, since he can owe none.

They who shut the gates that no one may dare seek a taste of this doctrine of predestination wrong us no less than God. For neither will anything else suffice to make us humble as we ought to be, nor shall we otherwise sincerely feel how much we are obliged to God.

26 May

Philip Neri

Founder of the Oratorians, Spiritual Guide, 1595

Born in 1515 in Florence, Philip Neri went to Rome when he was eighteen, resolved to give his life to God. He studied hard and led a noticeably austere life and, after a time living the life of a virtual hermit in the Roman catacombs, founded a fraternity to assist pilgrims and the sick. He was ordained in 1551 and he joined a company of priests working in San Girolamo Church, where he soon became a popular confessor and spiritual guide. As many regularly came to the oratory in that church, where he held spiritual conferences, other priests were attracted to his teaching and the Congregation of the Oratory was founded. It finally received papal approval in 1575. Philip was such a popular and revered person in Rome that he was treated almost like a living saint, even instructing the Pope to grant absolution to the French monarch, Henry IV, to prevent a political catastrophe. This kind and gentle priest gave his life for the service of others and died on this day in the year 1595.

A Reading from a letter of Philip Neri to his niece

What a destructive thing is avarice! We have received so much from God. He has given us, besides our being, and all created things from the angels downwards, his own Son. The sweet Christ, the incarnate Word, gave himself to us, without reserve even to the hard and shameful death of the cross. He has given himself to us in a sacrament, as at first he left heaven, humbling himself to become human for us. On the cross he was stripped of his garments, and shed his precious blood, and his soul was separated from his body.

All created things are open-hearted and liberal, and show forth the goodness of their creator; the sun pours abroad light, and fire gives out heat; every tree stretches forth its branches and reaches to us its fruit. The water, the air, and all nature declare the bounty of the creator. And yet we who are his living images do not represent him, but with base degeneracy deny him in our works however much we confess him with our mouths.

Now, if avarice is a monstrous thing in any one, what is it in a religious who has made a vow of poverty, abandoning everything for the love of God! We must, at whatever cost to ourselves, get rid of this foul pestilence of avarice; nor shall we feel the pain if we seriously reflect that as soon as we cast off this sordid garb, our soul is clothed with a regal and imperial garment. I mean not only that we must despise gold and silver and pleasure and all else that is so prized by a blind, deluded world, but that we are to give even the very life we love so much for the honour of God and the salvation of our neighbour. We should have our hearts ever ready to make this sacrifice in the strength of divine grace.

Love greatly holy obedience, and put this before and above every other thing. Never take anything to your own use unless it has been signed and sealed to you with the blessing of your Superior. Together with obedience, love and prayer; but carefully remember that while you love and desire prayer and holy communion with the utmost affection of your heart, you must be always ready to leave either or both at the call of obedience. Regard holy obedience as a true prayer and a real communion; for you must not desire prayer and communion for the sake of the sweetness of devotion you find in them – that would be seeking yourself and not God – but that you may become humble and obedient, gentle and patient. When you find these within you, then you will gather the fruit of prayer and communion, and above all, you will live in peace with all.

28 May

Melangell

Religious, seventh century

Melangell (or Monacella) is said to have been the daughter of an Irish king. In order to avoid an arranged marriage she fled to Wales, hiding in the remote valley of Pennant (now Pennant Melangell) in Montgomeryshire. There she lived a life of quiet prayer, which was interrupted one day by Brochwel Ysgythrog, prince of Powys. He was hunting a hare which took refuge under the folds of Melangell's cloak. Melangell made such an impression on Brochwel that, once he had heard her story, he gave her the valley of Pennant to be a sanctuary for ever. She gathered around her a community of holy women. Hares became known as 'ŵyn Melangell' ('Melangell's lambs') in Pennant Melangell and were specially protected there. Melangell's shrine has recently been restored and her beautiful and peaceful valley is once again a place of pilgrimage.

A Reading from *The Life of Saint Melangell*

One day in the year of our Lord 604, the illustrious prince went hunting in a certain place in Britain called Pennant, in the principality of Powys. Suddenly the hunting dogs of the said prince startled a hare. The dogs pursued the hare and he too gave chase until he came to a certain thicket of brambles, which was large and full of thorns. In this thicket he found a girl of beautiful appearance who, given up to divine contemplation, was praying with the greatest devotion, with the said hare lying boldly and fearlessly under the hem or fold of her garments, its face towards the dogs.

The prince cried, 'Get it, hounds, get it!' But the more he shouted, urging them on, the further the dogs retreated and, howling, fled from the little animal. Finally, the prince, altogether astonished, asked the girl how long she had lived on her own on his lands, and in such a lonely spot. In reply the girl said that she had not seen a human face for these fifteen years. Then he asked the girl who she was, her place of birth and origins, and in all humility she answered that she was the daughter of king Jowchel of Ireland and that 'because my father had intended me to be the wife of a certain great and generous Irishman, I fled from my native soil and with God leading me, came here in order that I might serve God and the immaculate Virgin with my heart and pure body until my dying day.'

Then the prince asked the girl her name. She replied that her name was Melangell. Then the prince, considering in his innermost heart the flourishing though solitary state of the girl, said, 'O most worthy virgin Melangell, I find that you are a handmaid of the true God and a most sincere follower of Christ. Therefore, because it has pleased the highest and all-powerful God to give refuge, for your merits, to this little wild hare with safe conduct and protection from the attack and pursuit of these savage and violent dogs, I give and present you most willingly these my lands for the service of God, that they may be a perpetual asylum, refuge, and defence, in honour of your name, excellent girl. Let neither king nor prince seek to be so rash or bold toward God that they presume to drag away any man or woman who has escaped here, desiring to enjoy protection in these your lands, as long as they in no way contaminate or pollute your sanctuary or asylum.'

This virgin Melangell, who was so very pleasing to God, led her solitary life for thirty-seven years in this very same place. And the hares, which are little wild creatures, surrounded her every day of her life just as if they had been tame or domesticated animals. Nor, by the aid of divine mercy, were miracles and various other signs lacking for those who called upon her help and the grace of her favour with an inner motion of the heart.

28 May

Lanfranc

Prior of Le Bec, Archbishop of Canterbury, Scholar, 1089

Lanfranc was born in Pavia, Italy, around the year 1005. At the age of thirty-five, he became a monk of Le Bec, in Normandy, where he founded the school which rose rapidly to renown throughout Europe. In 1062 William of Normandy appointed him Abbot of Caen, then in 1070 Archbishop of Canterbury. Lanfranc was a great ecclesiastical statesman, overseeing administrative, judicial and ecclesial reforms with the same energy and rigour that the Conqueror displayed in his new kingdom. Lanfranc did not forget his monastic formation: he wrote Constitutions for Christ Church, Canterbury, based on the customs of Le Bec, and appointed many Norman abbots to implement his vision in the English abbeys. He died in the year 1089.

A Reading from *Saints and Scholars* by David Knowles

From Lanfranc's arrival in England in 1070 till his death in 1089 his was the paramount influence in the monastic world of England. Wisdom was the quality that seemed most to distinguish Lanfranc in the eyes of his contemporaries, and by wisdom they perhaps understood that elevation of mind and calm foresight which enabled him to impose order upon men and institutions, for great as was his reputation as theologian even his own age realized that his disciples, rather than his writings, were his best monument. Yet we cannot read his letters, with their short, lucid, decisive sentences and their sane, masculine judgements, without submitting to his mental power. Out of the strong could come forth sweetness, as we can see if we care to read his letters to Anselm at Bec or to his monk-nephews, but strength was dominant even in his love. There is something Roman in his character and mind; a clarity, an order, a keenness, a genuine strength.

We may perhaps detect in more than one of his actions as Archbishop of Canterbury a prudence of this world that contrasts with the direct candour and simplicity of Anselm who was to succeed him. Yet his relations in later life with his aged abbot, his avoidance of all display when he visited Bec where he had been monk and Prior, and the affection with which he was now regarded by the children of the cloister, combine to show that by self-discipline he had made mellow what was harsh. Gilbert Crispin, who knew him intimately, speaks of his loving-kindness, and we have the most weighty testimony to his benignity at Christ Church, Canterbury, and to the fatherly care with which he ruled his English monks. He noticed at once if one was sad, spoke to him immediately and elicited the reason. It was by love, not by force, that he accomplished the necessary reforms, for he was a most skilled ruler of the human heart.

The monastic ideal Lanfranc brought to Canterbury was that of the Bec he had helped to create: a regular, liturgical life, with scope for study, and with the duty of raising the standard of religious life both by teaching and, when need arose, by going out to govern. This policy he developed as archbishop; the monasteries were to be the great powers in reorganizing the spiritual life of England. He wished for a strict, ordered, cloistered monasticism, but not one wholly separated by physical barriers from the life of the rest of the Church. Nowhere, perhaps, is his mind more clearly seen than in his organization and extension of the cathedral monasteries.

30 May

Josephine Butler

Social Reformer, 1906

Note: In Wales, Josephine Butler is commemorated on 29 July; and in Scotland, on 30 December.

Josephine Butler (née Grey) was born in April 1828, and baptized on this day that year, in Northumberland. She married an Anglican priest in 1852. She became incensed by the way contemporary society treated prostitutes, most of whom were forced into such activity through desperate poverty. From 1869, she campaigned for the repeal of the legislation which put all opprobrium onto the women concerned. The issue became international after she travelled in Europe addressing meetings in 1874–5. Her campaign succeeded with the repeal of the Contagious Diseases Act in 1883. She was a devout Anglican and a woman of prayer, basing her spirituality on that of Catherine of Siena, whose biography she wrote. She died on 30 December 1906.

A Reading from a biography of Josephine Butler by E. Moberly Bell

For some years Josephine had been greatly exercised by the question of the government regulation of prostitution. The system had been instituted by Napoleon in the French armies and had thence spread over all Europe; it was based on the theory that continence is impossible for men and that if the exigencies of public service necessitate long separation from their wives, it is the responsibility of the government to see to it that the women with whom they consort are free from disease. Regulationists affirmed that thus alone could the forces of any country be kept healthy and prevented from spreading infection through the rest of the population.

In 1866, by Act of Parliament a corps of special police was established, not in uniform, centrally appointed and not (as other police) under the control of the local authority. To these men was entrusted the business of making and keeping a list of licensed prostitutes, who must submit to regular medical examination. To secure the names for this list they were empowered to arrest any woman whom they had 'good cause to believe' to be a common prostitute. There was no definition of prostitution, and since the police were not required to prove the 'good cause', it put into their hands immense and corrupting power.

Josephine was horrified. She had seen the system at work in Paris, and observed the power of the police, the degradation of the unhappy women, and the general lowering of standards of decency which followed. She could not bear to think that this should be imposed on her own country. She was already heavily involved in the work of women's education in Liverpool, and in watching over the girls in the Industrial Home; but now she threw her energies into a campaign for the law to be repealed. She wrote:

> My motto is *no* legislation at all on prostitution, for all such legislation will press on women only. But even if it did not, I have no faith in it. For our legislative programme I would ask *only repeal.* No alternative, no substituted legislation, but let it be understood clearly that our *social* programme is not the same. As private or associated workers, societies etc., we are bound to do all we can to attack and heal the vices and miseries of

> society, and to reclaim the fallen, and prevent immorality. The very fact of leaving the State to do it by its laws will lessen the sense of personal responsibility and weaken the fervour of charity in all the best of us, so that our hands will hang down and we shall leave it to the State to do this deep, difficult, holy work.

Later, in giving evidence before the Select Committee of the House of Commons, her dignity and obvious sincerity made an enormous impression. Her views were firm:

> Negro slavery was abolished in our British possessions by a body of persons in England who had never seen a negro slave. They took their stand upon the principle that slavery was wrong; we take our stand entirely and purely on the principle that the State must not regulate prostitution; and no results given to us from year to year, as they are, no reports of this present Committee will in any respect or in the smallest degree alter our position, because we take our stand upon principles which are eternal.

30 May

Joan of Arc

Visionary, 1431

Joan of Arc was born at Domrémy in 1412, the daughter of a peasant farmer. She first heard voices of particular saints when she was fourteen years old, telling her to save France, which was caught up in the Hundred Years War with England. Though at first she was dismissed, her credibility increased when some of her predictions began to come true. She managed to identify the disguised Dauphin (who was later to become Charles VII) whose support and approval she gained. Joan persuaded troops to be sent to relieve Orléans and rode at their head, wearing white armour. Their success increased morale and enhanced her reputation. When the Dauphin was crowned king at Rheims, Joan stood at his side. Her voices warned her that her life would be short yet she was dangerously naïve in not seeing the jealousies she was provoking. After some failures in battle, she lost favour and was sold by the Duke of Burgundy to the English, tried in a court for heresy by the Bishop of Beauvais, and burned at the stake on this day in the year 1431. Twenty-five years later, the Pope formally declared Joan innocent. She was made second patron of France after her canonization in the year 1920.

A Reading from the report of the trial of Joan of Arc
held at Rouen in 1431, prepared for King Louis XII

Master Jean Estivet, appointed promoter at the trial by Pierre, Bishop of Beauvais, required Jeanne, known as the Pucelle, to be brought and questioned in accordance with the law. She had made a supplication that she might be allowed to hear Mass, but this the bishop refused in view of the crimes of which she was accused, and because she wore man's dress.

The bishop explained that she had been taken within the boundaries of his diocese. And since there was common report of a number of her deeds which were contrary to our faith, not only within the realm of France but in all the states in which they were known and published, and since she was accused of heresy, she had been handed over to him to be tried in a matter of faith.

He told her that she should tell the truth concerning the things which would be asked her, as much for the shortening of her trial as for the unburdening of her conscience, without subterfuge or craft; and that she should swear on the holy Gospels to tell the truth concerning everything she should be asked.

Jeanne answered that concerning her father and mother, and concerning everything she had done since she took the road for France, she would willingly swear. But as for revelations sent her from God, never had she told or revealed them save to Charles, who she said was her king.

She complained of the fetters which she had on her legs. She said also that there is a saying among little children that people are often hanged for telling the truth.

Asked if she knew whether she were in the grace of God, she answered: 'If I am not, may God put me there; if I am, may he keep me there.' She said further that if she knew she were not in the grace of God, she would be the most miserable person in the world. She said also that if she were in mortal sin, the voices would not come to her. And she would that everyone might hear them as well as she did. She also said that she thought she was thirteen years of age when the voices came to her the first time.

On Wednesday, the penultimate day of May, the trial was concluded and she was condemned as a heretic. After sentence was read, the bishop, the Inquisitor, and many of the judges went away, leaving Jeanne alone upon the scaffold. Then the Bailli of Rouen, an Englishman, ordered that she should be taken to the place where she was to be burned. When Jeanne heard this order given, she began to weep and lament in such a way that all the people present were themselves moved to tears.

And there in the market place of Rouen she was burned and martyred tragically, an act of unparalleled cruelty. And many, both noble and peasant, murmured greatly against the English.

alternative reading

A Reading from a sermon of Ronald Knox

Throughout the history of sanctity you find the persistence of a quality of realising that what we see and touch and feel are transitory things and unreal, and that the solid things are the things that appear not, a world we only grasp by faith. I think that this is a quality that stands out with quite extraordinary clearness in the life of Saint Joan of Arc: she did really live for a promise, and we know that the promise came true, but she did not – not in this life.

Joan was less than twenty years old when she was burnt at the stake. It is not true that she dressed as a man; she dressed as a boy. When she was only thirteen years old, at the age when the other boys and girls were fidgeting and playing the fool during mass, she could hardly go out of doors without hearing the voices of saints and angels talking to her. And these voices dominated her life; they echoed so loudly in her ears that all the world's noises were drowned for her.

People said: 'It is very silly of a small girl like you to think she can go and see the king' – she did not hear them. And the king disguised himself and hid among his courtiers, but she went straight up to him: 'I have come to raise the siege of Orleans and crown you king at

Rheims.' It was no good; the voices had told her about it. And I suppose when she had been appointed Chief of the Army, the General Staff would always be raising military difficulties, but it did not make a bit of difference to her, she always did what the voices told her.

After the first few victories, after the crowning of the king, the people she had come to save contented themselves with a partial conquest, and hung about making treaties and demobilising troops. But the ingratitude and apathy of the court affected her no more than its honours had done; she simply went on obeying the voices. And the French lords played her false, and she was taken prisoner. But she endured, as seeing him who is invisible.

And then came the hardest time of all. I do not think she minded being in prison; I do not think she minded the threat of execution; that was not why she tried to escape. No, it was simply that it seemed quite obvious to her she was to deliver France – the voices had told her so – and France was not yet delivered. And so she went to the stake, her hopes still unfulfilled, but never doubting for an instant that the voices were true.

Five years later the king entered Paris; twenty-two years later, England had no possessions left on French soil. She believed that he was faithful who had promised, not having received the promises, but beholding them afar off and saluting them. She could not foresee that her unjust condemnation would be reversed, point by point, twenty-five years after her death.

That, then, is her great witness, that is her capital contribution to our Christian hope – that it is the things of this world that are shams and shadows, and the real things and the solid things are the things we cannot see. Our Saviour Christ has ascended up into heaven, and a cloud received him from our sight, but we are not therefore to think of the spiritual world as something far removed from us, only to be reached by a supreme effort of thought. On the contrary, the spiritual world is all about us: the voices are still there, only Saint Joan could hear them and we cannot. But I wonder whose fault that is?

30 May

Apolo Kivebulaya

Priest, Evangelist in Central Africa, 1933

Apolo Kivebulaya's first contact with Christian teaching was in 1884 and he was baptized the following year, becoming a teacher in the Church of Uganda. He went as an evangelist and catechist to Boga in the Belgian Congo and was ordained priest in 1903. He built many churches and prepared countless catechumens for baptism. He spent the rest of his life at Boga, training teachers, supervising the school and evangelizing the people of the forest. His greatest achievement was the translation of St Mark's Gospel, apparently from the Lunyoro version, into the pygmy language. After his death on this day in the year 1933, the Church Missionary Society sent British missionaries to carry on his work.

A Reading from *Into the Great Forest: The Story of Apolo Kivebulaya of Central Africa* by Margaret Sinker

Apolo and his twin sister grew up in peace in a village, about forty miles from Mengo, the capital of Uganda. His was a beautiful country, richly covered with trees, where everything grew in profusion, and the banana, varied with fowls and sweet potatoes, served for every meal. After a series of fevers, his sister died. Only Apolo and his mother mourned her, and Apolo particularly, for even at an early age he hated death and disease, sorrow and all kinds of ugliness.

As a boy he came into contact with Christian teaching through a white missionary called Mackay, and in spite of threats of death and torture, he persevered in seeing him and learning from him. However, one day on returning to his native village, Apolo discovered that he was expected to join the Moslem army to fight for the possession of Uganda. He had also heard of Allah who was All Merciful and this seemed to remind him of the God of love whom Mackay had preached. But he found the All Merciful was forgotten when there was a village to be burned and women and children to be killed. The simple people were ordered to become Moslems and hardly given time to refuse before they were slaughtered and their houses burned over their heads.

Not in this faith was the truth and love which Apolo sought for his people. Thus it was as much in reaction to the atrocities of the war that Apolo became a Christian. In halting words, he described an experience in the forest to his friends, and how he was sure that Jesus had come to his aid: 'My brothers,' he said, 'I am not clever and I cannot read their book, but I tell you Jesus does come to those who call, and as he has come to me, will come to you too. This is the power of love, not of fear, and it is for all of us. We have his promise that he is with us always.'

Later in life Apolo ventured into unknown territory, into the great primeval forest to evangelise the Pygmies, tiny people no more than three or four feet high, but reputedly very dangerous. In the middle of a Pygmy village, Apolo found one hut standing solitary, and asked if this was the chief's house. 'No,' they replied, 'it is the temple to the great god.' 'What great god?' he asked. 'The great god who made us all,' they replied, 'you too, and the forest and all the wild beasts.' 'But why do you give him this fruit and these pots of honey?' Apolo asked. The Pygmies gazed from side to side in terror, until one said in a low voice in the Mboga tongue: 'We fear him because he hates us. He brings trouble to us, wild beasts and sickness and death. If we give him presents, and build him a temple, perhaps he will leave us alone.'

Apolo was moved with pity for these small people of the forest, and sitting down among them, he began to tell them of the God of love who was their Father and who had sent him to teach them. During the years that followed Apolo tried to write down some of the Pygmy words, for their language had never been written down. It took him many years to translate St Mark's Gospel, but eventually he succeeded, and to this day it remains his fitting memorial.

31 May

The Visit of the Blessed Virgin Mary to Elizabeth

Note: In England, the Feast of the Visitation may be celebrated on 2 July, if preferred.

The Church today recalls the visit of Mary to her cousin Elizabeth, as recorded in Luke's Gospel. The celebration of the feast first occurred at a Franciscan Order General Chapter in 1263, but quickly spread throughout Europe. Since it is a celebration clearly described in the gospel, the Churches of the Reformation were less inclined to proscribe it than they were other Marian feasts, particularly as it was the occasion for Mary to sing her great hymn of praise in honour of her Lord and God, the 'Magnificat'. Just as Luke sees John the Baptist as the last of the prophets of the old covenant, he uses John's leaping in Elizabeth's womb as the first time John bears witness to Christ as the promised Messiah. Thereby he links the old covenant with the new. He seems to be saying that just as the old covenant clearly points to Jesus, so does its last prophet, yet to be born.

A Reading from a sermon of the Venerable Bede

'My soul proclaims the greatness of the Lord, and my spirit rejoices in God my Saviour.' With these words Mary first acknowledges the special gifts she has been given. Then she recalls God's universal favours, bestowed unceasingly on the human race. When we devote all our thoughts to the praise and service of the Lord, we proclaim the greatness of God. Our observance of God's commands, moreover, shows that we have God's power and greatness always at heart. Our spirit rejoices in God our Saviour, and delights in the mere recollection of our creator who gives us hope for eternal salvation.

These words of praise, therefore, may be fittingly uttered by all of God's creatures, but it is especially appropriate that they should be spoken by the blessed Mother of God. She alone was chosen, and she burned with spiritual love for the son she so joyously conceived. Above all other saints, she alone could truly rejoice in Jesus, her Saviour, for she knew that he who was the source of eternal salvation would be born in time in her body, in one person both her own son and her Lord.

'For the Almighty has done great things for me, and holy is his name.' Mary attributes nothing to her own merits. She refers all her greatness to the gift of the one whose essence is power and whose nature is greatness, for he fills with greatness and strength the small and the weak who believe in him. She did well to add: 'and holy is his name,' to warn those who heard, and indeed all who would receive his words, that they must believe and call upon his name. For they too can share in everlasting holiness and true salvation according to the words of the prophet: 'and it will come to pass, that everyone who calls on the name of the Lord will be saved'.

Therefore it is an excellent and fruitful custom of holy Church that we should sing Mary's hymn at the time of evening prayer. By meditating upon the incarnation in this way, our devotion is kindled, and by remembering the example of the Mother of God, we are encouraged to lead a life of virtue.

alternative reading

A Reading from *The Life of our Blessed Lord and Saviour Jesus Christ* by Jeremy Taylor

When the eternal God meant to stoop so low as to be fixed in our centre, he chose for his mother a holy person and a maid. She received the angel's message with such sublimity of faith that her faith was turned into vision, her hopes into actual possession, and her grace into glory. She who was now full of God, bearing God in her virgin womb, and the Holy Spirit in her heart, arose with haste and gladness to communicate that joy which was designed for all the world; and she found no breast to pour forth the first emanations of her overjoyed heart so fit as her cousin's Elizabeth, for she was to be the mother of the Baptist, who was sent a forerunner to prepare the way of the Lord her son.

Let us notice how light and airy was the coming of the Virgin, as she made haste over the mountains; her very little burden which she bear hindered her not but that she might make haste enough; and as her spirit was full of cheerfulness and alacrity, so even her body was made airy and full of life. And there is this excellency in religion that when we carry Christ within us, his presence is neither so peevish as to disturb our health, nor so sad as to discompose our cheerfulness, but he recreates our body by charity and by securing God's providence over us while we are in the pursuit of the heavenly kingdom. For as the Virgin climbed mountains easily, so there is no difficulty in our life so great, but it may be managed by those assistances we receive from the holiest Jesus, when we carry him about us.

It is not easy to imagine what collision of joys was at this blessed meeting; two mothers of two great princes, the one the greatest that was born of woman, and the other his Lord. When these who were made mothers by two miracles came together, they met with joy and mysteriousness. The mother of our Lord went to visit the mother of his servant, and the Holy Ghost made the meeting festival. Never, but in heaven, was there more joy and ecstasy. For these women were not only hallowed, but made pregnant and big with religion, meeting together to compare and unite their joys and their eucharist.

By this God would have us know that when the blessings of God descend upon us, they should be published in the communion of the saints, so that the hopes of others may receive increase, that their faith may receive confirmation, that their charity and eucharist may grow up to become excellent and great, and the praises of God be sung aloud, till the sound strike at heaven and join with the alleluias which the morning stars in their orbs pay to their great creator.

alternative reading

A Reading from a poem by Gerard Manley Hopkins

The May Magnificat

May is Mary's month, and I
Muse at that and wonder why:
  Her feasts follow reason,
  Dated due to season –

Candlemas, Lady Day;
But the Lady Month, May,
  Why fasten that upon her,
  With a feasting in her honour?

Is it only its being brighter
Than the most are must delight
her?
  Is it opportunest
  And flowers finds soonest?

Ask of her, the mighty mother:
Her reply puts this other
   Question: What is Spring? –
   Growth in everything –

Flesh and fleece, fur and feather
Grass and greenworld all together;
   Star-eyed strawberry-breasted
   Throstle above her nested

Cluster of bugle blue eggs thin
Forms and warms the life within;
   And bird and blossom swell
   In sod or sheath or shell.

All things rising, all things sizing
Mary sees, sympathising
   With that world of good,
   Nature's motherhood.

Their magnifying of each its kind
With delight calls to mind
   How she did in her stored
   Magnify the Lord.

Well but there was more than this:
Spring's universal bliss
   Much, had much to say
   To offering Mary May.

When drop-of-blood-and-foam-dapple
Bloom lights the orchard-apple
   And thicket and thorp are merry
   With silver-surfèd cherry

And azuring-over greybell makes
Wood banks and brakes wash wet like lakes
   And magic cuckoocall
   Caps, clears, and clinches all –

This ecstasy all through mothering earth
Tells Mary her mirth till Christ's birth
   To remember and exultation
   In God who was her salvation.

June

1 June

Justin

Martyr at Rome, *c.*165

Justin was born at the beginning of the second century in Palestine. As a young man he explored many different philosophies before, at the age of thirty, embracing Christianity. He continued to wear the distinctive dress of a professional philosopher, and taught Christianity as a philosophy first at Ephesus, and later at Rome. He became an outstanding apologist for the Christian faith, and is honoured as the first Christian thinker to enter into serious dialogue with the other intellectual disciplines of his day, including Judaism. Justin always sought to reconcile the claims of faith and reason. It was at Rome in about 165 that he and some of his disciples were denounced as Christians, and beheaded. The authentic record of their martyrdom based on an official court report has survived. Traditionally, Justin is often surnamed 'Martyr' because of his two-fold witness to Christ, through his apologetic writings and his manner of death.

A Reading from the *First Apology* of Justin

Not only does sound reason direct us to reject the guidance of those who have done or taught what is wrong, but it is incumbent on every lover of truth, at whatever personal cost, even if his own life is at stake, to choose to do and to speak only what is right. I beg you, therefore, my readers, you who are called religious and philosophers, guardians of justice and lovers of learning, pay heed and attend to my address.

You call us Christians 'atheists'. We confess that we are atheists, in so far as the gods of this world are concerned, but not in respect to the most true God, the Father of righteousness, moderation and all other virtues, who is entirely pure. It is this God, and the Son (who came forth from God and taught us these things, and about the host of other good angels who follow and are made to be like him), and the prophetic Spirit, whom we worship and adore.

When you hear that we are looking for a kingdom, you rashly suppose that we mean something merely human. But we are speaking of a kingdom with God, as must be clear from our confession before you when you bring us to trial, though we know that death is the penalty for such a confession. For if we looked for a human kingdom we would deny our Christ in order to save our lives, and would try to remain in hiding in order to obtain the things we look for. But since we do not place our hopes on the present world, we are not troubled by being put to death, and we know we will have to die one day in any case.

Indeed, of all people we Christians are your best helpers and allies in securing good order, convinced as we are that no wicked person, no covetous person or conspirator (or virtuous person for that matter) can remain hidden from God, and that everyone goes to either eternal punishment or salvation in accordance with the character of their actions. If everyone knew this, nobody would choose vice even for a little time.

What sober-minded person, then, will not admit that we Christians are not atheists, worshipping as we do the creator of this universe, declaring as we have been taught, that God has no need of streams of blood and libations and incense? We praise God to the utmost of our power by prayer, by thanking God for the gift of life itself. We have been taught that the way to honour God is not by burning with fire the very things he has brought into being for our sustenance, but rather to use them for our good and those in need, expressing in psalms and hymns our gratitude to him for our creation, our health, for the sheer richness and diversity of life, for the changing seasons; and laying before him our prayers to live again in incorruption through faith in him.

Our teacher of these things is Jesus Christ, who was crucified under Pontius Pilate, procurator of Judea, in the time of Tiberius Caesar. Him we worship, having learned that he is the Son of the true God, and also the prophetic Spirit. Our detractors proclaim our madness because we honour a crucified man alongside the unchangeable and eternal God, the creator of all. They do not discern the mystery in this, and it is to this mystery that we beg you attend.

2 June

Blandina and her Companions

Martyrs, 177

Among the early persecutions of Christians, that at Lyons and Vienne stands out, partly because an account of it was written by survivors in a letter to the Churches in Asia and Phrygia. The Christians were first excluded from any public place, then seized by the mob and imprisoned on charges of incest and cannibalism. They were tortured, and sentenced to death in the arena, or, for those who were Roman citizens, by beheading. Bishop Pothinus, over ninety years old, was brutally beaten and died of his wounds. Blandina was a young slave-girl, who proclaimed under torture, 'I am a Christian, and we do nothing vile'. She was thrown to the wild beasts, and after a lengthy ordeal was gored to death by a bull. The bodies of the martyrs, who died on this day in the year 177, were burnt and their ashes thrown into the river Rhône, so that no relics should remain at all. In all, the names are known of forty-eight of these Christians who suffered such tribulation and fury as witnesses to their faith in Christ.

A Reading from a *Letter of the Churches of Lyons and Vienne* concerning the martyrdom of Blandina and her companions, as recorded by Eusebius

The whole fury of the mob, governor, and soldiers fell with crushing force on Sanctus, the deacon from Vienne, on Maturus, who although only recently baptized was nevertheless heroic in his ordeal; on Attakus, who had always been a pillar and buttress of the church in his native Pergamon; and on Blandina, through whom Christ was to prove that things deemed mean, ugly and contemptible in this world are deemed by God worthy of great glory, because her love for God shown in power and not merely in appearance.

When we were all afraid, and her earthly mistress who was herself facing the ordeal of martyrdom was in agony lest she should be unable to make a bold confession of Christ through her bodily weakness, Blandina was filled with such power that those who took it in turns to subject her to every kind of torture from morning to night were exhausted by their efforts and confessed themselves beaten. They could think of no other way to punish her. They were amazed that she was still breathing, for her whole body was mangled and her wounds were severe. They declared that torment of any one kind was enough to divide soul from body, let alone this succession of painful torments. But this blessed woman, wrestling magnificently, grew in strength as she proclaimed her faith, and found refreshment, rest, and insensibility to her sufferings in uttering the words, 'I am a Christian, and we do nothing vile.'

Blandina was then hung on a post and exposed as food for the wild beasts let loose in the arena. She looked as if she was hanging in the form of a cross, and through her ardent prayers she stimulated great enthusiasm in those undergoing their ordeal, who in their agony saw with their outward eyes in the person of their sister the One who was crucified for them, that he might convince those who believe in him that anyone who has suffered for the glory of Christ has fellowship for ever with the living God.

To crown all this, on the last day of the games, Blandina was again brought in, and with her Ponticus, a lad of about fifteen. Day after day they had been taken in to watch the others being punished, and attempts were made to make them swear by pagan idols. When they stood firm and treated these efforts with contempt, the mob was so infuriated that the boy's young age elicited no pity from them and the woman's sex no respect. They subjected them both to every horror and cruelty in turn, attempting again and again to get them to swear, but all to no avail. Ponticus was encouraged by his sister in Christ, and the crowd saw that she was urging him on, stiffening his resistance. He bravely endured every punishment until eventually he gave back his spirit to God.

Last of all, like a noble mother who had encouraged her children and sent them on ahead in triumph to the king, blessed Blandina herself passed through all the ordeals of her children and hastened to rejoin them, rejoicing and exulting at her departure as if invited to a wedding banquet instead of being thrown to wild beasts. After the whips, after the wild beasts, after the griddle, she was finally put in a basket and thrown to a bull. Time after time the animal tossed her, but she was insensible by this time to what was happening to her, because of her hope and sure hold on all that her faith meant to her, and her communing with Christ. Then she too was sacrificed and the pagans admitted among themselves that they had never known a woman suffer so much or for so long.

3 June

Kevin of Glendalough

Hermit, *c.*618

'Of gentle birth'. As his Irish name declares, Kevin is associated with the lovely Glendalough valley in the Wicklow hills where he lived a contemplative life, and which became the burial place of the kings of Leinster. A community gathered round this man of prayer, and the

monastery associated with him had a high reputation. He had a reputation as both poet and musician, and his influence was strong for many centuries, especially on Laurence O'Toole. He died on this day around the year 618.

A Reading from *The Life of Saint Kevin*

Towards the end of his life, blessed Kevin returned to his native country, and began to live in an isolated place, in the glen of the two lakes where he had been a hermit in his youth. That isolated place had been dear to him from the outset. In the lower part of the valley, where the two clear rivers meet, he founded a great monastery. Many came to him from the surrounding area, and Saint Kevin trained them in the monastic life.

The day came when Saint Kevin, having given his blessing to each monk, entrusted the care of his monastery to trustworthy brethren. He then journeyed on alone to the head of the glen, about a mile or so from the monastery, and there he built for himself a small hut on a narrow strip of land between the mountain and the lake, where the trees grew close and the streams flowed clear. He forbade his monks to bring him food of any kind, telling them not to visit him without urgent reason. Wild animals from the mountains and woods came and kept him company. They would even drink water from his hands like domesticated animals.

After seven years, Saint Kevin built a small oratory on the northern margin of the lake where he daily prayed to God. There, unknown, he lived but not on human food. One day a huntsman of the King of Leinster, Brandubh son of Eochaid (a descendant of Enna, who made such a slaughter in the great war that ravaged the northern provinces of Ireland) came down into the glen with his hounds in pursuit of a boar. The boar took refuge in Saint Kevin's oratory, but the hounds did not go in, but instead stayed outside by the gate, crouching down on the ground.

Saint Kevin was praying under a tree, with a great crowd of birds perched on his shoulders and his hands, and flitting all about him. The huntsman could not believe his eyes, and recalled his hounds, and in exchange of a blessing from the hermit, let the boar go free. He told the king and all he met of the marvel he had witnessed. Indeed there were times when the boughs and the leaves of the trees would sing sweet songs to Saint Kevin, that the melody of heaven might lighten his labours.

3 June

The Martyrs of Uganda

1885 and 1978

Note: The Ugandan martyrs are commemorated differently in England, Scotland and Wales. In addition to the reading below, see also the readings for:

Janani Luwum	17 February
James Hannington	29 October

In 1884, Mwanga became ruler (kabaka) of Buganda in Uganda. When three of his subjects, obeying a missionary's instruction, unwittingly disobeyed his orders, he had them executed: Yusufu Lugalama, Mako Kakumba and Nuwa Serwanga went to their deaths on

31 January 1885. In November, Joseph Mkasa Balikuddembe, a Roman Catholic courtier, was executed for protesting at the murder of Bishop James Hannington. The persecution reached its height in 1866, when some courtiers and palace officials refused Mwanga's sexual advances. Mwanga was enraged that the Christians acknowledged a higher authority than the kabaka and ordered their execution. Forty-six names are known, both Roman Catholic and Anglican, who were martyred. Most, led by Charles Lwanga, were burnt alive on Ascension Day, 3 June 1886. The last martyrdom was that of Jean-Marie Muzeyi in the following January. The description of the deaths of these Ugandans reads like a martyrdom narrative from the early Christian centuries.

The Churches in Uganda also came under extreme pressure during the presidency of Amin and the second presidency of Obote in the 1970s and 1980s. Among those who lost their lives at this time was Archbishop Janani Luwum. Christians in Uganda unite on this day to remember those who witnessed in their country for Christ, even unto death.

A Reading from a homily of Pope Paul VI on the occasion of the canonization of the Ugandan martyrs, Charles Lwanga and his companions, delivered on 18 October 1964

Every time we utter the word 'martyr' in the sense it has acquired in Christian hagiography, we should bring to our mind's eye a drama evoking horror and wonder. Horror, because of the injustice which unlooses such a drama with the instruments of power and cruelty; horror, again, because of the blood which is shed and of the death so unfeelingly inflicted; wonder, then, because of the simple strength which submits without struggle or physical resistance to torment, happy and proud to witness to the unconquerable truth of a faith which has fused itself with life.

Life, however, dies, faith lives on. We see brute as opposed to moral force; the first knowing in its very success defeat; the second, triumph in failure! Martyrdom, then, is a drama: an appalling drama, let it be said, but one rich in teaching. The unjust and evil violence which it brings about tends almost to be forgotten, while in the memory of centuries the gentleness which makes the offering of self a sacrifice, a holocaust, remains with all its lustre and attractiveness; a supreme act of love and faithfulness with regard to Christ; an example and a witnessing, and enduring message to contemporary and future generations alike. Such is martyrdom: such has been the glory of the Church through the centuries, and which we commemorate today.

These African martyrs add a new page to that list of victorious men and women that we call the martyrology, in which we find the most magnificent as well as the most tragic stories. The page that they add is worthy to take its place alongside those wonderful stories of ancient Africa, which we who live today, being of little faith, thought we should never see repeated.

We are familiar with the lives of the great saints, martyrs and confessors, of Africa, such as Cyprian, Felicity and Perpetua, and the great Augustine. Who would have imagined that one day we should be adding to that list those names of Charles Lwanga, Matthias Molumba Kalemba and their twenty companions? Nor should we forget those others of the Anglican Communion who died for the sake of Christ.

These martyrs of Africa have indeed laid the foundation of a new age. We should not dwell on the religious persecutions and conflicts, but rather on the rebirth of Christian and civil life that has begun.

For from the Africa that was sprinkled with the blood of these martyrs, the first of this new age (and, God willing, the last, so sublime, so precious was their sacrifice), there is emerging a free and independent Africa.

4 June

Petroc

Abbot of Padstow, sixth century

The large number of ancient church dedications to Petroc (also known as Pedrog) suggests that he was of outstanding importance among British Celtic saints, though little reliable historical information is available. He seems to have been the son of a Welsh chieftain who, on arrival in Cornwall, founded a monastery at Lanwethinoc, now called Padstow (from Petrockstowe), which became the chief centre for his monastic and missionary activities. He seems to have lived as a hermit for most of his life, and is said in later life to have withdrawn to a hermitage on Bodmin Moor. He died at Treravel and was buried at Padstow, though by the eleventh century the Augustinian Canons at Bodmin claimed to possess his relics. He is justly honoured as the 'captain of Cornish saints'.

A Reading from *The Life of Petroc* by an unknown medieval monastic author

The blessed Petroc, by nation a Welshman, sprang from royal stock. From childhood he lived in such a fashion that by holding to the faith and by imitating the works of Peter, the prince of the apostles, he showed himself to be the Rock on which the Truth himself had promised to build his Church, thus fulfilling the prophecy divinely given in the choice [by his parents] of his name: Petroc. And truly, God had bestowed on him such grace that he won favour in the eyes of all. For he was handsome in appearance, courteous in his speech, prudent, simple-minded, modest, humble, 'a cheerful giver', burning with ceaseless charity, always ready for all the works of religion because while still a youth he had attained by watchful care the wisdom of riper years.

Following the death of his father, the nobles of the whole province, with the unanimous acclamation of the people, demanded Petroc to be their king as was his by hereditary right. But he, not caring for high office, and solicitous rather for the salvation of his soul, resolved that he would not seek the glory of earthly dignity, seeing that he had set his heart on a heavenly kingdom. For there was in Petroc a spirit of humility, and he preferred to be by his own choice on a level with or even subject to others, over whom he could scarcely have ruled without becoming puffed up by a sense of greatness and vanity. He said, with the Apostle, 'Here we have no abiding city', and he sought so to serve God as not to 'entangle himself in the affairs of the world'. Petroc accordingly summoned his retainers and carefully explained to them what he had resolved in his mind to do, asking them also to follow the course he had decided on for himself. They all agreed to commit themselves and their fortunes, putting them at his disposal.

After this the youth, accompanied by sixty of his nobles, hastened to church where they all assumed the clerical state, and put on the new habit of the monastic life.

4 June

John XXIII

Bishop of Rome, Reformer, 1963

Angelo Giuseppe Roncalli was born in 1881 near Bergamo in Italy, and he became a priest, and subsequently a bishop. On the death of Pope Pius XII in 1958, an aged, caretaker pope was desired by the College of Cardinals, and Roncalli, Patriarch of Venice, was elected, and took the name John. Only three months after his election, John XXIII astounded the Roman Curia by calling a Council of the Roman Catholic Church, which he said was needed to 'open the windows of the Church and let in some fresh air'. The Council, known as the Second Vatican Council, laid the foundations for far-reaching reforms, which breathed new life into all the Churches. His personal piety was rather conservative but he had the foresight of a visionary and his brief pontificate left the Roman Catholic Church totally changed. He died, greatly mourned by the whole Christian world, on 3 June 1963.

A Reading from the opening address to the Second Vatican Council by Pope John XXIII, delivered on 1 October 1962

Today, venerable brethren, is a day of joy for Mother Church: through God's most kindly providence the longed-for day has dawned for the solemn opening of the Second Vatican Ecumenical Council, here at Saint Peter's shrine. And Mary, God's Virgin Mother, on this feast day of her noble motherhood, gives it her gracious protection.

We are convinced that the time spent in preparation for this ecumenical council was in itself an initial token of grace, a gift from heaven. For we have every confidence that the Church, in the light of this council, will gain in spiritual riches. New sources of energy will be opened for her, enabling her to face the future without fear. By introducing timely changes and a prudent system of mutual co-operation, we intend that the Church shall really succeed in bringing people, families and nations to the appreciation of supernatural values.

The major interest of the ecumenical council is this: that the sacred heritage of Christian truth be safeguarded and expounded with greater efficacy. That doctrine embraces the whole man, body and soul. It bids us live as pilgrims here on earth, as we journey towards our heavenly homeland. It demonstrates how we must use this mortal life of ours. If we are to achieve God's purpose in this regard we have a twofold obligation: as citizens of earth, and as citizens of heaven. That is to say, all people without exception, both individually and in society, have a life-long obligation to strive after heavenly values through the right use of the things of this earth. These temporal goods must be used in such a way as not to jeopardise eternal happiness.

If this doctine is to make its impact on the various spheres of human activity – in private, family, and social life – then it is absolutely vital that the Church shall never for an instant lose sight of that sacred patrimony of truth inherited from the Fathers. But it is equally necessary for her to keep up to date with the changing conditions of this modern world, and of modern living, for these have opened up entirely new avenues for the Catholic apostolate.

Our duty is not just to guard this treasure, as though it were some museum-piece and we the curators, but earnestly and fearlessly to dedicate ourselves to the work that needs to be done in this modern age of ours, pursuing the path which the Church has followed for almost twenty centuries. Nor are we here primarily to discuss certain fundamentals of Catholic doctrine, or to restate in greater detail the traditional teachings of the Fathers and of early and more recent theologians. There was no need to call a council merely to hold discussions of that sort.

What is needed at the present time is a new enthusiasm, a new joy and serenity of mind in the unreserved acceptance by all of the entire Christian faith. What is needed – and what everyone imbued with a truly Christian, Catholic, and apostolic spirit craves today – is that this doctrine shall be more widely known, more deeply understood, and more penetrating in its effects on people's moral lives. What is needed is that this certain and immutable doctrine, to which the faithful owe obedience, be studied afresh and reformulated in contemporary terms. For this deposit of faith, or truths which are contained in our time-honoured teaching, is one thing; the manner in which these truths are set forth (with their meaning preserved intact) is something else.

5 June

Boniface (Wynfrith) of Crediton

Bishop, Apostle of Germany, Martyr, 754

Born at Crediton in Devon in about the year 675, Wynfrith took the name Boniface when he entered the monastery in Exeter as a young man. He became a Latin scholar and poet and was ordained when he was thirty years old. He rejected a safe ecclesiastical career in England and, in the year 716, became a missionary to Frisia, following in the steps of Willibrord. He was eventually commissioned by the Pope to work in Hesse and Bavaria where he went after consecration as bishop in the year 722. He courageously felled a sacred oak at Geismar and, since the pagan gods did not come to the rescue, widespread conversion followed. He was the founder of a string of monasteries across southern Germany and made sure that they were places of learning, so that evangelizing could continue. Boniface was made Archbishop of Mainz in 732, where he consecrated many missionary bishops. He worked assiduously for the reform of the Church in France and managed to ensure that the more balanced Rule of Saint Benedict was adhered to in her monasteries. He crowned Pepin as the Frankish king in 751 but was already very old. While waiting for some new Christians to arrive for confirmation, he was murdered by a band of pagans on this day in the year 754. He has been judged as having a deeper influence on European history than any other Englishman.

A Reading from a letter of Boniface to Cuthbert, Archbishop of Canterbury, written in the year 747 on the establishment of the Church in Germany concerning the obstacles he was encountering

My dear brother, I fear we have undertaken to steer a ship through the waves of an angry sea, and we can neither succeed in our task, nor without sin abandon it. I am reminded of the statement of a certain wise man that 'If it is dangerous to be negligent when steering a ship on the open sea, how much more dangerous to let go of the rudder in a storm when the waves are running high. In her voyage across the ocean of this world, the Church is like such a great ship, pounded by the waves of temptation, and it is our duty not to abandon ship, but to control the rudder.'

As examples in this we have the early Fathers, Clement and Cornelius and many others in the city of Rome, Cyprian in Carthage, Athanasius in Alexandria. Living under pagan emperors, they steered the ship of Christ, that is the Church, his most dear spouse, teaching, defending, labouring and suffering, even to the point of shedding their own blood.

In the Church of which I have oversight, I have dug the ground over, manured the soil, but I am conscious that I have failed to guard it. Alas, all my labour seems to me like a dog barking at the approach of thieves and robbers, but because he has no one to help him in his defence, he can only sit there, whining and complaining.

According to the word of God to Ezekiel, when someone is entrusted with preaching the gospel, even though he live a holy life, nevertheless if he is afraid or ashamed to rebuke those who live wickedly, he will perish along with the rest because he remained silent. When I consider the example of such people, and those like them, I am filled with dread. 'Fear and trembling come upon me, and the darkness of my sins almost overwhelms me.' I would be only too glad to give up the task of guiding the Church which I had accepted, if I could have found some warrant for such a course of action in either the example of the Fathers or in holy Scripture.

Since this is not to be found, and since although the truth may be attacked it can never be ultimately defeated or falsified, with my tired mind I take refuge in the words of Solomon: 'Trust in the Lord with all your heart, and do not rely on your own insights. In all your ways, think on the Lord and he will guide your steps.'

Let us stand firm, then, in doing what is right and prepare ourselves to face trials. Let us wait upon the strength of God, and say to him: 'Lord, you have been our refuge from one generation to the next.' Let us trust in the One who laid this burden upon us. What we cannot bear on our own strength, let us bear with the help of the One who is all-powerful and who said, 'My yoke is easy and my burden is light.'

Let us never be dogs that do not bark, or silent bystanders, or hired servants who flee at the approach of the wolf. Instead let us be watchful shepherds, guarding the flock of Christ. And as God gives us strength, in season and out of season, let us preach to the powerful and powerless alike, to rich and poor alike, to all people of every rank and of whatever age, the saving purposes of God.

6 June

Jarlath of Tuam

Monk and Bishop (?), *c.*550

Very little is known of this saint. He is said to have belonged to a noble family in County Galway and to have been a disciple of Enda. He founded a monastery at Cluain Fois; later he moved two miles away to Tuam, of which he is asserted to have been bishop. His life and learning lie behind the Christian traditions in the diocese where St Mary's Cathedral stands on the site of the earliest place of worship. The chancel arch, which marks the entrance to the sanctuary, is strikingly composed of six semi-circular concentric and recessed arches. This impressive example of Hiberno-Romanesque architecture is justly famous. Jarlath died on this day in about the year 550.

A Reading from *The Rule of Carthage*,
a Celtic monastic Rule dating from the seventh century,
concerning the duties of a bishop

If you are a member of the noble order of bishops, take up your service wholeheartedly, be subject in all honesty to the Lord, and let all be obedient to you.

Cure all harmful ailments through the power of the good Lord, establish peace among the people, restrain the noble kings.

In your dealings with clergy and laity alike, act as becomes a pastor. Be assiduous in preaching, be gracious, be pleasant.

The suppression of the wicked who love to do evil, and the exaltation of the truth, are duties that become you.

When accepting holy orders you should be familiar with Scripture, for you will be a step-son of the Church if you are unprepared and ignorant.

It is true indeed that every ignorant person is uncouth, and someone who does not read the testament of the Lord is not a true successor of his.

Truly it belongs to you to condemn all heresy and all evil. Therefore be not yourself guilty of any evil, either in word or in deed.

The wicked will not rise at your approach, nor will they obey you. You yourself will be blameworthy if you are gentle with them.

It is certain that you will be answerable on the great judgement day for the sins of your subjects, as well as for your own faults.

6 June

Ini Kopuria

Founder of the Melanesian Brotherhood, 1945

As a native policeman, Ini Kopuria's job took him all over Guadalcanal in the Solomon Islands, but a vision of Jesus, calling him to do different work for his people, led him to a life of evangelism in which he aimed to take and live the gospel in the remotest villages and islands in Melanesia. He began a Brotherhood for Melanesians in 1925 and, with help from his bishop, prepared a Rule and made vows himself in which he dedicated his life and his land to God. Men were asked to make only a five-year commitment to service within the community and many came to join him and stayed for much longer. It quickly grew into one of the largest religious communities in the Anglican Communion and its method of evangelism proved highly effective. Ini died on this day in 1945, revered throughout the Pacific Islands and Papua New Guinea.

A Reading from the missionary journal of the Melanesian Mission, written by Dr Charles Fox and dated January 1946

There died in his own village in Maravovo in Guadalcanal on 6 June 1945 Ini Kopuria, founder of the Melanesian Brotherhood. He was, I think, one of the ablest Melanesians I have ever known. What things stood out about his character?

First I think his spirituality. Prayer was a very real thing for Ini: he was the most reverent Melanesian I have met, and that is saying a lot. God was all his thought. Second, his joyousness. He was almost always in high spirits, full of fun, full of the joy of being alive: it was good to live with him. Third, his deep understanding of the thoughts of Melanesians. At Brothers' Meetings when disputes were often hot, Ini always knew who was really in the wrong, and generally got that Brother to say so. Fourth, his common sense. He always knew what was practicable and kept discussions to that.

Reverent, joyful, sympathetic, wise, these the brothers knew him to be. He was not popular with the white staff who thought him conceited. There was a little truth in this, for he felt his own gifts, though I don't think the conceit went deep; but he was very sensitive to colour feeling. He thought it all wrong that *every* Melanesian because of his colour, should be inferior to every white man because of his colour. He felt that there was this feeling even within the Mission and the Church itself.

One of my strongest memories of Ini is of a baptism when Ini and I stood deep in the very cold water of a mountain river for several hours while streams of people came to us from the heathen side, were baptized by us and passed over to the Christian side where the bishop sat in his chair on a high grassy bank with the few already Christian around him. There the newly baptized dressed in white loin cloths, and finally a great procession, led by the cross, set off for the church – a procession so long that they were singing different hymns in different parts without realizing it, or caring either, so joyful did they feel. That is just one of my many memories of Ini. What great days those were!

In the end, in the early days of the war, Ini left the Brotherhood. He asked to be released from his vows and was released by the bishop. Then came the Americans in their thousands. It was a time of great unsettlement for everyone; and for a time Ini went, as the bishop wrote, 'into a far country'. There followed soon the sickness from which he died, but not before he had come back to full communion. The last period of failure was perhaps needed for the final lesson of humility, so hard for men of great gifts. The failure did not last long. It was as though God took his hand away for a moment in order that he might hold Ini for ever.

So on 6 June this brilliant, wayward, valiant leader of men found final happiness. As for us the Brotherhood, he always held our hearts and can never be forgotten. Rest in peace.

7 June

Colman of Dromore

Monk and Bishop, sixth century

It is said that there are as many as two hundred Colmans in the list of Irish saints. Colman of Dromore in the south of County Down is to be distinguished from Colman of Cloyne.

Dromore's Colman is included in the ancient calendars of both Scotland and Wales. Famed as a teacher of Finnian of Moville, Colman continued the pastoral and teaching traditions of Patrick. Dromore Cathedral, dedicated to Christ the Redeemer, has drawn inspiration through the centuries from Colman's zeal for faith and truth. He is thought to have died in the sixth century.

A Reading from *The Penitential of Cummean*

In the administration of penance, let this be observed: the length of time anyone remains in his faults, what education he has received, with what passion he is assailed, with what courage he resists, with what intensity of weeping he seems to be afflicted, and with what pressure he is driven to sin. For almighty God, who knows the hearts of all and has made us all different, will not weigh the burden of sins in an equal scale of penance, as this prophecy of Isaiah says: 'For dill is not threshed with a threshing sledge, nor is a cart wheel rolled over cummin; but dill is beaten out with a stick and the cummin with a rod, but bread corn shall be broken small'; or as in this passage: 'The mighty shall be tormented'.

For this reason a certain man, wise in the Lord, said, 'He to whom more is entrusted, from him more shall be exacted'. Thus priests of the Lord who preside over the churches should learn that not only is their share given to them, but also that of those whose faults they have caused to be forgiven. What does it mean to cause a fault to be forgiven unless, when you receive the sinner, by warning, exhortation, teaching and instruction, you lead him to penance, correcting him from error, improving him from his vices, and making him such a person that God becomes favourable to him after his conversion? It may then be truly said that you have caused his faults to be forgiven.

When you are a priest like this, therefore, and this is your teaching and your word, there is given to you the share of those whom you have corrected, that their merit may be your reward and their salvation your glory.

8 June

Thomas Ken

Bishop of Bath & Wells, Non-Juror, Hymn Writer, 1711

Note: In Scotland, Thomas Ken is commemorated on 22 March.

Thomas Ken was born at Berkhampstead in 1637 and educated at New College, Oxford. He was ordained priest in 1662 and worked first in a poor parish in the diocese of Winchester and then at Winchester College for ten years. He served as chaplain to King Charles II for two years and was then consecrated Bishop of Bath and Wells. After the king's death and the accession of the Roman Catholic James II, the new king proposed to rescind the Restoration penal laws, but Thomas and six of his fellow bishops refused to comply with this and were imprisoned on this day in 1688. Such was the integrity of Thomas that, when the king abandoned his throne and fled and the king's Protestant daughter Mary was offered the throne, together with her husband William of Orange, Thomas felt unable in good conscience to forswear his living, anointed monarch. He was deprived of his See, along with many other non-jurors, as they became known, and for a time there was schism in the Anglican fold. Thomas spent his final twenty years in quiet retirement, anxious not to make trouble, and renounced his rights to his bishopric. He wrote many hymns, still much used, and died on 19 March in the year 1711.

A Reading from a letter of Bishop Thomas Ken, to a fellow non-juror, George Hickes, Dean of Worcester, dated 7 March 1700

I wrote to you not long ago to recommend to your serious consideration the schism which has so long continued in our Church; and which I have often lamented to my Brother of Ely, now with God, and concerning which, I have many years had ill abodings. I need not tell you what pernicious consequences it may produce, and I fear has produced already; what advantage it yields to our enemies, what irreligion, the abandoning of the public assemblies may cause in some, and what vexation it creates to tender consciences in the country, where they live banished from the house of God.

I know you concur with me in hearty desires in closing the rupture; and methinks this is a happy juncture for it: the Lower House of Convocation do now worthily affect the rights of the clergy, and I dare say will gladly embrace a reconciliation. The question is, how it may be conscientiously effected? Give me leave to suggest my present thoughts.

If it is not judged advisable for my Brother of Norwich and myself, to resign up our canonical claims, which would be the shortest way, and which I am ready to do for the repose of the flock, having long ago maintained it to justify our character; if, I say, this is not thought advisable, then [I suggest] that a circular letter would be penned and dispersed which should modestly and yet resolutely assist the cause for which we suffer, and declare that our opinion is still the same, in regard to passive obedience, and specify the reasons which induce us to communicate in the public offices, the chiefest of which is to restore the peace of the Church, which is of that importance, that it ought to supersede all ecclesiastical canons, they being only of human, and not divine authority. A letter to this purpose would make our presence at some of the prayers rightly understood to be betraying of our cause; would guard us against any advantage our adversaries may take from our Christian condescension; would relieve fundamental charity, and give a general satisfaction to all well-minded persons.

I offer this with submission, and out of a sincere zeal for the good of the Church, and I beseech the divine goodness to guide both sides into the way of peace, that we may with one mind, and one mouth, glorify God.

alternative reading

A Reading from *An Exposition of the Church Catechism* by Thomas Ken

O my God, when in any of thy commands a duty is enjoined, love tells me the contrary evil is forbidden; when any evil is forbidden, love tells me the contrary duty is enjoined; O do thou daily increase my love to good, and my antipathy to evil.

Though thy commands and prohibitions, O Lord, are in general terms, yet let thy love direct my particular practice, and teach me, that in one general are implied all the kinds and degrees and occasions and incitements and approaches and allowances, relating to that good or evil which are also commanded or forbidden, and give me grace to pursue or to fly them.

O my God, keep my love always watchful and on its guard that in thy negative precepts I may continually resist evil; keep my love warm with an habitual zeal that in all thy affirmative precepts I may lay hold on all seasons and opportunities of doing good.

Let thy love, O thou that only art worthy to be beloved, make me careful to persuade and engage others to love thee, and to keep thy commandments as well as myself.

None can love thee, and endeavour to keep thy holy commands, but his daily failings in his duty, his frequent involuntary and unavoidable slips, and surreptitions and wanderings, afflict and humble him; the infirmities of lapsed nature create him a kind of perpetual martyrdom because he can love thee no more, because he can so little serve thee. But thou, O most compassionate Father, in thy covenant of grace dost require sincerity, not perfection; and therefore I praise and love thee.

O my God, though I cannot love and obey thee as much as I desire, I will do it as much as I am able: I will to the utmost of my power, keep all thy commandments with my whole heart and to the end. O accept of my imperfect duty, and supply all the defects of it by the merits and love and obedience of Jesus, thy beloved.

9 June

Ephrem of Syria

Deacon, Hymn Writer, Teacher of the Faith, 373

Note: In Scotland, Ephrem is commemorated on 8 June, and in Wales on 10 June.

Born of Christian parents in around the year 306, Ephrem was baptized as a young man and then ordained deacon. His early years were spent as a teacher in Nisibis in Mesopotamia until the city fell under Persian occupation in 363. Fleeing from his home, he settled in Edessa (Urfa in south-east Turkey) where he established a school of theology. Best known for his Syriac poetry, Ephrem is acclaimed as the greatest poet of the early Christian centuries, described by his contemporaries as the 'Harp of the Spirit'. His hymns, still used today, have found a place in liturgical traditions outside the East Syrian Church. He died on this day in Edessa in the year 373, ministering to victims of the plague.

A Reading from the *Hymns of Faith* of Ephrem of Syria

Truth and love are wings that cannot be separated,
for truth without love is unable to fly,
so too love without truth is unable to soar up:
their yoke is one harmony.

Lord, turn me back to your teaching:
I wanted to stand back,
but I saw that I became the poorer.
For the soul does not get any benefit
except through converse with you.

Whenever I have meditated upon you
I have acquired a veritable treasure from you;
Whatever aspect of you I have contemplated,
a stream has flowed from you.
There is no way in which I can contain it.

Your fountain, Lord, is hidden
from the person who does not thirst for you;
Your treasury seems empty
to the person who rejects you.
Love is the treasure of your heavenly store.

9 June

Columba (Columcille)

Abbot of Iona, Missionary, 597

Born in Ireland in about the year 521, Columba was trained as a monk by Finnian and then founded several monasteries himself, including probably that of Kells, before leaving Ireland to settle off the west coast of Scotland on the isle of Iona. He was accompanied by twelve companions and the number grew as the monastic life became more established and well known. Columba seems to have been an austere and, at times, harsh man who reputedly mellowed with age. He was concerned with building up both the monastery and its life and of enabling them to be instruments of mission in a heathen land. He converted kings and built churches, Iona becoming a starting point for the expansion of Christianity throughout Scotland. In the last four years of his life, when his health had failed, he spent the time transcribing books of the Gospels for them to be taken out and used. He died on this day in the year 597.

A Reading from *The Life of Columba* by Adamnán, a later abbot of Iona

Saint Columba was born of noble lineage. When he was forty-one he sailed away from Ireland to Britain, choosing to be a pilgrim for Christ. From boyhood he had devoted himself to training in the Christian life, and to the study of wisdom; with God's help, he had kept his body chaste and his mind pure, and shown himself, though placed on earth, fit for the life of heaven. He was like an angel in demeanour, blameless in what he said, godly in what he did, brilliant in intellect and great in counsel. He spent thirty-four years as an island soldier, and could not let even an hour pass without giving himself to praying or reading or writing or some other task. Fasts and vigils he performed day and night with tireless labour and no rest, to such a degree that the burden of even one seemed beyond human endurance. At the same time he was loving to all people, and his face showed a holy gladness because his heart was full of the joy of the Holy Spirit.

When his end was approaching, the venerable man and his faithful servant Diarmait went to bless the nearest barn. As he entered, the saint blessed it and the two heaps of grain stored there. With a gesture of thankfulness, he said: 'I am very glad for the monks of my community, knowing that if I have to go away somewhere you will have bread enough for a year.' Hearing this, the servant Diarmait was saddened and said: 'Father, this year you make us sad too often as you speak frequently about your passing.'

Later that night, when vespers was ended, Columba returned to his lodgings and rested on his bed, where at night instead of straw he had bare rock and a stone for a pillow, which today stands as a memorial beside his grave. There he gave his last commands to the brethren, with only his servant to hear: 'I commend to you, my little children, these my last words: Love one another unfeignedly. Peace. If you keep this course according to the example of the holy fathers, God, who strengthens the good, will help you, and I dwelling with him shall intercede for you. He will supply not only enough for the needs of this present life, but also the eternal things that are prepared as a reward for those who keep the Lord's commandments.'

As the bell rang out for the midnight office, the saint rose in haste and went to the church, running in ahead of the others and knelt alone in prayer before the altar. In the same moment his servant Diarmait following behind, saw from a distance the whole church filled inside with angelic light around the saint. As he reached the door, the light vanished. The lamps of the brethren had not yet been brought, but feeling his way in the dark he found the saint lying before the altar. Raising him up a little and sitting down at his side, he cradled the holy head on his bosom.

Meanwhile the monks and their lamps had gathered, and they began to lament at the sight of their father dying. Some of those who were present have related how, before his soul left him, the saint opened his eyes and looked about him with a wonderful joy and gladness in his face, for he could see the angels coming to meet him. Diarmait held up the saint's right hand to bless the choir of monks, and he gave up the ghost.

11 June

Barnabas

Apostle

Though not listed among the twelve apostles according to the evangelists, Barnabas emerges in the Acts of the Apostles as one of the most significant of their number. He sold his estate and gave the proceeds to the Church, since all things were to be held in common, and clearly became a leader. He is described as a Levite from Cyprus so, like his friend Paul, was from the Greek world rather than that of Palestine, and it was he who introduced Paul to the leaders of the Church in Jerusalem. He was sent to Antioch apparently to guide the Christians there in their relations with non-Jewish converts, promoting the concept of all being one in Christ. He broke with Paul to go to Cyprus and tradition has it that he was martyred there in the year 61.

A Reading from the commentary of Cyril of Alexandria
on St John's Gospel

Our Lord Jesus Christ has appointed certain people to be guides and teachers of the world and stewards of his divine mysteries. He bids them to shine out like the sun, the moon and the stars, and to cast their light not only over the land of the Jews, but on every country under the sun and on all people wherever they may be scattered, in whatever distant land they reside.

That person was indeed speaking the truth who said: 'No one takes this honour upon himself, but each one is called by God.' For our Lord Jesus Christ called his disciples before all others to this most glorious apostolate. These holy disciples became the pillars and buttresses of the truth, and Christ said that he was sending them just as he had been sent by his Father.

By these words he is making clear the dignity of the apostolate and the incomparable glory of the power given to them, but he is also, it would seem, giving them a hint about the methods they are to adopt in their apostolic mission. For if Christ thought it necessary to send out his intimate disciples in this fashion, just as the Father had sent him, then surely it was necessary that they whose mission was to be patterned on that of Jesus should see exactly why the Father had sent the Son. And so Christ interpreted the character of his mission to us in a variety of ways. Once he said: 'I have come to call not the righteous but sinners to repentance.' And then at another time he said: 'I have come down from heaven, not to do my own will, but the will of him who sent me. For God sent his Son into the world, not to condemn the world, but that the world might be saved through him.'

Accordingly, in affirming that they are sent as he was sent by the Father, Christ sums up in a few words the approach they themselves should take to their ministry. From what he said they would gather that it was their vocation to call sinners to repentance, to heal those who were sick whether in body or spirit, to seek in all their dealings never to do their own will but the will of him who sent them, and as far as possible to save the world by their teaching.

Surely it is in all these respects that we find his holy disciples striving to excel. To ascertain this is no great labour; a single reading of the Acts of the Apostles or of Saint Paul's writings is enough.

12 June

John Skinner and John Skinner

Priest, 1807; and Bishop, 1816

John Skinner the elder was born at Birse in Aberdeenshire in 1721. After studying at Aberdeen he was appointed schoolmaster at Monymusk, where he became an Episcopalian. He was ordained in 1742, and served the charge of Longside for sixty-five years. A devoted pastor and man of liberal sympathies, he was a noted historian and a considerable poet. In 1753 he was imprisoned under the Penal Laws for six months for conducting worship, and his son John, then nine, shared his imprisonment. He died in the year 1807.

This son, as incumbent of the Longacre Chapel in Aberdeen, was made coadjutor Bishop of Aberdeen in 1782, succeeding to the See in 1786. In 1788 he was elected Primus. Three notable events are associated with him: the consecration of Bishop Seabury for the Episcopal Church in America in 1784, the death of Prince Charles Edward shortly after he became Primus, and the repeal of the Penal Laws – largely as a result of his persistent efforts – in 1792. His wisdom and statesmanlike qualities guided the Episcopal Church as it emerged from long years of adversity, and laid the foundations for its future advance, not least by helping to make possible the union of many of the Qualified Chapels with the Scottish Episcopal Church. He died in the year 1816.

A Reading from *An Exposition of the Song of Solomon* by John Skinner the Elder

It is certain, our blessed Saviour, and his apostles after him, in all their argumentations, still looked back and referred to Moses and the prophets. And though it be lamented by some, and wondered at by many, that there are not more of their quotations and proofs out of these writers recorded, which it may be thought would have made everything plain, and silenced all controversy, we see now, and every humble Christian will admire, the gracious intention of this procedure, both to prevent the inconvenient bulk of our revelation code, and to awaken our curiosity, if such matters deserve our curiosity, to the diligent observance of that general precept, 'Search the scriptures.'

The scriptures recommended at this time, and by the author of this precept, were only that ancient collection I am speaking of, in which we are undoubtedly sure, this poem under consideration always stood as a part, and consequently is entitled, along with the rest, to the search, the investigation here enjoined. The enjoiner makes no distinctive exception and gives no preferable direction to one part of the received collection more than to another; as well knowing that they all pointed to the same view, and all uniformly concurred, according to their several modes, in the one gracious work of exhibiting to the studious searchers the consolatory prospect of eternal life, by their joint testifying of Jesus.

If after all there shall still remain in any or all of these sacred publications, and in this *Song* among the rest, any obscurity or unfathomable depth about which after all our attention and diligent examination we cannot attain to full satisfaction, let us trust the discovery of such hidden beauties, as beauties we are sure they are, to that happy state, with the prospect of which the apostle thus comforted himself: 'Now we see through a glass darkly, but then face to face; now I know in part, but then I shall know, even as I am known.' Till which time, let us gratefully adore where we do know, and reverently admire where we do not.

alternative reading

A Reading from *Biographical Studies in Scottish Church History* by Anthony Mitchell

It is related that before the younger Skinner was appointed Bishop, some of the older clergy waited upon his father and urged him to allow himself to be nominated for the office. He excused himself, according to the story, in this way: 'You wish me to be bishop, do you? Well then, elect John. I shall then be bishop all the same.'

Whether the words are authentic or not, they are not far wide of the mark as an expression of Skinner's influence upon general Church affairs in Scotland from this time forward. Able, energetic and sensible as the bishop was, his father's gifts were much greater, and it was to the younger man's credit and advantage that he relied upon him.

Hardly had the new bishop entered upon his duties when a matter of the greatest importance emerged. An English dignitary who was dwelling at St Andrews, Dr Berkeley, sub-dean of Canterbury and son of the famous bishop of Cloyne, wrote to him urging the Scottish bishops to consider a project for sending out an 'itinerant' bishop to America, now that the end of the War of Independence was in sight. This proposal the Scottish bishops wisely rejected, but a far happier result followed when on Sunday, 14 November 1784, Dr Samuel Seabury was consecrated as first Bishop of Connecticut and of the American Church, by three Scottish Bishops, Kilgour, Petrie, and Skinner, in an upper room in Longacre, Aberdeen. Of this important event the main management fell upon the shoulders of Bishop Skinner, and but for his firmness and energy the plan would probably have miscarried.

The Scottish Church is proud of its connection with the great Church of America, and well it may be. For the consecration of the first American bishop was more than the forging of a peculiarly intimate link between the two Churches. It proved to be the turning point in the depressed fortunes of the Church in Scotland. It brought a breath of new life and new hope into the minds of its members, and widened a horizon which had been narrowing for many years. It also brought into public prominence the almost forgotten fact of the Church's existence, and raised up in England friends whose zeal was afterwards enlisted in the repeal of the penal laws.

Note: Samuel Seabury is commemorated on 14 November.

14 June

Richard Baxter

Puritan Divine, 1691

Richard Baxter was born at Rowton in Shropshire in 1615. In 1633 he was at the court of Charles I, but was so disgusted with the low moral standards there that he returned home in order to study divinity. He was ordained but after the promulgation of an infamous Oath in 1640, which required obedience to a string of persons ending in the trite phrase 'et cetera', he rejected belief in episcopacy in its current English form, and went as a curate to a poor area of the West Midlands. He opposed the Civil War and played a prominent part in the recall of Charles II, but his continuing dissatisfaction with the way episcopacy was practised led him to decline the See of Hereford. This refusal led him to be debarred from further office in the Church, though he continued to contribute to its life as a prolific hymn writer. His writings breathe a spirit of deep unaffected piety and moderation, and his book The Reformed Pastor, published in 1656, illustrates the great care he took in his pastoral organization. He died in the year 1691.

A Reading from *The Reformed Pastor* by Richard Baxter

Our whole work must be carried on in a sense of our insufficiency, and in a pious believing dependence upon Christ. We must go to him for light, and life, and strength, who sends us on the work; and when we feel our own faith weak, and our hearts grown dull and unsuitable to so great a work as we have to do, we must have recourse to the Lord. Prayer must carry on our work as well as preaching.

We must also be very studious of union and communion among ourselves, and of the unity and peace of the churches that we oversee. We must be sensible how needful this is to the prosperity of the whole, the strengthening of our common cause, the good of the particular members of our flock, and the further enlargement of the kingdom of Christ. And, therefore, ministers must smart when the Church is wounded, and be so far from being the leaders in divisions, that they should take it as a principal part of their work to prevent and heal them. Day and night should they bend their studies to find out the means to close such breaches. They must not only hearken to motions for unity, but propound them and prosecute them; not only entertain an offered peace, but even follow it when it flieth from them. They must, therefore, keep close to the ancient simplicity of the Christian faith, and the foundation and centre of Catholic unity.

Do as much of God's work as you can in unanimity and holy concord. Blessed be the Lord that it is so well with us in this country in this regard as it is. We lose our authority with our people when we divide. They will yield to us when we go together who would resist and condemn the best of us alone. Maintain your meetings for communion. Though your own person might be without the benefit of such meetings yet the Church and our common work requireth them. Do not then show yourselves condemners or neglecters of such necessary work. Distance breedeth strangeness and fermenteth dividing flames and jealousies, which communion will prevent or cure. Ministers have need of one another and must improve the gifts of God in one another; and the self-sufficient are the most deficient, and commonly proud and empty men.

alternative reading

A Prayer of Richard Baxter

Keep me, O Lord,
while I tarry on this earth,
in a daily serious seeking after thee
and in a believing affectionate walking with thee;
that when thou comest,

I may be found not hiding my talent,
nor yet asleep with my lamp unfurnished;
but waiting and longing for my Lord,
my glorious God,
for ever and ever. Amen.

15 June

Evelyn Underhill

Spiritual Writer, 1941

Born in 1875, Evelyn Underhill was in her thirties before she began to explore religion. At first, she wrote on the mystics, most notably in her book Mysticism, published in 1911. Her spiritual journey brought her in 1921 back to the Church of England, in which she had been baptized and confirmed. From the mid-1920s, she became highly-regarded as a retreat conductor and an influential spiritual director. Of her many books Worship, published in 1936, embodied her approach to what she saw as the mystery of faith. She died on this day in 1941.

A Reading from *Worship* by Evelyn Underhill

Worship, in all its grades and kinds, is the response of the creature to the eternal: nor need we limit this definition to the human sphere. There is a sense in which we may think of the whole life of the universe, seen and unseen, conscious and unconscious, as an act of worship, glorifying its Origin, Sustainer, and End. Only in some such context, indeed, can we begin to understand the emergence and growth of the spirit of worship in men and women, or the influence which it exerts upon their concrete activities. Thus worship may be overt or direct, unconscious or conscious. Where conscious, its emotional colour can range from fear through to self-oblivious love. But whatever its form of expression may be, it is always a subject-object relationship; and its general existence therefore constitutes a damaging criticism of all merely subjective and immanental explanations of reality. For worship is an acknowledgement of transcendence; that is to say, of a reality independent of the worshipper, which is always more or less deeply coloured by mystery, and which is there first.

Directly we take this strange thing worship seriously, and give it the status it deserves among the various responses of men to their environment, we find that it obliges us to take up a particular attitude towards that environment. Even in its crudest form, the law of prayer – indeed the fact of prayer – is already the law of belief; since humanity's universal instinct to worship cannot be accounted for, if naturalism tells the whole truth about life. That instinct means the latent recognition of a metaphysical reality, standing over against physical reality, which human beings are driven to adore, and long to apprehend. In other words it is the implicit, even though unrecognised, vision of God that disclosure of the supernatural which is overwhelming, self-giving and attractive all at once, which is the first cause of all worship, from the puzzled upward glance of the primitive to the delighted self-oblation of the saint.

It is possible to regard worship as one of the greatest of humanity's mistakes; a form taken by the fantasy-life, the desperate effort of bewildered creatures to come to terms with the surrounding mystery. Or it may be accepted as the most profound of man's responses to reality; and more than this, the organ of his divine knowledge and the earnest of eternal life.

We are bound to take worship seriously, and ever more seriously with the deepening of our own spiritual sense. Worship points steadily towards the reality of God: gives, expresses, and maintains that which is the essence of all sane religion; namely, a theocentric basis to life. The first or central act of religion is *adoration,* the sense of God, his otherness though nearness, his distinctness from all finite beings though not separateness, his aloofness from them. In this great *sanctus*, all things justify their being and have their place. God alone matters, God alone is: creation only matters because of God.

alternative reading

A Prayer of Evelyn Underhill

For Wholeness

O Lord, penetrate those murky corners
where we hide memories and tendencies
on which we do not care to look,
but which we will not disinter
and yield freely up to you,
that you may purify and transmute them:
the persistent buried grudge,
the half-acknowledged enmity
which is still smouldering;
the bitterness of that loss
we have not turned into sacrifice;
the private comfort we cling to;
the secret fear of failure which saps our initiative
and is really inverted pride;
the pessimism which is an insult to your joy, Lord;
we bring all these to you,
and we review them with shame and penitence
in your steadfast light.

16 June

Richard

Bishop of Chichester, 1253

Richard de Wych (or of Droitwich as it is now known), was born there in 1197 and worked hard for his yeoman father to restore the family fortunes. Later he studied at Oxford and Paris and then in Bologna as an ecclesiastical lawyer. When he returned to England in 1235, he was made Chancellor of Oxford, and eventually Chancellor to the Archbishop of Canterbury, Edmund of Abingdon. When Richard eventually became Bishop of Chichester, he was seen as a model diocesan bishop: progressing around his diocese on foot, visiting and caring for his clergy and people, generally being accessible to all who needed his ministry. He insisted that the sacraments be administered without payment and with a proper dignity. Whilst on a recruitment campaign for the Crusades, he fell ill at Dover and died there on 3 April 1253. His mortal remains were translated to Chichester on this day in the year 1276.

A Reading from a contemporary *Life of Saint Richard* by Ralf Bocking

After a life shining with the glory of his miracles and renowned for the purity of his virtues in which, following Christ, blessed Richard learned constantly to bear the cross on which Christ was crucified for the world and the world for Christ, in order to make a glorious end to his life at the foot of the cross in service to and with Christ, he undertook the preaching of the cross for the relief of the Holy Land, a task entrusted to him by the Holy See. And so Christ's glorious priest and preacher set out, seeking to glory not in the commission which he had received from Rome but rather in the wounds of Christ, crying out with the Apostle: 'May God forbid that I should glory save in the cross of our Lord Jesus Christ.'

During his preaching tour he became very weak. They asked him to eat something and someone said to him, 'My Lord, are you having only one dish for supper? Eat as much as you like.' But he replied, 'It is enough. One dish should suffice for supper.' And he added, 'Do you know this text? It is what Saint Philip said to Christ, "Lord, show us the Father and it is sufficient for us." For he had already turned his whole mind upon God and could already taste the sweetness of the Lord's presence.

He embraced the image of the Crucified, which he had asked to be brought to him, for he knew that according to Saint Basil, the honour given to an image belongs to the subject which it represents. He devoutly kissed and tenderly caressed the wounds as if he had just seen them newly inflicted on his Saviour's dying body, and cried out: 'Thanks be to thee, Lord Jesus Christ, for all the benefits which thou hast granted to me, for all the pains and insults which thou hast suffered for me.'

And then he said to his attendants, 'Place this wretched body down on the ground.' And often repeating the words of the Psalmist, 'Into thy hands, O Lord, I commend my spirit,' and then turning with both heart and voice to the glorious Virgin, he said: 'Mary, mother of grace, mother of mercy, protect us from the enemy now and pray for us at the hour of our death.' Thus between the sighs of his pious devotions and the words of his holy prayers, surrounded by monks, priests, clerks and pious laymen, the blessed Richard rendered up his soul to his creator, soon to join those that dwell in the kingdom above. He passed from this world in about the fifty-sixth year of his age, in the ninth year of his episcopate.

16 June

Joseph Butler

Bishop of Durham, Philosopher, 1752

Born in 1692 at Wantage, Joseph Butler was the son of Presbyterian parents and studied at the dissenting academy of Tewkesbury. He abandoned Presbyterianism in 1714 for the Church of England and, after studying at Oxford, was ordained priest in 1718 and began preaching the sermons which won him his fine reputation. He became Bishop of Durham and is ranked among the greatest exponents of natural theology and ethics in England since the Reformation. He died on this day in 1752.

A Reading from *The Analogy of Religion* by Joseph Butler

Whatever account may be given of the strange inattention and disregard in some ages and countries to a matter of such importance as religion, it would, before experience, be incredible that there should be the like disregard in those who have had the moral system of the world laid before them as it is by Christianity, and often inculcated upon them: because this moral system carries in it a good degree of evidence for its truth, upon its being barely proposed to our thoughts. There is no need of abstruse reasonings and distinctions to convince an unprejudiced understanding that there is a God who made and governs the world, and will judge it in righteousness; though they may be necessary to answer abstruse difficulties when once such are raised; when the very meaning of those words which express most intelligibly the general doctrine of religion is pretended to be uncertain; and the clear truth of the thing itself is obscured by the intricacies of speculation.

To an unprejudiced mind, ten thousand thousand instances of design cannot but prove a designer. And it is intuitively manifest that creatures ought to live under a dutiful sense of their Maker; and that justice and charity must be his laws to creatures whom he has made social, and placed in society. Indeed the truth of revealed religion, peculiarly so called, is not self-evident, but requires external proof in order to its being received. Yet inattention among us to revealed religion will be found to imply the same dissolute immoral temper of mind as inattention to natural religion; because, when both are laid before us in the manner they are in Christian countries of liberty, our obligations to inquire into both, and to embrace both upon supposition of their truth, are obligations of the same nature.

For revelation claims to be the voice of God, and our obligation to attend to his voice is surely moral in all cases. And as it is insisted that its evidence is conclusive upon thorough consideration of it, so it offers itself to us with manifest obvious appearances of having something more than human in it, and therefore in all reason requires to have its claims most seriously examined into. It is to be added that though light and knowledge, in what manner soever afforded us, is equally from God, yet a miraculous revelation has a peculiar tendency from the first principles of our nature to awaken mankind, and inspire them with reverence and awe; and this is a peculiar obligation to attend to what claims to be so with such appearances of truth.

It is therefore most certain that our obligations to inquire seriously into the evidence of Christianity, and upon supposition of its truth, to embrace it, are of utmost importance.

17 June

Samuel and Henrietta Barnett

Social Reformers, 1913 & 1936

Samuel Augustus Barnett was born in Bristol in 1844 and educated at Wadham College, Oxford. To trace the beginnings of great movements is always difficult, but it is clear that following his ordination, Samuel was closely concerned with the inception of the Charity Organisation Society, and worked alongside Octavia Hill. From 1873 to 1894, he was Vicar of St Jude's Whitechapel, where his unorthodox methods, including evening schools and entertainments, aroused much criticism. However, he soon became recognized as a loyal priest, devoted to the religious and cultural improvement of the East End of London. In all his work, Samuel was ably assisted by Henrietta his wife. Henrietta Octavia Weston Rowland was born in Clapham in 1851 and, before her marriage to Samuel in 1873, had been a co-worker with Octavia Hill. In her later years she founded Hampstead Garden Suburb; a community in which all classes might live together. Samuel's spiritual gifts, combined with Henrietta's robust energy and assertive personality, made for a dynamic expression of Christian faith. Samuel died on this day at Hove in 1913; Henrietta died at Hampstead Garden Suburb on 10 June 1936.

A Reading concerning the life and work of Samuel Barnett by Lorraine Blair

> As soon as Samuel was shown a more excellent way, he immediately adopted it. Thus he grew more than anyone I have ever known. … It was of no consequence by what channel the suggestion came, be it lovingly by the voice of a friend, or rudely from the impersonal press.

These words, in a remembrance written by his wife, picture not only the character of the man, but the spirit which directed his life's work. 'A more excellent way' came to life as Toynbee Hall, the world's first University Settlement. Here students would live in the midst of the poor; each group challenged to learn from the other. Samuel hoped that the 'wealth of inheritance and opportunity stored up in Oxford (and Cambridge) would meet the poverty of the life lived amid the mean streets and monotonous labour of East London'. Furthermore,

> anything which mars the grandeur of human life must be brought under a converting influence. Such influences are the culture which opens to men's minds the enjoyment of art and literature, the knowledge which makes the whole world alive and binds together the human family by ties of common interest. … It is small links of friendship which bind classes together.

At the time of their marriage in 1872, the Barnetts could have taken the offer of a parish near Oxford, but instead fulfilled their mutual dream of going to East London. The offer came for Samuel to serve as Vicar of St Jude's, Whitechapel, which had been referred to as the worst parish in London. On a rainy day in January, just prior to their marriage, the couple stood alone, opposite the church in the midst of the gloomy squalor surrounding Commercial Street, and made the decision to accept the challenge of living and working there.

As their work grew, the Barnetts felt that their experience must be shared. University men were invited to 'come and see' and spend their holiday with the poor. The dream of a settlement began and Toynbee Hall opened in 1884. It has served to carry out Samuel Barnett's mission for over one hundred years.

Of the future, Samuel wrote:

> To those who love God, the kingdom of the future means a kingdom of love and peace – of truth and purity: no more war, no more strikes, no more prisons and workhouse, no children without their garden full of flowers to play in. There should be rest for all who are

weary, comfort for all who are sad. That is the kingdom of the future – that is the promised land to which men are travelling.

The perfect life is the life of him who lived and taught as One to whom that future was always present. If we can with steadfast heart follow in his footsteps, then we too shall have the happiness of those who are living to bring the kingdom of heaven into this sin stained world of ours.

alternative reading

A Reading concerning the life and work of Henrietta Barnett by Lorraine Blair

> When a man and a woman made one, bound together by perfect love, strong in the strength which each supplies, devote their common life to the service of all men, then doubt will grow weaker, joy come nearer to the earth, and evil lose some of its power.

This was part of a wedding address given by Samuel Barnett. No doubt he was reflecting on the perfect partnership of his own marriage. In the preface to Henrietta's biography of Samuel, the Archbishop of York wrote:

> There was only one person who could write this record. For the life which it presents was not a single life. It was with a singularly beautiful community of mind and spirit, shared, understood, interpreted, and sustained by his wife. Indeed, Canon Barnett used to say with a characteristic touch of humility, that he was but the mouthpiece of his wife and had the courage of her opinions.

One example of this courage was shown at St Jude's, Whitechapel, where Henrietta influenced her husband to bring worship to the people in a new way. 'The Worship Hour' was an innovative service with readings from modern writers as well as the Bible; service leaflets printed in bright colours to ease the dreariness, clergy unrobed and the church kept rather dark so the poor and dirty would not feel conspicuous.

Henrietta's strength was appreciated by many. Lord Beveridge said of her:

> The Canon had with him another creature of equal force. We young people of the Canon's House often spoke irreverently of Henrietta, but our irreverence was a cloak for profound respect.

Toynbee resident C. R. Ashbee wrote that:

> Mrs Barnett is … the Prior and Prioress of this place – the worthy head. A fine, noble bright-eyed, vigorous woman she appears; and one that will have her own way and not be sparing of her own opinion.

Henrietta's mission did not wane after the Toynbee Hall years. On her fifty-sixth birthday she turned the first spade of earth for the construction of Hampstead Garden Suburb. Here she created a community for people of all classes to live together in beauty and peace. At the opening of the Institute there, it was reported that Samuel said of his wife's efforts that he 'saw the growth of the gardens and streets, and felt the spirit of unity which was growing up, and was very proud that it was the work of a woman, and that that woman was my wife'.

Henrietta was a woman of bold faith who 'dreamed and did' both as her husband's partner, and on her own as well. The legacy of her life is clearly reflected in this letter which she received from the Bishop of Stepney at the time of her husband's death:

> He and you have stood side by side in it all, and all that is felt for him is felt for you. Your wise and tender love for the poor; your confidence in them and faith in their best; your work and your power of inspiring them have made all the difference! The best that is being done now is very largely the immediate result of your labours, and the good that shall be done will bear the constant impression of your touch.

18 June

Bernard Mizeki

Apostle of the MaShona, Martyr, 1896

Born in Portuguese East Africa, Bernard Mizeki went to work in Cape Town and there he was converted to the Christian faith by the Cowley Fathers (The Society of St John the Evangelist). He then gave his life as a translator and evangelist among the MaShona in what is present day Zimbabwe. He was murdered on this day in 1896 in a tribal uprising and is revered throughout Central Africa as a witness to the gospel of Christ. The site of his martyrdom has become an important place of pilgrimage for many Africans.

A Reading from *Mashonaland Martyr* by Jean Farrant

14 June 1896 was a Sunday, a crisp, clear day of the Mashonaland winter. Bernard Mizeki was troubled. Mutwa, his wife, now carried their child in her womb. Had he been right to disobey the orders of the priest in Umtali who had said that all catechists and teachers were to seek safety at Penhalonga? The priest had heard rumours that disturbed him, and feared that any Africans who were associated with the Europeans would be killed.

In his reply, Bernard had written: 'Chief Mangwende's people are suffering. The bishop has put me here and told me to remain. Until the bishop returns, here I must stay. I cannot leave my people now in a time of such darkness.'

As the hours passed, Bernard's wife became increasingly restless and kept saying that she had 'heard things' when she visited Mount Mahopo. She had become almost hysterical when Bernard had cut down the mukute trees and cleared a small plot of ground for growing wheat. She told him the trees were a sacred grove, the abode of the spirits of Chief Mangwende's ancestors. Bernard went out to the newly-cut stumps of the trees, and, thinking it would comfort her, cut a cross in each one saying: 'There! I cut the cross. The cross makes us safe from all spirits and sorcerers.' But it made no difference to Mutwa who begged him to flee saying that he was in great danger.

Two days later at about midnight, there came a loud knocking at the hut door. 'It is Ziute, Mangwende's son,' a voice shouted. 'Open this door. Mangwende has been killed. European troopers came to the village and shot him. They have beaten the people and driven away our cattle and goats!'

Startled and incredulous, Bernard opened the door. Ziute and another man, Saridjgo, came in. Bernard protested that they were lying or he would have heard news of it before. As he spoke the two men knocked him off balance and dragged him outside the hut where a third man was waiting, armed with a spear. While the two men held him down he drove the spear into Bernard's side.

Believing him to be dead, the attackers fled into the night. As soon as Mutwa was certain they had gone, she crept out of the hut, searching for her husband in the darkness. Eventually she and another woman found Bernard by the water spring where he was trying to wash his wound. He pleaded with the women to leave him, to flee and hide themselves. 'Your uncles have attacked me and I am dying,' he said to Mutwa. 'I wish you to be baptized and the child in your womb. Do not think that because your uncles have killed me the work of the priests and teachers is ended. No, when I am dead there will come many more priests, and one day all your people will be Christian.'

Bernard became weak and breathless. Together the two women stole down the hill to the hut to get food and blankets for him. As they began to climb the slope again, they were almost blinded by a great and brilliant white light. The whole of the hillside was lit up and there was a noise 'like many wings of great birds'. The noise came lower and lower, and as they crouched on the ground, covering their eyes, the women saw through their fingers that in the centre of the light where Bernard lay, there was a strange red glow.

After a long time the noise ceased. The light disappeared, but so had Bernard. They crept up the hillside to the rock above the spring. Bernard had gone. They never saw him again and his body was never found.

19 June

Sundar Singh of India

Sadhu (holy man), Evangelist, Teacher of the Faith, 1929

Born of wealthy Sikh parents, Sundar Singh was converted to Christianity after experiencing a vision. He was baptized in the Anglican Church at Simla in 1905. In an endeavour to present Christianity in a Hindu form, he donned the robes of a 'Sadhu' or holy man and travelled much around the Indian sub-continent. He even made a visit to Tibet, where he persisted in strenuous work, despite ill-health. He went missing there, presumed murdered, in April 1929.

Readings from the teaching of Sundar Singh

In Christ I have found what Hinduism and Buddhism could not give me: peace and joy in this world. People do not believe, because they are strangers to the experience. Once when I was wandering about in the Himalayas, in the region of eternal snow and ice, I came upon some hot springs, and I told a friend about them. He would not believe it. 'How can there be hot springs in the midst of ice and snow?' he said. I replied, 'Come and dip your hands in the water, and you will see that I am right.' He came, dipped his hands in the water, felt the heat and believed. Then he said, 'There must be a fire in the mountain.' So after he had been convinced by experience his brain began to help him to understand the matter. Faith and experience must come first, and understanding will follow. We cannot understand until we have some spiritual experience, and that comes through prayer.

As we practise prayer we shall come to know who the Father is and the Son, we shall become certain that Christ is everything to us and that nothing can separate us from him and from his love. Temptation and persecutions may come, but nothing can part us from Christ. Prayer is the only way to this glorious experience.

What is truth? Not a doctrine or dogma, but Jesus Christ himself. Some friends once asked me what I thought of Western civilisation. I told them I did not see real civilisation but animalism. People do not know Christ, do not live with him. They have learnt how to dress, eat and be punctual. They are trained animals.

The fact that Jesus Christ is spoken of in a book, even though it be the Bible, is not sufficient proof; this proof must be found in your own hearts. In your hearts you must find him, and then you will understand that he is your Saviour. I do not proclaim the gospel of Christ because it is written in a book, but because I know its power through experience. Christianity includes many truths which we do not understand if we simply learn about them in books; they only become clear when they are experienced. Christianity is no book-religion, but a religion of life.

Those who have seen Christ have no difficulty in understanding miracles. The great miracle is to receive life, to know the truth, to find heaven on earth.

20 June

Alban, Julius and Aaron

Martyrs, *c.*250

Note: In England, Alban is commemorated alone on 22 June.

Julius and Aaron are the first Welsh citizens whose names are known to us. Gildas records that they were citizens of Caerleon-on-Usk, who died for their faith during the persecution by the Emperor Diocletian (c.304–5). The Book of Llandaff mentions a church dedicated to them which was perhaps built over their graves. It is clear that the memory of these two Romano-British martyrs continued to be venerated without a gap from the Roman period through into medieval times and beyond. Their death provides us with a tenuous but potent link with the very beginnings of Christianity in Britain.

A Reading from *A History of the English Church and People* by the Venerable Bede

The Emperors Diocletian in the East and Maximianus Heculius in the West had ordered all churches to be destroyed and all Christians to be hunted out and killed. This was the tenth persecution since Nero, and it was more protracted and cruel than almost any that had preceded it. When these unbelieving rulers were issuing violent edicts against the Christians, Alban, though still a pagan at the time, gave shelter to a Christian priest who was fleeing from his persecutors. In the days that followed, Alban observed this man's constant faithfulness in prayer and vigil, and was touched by the grace of God and began to imitate the priest's example of faith and devotion. Little by little, he received instruction in the way of salvation until one day Alban renounced the darkness of idolatry, and wholeheartedly accepted Christ.

But when the priest had lived in his house some days, word came to the ears of the evil ruler that Christ's confessor, whose place of martyrdom had not yet been appointed, was hiding in Alban's house. Accordingly he gave orders to his soldiers to make a thorough search, and when they arrived at the martyr's house, Saint Alban, wearing the priest's long cloak, surrendered himself to the soldiers in the place of his guest and teacher, and was led bound before the judge.

When Alban was brought in, the judge happened to be standing before an altar, offering sacrifice to devils. Seeing Alban, he was furious that he had presumed to put himself in such danger by surrendering himself to the soldiers in place of his guest, and ordered him to be dragged before the idols where he was standing. 'Since you have chosen to conceal a sacrilegious rebel,' he said, 'rather than surrender him to my soldiers to pay the well-deserved penalty for his blasphemy against the gods, you shall undergo all the punishment due to him, if you dare to abandon the practice of our religion.'

But Saint Alban, who had freely confessed himself a Christian to the enemies of the faith, was not intimidated by such threats, and armed with spiritual strength, openly refused to obey this order. 'What is your family and race?' the judge asked. 'Of what concern is my family to you?' replied Alban. 'If you wish to know the truth about my religion, know that I am now a Christian, and am ready to do a Christian's duty.' The judge said, 'I insist on knowing your name. Tell me at once.' 'My parents named me Alban,' he answered, 'and I worship and adore the living and true God, who created all things.'

Incensed at his reply, the judge ordered God's holy confessor Alban to be flogged by the executioners, declaring that he would shake his constancy of heart by blows, since words had no effect. But Alban bore the most horrible torments patiently and even gladly for Christ's sake. When the judge realised that no torture could break him or make him renounce the worship of Christ, he ordered him to be executed.

And thus it was that Saint Alban suffered on 22 June near the city of Verulamium. Here, when the peace of Christian times was restored, a beautiful church worthy of his martyrdom was built, where sick folk are healed and frequent miracles take place to this day.

In the same persecution suffered Aaron and Julius, citizens of the City of Legions, and many others of both sexes throughout the land. After they had endured many horrible physical tortures, death brought an end to the struggle, and their souls entered the joys of the heavenly city.

20 June

Fillan

Abbot, eighth century

Fillan (Faelan, Fulan), a common Irish name, was borne by several saints. The eighth-century Fillan was of Irish birth, became a monk and accompanied his uncle Congan (Corrigan) to Scotland. He was a solitary at Pittenweem, Fife, where he was chosen as abbot. After some years he resigned and retreated to Glendochart. His name is associated also with Lochalsh, Renfrewshire and Strathfillan in the vicinity of Killin and Crianlarich, where an abbey bearing his name was built. A well with his name has long been associated with cures for mental ailments. His memory was held in great affection, and relics, especially his staff and bell, played an important part in later Scottish history.

A Reading from the *Instructions* of Columbanus

Who, I ask, will search out the Most High in his own being, for he is beyond words or understanding? Who will penetrate the secrets of God? Who will boast that he knows the infinite God, who fills all things, yet encompasses all things, who pervades all things, yet reaches beyond all things, who holds all things in his hand, yet escapes the grasp of all things? 'No one has ever seen God as he is.' No one must then presume to search for the unsearchable things of God: his nature, the manner of his existence, his selfhood. These are beyond telling, beyond scrutiny, beyond investigation. With simplicity, but also with fortitude, only believe that this is how God is and this is how he will be, for God is incapable of change.

Who then is God? He is Father, Son and Holy Spirit, one God. Do not look for any further answers concerning God. Those who want to understand the unfathomable depths of God must first consider the world of nature. Knowledge of the Trinity is rightly compared with the depth of the sea. Wisdom asks: 'Who will find out what is so very deep?' As the depths of the sea are invisible to human sight, so the Godhead of the Trinity is found to be beyond the grasp of human understanding. If anyone, I say, wants to know what you should believe, you must not imagine that you understand better through speech than through belief; the knowledge of God that you seek will be all the further off than it was before.

Seek then the highest wisdom, not by arguments in words but by the perfection of your life, not by speech but by the faith that comes from simplicity of heart, not from the learned speculations of the unrighteous. If you search by means of discussions for the God who cannot be defined in words, he will depart further from you than he was before. If you search for him by faith, wisdom will stand where wisdom lives, 'at the gates'. Where wisdom is, wisdom will be seen, at least in part. But wisdom is also to some extent truly attained when the invisible God is the object of faith, in a way beyond our understanding, for we must believe in God, invisible as he is, though he is partially seen by a heart that is pure.

22 June

Alban

First Martyr of Britain, *c.*250

Note: In Wales, Alban is commemorated jointly with Julius and Aaron on 20 June: see above for separate entry.

Alban was a citizen of the Roman city of Verulamium (now St Albans in Hertfordshire) who gave shelter to a Christian priest fleeing from persecution, hiding him in his house for several days. Greatly influenced by his devotion to prayer, Alban received instruction from the priest and was converted. When the priest's hiding-place was discovered, Alban dressed himself in the priest's cloak and was arrested in his place. Tortured by the Roman authorities, Alban refused to renounce his faith. He was beheaded on this day, probably in the year 250, and so is acknowledged as the first British martyr. The remains of his shrine stand today as a place of pilgrimage in the Cathedral and Abbey Church of St Alban.

A Reading from *A History of the English Church and People* by the Venerable Bede

In this country there occurred the suffering of Saint Alban, of whom the priest Fortunatus in his *Praise of the Virgins*, in which he mentions all the blessed martyrs who came to God from every quarter of the globe, says:

In fertile Britain's land
Was illustrious Alban born.

The Emperors Diocletian in the East and Maximianus Heculius in the West had ordered all churches to be destroyed and all Christians to be hunted out and killed. This was the tenth persecution since Nero, and it was more protracted and cruel than almost any that had preceded it. When these unbelieving rulers were issuing violent edicts against the Christians, Alban, though still a pagan at the time, gave shelter to a Christian priest who was fleeing from his persecutors. In the days that followed, Alban observed this man's constant faithfulness in prayer and vigil, and was touched by the grace of God and began to imitate the priest's example of faith and devotion. Little by little, he received instruction in the way of salvation until one day Alban renounced the darkness of idolatry, and wholeheartedly accepted Christ.

But when the priest had lived in his house some days, word came to the ears of the evil ruler that Christ's confessor, whose place of martyrdom had not yet been appointed, was hiding in Alban's house. Accordingly he gave orders to his soldiers to make a thorough search, and when they arrived at the martyr's house, Saint Alban, wearing the priest's long cloak, surrendered himself to the soldiers in the place of his guest and teacher, and was led bound before the judge.

When Alban was brought in, the judge happened to be standing before an altar, offering sacrifice to devils. Seeing Alban, he was furious that he had presumed to put himself in such danger by surrendering himself to the soldiers in place of his guest, and ordered him to be dragged before the idols where he was standing. 'Since you have chosen to conceal a sacrilegious rebel,' he said, 'rather than surrender him to my soldiers to pay the well-deserved penalty for his blasphemy against the gods, you shall undergo all the punishment due to him, if you dare to abandon the practice of our religion.'

But Saint Alban, who had freely confessed himself a Christian to the enemies of the faith, was not intimidated by such threats, and armed with spiritual strength, openly refused to obey this order. 'What is your family and race?' the judge asked. 'Of what concern is my family to you?' replied Alban. 'If you wish to know the truth about my religion, know that I am now a Christian, and am ready to do a Christian's duty.' The judge said, 'I insist on knowing your name. Tell me at once.' 'My parents named me Alban,' he answered, 'and I worship and adore the living and true God, who created all things.'

Incensed at his reply, the judge ordered God's holy confessor Alban to be flogged by the executioners, declaring that he would shake his constancy of heart by blows, since words had no effect. But Alban bore the most horrible torments patiently and even gladly for Christ's sake. When the judge realised that no torture could break him or make him renounce the worship of Christ, he ordered him to be executed.

And thus it was that Saint Alban suffered on 22 June near the city of Verulamium. Here, when the peace of Christian times was restored, a beautiful church worthy of his martyrdom was built, where sick folk are healed and frequent miracles take place to this day.

23 June

Etheldreda

Abbess of Ely, *c.*678

Etheldreda (Audrey) was born in Suffolk in the seventh century, a daughter of the king. She desired to commit her life to prayer and chastity and, after two arranged and unconsummated marriages, founded a religious house at Ely for both men and women, over which she ruled as Abbess. At her death on this day in around the year 678, she was revered as a woman of austerity, prayer and prophecy.

A Reading from *A History of the English Church and People*
by the Venerable Bede

Etheldreda was a daughter of Anna, King of the East Angles. She was married to King Egfrid, her former husband having died shortly after their wedding. For a long time Etheldreda begged her husband the king to allow her to relinquish worldly affairs and to serve Christ, the only true King, in monastic life. When at length and with difficulty she obtained his consent, she entered the monastery of the Abbess Ebba, King Egfrid's aunt, at Coldingham, where she received the veil and habit of a nun at the hands of Bishop Wilfrid.

A year later she was herself appointed abbess in the district called Ely, where she built a monastery and became by the example of her heavenly life and teaching, the virgin mother of many virgins dedicated to God. It is said that from the time of her entry into the monastery she would never wear linen but only woollen garments, and that she would seldom take a hot bath except on the eve of the greater festivals such as Easter, Pentecost, and the Epiphany, and only then after she and her assistants had first helped the other handmaids of Christ to wash. She seldom had more than one meal a day except at the greater festivals or because of urgent necessity, and she always remained at prayer in the church from the hour of matins until dawn unless prevented by serious illness.

There are some who say that she possessed the spirit of prophecy, and that in the presence of all the community, she not only foretold the plague that was to cause her death, but also openly declared the number who would die of it in the monastery. She was taken to the Lord in the presence of her sisters seven years after her appointment as abbess. When she died, in accordance with her instructions, she was buried in a wooden coffin among the ranks of the other nuns, as her turn came.

Ely lies in the province of the East Angles, an area of about six hundred hides. It resembles an island surrounded by water and marshes, and derives its name from the vast quantity of eels that are caught in the marshes. This servant of Christ wished to have her monastery in this place because her forebears came from the area.

24 June

The Birth of John the Baptist

The Biblical story of John, the son of Elizabeth and Zechariah, begins even before his birth. His leaping in his mother's womb is seen as a great alleluia in anticipation of the birth of his redeemer, and in all four Gospels, the good news of Jesus Christ is related as beginning with the emergence of John as the forerunner of Christ. He seemed to have a predestined rôle akin to that of the Old Testament prophets, particularly in encouraging the people of God to live lives worthy of their calling and in imminent anticipation of the coming of the Anointed One. In the tradition of the early Fathers, John was seen as endowed with grace from before his birth, and consequently the Church has always kept the celebration of this day with greater solemnity than that of his death.

A Reading from a sermon of Augustine

The Church observes the birth of John as a holy event. We have no such commemoration for any other of our forebears, and it is significant that we celebrate the birthdays of both John and Jesus. I cannot, therefore, let this day pass without a sermon, and even if my brief words fail to do justice to the dignity of the day, the profundity of the feast will itself give you food for thought.

John's mother was old and barren, while Christ's mother was young and a virgin. The news of John's birth was met with incredulity by his father, and he was struck dumb. The Virgin Mary believed, and Christ was conceived in faith. Such is the subject of our investigation and discourse. But as I have said, if I find myself incapable, either through lack of time or through lack of ability, to plumb the depths of this mystery, I know the Holy Spirit will enlighten you. The voice of the Spirit will make itself heard within you without any help from me, for it is he whom you contemplate in your hearts and minds, and whose temples you have become.

John marks the boundary between the Old and New Testaments. Indeed the Lord speaks of him as a sort of boundary line when he says that 'the Law and the prophets are valid until

John the Baptist'. John is both the representative of the past, and the herald of the new. As a representative of the past, it was fitting that he should have been born of elderly parents; and yet while still in his mother's womb he was declared to be a prophet in recognition of his future role. Although unborn, he leapt in his mother's womb at the arrival of blessed Mary. In the womb he was already designated Christ's precursor before they ever met in the flesh. These divine mysteries transcend the limits of our frail human reasoning. When at last John is born and receives his name, his father's tongue was loosened. Let us reflect on the event.

Zechariah had fallen silent and lost the power of speech until John, the Lord's precursor, is born and restores his voice. Is there not a prophetic dimension to Zechariah's silence, as if there were something hidden, kept secret until Christ could be proclaimed? Zechariah's voice is restored with the birth of John: his speech becomes clear when he is born as was foretold. This restoration can be paralleled to the rending of the veil of the Temple at Christ's crucifixion. If John were announcing his own coming, he could not have restored his father's speech. But Zechariah's tongue was loosened because a voice was born. For when John was preaching the coming of the Lord, he was asked: 'Who are you?' And he replied: 'I am the voice of one crying in the wilderness.' John was indeed a voice, but in the beginning was the Word. John was a voice that lasted only for a time; Christ, who is the Word from the beginning, is eternal.

alternative reading

A Reading from a homily of Rabanus Maurus, Archbishop of Mainz

Today we celebrate the birth of John the Baptist. It is right that the births of our Lord and Saint John should be celebrated throughout the world because each is a profound mystery worthy of our contemplation. A barren woman gave birth to John, a virgin conceived Christ; in Elizabeth barrenness was overcome, in Blessed Mary the way of human conception was changed. It was through knowing her husband that Elizabeth brought forth a son: Mary believed the angel and conceived a child. Elizabeth conceived a child who was a human being: Mary conceived both God and man.

Great then is John. Indeed, the Saviour himself testified to John's greatness when he said that 'among those born of woman there has arisen no one greater than John the Baptist'. He excels all, each and every one of us. He is greater than the prophets, he is superior to the patriarchs. Everyone born of woman is inferior to John, except the son of the Virgin who is greater still, as John himself said: 'He who comes after me ranks before me, and I am not worthy to undo the strap of his sandal.'

In the birth of our Lord's forerunner and in the birth of our redeemer there is this mystery: the prophet's birth signifies our humility, but the Lord's birth our ultimate exaltation. John was born as the days began to grow shorter: Christ was born in winter as the days were growing longer, because it was fitting that our status should grow smaller and the glory of God grow greater. John realised this when he said: 'I must grow smaller and he must grow greater.' John was sent ahead like a voice before a word, a lamp before the sun, a herald before a judge, a servant before his master, the best man before the bridegroom.

We have recognised the blessed forerunner of the Lord as a lamp which went ahead of the true light and who bore witness to the light so that all might believe through him. So let us have recourse to him and attend to his proclamation. Indeed his is the voice announced by the prophet Isaiah: 'A voice cries out in the wilderness: "Prepare the way of the Lord. Make straight his paths. Every valley shall be lifted up, and every mountain and hill be made low; the uneven ground shall become level, and the rough places a plain. And all flesh shall see the salvation of our God."'

Let us too, therefore, prepare a way for the Lord who is to come into our hearts. Let us remove the barriers of sin by confession and repentance; let us straighten the paths of our life which for too long have been undirected and devious; let us pave the way of true faith with good works. Let us rid ourselves of all arrogance and lift high our fainting hearts. Then, when all is in order, smoothed, and brought into harmony, we shall see the salvation of God as he is, for 'his home is in peace and his dwelling in Zion'.

alternative reading

A Reading from *God and Man* by Metropolitan Anthony of Sourozh

When you open Saint Mark's Gospel, you find that John the Baptist is defined as a voice that shouts in the wilderness. He is not even defined as a prophet or a messenger of God. He has got so identified with the message, he has become so one with God's own word which he has got to proclaim and to bring to people that one can no longer see him behind the message, hear the tune of his voice behind the thundering witness of God's own spirit speaking through him.

This is one thing we should learn. Too often when we bring a message, people can perceive us and a message which perhaps comes through us, because we are not sufficiently identified with what we have got to say. In order to be identified we must so read the gospel, make it so much ourselves, and ourselves so much the gospel, that when we speak from within it, in its name, it should be simply whatever words we use. I am not speaking of quotations – it should be simply the gospel that speaks and we should be like a voice – God's voice.

The second thing is that to attain to that state in which John could speak and not be noticed, in which all that people could perceive of him was a man who had been completely transformed into a message, into a vision, into a proclamation, meant that he was a man who consented to lay aside all that was selfish, grasping, all that was delighting selfishly in whatever he wanted to have. He had a pure heart, a clear mind, an unwavering will, a trained body, a complete mastery of self, so that when the message came, fear would not defeat him and make him silent; promises could not beguile him and make him silent, or simply the heaviness of the flesh, the heaviness of the mind, the heaviness of the heart, should not overcome the lightness and the lightening power of the spirit. This is something that is also our task.

25 June

Moluag of Lismore

Bishop, 592

Moluag was an Irish missionary who came to Scotland about the same time as Columba and established a missionary community on the island of Lismore, Loch Linnhe, where the

church of St Moluag subsequently became the seat of the bishopric of Argyll. He and his followers worked mainly in the Pictish areas. He was consecrated bishop and established other centres of mission at Rosemarkie on the Black Isle where, according to tradition, he died in the year 592.

A Reading from an Old Irish homily

It is our duty to give thanks to the Lord for his gifts. For the grateful soul who gives thanks to God for his grace is a temple and dwelling place of God; as Peter says, 'God makes the soul grateful and familiar to him.' That is, the man or woman who give thanks to God for his blessings is an estate that belongs to the King of all. But they who are not grateful for the blessings of God are a temple and dwelling place of the devil; as Peter says, 'The ungrateful soul is in possession of a demon.' The evil demon possesses and inhabits the soul of the ungrateful who do not give thanks to God for his blessings. It is that thanksgiving which is meant when they say, 'Our souls give thanks to you for your blessings without number.' That is, our souls give thanks to you, O Lord, for your blessings without number on heaven and earth.

And so may the blessing of the Lord of heaven and earth be on everyone with whom we have come into contact: on their possession of field and house, on their property both animate and inanimate, and on everyone who serves them and is obedient to them. May the earth give its fruits, may the air give its rainfall, may the sea give its fishes, may there be more grain and milk, more honey and wheat for everyone whose labour and goodwill we enjoy. May God give them a hundredfold on this earth and the kingdom of heaven in the life to come. For they who receive Christ's people actually receive Christ, as he himself says, 'Whoever hears you, hears me and whoever rejects you rejects me.' That is, he who receives you receives me, and he who despises you despises me.

26 June

Robert Leighton

Archbishop of Glasgow, 1684

Robert Leighton was born in 1611, the son of a puritanical physician. He studied at Edinburgh and on the continent where he was influenced by the piety and tolerance of the French Jansenists. In 1641 he became minister of Newbattle, but was highly critical of the Covenanting policy of those days. In 1652 he was sent to negotiate with Cromwell the release of Scots prisoners taken in battle at Worcester, and Cromwell's influence caused him to be appointed in the following year as Principal of Edinburgh University where he exercised a remarkable influence. At the Restoration he accepted the bishopric of Dunblane, the least remunerative, in the hope that he might use that office for the healing of the schisms within the Scottish Church. 'My sole object has been to procure peace and to advance the interests of true religion.' His plans for an accommodation with the Presbyterians led to his appointment as Archbishop of Glasgow in 1670. After four years he resigned the archbishopric following his failure of his efforts at reconciliation. He retired to the south of England where he died in the year 1684.

A Reading from *An Exposition of the Lord's Prayer* by Robert Leighton

This is the fault here: when the long continuance and much repetition in prayer is affected as a thing of itself available; when heaping on words and beating often over the same words, though the heart bear them not company, is judged to be prayer; and generally, whensoever the tongue outruns the affection, then is prayer turned into babbling. Yea, though a man use this very short form here prescribed, yet he may commit this very fault against which it was provided, he may babble in saying it; and it is to be feared the greatest part do so.

Men judge, and that rightly, a speech to be long or short, not so much by the quantity of words, as by the sense; so that a very short speech that is empty of sense, may be called long, and a long one that is full, and hath nothing impertinent, is truly short: thus, as men judge by the sense of speech, God judgeth by the affection of prayer, which is the true sense of it; so the quality is the rule of the quantity with him. There is no prayer too long to him, provided it be all enlivened with affection: no idle repetition, where the heart says every word over again as often, and more often than the tongue.

Therefore, those repetitions in the psalms, *Lord, hear; Lord, incline thine ear; Lord attend,* etc., were not idle on this account; God's own Spirit did dictate them, there was not one of them empty, but they came from the heart of the holy penmen, full fraught with the vehemency of their affections. And it is reported of Saint Augustine, that he prayed over for a whole night, 'Lord, let me know thee, let me know me': because his heart still followed the suit, all of it was prayer.

So that in truth, where the matter is new, and the words still diverse and very rich in sense, yet with God, it may be idle multiplying of words because the heart stays behind; and where the same words are repeated, so that a man seems poor and mean in the gift of prayer to others, yet if it be not defect of affection but the abundance of it, as it may be, that moves often the same request, it is not empty, but full of that sense that the Searcher of hearts alone can read. I had rather share with that publican in his own words, and say it often over, as if I had nothing else to say, 'God be merciful to me a sinner,' saying it with such a heart, rather than the most excellent prayer where the outside is the better half.

27 June

Cyril of Alexandria

Bishop of Alexandria, Teacher of the Faith, 444

Cyril was born in Alexandria and is first heard of as a young priest. He succeeded his uncle as Patriarch in the year 412 and began his great defence of the orthodox doctrines of God the Holy Trinity, and of the Incarnate Christ as a unique, single Person, at once God and human. His chief opponent was Nestorius, the Patriarch of Constantinople, who appears to have taught that there were two separate Persons co-existing in the Incarnate Christ, the one divine and the other human. The Nestorian Party thus rejected the description of Mary as Theotokos, 'the God-bearer', and also rejected the papal ruling that they comply with Cyril's doctrinal position that the union between divinity and humanity in Christ was total and real. The Council of Ephesus was convened in the year 431 to rule on the matter (see reading for 25 March) and eventually gave its full support to Cyril, making the term

Theotokos the touchstone of Christian orthodoxy. Cyril's writings reflect his outstanding qualities as a theologian. They are marked by precision in exposition, accuracy in thought and skill in reasoning. He died at Alexandria in the year 444.

A Reading from the commentary of Cyril of Alexandria on St John's Gospel

In a plan of surpassing beauty the creator of the universe decreed the renewal of all things in Christ. In his design for restoring human nature to its original condition, he gave a promise that he would pour out on it the Holy Spirit along with his other gifts, for otherwise our nature could not enter once more into the peaceful and secure possession of those gifts.

He therefore appointed a time for the Holy Spirit to come upon us: this was the time of Christ's coming. He gave this promise when he said: 'In those days,' that is, the days of the Saviour, 'I will pour out a share of my Spirit on all humanity.'

When the time came for this act of unforced generosity, which revealed in our midst the only-begotten Son, clothed with flesh on this earth, born of woman, in accordance with holy Scripture, God the Father gave the Spirit once again. Christ, as the first-fruits of our restored nature, was the first to receive the Spirit. John the Baptist bore witness to this when he said: 'I saw the Spirit coming down from heaven, and it rested on him.'

Christ 'received the Spirit' insofar as he was human, and insofar as a human being could receive the Spirit. He did so in such a way that, though he is the Son of God the Father, begotten of his substance, even before the incarnation, indeed before all ages, yet he was not offended at hearing the Father say to him after he had become human: 'You are my Son; today I have begotten you.'

The Father says of Christ, who was God, begotten of him before the ages, that he has been 'begotten today', for the Father is to accept us in Christ as his adopted children. The whole of our nature is present in Christ, insofar as he is human. So the Father can be said to give the Spirit again to the Son, though the Son possesses the Spirit as his own, in order that we may receive the Spirit in Christ. The Son, therefore, took to himself the seed of Abraham, as Scripture says, and became like us in all things.

The only-begotten Son receives the Spirit, but not for his own advantage, for the Spirit is his, and is given in him and through him, as we have already said. He receives it to renew our nature in its entirety and to make it whole again, for in becoming human he took our entire nature to himself. If we reason correctly, and use also the testimony of Scripture, we can see that Christ did not receive the Spirit for himself, but rather for us in him; for it is also through Christ that all gifts come down to us.

27 June

Richard FitzRalph

Archbishop of Armagh, Reformer, 1360

Popularly known as 'Saint Richard of Dundalk', Richard was a learned scholar who was Dean of Lichfield and Chancellor of Oxford University before becoming Archbishop of Armagh. He is affectionately honoured in Dundalk, County Louth, the place of his birth, for

his compassionate and caring nature. An important figure in Irish Church History, he was deeply concerned for the people of Dundalk and Drogheda who suffered during the Black Death, and for the welfare of the poor. This, however, did not prevent him from criticizing the mendicants of the day. Some of his teaching and writing influenced John Wyclif, later providing insights about a Christian stewardship of possessions. It is said of the pilgrims who visited his tomb, that they 'Many a mile did walk/ but had never seen so good a man/as Richard of Dundalk.' He died on this day in the year 1360.

A Reading from *A Fourteenth Century Scholar and Primate: Richard FitzRalph in Oxford, Avignon and Armagh* by Katherine Walsh

FitzRalph's activity as a preacher is almost unique in one important respect, in the detailed sermon diary which he kept, and the care and precision with which he revised and polished his formal Latin sermons, possibly with the intention of publishing them in collected form towards the end of his life, though he failed to complete the task. His diary provides an unusually complete and balanced picture of his work, as court theologian and plaintiff in Avignon, as pastor and administrator in Lichfield, and as prelate in the ecclesiastical province of Armagh, over a period of twenty-five years.

His sermons are forthright, committed, and often passionate to a degree which was impossible in the context of formal theological treatises, and they illuminate his personality, interests, and prejudices, his changing and developing views, his opportunism, his moods, hopes and fears. Furthermore, they reveal a concern for Church reform at all levels, from the curia through prelates and parish curates to the laity, long before he became embroiled in controversy with the friars. This concern was expressed in *ad hoc* terms, applied to specific situations, especially in Ireland where his sermons present a striking contrast to the conventional (and expected) denunciations of clerical vices in synodal and visitation sermons.

In the pulpit he did not mince his words, though he did tend to exercise discrimination in marrying theme and mood to audience, especially in Avignon where interests of self-preservation dictated a degree of prudence, at least in the early stages. He could and did express himself in elegant Latin, expounding complex theological themes in formally constructed discourses in accordance with the contemporary 'artes predicandi'. He was also capable of unleashing his wrath over contemporary abuses and injustices with forthright if not brutal clarity, even when his criticism was directed against curial courts and lawyers, prelates, and higher clergy. In this respect his tone became distinctly more moderate on being elevated to the episcopal dignity himself, when he learned to restrict much of his criticism to the privacy of provincial synods.

Nevertheless, his occasional outbursts in Avignon about place-hunters and pluralists, immoral prelates and double-dealing lawyers can be matched in England and Ireland with attacks on those who incite to and condone violence and dishonesty, fraudulent treatment of women and of the Gaelic Irish in matters of testamentary dispositions and inheritance laws, tithe-evasion and business malpractice, immorality, and neglect of their duties by the clergy. His strongly expressed views on racial tensions, in the case of England and France as well as in Anglo-Ireland, on the status of women, pastoral care, personal piety, honesty, and fair dealing, further enhance the value of his diary as a contemporary document, important and revealing on a wide range of social, political, and ecclesiastical issues.

27 June

Alexander Jolly

Bishop of Moray, 1838

Born in Stonehaven in 1756, Alexander Jolly was educated at Aberdeen, ordained in Peterhead and sent to minister at Turriff. After almost twelve years he moved to Fraserburgh where he spent the rest of his life. A man of great learning and deep personal devotion, he was consecrated in 1796 as coadjutor to Bishop Macfarlane, who had superintendence of Moray, Ross, Argyll and Caithness. In 1798 when Caithness was disjoined, Alexander was unanimously elected by the four presbyters of Moray as their diocesan. His wisdom guided the Church through the difficult years which followed the repeal of the Penal Laws, and his learning and saintly life brought considerable prestige to the Church he loved. He died in the year 1838.

A Reading from *The Christian Sacrifice in the Eucharist*
by Alexander Jolly

The great and general means of salvation, to which all the instrumental duties of holy living may be reduced, are Baptism and the blessed Eucharist.

These means of grace are indispensably necessary to salvation, wherever they may be had, according to Christ's institution, and from those duly commissioned stewards, whom he has appointed to give his family their portion of meat in due season. And, if we do at any time neglect them, when they are in our power, we can expect no favour from God; but, by disobeying his command, shall incur his displeasure.

Very strong, indeed, is our obligation to be constant communicants in the Christian sacrifice. It is bound upon us every tie of duty, love and gratitude, as well as regard to our own eternal interest – our advancement in grace and preparation for glory. Our divine Lord's command to priests and people is most express – to the priests to celebrate, and to the people to receive. 'Do this,' he said, 'in remembrance of me,' that is, offer this for my powerfully prevailing memorial: 'Take, eat, this is my body: drink ye all of this, for this is my blood.' In vain, then, we say or pray, Lord, Lord, or hope to enter into the kingdom of heaven, if we fail to do what is his Father's will, and his own. 'Why call ye me, Lord, Lord,' he asks, 'and do not the things that I say?'

28 June

Irenaeus

Bishop of Lyons, Teacher of the Faith, *c.*200

Irenaeus was probably a native of Smyrna, born in about the year 130. As a boy, he had heard Polycarp preach, who had in turn been a disciple of the Apostle John. Irenaeus is thus one of the important connections between the apostolic Church and the second century. He studied at Rome, and later became a priest at Lyons in Gaul, succeeding as bishop upon the martyrdom of his predecessor in 177. He contended against the mythological, unhistorical beliefs of the Gnostics, giving positive value to the full humanity of the Incarnate Christ, and affirmed the public teaching rôle of the episcopate to combat false doctrine. He is honoured as the first great Catholic theologian, one who drew upon the emerging traditions of East and West. Irenaeus died in about the year 200.

A Reading from the treatise *Against the Heresies* by Irenaeus

As those who see light stand within its compass and share its brilliancy, so those who see God are in God, and share his splendour. God's splendour is the source of life, and those who see God are sharing his life. Although beyond human comprehension, incomprehensible and invisible, God has made himself visible, comprehensible and knowable, so that those with faith might see him and live. His greatness is past searching out: his goodness is beyond the bounds of human language. Yet God allows himself to be seen, and in seeing God we come alive. Life is itself a gift, and the means of life is to be found in God alone, so as we come to share the life of God we are also coming to know God and to enjoy his favour.

Those who see God shall live: they will be made immortal by this vision and will be united with God. As Moses declared in Deuteronomy: 'Today we have seen that God may speak to someone and that person will live.' God sustains the universe in being. His nature and greatness cannot be seen or described by any of his creatures; but this does not mean he is unknowable. We learn from the Word that there is one God and Father who holds everything in being, and gives being to everything. Indeed, it is written in the gospel that 'no one has seen God at any time, except his only-begotten Son who is close to the Father's heart who has made him known'.

The Son has revealed the Father from the beginning, for he was with the Father in the beginning. He revealed God to the human race through the visions of the prophets, through various gifts, through his own ministry and the glory of the Father, at appropriate times and in order for our benefit. Where there is order, there is harmony; and where harmony exists we can be sure that the time is chosen; and when we know that, we can be sure that what is being revealed is for our benefit.

This is why the Word became the dispenser of the Father's grace for the benefit of humankind, and for our sake made these generous arrangements: revealing God to us, and raising us to God. In raising us to God, he shields the Father from human sight lest we ever undervalue God through familiarity, and also so that we always have something to strive after. On the other hand, he revealed God to us that we would not fall away and as a result, cease to exist. For the glory of God is a human being fully alive, and the life of humanity consists in the vision of God. Thus if the revelation of God in this world gives life to every living thing, how much more will the revelation of the Father by the Word give life to those who see God.

29 June

Peter and Paul

Apostles, *c.*64

Note: In Wales, provision for a separate commemoration of the Martyrdom of Paul, together with other martyrs of the early Church, is made on 30 June. In Ireland, only Saint Peter is commemorated today.

Peter has often been called the 'Prince of the Apostles' because of the words of Jesus renaming him Cephas instead of Simon. This was the Aramaic form of the Greek word Peter, which means 'rock'. Jesus said that on this rock he would build his Church. But both Peter and Paul came to be seen as having different rôles to play within the leadership of the Church: Peter in witnessing to the Lordship of Christ, and Paul developing an understanding of its meaning for Christ's followers, Jew and Gentile alike. Peter and Paul have been remembered jointly on this day from the very early days of the Church, it being honoured as the anniversary of their martyrdom in Rome in about the year 64.

A Reading from a sermon of Augustine

This day has been made holy by the martyrdom of the blessed apostles Peter and Paul. We are, therefore, not talking about some obscure martyrs. For as Scripture says, 'Their voice has gone forth to all the world, and their message to the ends of the earth.' These martyrs realised what they taught: they followed the path of integrity, they confessed the truth, and they died for it.

Saint Peter, the foremost of the apostles and a passionate lover of Christ, heard his merits acknowledged when the Lord addressed him: 'I say to you that you are Peter.' For he had himself said: 'You are the Christ, the Son of the living God.' Then Christ said: 'And I say to you that you are Peter, and on this rock I will build my Church.' He meant that 'Upon this rock I will build the faith that you now confess, for you have said to me, "You are the Christ, the Son of the living God." Therefore, I will build my Church on you, for you are Peter.' The name Peter comes from *petra*, the word for rock, just as the word Christian comes from Christ.

In a virtually unique way then, Peter can be said to represent the entire Church. And because of the role which he alone had, he merited to hear the words: 'To you I shall give the keys of the kingdom of heaven.' It was not an individual who received those keys, but the entire Church considered as one. Now insofar as he represented the unity and universality of the Church, Peter's preeminence is clear from the words: 'To you I give', for what was given was given to all. But it is clear that it was the Church that received the keys of the kingdom of God from what the Lord says elsewhere to all the apostles after his resurrection: 'Receive the Holy Spirit', adding immediately, 'whose sins you forgive, they are forgiven, and whose sins you retain, they are retained'.

It was logical, therefore, that the Lord after his resurrection should entrust Peter with the care of his sheep. He was not the only disciple who was worthy of this responsibility, but in speaking only to this one man, we should understand that Christ was speaking to all. Peter was addressed because he was foremost among the apostles. Therefore do not be disheartened, Peter; answer once, twice, yes three times. This threefold confession of love is necessary to recover what you lost three times by your fear. Untie by love the knot that you tied about yourself through fear.

Paul emerges out of Saul, the lamb out of the wolf; at first an enemy, he becomes an apostle; at first a persecutor, he becomes the preacher. The Lord showed him the things that he too had to suffer for his name: chains, beatings, imprisonment, shipwrecks. The Lord sustained Paul in his sufferings, and brought him to this day.

Both apostles share the same feast day, for these two were one, even though they were martyred on different days. Peter went ahead, Paul followed. Let our way, then, be made straight in the Lord. It is a narrow, stony, hard road we tread; and yet with so many gone before us, we shall find the way smoother. The Lord himself trod this way, the unshakeable apostles and the holy martyrs likewise. So let us celebrate this feast day made holy by the blood of these two apostles. Let us embrace their faith, their life, their labours, their sufferings, their preaching, and their teaching.

alternative reading

A Reading from a sermon of Leo the Great

The Apostle Paul has taught us that as many as are baptized into Christ have clothed themselves with Christ, for 'In Christ Jesus there is no longer Jew or Greek, slave or free, male or female; but all are one. And if you belong to Christ, you are Abraham's offspring, heirs of the promise.'

My friends, there can be no doubt that the Son of God took our human nature into so intimate a union with himself that one and the same Christ is present, not only in the firstborn of all creation, but in all his saints as well. The head cannot be separated from the members, nor the members from the head. And although it is true that not in this life, but only in eternity, will 'God be all in all', yet even now God dwells, whole and complete in his temple which is the Church. Indeed, this was his promise to us when Christ said: 'See, I am with you always, even to the end of the world.'

What the Son of God did and taught for the world's reconciliation is for us not simply a matter of past history. It is something we experience here and now through his power at work among us. Born of the Virgin Mother by the action of the Holy Spirit, Christ fertilises his spotless Church by the inspiration of the same Spirit. In baptism she brings to birth children for God beyond all numbering, of whom it is written: 'They are born not of blood, nor of the desire of the flesh, nor of human will, but of God.'

In Christ Abraham's posterity is blessed, because in him the whole world is receiving adoption as heirs, and in him the patriarch is becoming the father of all nations through a birth, not from human stock but by faith, of the descendants that were promised to him. From every nation on earth without exception, Christ is forming a single flock of those he has hallowed, daily fulfilling the promise he once made: 'I have other sheep, not of this fold, them also I must bring in; and there shall be one flock and one shepherd.'

Although it was primarily to Peter that Christ said: 'Feed my sheep,' yet the one Lord guides all pastors in the discharge of their office and leads to rich and fertile pastures all those who come to the rock. There is no counting the sheep who are nourished by the richness of his love, and who do not hesitate to lay down their lives for the sake of the Good Shepherd who died for them. But it is not only the martyrs who share in Christ's sufferings by their glorious courage; the same is true, by faith, of all of us who are born again in baptism. In our baptism we have renounced the devil and put our faith in God; we have passed from our former way of life and embraced a new life; we have cast off the earthly and been clothed with the heavenly – all these things are images of our dying and rising with Christ. In baptism we are welcomed by Christ and we welcome him into our hearts. We should remember that we are all called to become the flesh of the Crucified.

Note: For further alternatives, see below the readings for The Martyrdom of Paul.

30 June

The Martyrdom of Paul

Apostle, *c.*64

Note: In Wales, today may be observed as a more general commemoration of those other Christians, in addition to Peter and Paul, who were martyred in Rome under the Emperor Nero.

Since ancient times the apostles Peter and Paul have been venerated together on 29 June, the date on which, by tradition, they were both martyred. The first Book of Common Prayer (1549) broke with this custom, commemorating only Peter on that date. Modern revisions have restored the double festival, but this separate commemoration allows the witness of Paul, even unto death, to be celebrated in its own right.

A Reading from the *Ecclesiastical History* of Eusebius of Caesarea

Nero was the first emperor to be heralded above others an antagonist of God and was encouraged to murder the apostles. It is said that during his reign Paul was beheaded in Rome itself, and Peter was crucified. This story is supported by the attachment (which still prevails) of the names of Peter and Paul to the cemeteries there; and in no less degree also to a Christian named Gaius who lived in the time of Zephyrinus, Bishop of Rome. Gaius, in a written disputation with Proclus, a champion of the heresy of the Phygians, speaks of the places where the sacred remains of the apostles were laid.

Indeed, I can point out the shrines of the apostles. If you go to the Vatican, or to the Ostian Way, you will find the shrines of those who founded the church. The fact that they were both martyred on the same occasion is affirmed by Dionysius, Bishop of Corinth, who when writing to the Church in Rome says, 'In these ways you also, by such an admonition, have united the planting that came from Peter and Paul, of both the Romans and the Corinthians. For indeed, both apostles planted in our own Church in Corinth and taught us. In similar fashion they both taught in Italy, and were martyred on the same occasion.'

alternative reading

A Reading from *The Epitome of the Divine Institutes* by Lactantius

Things may be said with justice in this world. But who will hear them when those who exercise authority get angry and feel threatened by the exercise of personal liberty? In religion alone has liberty placed her dwelling. Here is an area of life which above all others should be a matter of free will: none should be put under compulsion to worship that which they do not wish to.

Thus, if some through fear of threats, or overwhelmed by pain when under torture, agree to offer detestable sacrifices, you should know that they are not doing so of their own free will. They will not do voluntarily what they are made to do under compulsion. As soon as the opportunity arises and their liberty is restored, they will flee to God, and with prayers and tears beseech his mercy for what they have had to endure; and pardon is never denied them. What then do those who mutilate the body but who cannot change the will, hope to accomplish by their actions?

If others, terrified neither by threats nor by torture, are prepared to maintain their faith and forfeit their life, against such people cruelty exerts all its strength, contriving unspeakable tortures, unbearable pain, just because it is known that death for the sake of God is deemed glorious, and that victory consists in rising above torment and in laying down one's life for faith and religion. Against such people the torturers go into competition: they will not risk allowing their victims to die; instead they devise new and subtle cruelties to compel the human spirit to submit to bodily pain. Should they fail, they pause, applying to the wounds they have inflicted every care, knowing that pain from repeated torture is worse when wounds are raw. In these ways they ply their trade against the innocent. They consider themselves pious, just and even religious (for with such rites they believe their gods will be pleased) and denigrate the martyrs as impious and wild people. What perversity this is, to call an innocent and tortured victim a desperate and impious creature, while the torturer is called just and pious!

It is said that those who revile the religious observances of the State which have been handed down by their ancestors, are rightly and deservedly punished. But what if those ancestors were fools in adopting empty religious rites? Are we Christians to be prohibited from pursuing a true and better course? Why should we abandon our liberty and become enslaved and addicted to what is false? Allow us to be wise and to seek after truth. If it suits the authorities to defend the practice of ancestral religion, then why, for example, are the Egyptians exempt who worship cattle and creatures of every kind as gods? Why are actors in the theatre allowed to ridicule the gods? Why is someone honoured because he has mocked the gods with a display of wit? Why are philosophers listened to when they argue that there are no gods, or that if they do exist, that they have no care or interest in human affairs, or that there is no providential ordering to the world?

Of all the human race it would seem that the only ones who are judged irreligious are Christians who follow after the truth of God. Since this truth is both justice and wisdom, these people brand it as a crime, counting it irreligion or folly; they obviously do not understand the nature of what is deceiving them, when they call evil good, and good evil.

July

1 July

Serf

Bishop, *c*.500

Serf is one of the heroes of the Celtic Church known to us only through fragments of his story which are not always consistent. Tradition locates his activity at Culross and in the foothills of the Ochils, where he evangelized the Pictish tribe occupying the land to the north of the Forth. Also associated with him is the village of Dysart, a name derived from his retreat or 'desertum'. Serf is thought to have been a disciple of Palladius and to have fostered and educated Kentigern, which would place his activity in the first half of the sixth century.

A Reading from an ancient Gaelic poem
'The Guardian Angel'

Thou angel of God who hast charge of me
From the dear Father of mercifulness,
The shepherding kind of the fold of the saints
To make round about me this night;

Drive from me every temptation and danger,
Surround me on the sea of unrighteousness,
And in the narrows, crooks and straits,
Keep thou my coracle, keep it always.

Be thou a bright flame before me,
Be thou a guiding star above me,
Be thou a smooth path below me,
And be a kindly shepherd behind me,
Today, tonight, and for ever.

I am tired and I am a stranger,
Lead thou me to the land of angels;
For me it is time to go home
To the court of Christ, to the peace of heaven.

1 July

Euddogwy

Bishop, c.500

Euddogwy (Oudoceus) is the third Celtic saint to whom Llandaff Cathedral is dedicated (The Cathedral Church of SS. Peter and Paul, with SS. Dyfrig, Teilo and Euddogwy). Little is known of him. It would seem that he was a nephew of Teilo, and a monk of Llantwit Major. On the death of Teilo, Euddogwy was elected Bishop of Llandaff by the abbots of the South Wales monasteries, and consecrated in the year 569.

A Reading from the *Conferences* of John Cassian

The whole purpose of the monk, and indeed the perfection of his heart, amount to this – total and uninterrupted dedication to prayer. He strives for unstirring calm of mind and for never-ending purity, and he does so to the extent that this is possible for human frailty. This is the reason for our tireless and unshakeable practice of both physical work and contrition of heart. Indeed, there is a mutual and undivided link between these. For just as the edifice of all the virtues strives upward toward perfect prayer so will all these virtues be neither sturdy nor enduring unless they are drawn firmly together by the crown of prayer. This endless, unstirring calm of prayer that I have mentioned can neither be achieved nor consummated without these virtues. And likewise virtues are the prerequisite foundation of prayer and cannot be effected without it.

It is pointless for me simply to talk about prayer, simply to direct attention to its ultimate reality, with its presupposition of the practice of all the virtues. The first task is to look at the succession of obstacles to be overcome and then to examine the necessary preliminaries to success. With the gospel parable for a guide, one must carefully calculate and gather together everything required for the construction of this most sublime tower of the spirit. And preliminary work will be necessary if the assembled materials are to be of any use, for they will not be able to support the sublime reality of perfection unless we unload all our vices and rid our souls of the wreck and rubble of passion. Then simplicity and humility must be laid as sure foundations on, as they say, the living solid earth of our hearts, on that rock of which Scripture speaks. There the tower to be built with our virtues may rest unshakeably and rise with utter assurance to the heights of the skies. That tower resting on such foundations will not crumble, will feel no shock even when mighty torrents of passion come pouring against it, when the raging tides of persecution are like a battering ram against its walls, when the cruel hurricane of devils pounds and thunders against it.

1 July

Henry Venn, John Venn and Henry Venn the younger

Priests, Evangelical Divines, 1797, 1813 & 1873

Henry Venn was born in Barnes in March 1725. After studying at Cambridge, he was ordained and served several parishes in the area. In 1750, he became a curate in Surrey, developing the evangelical principles for which he is known. He moved to London in 1753, becoming curate of Clapham the following year, and his son John Venn was born there in March 1759. Later that year, Henry took his family to Huddersfield where he had been appointed vicar. He worked assiduously to the point of exhaustion, and the family remained there until 1771 when Henry became Vicar of Yelling in Huntingdonshire. Although he became famous for his piety, he was always considered to be a cheerful and happy man, despising the traditionally regarded, gloomy disposition of his Calvinist leanings.

John Venn was educated at Sidney Sussex College, Cambridge, and became Rector of Little Dunham in Norfolk and eventually of Clapham in 1792. He was one of the founders of the Church Missionary Society in 1797. It was at Clapham that he became a central figure in the group of religious philanthropists known as the Clapham Sect. John was also an active participator in the movement for the abolition of the slave trade.

John's son, Henry Venn, was born at Clapham in 1796. After his time in Cambridge, he was ordained and held various livings, but in 1846 he devoted himself entirely to the work of the Church Missionary Society. He was secretary for thirty-two years and his organizing gifts and sound judgement made him the leading spirit in the Society. In his later years, he was recognized as a leader of the Evangelical body of the Church of England.

The elder Henry Venn died on 24 June 1797 at his son's rectory in Clapham. John Venn died at Clapham on this day in 1813; and his son Henry died at Mortlake on 13 January 1873.

A Reading from a sermon preached by John Venn in 1806 upon the anniversary of the departure of a group of missionaries for Africa

If Asia and Africa ever receive the faith of Christ, they must owe it to the successful labour of missionaries. A missionary is one who like Enoch walks with God, and derives from constant communion with him a portion of the divine likeness. With the world under his feet, with heaven in his eye, with the gospel in his hands and Christ in his heart, he pleads as an ambassador for God, knowing nothing but Jesus Christ, enjoying nothing but the conversion of sinners, hoping for nothing but the promotion of the kingdom of Christ, and glorifying in nothing but in the cross of Christ Jesus by which he is crucified to the world and the world to him. Daily studying the word of life, and transformed more and more into the image which it sets before him, he holds it forth to others as a light to illuminate the darkness of the world around him, as an exhibition of the light and glory of a power and higher world above.

We must fix our hope of success chiefly upon God, on the nature of divine truth, and on the spirit and temper of the men who preach it. And though we have not met with immediate success, are we not laying a foundation on which much may be successfully built hereafter? But what have we to do with success? Success as I say belongs to God – duty is our part. Shall we sit still and make no effort for the conversion of our fellow-creatures? Can we acquit ourselves of guilt by waiting longer till we see a more favourable prospect? Our duty, our indispensable duty, is to endeavour; nor are our endeavours at all less acceptable to God, even though they may be unsuccessful.

alternative reading

A Reading from *Henry Venn: Missionary and Statesman* by Wilbert Shenk

Although missions were no longer a novelty by the time Henry Venn became the secretary of the Church Missionary Society in 1841, no one had yet conceived a formal theoretical framework of mission. Venn became a central figure in the forging of mission theory. He used the term 'principle' to mean both axiom and goal. He established no ranking of principles, and indeed expected that 'working' principles would be modified by time and place. Communicating Christ as Saviour was an infinitely varied and complex process.

His working principles were in many ways interrelated. The first was preaching. He saw preaching as the engine of mission, but not to be misused. The preacher could cheapen the gospel by proclaiming it in the wrong manner or place. The cross of Christ was the centre of Christian preaching. His second working principle was that the missionary must master the vernacular languages. He insisted that preaching through an interpreter was not missionary work. And thirdly, in relation to this, he stressed the importance of giving people the Scriptures in their own language as early as possible. The Bible possessed a 'living energy'.

Venn felt that education was basic to missionary work. From the very beginning the Church Missionary Society set as a goal the training of an indigenous leadership. In 1846, writing to teachers in Sierra Leone, he said: 'It has been our constant aim and prayer that we might be enabled to train up a body of native teachers to whom we may turn over the pastoral charge of those of your countrymen who have embraced the gospel of Christ.' He saw the unique task of the Society as pioneering rather than pastoring. In all his statements we find the principles of native agency, education, self-reliance, and continuous advance intertwined.

Venn was concerned to inculcate self-reliance rather than dependence. 'Do not let them lean too much on the Society,' he wrote. 'Draw out their native resources. Let them feel their own powers and responsibilities.' This admonition was given as much for the benefit of the missionary as for the young church. The missionary was too inclined to take the lead. Venn always insisted that 'prompting to self-action is more important than inducing people to follow a leader'.

In a paternalistic age, which assumed Western nations were trustees of the welfare of the rest of the world, Venn saw how this attitude inhibited self-respect and self-reliance in the young church. He recognised that self-respect and dignity cannot be built through subjugation. He was always on guard against tendencies in missionary activity to Westernise young people because this would destroy pride in their own culture. Writing to an African missionary Venn admonished him to 'let all European habits, European tastes, European ideas, be left behind you. Let no other change be visible in your tone of mind or behaviour than that of a growth in grace and in the knowledge and love of God.'

3 July

Thomas

Apostle

Thomas is mentioned among the number of the apostles in the Gospels of Matthew, Mark and Luke; but it is in John's Gospel that his significance is revealed. Firstly, he is heard encouraging the other disciples to go to Judea with Jesus; then, not knowing what Jesus meant when he talked about where he was to go elicited the answer that Jesus was himself the Way. But probably most famously he was the apostle notably unconvinced by reports of the resurrection of Jesus, causing Jesus to show him the marks in his hands and feet and side. Thomas then proclaims the words that have been described as the great climax to John's Gospel by saying to Jesus, 'My Lord and my God!'

A Reading from a homily of Gregory the Great

'Thomas, called the Twin, who was one of the twelve, was not with them when Jesus came.' Thomas was the only disciple missing. When he returned and heard what had happened, he refused to believe what he heard. The Lord came again and offered his side to his sceptical disciple to touch. He showed his hands; and by showing the scars of his wounds he healed the wound of Thomas' unbelief.

What conclusion, dear sisters and brothers, do you draw from this? Do you think it was by chance that this chosen disciple was absent? Or that on his return he heard, that hearing he doubted, that doubting he touched, and touching he believed? This did not happen by chance, but by the providence of God. Divine mercy brought it about most wonderfully, so that when that doubting disciple touched his Master's wounded flesh he healed the wound of our unbelief as well as his own. Thomas' scepticism was more advantageous to us than was the faith of the other disciples who believed. When he was led to faith by actually touching Jesus, our hearts were relieved of all doubt, for our faith is made whole.

After his resurrection Jesus allowed this disciple to doubt, and he did not desert him in his doubt. He became a witness to the reality of the resurrection. Thomas touched him and cried out: 'My Lord and my God.' Jesus said to him: 'Because you have seen me, Thomas, you have believed.' When the apostle Paul says that 'faith is the guarantee of the blessings that we hope for, the proof of the realities that are unseen', it is clear that faith provides the proof of those things that are not evident; visible things do not require faith, they command recognition. Why, when Thomas saw and touched him, did Jesus say: 'Because you have seen me, you have believed'? What Thomas saw was one thing; what he believed, was another. A mortal could not have seen God. Thomas saw a human being, but by his words, 'My Lord and my God', he acknowledged his divinity. It was by seeing that he believed. He recognised the reality of the man and testified that he was the invisible God.

Let us rejoice at what follows: 'Blessed are they who have not seen and have believed.' This expression makes special reference to us for we have not seen him in the flesh but know him in the mind. The reference is for us, but only if we follow up our faith with good works. Those who give expression to their faith are the genuine believers.

4 July

Peblig

Abbot, fourth century

Tradition has it that Peblig was the son of the would-be Roman Emperor Macsen Wledig (Magnus Maximus) and his wife Elen or Helen. Macsen left Britain in 383 at the start of an ultimately unsuccessful attempt to seize the throne of the Western Empire. Sulpicius Severus describes Macsen's wife as a devoted disciple of Martin, the ascetic Bishop of Tours. If Peblig was indeed her son he may have embraced some of Martin's teachings and practices. Peblig (the Welsh form of Publicius) is remembered as the founder of the Church of Llanbeblig, within the walls of the Roman settlement of Segontium near the later Caernarfon. He seems to have played an important part in ensuring the survival of Christianity in that area of Wales in the troubled period during and after the withdrawal of the Roman legions.

A Reading from *The Welsh and their Religion* by Glanmor Williams

Christianity was first introduced into Wales before the Welsh, as a separate people, can properly be said to exist. It was brought by anonymous Roman traders and soldiers when Britain was still a remote province of the Empire. During the era of imperial rule it remained very much a religion of the towns and civilian settlements, of which there were relatively few in Wales.

In the course of the two or three hundred years following the end of Roman rule, from the fifth to about the eighth century, the inhabitants of Wales, Celtic in speech and culture, came to be cut off from their fellows elsewhere in northern and south-western Britain as a result of Anglo-Saxon intrusions. It was at this time that they began to envisage themselves, however dimly and uncertainly in the early stages, as a separate people. In the process, they underwent a more thorough conversion to Christianity which left a profound impact on them for centuries afterwards. This resulted from the activities of the 'Celtic saints', who worked among them during these formative centuries of their history.

These 'saints' were mostly natives of Wales; enthusiastic, peripatetic evangelizers, mainly monks, some of whom were associated with a number of lands, all of which then spoke Celtic languages – Ireland, western Scotland and the Isles, the Isle of Man, parts of northern England, Wales, Cornwall, and Brittany – most of which we still think of as the Celtic countries and regions. It was the impetus given by these monks as itinerant missionaries and preachers which did a great deal to strengthen and extend Christian belief and worship among the population of Wales. They not only inherited the earlier Christian tradition from Roman Britain but were also candescently inspired by the infusion into their midst of the ascetic ideals of eastern Christianity, which spread into Britain via France.

Their ranks may also have been augmented by the arrival among them of Christian refugees moving westward from those parts of Britain which were coming under pressure from pagan Anglo-Saxons. Indeed, one of the most powerful incentives inducing the Britons to identify themselves with the Christian faith may have been the way in which it distinguished them from their hated enemies. Certainly, there survived among them long afterwards an intense awareness of what they believed to be their association with *Romanitas*; their Christian superiority over the pagan and barbarian milieu of the Anglo-Saxons.

6 July

Palladius

Bishop, *c*.450

According to tradition, Palladius, a deacon at Rome but probably a native of Gaul, urged Pope Celestine to send Bishop Germanus of Auxerre to the British Isles to combat the Pelagian heresy. He was himself sent as bishop two years later in 431 to continue this work. He landed in Ireland before the beginning of Patrick's mission. He appears to have been expelled from Ireland after a short time. He continued his work in Scotland where his name is linked with Airthrey near Stirling, with which Serf, possibly a disciple of his, is also associated. He is also linked with Fordoun in the Mearns, where he is said to have died. He is thought to have been the teacher of Ternan.

A Reading from the treatise *Concerning Heresie*s by Augustine

The Pelagian heresy, at this current time the most recent of heresies to have emerged, owes its rise to a monk called Pelagius. He and his followers are opponents of the grace of God inasmuch as they suggest that we can achieve the commandments of God without recourse to his grace. If this were true, why should God ever have said, 'Without me, you can do nothing'?

After some time teaching this doctrine, Pelagius was accused of ascribing nothing to the grace of God. He admitted the charge. Indeed, in his teaching not only did he put grace before free will, but by suggesting that the function of grace was merely to assist our free will in accomplishing what we are commanded by God, he was subtly supplanting grace. By saying that with grace we 'are able the more easily' to fulfil the commandments of God, he implied that it is possible (albeit harder) for us to do so without grace.

The grace of God without which we cannot do anything that is good, they say consists simply in the unfettered exercise of our free will which is part of our human nature created by God. God (they say) is merely in the role of our assistant: he has given us his law and doctrine in order that we can learn what to do and what to hope for – rather than through the gift of his Spirit, we are able to bring to good effect what we have learned ought to be done.

They teach that divine knowledge is given to us, dispelling human ignorance, but then deny the love that is given to us whereby we may lead a religious life. But as Paul reminds us, knowledge without love puffs up. They teach that whereas knowledge is the gift of God, love is not. And in so doing they are emptying the prayers of the Church of meaning, whether prayer for the unbelieving and those who refuse the doctrine of God that they may return to God; or for the faithful that their faith may be increased and that they may persevere. Such things, they argue, we do not receive from God, but from ourselves; and the grace of God whereby we are delivered from irreligion, is given to us according to our merits.

At his trial before the bishops in Palestine, Pelagius was confronted with his teachings. Initially, through fear of being condemned, he admitted his error; but in his subsequent writings, it is clear that he continued to teach them. He even went so far as to suggest that that it is possible for the righteous to live free from sin, and that the Church of Christ in this mortal life can become so perfect as to be 'without spot or stain'. If this were so, why is it that the Church of Christ throughout the world cries out to God, 'Forgive us our debts'?

6 July

Moninne of Killeavy

Abbess, *c.*518

Sometimes called Darerca or Bline, Moninne founded a small monastery for women (eight virgins and one widow, according to one tradition). She continued in Killeavy, not far from Newry, the spirit of the teaching and pastoral concern of Patrick and Brigid. She died on this day in about the year 518.

A Reading from a letter of Sulpicius Severus *'In praise of virginity'*

Of all the heavenly gifts of God, what blessings are accorded to holy virginity! Besides the testimony of scripture, we also learn from the practice of the Church that a particular merit belongs to those who consecrate themselves to God in this way. For while the whole people of God receive equal gifts of grace, and all rejoice in the blessings of the sacraments, those who are virgins possess something over and above the rest, since they have been chosen by the Holy Spirit out of the holy and unstained company of the Church to be presented by the bishop at the altar of God as holy and pure sacrifices, on account of their voluntary dedication. Theirs is a true sacrifice worthy of God because it represents the precious self-offering of one made in the image of God, and nothing delights God more. I think the apostle Paul was referring to this kind of sacrifice when he wrote, 'Now I entreat you brothers and sisters, by the mercy of God, to present your bodies a living sacrifice, holy and acceptable to God.' Virginity possesses both that which others have and that which they have not; it obtains both common and special grace, and rejoices (so to speak) in its own special privilege of consecration.

The authority of the Church also permits us to style virgins as 'brides of Christ'. After the manner of brides, the Church veils those whom it consecrates to the Lord, openly proclaiming those who have turned their back on physical fellowship as possessing a spiritual marriage. They are worthily united to God (in a spiritual way), in accordance with the analogy of marriage, who, for love of God, set aside human alliances. In their case, that saying of the apostle finds its fullest expression: 'Those who are joined to the Lord, are of one spirit.'

For it is a great and a divine gift to be able to transcend our bodily nature, to set aside luxury and by strength of mind to extinguish the flame of sexual desire which ignites in our youth, to live in a way counter to the general practice of the human race, to despise the comfort of marriage, to turn your back on the delights derived from children, and to regard as nothing all that is acknowledged as advantageous in this life in hope of future blessedness. This, as I have said, is a great and admirable virtue, and therefore it is not without reason destined for a great reward in proportion to the greatness of the offering.

6 July

Thomas More and John Fisher

Reformation Martyrs, 1535

Note: In Wales, only Thomas More is commemorated.

Born in London in 1478, Thomas More studied classics and law, being called to the Bar when he was twenty-three years old. His clear honesty and integrity impressed Henry VIII and he appointed Thomas as his Chancellor. He supported the king in his efforts to reform the clergy but disagreed over Henry's disputes with the papacy, caused by the king's desire to annul his marriage to Catherine of Aragon and to find another queen who might provide him with a male heir. Henry could stand no such act of defiance and imprisoned his Chancellor in the hope that he would renege. Thomas refused to take the Oath of the Act of Succession, which declared the king to be the only protector and supreme head of the Church in England, and was executed for treason on this day in 1535, declaring that he died 'the king's good servant but God's first'.

John Fisher was Thomas More's close friend and ally. A brilliant academic, he had substantially reformed the life of the University of Cambridge, through the wealth and influence of his patron, Lady Margaret Beaufort, the mother of Henry VII. He was made Bishop of Rochester and proved himself to be a good pastor to his small diocese. As with Thomas, Henry VIII much admired him at first, but when he opposed the king their relationship deteriorated. Aged sixty-six and in indifferent health, he nevertheless endured the trauma of imprisonment in the Tower of London. He was executed just two weeks before Thomas on 22 June 1535.

A Reading from a letter of Thomas More to his daughter, Margaret Roper, written from the Tower of London in 1534

That you fear your own frailty Margaret, I do not disapprove. God give us both the grace to despair of our own self, and wholly to depend and hang upon the hope and strength of God. The blessed apostle Saint Paul found such strength in himself that in his temptation he was thrice to call and cry out to God to take that temptation from him. And yet attained he not his prayer in the manner he required. Of himself never so feeble and faint was he, nor never so likely to fall, yet the grace of God was sufficient to keep him up and make him stand. The more weak that man is, the more is the strength of God in his safeguard declared.

Surely, Meg, a fainter heart than thy frail father hath, canst you not have. And yet I verily trust in the great mercy of God, that he shall of his goodness so stay me with his holy hand that he shall not finally suffer me to fall wretchedly from his favour. And the like trust (dear daughter) in his high goodness I verily conceive of you. And so much the more, in that there is neither of us both, but that if we call his benefits to mind and give him oft thanks for them, we may find tokens many, to give us good hope for all our manifold offences toward him; and that his great mercy, when we will heartily call therefore, shall not be withdrawn from us.

And verily, my dear daughter, in this is my great comfort, that albeit I am of nature so shrinking from pain that I am almost afeard of a cut on my finger, yet in all the agonies that I have had, whereof before my coming hither (as I have showed you ere this) I have had neither small nor few, with heavy fearful heart, forecasting all such perils and painful deaths, as by any manner of possibility might after fall unto me, and in such thought lain long restless and waking, while my wife had thought I was asleep; yet in any such fear and heavy pensiveness (I thank the mighty mercy of God) I never in my mind intended to consent that I would for the enduring of the uttermost do any such thing as I should in mine own conscience (for with other men's consciences I am not a man meet to take upon me to meddle) think to be to myself, such as should damnably cast me in the displeasure of God.

And this is the least point that any man may with his salvation come to, as far as I can see, and is bounden if he see peril to examine his conscience surely by learning and by good counsel and be sure that his conscience be such as it may stand with his salvation, or else reform it. And if the matter be such as both the parties may stand with salvation, then on whither side his conscience fall, he is safe enough before God. But that mine own may stand with my own salvation, thereof I thank our Lord I am very sure. I beseech our Lord bring all parts to his bliss.

It is now, my good daughter, late. And therefore thus I commend you to the Holy Trinity, to guide you, comfort you and direct you with his Holy Spirit, and all ours and my wife with all my children and all our other friends.

alternative reading

A Reading from a treatise *The Ways to Perfect Religion,* written in the Tower of London by John Fisher for his sister, Elizabeth, in 1535, shortly before his execution

Sister Elizabeth, gladly I would write unto you something that might be to the health of your soul and furtherance of it in holy religion. But well I know that without some fervour in the love of Christ, religion cannot be to you savoury, nor any work of goodness can be delectable, but every virtuous deed shall seem laborious and painful. For love maketh every work appear easy and pleasant, though it be right displeasant of itself.

The consideration that you should call well to remembrance is that in our Saviour Christ, the Son of God, is no deformity, for he is all goodly and surmounteth all others in goodliness. And therefore of him the prophet David affirmeth in this manner: 'He is goodly before the children of men.' And of truth, much goodly must he needs be that hath made so many goodly creatures. Behold the rose, the lily, the violet; behold the peacocks, the pheasant, the popinjay; behold all the other creatures of this world: all these were of his making, all their beauty and goodliness of him they received it. Wherefore this goodliness describeth that he himself must needs of necessity be very goodly and beautiful. And for that in the Book of Canticles, the Spouse describeth his goodliness saying: 'He that I love is all white and red, chosen out of thousands.' And this beauty and goodliness is not mortal; it cannot fade nor perish as doth the goodliness of other men, which like a flower today is fresh and lovely, and tomorrow with a little sickness is withered and vanishes away.

And yet it is sensible to the goodliness of man's nature, for the which also Christ is more naturally to be beloved of many. For likeness is the ground of love: like always doth covet like; and the nearer in likeness that any person be, the sooner they may be knit together in love. The same likeness he hath and you have, like body and like soul, touching his manhood, your soul is also like unto him in his Godhead: for after the image and similitude of it your soul is made.

Furthermore, of his might and power you may be likewise certain. He made this world by the only commandment of his mouth, and gave to the herbs and all other creatures their virtue, and might that they have. And may also by his power save and damn creatures either to lift them up in body and soul into heaven above, or else to throw them down into ever-during pains of hell.

If you doubt of his wisdom, then behold all this world: how the heavens are apparelled with stars, the air with fowls, the water with fishes, the earth with herbs, trees and beasts; how the stars be clad with light, the fowls with feathers, the fish with scales, the beasts with hair, herbs and trees with leaves, and flowers with scent, wherein doth well appear a great and marvellous wisdom of him that made them.

Finally, his good and gentle manner is all full of pleasure and comfort so kind, so friendly, so liberal and beneficious, so piteous and merciful, so ready in all opportunities, so mindful and circumspect, so dulcet and sweet in communication. For as scripture saith 'His manners are sweet and pleasant, and his conversation hath no bitterness, and his company hath no loathsomeness.'

7 July

Boisil of Melrose

Religious, *c.*642

Boisil, or Boswell, became Abbot of the Abbey of Melrose which Aidan had founded. Bede describes him as a man of great virtue. Among his disciples were Cuthbert and Egbert. He died around the year 642.

A Reading from *A History of the English Church and People* by the Venerable Bede

In the year of his death, King Egfrid appointed as Bishop of Lindisfarne the holy and venerable Cuthbert, who for many years had lived a solitary life of great self-mastery of mind and body on the tiny island known as Farne, which lies in the ocean about nine miles from the church. From his earliest boyhood he had always longed to enter the religious life, and as soon as he became a youth was clothed and professed as a monk.

He first entered the monastery of Melrose on the banks of the River Tweed, then ruled by Abbot Eata, the gentlest and simplest of men, who later became Bishop of the church of Hexham or Lindisfarne. The prior of Melrose was Boisil, a priest of great virtues and prophetic spirit. Cuthbert humbly submitted himself to the direction of Boisil, who gave him instruction in the Scriptures and showed him an example of holy life. When Boisil departed to our Lord, Cuthbert was appointed prior in his place, and trained many men in monastic life with masterly authority and by his personal example. It was God's servant Boisil who, with prophetic insight, had foretold all that was to happen to Cuthbert, and had said that one day he would become a bishop.

8 July

Kilian

Bishop & Martyr, 689

Kilian from County Cavan was a missionary to Franconia and rebuilt the Church in Baden and Bavaria. Many pre-Reformation cathedrals in Germany and Austria were dedicated in honour of Kilian, pre-eminent among them being that at Würzburg, where with two companions he was murdered on this day in the year 689.

A Reading from a sermon of Augustine

When we talk of death, we speak in terms of the body and the soul. In one sense, the soul cannot die, but in another it can. It cannot die inasmuch as the awareness of itself endures; yet it can die if it loses God. For just as the soul is the life of the body, so God is the life of the soul. The body perishes when the soul that is its life departs: the soul perishes when God casts it away. So lest God cast our souls away, let us always live in faith. Only so will we not fear to die for God, and not die abandoned by God.

The death of the body will always remain a fear. And yet Christ the Lord has made his martyrs a counter-balance to our fear. Why worry about the safety of limbs when we have been reassured that the hairs on our head are secure? Does not Scripture say that 'the very hairs on your head are numbered'? Why should our human frailty cause us to be so frightened when the truth has spoken thus?

Blessed indeed then, are the saints whose memory we commemorate on the day of their passion. In surrendering their security in this world, they received an eternal crown and immortality without end. As we gather to remember them in prayer, their example sends us messages of encouragement. When we hear how the martyrs suffered, we rejoice and glorify God in them. We do not grieve because they died. If they had not died, do you think they would still be alive today? Their confession of faith served to consummate what sickness would one day also have brought about.

Therefore, my dear friends, let us rejoice in their commemoration. Let us pray to God that we may follow in the steps of his martyrs. They were mortal like you: their manner of birth no different from yours. They had bodies no different from your own. We are all descended from Adam: we should all seek to return to Christ.

Honour the martyrs; praise, love, preach and honour them. But remember, worship only the God of the martyrs.

11 July

Benedict of Nursia

Abbot of Monte Cassino, Father of Western Monasticism, Patron of Europe, *c.*550

Note: See also The Passing of Benedict on 21 March.

Benedict was born in Nursia, in central Italy, around the year 480. As a young man he was sent to study in Rome, but appalled by the corruption in society, he withdrew to live as a hermit at Subiaco. He quickly attracted disciples and began to establish small monasteries in the neighbourhood. Around the year 525, a disaffected faction tried to poison him, so Benedict moved south to Monte Cassino with a band of monks loyal to him. Later in life Benedict wrote his 'Rule for Monks', based on his own experience of fallible people striving to live out the gospel. He never intended to found an 'Order' as such, but his Rule proved to be so good and well-balanced that it was disseminated widely, becoming in time the model for all Western monasticism. Benedict died at Monte Cassino in about the year 550.

A Reading from the prologue to his *Rule for Monks* by Benedict of Nursia

Listen carefully, my son, to the instructions of your teacher, and attend with the ear of your heart to the advice of a loving father. Welcome it and faithfully put it into practice; so that through the labour of obedience you may return to the God from whom you have drifted through the sloth of disobedience. To you, then, whomever you may be, are my words addressed, that renouncing your own will, and taking up the strong and glorious weapons of obedience, you may do battle in the service of Christ the Lord, our true King.

First of all, whenever you begin a good work, you must pray to God most urgently to bring it to perfection, so that he who has delighted to count us his children, may never be saddened by our evil lives. For we must serve God with the gifts he has given us that he may never as an angry father disinherit us or like some dreaded master, enraged by our sins, hand us over to eternal punishment as worthless servants who have refused to follow him in the way to glory.

Let us then at last arouse ourselves! For the Scriptures challenge us to do so in these words: 'Now is the time for us to rise from sleep.' Let us open wide our eyes to the light that transfigures, and unstop our ears to the sound of God's voice which daily cries out to us: 'O that today you would listen to his voice and harden not your hearts.' And again as Scripture says: 'You that have ears to hear, listen to what the Spirit is saying to the churches.' And what is the Spirit saying? 'Come, my children, listen to me and I will teach you the fear of the Lord.' 'Run while you have the light of life, lest the darkness of death overtake you.'

Dear friends, what can be more delightful than this voice of the Lord inviting us? Behold, in his loving mercy, the Lord is showing us the way of life. Clothed then with faith and the performance of good works, and with the gospel as our guide, let us set out on this way of life that we may deserve to see the God 'who is calling us in his kingdom'.

We propose to establish a school of the Lord's service. In founding this we hope that we shall not make rules that are harsh or burdensome. But if, for the good of all concerned, for the correction of faults or the preservation of charity, there be some strictness of discipline, do not be immediately daunted and run away from the way that leads to salvation. Its entrance is inevitably narrow. But as we progress in this way of life and in faith, our hearts will be enlarged, and we shall run in the way of God's commandments with an inexpressible delight of love. Let us then never swerve from his instructions but rather persevere in God's teaching in the monastery until death. Thus shall we share by patience in the sufferings of Christ, and so deserve to share in his kingdom. Amen.

12 July

Drostan (Tristan) of Deer

Abbot, *c.*600

Little is known of Drostan (Tristan). He is said to have been of royal descent, a nephew or companion of Columba, with whom he visited Buchan, and who left him in charge of the new monastic foundation at Deer (Aberdeenshire); but his name suggests he was of Pictish origin. His name occurs in many dedications in the north-east of Scotland. He seems also to have been venerated in Galloway and Glen Urquhart.

A Reading from the *Conferences* of John Cassian

My sons, when a person wishes to acquire the skills of a particular art he needs to devote all possible care and attention to the activities characteristic of his chosen profession. He must observe the precepts and, indeed, the advice of the most successful practitioners of this work or of this way of knowledge. Otherwise he will be dealing in empty dreams. One does not come to resemble those whose hard work and zeal one declines to imitate.

I have known some people who have come to our monastery in the past from where you live, and who have travelled round countless monasteries, and all for the sake of acquiring knowledge. But it never occurred to them to practise the rules or customs they encountered which were the objective of their travels. Nor would they withdraw into a cell where they could try to practise what they had seen and heard. Instead, they stuck to their old habits and practices, just as they had left their own provinces not for the sake of their own progress, but to avoid the presence of poverty. Not only were they unable to acquire any learning, but they could not even stay here because of the sheer stubbornness of their disposition. They would make no changes in their habits of fasting, in the order in which they recited the psalms, or even in the clothes they wore. What else could we think except that they had come here solely for the purpose of getting fed?

Now I believe that it is for the sake of God that you have come here to our monastery to get to know us. You must, therefore, abandon all those teachings which marked your beginning as monks. You must take to yourselves, completely and humbly, all the practices and teachings of our old masters in the monastic life. It may be that a moment will come when you fail to grasp the deep meaning of a certain statement or mode of conduct. Do not be put off, and do not fail to conform. Those seeking profit only, and struggling to imitate faithfully what they have seen their masters doing and saying, and have not argued endlessly about them, these will receive a knowledge of everything, even while they are still undergoing the experience. But the man who teaches himself by engaging in arguments will never reach the truth.

14 July

John Keble

Priest, Tractarian, Poet, 1866

Note: In Scotland, John Keble is commemorated on 29 March.

Born in 1792, the son of a priest, John Keble showed early brilliance as a scholar, becoming a Fellow of Oriel College, Oxford, at the age of nineteen, a few years before his ordination. He won great praise for his collection of poems, The Christian Year, issued in 1827, and was elected Professor of Poetry in Oxford in 1831. A leader of the Tractarian movement, which protested at the threats to the Church from liberal developments in both politics and theology, he nevertheless did not seek preferment and in 1836 became a parish priest near Winchester, a position he held until his death in 1866. He continued to write scholarly books and was praised for his character and spiritual counsel. Yet he is still best remembered for the Assize Sermon 'On National Apostasy' he preached in Oxford, considered by some the beginning of the Oxford Movement, delivered on this day in the year 1833.

A Reading from the *Assize Sermon* 'On National Apostasy' preached by John Keble in the University Church of Saint Mary the Virgin, Oxford, 14 July 1833

What are the symptoms by which one may judge most fairly, whether or not a nation is becoming alienated from God and Christ?

The case is at least possible of a nation, having for centuries acknowledged as an essential part of its theory of government, that as a Christian nation, she is also a part of Christ's Church, and bound in all her legislation and policy, by the fundamental rules of that Church – the case is, I say, conceivable, of a government and people so constituted, deliberately throwing off the restraint which in many respects such a principle would impose on them, disavowing the principle itself; and that, on the plea that other states, as flourishing or more so in regard of wealth and dominion, do well enough without it.

What should be the tenor of their conduct, who find themselves cast on such times of decay and danger? How may a man best reconcile his allegiance to God and his Church with his duty to his country, that country which now by the supposition is fast becoming hostile to the Church, and cannot therefore long be the friend of God?

Should it ever happen (which God avert, but we cannot shut our eyes to the danger) that the Apostolical Church should be forsaken, degraded, nay trampled on and despoiled by the State and people of England, I cannot conceive of a kinder wish for her, on the part of her most affectionate and dutiful children, than that she may consistently act in the spirit of that most noble sentence of the prophet Samuel: 'God forbid that I should sin against the Lord in ceasing to pray for you: but I will teach you the good and the right way.' In speaking of the Church, I mean, of course, the laity as well as the clergy in their three orders – the whole body of Christians united, according to the will of Jesus Christ, under the successors of the apostles.

The Church would, first of all, have to be constant in intercession. No despiteful usage, no persecution, could warrant her in ceasing to pray, as did her first fathers and patterns, for the State and all who are in authority. That duty once well and cordially performed, all other duties are secured.

Secondly, remonstrance – calm, distinct, and persevering, in public and in private, direct and indirect, by word, look and demeanour, is the unequivocal duty of every Christian, according to his opportunities when the Church's landmarks are being broken down.

Finally, the surest way to uphold or restore our endangered Church, will be for each of her anxious children, in his own place and station, to resign himself more thoroughly to his God and Saviour in those duties, public and private, which are not immediately affected by the emergencies of the moment: the daily and hourly duties, I mean, of piety, purity, charity and justice. It will be no unworthy principle, if any man be more circumspect in his behaviour, more watchful and fearful of himself, more earnest in his petitions for spiritual aid, from a dread of disparaging the holy name of the English Church, in her hour of peril, by his own personal fault or negligence.

alternative reading

A Reading from a sermon of John Keble preached at Coln St Aldwyn's, Gloucestershire, in 1829

The thing which hinders us from seeing and feeling things as we ought to do I apprehend to be nothing else than our great carelessness about our Christian calling; our want of faith in the blessings which Jesus Christ provided for us when he received us into his Church. If we had anything like a worthy notion of our near relation to God, adopted as we are by baptism to be his own children in Christ Jesus, we should then understand how very near the same adoption brings us to one another.

But whether we choose to recollect it or no, certain it is that we are all brethren, and as brethren are bound to love and serve one another. By which one consideration, if men would but bear it in mind, a whole host of unkindly thoughts and expressions would at once be silenced and done away with.

Saint Paul's brotherly love, the love he expressed and taught in his epistles, was not merely that he watched for every opportunity of doing good to the Christians among whom he lived; he found leisure to extend his brotherly care and charity to those who were far out of his reach, whom he had never seen, and very likely never might see. Surely we ought to be ashamed, when we compare our brotherly love with his; we who think it a great matter to take some small care of the spiritual good of our nearest relations or children.

And as the term 'brotherly love one towards another', shows us how far our kindness to our fellow-Christians should extend, so another expression of Saint Paul shows us in what manner that kindness should be exercised. 'Be kindly affectioned one to another with brotherly love.' The word literally and properly means, 'delighting' in brotherly love, as in an exercise of natural affection; as a mother for instance, delights in showing fondness to her infant or a brother to his sister, or a dutiful child to a tender parent. The love and affection in each of these cases, comes as it were naturally of itself. A mother does not want to be taught that she is to love, and nurse, and watch her child. God has put an instinct into her heart, a silent teacher, which inclines her to perform those duties for her own pleasure. So will brotherly love – love unfeigned towards the meanest of our fellow Christians – arise naturally and without an express call, in the mind of every sincere and practical believer in Jesus Christ. He will be restless and uneasy in mind till he has done, to all within his reach, all the good which lies in his power. His labour will always be fresh, always beginning; and yet he is never over-weary of it, because it is a labour of love.

15 July

Swithun

Bishop of Winchester, *c.*862

Swithun was Bishop of Winchester in the ninth century, though little is known of his life. He was bishop for ten years and appears to have been the trusted adviser of King Egbert of Wessex. According to William of Malmesbury, at the end of his life Swithun 'commanded that his body should be buried outside the church, where it would be trodden by the feet of passers-by and made wet by the rain that falls from heaven'. When he died on 2 July 862 his request was fulfilled. However, when a new cathedral was being built, Ethelwold, the new bishop, decided to move Swithun's remains into a shrine in the cathedral, despite dire warnings that to move the bones would bring about terrible storms. He was duly translated on this day in the year 971, and though many cures were claimed and other miracles observed it apparently rained for forty days, as forecast. Thus the feast day of Swithun became synonymous with long, summer storms, rather than as an occasion for celebrating Christian simplicity and holiness.

A Reading from a sermon of Caesarius of Arles

Ever since the day when the burden of episcopacy was placed on my shoulders, a burden to which it is so difficult to do justice, I have been troubled by the anxieties that go hand in hand with the honour. Today, which is the anniversary of my ordination to the episcopate, I am troubled by these concerns more than ever, for I am reminded once again of my duties, but also I get the feeling that I have only just begun.

What is it that I fear in being a bishop, if not that I take more pleasure in the dangers of the honour than in the fruits that go with your salvation? I ask for the help of your prayers that the Lord may help me bear this burden. Indeed, when you are praying for me, you are praying for yourselves. For what is this burden that I carry if not yourselves? Pray then, just as I pray, that you will not become too heavy for me to bear. Our Lord Jesus Christ would never speak of a burden as light unless he were prepared to assist in carrying it. But you too should lift me up, so that in obedience to the commandment of the apostle Paul, we may 'bear one another's burdens, and so fulfil the Law of Christ'.

If Christ does not help me with this burden, I will surely fall beneath its weight. If he does not support me, I will sink to the ground. I am so afraid of what I am called to be for you, and yet I am comforted by what I am with you. To you I must be a bishop, and with you I am a Christian. The former I have from the office I hold, the latter I have from grace. One is a source of danger, the other a source of salvation. I am tossed about by the storms of this office as though I were adrift on the open sea. But when I recall by whose blood we have been redeemed, I discover a safe harbour of tranquillity. After struggling in the performance of my duties, I find rest in our common well-being. If, therefore, I find more joy in having been redeemed with you than in having been placed over you, I shall be (as the Lord has commanded) all the more willingly your servant.

We fail as pastors – and God forbid that we should – because of our failings. We succeed as pastors – and God helps us to this goal – only by his grace. It for this reason, my dear friends, that 'we entreat you not to receive the grace of God in vain'. Make my ministry among you fruitful.

Let us pray then, that my episcopate may bear fruit both for you and for me. It will be fruitful for me if I can instruct you about what needs to be done, and it will be fruitful for you if you carry out what you learn from me. If, in the perfect love of God, you pray unceasingly for me and I pray unceasingly for you, then, with the help of God, we shall together achieve eternal blessedness.

15 July

Bonaventure

Friar, Bishop, Teacher of the Faith, 1274

Born at Bagnoreggio in Italy in about the year 1218, Bonaventure became a Franciscan Friar in 1243 and his intellectual ability was soon recognized by his Order and by the Church. At the age of thirty-six he was elected Minister General of the Franciscans and virtually re-founded the Order, giving it a stability in training and administration previously unknown. He upheld all the teachings of Saint Francis except in the founder's attitude to study, since Francis felt the Order should possess no books. He clearly saw, with Francis, that the rôle of the Friars was to support the Church through its contemporary structures rather than to be an instrument for reform. He also believed that the best conversions came from the good example of those anxious to renew the Church, rather than by haranguing or passing laws. He was appointed a cardinal-bishop against his will, and kept the papal messengers waiting while he finished the washing up. He brought about a temporary reunion of the Churches in the East and the West but, before it was repudiated, he died on this day at Lyons in the year 1274.

A Reading from the treatise *The Soul's Journey into God* by Bonaventure

Christ is the way and the door; Christ is the ladder and the vehicle by which we journey to God, like the mercy-seat placed above the ark of God, and the mystery hidden from eternity. Whoever turns to face fully the mercy-seat, and with faith, hope and love, with wonder, devotion and admiration, with appreciation, praise and joy beholds Christ hanging upon the cross, such a one makes the Pasch, that is, his Passover with Christ.

By the staff of the cross he passes over the Red Sea, journeying from Egypt into the desert, there to taste the hidden manna. He will lie with Christ in the tomb, as if dead to the world, but will experience (as far as is possible in this pilgrim life) what was said on the cross to the thief who aligned himself with Christ: 'Today you shall be with me in paradise.'

In this Passover, if it is to be complete, it is vital that all intellectual activity be left behind, and that the height of our affections be totally transferred and transformed into God. This process is highly mystical and hidden, and no one knows it is happening except the person who has undergone it. No one understands it except the person who longs for it, and no one longs for it except they be penetrated to the very marrow of their being by the fire of the Holy Spirit whom Christ sent into the world. This is why the Apostle Paul says that this mystical wisdom is revealed through the Holy Spirit.

In regard to this transformation, nature can do nothing, and will-power achieve but little. Thus little importance should be attached to intellectual inquiry, but much to the anointing of the Spirit; little importance should be attached to the power of the tongue, but much to inner joy; little importance should be attached to words and writing, but everything to the gift of God, the Holy Spirit.

If you wish to know how this transformation comes about, then ask for grace, not learning; ask to long for it, not merely to understand what is happening; ask for it in prayer too deep for words rather than in diligent reading; ask it of Christ your Spouse, not of a human teacher; ask it of God not mortals; ask it of darkness not clarity. Ask it not of light but of that fire which totally inflames and carries us into God by ecstatic anointing and burning affection. This fire is God and its furnace is in Jerusalem; and it is Christ who kindles it through the burning heat of his passion.

All this can only be grasped by those who echo the words of Job when he said: 'My soul chooses hanging, and my bones death.' For it is clear that those who choose death in this way can see God because it is beyond doubt that 'no mortal can see me and live'. Let us die, then, and enter into the darkness. Let us silence our anxieties, our longings and our fantasies. Only with Christ crucified can we Passover 'out of this world to the Father'. Then with Philip, when the Father is before us, we too will say: 'It is enough for us.' With Paul we too will hear: 'My grace is sufficient for you.' With David we too will rejoice and say: 'My flesh and my heart may fail, but you, O God, are the strength of my heart, and my portion for ever. Blessed be the Lord forever, and let all the people say, Amen, Amen.'

16 July

Osmund

Bishop of Salisbury, 1099

Born the son of a Norman count, Osmund came to England in the wake of William the Conqueror, his mother's half-brother, and was quickly promoted to Chancellor in 1072. Six years later he became Bishop of Salisbury and completed the building of the new cathedral at Old Sarum. He was a scholar and a good administrator but was best loved for his lack of avarice and ambition, traits apparently not common in the new hierarchy of Church and State. He took part in collecting the information for the Domesday Book and was present at Sarum when it was presented to the king in 1086. He is said to have compiled the Sarum Use. Osmund died on 4 December 1099 and his remains were translated to the new cathedral in Salisbury on this day in the year 1457.

A Reading from a homily of Gregory the Great

A person is called a hired hand, and not a shepherd, who provides pasture for God's sheep when motivated by the love of personal gain rather than love of the sheep. He is a hired hand occupying the place of shepherd when he is not concerned for the welfare of those in his care. He desires worldy comforts, and takes pride in his status. He is pastoring the sheep solely for the sake of temporal rewards, and is flattered by the adulation of others. Such are the rewards for which hired hands crave. They have already received payment for their labours, but hereafter, they will be excluded by God from any share in the inheritance of the sheep.

Let it be said that except in very exceptional circumstances, we cannot distinguish a true shepherd from a hired hand. In times of peace and tranquillity, the sheep are guarded by a hired hand with an identical fidelity to that of a shepherd. However, the approach of a wolf is sufficient to expose the motives of each. The wolf descends upon the sheep when any corrupt or predatory person oppresses the faithful and persecutes the poor. Then, the person who had seemed to be a shepherd, but in fact was just a hired hand, immediately abandons the sheep and runs away. Why? because as soon as he senses danger to himself, he is off: he will not stand up to injustice. He runs away – I do not mean necessarily literally – every time he refuses to console his sheep. He runs away every time he takes refuge behind a wall of silence.

Of such people the prophet Ezekiel said: 'You have not confronted the enemy, nor have you repaired a wall for the house of Israel so that it might stand firm in battle on the day of the Lord.' To confront the enemy necessitates upholding rightful liberties in the face of any oppressive force. We stand firm in battle for the house of Israel, raising up a wall around it on the day of the Lord, if with all the strength of justice, we defend the faithful innocent against the injustice of the wicked. Hired hands will never do this, so we can truly say that they run away.

There is also another kind of wolf, the type that ravages the mind, rather than the body. I refer to evil spirits which surround the sheepfold, seeking the death of their souls. Of such Christ says: 'The wolf comes and scatters the sheep.' The wolf comes and the hired hand runs away each time the faithful are tortured by temptation, and their pastor exhibits no concern for them. Souls are perishing while he dallies with worldly endearments.

Our redeemer notes the weaknesses of such false shepherds, and in the face of them he gives us the model which every pastor is called upon to imitate. He says, 'I am the Good Shepherd: I know my sheep, and my sheep know me.' He adds, 'I know my sheep', meaning he truly loves them. Moreover 'they know me', because the sheep will follow those who love them.

18 July

Elizabeth Ferard

First Deaconess of the Church of England, Founder of the Community of St Andrew, 1883

Elizabeth Catherine Ferard was encouraged by Bishop Tait of London to visit deaconess institutions in Germany, notably at Kaiserwerth on the Rhine. Some three years later in November 1861, she and a group of women dedicated themselves 'to minister to the necessities of the Church, as servants in the Church'. On this day in 1862, Elizabeth Ferard received the first deaconess licence from Bishop Tait. She went on to found a community with a dual vocation of being deaconesses and religious sisters, working first in a poor parish in the King's Cross area of London, and then moving to Notting Hill in 1873. When her health failed, she passed on the leadership to others and died on Easter Day in the year 1883.

A Reading from *Of the Deaconess Office in General* written by Elizabeth Ferard and dated 1861

Deaconesses have, according to the apostolical regulations, the office of serving the Christian congregation as Phoebe served the Church at Cenchrea. To them is committed the care of the sick, the poor, the education of young children, and generally the help of the needy of whatever kind. And also it is their office to be helpers, either directly or indirectly, to the ministers of the Church.

They must, therefore, have the qualities which the Apostle requires from deacons (Acts 6:8). They must first, be of good report; and second, be full of faith and good works.

Deaconesses who desire to fulfil their calling in a Christian spirit, must above all remember that they are to tend and to teach the poor, the sick and children as *servers* according to the signification of their name of 'deaconess': first, as servants of the Lord Jesus; second, as servants of the poor and needy for Christ's sake; and third, as servants of one another.

A great privilege which deaconesses possess above other Christians is, that belonging to a Sisterhood, they associate with believers like minded with themselves, and are not exposed to the dangers of those who, living amongst unbelievers, may be tempted to luke-warmness, in the love of God or their neighbour, and thus be in danger of making shipwreck of faith and a good conscience.

It is for this reason that deaconesses employed in a parish, or in the training and education of children, are where practicable sent out in companies of at least two, that thus one sister may have the help and support of a fellow-worker.

alternative reading

A Reading from the *Form of Service for the Admission of Deaconesses into the Community*, recorded by the Chaplain in his manuscript notebook

Dearly beloved, we are met together to admit into the Community of the London Diocesan Deaconess Institution these (two) women, who have been lately set apart by the Bishop for the Office of Deaconess in the Church. There are various advantages to be derived from the banding together of Deaconesses in an organised Society. The cause itself is strengthened by a concentration of the members, and the members themselves must receive great benefit from sisterly conference, counsel and sympathy, from mutual encouragement in good works, and from the holy concert and combination in resisting the snares and temptations of human life. We ask prayers for these Deaconesses, and for the Society, that it may be by God's blessing extended and quickened with fresh zeal and activity in the service of our Lord and Master Jesus Christ.

18 July

Elizabeth of Russia

Religious and Martyr, 1918

Elizabeth of Hesse-Darmstadt was born in 1864 and embraced Russian Orthodoxy upon her marriage to Grand Duke Sergei, the fifth son of the Tsar of Russia. In 1905 Sergei was assassinated, and Elizabeth gave away her jewellery, sold her most luxurious possessions, and opened the Martha and Mary home in Moscow, to foster the prayer and charity of devout women. Elizabeth and seventeen women were dedicated as Sisters of Love and Mercy. Their work flourished: soon they opened a hospital and engaged in a variety of philanthropic ventures.

After the 1917 Revolution, amid the terrible persecution of the Church, Elizabeth and two sisters from her convent were arrested and transported to Alapaevsk. On 17 July 1918 the Tsar and his family were shot dead, and the following night Elizabeth, a sister named Varvara, and members of the royal family, were murdered in a mineshaft. In 1984 Elizabeth was recognized as a saint by the Russian Orthodox Church Abroad, and then by the Moscow Patriarchate in 1992.

A Reading from *The holy new martyr: Grand Duchess Elizabeth Feodorovna* by Metropolitan Anastassy

The main task of the grand duchess became the building of a sisterhood in which inner service to God was integrated with active service to one's neighbour in the name of Christ. This was a completely new form of organized charitable church activity, and consequently drew general attention to itself. At its foundation was placed a deep and immutable idea: no one could give to another more than he himself already possessed. We all draw upon God and therefore only in God can we love our neighbour. Natural love so-called or humanism quickly evaporates, replaced by coldness and disappointment, but those who live in Christ can rise to the heights of complete self-denial and lay down their life for their friends. The grand duchess not only wanted to impart to charitable activities the spirit of the Gospel, but to place them under the protection of the Church. Thus she hoped to attract gradually to the Church those levels of Russian society which up until that time had remained largely indifferent to the faith. Highly significant was the very name the grand duchess bestowed upon the institution she established – the Martha and Mary Convent, which name contains within itself the mission, the life of its holy patrons.

The community was intended to be like the home of Lazarus which our Saviour so often visited. The sisters of the convent were called to unite both the high lot of Mary, attending to the eternal word of life, and the service of Martha, to that degree in which they found Christ in the person of his less fortunate brethren. In justifying and explaining her thought, she said that Christ could not judge Martha for showing him hospitality, since the latter was a sign of her love for him. He only cautioned Martha, and in her all women in general, against that excessive fussing and triviality which draw them away from the higher needs of the spirit.

To be not of this world, and at the same time live and act in the world in order to transform it – this was the foundation upon which she desired to establish her convent.

During the course of the last months of 1917 and the beginning of 1918, the Soviet power to everyone's amazement granted the Martha and Mary Convent and its abbess complete freedom to live as they wished and even supported them by supplying essentials. This made the blow even heavier and unexpected for them when on Pascha the grand duchess was suddenly arrested and transported to Ekaterinburg.

However, in the face of captivity and ridicule she did not lose her abiding firmness of spirit. And so it continued until the fateful night of 5th July. On that night together with the other royal captives striving with her and her valiant fellow-struggler Sister Barbara, she was suddenly taken outside the city and apparently buried alive with them in one of the local mine shafts. The results of later excavations there have shown that she strived until the last moment to serve the grand dukes who were severely injured by the fall. Local peasants who carried out the sentence on these people whom they did not know, reported that for a long time there was heard a mysterious singing from below the earth.

This was Elizabeth, the great-passion-bearer, singing funeral hymns to herself and the others until the songs of heaven began to resound for her.

19 July

Gregory of Nyssa and his sister Macrina

Bishop of Nyssa, and Deaconess, Teachers of the Faith, 394 & 379

Note: In Scotland, Gregory of Nyssa is commemorated jointly with Basil the Great and Gregory of Nazianzus on 14 June.

Gregory of Nyssa was born at Caesarea in what is now Turkey around the year 330, the child of an aristocratic Christian family. Unlike his elder brother Basil, he was academically undistinguished, but ultimately proved to be the most original of the group of theologians known as the Cappadocian Fathers. He was introduced to the spiritual life by his elder sister Macrina who exercised a formative influence upon him, and with whom he maintained close bonds of friendship throughout his life. It was she who, after the death of their father, converted the household into a sort of monastery on one of the family estates. Gregory married a deeply spiritual woman, Theosebia, and at first refused ordination, choosing to pursue a secular career. He was ordained only later in life, and in 372 was chosen to be Bishop of Nyssa. In the year 379 both his brother Basil and his sister Macrina died, and this deeply affected him; but out of this darkness emerged a profound spirituality. For Gregory, God is met not as an object to be understood, but as a mystery to be loved. He died in the year 394.

A Reading from a homily of Gregory of Nyssa

When we look down from the sublime words of the Lord into the ineffable depths of his thoughts, we have an experience similar to that of gazing down from a high cliff into the immense sea below. On the coastline one can often see rocky cliffs where the seaward face has been sliced off sheer from top to bottom, with the tops of the cliffs projecting outwards forming a promontory overhanging the depths. If anyone were to look down from such a lofty height into the sea below they would feel giddy. This is exactly how my soul feels now, as it is raised from the ground by this mighty word of the Lord: 'Blessed are the pure in heart, for they shall see God.'

God offers himself to the vision of those whose hearts have been purified. And yet, as the great John says: 'No one has seen God at any time.' And the sublime mind of Paul confirms this opinion when he says that 'no one has seen or can see God'. God is this slippery, steep crag which yields no footholds for our imagination. Moses too, in his teaching, declares that God is so inaccessible that our mind cannot approach him. He explicitly discourages any attempt to apprehend God, saying: 'No one can see the Lord and live.' To see the Lord is eternal life, and yet these pillars of the faith, John, Paul and Moses, all declare it to be impossible! What vertigo in the soul this causes! Confronted by the profundity of these words I am confounded.

If God is life, then they who do not see God do not see life. On the other hand, the divinely inspired prophets and apostles assert that it is impossible to see God. Is not all human hope thus destroyed? But the Lord supports our faltering hope, just as he grasped Peter when he was in danger of sinking and stood him on the waves as though it were solid ground. If, then, the hand of the Word is extended to us also, supporting those who are at sea in the midst of conflicting speculations, we can be without fear. We are gripped by the guiding hand of the Word who says to us: 'Blessed are the pure in heart, for they shall see God.'

Those who see God shall possess in this act of seeing everything that is good: eternal life, eternal incorruption, unending bliss. With these things we shall experience the joy of the eternal kingdom in which happiness is secure; we shall see the true light and hear the delightful voice of the Spirit; we shall rejoice unceasingly in all that is good in the inaccessible glory of God. This is the magnificent consummation of our hope held out to us by the promise of this Beatitude.

A Reading from the *Life of Macrina* by her brother, Gregory of Nyssa

Barely nine months after the death of our dear brother Basil, a synod of bishops was held in Antioch. Before returning to my diocese I determined to visit my sister, Macrina, whom I had not seen for over eight years.

When I arrived I found her very ill. She was not resting on a couch or in bed, but on the ground, lying on a simple board covered with some coarse material, with another board to support her head. When she saw me standing at the door, she raised herself up on her elbow; her strength was already dissipated by the fever and she was unable to walk. I ran to her and lifting her head, gently lowered her body to her previous reclining position. She raised her hand to heaven and said, 'Thank you Lord, for not depriving me of my desire, and for sending your servant to see your handmaid.'

In order not to alarm me, she tried to stifle her pain and gloss over the fact that she was obviously having great difficulty in breathing. We talked about various things, but she longed to hear my news and asked me various questions. As we talked we shared our memories of the great Basil, and immediately my soul was troubled, my face fell and I burst into tears. But dear Macrina, far from being downcast by our grief, made mention of that holy man the starting point for a profound conversation. She always discussed our human predicament, even in misfortune, in the light of the hidden providence of God. And went on to speak of the future life like one inspired by the Holy Spirit. As usual I found my soul lifted up out of the human sphere by her conversation, and under her guidance, I found myself thinking of heavenly realities.

Later, after her rest, I returned to her and she began to tell me the story of her childhood, what she remembered about our parents, what happened before I was born and immediately after my birth. What characterised her own story was the way she always gave thanks to God for all that had happened.

The next day it became clear to me that this was to be her last. The fever had consumed the last vestiges of her strength. As evening came she asked for her couch to be turned toward the east and, drawing our conversation to a close, with her remaining time she gave herself to God in prayer. She said:

> O Lord, you have freed us from the fear of death; you have made the end of life here the beginning of true life for us. For a period you give rest to our bodies in sleep, but then awaken us with the call of the last trumpet. Our earthly body, formed by your hands, you consign in trust to the earth; and then once more you reclaim it, transfiguring with immortality and grace whatever in us is mortal or deformed. You have opened for us the way to resurrection, and given to those who fear you the sign of the holy cross as their emblem, to destroy the enemy and to save our life.
>
> O eternal God, on you I have depended since my mother's womb; you my soul has loved with all its strength; to you I dedicated my body and my soul from childhood. Set by my side an angel of light to lead me to the place of refreshment where there are restful waters in the midst of your holy ones. You have shattered the flaming sword, and in your compassion, you restored the thief who was crucified with you to paradise. Remember me also in your kingdom, for I too have been crucified with you. Let not the terrible abyss of

the dead separate me from your chosen ones; let not the accuser bar my way. Forgive me my sins that my soul may be received in your sight, blameless and spotless.

As she ended her prayer she made the sign of the cross upon her eyes and mouth and heart, and little by little, as the fever dried up her tongue, she was no longer able to speak clearly; her voice gave out and only from the trembling of her lips and the motion of her hands did we know that she was continuing to pray. Eventually she breathed a deep breath and with that prayer, her life came to an end.

20 July

Margaret of Antioch

Martyr, fourth century

Margaret, also called Marina, gave her life during the Diocletian persecutions at the beginning of the fourth century. Her preaching before her death is said to have converted many to the Christian faith.

A Reading from a sermon of Leo the Great

Those of you who think that because the persecutions are over there is no struggle against our enemies, I challenge to search the intimate hidden places of your heart. Become discerning inspectors of your soul, explore its byways: check that there lurks no opposing force ready to attack you, no tyrant waiting to dominate the fortress of your mind. I beg you, make no peace with avarice, and despise all wealth gained from unjust practices. Refuse any pact with pride, and fear more to be received in honour than to be walked over in lowliness! Distance yourself from anger, do not allow the thirst for vengeance to awaken in you the torment of envy. Renounce the pursuit of pleasure, turn away from impurity, reject luxury, fly from evil, resist colluding with falsehood. Once you recognise that you too have to wage war on many fronts, then as the martyrs before us, you will secure a glorious victory.

As often as we die to sin, so sin dies in us. 'Precious in the sight of the Lord' is even this 'death of his saints' for a person is slain to the world, not by the destruction of their mortal frame, but by the destruction of vices. You can only honourably celebrate this solemn day of the martyrs, dear friends, if you stop entering into partnerships with unbelievers, if you stop living sinful lives, if you cease to be controlled by the temptation to indulge every sexual desire.

Therefore, my dearest brothers and sisters, receive what you see with your eyes, and reflect on the example of the martyrs for your own spiritual growth. May each of you so honour this dwelling built by previous generations that you remember that you yourselves are temples of God. Let no one desecrate or weaken the sacred space of their being; but by agreeing with the living and chosen stones through the way you live, you will form an indissoluble bond with those who have gone before us, thus growing into the unity of the Lord's body; and this we shall accomplish with the help of the Cornerstone, Jesus Christ our Lord.

20 July

Bartolomé de las Casas

Apostle to the Indies, 1566

Bartolomé de las Casas was a sixteenth-century Dominican priest who became known as 'the defender of the Indians' in 'the new world' of America. Born in 1484 at Las Casas in Seville, Bartolomé arrived in Haiti in 1502 and underwent a conversion after witnessing the injustices inflicted on the Indians. Proclaiming that Jesus Christ was being crucified in the poor, he went on to spend a lifetime challenging the Church and the Empire of his day. He was consecrated Bishop of Chiapa in Mexico in 1543 where he continued his prophetic rôle and emerged as a man of unquestioned courage and a theologian of remarkable depth, whose vision continues to set in relief the challenge of the Gospel in a world of injustice. He died on 18 July in the year 1566.

A Reading from *Las Casas: In Search of the Poor of Jesus Christ* by Gustavo Gutiérrez

From the very beginning, Bartolomé de las Casas had a clear consciousness that the oppression of the Indian was contrary to the 'intention of Jesus Christ and to the whole of Scripture', and that what God wished instead was the 'liberation of the oppressed'.

This conviction took such deep root in him that it motivated the struggle he waged for the rest of his life. The poor are the beloved of God with a love of predilection because 'God has a very fresh and living memory of the smallest and most forgotten.' This preference, then, ought to be the norm of life for the Christian. He reminded people that those who exploited and murdered the Indians 'have gold as their actual, principal end'. He refused them the name of Christian, stating that 'Christ did not come into the world to die for gold'.

In his *History of the Indies* Las Casas recounts his endeavour 'to protect these miserable people and prevent them from perishing'. He wrote:

> I leave, in the Indies, Jesus Christ, our God, scourged and afflicted and buffeted and crucified, not once but thousands of times, on the part of all the Spaniards who ruin and destroy these people and deprive them of the space they require for their conversion and repentance, depriving them of life before their time so that they die without faith and without the sacraments. Many times have I besought the King's Council to provide them with a remedy and remove the impediments to their salvation, which consist in the Spaniards holding in captivity those whom they already have, and where they still do not, to send Spaniards to go to a certain part of the continent where religious servants of God have commenced to preach the Gospel. The Spaniards who traverse that land with their violence and wicked example prevent them from doing so and make the name of Christ into a blasphemy. They have replied that there is no room there, that is, if the friars were to occupy the land, the King would have no income from it.

Bartolomé was seized with a passion: his love for the living Jesus Christ, scourged, buffeted, crucified, and murdered in the 'captive poor' of the Indies 'not once, but thousands of times'. Their spoilation, exploitation, and murder was 'blasphemy of the name of Christ'.

His definitive argument is drawn from the Parable of the Sheep and Goats in the Gospel of Matthew. He argues that an act addressed to the poor always reaches the God present in the poor. And in a commentary on the words of Christ 'You fed me nothing … you gave me no water …' Bartolomé insists: 'They are damned, not for doing evil, but for not doing good.' The poor of the Indies are being robbed, he argued, and in them, Christ himself.

21 July

Howell Harris

Preacher, 1773

Howell Harris was born at Talgarth in 1714, becoming a schoolmaster at Llangors and Llangasty between 1732 and 1735. On Whitsunday 1735 he underwent a profound religious experience after receiving holy communion. This led him to become an 'exhorter', holding informal services among his neighbours and urging them to pray and receive the sacrament. His request for ordination was turned down, but he continued to preach. In 1737 he met Daniel Rowland at Llangeitho, and the two began to work together, developing a Welsh Methodist movement within the Anglican Church. In 1750 the two leaders quarrelled and Harris retired to Trefeca, where he set up a Christian community or 'family' on Moravian lines. In 1762 Harris and Rowland were reconciled. Harris was a complex and difficult character, but his powerful and enthusiastic preaching left an indelible mark on the spiritual history of Wales. He died in the year 1773 and was buried near the altar rails of Talgarth church.

A Reading from the diary of Howell Harris

June 18th 1735, being in secret prayer, I felt suddenly my heart melting within me like wax before the fire with love to God my Saviour; and I also felt not only love, peace, etc. but longing to be dissolved, and to be with Christ. Then was a cry in my inmost soul, which I was totally unacquainted with before, Abba, Father! Abba, Father! I could not help calling God my Father; I knew that I was his child, and that he loved me, and heard me. My soul being filled and satiated, crying, 'Tis enough, I am satisfied. Give me strength, and I will follow thee through fire and water.' I could say I was happy indeed! There was in me a well of water, springing up to everlasting life. The love of God was shed abroad in my heart by the Holy Ghost.

alternative reading

A Reading from the spiritual advice given to an acquaintance by Howell Harris

Rest not till you have the Spirit of God continually bearing witness with your spirit that you are born of God, till you can say I know on whom I have believed; – see that faith grows, and then love, meekness, brokenness of heart, godly sorrow, resignation of will, humility, holy fear, watchfulness, tenderness of conscience, and all other graces will grow, which are all destroyed by unbelief and doubts: – O beware of this hellish root, this hardens the heart, and alienates the soul from God. Still look up to Jesus, in him alone salvation is laid up, and can be conveyed to us by faith alone.

O glorious faith, when shall I hear thee preached up fully? All talking of holiness before faith is fruitless; but let us first lay the spring of it in our hearts, Christ living in us by faith, and the tree being once made good, the fruit will be so of course; and without this heart-purifying faith, this world-overcoming newborn creature of God, we may strive, and watch, and pray, but we shall be whited sepulchres at last.

O see to the growth of this heavenly flower, and then all the wheels in your soul will keep a regular motion. Beware of false rests, and false peace. Rather, be wounded and mourning, till Christ speaks peace to your soul.

22 July

Mary Magdalene

All four gospels give Mary Magdalene a unique place among Jesus' followers. Probably from Magdala by the Sea of Galilee, she is described as having been healed by Jesus before accompanying him during his ministry. Along with other faithful women, she stayed beside the cross during the crucifixion and was the first disciple to discover the empty tomb on Easter morning. She was privileged with the first appearance of the risen Lord, who sent her to take the good news of the resurrection to the other disciples. This commission earned her the title 'Apostle to the Apostles' in the early Church.

A Reading from a homily of Gregory the Great

Mary Magdalen had been a 'sinner in the city'. She loved Jesus, the Truth, and washed away the stain of her wickedness with her tears. In this way the word of truth was fulfilled: 'Her many sins have been forgiven her because she has shown great love.' Her sins had indeed chilled her heart, but now she was burning inside with an unquenchable love. When she came to the tomb and did not find the Lord's body, she imagined that it had been taken away, and she went and reported it to the disciples. They came, and saw, and they believed that it had actually happened as she had told them. Then the gospel narrative continues: 'The disciples went away again to their homes. But Mary stayed behind, standing by the tomb, weeping.'

At this point let us pause and reflect upon Mary's state of mind, upon the intense love of this woman who would not leave the Lord's tomb even after the disciples had gone away. She carried on seeking him whom she had not found, weeping as she searched; and ablaze with love, she yearned for him whom she believed had been taken away. Thus it happened that she was alone when she saw Jesus, she who had stayed behind to seek him. From this we learn that at the heart of every good work is to be found the virtue of perseverance. Indeed, the lips of truth itself have said: 'Those who persevere to the end will be saved.'

'And as she wept, she stooped down and looked into the tomb.' Mary had already seen that the tomb was empty and she had told the disciples that the Lord had been taken away; so why did she stoop down again? Why did she want to look a second time? The truth is that it is never enough for a lover to look merely once; the sheer intensity of love will not allow a lover to give up searching. Mary had sought and found nothing. But she persevered, and therefore she found the object of her love.

While she was seeking, her unfulfilled desires grew stronger and stronger until at their most intense moment they were quenched in the embrace of him whom she sought. Holy desires grow with waiting: if they fade through waiting then they cannot be genuine. This must be the quality of love that inflames anyone who reaches out for the truth. It is why David says [in the psalms]: 'My soul is thirsting for the living God; when shall I come and behold the face of God?' And the Church says in the Song of Songs: 'I am wounded by love,' and again, 'My soul faints within me.'

'Woman, why are you weeping? Whom do you seek?' Mary is asked the cause of her sorrow so that her desire may increase, for as she names the one she seeks, she discovers herself burning with yet greater love for him. 'And Jesus said to her: "Mary."' First of all he called her 'woman', the common address at that time for one of her sex, and she did not recognise him. But now he calls her by her own name, as if to say: 'Recognise the one who recognises you.' You will remember that the Lord had said to Moses, 'I know you by name.' Moses was his own name, and the Lord told him that he knew him by name, as if saying 'I do not know you in some general way, I know you personally.' In the same way, addressed by her own name, Mary too recognised her creator and immediately calls out 'Rabboni', that is 'teacher'. Outwardly, it was he who was the object of her search, but inwardly it was he who was leading her to search for him.

alternative reading

A Reading from a poem by Janet Morley

They have taken away my Lord

It was unfinished.
We stayed there, fixed, until the end,
women waiting for the body that we loved;
and then it was unfinished.
There was no time to cherish, cleanse, anoint;
no time to handle him with love,
no farewell.

Since then, my hands have waited,
aching to touch even his deadness,
smoothe oil into bruises that no longer hurt,
offer his silent flesh my finished act of love.

I came early, as the darkness lifted,
to find the grave ripped open and his body gone;
container of my grief smashed, looted,
leaving my hands still empty.

I turned on the man who came:
'They have taken away my Lord – where is his corpse?
Where is the body that is mine to greet?
He is not gone

I am not ready yet, I am not finished –
I cannot let him go
I am not whole.'

And then he spoke, no corpse,
and breathed,
and offered me my name.
My hands rushed to grasp him;
to hold and hug and grip his body close;
to give myself again, to cling to him,
and lose my self in love.
'Don't touch me now.'
I stopped, and waited, my rejected passion
hovering between us like some dying thing.
I, Mary, stood and grieved, and then departed.

I have a gospel to proclaim.

23 July

Declan

Bishop, fifth century

Declan of Ardmore in County Waterford, was a prince of the tribe of Decies, among whom there were Christians prior to the coming of Patrick. It is believed that when Patrick was escaping from slavery, he received hospitality among the Christian Decies. The round tower (over thirty metres in height) at Ardmore is probably the best surviving example of its kind. Declan is believed to have lived and died in the fifth century.

A Reading from a treatise *On the Consummation of the World* attributed to Hippolytus of Rome

In the holy gospel we are told that the Son of Man will gather together all nations; and that 'He will separate people one from another, as a shepherd separates sheep from goats. The sheep he will place at his right hand, the goats at his left. Then he will say to those at his right: Come, you blessed of my Father, inherit the kingdom that has been prepared for you from the foundation of the world.' Come, you lovers of the poor and strangers. Come, you who fostered my love, for I am Love. Come, you who shared peace, for I am Peace.

Come, you blessed of my Father, inherit the kingdom prepared for you who did not make an idol of wealth, who gave alms to the poor, help to orphans and widows, drink to the thirsty, and food to the hungry. Come, you who welcomed strangers, clothed the naked, visited the sick, comforted prisoners, helped the blind. Come, you who maintained your seal of faith unblemished, who were quick to assemble in the churches, who listened to my Scriptures, who attended to my words, observed my law day and night, and like good soldiers shared in my suffering because you wanted to please me, your heavenly King. 'Come, inherit the kingdom prepared for you from the foundation of the world.' Behold, my kingdom is ready, the gates of paradise stand open, my immortality is displayed in all its beauty.

Then, astonished at so magnificent a spectacle, at being called friends by him whom the angelic hosts are unable to behold entirely, the righteous will reply: 'Lord, when did we see you hungry and feed you? When did we see you thirsty and give you drink? When did we see you, whom we hold in awe, naked and clothe you? When did we see you, the immortal One, a stranger and welcome you? When did we see you, lover of our race, sick or in prison and come to visit you? You are eternal without beginning like the Father, and co-eternal with the Spirit. You are the One who created all things out of nothing; you are the King of angels; you make the depths tremble; you are clothed in light as in a garment; you are our Creator who fashioned us from the earth; you are the ruler of the invisible world. The whole earth flies from your presence. How could we possibly have received your kingly presence, your royal majesty, as our guest?'

Then the King of Kings shall say to them in reply: 'Inasmuch as you did this to one of the least of these my brothers and sisters, you did it to me.' Inasmuch as you received, clothed, fed, and gave drink to those members of my body about whom I have spoken, that is, the poor, then you did it to me. So come, enter 'the kingdom prepared for you from the foundation of the world'; enjoy for eternity the gifts of my heavenly Father, and of the most holy and life-giving Spirit. What tongue can indeed describe those blessings? For as Scripture says: 'Eye has not seen, nor ear heard, nor has the human heart conceived what God has prepared for those who love him.'

23 July

Bridget of Sweden

Abbess of Vadstena, 1373

Bridget's father was governor of Uppland when she was born in about the year 1303. She married at the age of fourteen, had eight children and often attended the royal court, where she continued to experience the mystical revelations she had known since childhood. These increased in intensity after her husband's death and, three years later, she responded by founding a monastery for nuns and monks at Vadstena in 1346. Bridget's daughter Catherine was the first abbess of the so-called Brigettine Order, which became very influential in northern Europe. After travelling to Rome to obtain the Pope's approval for her plans, Bridget never returned to Sweden but spent the rest of her life as a pilgrim, an adviser to rulers and Church leaders, and a minister to all in need. Her Revelations were recorded by her confessors before her death, which occurred on this day in the year 1373.

A Reading from the *Revelations* of Bridget of Sweden

On the day of Pentecost a priest was saying mass in the monastery and when the Body of God was elevated the bride of Christ saw fire come down from heaven over the altar, and behold in the bread in the priest's hands was a living Lamb, and in the Lamb a flaming face.

And she heard a voice speaking to her: 'As you see fire descend over the altar, so my Spirit fell over the apostles on a day like this, enflaming their hearts. And the bread becomes through the Word a Living Lamb, that is my Body, and the Face in the Lamb and the Lamb in the Face, just as the Father is in the Son and the Son in the Father, and the Holy Spirit in both.' And when the Body of God was again elevated in the priest's hands, she saw a very beautiful young man who said to her: 'I bless you who believe, but to those who do not believe I will be a judge.'

One day our Lady said to the bride: 'Do not be saddened if you must preach the Word of God to those who do not want to listen, because anyone who is slandered or contradicted when doing so but perseveres with patience, is adorning his soul with all beauty. The soul of a person who is thus slandered but refuses to think ill of the slanderer, is clothed with the most beautiful garment which makes her Bridegroom (who is God in Three Persons) long for her to enter the eternal bliss of the Godhead. That is why the friends of God must labour to convert those whose love is pride and avarice more than the love of God, that they may be saved to life, because as it is they are trapped underneath a heavy rock.'

'Just as anyone who saw a brother or sister crushed underneath a fallen rock would immediately try to break the rock into smaller pieces in order to remove it, working with all care so as not to inflict further pain, but sometimes of necessity having to make heavy cuts to lessen the weight, and all the time never thinking of themselves and their labours but only of the other person and saving their life, so the friends of God must work for the salvation of souls in peril.'

25 July

James

Apostle

James, often called 'the Great', was a Galilean fisherman who, with his brother John, was one of the first apostles called by Jesus to follow him. The two brothers were with Jesus at his transfiguration and with him again in the garden of Gethsemane. They annoyed the other followers of Jesus by asking 'to sit one on his left and the other on his right when he came into his glory' and they were present for the appearances of Christ after the resurrection. James was put to death by the sword on the order of Herod Agrippa, who hoped in vain that, by disposing of the Christian leaders, he could stem the flow of those hearing the good news and becoming followers in the Way. James' martyrdom is believed to have taken place in the year 44.

A Reading from a homily of John Chrysostom

The sons of Zebedee press Christ as follows: 'Promise that one of us may sit at your right hand and the other at your left.' How does Christ deal with this request? We should note that their demand comes as a response to an earlier question of Christ: 'What would you have me do for you?' It is not that Christ was ignorant of what was going through their minds, but that he wanted them to speak their mind, to lay open their wound so that he could apply healing ointment. Furthermore, he wants to show them that it is not a spiritual gift for which they are asking, and that if they knew just what their request involved, they would never dare make it. This is why he says: 'You do not know what you are asking,' in other words, you do not know what a great and splendid thing it is, and how much beyond the reach even of the heavenly powers.

Then Christ continues: 'Can you drink the cup which I must drink and be baptized with the baptism which I must undergo?' He is saying: 'You talk of sharing honours and trophies with me, but I must talk of struggle and toil. Now is not the time for rewards or the time for my glory to be revealed. The present time is one of bloodshed, war and danger.'

Notice how, by the manner of his questioning, he exhorts and challenges them. He does not say: 'Can you face being slaughtered? Are you prepared to shed your blood?' Instead he puts a different question: 'Can you drink the cup?' And then he coaxes them, saying: 'The cup which I must drink', so that the prospect of sharing it with him may make them more eager. He also calls his suffering a baptism, to show that it will effect a great cleansing of the whole world. The disciples answer him: 'We can!' Zeal makes them answer immediately, even though they really do not know what they are saying, but still think they will receive what they ask for.

How does Christ respond to their zealous reply? 'You will indeed drink my cup and be baptized with my baptism.' He is really prophesying a great blessing for them, since effectively he is telling them: 'You will be found worthy of martyrdom; you will suffer what I suffer and end your life with a violent death, thus sharing everything with me. But seats at my right and left side are not mine to give; they belong to those for whom the Father has prepared them.' Thus, after lifting their minds to higher goals and preparing them to meet and overcome all that could make them dejected, he corrects their request.

'Then the other ten became angry at the two brothers.' See how imperfect all the disciples were: the two who tried to receive preferential treatment over the other ten, and the ten's jealousy of the two disciples. And yet, as I said earlier on, when we look at these two disciples later on in their lives, we observe how free they were of these impulses. In the Acts of the Apostles we read how John, whom here is recorded as the one who asks for preferential treatment, in fact yields to Peter when it comes to preaching and in working miracles. And James, for his part, was not to live long. From the beginning he was inspired by so great a zeal, that setting aside all earthly interests, he rose to such pre-eminence that it was inevitable that he would be killed straight away.

26 July

Anne and Joachim

Parents of the Blessed Virgin Mary

Note: In Wales, only Anne is commemorated.

In the Proto-Gospel of James, written in the middle of the second century, the parents of Mary the mother of Jesus are named as Anne and Joachim. The story appears to be based heavily on that of Hannah, the mother of Samuel. The Church maintains their feast day both to emphasise God's plan from the beginning to send his Son, born of a woman, born under the Law, to redeem fallen humanity; and also to show God's faithfulness in keeping his covenant with all generations.

A Reading from an oration of John of Damascus

Anne was to be the mother of the Virgin Mother of God, and hence nature did not dare to anticipate the flowering of grace. Thus nature remained barren, until grace produced its fruit. For she who was to be born had to be a first-born daughter, since she would be the mother of the first-born of all creation, 'in whom all things are held together'.

Joachim and Anne, how blessed a couple! All creation is indebted to you. For at your hands the creator was offered a gift excelling all other gifts: a chaste mother, who alone was worthy of the creator.

And so rejoice, Anne, O barren one who 'has not borne children; break forth into shouts, you who have not given birth'. Rejoice, Joachim, because from your daughter 'a child is born for us, a Son is given us, whose name is messenger of great counsel and universal salvation, mighty God'. For this child is God.

Joachim and Anne, how blessed and spotless a couple! You will be known by the fruit you have borne, as the Lord says: 'By their fruits you will know them.' The conduct of your life pleased God and was worthy of your daughter. For by the chaste and holy life you led together, you have fashioned a jewel of virginity: she who remained a virgin before, during and after giving birth. She alone for all time would maintain her virginity in mind and soul, as well as in body.

Joachim and Anne, how chaste a couple! While safeguarding the chastity prescribed by the law of nature, you achieved with God's help something which transcends nature in giving the world the Virgin Mother of God as your daughter. While leading a devout and holy life in your human nature, you gave birth to a daughter nobler than the angels, whose queen she now is. Girl of utter beauty and delight, daughter of Adam and Mother of God, blessed are the loins and blessed is the womb from which you come! Blessed are the arms that carried you, and blessed are your parents' lips.

'Rejoice in God, all the earth. Shout, exult and sing hymns.' Raise up your voice, raise it up, and be not afraid.

Note: For alternative reading, see The Birth of the Blessed Virgin Mary (8 September).

27 July

Brooke Foss Westcott

Bishop, Teacher of the Faith, 1901

Born in 1825, Westcott was first ordained and then became a master at Harrow School. Whilst there, he published a series of scholarly works on the Bible, his expertise eventually leading to his election as Regius Professor of Divinity at the University of Cambridge in 1870. With Fenton Hort and J. B. Lightfoot, he led a revival in British Biblical studies and theology. He became influential too in the field of Anglican social thought and was significant in the founding of the Clergy Training School in Cambridge (later renamed Westcott House in his memory). In 1890, he was consecrated Bishop of Durham, where he died on this day in the year 1901.

A Reading from *Christus Consummator* by Brooke Foss Westcott

If the outward were the measure of the Church of Christ, we might well despair. But side by side with us, when we fondly think like Elijah or Elijah's servant, that we stand alone, are countless multitudes whom we know not, angels whom we have no power to discern, children of God whom we have not learnt to recognise. We have come to the kingdom of God, peopled with armies of angels and men working for us and with us because they are working for him. And though we cannot grasp the fullness of the truth, and free ourselves from the fetters of sense, yet we can, in the light of the Incarnation, feel the fact of this unseen fellowship; we can feel that heaven has been re-opened to us by Christ; that the hosts who were separated from Israel at Sinai by the fire and the darkness are now joined with us under our Saviour King, ascending and descending upon the Son of Man; that no external tests are final in spiritual things; that while we are separated one from another by barriers which we dare not overpass, by difference of opinion which we dare not conceal or extenuate, there still may be a deeper-lying bond in righteousness, peace, and joy in the Holy Ghost, the apostolic notes of the kingdom of God, which nothing that is of earth can for ever overpower.

Such convictions are sufficient to bring calm to the believer in the sad conflicts of a restless age, widely different from the blind complacency which is able to forget the larger sorrows of the world in the confidence of selfish security, and from the superficial indifference which regards diversities as trivial which for good or evil modify the temporal workings of faith. They enable us to preserve a true balance between the elements of our life. They teach us to maintain the grave, if limited, issues of the forms in which men receive the truth, and to vindicate for the Spirit perfect freedom and absolute sovereignty. They guard us from that deceitful impatience which is eager to anticipate the last results of the discipline of the world and gain outward unity by compromise, which is hasty to abandon treasures of our inheritance because we have forgotten or misunderstood their use. They inspire us with the ennobling hope that in the wisdom of God we shall become one, not by narrowing and defining the faith which is committed to us, but by rising through the help of the Spirit, to a worthier sense of its immeasurable grandeur.

27 July

John Comper

Priest, 1903

John Comper was born in 1823 at Pulborough, Sussex and moved to Scotland in 1848 to become master of the newly founded church school at Kirriemuir. In 1849 he moved to St Margaret's College, Crieff, and in 1850, in the week following the Consecration of St Ninian's Cathedral in Perth, he was made deacon by Bishop Forbes of Brechin. One of his examiners, impressed by the quality of his answers, sent these to John Mason Neale, with whom a life-long friendship developed. He was ordained priest in 1852 and in the following year moved to Nairn. As Chaplain to Bishop Eden at Inverness, he started a mission which ultimately developed into the congregation of Inverness Cathedral. In 1857 he was given the charge of Stonehaven. Four years later he became Rector of St John's, Aberdeen, where he set up a day school. He was instrumental in establishing a community of nuns in Aberdeen's Gallowgate, from which in 1870 St Margaret's Church was founded. His work among the poor led him to establish a school in the Gallowgate. He published several works on liturgy. He died on this day in 1903 in the Duthie Park, Aberdeen, apparently whilst giving a strawberry to a little child. The strawberry became the insignia of the work of his son, Sir Ninian Comper, the noted church Architect.

A Reading from an essay 'Of the atmosphere of a church'
by Sir Ninian Comper

A church built with hands, as we are reminded at every consecration and dedication feast, is the outward expression here on earth of that spiritual Church built of living stones, the bride of Christ, *urbis beata Jerusalem,* which stretches back to the foundation of the world and onwards to all eternity. With her Lord she lays claim to the whole of his creation and to every philosophy and creed and work of man which his Holy Spirit has inspired. And so the temple here on earth, in different lands and in different shapes, in the East and in the West, has developed or added to itself fresh forms of beauty and, though it has suffered from iconoclasts and destroyers both within and without, and perhaps nowhere more than in this land, it has never broken with the past: it has never renounced its claim to continuity.

To enter therefore a Christian church is to enter none other than the house of God and the gate of heaven. It is to leave all strife, all disputes of the manner of church government and doctrine outside – 'Thou shalt keep them secretly in thy tabernacle from the strife of tongues' – and to enter here on earth into the unity of the Church triumphant in heaven. It cannot be otherwise, since he himself, who is the temple of it, the Lamb slain from the foundation of the world, is there also.

28 July

Samson

Bishop, 565

Samson was born in Dyfed about the year 485. He was sent as a young boy to Illtud's school at Llantwit Major, and at the age of twenty-three ordained deacon there by Dyfrig. He left soon after for the monastery on Caldey Island, where he was made first cellarer and then abbot. About eighteen months later Samson went on a missionary journey to Ireland, and on his return to Wales became a hermit, living in a cave near Stackpole on the south Pembrokeshire coast. In 521 Samson was summoned by Dyfrig to attend a synod at Llantwit Major, where he was elected abbot and consecrated bishop. He did not remain long at Llantwit Major, leaving for Cornwall where he spent twenty-five years founding monastic communities, and then crossing to Brittany, establishing a monastery at Dol. This became a great centre for evangelism and it was here that Samson died in the year 565.

A Reading from *The Life of Petroc*
by an unknown medieval monastic author

Close to the shore [of Cornwall], on the estuary of the river Haile, a certain Samson, a worthy servant of God, had his hermitage in the wilderness. This man, with zealous self-denial and continual prayers, offered himself with much penitential discipline as a living sacrifice to God, and endeavoured by daily labour to build in his soul a fitting temple for God.

One day blessed Petroc, arriving on shore from his boat, inquired of some men harvesting in the fields and who were entirely ignorant of the Christian religion, whether there was any Christian person in the province. They pointed out to him the aforesaid Samson, telling him of Samson's solitary life, and strict abstinence, and how he spent the night in prayer, and was entirely devoted to God's service, eating nothing but a little barley bread.

The servant of God, hearing these things, and perceiving where Samson was, with glad mind began to walk towards him, praying to the Lord that Samson might not leave his cell before he arrived, so that he might talk with him – so greatly did this holy soul desire to converse with this holy man. The Lord granted the desire of his soul, 'adding to his wish that which he had not presumed to ask' because immediately Samson's limbs became as stiff as stone. In vain he attempted to put his hands to the spade with which he was turning over the soil. But he was bound fast by the prayer of the man of God. But when holy Petroc reached him, at the voice of his greeting Samson was freed from his stone-like rigidity. After they had exchanged the kiss of peace, Samson gave glory to God for the virtue and holiness which had been revealed by so wonderful a miracle.

29 July

Mary, Martha and Lazarus

Companions of our Lord

Note: In Scotland, only Mary and Martha are commemorated.

The Gospels of Luke and John variously describe how Mary, Martha and their brother Lazarus gave Jesus hospitality at their home at Bethany outside Jerusalem. Jesus is said to have loved all three. After Lazarus' death, he wept and was moved by the sisters' grief: he brought Lazarus back from the dead that the glory of God might be shown. It was Martha who recognized Jesus as the Messiah, while Mary anointed his feet. On another occasion, Mary was commended by Jesus for her attentiveness to his teaching while Martha served. From this, Mary is traditionally taken to be an example of the contemplative spiritual life and Martha an example of the active spiritual life.

A Reading from a sermon of Augustine

The words of our Lord Jesus Christ teach us that there is one goal towards which we should be travelling while we toil among the countless distractions of this world. We make our way like pilgrims on a journey, people of no fixed abode; we are on the road, not yet home; still aiming for our goal, though yet to arrive. So let us press on, never wearying, never giving up, so that one day we may reach our destination.

Martha and Mary were sisters, related not only by blood, but also by a shared desire for holiness. Both were devoted to the Lord, and together served him when he was here among us. Martha welcomed him as a pilgrim would be received. But in her case, the reality was that the servant was receiving her Lord, a sick woman receiving her Saviour, the creature receiving her creator. She who was to be fed with the Spirit welcomed him whom she served with bodily food. For it was the will of the Lord to take the form of a servant and while in the form of a servant to be fed by his own servants, for whom it became an honour not a duty. It was an honour that he should present himself to them needing to be fed. He had flesh in which he hungered and became thirsty.

Thus our Lord was received as a guest, who 'came to his own home, and his own people received him not. But to all who received him, he gave power to become children of God.' He chose servants and raised them to the status of sisters and brothers; he set captives free and made them joint heirs with himself.

Now if any of you happen to say: 'How blessed are those who were found worthy to receive Christ into their own homes,' do not murmur because you were born in a later age when you no longer see the Lord in the flesh: he has not robbed you of that honour. For he says, 'Truly, as you did it to one of the least of these my brothers and sisters, you did it also to me.'

You dear Martha, if I may say so, are blessed for your good service; you are seeking the reward of your labours, namely, rest. For the moment you are preoccupied with the demands of service, feeding a mortal body, albeit a holy one. But when you reach your heavenly homeland, will you find a pilgrim to welcome, someone hungry to feed, someone thirsty to whom you may give a drink, someone ill whom you can visit, someone quarrelsome whom you could reconcile, a dead body to bury? Martha, none of these tasks will be there. But what will you find?

You will find what Mary chose. There we shall not have to feed other people: we shall be fed. What Mary chose in this life will on that day be realised in its fullness. She was gathering the crumbs from a rich banquet, the Word of God. And do you wish to know what will happen when we arrive there? The Lord himself tells us when he says of his servants: 'Truly, I say to you, he will have them sit at table, and he will come and serve them himself.'

alternative reading

A Reading from the treatise *On Spiritual Friendship* by Aelred of Rievaulx

Spiritual friendship should be desired not for consideration of any worldly advantage or for any extrinsic cause, but for the dignity of its own nature and the feelings of the human heart, so that its fruition and reward is nothing other than itself. That is why the Lord in the gospel says: 'I have appointed you that you should go, and should bring forth fruit,' that is, that you should love one another. For true friendship advances by perfecting itself, and the fruit is derived from experiencing the sweetness of that perfection. Thus spiritual friendship among the righteous is born of a similarity in life, morals, and pursuits, that is, it consists in a mutual conformity in matters human and divine united with generosity and charity.

Have you forgotten that in the Book of Proverbs it says: 'He that is a friend loves at all times'? Saint Jerome also, as you may recall, says that 'Friendship which can end was never true friendship.' That friendship cannot endure without charity has been more than adequately established. Since then in friendship eternity blossoms, truth shines forth, and charity grows sweet, consider whether you ought to separate the name of wisdom from these three things.

And what does all this add up to? Dare I say of friendship what John, the friend of Jesus, says of charity, namely that 'God is friendship'?

That would be unusual, to be sure, nor does it have the sanction of the Scriptures. And yet what is true of charity, I surely do not hesitate to grant to friendship, since 'those who abide in friendship, abide in God, and God in them'.

30 July

Silas

Companion of Paul

Silas (or Silvanus) appears in the Acts of the Apostles and the New Testament epistles as a companion and fellow-worker of Paul. He was chosen by the Council of Jerusalem to accompany Paul and Barnabas to Antioch with the Council's decision on the admission of Gentiles. He was freed from gaol in Philippi with Paul, and at Rome worked with both Paul and Peter. There is a tradition that he died in Macedonia.

A Reading from a homily of John Chrysostom

In my view there is nothing so frigid as a Christian who does not care about the salvation of other people. It is useless to plead poverty in this respect, for the poor widow who put two copper coins in the treasury will be your accuser. So will Peter who said, 'Silver and gold have I none,' and indeed Paul was so poor that he often went hungry and without the basic necessities of life. Nor can you plead humble birth because the apostles were of humble origin and from obscure families. You cannot claim lack of education because they too were illiterate. And do not plead sickness because Timothy suffered poor health and was often ill. All of us can be of service to our neighbour if only we exercise our responsibilities.

Look at the trees of the forest. See how sturdy they are, how beautiful, how tall, and how smooth their bark; but they do not bear fruit. If we had a garden we would prefer to plant pomegranates or olive trees. The other trees may be delightful to look at but they are not grown for profit, or if they are, it is very small. Those who are concerned only for themselves are like trees of the forest – no, they are not even as worthwhile. At least forest timber can be used for building houses and fortifications, whereas they are good only for the bonfire. They are like the foolish virgins in the parable: chaste certainly, discreet and modest too, but useless. That is why they were rejected. Such is the fate of all who do not nourish Christ.

You should reflect on the fact that none of them is charged with specific sins such as fornication or perjury; they are charged simply with being of no service to their fellow men and women. Take the example of the man who went and buried his talent. He led a blameless life but a life that was not of service to others. How can such a person be called a Christian? If yeast when it is mixed with the flour fails to leaven the dough, how can it be called yeast? Or again, if perfume cannot be sensed by those present, how can it be called perfume in any meaningful sense? So do not say, 'I cannot encourage others to become Christians; it is impossible;' because if you were really a Christian, it would be impossible for you not to do so.

In the natural world, the way things behave is an expression of their properties. It is the same situation here: what I am describing belongs to the very nature of being a Christian. So do not insult God. To claim that the sun cannot shine or that a Christian cannot do good is insulting to God and reveals you as a liar. If we get our lives ordered the rest will follow as a natural consequence. It is impossible for the light of a Christian to be hidden; it is impossible for so resplendent a lamp to be concealed.

30 July

William Wilberforce

Social Reformer, 1833

Olaudah Equiano and Thomas Clarkson

Anti-slavery campaigners, 1797 and 1846

William Wilberforce was born in 1759 in Hull. Converted to an Evangelical piety within the Church of England, Wilberforce decided to serve the faith in Parliament instead of being ordained, becoming a Member of Parliament at the age of twenty-one. He was a supporter of missionary initiatives and helped found The Bible Society. Settling in Clapham in London, he became a leader of the reforming group of Evangelicals known as the 'Clapham Sect'. Of all the causes for which he fought, he is remembered best for his crusade against slavery. After years of effort, the trade in slaves was made illegal in the British Empire in 1807 and Wilberforce lived to see the complete abolition of slavery, just before his death on this day in the year 1833.

According to his autobiography, Olaudah Equiano was born in Essaka (modern-day Nigeria) circa 1745. When he was about eleven he was captured and sold into slavery, and was taken as an enslaved African to the Americas. Equiano was first sold to a British naval officer, who changed his name to Gustavus Vassa, and was then purchased by a Quaker merchant. Equiano purchased his freedom for £40 in 1766. Having served as a seaman, he journeyed to the West Indies, the Mediterranean and Canada. (He was the first Black man known to have attempted to travel to the North Pole.) Equiano subsequently settled in England and joined in the campaign to end the slave trade. His celebrated autobiography The Interesting Narrative of the Life of Olaudah Equiano, or Gustavus Vassa the African (1789) became a runaway success, helping to advance the cause of the anti-slavery movement in Britain. During his lifetime, the book went through nine British editions and many others followed after his death in 1797. In it Equiano notes that he was baptized in St Margaret's Church, Westminster, and that his Christian faith underpinned all his life's work.

Thomas Clarkson was born in Wisbech, Cambridgeshire, in 1760. After winning a Cambridge University prize for an essay on slavery in 1785, he travelled to London and helped form the anti-slave trade movement. Clarkson became its chief researcher, responsible for gathering the evidence, while William Wilberforce became its public voice. One of the most enduring anti-slavery images is Clarkson's diagram of the slave ship Brookes. Ill health in the 1790s forced him to withdraw from the campaign for nearly a decade. On his return in 1804, he supported Wilberforce in navigating the Abolition of the Slave Trade Bill successfully through Parliament in 1807. William Wordsworth subsequently wrote a sonnet in honour of his efforts and Clarkson wrote his own account of the abolition of the slave trade in 1808. Moving to Playford near Ipswich in 1816, he turned his attention to the ending of slavery itself and in 1823 joined a new generation of younger abolitionists such as Thomas Fowell Buxton MP in founding the British Anti-Slavery Society. It was as a result of this group's activities that an Act emancipating slaves in British colonies was passed in 1833. Clarkson died in Playford in 1846.

A Reading from a speech of William Wilberforce delivered to the House of Commons in May 1789 on the total abolition of slavery

I mean not to accuse anyone, but to take the shame upon myself, in common indeed with the whole Parliament of Britain, for having suffered this horrid trade of slavery to be carried on under their authority. We are all guilty – we ought to all plead guilty, and not to exculpate ourselves by throwing the blame on others.

[In the facts that I have laid before you,] I trust that I have proved that, upon every ground, total abolition ought to take place. I have urged many things which are not my own leading motives for proposing it, since I have wished to show every description of gentlemen, and particularly the West India planters, who deserve every attention, that the abolition is politic upon their own principles. Policy, however, Sir, is not my principle; and I am not ashamed to say it. There is a principle above everything that is politic, and when I reflect on the command which says: 'Thou shalt do no murder,' believing its authority to be divine, how can I dare to set up any reasonings of my own against it?

Sir, the nature and all the circumstances of this trade are now laid open to us. We can no longer plead ignorance. We cannot evade it. We may spurn it. We may kick it out of the way. But we cannot turn aside so as to avoid seeing it. For it is brought now so directly before our eyes that this House must decide, and must justify to all the world and to its own conscience, the rectitude of all the grounds of its decision.

Let not Parliament be the only body that is insensible to the principles of natural justice. Let us make reparation to Africa, as far as we can, by establishing trade upon true commercial principles, and we shall soon find the rectitude of our conduct rewarded by the benefits of a regular and growing commerce.

alternative reading

A Reading of extracts from *The Interesting Narrative of the Life of Olaudah Equiano, or Gustavus Vassa, the African, Written by Himself*

In my deep consternation the Lord was pleased to break in upon my soul with his bright beams of heavenly light; and in an instant as it were, removing the veil, and letting light into a dark place, I saw clearly with the eye of faith the crucified Saviour bleeding on the cross on mount Calvary: the scriptures became an unsealed book…. I was sensible of the invisible hand of God, which guided and protected me when in truth I knew it not: still the Lord pursued me although I slighted and disregarded it; his mercy melted me down.

I early accustomed myself to look at the hand of God in the minutest occurrence, and to learn from it a lesson of morality and religion; and in this light every circumstance I have related was to me of importance. After all, what makes any event important, unless by its observation we become better and wiser, and learn 'to do justly, to love mercy, and to walk humbly before God'?

Tortures, murder, and every other imaginable barbarity and iniquity, are practised upon the poor slaves with impunity. I hope the slave trade will be abolished. I pray it may be an event at hand. … In a short time one sentiment alone will prevail, from motives of interest as well as justice and humanity.

alternative reading

A Reading from *History of the Rise, Progress, and Accomplishment of the Abolition of the African Slave-Trade by the British Parliament*, by Thomas Clarkson

The author of our religion was the first who taught that, however in a legal point of view the talent of individuals might belong exclusively to themselves, so that no other person had a right to demand the use of it by force, yet in the Christian dispensation they were but the stewards of it for good.

If the great evil of the Slave-trade, so deeply entrenched by its hundred interests, has fallen prostrate before the efforts of those who attacked it, what evil of a less magnitude shall not be more easily subdued? O may reflections of this sort always enliven us, always encourage us, always stimulate us to our duty! May we never cease to believe, that many of the miseries of life are still to be remedied, or to rejoice that we may be permitted, if we will only make ourselves worthy by our endeavours, to heal them! May we encourage for this purpose every generous sympathy that arises in our hearts, as the offspring of the Divine influence for our good, convinced that we are not born for ourselves alone, and that the Divinity never so fully dwells in us, as when we do his will; and that we never do his will more agreeably, as far as it has been revealed to us, than when we employ our time in works of charity towards the rest of our fellow-creatures!

31 July

Joseph of Arimathea

All four Gospels tell us that it was Joseph of Arimathea who recovered the body of Jesus and arranged for its burial. He is described as a rich man, as a member of the Council, the Jewish Sanhedrin, and as a follower of Jesus. According to John's Gospel, his discipleship was secret because he was afraid. Nonetheless, when Jesus' closest friends had deserted him, Joseph went boldly to Pontius Pilate and asked for and received the body, wrapped it in a linen shroud, and laid it in a new tomb. In John he is helped by Nicodemus, and in Matthew and Mark a stone is rolled across the entrance. He thus plays a small but significant part in the narrative of the passion and resurrection of our Lord. Later romantic legend provides a much fuller story, but it is for his selfless act in giving to Jesus just what was needed, at some risk to himself, that he is remembered today.

A Reading from a treatise *On the Holy Spirit*
by Basil the Great

To attain holiness we must not only pattern our lives on that of Christ by being gentle, humble and patient, but we must also imitate him in his death. Taking Christ for his model, Paul said that he wanted to become like him in his death in the hope that he too would be raised from death to life.

We imitate Christ's death by being buried with him in baptism. If we ask what this kind of burial means and what benefit we may hope to derive from it, it means first of all making a complete break with our former way of life, and our Lord himself said that this cannot be done unless we are born again. In other words, we have to begin a new life, and we cannot do so until our previous life has been brought to an end. When runners reach the turning point on a racecourse, they have to pause briefly before they can go back in the opposite direction. So also when we wish to reverse the direction of our lives there must be a pause, or a death, to mark the end of one life and the beginning of another.

Our descent into hell takes place when we imitate the burial of Christ by our baptism. The bodies of the baptized are in a sense buried in the water as a symbol of their renunciation of the sins of their unregenerate nature. As the Apostle says: 'The circumcision you have undergone is not an operation performed by human hands, but the complete stripping away of your unregenerate nature. This is the circumcision that Christ gave us, and it is accomplished by our burial with him in baptism.' Baptism cleanses the soul from the pollution of worldly thoughts and inclinations: 'You will wash me,' says the psalmist, 'and I shall be whiter than snow.' We receive this saving baptism only once because there was only one death and one resurrection for the salvation of the world, and baptism is its symbol.

31 July

Ignatius of Loyola

Founder of the Society of Jesus, 1556

Born in 1491, the son of a Basque nobleman, Ignatius served as a soldier and was wounded at the siege of Pamplona in 1521. During his convalescence he read a Life of Christ, was converted and lived a life of prayer and penance, during which he wrote the first draft of his Spiritual Exercises. He gathered six disciples, and together they took vows of poverty and chastity and promised to serve the Church either by preaching in Palestine or in other ways that the Pope thought fit. By 1540, Ignatius had won papal approval for his embryonic Order and the Society of Jesus was born. For the next sixteen years he directed the work of the Jesuits as it spread around the world, until his sudden death on this day in the year 1556.

A Reading from the *Spiritual Exercises* of Ignatius of Loyola, their 'Principle and Foundation'

The human person is created to praise, reverence and serve God Our Lord, and by so doing to save his or her soul. The other things on the face of the earth are created for human beings in order to help them pursue the end for which they are created. It follows from this that one must use other created things in so far as they help towards one's end, and free oneself from them in so far as they are obstacles to one's end. To do this we need to make ourselves indifferent to all created things, provided the matter is subject to our free choice and there is no prohibition. Thus as far as we are concerned, we should not want health more than illness, wealth more than poverty, fame more than disgrace, a long life more than a short one, and similarly for all the rest, but we should desire and choose only what helps us more towards the end for which we are created.

alternative reading

A Reading from the *Reminiscences* or *The Life of Ignatius of Loyola* as heard and recorded by Luis Gonzalez da Camara

Ignatius was badly wounded in battle, with one leg completely shattered. He was carried home to Loyola on a litter. Upon arrival it was discovered that the leg had been badly set, and would need to be broken, cut and re-set, and that the pain would be greater than all those he had undergone before. Once the flesh and excess bone had been cut, the concern was to use remedies whereby the leg would not be left so short, applying many ointments to it and stretching it continually with appliances, which on many days were making a martyr of him.

But Our Lord was gradually giving him health, and Ignatius was in such a good state that he was cured in all other respects except that he could not hold himself well on his leg, and thus he was forced to be in bed. And because he was much given to reading worldly and false books, which they normally call 'tales of chivalry', he asked, once he was feeling well, that they give him some of these to pass the time. But in that house none of those books which he normally read could be found, and so they gave him a life of Christ and a book of the lives of the saints in Spanish.

Reading through these often, he was becoming rather attached to what he found written there. But, on ceasing to read them, he would stop to think: sometimes about the things he had read, at other times about the things of the world he had been accustomed to think about before. Our Lord was helping him, causing other thoughts, which were born of the things he was reading, to follow these. For, while reading the lives of Our Lord and the saints, he would stop to think, reasoning with himself, 'How would it be, if I did this which Saint Francis did, and this which Saint Dominic did?' And thus he used to think over many things which he was finding good, always proposing to himself difficult and laborious things. And as he was proposing these, it seemed to him he was finding in himself an ease as regards putting them into practice.

But his whole way of thinking was to say to himself: 'Saint Francis did this, so I must do it; Saint Dominic did this, so I must do it.'

These thoughts too used to last a good space, and, after other things in between, the thoughts of the world would follow, and on these too he would stop for a long while. And this succession of such different kinds of thoughts lasted a considerable time for him, with him always dwelling on the thought whose turn it was, whether this was of the former worldly deeds which he wanted to do, or of these latter from God which were occurring to his imagination, until the point came when he would leave them because of tiredness and attend to other things.

Still, there was this difference: that when he was thinking about worldly stuff he would take much delight, but when he left it aside after getting tired, he would find himself dry and discontented. But when about doing the various austerities which the saints had done, not only used he to be consoled while in such thoughts, but he would remain content and happy even after having left them aside. But he wasn't investigating this, nor stopping to ponder this difference, until one time when his eyes were opened a little, and he began to marvel at this difference in kind and to reflect on it, picking it up from experience that from some thoughts he would be left sad and from others happy; and little by little coming to know the difference in kind of spirits that were stirring: the one from the devil, and the other from God.

This was the first reflection he made on the things of God; and later, when he produced the *Spiritual Exercises,* this experience was the starting point for teaching his followers the discernment of spirits.

August

3 August

Germanus

Bishop, 448

Germanus became Bishop of Auxerre in Gaul in 418. Eleven years later some British clergy invited him to cross the Channel and help them combat the spread of Pelagianism. During his visit he helped the Britons to ambush an army of invading Saxons and Picts. The battle took place at Eastertide and Germanus taught the British soldiers, many of whom he had newly baptized, to use 'Alleluia' as their war cry. Archbishop Ussher suggested that the scene of this 'Alleluia Victory' was Maes Garmon near Mold in Flintshire, but a more recent scholar has located it in north Kent. Germanus died in Ravenna in the year 448, not long after a second brief visit to the beleaguered British Christians. He has been traditionally identified with the Garmon to whom a string of churches are dedicated in North Wales. This has been disputed, on philological grounds, by several modern authors.

A Reading from *A History of the English Church and People* by the Venerable Bede

The Pelagian heresy was introduced into Britain by Agricola, the son of a Pelagian bishop called Severianus, and as a result seriously infected the faith of the British Church. Although the British rejected this perverse teaching which was so blasphemous in its repudiation of the grace of Christ, they were unable to refute its plausible arguments in disputation, and wisely decided to seek help from the bishops of Gaul in this spiritual conflict. The bishops summoned a great synod, and consulted about whom they should send to uphold the faith. Their unanimous choice fell upon the apostolic bishops Germanus of Auxerre and Lupus of Troyes, whom they appointed to send to the Britons to confirm their belief in God's grace.

And so it was that the island of Britain was steadily influenced by the arguments, the preaching, and indeed the virtues of these apostolic bishops. The word of God was preached daily not only in the churches, but also in the streets and fields, so that Catholic Christians everywhere were strengthened and heretics corrected. Theirs was the honour and authority of apostles by virtue of their holy witness, the truth of their learning, and the virtue of their merits. The majority of the people readily accepted their teaching, while the authors of false doctrine made themselves scarce.

Once this abominable heresy had been routed and its authors refuted, and with the people once again settled in the true faith of Christ, the bishops paid a visit to the tomb of the blessed martyr Alban to return thanks to God through him. Germanus, who had with him relics of all the apostles and several martyrs, first offered prayer, and then directed the tomb

, so that he could deposit these precious gifts within it. For he thought it fitting equal merits of the saints had won them a place in heaven, so their relics should ed together from different lands into a common resting-place.

all matters were settled, the blessed bishops returned home as successfully as they .ad come. Subsequently, Germanus visited Ravenna to obtain peace for the people of Brittany. There he was received with honour by the Emperor Valentinian and his mother Placidia, and while still in this city, Germanus departed to Christ.

4 August

Jean-Baptiste Vianney

Curé d'Ars, Spiritual Guide, 1859

Jean-Baptiste Marie Vianney was born in Dardilly near Lyons in 1786, the son of a farmer, and he spent much of his childhood working as a shepherd on his father's farm. He had little formal education but, at the age of twenty, he began studying for the priesthood which he found extremely difficult. Despite his poor academic performance, he was ordained in 1815, mainly because of his devotion and holiness. He served as assistant priest at Ecully and, in 1818, was appointed curé, or parish priest, of the remote, unimportant village of Ars-en-Dombes. From this backwater, his fame was to spread worldwide. His skills in preaching and spiritual counsel earned him a reputation as a discerning and wise priest. His visiting penitents soon numbered three hundred a day. He would preach at eleven o'clock each morning and then spend up to sixteen hours in the confessional. His love of God and his people ensured that he remained in Ars the rest of his life, despite a call to the religious life and many offers of promotion in the Church. He died on this day in the year 1859.

A Reading from the catechetical instructions of Jean-Baptiste Vianney

My children, reflect that a Christian's treasure is not on earth but in heaven. Therefore our thoughts should turn to where our treasure is. Ours is a noble task: that of prayer and love. To pray and to love, that constitutes the greatest possible happiness for us in this life.

Prayer is nothing less than union with God. When the heart is pure and united with God it is consoled and filled with sweetness; it is transfigured by a wonderful light. In this intimate union with God it is as if two pieces of wax were moulded together; they can no longer be separated. This union of God with us, insignificant creatures that we are, is a truly wonderful thing, a happiness beyond our comprehension.

We had deserved to be left abandoned, unable to pray; but in his goodness, God has permitted us to speak with him. Our prayer is an incense that is delightful to God.

My children, I know your hearts are small, but prayer will enlarge them and make them capable of loving God. Prayer is a foretaste of heaven, an overflowing of heaven. It never leaves us without sweetness; it's like honey, running down into the soul and sweetening everything with which it comes into contact. When we pray truly, difficulties melt like snow in the sunshine.

Prayer makes time pass quickly, and is so pleasant that one loses all sense of time. When I was parish priest of Bresse, it happened once that virtually all my colleagues were ill, and as a result I had to make long journeys during which I used to pray to God; and I can assure you, the time did not seem long to me. Indeed, there are those who completely lose themselves in prayer, like fish in water, because they are absorbed in God. There is no division in their hearts. How I love such noble souls!

As for ourselves, how often do we come casually into church without the slightest idea of why we have come or what we need to ask God for. And yet when we call on a neighbour we suddenly have no difficulty in remembering why we've called. It was as if we are saying to God: 'Sorry, I can only spare a couple of words now because I need to get on.' And yet, it is my belief, that if we were to speak to God out of a living faith and a pure heart, we should receive all we ask.

5 August

Oswald

King of Northumbria, Martyr, 642

Born around the year 605, the son of King Ælfrith of Northumbria, Oswald was forced to leave home after his father's death and move to Iona where, influenced by the monks of Saint Columba, he was baptized. Returning to Northumbria in 634, Oswald defeated the British king, setting up a cross as his standard and gathering his men around it to pray the night before the battle. A man of humility and generosity, Oswald worked closely with his friend Saint Aidan, travelling with him on his missionary journeys and acting as his interpreter. He died in battle on this day in the year 642 defending his kingdom from the Mercians.

A Reading from *The History of the English Church and People* by the Venerable Bede

When King Oswald was about to engage in battle with the heathen, he set up the sign of the holy cross and, kneeling down, prayed God to send his heavenly aid to those who trusted in him in their dire need. The place is pointed out to this day and held in great veneration. It is said that, when the cross had been hurriedly made and the hole dug in which it was to stand, the devout king with ardent faith seized the cross and placed it in position himself, holding it upright with his own hands until the soldiers had heaped up sufficient earth so that it stood firm. This done he raised his voice, and calling out to his army, said: 'Let us all kneel together, and pray the true, the ever-living and almighty God to protect us in his mercy from the arrogant savagery of our enemies, for he knows that we fight in a just cause for the preservation of our nation.'

The whole army did as he ordered and, advancing against the enemy as dawn was breaking, they won the victory that their faith deserved. At this spot where the king prayed, innumerable miracles of healing are known to have been occurred which serve as a reminder and memorial of the king's faith. This place is known as 'the heavenly field', which name, bestowed upon it a long time ago, was a sure omen of future events, indicating that there the heavenly sign would be set up, a heavenly victory won, and heavenly miracles take place. It lies on the northern side of the wall which the Romans built from sea to sea.

King Oswald had been instructed in the Christian faith by Bishop Aidan, with the result that the king and the English people under his rule, not only learned to hope for the kingdom of heaven, which had been unknown to his ancestors, but were also granted by almighty God, creator of heaven and earth, an earthly kingdom greater than anything they had possessed. For Oswald gradually brought under his sceptre all the peoples and provinces of Britain speaking the four languages, British, Pictish, Irish and English.

Although he wielded supreme power over the whole land, Oswald was always wonderfully humble, kind, and generous to the poor and to strangers. Eventually, he fell in a fierce battle fought at the place called Oswestry against the same heathen Mercians and their heathen king who had slain his predecessor Edwin. He died on the fifth day of August in the year 642 when he was thirty-eight years of age.

6 August

The Transfiguration of our Lord

The story of the transfiguration of Jesus on the mount is recorded in the Gospels of Matthew, Mark and Luke, and Peter refers to it in his Second Epistle. Each time it is made clear that God's salvation is for all and that Jesus is the Chosen One of God who brings that salvation. Tradition locates the transfiguration on Mount Tabor. The testimony of the law and the prophets to Jesus is indicated by the figures of Moses and Elijah, and the event is seen as prefiguring the resurrection, giving a foretaste of the life of glory.

A Reading from an address on the transfiguration of Christ by Anastasius, Abbot of Saint Catherine's Monastery, Mount Sinai

Upon Mount Tabor, Jesus revealed to his disciples a heavenly mystery. While living among them he had spoken of the kingdom and of his second coming in glory, but to banish from their hearts any possible doubt concerning the kingdom and to confirm their faith in what lay in the future by its prefiguration in the present, he gave them on Mount Tabor a wonderful vision of his glory, a foreshadowing of the kingdom of heaven. It was as if he said to them: As time goes by you may be in danger of losing your faith. To save you from this I tell you now that some standing here listening to me, 'will not taste death until they have seen the Son of Man coming in the glory of his Father'.

Moreover, in order to assure us that Christ could command such power when he wished, the evangelist continues: 'Six days later, Jesus took with him Peter, James and John, and led them up a high mountain where they were alone. There, before their eyes, he was transfigured. His face shone like the sun, and his clothes became as white as light. Then the disciples saw Moses and Elijah appear, and they were talking to Jesus.'

These are the divine wonders we celebrate today; this is the saving revelation given us upon the mountain; this is the festival of Christ that has drawn us here. Let us listen, then, to the sacred voice of God so compellingly calling us from on high, from the summit of the mountain, so that with the Lord's chosen disciples we may penetrate the deep meaning of these holy mysteries, so far beyond our capacity to express. Jesus goes before us to show us the way, both up the mountain and into heaven, and – I speak boldly – it is for us now to follow him with all speed, yearning for the heavenly vision that will give us a share in his radiance, renew our spiritual nature and transform us into his own likeness, making us for ever sharers in his Godhead and raising us to heights as yet undreamed of.

Let us run with confidence and joy to enter into the cloud like Moses and Elijah, or like James and John. Let us be caught up like Peter to behold the divine vision and to be transfigured by that glorious transfiguration. Let us retire from the world, stand aloof from the earth, rise above the body, detach ourselves from creatures and turn to the creator, to whom Peter in ecstasy exclaimed: 'Lord, it is good for us to be here.'

It is indeed good to be here, as you have said, Peter. It is good to be with Jesus and to remain here for ever. What greater happiness or higher honour could we have than to be with God, to be made like him and to live in his light? Therefore, since each of us who possesses God in our heart is being transformed into the divine image, we also should cry out with joy: 'It is good for us to be here' – here where all things shine with divine radiance, where there is joy and gladness and exultation; where there is nothing in our hearts but peace, serenity and stillness; where God is seen. For here, in our hearts, Christ takes up his abode together with the Father, saying as he enters: 'Today salvation has come to this house.' With Christ, our hearts receive all the wealth of his eternal blessings, and there where they are stored up for us in him, we see reflected as in a mirror both the firstfruits and the whole of the world to come.

alternative reading

A Reading from the *Spiritual Homilies* of Pseudo-Macarius

When the soul is counted worthy to enjoy communion with the Spirit of the light of God, and when God shines upon the soul with the beauty of his ineffable glory, preparing her as a throne and dwelling for himself, she becomes all light, all face, all eye. Then there is no part of her that is not full of the spiritual eyes of light. There is no part of her that is in darkness, but she is transfigured wholly and in every part with light and spirit.

Just as the sun is the same throughout, having neither back nor anything irregular, but is wholly glorified with light and is all light, being transformed in every part; or as fire, with its burning sheath of flame, is constant throughout, having neither a beginning nor an end, being neither larger nor smaller in any part, so also when the soul is perfectly illumined with the ineffable beauty and glory of the light of Christ's countenance, and granted perfect communion with the Holy Spirit and counted worthy to become the dwelling-place and throne of God, then the soul becomes all eye, all light, all face, all glory, all spirit.

alternative reading

A Reading from *Be Still and Know* by Michael Ramsey

In Saint Luke's account of the transfiguration of our Lord, we see his characteristic relating of a scene to prayer and to the mission of Jesus as he moves towards death and glory. Jesus is praying, and the light shines on his face. We do not know that it is a prayer of agony and conflict like the prayer in Gethsemane, but we know that it is a prayer near to the radiance of God and the prayer of one who has chosen the way of death. Luke tells us that the two witnesses Moses and Elijah were conversing about the exodus which Jesus would accomplish in Jerusalem: not death alone, but the passing through death to glory, the whole going forth of Jesus as well as the leading forth of the new people of God in the freedom of the new covenant. Luke tells us that after the resurrection Jesus spoke of the witness of Moses and of all the prophets to his suffering and glory.

It was not a glory which the disciples at the time could fathom. No doubt they would have welcomed a glory on the mountain far away from the conflicts which had happened and the conflicts which were going to happen as Jesus sets his face towards Jerusalem. Yet when Jesus went up the mountain to be transfigured he did not leave these conflicts behind, but rather carried them up the mountain so that they were transfigured with him. It was the transfiguration of the whole Christ, from his first obedience in childhood right through to the final obedience of Gethsemane and Calvary.

The disciples could not grasp this at the time, but the writings of the apostolic age were to show that the link between the suffering and the glory came to be understood as belonging to the heart of the Christian message. Glory belongs to the plain as well as to the mountain. The scene on the mount speaks to us today, but we are not allowed to linger there. We are bidden to journey on to Calvary and there learn of the darkness and the desolation which are the cost of the glory. But from Calvary and Easter there comes a Christian hope of immense range: the hope of the transformation not only of mankind but of the cosmos too.

In Eastern Christianity especially there has been the continuing belief that Easter is the beginning of a transformed cosmos. There is a glimpse of this hope in Saint Paul's Letter to the Romans, a hope that the creation itself will be set free from its bondage to decay and obtain 'the glorious liberty of the children of God'. The bringing of mankind to glory will be the prelude to the bringing of all creation. Is this hope mere fantasy? At its root there is the belief in the divine sovereignty of sacrificial love, a sovereignty made credible only by transfigured lives.

7 August

John Mason Neale

Priest, Hymn Writer, 1866

John Mason Neale was born in 1818 and, whilst an undergraduate at Cambridge, was influenced by the ideas of the Tractarians. He was a founder of the Cambridge Camden Society, which stimulated interest in ecclesiastical art and which played a part in the revival of Catholic ritual in the Church of England. Whilst Warden of Sackville College, East Grinstead, a post he held from 1846, Neale founded the Society of St Margaret, which grew into one of the largest of Anglican women's Religious communities. Neale is remembered as an accomplished hymn writer and his influence on Anglican worship has been considerable. He suffered frail health for many years and died on the Feast of the Transfiguration in 1866.

A Reading from a sermon of John Mason Neale preached at Sackville College on All Saints' Day

'In my Father's house are many mansions; if it were not so, I would have told you,' says our Lord. A mansion for every one of us, if we really choose to have it. Wishing will not serve the turn; trying a little will not serve the turn; trying a great deal and then leaving off will not serve the turn; but resolving with the grace of the Holy Ghost will.

Great cause have we to rejoice in this Feast of the Saints; good cause have we to think it one of the greatest in the whole year. We keep in memory the saints and righteous persons, known and unknown, not of one nation, not of one kingdom, not of one age, but of every kindred and tongue and people, from just Abel who was slain for the truth, down to the last Christian that has this very day died the death of the righteous. This feast belongs to us.

There is no Christian family so unhappy as not to have some of its ancestors in paradise. Some of you have lost baptized children in infancy. Then we keep them in memory too; seeing that God hath embraced them with the arms of his mercy, and made them partakers of everlasting life. Is the day ours in a more particular sense still? Yes, it is: for if of God's great goodness we ever merit to enter into life eternal, the time will come, and not long hence, when we also shall be of the number of the saints. Now we keep others in memory – then we shall be kept in memory ourselves: now we celebrate others – then others will celebrate us.

This can only be if we walk and live like the saints, thinking no labour too great, no battle too hard, forgetting that there is such a word in the language as 'cannot'. Cannot has kept many a soul out of heaven. We *can* do all things through Christ who strengthens us. And if we resolve, by the help of the Holy Ghost, to take heaven by violence, and persevere in our resolve, we shall receive from him grace in this life, and in the life to come, the reward of grace which is glory.

alternative reading

A Reading from an essay on *English Hymnology: Its History and Prospects* by John Mason Neale

Among the most pressing of the inconveniences consequent on the adoption of the vernacular language in the office-books of the Reformation, must be reckoned the immediate disuse of all the hymns of the Western Church. That treasury, into which the saints of every age and country had poured their contributions, delighting, each in his generation, to express their hopes and fears, their joys and sorrows, in language which should be the heritage of their holy Mother to the end of time – those noble hymns, which had solaced anchorites on their mountains, monks in their cells, priests in bearing up against the burden and heat of the day, missionaries in girding themselves for martyrdom – henceforth they became as a sealed book and as a dead letter. The prayers and collects, the versicles and responses, of the earlier Church might, without any great loss of beauty, be preserved; but the hymns, whether of the sevenfold daily office, of the weekly commemoration of creation and redemption, of the yearly revolution of the Church's seasons, or of the birthdays to glory of martyrs and confessors – those hymns by which day unto day had uttered speech, and night unto night had taught knowledge – they could not, by the hands then employed in ecclesiastical matters, be rendered into another, and that a then comparatively barbarous tongue. One attempt the Reformers made – the version of the *Veni Creator Spiritus* in the Ordinal; and that, so far perhaps fortunately, was the only one. Cranmer, indeed, expressed some casual hope that men fit for the office might be induced to come forward; but the very idea of a hymnology of the time of Henry VIII may make us feel thankful that the primate's wish was not carried out.

The Church of England had, then, to wait. She had, as it has been well said, to begin over again. There might arise saints within herself, who, one by one, should enrich her with hymns in her own language; there might arise poets, who should be capable of supplying her office-books with versions of hymns of earlier times. In the meantime the psalms were her own; and grievous as was the loss she had sustained, she might be content to suffice herself with those, and expect in patience the rest.

8 August

Dominic

Priest, Founder of the Order of Preachers, 1221

Born at Calaruega in Castile, of the ancient Guzman family in 1170, Dominic became an Augustinian or Austin Friar and led a disciplined life of prayer and penance. He became prior in 1201 but three years later, whilst on a trip to Denmark with his bishop, he passed through France and came across Cathars or Albigenses. They claimed to be Christians but held the heterodox belief that flesh and material things were evil, that the spirit was of God, and that flesh and spirit were therefore in permanent conflict. Dominic formed an Order of Preachers to combat this belief, although he would have nothing to do with the vengeful Crusade that began to be waged against the Albigenses. The Dominican Order spread to many countries in just a few years and did much to maintain the credibility of the orthodox faith in late medieval Europe. Dominic died on this day at Bologna in the year 1221.

A Reading from selected sources of the history
of the Order of Preachers

Dominic possessed such great integrity and was so strongly motivated by divine love, that without a doubt he proved to be a bearer of honour and grace. He was a man of great serenity, except when moved to compassion and mercy. And since a joyful heart animates the face, he displayed the peaceful composure of a spiritual person in the kindness he manifested outwardly and by the cheerfulness of his countenance.

Wherever he went he showed himself in word and deed to be a follower of the Gospel. During the day no one was more community-minded or pleasant toward associates. During the night hours no one was more persistent in every kind of vigil and supplication. Dominic seldom spoke unless it was with God, that is, in prayer, or about God; and in this matter he instructed his brothers.

Frequently Dominic made a special personal petition that God would deign to grant him a genuine charity, effective in caring for and in obtaining the salvation of humankind. For he believed that only then would he be truly a member of Christ, when he had given himself totally for the salvation of all, just as the Lord Jesus, the Saviour of all, had offered himself completely for our salvation. So, for this work, after a lengthy period of careful and provident planning, Dominic founded the Order of Friars Preachers.

In his conversations and letters he often urged the brothers of the Order to study constantly the Old and New Testaments. He always carried with him the Gospel according to Matthew and the Epistles of Paul, and so well did he study them that he almost knew them from memory. Two or three times Dominic was chosen bishop, but he always refused, preferring to live with his brothers in poverty.

9 August

Felim

Father of Columba, *c.*560

According to tradition, Felim ('Fedilimth' in Adamnán's life of Columba) was the father of Columba. The abbey on Trinity Island in Lough Oughter, not far from the diocesan cathedral, recalls the early days of Christianity in Cavan and the neighbourhood. A later Norman doorway from the island is now incorporated in the present cathedral at Kilmore. Felim died on this day in about the year 560.

A Reading from *The Life of Columba* by Adamnán, a later abbot of Iona

There was a man of venerable life and blessed memory, the father and founder of monasteries, whose name was the same as the prophet Jonah's. For though the sound is different in three different languages, in Hebrew *Jona*, in Greek *Perister*, in Latin *Columba*, the meaning is the same, 'dove'. So great a name cannot have been given to the man of God but by divine providence. For it is shown by the Gospels that the Holy Spirit descended upon the only begotten Son of the everlasting Father in the form of that little bird. For this reason, in the Scriptures the dove is generally taken allegorically to represent the Holy Spirit.

Earlier still, many years before the time of his birth, by revelation of the Holy Spirit to a soldier of Christ, Columba was marked out as a son of promise in a marvellous prophecy. A certain pilgrim from Britain, named Mochta, a holy disciple of the holy bishop Patrick, made this prophecy about our patron, which has been passed down by those who learnt it of old and held it to be genuine:

'In the last days of the world, a son will be born whose name Columba will become famous through all the provinces of the ocean's islands, and he will be a bright flight in the last days of the world. The fields of our two monasteries, mine and his, will be separated by only a little hedge. A man very dear to God and of great merit in his sight.'

Saint Columba was born of noble lineage. His father was Fedilimth mac Ferguso, his mother was called Eithne and her father Mac Naue which means 'son of a ship'. In the second year following the battle of Cúl Drebene, when he was forty-one Columba sailed away from Ireland to Britain, choosing to be a pilgrim for Christ.

From boyhood he had devoted himself to training in the Christian life, and to the study of wisdom; with God's help, he had kept his body chaste and his mind pure, and shown himself, though placed on earth, fit for the life of heaven. He was like an angel in demeanour, blameless in what he said, godly in what he did, brilliant in intellect and great in counsel.

9 August

Crumnathy (Nathi)

Religious, *c.*610

The Monastery at Achonry in County Sligo was founded by Finnian of Clonard at some date in the sixth century, and was established under Nathi as a centre of prayer and study. Nathi died on this day in about the year 610.

A Reading from the *Conferences* of John Cassian

Every art and every discipline has a particular objective, that is to say, a target and an end peculiarly its own. Someone keenly engaged in any one art calmly and freely endures every toil, danger, and loss. The farmer, for instance, does not shirk the burning rays of the sun or the frosts and the ice as he tirelessly cuts through the earth, as, over and over again, he ploughs the untamed clods of soil. All the time he is pursuing his objective, clearing all brambles from the field, clearing away all grass, breaking up the earth until it is like fine sand. He is aware that there is no other way to achieve his aim, which is the prospect of an abundant harvest and a rich yield of crops so that he may live securely or add to his possessions. He draws the grain willingly from the fullness of his barns and, working intensively, he invests it in the loosened soil. He pays no attention to what he is losing now because he is thinking ahead to the coming harvests.

Again, there are those who engage in commerce. They are not frightened by the hazards of the sea. No dangers terrify them. Borne up by their hope of profit they are carried toward their goal.

It is the same with those inflamed by military ambitions. They look toward the goal of honours and power and as they do so they shrug off doom and danger while they venture afar. They are brought down neither by the sufferings of the moment nor by wars, so long as they keep before themselves the honoured plan to which they aspire.

So also our monastic profession. It too has its own objective and goal to which, not just tirelessly but with true joy, we devote all our labours. The hunger of fasts does not weary us. The tiredness from keeping vigil is a delight to us. The reading and the endless meditation on Scripture are never enough for us. The unfinished toil, the nakedness, the complete deprivation, the fear that goes with this enormous loneliness, do not frighten us off.

The objective of our life and labours is the kingdom of God, but we should carefully ask what we should aim for. If we do not look very carefully into this we will wear ourselves out in useless strivings. For those who travel without a marked road there is the toil of the journey – and no arrival at a destination. Our point of reference, our objective, is a clean heart, without this it is impossible for anyone to reach our target.

9 August

Augustine Baker

Priest and Monk, 1641

Augustine Baker was born David Baker in Abergavenny in 1575. After studying at Oxford, he became a lawyer and was made Recorder of his home town. In 1600, he narrowly escaped death when crossing a dangerous bridge, an escape he attributed to divine providence, and he turned from a faithless life to Christianity. His parents had been sympathetic to Rome, and David Baker became a Roman Catholic in 1603. He was clothed as a Benedictine monk in Italy, taking the name Augustine, and was ordained priest. He travelled much between England and the Continent, recording the history of the English Benedictines from the earliest times, and wrote extensive works on spirituality in which he explored the life of prayer. His writings were subsequently edited into a classic of mystical theology Sacra Sancta, or Holy Wisdom. He died in London of the plague on 9 August 1641, and was buried in the churchyard of St Andrew's, Holborn.

A Reading from *Holy Wisdom* by Augustine Baker

The whole employment of an internal contemplative life having been by me comprehended under two duties, to wit, mortification and prayer, we have discoursed upon the former. We are now henceforward to treat of the other most noble and divine instrument of perfection, which is prayer; by which and in which alone we attain to the reward of all our endeavours, the end of our creation and redemption – to wit, union with God, in which alone consists our happiness and perfection.

By prayer, in this place, I do not understand petition or supplication, which according to the doctrine of the schools, is exercised principally by the understanding, being a signification of what a person desires to receive from God. But prayer here especially is meant rather an offering and giving to God whatsoever he may justly require from us – that is, all duty, love, obedience; and it is principally, yea, almost only exercised by the affective part of the soul.

Now prayer may be defined to be an elevation of the mind to God, or more largely and expressly thus: prayer is an affectuous actuation of an intellective soul towards God, expressing or at least implying an entire dependence on him as the author and fountain of all good, a will and readiness to give him his due, which is no less than all love, obedience, adoration, glory, and worship, by humbling and annihilating of herself and all creatures in his presence; and lastly, a desire and intention to aspire to an union of spirit with him.

This is the nature and these the necessary qualities which are all, at least virtually, involved in all prayer, whether it be made interiorly in the soul only, or withal expressed by words or outward signs.

Hence it appears that prayer is the most perfect and most divine action that a rational soul is capable of; yea, it is the only principal action for the exercising of which the soul was created, since in prayer alone the soul is united to God. And by consequence, it is of all other actions and duties the most indispensably necessary.

Hence it is also that all the devil's quarrels and assaults are chiefly, if not only, against prayer; the which if he can extinguish, he has all that he aims at – separating us from the fruition and adhesion to God, and therewith from all good. And hence likewise it is that the duty of prayer is enjoined after such a manner as no other duty is, for we are commanded to exercise it without intermission: 'We must needs pray continually and never lose heart'.

9 August

Mary Sumner

Founder of the Mothers' Union, 1921

Mary Elizabeth Sumner (née Heywood) was born in 1828 at Swinton. In 1848, she married a young curate, George Henry Sumner, nephew of Archbishop Sumner, who was himself to become Bishop of Guildford in 1888. A mother of three children, Mary called a meeting in 1876 at which the Mothers' Union was founded, providing a forum in which to unite mothers of all classes in the aim of bringing up children in the Christian faith. Baptism and parental example were its two basic principles. At first a parochial organization, it grew steadily into an international concern, encouraging the ideal of a Christian home. Mary died on this day in the year 1921.

A Reading from *Mary Sumner: Her Life and Work*
compiled by Mary Porter

It was a heavy task Mary Sumner set herself in the launching of the Mothers' Union. Once or twice she owned that the strain of those first years was sometimes not far from breaking her down. It was her way, however, to constantly relieve the strain of her own efforts by the worship of God's glory. Addressing a group in Winchester she said:

> Let us settle it in our hearts that the greatest work we can do for the nation is to strive to bring the Church into the home; which means Christ himself into hearts and homes. Christ must be in every home, if it is to be in any way a home of peace and love.
>
> God's plans are better than our own, and he has ordained that the training-place for his human creatures should be the *home*; the training-place for *parents* as well as children.
>
> Our task is to restore true family life – for it is God's own institution, and therefore a divine thing – and to convince all our members that there are these two divine institutions in the world: the Church and the home. The home is God's institution as truly as is the Church: let that be the truth that we proclaim!

In November 1887 the first Diocesan Conference of the Mothers' Union was held in Winchester at which Mary Sumner was able to report a beginning full of promise. At the Conference the following statement was accepted which was to form the basis of the Mothers' Union:

The Principles upon which we would build our work are these:
That the prosperity of a nation springs from the family life of the homes;

That family life is the greatest institution in the world for the formation of the character of children;

That the tone of family life depends in great measure upon the married life of the parents – their mutual love, loyalty and faithfulness the one to the other;

That religion is the indispensable foundation of family life, and that the truths of the Christian faith should be taught definitely at home as well as at school;

That parents are themselves responsible for the religious teaching of their children;

That character is formed during the first ten years of life by the example and habits of the home;

That example is stronger than precept, and parents therefore must be themselves what they wish their children to be;

That the history of the world proves the divine power given by God to parents, and to mothers especially, because children are placed in their arms from infancy, in a more intimate and closer relationship with the mother than with the father, and this moreover, during the time when character is formed;

That the training of children is a profession;

That it needs faith, love, patience, method, self-control, and some knowledge of the principles of character-training;

That it is the duty of every mother with her own lips to teach her child that he is God's child, consecrated body and soul in Holy Baptism to be our Lord Jesus Christ's soldier and servant unto his life's end;

That every baptized child should be taught the Creed, the Lord's Prayer and the Ten Commandments and all other things which a Christian ought to know and believe to his soul's health.

9 August

Edith Stein

Teacher of the Faith, Religious and Martyr, 1942

Edith Stein was born into a devout Jewish family in 1891 in Breslau, Germany (now Wroclaw, Poland). She considered herself an atheist until in 1921 she read the autobiography of Teresa of Avila and was convinced of the truth of Christianity. She was baptized and became a leading voice in the Catholic Women's Movement in Germany. With Hitler's rise to power, Edith was concerned with the mounting tide of anti-Semitism. She became a Carmelite, taking the name Teresa Benedicta of the Cross. After the terror of Kristallnacht (9 November 1938), she was sent secretly to the Netherlands, but when that country fell to the Nazis the Gestapo rounded up all Roman Catholic Jews to be sent to the death camps. Edith Stein was arrested on 2 August 1942, saying as she was taken from her convent, 'We go for our people'. Edith Stein was deported to Auschwitz and was executed just a week later.

A Reading from *The Scholar and the Cross: The Life and Work of Edith Stein* by Hilda C. Graef

On 2 August 1942, as a reprisal for the pastoral letter promulgated by the bishops, all non-Aryan Catholics were arrested throughout Holland. Among them was Edith Stein. It was there, in the camp of utter human misery and despair, that she grew to the full stature of Christian charity. The simple statement of a Jewish businessman who had the good fortune to escape deportation and death is the most eloquent testimony of the height she had reached. He wrote:

> Among the prisoners who arrived at Auschwitz on 5th August, Sister Benedicta made a striking impression by her great calm and composure. The misery in the camp and the excitement among the newcomers were indescribable. Sister Benedicta walked about among the women, comforting, helping, soothing like an angel. Many mothers were almost demented and had for days not been looking after their children, but had been sitting brooding in listless despair. Sister Benedicta at once took care of the poor little ones, washed and combed them, and saw to it that they got food and attention. As long as she was in the camp she made washing and cleaning one of her principal charitable activities, so that everyone was amazed.

When she was not occupied with these, the contemplative side of her was allowed to show itself. Another prisoner gave this account:

> The great difference between Edith Stein and the others lay in her silence. My personal impression is that she was most deeply sorrowful, but without anxiety. I cannot express it better than by saying that she gave the impression of bearing such an enormous load of sorrow that even when she did smile it only made one more sorrowful. She hardly ever spoke, but she often looked at her sister Rosa with indescribable sadness… She was thinking of their sorrow she foresaw, not her own sorrow, for that she was far too calm, she thought of the sorrow that awaited the others. Her whole appearance, as I picture her in my memory sitting in that hut, suggested only one thought to me: a Pietà without Christ.

Once her attitude at prayer had reminded a Benedictine monk of one of the Orantes of ancient Christian art; now Sister Benedicta of the Cross was being transformed into an image of the Mater Dolorosa whom she had loved so much. At her profession the virgin had become a bride; now her course was complete, she had truly become a mother – a mother tending little children whose natural mothers neglected them; a sorrowful mother, suffering with and for her children, who like herself, would soon be driven into the gas chambers to be liquidated like vermin.

alternative reading

A Reading from an essay on 'The Knowledge of God' by Edith Stein

In all true knowledge of God, God himself comes to us, though his presence is not actually felt except when it is a case of experimental knowledge. In natural knowledge, God approaches man through images, words and various effects; in faith through his self-revelation in his Word. Whenever we are concerned with the question of knowing a person, there is not only the possibility of self-manifestation, but also of its opposite, barring the approach to knowledge, and further the possibility of hiding behind one's work. This work will then still have its real meaning and significance, but it will no longer be the means of contact between two minds. God will let himself be found by those who seek him. Therefore he desires to be sought. Hence we shall understand why natural revelation is not perfectly clear and unequivocal, but rather a spur inviting further search, whereas supernatural revelation answers the questions raised by natural revelation.

Faith is already finding God and means that God lets himself be found to a certain extent, not only in the sense that he allows us to be told something about him by his Word, but also that he actually lets himself be found in it. Faith is a gift that must be accepted; here divine and human freedom meet. But it belongs to its nature that it must ask for more. Being a dark knowledge lacking true insight, faith arouses the desire for unveiled brightness; being an indirect meeting it makes us wish to meet God directly, the very content of faith excites this longing by promising the beatific vision.

10 August

Laurence

Deacon at Rome, Martyr, 258

The sources for the martyrdom of Laurence are among the earliest, though the details are thin. Laurence was one of the seven deacons at Rome and closely associated with Pope Sixtus II, martyred just a few days before him. His examiners insisted he produce the Church treasures. He promptly did so: assembling all the poor, he is reputed to have said, 'These are the treasures of the Church.' The tradition of his being put to death on a gridiron is probably a later addition to the story. He died on this day in the year 258.

A Reading from a sermon of Leo the Great

No model is more useful in teaching God's people than that of the martyrs. Eloquence may enable intercession, reasoning may succeed in persuading; but in the end examples are always more powerful than words, and teaching communicates better through practice than precept. In this respect, how gloriously powerful is the blessed martyr Laurence whose sufferings we commemorate today. Even his persecutors felt the power of his teaching when they were confronted by his courage, a courage born of love for Christ, which not only refused to yield to them, but actually gave strength to those around him.

When the fury of the pagans was raging against Christ's most chosen members and attacking those especially who were ordained, the wicked persecutor's wrath was vented on Laurence the deacon, who was outstanding not only in the performance of the liturgy, but also in the management of the church's property. The persecutor promised himself a double spoil from this man's capture, reasoning that if once he could force Laurence to surrender the Church's treasures, his action would also discredit him irredeemably. Greedy for money and an enemy to the truth, the persecutor armed himself with a double weapon: with avarice to plunder the gold, and with impiety to carry off Christ.

And so it was that he demanded that the Church's wealth, on which his greedy mind was set, should be brought out to him. The holy deacon then showed him where he had it stored. He pointed to a crowd of holy poor people, in the feeding and clothing of whom, he said, was to be found a treasury of riches which could never be lost, and which was entirely secure because the money had been spent on so holy a cause. At first the plunderer was completely baffled, but then his anger blazed out into hatred for a religion which should put its wealth to such a use. Determined to pillage the Church's treasury, and finding no hoard of money, he resolved then to carry off a still greater prize by carrying off that sacred deposit of faith with which the Church was enriched.

He ordered Laurence to renounce Christ, and prepared to test the deacon's stout courage with terrifying tortures. The deacon's limbs, already torn and wounded by many beatings, were ordered to be roasted alive on an iron grid. The grid was already hot enough to burn anyone, but to prolong his agony and to make his death more lingering, they turned the grid from time to time in the fire so that only one limb at a time was in the flames.

You gain nothing by this, O savage cruelty. When his poor mortal frame is released from your devices, and Laurence departs for heaven, you are vanquished! The flame of Christ's love could not be overcome by your flames, and the fire which burnt outside was weaker than the fire that burnt within Laurence's heart.

11 August

Clare of Assisi

Founder of the Minoresses (Poor Clares), 1253

Born in 1193 in Assisi of a wealthy family, Clare caught the joy of a new vision of the gospel from Francis' preaching. Escaping from home, first to the Benedictines and then to a Béguine-style group, she chose a contemplative way of life when she founded her own community, which lived in corporate poverty understood as dependence on God, with a fresh, democratic lifestyle. Clare became the first woman to write a religious Rule for women, and in it showed great liberty of spirit in dealing with earlier prescriptions. During the long years after Francis' death, she supported his earlier companions in their desire to remain faithful to his vision, as she did. Some of her last words were: 'Blessed be God, for having created me.'

A Reading from the last letter of Clare to Blessed Agnes of Prague, written in 1253 shortly before Clare's death

If I have not written to you as often as your soul and mine well desire and long for, do not wonder or think that the fire of love for you glows less sweetly in the heart of your mother. No, this is the difficulty: the lack of messengers and the obvious dangers of the roads. Now, however, as I write to your love, I rejoice and exult with you in the joy of the Spirit, O bride of Christ, because since you have totally abandoned the vanities of this world, like another most holy virgin, Saint Agnes, you have been marvellously espoused to the spotless Lamb who takes away the sins of the world.

Happy indeed is she to whom it is given to share this banquet, to cling with all her heart to him whose beauty all the heavenly hosts admire unceasingly, whose love inflames our love, whose contemplation is our refreshment, whose graciousness is our joy, whose gentleness fills us to overflowing, whose remembrance brings a gentle light, whose fragrance will revive the dead, whose glorious vision will be the happiness of all the citizens of the heavenly Jerusalem.

Inasmuch as this vision is the splendour of eternal glory, the brilliance of eternal light and the mirror without blemish, look upon that mirror each day, O queen and spouse of Jesus Christ; and continually study your face in it so that you may adorn yourself within and without with beautiful robes, and cover yourself with the flowers and garments of all the virtues as becomes the daughter and most chaste bride of the Most High King. Indeed, blessed poverty, holy humility, and ineffable charity are reflected in that mirror as, by the grace of God, you can contemplate them throughout the entire mirror.

Look at the parameters of the mirror, that is the poverty of him who was placed in a manger and wrapped in swaddling clothes. O marvellous humility! O astonishing poverty! The King of the angels, the Lord of heaven and earth, is laid in a manger! Then, look at the surface of the mirror, dwell on the holy humility, the blessed poverty, the untold labours and burdens which he endured for the redemption of the world. Then, in the depths of this same mirror, contemplate the ineffable charity which led him to suffer on the wood of the cross and to die thereon the most shameful kind of death.

Therefore that mirror, suspended on the wood of the cross, urged those who passed by to reflect, saying, 'All you who pass by the way, look and see if there is any suffering like my suffering!' Let us answer his cry with one voice and spirit for he said, 'Remembering this over and over leaves my soul downcast within me.' In this way, O queen of our heavenly King, let yourself be inflamed more strongly with the fervour of charity.

And as you contemplate further his ineffable delights, his eternal riches and honours, and sigh for them in the great desire and love of your heart, may you cry out in the words of Solomon: 'Draw me after you! We will run in the fragrance of your perfumes, O heavenly spouse! I will run and not tire, until you bring me into the wine-cellar, until your left hand is under my head and your right hand will embrace me happily, and you kiss me with the happiest kiss of your mouth.'

In this contemplation may you remember your poor mother, knowing that I have inscribed the happy memory of you indelibly on the tablets of my heart, holding you dearer than all the others.

11 August

John Henry Newman

Priest, Tractarian, 1890

John Henry Newman was born in 1801. His intellectual brilliance saw him appointed to a Fellowship in Oxford at the young age of twenty-one. His Evangelical roots gradually gave way to a more Catholic view of the Church, particularly after liberal trends both in politics and theology appeared to undermine the Church of England's authority. Newman was one of the leaders of the Tractarians who defended the Church and he is associated especially with the idea of Anglicanism as a via media or middle way between Roman Catholicism and Protestantism. He continued to make an original and influential contribution to theology after he joined the Roman Catholic Church in 1845. He established an Oratorian community in Birmingham in 1849 and towards the end of his life was made a Cardinal. He died on this day in the year 1890.

A Reading from a sermon of John Henry Newman preached in December 1831

How are we the better for being members of the Christian Church? This is a question which has ever claims on our attention; but it is right from time to time to examine our hearts with more than usual care. I ask, then, how are we the better for being Christ's disciples? Have we received the kingdom of God in word or power?

If we would form a just notion how far we are influenced by the power of the gospel, we must evidently put aside everything which we do merely in imitation of others, and not from religious principle. Not that we can actually separate our good words and works into two classes, and say what is done from faith, and what is done only by accident, and in a random way. Nevertheless, without being able to draw the line, it is quite evident that so very much of our apparent obedience to God arises from mere obedience to the world and its fashions; or rather, that it is difficult to say what *is* done in the spirit of faith. Let a person merely reflect on the number and variety of bad or foolish thoughts which he suffers and dwells on in private which he would be ashamed to put into words, and he will at once see how very poor a test his outward demeanour in life is of his real holiness in the sight of God. Or again, let him consider the number of times he has attended public worship as a matter of course because others do, and without seriousness of mind.

Now when I say this, am I condemning all that we do without thinking expressly of the duty of obedience at the very time we are doing it? Far from it; a religious person, in proportion as obedience becomes more and more easy to him, will doubtless do his duty unconsciously. It will be *natural* to him to obey, and therefore he will do it naturally, without effort or deliberation. It is difficult things we are obliged to think about before doing them. But when we have mastered our hearts we no more think of the duty while we obey, than we think how to walk when we walk. Separate acts of faith aid us only while we are *unstable.* This is where we begin. And as we grow in grace, we throw away childish things; then we are able to stand upright like grown-ups, without the props and aids which our infancy required. This is the noble manner of serving God, to do good without thinking about it, without any calculation or reasoning, from love of the good, and hatred of evil.

With others we have no concern; we do not know what their opportunities are. There may be thousands in this populous land who never had the means of hearing Christ's voice fully. Nor can we know the hearts of any, or tell what is the degree in which they have improved their talents. It is enough that we keep to ourselves. We dwell in the full light of the gospel, and the full grace of the sacraments. We ought, therefore, to have the holiness of the apostles, following them as they followed Christ.

12 August

Muredach (Murtagh)

Bishop, *c.*480

Muredach was an 'old man', perhaps a presbyter, in Patrick's household. At the conclusion of his mission to the West, Patrick left his companion to be bishop in west Sligo and Mayo. One tradition says that, at the end of his life, he went to live as a hermit on the island of Innishmurray. He died on this day in about the year 480.

A Reading from the *Confession* of Saint Patrick

It is in Ireland that I desire to wait for the promise of the God who never deceives us and who repeatedly promises us in the gospel that 'they will come from east and west, and from south and north, and sit at table with Abraham, Isaac, and Jacob.'

So it is right and proper that we should fish well and carefully, as the Lord warns and teaches us, saying: 'Follow me and I will make you fish for people.' And again he says through the mouth of the prophets: 'Behold! I send out fishermen and hunters, says God,' and so forth. Truly it is our task to cast our nets and catch 'a great multitude', a crowd for God. Equally, it is our task to ensure that there are clergy everywhere to baptize and preach to people who are in want and need. This is exactly what the Lord warns and teaches about in the gospel when he says, 'Go therefore, and teach all the nations, baptizing them in the name of the Father, and of the Son, and of the Holy Spirit, teaching them to observe all that I have commanded you. And behold, I am with you always, even to the close of the age.' And again, 'Go into all the world and preach the gospel to the entire universe. Those who believe and are baptized will be saved; but those who do not believe will be condemned.' And again, 'This gospel of the kingdom must be preached throughout the entire universe, as a testimony to all nations; and then the end will come.' The Lord also foretold this through the prophet when he said, 'And in the last days it shall come to pass, says the Lord, that I will pour out my Spirit upon all flesh. Your sons and daughters shall prophesy; your young men shall see visions, and your old men shall dream dreams; and indeed, on my male and female servants in those days I will pour out my spirit; and they shall prophesy.' Again, the prophet Hosea says, 'Those who were not my people, I shall call "my people", and she who was not beloved I will call "my beloved". And in the very place where it was said to them, "You are not my people," they will be called "sons and daughters of the living God".'

Such indeed is the case with Ireland where until now they have never enjoyed the knowledge of God, but have simply had idols and unclean things with which to celebrate. But recently, what a change has taken place! They have become a 'prepared people' of the Lord and 'children of God'. We see the sons and daughters of Irish chieftains becoming monks and virgins of Christ.

12 August

Blane

Missionary, 590

Blane received his education at Bangor in County Down under Comgall. He came to the island of Bute to work with his uncle, Catan, the centre of whose missionary operations was a settlement at Kingarth on Kilchattan Bay. There are many indications of the work of these two missionaries in Argyll, and Blane moved eastwards to Strathearn, where the medieval Dunblane Cathedral stands on the site of one of his foundations. The place and date of his death are uncertain, although the year 590 is now generally accepted.

A Reading from *The Rule of Comgall*

Be faithful to the rule of the gentle Lord, because therein lies your salvation. Far better that you not violate it while in this present life.

In this lies the heart of the rule: to love Christ, to shun wealth, to remain close to the heavenly king, and to be gentle towards all people.

What a wonderful road it is to remain faithful to self-denial, and to be eager for it. Let the monk daily bear in mind that he will die, and let him be zealous in his concern for every person.

The monk should make one hundred genuflections while chanting the psalm 'Blessed are those whose way is blameless', morning and evening. If this is done his reward will be great in the kingdom of heaven.

Let him, each morning, at the proper time, and with alacrity, completely prostrate himself three times, and let him make the sign of the cross over breast and face.

Do not practise long drawn-out devotions, but rather give yourself to prayer at intervals, as you would to food. Pious humbug is an invention of the devil.

A fire built of fern soon dies out. Do not be like flotsam, going with every current, if you wish to persevere in devotion.

When faced with innumerable battles against many vices, against the devil, or against the body, it is essential that you be resolute.

These three following counsels should be your guide, and nothing should be allowed to separate you from them: namely, have forbearance, humility, and the love of God in your heart.

Through fear comes the love of the king who heals every ill; for love of him we carry out his will and cherish his commandments.

The love of God embraces the whole world and powerfully restrains wandering thoughts. Fear is the master of repentance. The love of God determines the fervour of our piety.

Let us pray, then, to Christ in times of fear and hurt, that we may be granted relief.

12 August

Ann Griffiths

Poet, 1805

Ann Thomas was born at Dolwar Fach, Llanfihangel-yng-Ngwynfa, in 1776. At the age of twenty, Ann underwent an experience of conversion and she joined the Methodist Society in Pontrobert the following year. After her father's death in 1804 Ann married Thomas Griffiths, but died in August 1805, shortly after the birth of their child. Ann's hymns are among the greatest treasures of Welsh Christian literature. Most of them were learnt by heart by her illiterate maid, Ruth Evans. She repeated them to her husband, John Hughes, who wrote them down. Ann's verses combine a depth of personal spiritual experience with a profound understanding of the central truths of the Christian faith. Eight of her letters also survive and give an insight into the depths of her character and her beliefs.

A Reading from a hymn of Ann Griffiths

Rhyfedd, rhyfedd gan angylion,
Rhyfeddod fawr yng ngolwg ffydd,
Gweld rhoddwr bod, cynhaliwr helaeth
A rheolwr pob peth sydd,
Yn y preseb mewn cadachau
Aroi'i heb le i roi ben i lawr,
Ac eto disglair lu'r gogoniant
Yn ei addoli ef yn awr.

Pan o Sinai i gyd yn mygu,
A swn yr utgorn uch'i radd
Caf fynd i wledda tros y terfyn
Yng Nghrist y Gair heb gael fy lladd;
Mae yno'n trigo bob cyflawnder,
Llond gwagle colledigaeth dyn;
Ar yr adwy rhwng y ddwyblaid
Gwnaeth gymod trwy ei offrymu ei hun.

Efe yw'r Lawn fu rhwng y lladron,
Efe ddioddefodd angau loes,
Efe a nerthodd freichiau ei ddenyddwyr
I'w hoelio yno ar y groes;
Wrth dalu dyled pentewynion
Ac anrhydeddu deddf ei Dad,
Cyfiawnder, mae'n disgleirio'n danbaid
Wrth faddau yn nhrefn y cymod rhad.

O f'enaid, gwêl y an gorweddodd
Pen brenhinoedd, awdwr hedd,
Y greadigaeth ynddo'n symud,
Yntau'n farw yn y bedd;
Cân a bywyd colledigion,
Rhyfeddod mwya' angylion nef,
Gweld Duw mewn cnawd a'i gydaddoli
Mae'r côr dan weiddi 'Iddo Ef'.

Diolch byth, a chanmil diolch,
Diolch tra bo ynof chwyth
Am fod gwrthrych i'w addoli
A thestun cân i bara byth;
Yn fy natur wedi ei demtio
Fel y gwaela'o ddynol-ryw,
Yn ddyn bach, yn wan, yn ddinerth, \
Yn anfeidrol wir a bywiol Dduw.

Yn llcario corff o lygredd,
Cyd-dreiddio â'r côr yn danllyd fry
I ddiderfyn ryfeddodau
Lachawdwriaeth Calfari,
Byw i weld yr Anweledig
Fu farw ac sy'n awr yn fyw,
Tragwyddol anwahanol undeb
A chymundeb â fy Nuw.

Yno caf ddyrchafu'r Enw
A osododd Duw yn lawn
Heb ddychymyg' llen na gorchudd,
A'm henaid ar ei ddelw'n llawn;
Yng nghymdeithas y dirgelwch
Datgnddiedig yn ei glwy',
Cusanu'r mab i dragwyddoldeb
Heb im gefnu arno mwy.

Wonderful, wonderful in the sight of angels,
a great wonder in the eyes of faith,
to see the giver of being,
the generous sustainer and ruler of everything that is,
in the manger in swaddling clothes
and with nowhere to lay his head,
and yet the bright host of glory
worshipping him now.

When Sinai is altogether on smoke,
and the sound of the trumpet at its loudest,
in Christ the Word I can go to feast
across the boundary without being slain;
in him all fullness dwells,
enough to fill the gulf of man's perdition;
in the breach, between the parties,
he made reconciliation through his self-offering.

He is the Satisfaction that was between the thieves,
he suffers the pains of death,
it was he who gave to the arms of his executioners

the power to nail him there to the cross;
when he pays the debt of brands plucked out of the burning,
and honours his Father's law,
Righteousness shines with fiery blaze
as it pardons within the terms of the free reconciliation.

O my soul, behold the place where lay the chief of kings,
the author of peace,
all creation moving in him,
and he lying dead in the tomb;
song and life of the lost,
greatest wonder of the angels of heaven,
the choir of them sees God in flesh and worships him together,
crying out 'Unto him'.

Thanks for ever, and a hundred thousand thanks,
thanks while there is breath in me,
that there is an object to worship
and a theme for a song to last for ever;
in my nature, tempted
like the lowest of mankind,
a babe, weak, powerless,
the infinite true and living God.

Instead of carrying a body of corruption,
to penetrate ardently with the choir above
into the endless wonders of the salvation
wrought on Calvary,
to live to see the Invisible
who was dead and now is alive –
eternal inseparable union
and communion with my God!

There I shall exalt the Name
which God has set forth to be a Propitiation,
without imagination, curtain or covering
and with my soul fully in his likeness;
in the fellowship of the mystery revealed in his wounds,
I shall kiss the Son to all eternity,
and never turn from him any more.

13 August

Jeremy Taylor

Bishop of Down and Connor, Teacher of the Faith, 1667

Jeremy Taylor was born in Cambridge in 1613 and educated there at Gonville and Caius College. He was ordained in 1633 and, as the Civil War got under way, he became a chaplain with the Royalist forces. He was captured and imprisoned briefly but after his release went to Wales, where the Earl of Carbery gave him refuge. He wrote prolifically whilst there, notably The Rule and Exercise of Holy Living in 1650 and of Holy Dying the following year. In 1658 he went to Ireland to lecture and two years later was made Bishop of Down and Connor. He found many of his clergy held to Presbyterianism and so ignored him; and the Roman Catholics rejected him as a Protestant. In turn, he treated both sides harshly. His health was worn down by the protracted conflicts and he died on this day in the year 1667.

A Reading from *Holy Living* by Jeremy Taylor

When religion puts on armour, it may have the power of the sword, but not the power of godliness, and we have no remedy but the fellowship of Christ's sufferings, and the returns of the God of peace. Men are apt to prefer a prosperous error before an afflicted truth; and that those few who have no other plot in their religion but to serve God and save their souls, do want such assistance of ghostly counsel as may assist their endeavours in the acquist of virtues, and relieve their dangers when they are tempted to sin and death; I thought I had reasons enough inviting me to draw into one body those advices: that a collection of holy precepts and the rules for conduct might be committed to a book which they might always have.

A man does certainly belong to God who believes and is baptized into all the articles of the Christian faith, and studies to improve his knowledge in the matters of God, so as may best make him to live a holy life; he that, in obedience to Christ, worships God diligently, frequently, and constantly, with natural religion, that is of prayer, praises, and thanksgiving; he that takes all opportunities to remember Christ's death by a frequent sacrament, as it can be had, or else by inward acts of understanding, will and memory (which is spiritual communion) supplies the want of the external rite; he that lives chastely; and is merciful; and despises the world, using it as a man, but never suffering it to rifle a duty; and is just in his dealing, and diligent in his calling; he that is humble in spirit; and obedient to government; and is content in his fortune and employment; he that does his duty because he loves God;

and especially if after all this he be afflicted, and patient, or prepared to suffer affliction for the cause of God: the man that has these twelve signs of grace does as certainly belong to God, and is his son as surely, as he is his creature.

These are the marks of the Lord Jesus, and the characters of a Christian: this is a good religion; and these things God's grace hath put into our powers, and God's laws have made to be our duty, and the nature of man, and the needs of commonwealths, have made to be necessary.

13 August

Florence Nightingale

Nurse, Social Reformer, 1910

Florence Nightingale was born in 1820 into a wealthy family. In the face of their opposition, she insisted that she wished to train in nursing. In 1853, she finally achieved her wish and headed her own private nursing institute in London. Her efforts at improving conditions for the wounded during the Crimean War won her great acclaim and she devoted the rest of her life to reforming nursing care. Her school at St Thomas's Hospital became significant in helping to elevate nursing into a profession. An Anglican, she remained committed to a personal mystical religion which sustained her through many years of poor health until her death in the year 1910.

A Reading from *The Silent Rebellion* by A. M. Allchin

The heroism and ability of Florence Nightingale, and of the nurses who worked with her in the Crimea, caught the imagination of mid-nineteenth century England, and suddenly drew attention to the problem of the position and rights of women in society. A great many difficult questions were raised. Was it right, for instance, for an unmarried lady to make a career for herself in public life? If it were, what professions might she suitably take up? How far, if at all, should the mother of a family engage in activities outside her home? What should be the nature of women's education? These were all issues which had been thought about before 1854, but the events in the Crimea made them the centre of widespread and insistent discussion.

It is not easy at this length of time to envisage quite how restricted were the activities of a mid-Victorian lady. The case of Florence Nightingale, because of the outstanding quality of her character, and her exceptional outspokenness, reveals the situation to us in all its difficulty; and although she herself never became a member, or should one say the superior, of a community, her problems are very similar to those of her contemporaries who in fact entered the Anglican sisterhoods. She was facing all the weight of social convention, and the pitch of her feelings is plain in a private note which she wrote in 1851:

> Women don't consider themselves as human beings at all. There is absolutely no God, no country, no duty to them at all, except family. … I have known a good deal of convents. And, of course, everyone has talked of the petty tyrannies supposed to be exercised there. But I know nothing like the petty grinding tyranny of a good English family.

or again:

> What I complain of the Evangelical party for, is the degree to which they have raised the claims upon women of 'Family' – the idol they have made of it.

This intense dissatisfaction with the Evangelical party was in fact extended to the Church of England as a whole. In a letter written in 1852 she exclaims:

> The Church of England has for men bishoprics, archbishoprics, and a little work. … For women she has – what? I had no taste for theological discoveries. I would have given her my head, my hand, my heart. She would not have them. She did not know what to do with them. She told me to go back and do crochet in my mother's drawing room; or, if I were tired of that, to marry and look well at the head of my husband's table. You may go to the Sunday School if you like it, she said. But she gave me no training even for that. She gave me neither work to do for her, nor education for it.

Florence Nightingale was only able to break out of the restrictions of Victorian family life by force of character and exceptional perseverance.

13 August

Octavia Hill

Social Reformer, 1912

Octavia Hill was born in 1838 into a family active in social work, and, during her teens, she was influenced by the friendship of F. D. Maurice and John Ruskin. Earning her living through teaching, Octavia was appalled at the conditions in which most of her pupils lived. Borrowing money, she bought some slum properties and began to manage them in a more sympathetic way, insisting on financial viability rather than mere charity. The success of the scheme led to its extension and Octavia became a pioneer of housing reform. Strongly motivated by her faith, she never allowed her growing fame to undermine her personal humility. She continued her work until her death on this day in the year 1912.

A Reading from *Homes of the London Poor* by Octavia Hill

Two years ago I first had an opportunity of carrying out the plan I had long contemplated, that of obtaining possession of houses to be let in weekly tenements to the poor. That the spiritual elevation of a large class depended to a considerable extent on sanitary reform was, I considered, proved; but I was equally certain that sanitary improvement itself depended upon educational work among grown-up people.

I desired to be in a condition to free a few poor people from the tyranny and influence of a low-class of landlords and landladies; from the corrupting effect of continual forced communication with very degraded fellow-lodgers; from the heavy incubus of accumulated dirt: that so the never-dying hope which I find characteristic of the poor might have leave to spring, and with it such energy as might help them to help themselves.

It should be observed that well-built houses were chosen, but they were in a dreadful state of dirt and neglect. The repairs required were mainly of a superficial and slight character: slight in regard to expense – vital as to health and comfort. The place swarmed with vermin; the paper, black with dirt, hung in long strips from the walls; the drains were stopped, the water supply out of order. All these things were put in order, but no new appliances of any kind were added, as we had determined that our tenants should wait for these until they had proved themselves capable of taking care of them. A regular sum is set aside for repairs, and after breakage and damage have been attended to, each tenant decides in turn in what way any surplus shall be spent, so as to add to the comfort of the house. This regime has given our tenants a dignity and glad feeling of honourable behaviour.

I am also of the opinion that there is no need of the poor of London which more prominently forces itself on the notice of anyone working among them than that of space. To most men this is an inheritance to which they were born, and which they accept straight from God as they do the earth they tread on, and light and air, its companion gifts. Space it seems is a common gift to man, a thing he is not specially bound to provide for himself and his family; where it is not easily inherited, however, it seems to me it may be given by the state, the city, the millionaire, without danger of destroying the individual's power and habit of energetic self-help. We all need four things: places to sit in, places to play in, places to stroll in, and places to spend a day in.

I wish to urge the immense value to the education and reformation of our poorest people of some space near their homes, or within reasonable distance of them. We all need space; unless we have it we cannot reach that sense of quiet in which whispers of better things come to us gently. Our lives in London are over-crowded, over-excited, over-strained. This is true of all classes; we all want quiet; we all want beauty for the refreshment of our souls. Sometimes we think of it as a luxury, but when God made the world, he made it very beautiful, and meant that we should be amongst its beauties, and that they should speak to us in our daily lives.

14 August

Fachtna (Fachanan)

Bishop of Ross, sixth century

Fachtna was described as being 'a wise and upright man' and one with a great gift for preaching. He was founder of the community of Rosscarbery in West Cork. He lived and died in the sixth century.

A Reading from the treatise *Pastoral Care* by Gregory the Great

It often occurs when a sermon has been delivered well and with a powerful message, that afterwards the mind of the preacher is elated with a sense of joy at his own performance. In such circumstances, take great care to examine yourself rigorously, lest in restoring others to health by healing their inner wounds, you disregard your own inner well-being, and foster the cancer of pride. While helping your neighbour, never neglect to examine yourself; never raise up others, but fall yourself.

In many cases, the very greatness of a preacher's virtue can be the occasion of his downfall because he has felt over-confident in his own ability, and has perished through negligence. Indeed, in the struggle of virtue against vice, the mind can sometimes flatter itself. It is almost as if it becomes exhilarated by the contest with the result that the soul ceases to be cautious or circumspect, and puts its confidence in its own ability to perform well. It is at this juncture that the cunning Seducer infiltrates himself, enumerating to the soul a catalogue of our successes, enlarging the ego with conceited thoughts about superiority over others.

This is why it is so important that when a wealth of virtues flatter us, we should turn the eye of our soul to gaze upon our weaknesses, and that for our own good, we should constantly stand in humility before God. We should attend not to the good we have done, but to the good we have failed to do, so that while the heart becomes contrite in recollecting its frailty, it may be the more solidly established in the eyes of the Author of humility. For although almighty God will bring to perfection in large measure the minds of those whose task it is to lead, he will always leave them in some sense unfinished in order that, when they are resplendent in their marvellous achievements, they may still grieve their imperfections; and because they constantly have to struggle over trivial things that plague them, they will not be tempted to over-estimate themselves when confronted by major things. If they cannot overcome the little things of life that afflict them, they will be less likely to pride themselves on the great things they may accomplish.

14 August

Maximilian Kolbe

Friar, Martyr, 1941

Maximilian Kolbe was born at Zdunska Wola near Lodz in Poland in 1894. His parents were Franciscan Tertiaries and, beginning his training for ordination in 1907, Maximilian joined the Franciscan noviciate in 1910. He studied at Rome but, suffering from tuberculosis, he returned to Poland and became a lecturer in Church History. After suffering a severe illness, he resolved to publish a magazine for Christian readers and this soon gained a huge circulation. Soon his community was producing daily and weekly journals. After the Nazi invasion of Poland, Maximilian was arrested as an 'intellectual' and taken to Auschwitz in May 1941. There he continued his priestly ministry, secretly celebrating the Eucharist. When, after an escape, a prisoner was chosen to forfeit his life as an example, Maximilian stepped forward to take his place and be put to death. Two weeks later he was injected with phenol and died on this day in 1941.

A Reading from the homily of Pope John Paul II preached at the canonization of Maximilian Kolbe, 10 October 1982

'How can I repay the Lord for all his goodness to me? I will take up the cup of salvation and call upon the name of the Lord.' These are words of thankfulness. Death undergone for love, in place of a brother, is Father Kolbe's heroic act, by which we glorify God at the same time as his saint. For it is from God that the grace of such heroism, the grace of this martyrdom, comes.

Today, then, we glorify the great work of God in this man. Before all of us gathered here, Father Maximilian Kolbe raises his 'cup of salvation', in which is brought together the sacrifice of his whole life, sealed by his death as a martyr 'for his brother'. The world looked at what went on in the camp at Auschwitz. Even if it seemed to some eyes that one of their companions died in torture, even if humanly they could consider his 'going from them to be destruction', in reality they were aware that it was not merely death.

Maximilian is not dead, but he has 'given his life for his brother'. There was in that death, humanly so terrible, all the absolute greatness of the human act and human choice: he, himself, on his very own, had offered himself to death out of love.

And in this human death there was the transparent witness given to Christ: witness given in Christ to the dignity of humanity, to the sanctity of life, and to the saving power of death in which is revealed the strength of love. It is precisely on this account that the death of Maximilian Kolbe has become a sign of victory. It was a victory achieved over a whole system of outrage and hatred towards men and women, and towards what is divine in us, a victory like to that which our Lord Jesus Christ achieved on Calvary.

alternative reading

A Reading from *A Theology of Auschwitz* by Ulrich Simon

Theology is the science of divine reality. Auschwitz is a place in Poland where millions of human beings were killed between 1942 and 1945. This Konzentrationslager occupied about fifteen square miles and consisted of three main and thirty-nine subsidiary camps. The first prisoner arrived on 14 July 1940. The camp was evacuated and for the most part destroyed by 27 January 1945, before Russian troops liberated what was left of it. There were only forty thousand registered prisoners among the millions who perished there without leaving a name.

At first sight theology and Auschwitz have nothing in common. The former articulates a joyful tradition, the latter evokes the memory of untold suffering. Theology speaks of eternal light, Auschwitz perpetuates the horror of darkness. Nevertheless, as light and darkness are complementary in our experience, and as the glory and the shame must be apprehended together, so the momentous outrage of Auschwitz cannot be allowed to stand, as it has done, in an isolation such as the leprous outcast used to inspire in the past. The evils that we do live after us; unless they are understood they may recur.

Such an understanding meets with endless obstacles. It is easy enough to present the documentation of what happened in Auschwitz between 1942 and 1945. The facts are available to all who care to open the files. The lawyers have put us in their debt by enabling us to see the scene of unprecedented crime in as unemotional a light as possible. The pictures of the tormented, the dying, and the dead, as well as of the death factories, have become the exhibits in the many trials which have been held to bring the guilty to justice. The subject has thus been frozen with the unemotional air of the dispassionate procedure of justice. These cases were listed, heard, and concluded under criminal law.

The theologian's enquiry, however, goes beyond the terms of criminal investigation and the sifting of evidence. Unlike the court the theologian is not satisfied by the elucidation of the facts.

He must ask the great 'Why?', rather than be content to know how and when certain crimes were perpetrated. He extends the 'Why?' to the root of the historical drama and to the actors in it. The theologian will compare and contrast his findings with the declared Christian doctrines. How does Auschwitz stand in the light of the Fatherhood of God, the person and work of Christ, and the coming of the Holy Ghost? These norms of Christian theology govern our enquiry and rule out an untidy or hysterical survey. They exclude a morbid fascination with facts which the human eye finds too repulsive to see and which the mind cannot fathom.

Auschwitz belongs to the past, thank God. But its multidimensional range of evil extends to the present and throws its shadow over the future. It is the comprehensive and realistic symbol of the greatest possible evil which still threatens humankind. A theology of Auschwitz, therefore, is an attempt to interpret this evil responsibly for the present.

15 August

The Blessed Virgin Mary

Note: In Ireland, The Birth of the Blessed Virgin Mary on the 8 September is observed as the major festival of Mary.

Nothing for sure is known of the parentage or the place of birth of the Mother of the Lord. Only her name is known for certain – Mary or Miriam (in Hebrew) – and that she had an aged relative called Elizabeth. According to the Gospel of Luke, Mary was a young Jewish girl living in Nazareth, engaged to a man called Joseph, when a messenger from the Lord announced that she was to be the bearer of the Son of God to the world. Her response, 'Let it be to me according to your word', and her life of obedience and faithfulness have been upheld ever since as a model for all who hear and obey God's word. In Christian tradition Mary is often described as 'the second Eve' who unlocks Eve's disobedience. Mary was present at the crucifixion of her Son, and was with the apostles and others at Pentecost. According to the Gospel of John, at the time of his death Jesus commended the care of his mother to the beloved disciple which may explain why in Christian tradition her final years are associated with both Jerusalem and Ephesus. This day is now celebrated as the major feast of the Blessed Virgin Mary throughout most of Christendom.

A Reading from *Revelations of Divine Love* by Julian of Norwich

With the same cheerful joy our good Lord looked down to his right and thereby brought to mind the place where our Lady was standing during his passion. 'Do you want to see her?' he said, saying in effect, 'I know quite well you want to see my blessed Mother, for, after myself, she is the greatest joy I can show you, and most like me and worthy of me. Of all my creation, she is the most desirable sight.' And because of his great, wonderful, unique love for this sweet maiden, his blessed Mother our Lady Saint Mary, he showed her to be rejoicing greatly. This is the meaning of the sweet words. It was as if he were saying, 'Do you want to see how I love her, so that you can rejoice with me in my love for her, and hers for me?'

Here – to understand this word further – our Lord God is speaking to all who are going to be saved, as it were to all humankind in the person of one individual. He is saying, 'Can you see in her how greatly you are loved? For love of you made her so exalted, so noble, so worthy. This pleases me, and I want it to please you too.' For after himself she is the most blessed of all sights.

But, for all that, I am not expected to want to see her physically present here on earth, but rather to see the virtues of her blessed soul, her truth, her wisdom, her charity, so that I can learn to know myself, and reverently fear my God.

When our good Lord had showed me this and said, 'Do you want to see her?' I answered, 'Yes, good Lord, thank you very much. Yes, good Lord, if it is your will.' I prayed this often, and I thought I was going to see her in person. But I did not see her in this way. Jesus, in that word, gave me a spiritual sight of her. Just as I had seen her before, lowly and unaffected, so now he showed her, exalted, noble, glorious, and pleasing to him above all creation.

He wills it to be known that all who delight in him should delight in her too, with the same pleasure he has in her, and she in him. To help understand it better he gave this example. If you love one particular thing above everything else, you will try to make everyone else love and like what it is you love so greatly. When Jesus said, 'Do you want to see her?' I thought it was the nicest word about her that he could possibly have said, together with the spiritual revelation that he gave me of her. Except in the case of our Lady, Saint Mary, our Lord showed me no one specially – and her he showed three times. The first occasion was when she was big with child, the second sorrowing under the cross, and the third as she is now, delightful, glorious, and rejoicing.

alternative reading

A Responsory and Alleluia for the Blessed Virgin Mary by Hildegard of Bingen

Sweet branch,
From the stock of Jesse,
How magnificent
That God saw the girl's beauty,
Like an eagle,
Fixing its eye on the sun:

When the highest Father saw
The girl's radiance
And desired his Word
To take flesh in her.

For in the hidden mystery of God,
Her mind was filled with light,
And there emerged from the Virgin
A bright flower,
Wonderfully:

When the highest Father saw
The girl's radiance
And desired his Word
To take flesh in her.

Alleluia!
O branch mediatrix,
Your sacred womb
Overcame death
And illumined
All creatures
In the fair flower
Born of the sweetest integrity
Of your sealed chastity.
Alleluia!

alternative reading

A Reading from *Mary, Mother of God, Mother of the Poor* by Ivone Gebara and Maria Bingemer

Mary's assumption brings a new and promising future for women. Excluded from Jewish initiation rites because of their anatomy, banned from full participation in worship and the synagogue by their menstrual cycles, for a long time women – even in Christianity – subtly or explicitly have been second-class citizens in the world of faith because of the 'inferiority' and the 'poverty' of their bodies.

Mary's assumption, however, restores and reintegrates woman's bodiliness into the very mystery of God. Starting with Mary, the dignity of women's condition is recognised and safeguarded by the creator of that very bodiliness. In Jesus Christ and Mary the feminine is respectively resurrected and assumed into heaven – definitively sharing in the glory of the Trinitarian mystery from which all proceeds and to which all returns.

Her assumption is intimately connected to Jesus' resurrection. Both events of faith are about the same mystery: the triumph of God's justice over human injustice, the victory of grace over sin. Just as proclaiming the resurrection of Jesus means continuing to announce his passion which continues in those who are crucified and suffer injustice in this world, by analogy, believing in Mary's assumption means proclaiming that the woman who gave birth in a stable among animals, whose heart was pierced with a sword of sorrow, who shared in her son's poverty, humiliation, persecution, and violent death, who stood at the foot of the cross, the mother of the condemned, has been exalted. Just as the crucified one is the risen one, so the sorrowing one is the one assumed into heaven, the one in glory. She who, while a disciple herself, shared persecutions, fear and anxiety with other disciples in the early years of the Church, is the same one who, after a death that was certainly humble and anonymous, was raised to heaven. The assumption is the glorious culmination of the mystery of God's preference for what is poor, small, and unprotected in this world, so as to make God's presence and glory shine there.

The virgin of the *Magnificat*, on whose lips is placed the message that God is exalting the humble and casting down the powerful, finds her life confirmed and glorified by the Father of Jesus. Mary's assumption – seen in the light of Jesus' resurrection – is hope and promise for the poor of all times and for those who stand in solidarity with them; it is hope and promise that they will share in the final victory of the incarnate God.

16 August

Charles Inglis

Bishop of Nova Scotia, 1816

Charles Inglis was the son of a rector of Glencolumbkille in County Donegal in the Diocese of Raphoe. He emigrated to Pennsylvania where he studied for ordination and served at Trinity Church, New York. After the American Revolution, on 12 August 1787, he was consecrated at Lambeth Palace as the first Bishop of Nova Scotia (a diocese which then included the provinces of Quebec and Ontario) and the first bishop in the British Empire overseas. He died in the year 1816 and is commemorated on this day in his home parish at Glencolumbkille.

A Reading from *The Life and Letters of Charles Inglis*
by John Wolfe Lydekker

In America Dr White and his brethren in Pennsylvania had decided to approach the English Primates with a view to obtaining the consecration of selected candidates from the United States. Among many American churchmen Dr Seabury's consecration by the Scottish Non-Juring bishops was viewed with some apprehension, and the ecclesiastical Convention of Pennsylvania was strongly in favour of an English episcopal succession.

The Convention's Address, supported by a recommendatory letter from the President of Congress, was sent to John Adams, then American Ambassador in London, who presented it to the Archbishop of Canterbury on 3 January 1786. A few days later Charles Inglis received a summons from the Primate to attend him at a private interview, and asked for his opinion. Apart from his appreciation of Inglis' wide knowledge of the intricate ecclesiastical affairs in America, Dr Moore had already formed a high opinion of his character and abilities, and rightly considered that Inglis could supply the best advice on the subject.

At this interview the question of a bishop for Nova Scotia was again mentioned by Dr Moore, through whose far-sighted influence the scheme was in due time to be adopted. The original choice of Dr Chandler as bishop-designate of the new diocese was now no longer applicable through his ill-health. The next obvious person for the post was Charles Inglis himself, and the Primate now told him that the appointment would in all probability be offered to him. Further, that he had already presented an Address to the King petitioning for the appointment of a bishop for the Canadian colonies, and that he intended to apply for an Act of Parliament authorising the English bishops to consecrate American bishops.

The same evening on his return from Lambeth, Inglis wrote to Dr White as follows:

> I consider the interposition of the Bishops here on this head, as a great advantage to the Church and clergy with you; for it gives the clergy ground to stand on which they had not before.
>
> The authority of bishops is purely spiritual; it has nothing to do with civil constitutions, or their different forms. It existed as fully when Christianity was persecuted by heathen emperors, as when emperors became nursing fathers of the Church – it exists as fully now in the Roman Cantons or Republics of Switzerland, as it does in the Kingdom of France. It

is therefore idle to say, that because the American States are Republics, therefore bishops residing in them must be stripped of their spiritual or ecclesiastical powers; for the one is no reason for the other, nor does the consequence by any means follow. The purely spiritual or ecclesiastical authority of a bishop, and you should aim at no more, may be well allowed and exercised in a democratic state, as in an absolute monarchy.

The bishops here have no right to interpose authoritatively – they can only admonish and advise; but when they do this in matters which are for your benefit, and which are necessary to enable them to serve you, consistently with their duty and conscience, their advice should have great weight. You will find a benevolent, brotherly, Christian spirit breathes through their letter of response, joined in a proper regard for the interests of religion. I sincerely wish their letters may have the desired effect, as it will tend much to the benefit of the Church.

20 August

Bernard

Abbot of Clairvaux, Teacher of the Faith, 1153

Bernard was born at Fontaines, near Dijon, in France in the year 1090. He entered the Benedictine abbey at Cîteaux in 1112, taking with him many of his young companions, some of whom were his own brothers. He was a leader of the reform within Benedictinism at this time, and in 1115 was sent to establish a new monastery at a place he named Clairvaux, or 'Valley of Light'. Though times were hard, he built up the community through his remarkable qualities of leadership. Bernard preached widely and powerfully, and proved himself a theologian of renown. Literally hundreds of houses were founded on the Cîteaux or Cistercian system and Bernard's influence on his own generation and beyond was immense. He died on this day in the year 1153.

A Reading from the treatise *On the Love of God* by Bernard of Clairvaux

God deserves of us all our love, a love which knows no bounds. This is the first thing to understand. The reason is because God was the first to love. God, who is so great, loves us so much; he loves us freely, poor, pathetic, worthless creatures though we be. This is why I insist that our love for God should know no bounds. And since love given to God is given to the One who is infinite and without boundary, what measure or boundary could we make anyway?

Furthermore, our love is not bestowed for no reason, as God's love is for us: we render it in payment of a debt. God, infinite and eternal, who is love beyond our human capacity to comprehend, whose greatness knows no bounds, whose wisdom has no end, simply loves. Should we, for our part then, set limits on our love for God?

'I will love you, O Lord my strength, my strong rock and my defence, my Saviour, my sole desire and love.' My God, my helper, I will love you with all the power you have given me; not worthily, because that is impossible, but nevertheless to the best of my ability. Do what I will in life, I can never discharge my debt to you, and I can love you only according to the power you have given me. But I will endeavour to love you more and more, as you see fit to enable me to do so; and yet, never, never, as you should be loved. 'Your eyes saw my unformed substance.' In your book are written all who do the best they can, though they never pay their debt to you in full.

The reason, then, for our loving God *is* God. He is the initiator of our love and its final goal. He is himself the occasion of human love; he gives us the power to love, and brings our desire to consummation. God is loveable in himself, and gives himself to us as the object of our love. He desires that our love for him should bring us happiness, and not be arid and barren. His love for us opens up inside us the way to love, and is the reward of our own reaching out in love. How gently he leads us in love's way, how generously he returns the love we give, how sweet he is to those who wait for him!

God is indeed rich to all who call to him, for he can give them nothing better than to give them himself. He gave himself to be our righteousness, and he keeps himself to be our great reward. He offers himself as refreshment to our souls, and spends himself to set free those in prison. You are good, Lord, to the soul that seeks you. What, then, are you to the soul that finds you? The marvel is, no one can seek you who has not already found you. You want us to find you so that we may seek you, but we can never anticipate your coming, for though we say 'Early shall my prayer come before you,' a chilly, loveless thing that prayer would be, were it not warmed by your own breath and born of your own Spirit.

20 August

William and Catherine Booth

Founders of the Salvation Army, 1912 & 1890

William Booth was born in Nottingham in 1829, the same year as Catherine Mumford was born in Ashbourne, Derbyshire. They were married in 1855. A passionate preacher, William's style was criticised by his fellow Methodists and he left them in 1861, founding his own revivalist mission in Whitechapel, London, four years later. The Christian Mission, as it was then known, evolved into the Salvation Army by 1878. Both William and Catherine were famous for preaching and their movement developed into a world-wide denomination. It coupled moral fervour with a strong social commitment to the poor. Catherine died on 4 October 1890 and William on this day in 1912.

A Reading from *In Darkest England and the Way Out* by William Booth

I want it to be clearly understood that it is not in my own strength, nor at my own charge, that I propose to embark upon this great undertaking. Unless God wills that I should work out the idea of which I believe he has given me the conception, nothing can come of any attempt at its execution but confusion, disaster and disappointment.

I do not run without being called. I do not press forward to fill this breach without being urgently pushed from behind. Whether or not I am called of God, as well as by the agonising cries of suffering men and women and children, God will make plain.

That you do not like the Salvation Army I venture to say, is no justification for withholding your sympathy and practical co-operation in carrying out a scheme which promises so much blessedness to your fellow-men. You may not like our government, our methods, our faith. Your feeling towards us might perhaps be duly described by an observation that slipped unwittingly from the tongue of a somewhat celebrated leader the evangelistic world some time ago, who when asked what he thought of the Salvation Army, replied that he 'did not like it all, but he believed that God Almighty did'. Perhaps, as an agency, we may not be exactly of your way of thinking, but that is hardly the point. Look at that dark ocean, full of human wrecks, writhing in anguish and despair. How to rescue those unfortunates is the question. The particular character of the methods employed, the peculiar uniforms worn by the lifeboat crew, the noises made by the rocket apparatus, and the mingled shouting of the rescued and the rescuers, may all be contrary to your taste and traditions. But all these objections and antipathies, I submit, are as nothing compared with the delivering of the people out of that dark sea.

The responsibility is no longer mine alone. It is yours as much as mine. It is yours even more than mine if you withhold the means by which I may carry out the scheme. I give what I have. If you give what you have the work will be done. If it is not done, and the dark river of wretchedness rolls on, as wide and deep as ever, the consequences will lie at the door of those who hold back.

I am only one man among my fellows, the same as you. The obligation to care for these lost and perishing multitudes does not rest on me any more than it does on you. To me has been given the idea, but to you the means by which it may be realised.

23 August

Tydfil

Martyr, fifth century

The early Welsh genealogies claim that Tydfil was one of the twenty-five daughters of Brychan Brycheiniog, whose family formed one of the three saintly tribes of Wales, and who also had eleven sons. She was buried at what became Merthyr Tydfil. It is said that she was on the way to visit her aged father when she was murdered by pagans. Her brother Rhun avenged her, but was killed at the moment of victory. Unfortunately, this story derives from the creative pen of the romantic poet and literary forger Iolo Morganwg. It may contain elements of folk tradition, but it is more probably the result of imaginative speculation about local place names.

A Reading from a commentary on St John's Gospel by Augustine

'If any would serve me, they must follow me.' What is meant by this saying of Jesus if not that we must imitate him? For as the apostle Peter says, Christ suffered for us, leaving us an example that we should follow in his footsteps. But with what consequence or prize? Jesus says, 'Where I am, there shall my servant be also.' Christ must be loved gladly if we are to be rewarded in such a way. For where can one be well off without Christ, or where can one be badly off if we are with him?

'If any serve me, my Father will honour them.' What greater honour can one conceive of beyond that of being with the Son? Indeed, what Jesus said earlier should be understood in relation to these words. For what greater honour can an adopted child receive, than that he or she be where the only-begotten is, not made equal to the divine nature, but sharing in eternity?

So what work is required of us if we are to be rewarded in such a way? We serve Jesus Christ when we do not seek our own interests, but those of Jesus Christ. For when Jesus says we must follow him, he means that we must walk in his ways. As it is written elsewhere in Scripture, 'they must walk in the same way as he walked'. Christ's followers ought also, if he or she gives bread to the hungry, act out of mercy and not out of ostentation, seeking nothing else other than the good work itself, the left hand not knowing what the right hand is doing. We are servants of Christ when we not only carry out the corporal works of mercy, but do all good works on account of Christ, up to and including the supreme work of love, that of laying down one's life for one's friends: for it is to lay it down for Christ. For such a thing Jesus prepared himself, calling himself a servant, as he says, 'The Son of Man did not come to be served but to serve, and to lay down his life for many.'

When you hear the Lord saying, 'where I am there shall my servant be also', it follows that you are not to think only of good bishops and clergy. All of us, in our own way, are to serve Christ: by living well, by giving alms, by spreading his name and teaching to the best of your ability. As for the greatest act of service, that of suffering, many of you have already offered yourselves, many who were not bishops or clergy: young men and women, old people and youths, married men and women, many fathers and mothers of families: all in their service of Christ have been called upon to lay down their lives in witness, and as a result have received the most glorious crowns from the Father as he honoured them.

24 August

Bartholomew

Apostle

It has long been assumed that Bartholomew is the same as Nathanael though it is not certain. The Gospel according to John speaks of Philip bringing Nathanael to Jesus who calls him 'an Israelite worthy of the name'. He is also present beside the Sea of Galilee at the resurrection. Although he seems initially a somewhat cynical man, he recognizes Jesus for who he is and proclaims him as Son of God and King of Israel.

A Reading from the treatise *On Prescription against Heresies*
by Tertullian

The apostles (whose name means 'sent') first bore witness to their faith in Jesus Christ throughout Judea, and established churches there. After this they went out into the rest of the world, proclaiming the same doctrine of the same faith to the nations. In the same way they established churches in every city, from which other churches derived the shoots of faith and the seeds of doctrine, and are still deriving them, in order that they may become churches.

It is through this process that these churches are accredited 'apostolic', in that they are the offspring of apostolic churches.

Every kind of thing is classified according to its origin. For this reason, the churches, however numerous and significant they are, are ultimately identical with that one primitive church which derives from the apostles, and from which all have their origins. All are primitive and all are apostolic, provided all are one. And this unity is demonstrated by their sharing of peace, by their title of 'brother' and 'sister', and by a mutual obligation of hospitality. Such rights have no basis other than in the one tradition of a common creed.

It is on this basis, therefore, that we lay down this ruling: if the Lord Jesus Christ sent out the apostles to preach, no preachers other than those which are appointed by Christ are to be received, since 'no one knows the Father except the Son and those to whom the Son has revealed him', and the Son appears to have revealed him to no one except the apostles whom he sent to preach what he had revealed to them. What they preached – that is, what Christ revealed to them – ought, by this ruling, to be verified only by those churches which those apostles founded by their preaching either (as they say) by their living voice, or subsequently through their letters. If this is true, all doctrine which is in agreement with those apostolic churches, the wombs and original sources of the faith, must be reckoned as the truth, since it undoubtedly preserves what the churches received from the apostles, the apostles from Christ, and Christ from God.

On one occasion, it is true, the Lord did say: 'I still have many things to say to you, but you cannot bear them now'; but by adding, 'when the Spirit of truth comes, he will guide you into all truth,' he showed that they would receive the whole truth through the Spirit of truth.

So if there are any heresies that dare to trace their origins back to the apostolic era, so that it might appear that they had been handed down by the apostles because they existed under the apostles, we are able to say: let them declare the origins of their churches; let them declare the list of their bishops, showing that there is indeed a succession from the beginning, that their first bishop had as his precursor and predecessor an apostle or some apostolic man who was closely associated with the apostles. For this is the way that apostolic churches pass on and legitimise their successors. The Church of Smyrna, for example, records that Polycarp was placed in office by the apostle John; the Church of Rome records that Clement was ordained by Peter. In just the same way other churches can show how their current bishops were and are to be regarded as the transmitters of the apostolic seed.

alternative reading

A Reading from a sermon of John Henry Newman

An even, unvaried life is the lot of most men, in spite of occasional troubles or other accidents; and we are apt to despise it, and to get tired of it, and to long to see the world, or at all events we think such a life affords no great opportunity for religious obedience. To rise up, and go through the same duties, and then to rest again, day after day; to pass week after week, beginning with God's service on Sunday, and then to our worldly tasks: so to continue till year follows year, and we gradually get old – an unvaried life like this is apt to seem unprofitable to us when we dwell upon the thought of it.

Many indeed there are who do not think at all, but live in their round of employments without care about God and religion, driven on by the natural course of things in a dull irrational way like the beasts that perish. But when a man begins to feel he has a soul, and a work to do, and a reward to be gained, greater or less, according as he improves the talents committed to him, then he is naturally tempted to be anxious from his very wish to be saved, and he says, 'What must I do to please God?' And sometimes he is led to think he ought to be useful on a large scale, and goes out of his line of life, that he may be doing something worth doing, as he considers it.

Here we have the history of Saint Bartholomew and the other apostles to recall us to ourselves, and to assure us that we need not give up our usual manner of life, in order to serve God; that the most humble and quietest station is acceptable to him, if improved duly – nay, affords means for maturing the highest Christian character, even that of an apostle. Bartholomew read the Scriptures and prayed to God; and thus was trained at length to give up his life for Christ, when he demanded it.

But further, let us consider the particular praise which our Saviour gives him. 'Behold an Israelite indeed, in whom there is no guile!' This is just the character which, through God's grace, they may attain most fully, who live out of the world in the private way I have been describing – which is made least account of by man, and thought to be in the way of success in life, though our Saviour chose it to make head against all the power and wisdom of the world.

David describes his character in the fifteenth psalm; and, taken in all its parts, it is a rare one. He asks, 'Lord, who shall abide in thy tabernacle? Who shall dwell in thy holy hill? He that walketh uprightly, and worketh righteousness, and speaketh the truth in his heart. He that backbiteth not with his tongue, nor doeth evil to his neighbour, nor taketh up a reproach against his neighbour. In whose eyes a vile person is condemned; but he honoureth them that fear the Lord. He that sweareth to his own hurt, and changeth not.'

I say it is difficult and rare virtue, to mean what we say, to love without dissimulation, to think no evil, to bear no grudge, to be free from selfishness, to be innocent and straightforward. This character of mind is something far above the generality of people; and when realised in due measure, one of the surest marks of Christ's elect.

25 August

Ebba of Coldingham

Abbess, *c.*683

Ebba was the sister of the Northumbrian prince Oswald and shared his exile on Iona. She refused to marry, received the veil from Finan of Lindisfarne, and was granted land for a convent, but withdrew to establish a mixed community on the Northumbrian coast near Coldingham. Such communities were not uncommon in the Celtic tradition, but this one developed a name for laxity and luxury, possibly because Ebba, whom Bede calls a 'pious woman and handmaid of Christ' was not able to exert the strong leadership which such a community required. She died about the year 683, and around the time of her death the monastery was destroyed by lightning.

A Reading from *The History of the English Church and People* by the Venerable Bede

The convent of the Abbess Ebba, King Egfrid's aunt, was at Coldingham. It was burned down through carelessness. However, all who knew the facts of the case think that this occurred because of the wickedness of its members, and in particular of those who were supposed to be in authority. God's mercy had given them due warning of punishment, and if only they had followed the example of the people of Nineveh in fasting, prayers and tears, they could have averted the anger of the just judge.

One day a man of God by the name of Adamnán, on returning to the monastery, as he approached its buildings towering high, suddenly burst into tears. His companion inquired of him the reason for his tears, and he replied, 'The time is near when all the public and private buildings in front of us will be burned to ashes.' On hearing this, his companion informed Ebba, the Mother of the Community, as soon as they arrived. She was naturally alarmed, and summoning Adamnàn, pressed him to explain his vision.

'One night,' he said, 'when I was in vigil and reciting the psalms, a stranger suddenly appeared at my side. He said to me, "I have visited every room and every bed in this monastery, and entered every building and dormitory. But nowhere have I found anyone except yourself concerned with the health of his own soul. All of them, men and women alike, are either sunk in unprofitable sleep, or else awake early, but only to sin. Even the cells which were built for prayer and study, are now converted into places of eating, drinking, gossip and amusement. When they have leisure, even the nuns vowed to God abandon the propriety of their calling, and spend their time weaving fine clothes."'

The abbess asked, 'Why did you not reveal all this to me earlier?' Adamnán replied, 'I hesitated out of regard for you, lest it should cause you distress. But take some comfort, for no calamity will befall the monastery in your lifetime.'

Once this vision became known, the Community was somewhat alarmed for a few days: they began to refrain from wrong-doing and underwent penance. But after the death of Abbess Ebba they relapsed into their former sinful ways and became even more debauched. They cried 'Peace and safety', and behold, sudden destruction came upon them.

27 August

Monica

Mother of Augustine of Hippo, 387

Monica was born in North Africa of Christian parents in 332. She was married to a pagan, Patricius, whom she converted to Christianity. They had three children of whom the most famous was her eldest child, Augustine. Indeed, Augustine ascribed his conversion to the example and devotion of his mother: 'She never let me out of her prayers that you, O God, might say to the widow's son "Young man, I tell you arise"' – which is why the Gospel of the widow of Nain is customarily read at the Eucharist today as her memorial. Monica's husband died when she was forty. Her desire had been to be buried alongside him, but this was not to be. She died in Italy, at Ostia, in the year 387 on her way home to North Africa with her two sons.

A Reading from the *Confessions* of Augustine

Monica was the kind of person she was because she was taught by you Lord, her inward teacher, in the school of her heart. The day was imminent when she was to depart this life (the day which you knew and we did not). It came about, as I believe by your providence through your hidden ways, that she and I were standing leaning out of a window overlooking a garden. It was at the house where we were staying at Ostia on the Tiber, where, far removed from the crowds, after the exhaustion of a long journey, we were recovering our strength for the voyage.

[Alone with each other, we talked very intimately. 'Forgetting the past and reaching forward to what lies ahead', we were searching together in the presence of the truth which is you yourself. We asked what quality of life the eternal life of the saints will have, a life which 'neither eye has seen nor ear heard, nor has it entered into the heart of man'. But with the mouth of the heart wide open, we drank in the waters flowing from your spring on high, the spring of life which is with you. Sprinkled with this dew to the limit of our capacity, our minds attempted in some degree to reflect on so great a reality. The conversation led us towards the conclusion that the pleasure of the bodily senses, however delightful in the radiant light of this physical world, is seen by comparison with the life of eternity to be not even worth considering.]

As we talked on, my mother said, 'My son, as for myself, I now find no pleasure in this life. What I have still to do here and why I am here, I do not know. My hope in this world is already fulfilled. The one reason why I wanted to stay longer in this life was my desire to see you a Catholic Christian before I die. My God has granted this in a way more than I had hoped. For I see you despising this world's success to become his servant. What have I to do here?'

The reply I made to this I do not well recall, for within five days or not much more she fell sick of a fever. While she was ill, on one day she suffered loss of consciousness and gradually became unaware of things around her. We ran to be with her, but she quickly recovered consciousness. She looked at me and my brother standing beside her, and said to us in the manner of someone looking for something, 'Where was I?' Then seeing us struck dumb with grief, she said: 'Bury your mother here.'

I kept silence and fought back my tears. But my brother, as if to cheer her up, said something to the effect that he hoped she would be buried not in a foreign land but in her home country. When she heard that, her face became worried and her eyes looked at him in reproach that he should think that. She looked in my direction and said, 'See what he says,' and soon said to both of us 'Bury my body anywhere you like. Let no anxiety about that disturb you. I have only one request to make of you, that you remember me at the altar of the Lord, wherever you may be.' She explained her thought in such words as she could speak, then fell silent as the pain of her sickness became worse. 'Nothing,' she said, 'is distant from God, and there is no ground for fear that he may not acknowledge me at the end of the world and raise me up.'

On the ninth day of her illness, when she was aged fifty-six, and I was thirty-three, this religious and devout soul was released from the body.

28 August

Augustine of Hippo

Bishop, Teacher of the Faith, 430

Augustine was born in North Africa in the year 354. His career as an orator and rhetorician led him from Carthage to Rome, and from there to Milan where the Imperial court at that time resided. By temperament, he was passionate and sensual, and as a young man he rejected Christianity. Gradually, however, under the influence first of Monica, his mother, and then of Ambrose, Bishop of Milan, Augustine began to look afresh at the Scriptures. He was baptized by Ambrose at the Easter Vigil in the year 387. Not long after returning to North Africa he was ordained priest, and then became Bishop of Hippo. It is difficult to overestimate the influence of Augustine on the subsequent development of European thought. A huge body of his sermons and writings has been preserved, through all of which runs the theme of the sovereignty of the grace of God. He died in the year 430.

A Reading from the *Confessions* of Augustine

With you as my guide I entered into my innermost citadel, and was given power to do so because you had become my helper. I entered and with my soul's eye, such as it was, saw above that same eye of my soul the immutable light higher than my mind – not the light of every day, obvious to anyone, nor a larger version of the same kind which would, as it were, have given out a much brighter light and filled everything with its magnitude. It was not that light, but a different thing, utterly different from all our kinds of light. It transcended my mind, not in the way that oil floats on water, nor as heaven is above earth. It was superior because it made me, and I was inferior because I was made by it. The person who knows the truth knows it, and he who knows it knows eternity. Love knows it.

Eternal truth and true love and beloved eternity: you are my God. To you I sigh 'day and night'. When I first came to know you, you raised me up to make me see that what I saw is Being, and that I who saw am not yet Being. And you gave a shock to the weakness of my sight by the strong radiance of your rays, and I trembled with love and awe. And I found myself far from you 'in the region of dissimilarity', and heard as it were your voice from on high: 'I am the food of the fully grown; grow and you will feed on me. And you will not change me into you like the food your flesh eats, but you will be changed into me.'

I sought a way to obtain strength enough to enjoy you; but I did not find it until I embraced the mediator between God and man, the man Christ Jesus, who is above all things, God blessed for ever. He called and said 'I am the way and the truth and the life.' The food which I was too weak to accept he mingled with flesh, in that 'The Word was made flesh', so that our infant condition might come to suck milk from your wisdom by which you created all things.

Late have I loved you, beauty so old and so new; late have I loved you. And see, you were within me and I was in the external world and sought you there, and in my unlovely state I plunged into those lovely created things which you made. You were with me, and I was not with you. The lovely things kept me from you, though if they did not have their existence in you, they would have had no existence at all. You called and cried out loud to me and shattered my deafness. You were radiant and resplendent, you put to flight my blindness. You were fragrant, and I drew in my breath and now pant after you. I tasted you, and now I feel nothing but hunger and thirst for you. You touched me, and I am set on fire to attain the peace which is yours.

29 August

The Beheading of John the Baptist

The principal celebration for John the Baptist is held on 24 June, the date observing his birth. But John was the forerunner of Christ in his death as well as his birth which, as the Gospels according to Matthew and Mark relate it, followed his denunciation of immorality and his call to repentance, and in particular his condemnation of Herod's marriage. On hearing of John's arrest, Christ's first words immediately take up John's call: 'Repent, for the kingdom of heaven has come near; repent, and believe the good news.'

A Reading from a sermon of the Venerable Bede

As forerunner of our Lord's birth, preaching and death, the blessed John showed in his struggle a goodness worthy of the sight of heaven. In the words of Scripture: 'Though in the sight of the people he suffered torments, yet his hope is full of immortality.' We justly commemorate the day of his birth with a joyful celebration, a day which he himself made festive for us through his suffering, and which he adorned with the crimson splendour of his own blood. We do rightly to revere his memory with joyful hearts, for he stamped with the seal of martyrdom the testimony which he delivered on behalf of our Lord.

There is no doubt that blessed John suffered imprisonment and chains as a witness to our redeemer, whose forerunner he was, and gave his life for him. His persecutor had demanded not that he should deny Christ, but only that he should keep silent about the truth. Nevertheless, he died for Christ. Does Christ not say: 'I am the truth.' Therefore, because John shed his blood for the truth, he surely died for Christ. Through his birth, preaching and baptizing, he bore witness to the coming birth, preaching and baptism of Christ, and by his own suffering he showed that Christ also would suffer.

Such was the quality and strength of the one who accepted the end of this present life by shedding his blood after the long imprisonment. He preached the freedom of heavenly peace, yet was thrown into irons by the ungodly; he was locked away in the darkness of prison, though he came bearing witness to the Light of life and deserved to be called a bright and shining lamp by that Light itself, which is Christ. John was baptized in his own blood, though he had been privileged to baptize the redeemer of the world, to hear the voice of the Father above him, and to see the grace of the Holy Spirit descending upon him. But to endure temporal agonies for the sake of the truth was not a heavy burden for such as John; rather it was easily borne and even desirable, for he knew eternal joy would be his reward.

Since death was ever near at hand through the inescapable necessity of nature, such people considered it a blessing to embrace it and thus gain the reward of eternal life by acknowledging Christ's name. Hence the Apostle Paul rightly says: 'You have been granted the privilege not only to believe in Christ but also to suffer for his sake.' And he tells us why it is Christ's gift that his chosen ones should suffer for him: 'The sufferings of this present time are not worthy to be compared with the glory that is to be revealed in us.'

30 August

John Bunyan

Spiritual Writer, 1688

Born at Elstow in Bedfordshire in 1628, John Bunyan was largely self-educated and used the Bible as his grammar. He read very few other books, and they were all piously Protestant in nature, yet he produced The Pilgrim's Progress, probably the most original text of spiritual genius that century, telling the story of the man Christian on his journey through life to God. It was not written while he was a prisoner in Bedford gaol, as often stated, but during a confinement some years later. History tells us little of the man but what is clear from his writings is that the salvation of the soul was what mattered most to him. He died on this day in the year 1688.

A Reading from *The Pilgrim's Progress* by John Bunyan

Then it came to pass, a while after, that there was a post in the town that inquired for Mr Honest. So he came to his house where he was, and delivered to his hand these lines: 'Thou art commanded to be ready against this day seven-night, to present thyself before thy Lord, at his Father's house. And for a token that my message is true, "All thy daughters of music shall be brought low."' Then Mr Honest called for his friends, and said unto them, 'I die, but shall make no will. As for my honesty, it shall go with me; let him that comes after be told of this.' When the day that he was to be gone was come, he addressed himself to go over the river. Now the river at that time overflowed the banks in some places; but Mr Honest in his lifetime had spoken to one Good-conscience to meet him there, the which he also did, and lent him his hand, and so helped him over. The last words of Mr Honest were, 'Grace reigns.' So he left the world.

After this it was noised abroad, that Mr Valiant-for-truth was taken with a summons by the same post as the other; and had this for a token that the summons was true, 'That his pitcher was broken at the fountain.' When he understood it, he called for his friends, and told them of it. Then, said he, 'I am going to my Father's; and though with great difficulty I am got hither, yet now I do not repent me of all the trouble I have been at to arrive where I am. My sword I give to him that shall succeed me in my pilgrimage, and my courage and skill to him that can get it. My marks and scars I carry with me, to be a witness for me, that I have fought his battles who now will be my rewarder.' When the day that he must go hence was come, many accompanied him to the river side, into which as he went he said, 'Death, where is thy sting?' And as he went down deeper, he said, 'Grave, where is thy victory?' So he passed over, and all the trumpets sounded for him on the other side.

31 August

Aidan

Abbot, Bishop of Lindisfarne, Missionary, 651

One of Columba's monks from the monastery of Iona, Aidan was sent as a missionary to Northumbria at the request of King Oswald, who was later to become his friend and interpreter. Consecrated Bishop of Lindisfarne in 635, Aidan worked closely with Oswald and became involved with the training of priests. From the island of Lindisfarne he was able to combine a monastic lifestyle with missionary journeys to the mainland where, through his concern for the poor and enthusiasm for preaching, he won popular support. This enabled him to strengthen the Church beyond the boundaries of Northumbria. He died on this day in the year 651.

A Reading from *The History of the English Church and People* by the Venerable Bede

As soon as he came to the throne, King Oswald was anxious that all the people whom he ruled should be filled with the grace of the Christian faith, of which he had had so wonderful an experience in his victory over the heathen. So he sent to the Irish elders among whom he and his companions had received the sacrament of baptism when in exile, asking them to send him a bishop by whose teaching and ministry the English people over whom he now ruled might receive the blessings of the Christian faith and the sacraments. His request was granted without delay, and they sent him Bishop Aidan, a man of outstanding gentleness, holiness, and moderation.

On Aidan's arrival, the king appointed the island of Lindisfarne to be his see at his own request. As the tide ebbs and flows, this place is surrounded by sea twice a day like an island, and twice a day the sand dries and joins it to the mainland. The king always listened humbly and gladly to Aidan's advice in all things, and diligently set himself to establish and extend the Church of Christ throughout his kingdom. Indeed, when the bishop, who was not fluent in the English language, preached the gospel, it was most beautiful to see the king himself acting as interpreter of the heavenly word for his earldormen and thanes; for he himself had obtained perfect command of Irish during his long exile.

Aidan himself was a monk from the island of Iona. He gave his clergy an inspiring example of self-discipline and continence, and the best recommendation of his teaching to all was that he taught them no other way of life than that which he himself and his followers practised. He never sought or cared for any worldly possessions, and loved to give away to the poor who chanced to meet him whatever he received from kings or wealthy folk. Whether in town or country, he always travelled on foot unless compelled by urgent necessity to ride; and whatever people he met on his walks, whether rich or poor, he stopped and talked with them. If they were heathen, he invited them to accept the mystery of the faith; if they were Christians, he strengthened their faith, and inspired them by word and deed to live a good life and to be generous to others.

Aidan's life was in marked contrast to the apathy of our own times, for all who walked with him, whether monks or layfolk, were required to meditate, that is, either to read the

Scriptures or to learn the psalms by heart. This was their daily occupation wherever they went. If wealthy people did wrong, he never kept silent out of respect or fear, but corrected them publicly. He would never offer money to influential people, but would always offer them food whenever he entertained them. And if the wealthy ever gave him gifts of money, he either distributed it for the needs of the poor, or else used it to ransom any who had unjustly been sold into slavery. In fact, many of those whom he ransomed in this way afterwards became his disciples; and when they had been instructed and trained, he ordained them to the priesthood.

Death came to Aidan when he had completed sixteen years as a bishop while he was staying at a royal residence near Bamburgh. Having a church and cell there, he often used to go and stay at the place, travelling around the surrounding countryside to preach. When he fell ill, a tent was erected for him on the west side of the church, so that the tent was actually attached to the church wall. And so it happened that, as he drew his last breath, he was leaning against a post that buttressed the wall on the outside. He passed away on the last day of August 651, in the seventeenth year of his episcopate, and his body was taken across to Lindisfarne and buried in the monks' cemetery.

September

1 September

Giles

Hermit, *c.*710

Giles was a hermit who died in about the year 710. He founded a monastery at the place now called Saint-Gilles in Provence which became an important place on the pilgrimage routes both to Compostela and to the Holy Land. His care for the wounded and those crippled by disease resulted in his becoming the patron saint of such people, particularly of those with leprosy. Leprosy sufferers were not permitted to enter towns and cities, and therefore often congregated on the outskirts, where churches built to meet their needs were regularly dedicated to Giles.

A Reading from *The Sayings of the Desert Fathers*

Abba Agathon said, 'If I could meet a leper, give him my body and take his, I should be very happy.' That indeed is perfect charity.

It was also said that going to town one day to sell some small articles, Abba Agathon met a cripple on the roadside, paralysed in both legs, who asked him where he was going. Abba Agathon replied, 'To town in order to sell some things.' The other said, 'Do me a favour of carrying me there.' So he carried him to the town. The cripple said to him, 'Put me down where you sell your wares.' He did so.

When he had sold an article, the cripple asked, 'What did you sell it for?' and he told him the price. The other said, 'Buy me a cake,' and he bought it. When Abba Agathon had sold a second article, the sick man asked, 'How much did you sell it for?' And he told him the price of it. Then the other said, 'Buy me this,' and he bought it. When Agathon, having sold all his wares, wanted to go, he said to him, 'Are you going back?' and he replied 'Yes.' Then said he, 'Do me the favour of carrying me back to the place where you found me.'

Once more picking him up, he carried him back to that place. Then the cripple said, 'Agathon, you are filled with divine blessings, in heaven and on earth.' Raising his eyes, Agathon saw no one; it was an angel of the Lord, come to try him.

2 September

Lucian Tapiedi and the Martyrs of Papua New Guinea

1901 and 1942

The Church in Papua New Guinea has been enriched by martyrdom twice in the twentieth century. James Chalmers, Oliver Tomkins and some companions were sent to New Guinea by the London Missionary Society. They met their death by martyrdom in 1901. Forty years later, during the Second World War, New Guinea was occupied by the Imperial Japanese Army, and 333 Christians of all denominations died for the faith. Among them were priests, Henry Holland, John Duffill, and Vivian Redlich who remained with their people after the invasion of 1942; evangelists Leslie Gariadi, Lucian Tapiedi and John Barge; May Hayman, a nurse; and teachers Margaret Brenchley, Lilla Lashman, and Mavis Parkinson. Also remembered is Bernard Moore, shot while presiding at the Eucharist in New Britain.

A Reading from *The White-Robed Army of Martyrs*
by David Hand, first Archbishop of Papua New Guinea

As the thrust of the Japanese invasion approached Papua New Guinea in 1942, Bishop Philip Strong broadcast over the radio a message to his staff which has become famous in the annals of missionary history. He said:

> We could never hold up our faces again, if for our own safety, we all forsook him and fled when the shadows of the passion began to gather around him in his spiritual body, the Church in Papua. Our life in the future would be burdened with shame and we could not come back here and face our people again; and we would be conscious always of rejected opportunities. The history of the church tells us that missionaries do not think of themselves in the hour of danger and crisis, but of the Master who called them to give their all, and of the people they have been trusted to serve and love to the uttermost. His watchword is none the less true today, as it was when he gave it to the first disciples: 'Whosoever would save his life will lose it, and whosoever will lose his life for my sake and the gospel's shall find it.'
>
> We could not leave unless God, who called us, required it of us, and our spiritual instinct tells us he would never require such a thing at such an hour. No, my brothers and sisters, fellow workers in Christ, whatever others may do, we cannot leave. We shall not leave. We shall stand by our trust. We shall stand by our vocation.
>
> Papua is a body, the Church: God will not forsake us. He will uphold us; he will strengthen us and he will guide us and keep us through the days that lie ahead. If we all left, it would take years for the Church to recover from our betrayal of our trust. If we remain – and even if the worst came to the worst and we were all to perish in remaining – the Church will not perish, for there would have been no breach of trust in its walls, but its foundations and structure would have received added strength for the future building by our faithfulness unto death. This, I believe, is the resolution of you all.
>
> I know there are special circumstances which may make it imperative for one or two to go (if arrangements can be made for them to do so). For the rest of us, we have made our

resolution to stay. Let us not shrink from it. Let us trust and not be afraid. To you all I send my blessing. The Lord be with you.

What happened?

To a man and woman, all the bishop's staff stood by their people until it became clear that that course might imperil their people. The bishop himself was bombed and machine-gunned. He escaped injury, despite travelling freely and fearlessly around his diocese to care for, and encouraged his staff and people, as well as acting as senior chaplain to the military.

Among those who died were the two Gona sisters, teacher Mavis Parkinson and nurse May Hayman. They were handed over to the Japanese, and bayoneted to death at Ururu where an altar-shrine now marks the spot.

Elderly and holy Father Henry Holland, having served in Papua New Guinea for twenty-five years, first as a lay evangelist, and latterly as a priest at Isivita, stacks of whose translations of the Scriptures into the Orokaiva language were scattered and lost when the Japanese looted his station; he and John Duffill, his close colleague, were both killed.

Father Vivian Redlich of Sangara, who refused to abandon his Sunday Mass when warning came that the Japanese arrival at his camp was imminent and Lucian Tapiedi, his devoted teacher-evangelist who had said to his married colleagues: 'Take your wives and families to the bush and hide. I am single; I'll stay with the fathers and sisters; it doesn't matter if the Japanese get me'; the Sangara missionary-teachers Lilla Lashmar and Margery Brenchley, who had laid the foundations of the Church's educational work in the Orokaiva area, all perished.

John Barge, recently posted to open up work in a totally unevangelized area, refused to 'go bush' with the nearest Roman Catholic priest. Forced to dig his own grave he was then shot into it by Japanese guns.

Many people blamed Bishop Strong for not taking out all his staff to safety. But it was, ultimately, their own choice. To the world, it seemed a waste, a tragedy, a failure – like Calvary. But look what God has done with it – with their 'defeat'. He has turned it into victory. Look at the rise of the Martyrs' School in their honour – a living organism, not just a memorial, serving God and the nation. Look at the fruit of martyrdom in the ability of the Orokaiva Church to resurrect after the Lamington eruption. Look at the post-World War II leap forward into inland Papuan areas, the New Britain Resurrection and the great 'putsch' into the New Guinea Highlands.

Yes, 'the blood of the martyrs' has once again proved to be 'the seed of the Church' – here, in this country. Thanks be to God.

3 September

Gregory the Great

Bishop of Rome, Teacher of the Faith, 604

Gregory was born in 540, the son of a Roman senator. As a young man he pursued a governmental career, and in 573 was made Prefect of the city of Rome. Following the death of his father, he resigned his office, sold his inheritance, and became a monk. In 579 he was sent by the Pope to Constantinople to be his representative to the Patriarch. He returned to Rome in 586, and was himself elected Pope in 590. At a time of political turmoil, Gregory proved an astute administrator and diplomat, securing peace with the Lombards. He initiated the mission to England, sending Augustine and forty monks from his own monastery to re-found the English Church. His writings were pastorally oriented. His spirituality was animated by a dynamic of love and desire for God. Indeed, he is sometimes called the 'Doctor of desire'. For Gregory, desire was a metaphor for the journey into God. As Pope, he styled himself 'Servant of the servants of God' – a title which typified both his personality and ministry. He died in the year 604.

A Reading from a homily of Gregory the Great

The prophet Ezekiel, whom the Lord sent to preach his Word, is described as a watchman. A watchman always selects a high vantage point in order to be able to observe things better. In the same way, whoever is appointed watchman to a people should live on the heights so that he can help his people by having a broad perspective. I find it hard to make such a statement because such words are a reproach to myself. My preaching is mediocre, and my life does not cohere with the values I preach so inadequately. I do not deny that I am guilty, for I recognise in myself lethargy and negligence. Perhaps my very awareness of my failings will gain me pardon from a sympathetic judge.

When I lived in a monastic community I could keep my tongue from idle chatter and devote my mind almost continually to the discipline of prayer. However, since assuming the burden of pastoral care, I find it difficult to keep steadily recollected because my mind is distracted by numerous responsibilities. I am required to deal with matters affecting churches and monasteries, and often I must judge the lives and actions of individuals. One moment I am required to participate in civil life, and the next moment to worry over the incursions of barbarians. I fear these wolves who menace the flock entrusted to my care. At another time I have to exercise political responsibility in order to give support to those who uphold the rule of law; I have to cope with the wickedness of criminals, and the next moment I am asked to confront them, but yet in all charity.

My mind is in chaos, fragmented by the many and serious matters I am required to give attention to. When I try to concentrate and focus my intellectual resources for preaching, how can I do justice to the sacred ministry of the Word? I am often compelled by virtue of my office to socialise with people of the world and sometimes I have to relax the discipline of my speech. I realise that if I were to maintain the inflexible pattern of conversation that my conscience dictates, certain weaker individuals would simply shun my company, with the result that I would never be able to attract them to the goal I desire for them. So inevitably, I find myself listening to their mindless chatter. And because I am weak myself, I find myself gradually being sucked into their idle talk and saying the very things that I recoiled from listening to before. I enjoy lying back where beforehand I was conscious lest I fall myself.

Who am I? What kind of watchman am I? I do not stand on the pinnacle of achievement; I languish in the pit of my frailty. And yet although I am unworthy, the creator and redeemer of us all has given me the grace to see life whole and an ability to speak effectively of it. It is for the love of God that I do not spare myself preaching him.

4 September

Oengus Mac Nisse of Dalriada

Bishop of Connor, 514

Oengus Mac Nisse (or Macanisius), the first Bishop of Connor in County Antrim, is thought to have been at Kells as a hermit earlier in his life. The story told of him may reveal his sense of dedication: instead of carrying his Gospel-book in his satchel as was customary, he bore it on his shoulders 'hunched up or on all fours'. He died on this day in the year 514.

A Reading from a sermon of Augustine

Let us sing 'Alleluia' here and now in this life, even though we are oppressed by various worries, so that we may sing it one day in the world to come when we are set free from all anxiety. Why is it that we worry so much in this life? I suppose it is hardly surprising that we should worry when I read in the Scriptures: 'Are not the days of our life full of trouble?' Are you surprised that I am worried when I hear the words: 'Watch and pray that you enter not into temptation'? Are you surprised that I am worried when in the face of so many temptations and troubles the Lord's Prayer orders us to pray: 'Forgive us our debts as we also forgive our debtors'? Every day we pray and every day we sin.

But how happy will be our shout of 'Alleluia' as we enter heaven, how carefree, how secure from any assault, where no enemy lurks and no friend dies. There praise is offered to God, and here also; but here it is offered by anxious people, there by those who have been freed from all anxiety; here by those who must die, there by those who will live for ever. Here praise is offered in hope, there by those who enjoy the reality; here by pilgrims in transit, there by those who have reached their homeland.

So my dear friends, let us sing 'Alleluia', albeit not yet in the enjoyment of our heavenly rest, but in order to sweeten our toil in this life. Let us sing as travellers sing on a journey in order to help them keep on walking. Lighten your toil by singing and never be idle. Sing and keep on walking. And what do I mean by walking? I mean press on from good to better in this life. The Apostle Paul says that there will be those who go from bad to worse; but if you persevere, you will indeed keep on walking. Advance in virtue, in true faith and in right conduct. Sing up – and keep on walking!

4 September

Birinus

Bishop of Dorchester (Oxon), Apostle of Wessex, *c.*650

Birinus was born in the mid sixth century, probably of northern European origin, but he became a priest in Rome. Feeling called by God to serve as a missionary, he was consecrated bishop, and sent to Britain by the Pope. He intended to evangelize inland where no Christian had been before but, arriving in Wessex in 634, he found such prevalent idolatry that he looked no further to begin work. One of his early converts was King Cynegils and thereafter he gained much support in his mission, as well as the town of Dorchester for his See. He died in about the year 650 having earned the title 'Apostle of the West Saxons'.

A Reading from *The History of the English Church and People* by the Venerable Bede

About this time, during the reign of Cynegils, the West Saxons accepted the faith of Christ through the preaching of Bishop Birinus. He had come to Britain at the direction of Pope Honorius, having promised in the pope's presence that he would scatter the seeds of our holy faith in the most inland and remote regions of the English, where no other teacher had been before him.

He was accordingly consecrated bishop, at the pope's command, by Asterius, Bishop of Genoa. But when Birinus reached Britain and entered the territory of Wessex, he found the people completely heathen, and decided that it would be better to begin to preach the word among them rather than seek more distant converts. He therefore evangelized that province, and when he had instructed its king, he baptized him and his people.

It happened at the time that Oswald, the most holy and victorious king of the Northumbrians, was present, and greeted King Cynegils as he came from the font, and offered him an alliance most acceptable to God, taking him as his godson and his daughter as wife. The two kings gave Bishop Birinus the city of Dorchester for his episcopal see, and there he built and dedicated several churches and brought many people to the Lord by his holy labours. He also died and was buried there. Many years later, when Haeddi was bishop, the body of Birinus was translated to Winchester and laid in the church of the blessed apostles Peter and Paul.

6 September

Allen Gardiner

Founder of the South American Mission Society, 1851

Allen Francis Gardiner was born in 1794 and joined the Royal Navy as a young man. He resigned in 1826 and, on the death of his wife in 1834, dedicated himself to missionary work. He pioneered a mission to the Zulus in South Africa for the Church Missionary Society and founded the city of Durban. He then went to South America to investigate the possibility of evangelism amongst the indigenous tribes. He travelled extensively and founded the South American Mission Society in 1844. With seven other missionaries, he died of starvation in the year 1851 on the shores of Tierra del Fuego.

A Reading from the diary of Allen Gardiner

Captain Allen Gardiner was absorbed in his desire to evangelise the South American tribes. The fact that all his efforts to do so had ended in failure was no reason for giving up the attempt. On 7 August 1851, a month before he died of cold, hunger and thirst, shipwrecked on the desolate shores of Tierra del Fuego, he wrote in his journal:

Eleven months to the day we left England for this country, and have been graciously preserved through many dangers and troubles. The Lord, in his providence, has seen fit to bring us very low. In his infinite wisdom, mercy and love, he has removed many of his blessings – but for our good.

For my part, I have abused the manifold gifts of God. I have taken for granted his daily mercies. Lord, have mercy upon me a sinner and keep me so humble under your mighty hand that I may not despise your goodness or faint, but rather wait upon your grace to profit from this and every other act of your providence.

For I sense that there is a deep purpose in my present trial and I pray that I may discern it for my own good. Help me to see myself in the light of your holy word, and to search and try my heart by it. May your Holy Spirit bring within me a true repentance which will bear fruit in the graces of love and faith and obedience.

And, let not this mission fail, even if we are not permitted to labour in it. But raise up others who will bring the saving truths of the gospel to the poor, blind heathen around us.

The South American Mission Society seeks to fulfil this vision of Allen Gardiner, and continues to make known the gospel of our Lord Jesus Christ to the peoples of Latin America and the Iberian Peninsula.

8 September

The Birth of the Blessed Virgin Mary

This festival in honour of the birth of the mother of our Lord is celebrated on this day in both the Eastern and the Western Churches. Falling just nine months after the Feast of the Conception of Mary, the feast stands on the boundary between the old and the new covenants, and ushers in the dispensation of grace. Today, with the birth of Mary, 'a shrine is built for the creator of the universe'.

A Reading from a homily of Andrew of Crete

The law has achieved its goal with Christ, who leads us away from the letter of the law so as to bring us to the spirit. The law is fulfilled because the lawgiver himself has brought it to completion, transforming in his own person the letter into the spirit, summing up all things in himself and living the law of love. He has made law subject to love, and brought love and law into harmony. He has not fused the particular qualities of each, but in a wonderful way has lightened and set on a new foundation what beforehand was experienced by us as burdensome, servile and repressive. For, as the Apostle Paul says, 'we are no longer to be enslaved by the elemental spirits of the world' or to be trapped in the yoke of slavery to the letter of the law.

This is the summary of the benefits Christ has secured for us. In Christ the mystery is unveiled, nature is made new, divine and human, and the deification of our human nature is assumed by God. But so radiant, so glorious a visitation of God among mortals required some prelude of joy to introduce to us the great gift of salvation. Today's feast, celebrating the birth of the God-bearer, is that prelude, and the final act is the destined union between the Word and human nature.

Today a virgin is born, suckled and nurtured, and is being made ready to be the God-bearer, the king of all. With justification we should celebrate the mystery of this day, for if we do our gain will be twofold: we shall be led towards the truth, and we shall be led away from a life of slavery to the letter of the law. How can this be? In the same way that the shadow gives way to the presence of the light, grace introduces freedom in place of the letter of the law. Today's feast stands on the boundary between these two dispensations: it joins us to the truth instead of to signs and figures, and it ushers in the new in place of the old.

Let the whole creation, therefore, sing praise and dance and unite in celebrating the glories of this day. Today let there be one common feast of all in heaven and earth. Let everything that is, in and above the earth, join together in rejoicing. For today a shrine is built for the creator of the universe. The creature is newly ready as a divine dwelling for the creator.

alternative reading

A Reading from the Office for the *Feast of the Nativity of our Most Holy Lady the Theotokos* in the Orthodox Church

What is this sound of feasting that we hear?
Joachim and Anna mystically keep festival.
'O Adam and Eve,' they cry, 'rejoice with us today:
For if by your transgressions you closed the gates of Paradise
to those of old,
We have now been given a glorious fruit,
Mary the Child of God
Who opens its entrance to us all.'

Thy nativity, O Theotokos,
Has brought joy to all the world:
For from thee has shone forth
The Sun of Righteousness, Christ our God.
He has loosed us from the curse and given the blessing:
He has vanquished death, and bestowed on us eternal life.

By thy holy nativity,
O most pure Virgin,
Joachim and Anna were set free from the
reproach of childlessness,
And Adam and Eve from the corruption of death.
Delivered from the guilt of sin,
Thy people keep the feast and sing:
'The barren woman bears the Theotokos,
the Sustainer of our life.'

Be renewed, O Adam, and be magnified, O Eve;
You prophets, dance with the apostles and the righteous;

Let there be common joy in the world
among angels and mortals
For the Theotokos is born today of
righteous Joachim and Anna.

9 September

Ciaran of Clonmacnoise

Monk, *c.*545

Ciaran from Connaught was the founder of the great monastery on the east bank of the river Shannon at Clonmacnoise, where the ancient chariot-road through the centre of Ireland crossed the river. It was an outstanding centre of prayer and study and monastic life. Many missionaries went out from there to the European continent, including Virgilius (Fergal), Archbishop of Salzburg, and Alcuin's teacher, Colgu. Among the books written there were the Annals of Clonmacnoise, the Book of the Dun Cow, and the Annals of Tigernach (Tierney). The stones, the cross of the scriptures and the stone churches encircling 'the great stone church', a thousand years old, make an impressive sight. Ciaran died on this day in about the year 545.

A Reading from *The Litany of Confession*
attributed to Ciaran of Clonmacnoise

'According to the multitude of your mercies, cleanse my iniquity.'

O star-like sun,
O guiding light,
O home of the planets,
O fiery-maned and marvellous one,
O fertile, undulating, fiery sea,
Forgive.

O fiery glow,
O fiery flame of judgement,
Forgive.
O holy story-teller, holy scholar,
O full of holy grace, of holy strength,
O overflowing, loving, silent one,
O generous and thunderous giver of gifts,
Forgive.

O rock-like warrior of a hundred hosts,
O fair crowned one, victorious, skilled in battle,
Forgive.

9 September

Charles Fuge Lowder

Priest, 1880

Charles Lowder was born in 1820 and came under the influence of the Oxford Movement during his studies at Exeter College, Oxford, in the early 1840s. After ordination, he became increasingly drawn to a Tractarian and ritualist expression of the faith, especially after his move to London in 1851, despite the fierce opposition such Catholic spirituality faced within the Church. As a curate in Pimlico and Stepney, and then as the first Vicar of St Peter's, London Docks, Lowder came to epitomize the nineteenth-century Anglo-Catholic 'slum priest'. Dedicated to the poor and destitute, he was tireless in his parish work. His health gave way and he died at the age of sixty on this day in the year 1880.

A Reading from a reply of Charles Lowder to his parishioners and congegation at St Peter's, London Docks, on 22 June 1878, thanking them for their support following complaints to the Bishop of London concerning Lowder's ritualistic practices

I hope those of you who signed the address to our bishop did so not merely out of respect or regard for me personally, but because you believe that during these twenty-two years I have been endeavouring to teach the truth, and that our services in church, our sermons and instructions, have been faithful to the Church of England, profitable to salvation, and blessed in the conversion of souls.

Now, this is the system of teaching which our opponents want to put down. Our daily services and communions, fasts and festivals regularly observed, ever open church free to all, orderly and reverent and beautiful ceremonial, congregational singing and worship, the Creeds faithfully taught, catechisings and instructions, are a constant witness to our strict observance of the laws of the Church. It is because we keep these rules so faithfully that we are complained of. If we had our church closed from Sunday to Sunday – as so many churches are – made our services dull, heartless and dreary, or as like as possible to those in Dissenting Chapels, no complaints would be made, we should be left in peace. It is because we have, by God's blessing, taught people to love the Church and her services and to keep her rules that we are now attacked.

Now I do not wish to attack or interfere with others. I am content to go on quietly and steadily doing my duty to God and to you if they will kindly leave me alone. If I must go to prison for doing this duty, and trying my best to save your souls, I shall give no trouble to the policeman, but go quietly; but I had rather stay at my post in Saint Peter's and minister to you there, and in your houses when you need my visits. But maintain the laws of the Church I will, for I vowed to do this when I was ordained thirty-five years ago.

But the main object of this address is to impress upon you, my friends, the great duty of showing by your lives that you really value these Church privileges. That is, after all, the best answer to these complaints – the witness of our own lives and those of our people. Let those of you who are already communicants consider this Festival of Petertide a call to dedicate yourselves more strictly to God's service. Prepare to make a good communion, resolving to serve God more faithfully than ever. If you have been careless or lukewarm in your religious duties, remember that you are not only doing harm to your own soul, but also to the souls of others who make your careless lives an excuse for going on themselves carelessly and without religion.

And to you who are not communicants, and some of whom perhaps seldom come to church, let me say this, that though I thank you very sincerely for your kind feelings to me in signing the address, yet I should be far more thankful – O how thankful to Almighty God – if I might see you henceforth giving yourselves heartily and entirely to his service, loving the Church and religion yourselves, and bringing up your children to love God and their religious duties. Then I should indeed feel that this persecution was blessed to us. I would willingly go to prison – nay, even if it were needed to death itself – if I believed it were to lead to your salvation and sanctification.

10 September

Finnian of Movilla in the Ards

Missionary, 579

Note: See also the Scottish commemoration of Finnbar of Caithness on 25 September.

Finnian was educated at the Abbey of Nendrum on Mahee Island on Strangford Lough in County Down. After spending twenty years in Scotland as student and missionary he came to Movilla (some five miles from Bangor) to found his monastery. There is a tradition that the Psalter, called the Cathach (the 'battle-book'), now in the Royal Irish Academy, was one of Finnian's books. Some scholars say that Finnian introduced to Ireland its first copy of Jerome's Vulgate version of the Scriptures. Several Finnians are associated with the famous story of Columba's secret copying of the manuscript without permission; the king's judgement against Columba was supposed to have led to his exile in Iona. Finnian died on this day in the year 579.

A Reading from the *Conferences* of John Cassian

If you wish to achieve true knowledge of Scripture you must hurry to achieve unshakeable humility of heart. This is what will lead you not to the knowledge which puffs up a man, but to the lore which illuminates through the achievement of love. It is impossible for the unclean of heart to acquire the gift of spiritual knowledge. Therefore be very careful that your zeal for scriptural reading does not, because of empty pretentiousness, prove to be a cause of perdition, instead of being for you the source of knowledge, light, and of the endless glory promised to those enlightened by knowledge.

Having banished all worldly concerns and thoughts, strive in every way to devote yourself constantly to the sacred reading so that continuous meditation will seep into your soul and, as it were, shape it to its image. Somehow it will form that 'ark' of the Scriptures and will contain the two stone tablets, that is, the perpetual strength of the two testaments. There will be the golden urn which is a pure and unstained memory and which will preserve firmly within itself the everlasting manna, that is, the eternal, heavenly sweetness of spiritual meanings and of that bread which belongs to the angels. The branch of Aaron is the saving standard of our exalted and true high priest Jesus Christ. It leafs out forever in the greenness of undying memory. This is the branch which was cut from the root of Jesse and which after death comes more truly alive.

As our mind is increasingly renewed by such study, Scripture begins to take on a new face. A mysteriously deeper sense of it comes to us and somehow the beauty of it stands out more and more as we get farther into it. Scripture shapes itself to human capacity. It will be earthly for those of the flesh, but divine for those of the spirit. Those who once thought of it as somehow wrapped up in thick clouds of obscurity, find themselves unable to grasp either its subtlety or to endure its brilliance.

10 September

William Salesbury and William Morgan

Translator, 1584; and Bishop and Translator, 1604

William Salesbury was born in Llansannan, Denbighshire, around the year 1520, and was educated at Oxford. In 1551 he published Kynniver llith a ban, a version of the epistles and gospels from the 1549 Book of Common Prayer, the first substantial translation of the Scriptures into Welsh. He co-operated with Bishop Richard Davies on the 1567 translations of the New Testament and the Prayer Book, most of the work being done by Salesbury. He probably died in the year 1584. His linguistic ideas, though sometimes eccentric and criticized, nevertheless provided a good foundation for the work of others, and his sincerity and profound Christian devotion were never in doubt.

William Morgan was born at Tŷ Mawr, Wybrnant, Penmachno, in 1545, and educated at St John's College, Cambridge. In 1572 he became Vicar of Llanbadarn Fawr and six years later Rector of Llanrhaeadr-ym-Mochnant. His life there was difficult. He had many bitter enemies in the parish, was under financial pressure and had no great library nearby, but here he worked on the first complete translation of the Bible into Welsh, published in 1588. This masterpiece, as Gwenallt remarked, turned the Welsh language into 'one of the dialects of God's Revelation'. Morgan was consecrated Bishop of Llandaff in 1595, and encouraged scholarship and preaching in his diocese. In 1601 he moved to the see of St Asaph, and he died in the year 1604. His translation of the Bible had a lasting impact on the spiritual life, language, literature and national consciousness of Wales.

A Reading from *Wales and the Reformation*
by Glanmor Williams

The most insurmountable obstacle to the progress of the Reformation in Wales was the absence of a Welsh Bible and Prayer Book. The word of God, as William Salesbury had written in 1551, was 'bound in fetters', or else, to quote Bishop Robinson, it was 'closed up in an unknown tongue'. Just as the Danish kingdom had brought the 'cultural imperialism' of a Danish Bible to the Norwegians, or the Swedes a Swedish text to the Finns, so the English had done to the Welsh, not even allowing them the use of a Latin text as they had done with the Irish. Salesbury took up the cry in his home diocese of St Asaph. Here, he found a small, but intensely enthusiastic band of supporters responding to his appeal. The arrival of a new bishop there in 1560 may have given his hopes a fresh fillip. Richard Davies was a returned exile, a convinced Protestant, who had seen for himself in many parts of Europe the beneficial effect of scriptural translations. He and Salesbury may have been joined by other enthusiasts like Humphrey Lhuyd, Renaissance scholar and literary enthusiast, Gruffudd Hiraethog, friend of William Salesbury and literary tutor of Richard Davies, and members of the influential Myddleton family.

The effects soon became apparent. Davies and/or Salesbury were almost certainly responsible for the articles drawn up at this time which suggested, though without success, that it might be made 'lawful for such Welsh or Cornish children, as could speak no English, to learn the catechism in the Welsh tongue or the Cornish language'.

Although Welsh prose had a tradition that was centuries-old, these authors of the sixteenth century constantly complained about the paucity of Welsh texts to which they had access and the fewness of the patterns on which to base their own writings. Welsh, like many other European languages, was at this time going through a difficult transitional stage between its medieval and its modern form, and handling it effectively was a delicate operation. If possible, the language ought to be freed from outmoded terms and usages; not overdependent on any one dialect; flexible and intelligible, yet dignified, resonant, and preserving the classic qualities of uniformity, strength, and purity associated with the old literary tradition. It was a Herculean labour to translate the Prayer Book, Psalter, and Bible within the three or fear years dictated by Parliament. The enterprise demanded of the men who proposed to embark upon it a daunting combination of virtues. They would need a clear vision, an unswerving dedication, and a readiness to commit themselves wholeheartedly to what they saw as the highest service of God and the greatest good of their countrymen. With the human resources of a small nation numbering not much more than a quarter of a million on which to draw, the Welsh were singularly fortunate to find that men of this calibre appeared at the right time. As Salesbury had earlier predicted, if the task were postponed for another generation, it would be too late.

alternative reading

A Reading from *Wales and the Reformation* by Glanmor Williams

Of the excellence of Morgan's translation [of the Bible] much has been written. Three qualities have been especially singled out for commendation: his talents as a scholar; his revision of Salesbury's New Testament and Prayer Book; and his gifts as a writer of Welsh.

Morgan proved himself to be a consummate scholar, who made use of the best Hebrew and Greek texts available to him with exceptional skill and discernment. He set out to translate the original wording as faithfully and accurately as he could, but without in any way sacrificing intelligibility in the process. Much as he admired the fine scholars who had preceded him, he was not afraid to choose his own path and back his individual judgement. He was rarely wrong and, in some instances, he offered translations which anticipated the mature scholarship of the Revised Version of the English Bible of 1882. He was a singular master of the rare art of turning the 'spare, muscular, direct language of the Hebrew original into Welsh that is distinguished by the same qualities'. Even John Wynn, exasperated by Morgan's stubborn opposition to him and reluctant to pay him any compliments, grudgingly admitted that he was 'a good scholar, both a Grecian and Hebrician'.

Morgan was only too conscious of the infelicities of earlier Welsh versions. Although he accepted about three-quarters of Salesbury's actual translation of the New Testament, he comprehensively revised its whole text, as far as orthography and vocabulary were concerned. In relation to vocabulary he showed his preference for living words rather than the less familiar archaisms; he rejected many of Salesbury's loan-words, derived either from English or Latin; and he cut down drastically on those excessive variations in the text and margin so beloved of Salesbury in his quest for 'copiousness'. Throughout, he aimed at fidelity to the original texts, consistency, and regularity. In short, he made a point of eliminating Salesbury's archaisms, Latinizations, and other idiosyncrasies, which had caused the versions of 1567 to be so difficult to understand and so badly read.

Finally, and most commendable of all, perhaps, Morgan's handling of the Welsh language bore all the hallmarks of a superb writer as well as an erudite scholar. He had the instinctive sureness and intuitive grasp of a man to whom his native tongue was an heirloom to treasure as well as a tool to use.

11 September

Deiniol

Bishop, 584

Deiniol Wyn ('Deiniol the Blessed') was a grandson of Pabo Post Prydain. He helped his father, Dunawd, to found the famous monastery of Bangor Is-coed on the banks of the Dee in Flintshire. There is a suggestion (possibly the product of medieval ecclesiastical politics) that he then went to South Wales and was consecrated bishop there by Dyfrig. What is certain is that Deiniol founded a monastic school at Bangor Fawr in Arfon from which the Diocese of Bangor derives its origin. David's biographer records that Deiniol was present at the great Synod of Llanddewibrefi. He may also have spent some time in Ireland and in Brittany. He is said to have died in 584 and to have been buried on Bardsey Island. His cult was widespread in North Wales and there are also a few churches and holy wells in the south that bear his name.

A Reading from *The Life of Saint David* by Rhigyfarch the Wise

Since even after Saint Germanus had come to our aid a second time, the Pelagian heresy was recovering its strength and obstinacy, again implanting the poison of a deadly serpent in the heart of our country, a general synod of all the bishops of Britain was called. And so one hundred and eighteen bishops came together, as well as an innumerable multitude of priests, abbots, clergy of other ranks, kings, princes, lay men and women, so that this very great crowd completely covered the surrounding land.

Such were the numbers that the speakers' voices could barely reach those who were nearest to them. The people awaited the Word, but the majority could not hear it. One after another tried to preach, but to no avail. They felt a great anxiety and fear that the people would return with the heresy still unopposed.

Messengers were sent out a second and third time to encourage holy Dewi to come to the synod, but he withheld his consent. Finally, the holiest and most faithful men were sent, the brothers Deiniol and Dubritius. But the holy bishop Dewi foresaw this with prophetic spirit and said to his brethren, 'Today, my brethren, very holy men are coming to visit us. Receive them gladly, and procure fish to have with the bread and water for their meal.' The brothers arrived, all exchanged greetings and conversed about holy things. To them the saint said, 'I cannot refuse you. Eat, and I will go with you to the synod. But I cannot preach there, though I shall assist you, however little, with my prayers.'

When he entered the synod, the company of bishops rejoiced, the people were glad, and the whole assembly exulted. They begged him to preach, and he did not spurn the council's will.

Thus was the heresy driven out, the faith strengthened in sound hearts, and all were of one accord. Thanks be given to God and to holy David.

12 September

Ailbhe

Bishop, *c.*526

Much of the recorded life of Ailbhe is a confusion of valueless legends and contradictory versions. Yet the tradition of a holy man, a powerful preacher and teacher in the region of Cashel, cannot be set aside lightly. There is just a possibility that Ailbhe may represent an evangelistic initiative arising from a Christian British colony in Ireland independent from that of Patrick. The monastic Rule attributed to Ailbhe was probably composed some two hundred years after the saint's death. The original was in metrical form, and it is likely that the author attributed it to Ailbhe out of respect for his doctrine and leadership of the Church. Ailbhe died around the year 526.

A Reading from *The Rule of Ailbhe*

A monk should be imperturbable, never agitated. He should be wise, studious, and devout. Let him keep vigil; let him not be reproachful. Let him be the servant of all, humble and kind.

He should be disciplined and reserved but nevertheless zealous. Let him be honourable, generous, and hospitable. Let him beware of the temptations of the world, and let him be warlike against the worldly.

Let him be nimble as a serpent, and like a dove in his affection. Let him be gentle in his vigils, and like a fortress in his prayer.

Even though he have possession of the unsavoury world, he should not love its treasures. Let him cultivate and share the fruits of the earth. He should not be cruel since that will not bring him to bright heaven.

He shall accept the jewels both of baptism and communion, and he should be faithful to the obligation of intercession. Let him receive the confessions of those who so wish, and let him be silent about what he hears therein.

He should bewail with everyone his sins. When there is cause for shame let him be silent about it. The poor and the needy are to be helped as far as lies within his power.

He should not speak evil of, or harshly reproach, another, nor should he cause anyone to blush. Never should he violently rebuke anyone or carry on a conversation with a boorish person, and his speech at all times should be noted for its lack of boastfulness.

He should never refuse assistance to a person who calls with insistence for it. Let him share generously and without measure with one who asks.

His manner should be full of affection, lacking harshness and contention on the one hand, and lust on the other. His deportment should rather be humble, patient and mild.

He should be constant in prayer, never forgetting his canonical hours. Let him give his mind to his prayer with humility and with great peace.

13 September

John Chrysostom

Bishop of Constantinople, Teacher of the Faith, 407

Note: John Chrysostom is commemorated on 27 January in Scotland and Wales.

John was born in Antioch, the third city of the Roman Empire, in about 347. He was a brilliant preacher which earned him in the sixth century the surname 'Chrysostom', literally 'golden-mouthed'. He is honoured as one of the four Greek Doctors of the Church. Against his wish he was made Patriarch of Constantinople in 398. He set about reforming the Church and exposing corruption amongst the clergy and in the Imperial administration. 'Mules bear fortunes and Christ dies of hunger at your gate,' he is alleged to have cried out. He fell foul of the Empress Eudoxia, and in spite of the support of Pope Innocent I of Rome, was sent into exile twice, finally dying of exhaustion and starvation in September 407, with the words 'Glory be to God for everything' on his lips.

A Reading from the last homily preached by John Chrysostom in Constantinople before he went into exile

The waves have risen and the surging sea is dangerous, but we do not fear drowning for we stand upon the rock. Let the sea surge! It cannot destroy the rock. Let the waves rise! They cannot sink the boat of Jesus. Tell me, what are we to fear? Is it death? But 'for me life is Christ, and death is gain'. So tell me, is it exile? 'The earth is the Lord's and all that it contains.' Is it the confiscation of property? 'We brought nothing into the world and it is certain we can take nothing out of it.' I have nothing but contempt for the threats of this world; its treasures I ridicule. I am not afraid of poverty, I do not crave after wealth, I am not afraid of death, and I do not seek to live except it be of help to you. So I simply mention my present circumstances and call on you, my dear people, to remain steadfast in your love.

Do you not hear the Lord saying, 'Where two or three are gathered together in my name, there I am among them'? Where will he be absent, for where will there not be two or three bound together by love? I have his pledge, so I do not have to rely on my own strength. I cling to his promise: it is my staff, my security, it is my peaceful harbour. Even though the entire world be in turmoil, I cling to his promise and read it. It is my rampart and my shield. What promise is this? 'I am with you always, even to the end of time.'

Christ is with me, whom then shall I fear? Let the waves rise up against me, the seas, the wrath of rulers: these things to me are mere cobwebs. And if you, my dear people, had not held me back I would have left this very day. I always say, 'Lord, your will be done'; not what this person or that person wishes, but as you wish. This is my fortress, this is my immovable rock, this is my firm staff. If God wishes this to be, then so be it. If he wishes me to be here, I thank him. Wherever he wants me to be, I thank him. Wherever I am, there are you also; where you are, there am I too; we are one body. And the body cannot be separated from its head, nor the head from the rest of the body. We may be separated by space, but we are united by love. Not even death can sever us. For even if my body dies, my soul will live on, and my soul will remember you, my people.

You are my fellow-citizens, my fathers, my brothers, my children, my limbs, my body, my light, and yes, dearer to me than light. For what can the rays of the sun give me when compared with the gift of your love? Its rays are useful to me in this present life, but your love is weaving for me a crown for the life that is to come.

14 September

Holy Cross Day

The cross on which our Lord was crucified has become the universal symbol for Christianity, replacing the fish symbol of the early Church, though the latter has been revived in recent times. After the end of the persecution era, early in the fourth century, pilgrims began to travel to Jerusalem to visit and pray at the places associated with the life of Jesus. Helena, the mother of the emperor, was a Christian and, whilst overseeing excavations in the city, is said to have uncovered a cross, which many believed to be the Cross of Christ (see also 21 May). A basilica was built on the site of the Holy Sepulchre and dedicated on this day in the year 335.

A Reading from a homily on the Exaltation of the Holy Cross
by Andrew of Crete

We are celebrating the feast of the cross which drove away darkness and brought in the light. As we keep this feast, we are lifted up with the crucified Christ, leaving behind us earth and sin so that we may gain the things above. So great and outstanding a possession is the cross that whoever wins it has won a treasure. Rightly could I call this treasure the fairest of all fair things and the costliest, in fact as well as in name, for on it and through it, and for its sake, the riches of salvation that had been lost were restored to us.

Had there been no cross, Christ could not have been crucified. Had there been no cross, life itself could not have been nailed to the tree. And if life had not been nailed to it, there would be no streams of immortality pouring from Christ's side, blood and water for the world's cleansing. The bond of our sin would not be cancelled, we should not have obtained our freedom, we should not have enjoyed the fruit of the tree of life and the gates of paradise would not stand open. Had there been no cross, death would not have been trodden underfoot, nor hell despoiled.

Therefore, the cross is something wonderfully great and honourable. It is great because through the cross the many noble acts of Christ found their consummation – very many indeed, for both his miracles and his sufferings were fully rewarded with victory. The cross is honourable because it is both the sign of God's suffering and the trophy of his victory. It stands for his suffering because on it he freely suffered unto death. But it is also his trophy because it was the means by which the devil was wounded and death conquered; the barred gates of hell were smashed, and the cross became the one common salvation of the whole world.

The cross is called Christ's glory; it is saluted as his triumph. We recognise it as the cup he longed to drink and the climax of the sufferings he endured for our sake. As to the cross being Christ's glory, listen to his words: 'Now is the Son of Man glorified, and in him God is glorified, and God will glorify him at once.' And again, 'Father, glorify me with the glory that I had with you before the world came to be.' And once more: 'Father, glorify your name.' Then a voice came from heaven: 'I have glorified it and I will glorify it again.' Here he speaks of the glory that would accrue to him through the cross. And if you would understand that the cross is Christ's triumph, then hear what he himself also said: 'When I am lifted up, then I will draw all people to myself.'

Now you can see that the cross is Christ's glory and his triumph.

alternative reading

A Reading from the anonymous Anglo-Saxon poem *The Dream of the Rood*

Many years ago – the memory abides –
I was felled to the ground at the forest's edge,
Severed from my roots. Enemies seized me,
Made of me a mark of scorn for criminals to mount on;
Shoulder-high they carried me and set me on a hill.
Many foes made me fast there. Far off then I saw
The King of all mankind coming in great haste,
With courage keen, eager to climb me.
I did not dare, against my Lord's dictate,
To bow down or break, though I beheld tremble
The earth's four corners. I could easily
Have felled his foes; yet fixed and firm I stood.
Then the young Warrior – it was God Almighty –
Strong and steadfast, stripped himself for battle;
He climbed up on the high gallows, constant in his purpose,
Mounted it in sight of many, mankind to ransom.

Horror seized me when the Hero clasped me,
But I dared not bow or bend down to earth,
Nor falter, nor fall; firm I needs must stand.
I was raised up a Rood, a royal King I bore,
The High King of Heaven: hold firm I must.
They drove dark nails through me, the dire wounds still show,
Cruel gaping gashes, yet I dared not give as good.
They taunted the two of us; I was wet with teeming blood,
Streaming from the Warrior's side when he sent forth his spirit.
High upon that hill helpless I suffered
Long hours of torment; I saw the Lord of Hosts
Outstretched in agony; all embracing darkness
Covered with thick clouds the corpse of the world's Ruler;
The bright day was darkened by a deep shadow,
All its colours clouded; the whole creation wept,
Bewailing its King's fall; Christ was on the Rood.

And now I give you bidding, O man beloved,
Reveal this Vision to the children of men,
And clearly tell of the Tree of glory
Whereon God suffered for man's many sins
And the evil that Adam once wrought of old.

15 September

Cyprian

Bishop of Carthage, Martyr, 258

Note: Cyprian is commemorated on 13 September in Scotland.

Born in Carthage in about the year 200, Cyprian was a teacher of rhetoric and a lawyer in the city before his conversion to Christianity. He gave away his pagan library and set his mind to study the sacred Scriptures and the commentaries that were beginning to proliferate. He became a priest and then, in the year 248, was elected Bishop of Carthage by the people of the city, together with the assembled priests and other bishops present. He showed compassion to returning apostates, whilst always insisting on the need for unity in the Church. During the persecution of Valerian, the Christian clergy were required to participate in pagan worship; Cyprian refused and was first exiled and then condemned to death. He died on this day in the year 258.

A Reading from the letter of Cyprian to Donatus

As I write to you I am aware of the mediocrity of much of my thinking and how shallow a lot of my understanding is. I have gathered a poor harvest. I have little to enrich the soil of your heart. If one is in court, or having to address a public assembly or the senate, a lavish and extravagant eloquence is appropriate. But when speaking of God, our master, the absolute sincerity of what we say will communicate to others not by our eloquence but by the substance of our lives. And so please accept these words that carry conviction rather than charm, and are designed not to win over a popular audience by their cultivated rhetoric, but simply to preach the mercy of God by their unvarnished truth. Accept that which has been sincerely felt rather than merely learned, that which has not been laboriously accumulated over the course of a long apprenticeship, but inhaled in one gulp by a sudden act of grace.

When I was younger I lay in darkness and in the depths of night, tossed to and fro in the waves of this turbulent world, uncertain which path to take, ignorant of my true life and a stranger to the light of truth. At that time, and on account of the life I then led, it seemed difficult to believe what divine mercy promised for my salvation, namely, that it was possible for someone to be born again to a new life by being immersed in the healing waters of baptism. It was difficult to believe that a person though physically the same, could be changed in heart and mind.

How was it possible, I thought, that a change could be great enough to strip us in a single moment of the innate hardness of our nature? How could the bad habits acquired over the course of years disappear, since these are invariably deeply rooted within us? If someone is used to feasting and lavish entertainment, how can they learn the discipline of a simpler lifestyle? If someone is used to dressing ostentatiously in gold and purple, and been admired for their good taste, how can they cast them aside for ordinary clothes? Someone who loves the trappings of public office cannot easily retire into the anonymity of private life. Someone who is surrounded by great crowds of supporters and is honoured by an entourage of attendants will consider solitude a punishment. As long as we allow ourselves to be trapped by these outward allurements we will be the more easily seduced by wine, inflated with pride, inflamed by anger, be eaten up with greed, be excited by cruelty, be controlled by ambition, and a prey to our lusts.

These were my frequent thoughts. I was trapped by the past errors of my life from which it seemed impossible to escape. I gave in to my sins which clung fast to me. Since I despaired of improvement I took an indulgent view of my faults and regarded them as if they were permanent occupants in my house.

But after the life-giving water of baptism came to my rescue and washed away the stain of my former years, and the light which comes from above, serene and pure, was poured into my cleansed and reconciled heart, and after the Heavenly Spirit was breathed into me, and I was made a new man by a second birth, then amazingly what I had previously doubted became clear to me. What had been hidden was revealed. What had been in the dark became clear to me. What previously had seemed impossible now seemed possible. What was in me of the guilty flesh I now acknowledged to be earthly. What was made alive in me by God was now animated by the Spirit of holiness.

All our power is of God; I repeat, it is of God. From God we receive the gift of life and strength. By the power derived from God we are able, while still living in this world, to glimpse the things of eternity. But let fear be the guardian of our conscience, so that the Lord, who in his great mercy has infused our hearts abundantly with his grace, may always be honoured by the hospitality of a grateful mind, lest the assurance we have received lead us to become careless, and our old enemies creep up on us again.

16 September

Ninian

Bishop of Galloway, Apostle of the Picts, *c.*432

Ninian was born in about the year 360 and was the son of a Cumbrian chieftain who had himself converted to Christianity. It seems he visited Rome in his youth, where he received training in the faith. He was consecrated bishop in the year 394 and returned to Britain, where he set up a community of monks at Candida Casa (Whithorn) from where they went out on missionary journeys as far as Perth and Sterling. Ninian died in about the year 432.

A Reading from *The History of the English Church and People* by the Venerable Bede

In the year of our Lord 565, when Justin the Younger succeeded Justinian and ruled as Emperor of Rome, there came from Ireland to Britain a priest and abbot named Columba, a true monk in life no less than habit, to preach the Word of God in the provinces of the Northern Picts, which are separated from those of the Southern Picts by a range of steep and rugged mountains.

The Southern Picts, who live on this side of the mountains, are said to have abandoned the errors of idolatry long before this date and accepted the true faith through the preaching of the Word by Bishop Ninian, a most revered and holy man of British race, who had been regularly instructed in the mysteries of the Christian faith in Rome.

Ninian's own episcopal See, named after Saint Martin and famous for its stately church, is now held by the English, and it is there that his body and those of many saints lie at rest. The place belongs to the province of Bernicia and is commonly known as *Candida Casa*, the 'White House', because he built a church of stone, using a method which was unusual among the Britons.

alternative reading

A Reading from *The Life of Saint Ninian* by Aelred of Rievaulx

As a young man Ninian travelled to Rome, and there the pope placed him in the care of good teachers of the truth to be instructed in the disciplines of the faith and in the meaning of Scripture. The young man, full of God, did not labour in vain or to no purpose. In the course of his studies he came to realise how much of his previous education at the hands of unskilled teachers had been at variance with sound doctrine. Therefore with all eagerness Ninian opened wide the mouth of his soul to receive the word of God. Like a bee which sucks nectar from many different flowers, he formed in his mind honeycombs of wisdom constructed from the arguments he gathered from his various teachers. He stored them in the secret recesses of his heart, preserving them until they had been thoroughly digested, with the result that in later years he could bring forth from his inner person a wisdom that not only nurtured his own soul, but also brought comfort to others. Truly, it was the due reward for one who for the love of truth had been prepared to forsake his native land, wealth and pleasure.

Having lived for many years in the city, it came to the knowledge of the Bishop of Rome that in certain western parts of Britain were yet many who had not received the faith of our Saviour, and that some were hearing the word of the gospel from the lips of heretics and those poorly instructed in the law of God. Moved by the Spirit of God, the pope with his own hands therefore ordained the man of God to the episcopate, and having bestowed on him his blessing, appointed him apostle to his native land.

Ninian travelled home via the city of Tours, for at this time the most blessed Martin was its bishop, and he had long been desirous to meet him. There he stayed for a while consulting the holy man. On reaching his native land a great crowd of people went about to meet him. Great was the joy of all, wonderful the devotion; everywhere resounded with the praise of Christ, for everyone regarded Ninian as a prophet. Straight away this diligent workman entered upon the field of his Lord, rooting out what had been wrongly planted, scattering what had been wrongly collected, and pulling down that which had been wrongly built. Then, with the minds of his people purged of error, Ninian began to lay in them the foundations of the true faith, building with the gold of wisdom, the silver of knowledge, and the precious stones of good works.

He chose a site for his church at a place which is now called Whithorn. It is situated on the shore of the ocean, the land running far out to sea so that it is enclosed by the sea on three sides, with access only from the north. Here, by the command of the man of God, stonemasons whom he had brought with him from Tours built a church of stone, before which (it is said) no other had ever been built in Britain.

When Blessed Ninian died, perfect in life and full of years, he left this world a happy man, and accompanied by the angels his soul was carried to heaven there to receive his eternal reward.

16 September

Edward Bouverie Pusey

Priest, Tractarian, 1882

Edward Pusey was born in 1800 and educated at Oxford, where he became a Fellow of Oriel College in 1823. He became an expert in Biblical languages and criticism and in 1828 he was appointed Regius Professor of Hebrew in Oxford, the same year he was ordained. His patristic studies and firm adherence to a Catholic interpretation of doctrine made him one of the leaders of the Oxford Movement. He was significant in encouraging the revival of Religious Life within the Church of England and was a noted preacher. His austere way of life made him much revered by his contemporaries and they founded Pusey House and Library in Oxford in his memory, following his death on this day in the year 1882.

A Reading from a sermon of Edward Bouverie Pusey

Holiness is made for all. It is the end for which we were made; for which we were redeemed; for which God the Holy Ghost is sent down and 'shed abroad in the hearts' which will receive him. God willed not to create us as perfect. He willed that we, through grace, should become perfect. We know not why our freewill is so precious in the eyes of God that he waits for us, pleads with us, draws us, allures us, wins us, overpowers us with his love; but he will not force us. He made us to be like him. And what is this but to be holy? 'Be ye holy, for I your God am holy.'

The mistake of mistakes is to think that holiness consists in great or extraordinary things beyond the reach of ordinary people. It has been well said, 'Holiness does not consist in doing uncommon things, but in doing common things uncommonly well.' Even in those great saints of God, the things which dazzle us most are not perhaps those which are the most precious in the sight of God. Great was the faith of Joshua, for example, when he said: 'Sun, stand thou still upon Gibeon, and thou moon, in the valley of Ajalon.' God himself speaks of it that 'there was no day before it nor after it, that the Lord hearkened unto the voice of a man'. Yet nearer to the heart of God were those words of Joshua's aged love: 'As for me and my house, we will serve the Lord.'

So too now. It is not by great things, but by great diligence in little everyday things that thou canst show great love for God, and become greatly holy, and a saint of God. Few ever do great things, and the few who can do them can each do but few. But every one can study the will of God and can give great diligence to know it and to do what he knows. Everyone can, by the grace of God, be faithful to what he knows. Your daily round of duty is your daily path to come nearer unto God.

alternative reading

A Reading from a sermon of Edward Bouverie Pusey preached before the University of Oxford at Christ Church in 1851, concerning 'The Rule of Faith as maintained by the Fathers and the Church of England'

We acknowledge that Holy Scripture is the source of all saving truth; but it does not therefore follow that everyone, unguided, is to draw for himself the truth out of that living well. This being so, has the Church herself any guide external to herself, except the Holy Scripture as illumined by the light of God's Holy Spirit? Saint Paul writing to Saint Timothy has always been understood to say that she has: 'Hold fast the form of sound words which thou hast heard of me, that good thing which was committed unto thee, the good deposit, keep by the Holy Ghost which dwelleth in us.'

The word 'deposit' became a word set apart to denote the body of the Christian faith, committed to the Church; a sacred deposit to be faithfully guarded and not tampered with, not to be lessened, not to be adulterated, but to be kept for him who left it to her trust. 'Keep,' Vincentius paraphrases, 'that which is committed to thee, not that which is invented of thee: that which thou hast received, not that which thou hast devised; a thing not of wit but of learning: not of private assumption but of public tradition; a thing brought to thee not brought forth of thee; wherein thou must not be an author but a keeper; not a master but a disciple; not a leader but a follower. Keep the deposit. Preserve the talent of the Catholic Faith safe and undiminished; that which is committed to thee, let that remain with thee, and that deliver. Thou hast received gold, render then gold.'

The Church of England has, from the Reformation, held implicitly in purpose of heart, all which the ancient Church ever held. The rule of Vincentius was ever held. Discordant voices, as far as they are discordant, cannot be the one voice of truth. One body of truth and faith and morals there can alone be, in which every declaration of Holy Scripture would meet and be combined and fulfilled. It does seem to be a paradox, therefore, when some have put forth that the faith is less faith because not received from a living, infallible authority. Faith is that which rests on him who is the truth – God. Faith is from God to God. It is not gained by man's own toil or search or study, but is given by God.

These are heavy times. Darkly did the last year close; darker has the present begun. Contention has taken the place of love; suspicion of trust. We all desire to know and to teach the Faith; we all believe that we have it; I do trust that if we could understand one another we might meet in one truth. But it cannot be the sound and healthy and normal state of a Church which we have been wont thankfully to call pure and apostolic, that we should be contradicting one another, condemning one another. This is not like the time of the apostles when all 'were of one heart and mind'. This is not to fulfil the apostolic precept 'let the peace of God rule in your hearts to the which also ye are called in one body' when some are ready to cast others out of that body. Instead of this strife, let us rather seek one another, be at pains to understand one another, harmonise what all believe truly, not by abandoning any truth, but by affirming together all which is the truth.

17 September

Hildegard

Abbess of Bingen, Visionary, 1179

Hildegard was born in 1098 at Böckelheim in Germany. From her earliest years she had a powerful, visionary life, becoming a nun at the age of eighteen, much influenced by her foster-mother, Jutta, who had set up the community and whom she succeeded as abbess in 1136. Her visions of light, which she described as 'the reflection of the Living Light', deepened her understanding of God and creation, sin and redemption. They were, however, accompanied by repeated illness and physical weakness. About twenty years later, she moved her sisters to a new Abbey at Bingen. She travelled much in the Rhineland, founding a daughter house and influencing many, including the Emperor Frederick Barbarossa. She was a pastor, a composer and teacher, seeing herself as a 'feather on the breath of God'. She wrote three visionary works, a natural history and a medical compendium. She died on this day in the year 1179.

A Reading from *The Book of Life's Merits* by Hildegard of Bingen

Forgetting about God leads to harmful and idle chatter such as: 'How can we know about God if we have never seen him? And why should we have any regard for him if we have never set eyes on him?' People who talk like that are no longer mindful of their creator, and their minds are in the darkness of unbelief. For when man fell, darkness fell on the whole of creation. But God had created human beings to be full of light so that they could see the radiance of pure ether and hear the songs of angels. He had clothed them in such radiance that they shone with the splendour of it. But all this was lost when man disobeyed God's commandment and so caused nature to fall with him. Yet the natural elements retained a glimmering of their former pristine position, which human sin could not destroy completely. For which reason people should retain a glimmering of their knowledge of God. They should allow God to return to the centre of their lives, recognising that they owe their very existence to no one else save God alone, who is the creator of all.

alternative reading

A Reading from a letter of Hildegard to Adam, Abbot of Ebrach, written before 1166

In a true vision of the spirit, my body fully awake, I saw, as it were, a beautiful girl of such great brightness, with so shining a face, that I could hardly gaze upon her. She had a cloak whiter than snow and brighter than the stars, and she had on shoes of the purest gold. And she held the moon and the sun in her right hand, and she embraced them lovingly. On her breast there was an ivory tablet, and on this tablet there was an image of man coloured like sapphire. Every creature called this girl sovereign lady. And to the image on her breast, she said: 'With thee is the beginning in the day of thy strength: in the brightness of the saints: from the womb before the day-star I begot thee.'

And I heard a voice saying to me: This girl that you see is Divine Love, and she has her dwelling place in eternity. For when God wished to create the world, he bent down in sweetest love, and he provided for all necessary things, just as a father prepares the inheritance for his son. Thus it was that in great ardour he established all his works in order. Then all creation in its various kinds and forms acknowledged its creator, for in the beginning divine love was the matrix from which he created all things, when he said, 'Let there be, and it was done.' Thus every creature was formed through divine love in the twinkling of an eye.

And this figure shines with such great brightness, with so shining a face, that one can scarcely gaze upon her because she displays the fear of the Lord in such pure knowledge that mortal man will never be able to fully realise it. She has a cloak whiter than snow and brighter than the stars because, in pure innocence and without pretence, she embraces all things with the refulgent works of the saints. And she wears shoes of the purest gold, because her paths lead through the best part of God's election. And she holds the sun and the moon in her right hand, embracing them lovingly, because God's right hand embraces all creatures and because divine love is dispersed among the good of all nations and all realms. Moreover, the ivory tablet is on her breast because, in the knowledge of God, the hand of integrity flourished always in the Virgin Mary, so that, in her, the image of man appears coloured like sapphire, because the Son of God, in divine love, radiated forth from the ancient of days in divine love.

For when all creation was fulfilled by God's commandment – just as he himself said: 'Increase and multiply, and fill the earth' – the heat of the true sun descended like dew into the womb of the Virgin and made man from her flesh, just as also he formed Adam's flesh and blood from the mud of the earth. And the Virgin gave birth to him immaculately.

19 September

Theodore of Tarsus

Archbishop of Canterbury, 690

Theodore was born at Tarsus in Cilicia in about the year 602. He was an Asiatic Greek and had been educated in Athens before being appointed Archbishop of Canterbury by the Pope. He was raised straight from being a sub-deacon to the archiepiscopal see but proved his worth by immediately undertaking a visitation of the whole of England soon after his arrival. He set about reforming the Church in England with the division of dioceses and summoned the Synod of Hertford on 24 September 673, probably the most important Church council in the land, as it issued canons dealing with the rights and obligations of both clergy and Religious: it restricted bishops to working in their own diocese and not intruding on the ministry of their prelate neighbours; it established precedence within the episcopacy; it ensured that monks remained stable to their monastery and obedient to their abbot; and many other matters were dealt with to effect the good order of the Church. The canons were based on those of the Council of Chalcedon. Theodore proved to be the first Archbishop of Canterbury to have the willing allegiance of all Anglo-Saxon England. He died on this day in the year 690.

A Reading from *The History of the English Church and People* by the Venerable Bede

Following the death of Deusdedit, the sixth Archbishop of the church at Canterbury, the see of Canterbury was vacant for a considerable time. Egbert, King of Kent, and Oswy, King of Northumbria, jointly sent a priest called Wigheard to Rome, with a request that he might be consecrated archbishop of the English. However, not long after his arrival in Rome, he and almost all of his companions died in a outbreak of the plague.

Pope Vitalian took counsel about the matter and tried hard to find someone worthy to send as archbishop of the English Church. Now there was in Rome at this time a monk named Theodore, a native of Tarsus in Cilicia. He was learned both in sacred and secular literature, in Greek and Latin, of proven integrity, and of the venerable age of sixty-six. Hadrian, a native of Africa and abbot of a monastery near Naples, suggested the name of Theodore to the pope, who agreed to consecrate him on condition that Hadrian himself should accompany Theodore to Britain, since he had already travelled through Gaul twice on various missions and was not only better acquainted with the road, but had sufficient followers of his own available. The pope also ordered Hadrian to give full support to Theodore in his teaching, but to ensure that he did not introduce into the Church which he was to rule any Greek customs which conflicted with the teachings of the true faith.

Theodore arrived in Canterbury on Sunday 27 May, in the second year after his consecration, and he held the see for twenty-one years, three months, and twenty-six days. Soon after his arrival, he visited every part of the island occupied by the English peoples, and received a ready welcome and hearing everywhere. He was accompanied and assisted throughout his journey by Hadrian, and he taught the Christian way of life and the canonical method of keeping Easter.

Theodore was the first archbishop whom the entire Church of the English consented to obey. And since, as I have observed, both he and Hadrian were men of learning in sacred and secular literature, they attracted a large number of students, into whose minds they poured the waters of wholesome learning day by day. In addition to instructing them in the holy Scriptures, they also taught their pupils poetry, astronomy and the calculation of the church calendar. In proof of this, some of their students still alive today are as proficient in Latin and Greek as in their native tongue.

Never had there been such happy times as these since the English settled in Britain; for the Christian kings were so strong that they daunted all the barbarous tribes. The people eagerly sought the new-found joys of the kingdom of heaven, and all who wished for instruction in the reading of the Scriptures found teachers ready to hand.

20 September

Saints, Martyrs and Missionaries of Australasia and the Pacific

The gospel of Jesus Christ was brought to Australasia and the Pacific largely by European and American missionaries over the last two centuries. They worked in difficult, often hostile, conditions amongst native peoples and settlers. Many gave long years of their lives, travelling enormous distances between islands, or across the Australian continent, preaching and ministering to their charges. We give thanks for the work of people like Peter Chanel, missionary in Fiji, and the first martyr of this region; John Coleridge Patteson, martyred in Melanesia on this day; and those martyred in New Guinea. We remember the example of George Augustus Selwyn, first bishop and one of the founding fathers of New Zealand; and of Ini Kopuria, a native policeman who founded a thriving religious community in Melanesia. In commemorating these lives we celebrate all who have witnessed to the faith of Christ in Australasia and the Pacific.

Note: For readings on the above mentioned saints, see their individual entries as follows:

Peter Chanel	28 April
Caroline Chisholm	16 May
John Coleridge Patteson	see below
George Augustus Selwyn	11 April
Ini Kopuria	6 June
Lucian Tapiedi	2 September

A Reading from *The Cost of Discipleship* by Dietrich Bonhoeffer

In the fellowship of the crucified and glorified body of Christ, we participate in his suffering and glory. His cross is the burden which is laid on his Body, the Church. All its sufferings borne beneath this cross are the sufferings of Christ himself. This suffering first takes the form of the baptismal death, and after that the daily dying of the Christians in the power of their baptism. But there is a far greater form of suffering than this, one which bears an ineffable promise. For while it is true that only the suffering of Christ himself can atone for sin, and that his suffering and triumph took place 'for us', yet to some, who are not ashamed of their fellowship in his body, he vouchsafes the immeasurable grace and privilege of suffering 'for him', as he did for them. No greater glory could he have granted to his own, no higher privilege can the Christian enjoy, than to suffer 'for Christ'. When that happens, something comes to pass which is inconceivable under the law. For according to the law we can only be punished for our own sins. Under the law there is nothing that a person can suffer for his own good, still less for the good of another, and least of all for the good of Christ. The body of Christ, which was given for us, which suffered the punishment of our sins, makes us free to take our share of suffering and death 'for Christ'. Now we may work and suffer for Christ, for the sake of him who did everything possible for us. This is the miracle of grace we enjoy in our fellowship in the Body of Christ.

Although Christ has fulfilled all the vicarious suffering necessary for our redemption, his suffering on earth is not yet finished. The Body of Christ has its own allotted portion of suffering. God grants one person the grace to bear special suffering in place of another, and this suffering must at all costs be endured and overcome. Blessed are they whom God deems worthy to suffer for the Body of Christ. Such suffering is joy indeed, enabling the believer to boast that he bears the dying of Jesus Christ and the marks of Christ in his body.

20 September

John Coleridge Patteson and his Companions

First Bishop of Melanesia, Martyrs, 1871

Born in London in 1827, John Coleridge Patteson came under the influence of George Augustus Selwyn while John was a scholar at Eton. Patteson was ordained and, in 1855 at the age of twenty-eight, left Britain to begin his life's work among the Islanders of the South Pacific, becoming their first bishop. His system of evangelization was to train indigenous evangelists in the hope that some would be ordained, and so to equip local people to share the gospel in a way that was within their own culture. This bore fruit and Christianity spread rapidly. Also working in Melanesia were 'thief ships' or 'blackbirders', essentially European slave-traders who carried off Islanders to work in British and other colonies. When Patteson landed alone on the island of Nukapu in the hope of showing that not all white men were deceivers, he was killed, probably in revenge for the stealing of five young men by the blackbirders. His fellow-workers were also attacked in their boat, two of them later dying of tetanus. John Coleridge Patteson gave his life for the gospel on this day in the year 1871.

A Reading from the life of Bishop John Coleridge Patteson
by Margaret Cropper

It had become increasingly clear to Bishop Selwyn that there must be a separate Bishop of Melanesia, and who more suitable than John Patteson, this man of God whom God had given him? Thus it was that on Saint Matthias' Day 1861, John Coleridge Patteson was consecrated first Bishop of Melanesia. Confiding to his diary he wrote:

> I feel the sense of responsibility deepening on me. I must go out to work without Selwyn, and very anxious I am sometimes, and almost oppressed by it. But strength will come, and it is not one's own work, which is a comfort; and if I fail – which is very likely – God will place some other man in my position, and the work will go on, whether in my hands or not, and that is the real point.
>
> Indeed I do wonder that I am as calm as I am. When I look at the map, the countless islands overwhelm me. Where to begin? How to decide on the best method of teaching? I must try to be patient, and be content with very small beginnings, and endings too, perhaps.

Later, in a letter to his cousin, he recorded impressions of his work:

> I see everywhere signs of a really extraordinary change in the last few years. I know of twenty or thirty or perhaps forty places where a year ago, no white man could land without some little uncertainty as to his reception, but where I can feel confident now of meeting with friends. I can walk inland, a thing never dreamt of in the old days, sleep ashore, and put myself entirely in their hands and meet with a return of confidence on their part.

Mota was the language that Patteson had chosen for the translations from the Gospels and parts of the Prayer Book, the product of his genius and devotion. But in the wake of the Church's mission to Melanesia, there came traders, and worse, slave traders. 'Thief ships' the islanders called them. Some of the people even asked one of the bishop's staff: 'How was it that you and the bishop came first and then the slaughterers? Did you send them?'

On 20 September 1871 Patteson and four companions went ashore the island of Nu Kapu. As he stepped ashore the group was attacked by islanders. Later the ship's crew discovered the body of the bishop with five wounds, inflicted with club and arrow; only his face was untouched. Across his breast his murderers had laid a palm branch with five knots in the leaves which led the Melanesians to believe that his death was an act of vengeance for five men whom the traders had killed. He was buried at sea. Later two of his companions also died from the effects of poisoned arrows received in the attack.

One of the Melanesians wrote: 'The bishop did nothing for himself alone, but always sought what he might keep others with, and the reason was his pitifulness and his love. He never despised anyone, or rejected anyone with scorn, whether it was a white person or a black person. He thought of them all as one, and treated them all alike.' Patteson's murder was brutal, but it proved to be the seed of the Melanesian Church which grew and continues to grow from strength to strength.

21 September

Matthew

Apostle and Evangelist

Matthew appears in the list of the twelve apostles of Jesus and, according to the Gospel written under his name, was a tax-collector. Mark and Luke called the tax-collector Levi, and it has been assumed that they are one and the same person. This occupation was despised by his fellow Jews as a betrayal to the occupying Roman force, but Christ showed that judging by outward appearance was not what he was about. He ate with Matthew and with his friends, scandalizing those around him. Matthew followed at his call and this was enough for Jesus, for he had drawn someone back to God. He was forgiven, therefore he was acceptable, therefore he was received.

A Reading from a homily of the Venerable Bede

'Jesus saw a man called Matthew sitting at the tax office, and he said to him: Follow me.' Jesus saw Matthew, not merely in the usual sense, but more significantly with his merciful understanding of humankind. He saw the tax collector and, because he saw him through the eyes of mercy and chose him, he said to him: 'Follow me.' This following meant imitating the pattern of his life – not just walking after him. Saint John tells us: 'Whoever says he abides in Christ ought to walk in the same way in which he walked.'

'And he rose and followed him.' There is no reason for surprise that the tax collector abandoned earthly wealth as soon as the Lord commanded him. Nor should one be amazed that neglecting his wealth, he joined a band whose leader had, on Matthew's assessment, no riches at all. Our Lord summoned Matthew by speaking to him in words. By an invisible, interior impulse flooding his mind with the light of grace, he instructed him to walk in his footsteps. In this way Matthew could understand that Christ, who was summoning him away from earthly possessions, had incorruptible treasures of heaven in his gift.

'And as he sat at table in the house, behold many tax collectors and sinners came and sat down with Jesus and his disciples.' The conversion of one tax collector provided many, those from his own profession and other sinners, with an example of repentance and pardon. Notice also the happy and true anticipation of his future status as apostle and teacher of the nations. No sooner was he converted than Matthew drew after him a whole crowd of sinners along the same road to salvation. He took up his appointed duties while still taking his first steps in the faith, and from that he fulfilled his obligation, and thus grew in merit.

To see a deeper understanding of the great celebration Matthew held at his house, we must realise that he not only gave a banquet for the Lord at his earthly residence, but far more pleasing was the banquet set in his own heart which he provided through faith and love. Our Saviour attests to this: 'Behold I stand at the door and knock; if any hear my voice and open the door, I will come in to them and eat with them, and they with me.'

On hearing Christ's voice, we open the door to receive him, as it were, when we freely assent to his prompting and when we give ourselves over to doing what must be done. Christ, since he dwells in the hearts of his chosen ones through the grace of his love, enters so that he might eat with us and we with him. He ever refreshes us by the light of his presence insofar as we progress in our devotion to and longing for the things of heaven. He himself is delighted by such a pleasing banquet.

23 September

Adamnán (Eunan)

Abbot of Iona, 704

Adamnán, Eunan, ninth Abbot of Iona, was born near Raphoe, in County Donegal about the year 624, a relation of Columba whose Life he wrote – a vivid and warmly human account of the famous saint of Iona. At the age of fifty-five, he was elected Abbot of Iona. He travelled widely, in Evangelistic endeavours and on political missions. He was concerned to bridge the gulf between the Celtic and Roman traditions and travelled between Scotland and England in negotiation. He accepted the Roman way of dating Easter and abandoned the Celtic style of tonsure, but these reforms were strongly resisted by his own community. At the Synod of Birr in 697 he played a leading part, drawing up the law code which bears his name. It was designed to raise the status of women and was enacted by the Synod. It is possible that he remained in Ireland for the rest of his life, returning to Iona just before his death on this day in the year 704.

A Reading from the first preface of *The Life of Saint Columba* by Adamnán, Abbot of Iona

Our blessed patron's life I shall now, with Christ's help, describe in response to the entreaties of the brethren. First, I am minded to warn all who read it that they should put their faith in accounts which are attested, and give more thought to my subject than to my words which I consider rough and of little worth. They should remember that the kingdom of God stands not on the flow of eloquence but in the flowering of faith. There are words here in the poor Irish language, strange names of men and peoples and places, names which I think are crude in comparison with the different tongues of foreign races. But let no one think this is a reason to despise the proclamation of profitable deeds, which were not achieved without the help of God.

The reader should also be reminded of this, that many things worth recording about Columba, a man of blessed memory, are left out here for the sake of brevity, and only a few things out of many are written down so as not to try the patience of those who will read them. But even in comparison with the little we now propose to write, popular report has spread almost nothing of the very great things that can be told about this blessed man.

alternative reading

A Reading from *A History of the English Church and People* by the Venerable Bede

Adamnán, priest and abbot of the monks who lived on the Isle of Iona, was sent by his nation on a mission to Aldfrid, King of the English, and remained in his province for some while, where he observed the rites of the Church canonically performed. He was earnestly advised by many who were more learned than himself not to presume to act contrary to the universal customs of the Church, whether in the keeping of Easter or in any other observances, seeing that his following was very small and situated in a remote corner of the world. As a result Adamnán changed his opinions, and readily adopted what he saw and heard in the churches of the English in place of the customs of his own people. For he was a wise and worthy man, well grounded in the knowledge of the Scriptures.

On his return home, he tried to lead his own people in Iona and those who were under the jurisdiction of that monastery into the correct ways that he had himself learned and wholeheartedly embraced; but in this he failed. Then he sailed over to preach in Ireland, and by his simple teaching showed its people the proper time of Easter. He corrected their ancient error and restored nearly all who were not under the jurisdiction of Iona to Catholic unity, teaching them to observe Easter at the proper time.

Adamnán also wrote a book about the Holy Places, which is most valuable to many readers. The man who dictated the information it contains was Arculf, a bishop from Gaul who had visited Jerusalem to see the holy places for himself. Having toured throughout the Promised Land, Arculf then journeyed to Damascus, Constantinople, Alexandria, and many islands; but as he was returning home, his ship was blown off course by a violent storm to the west coast of Britain. After various adventures, he visited Adamnán, who, finding him learned in the Scriptures and well acquainted with the holy places, was glad to welcome him and listen to him.

25 September

Fin Barre of Cork

Hermit and Abbot, 623

From his hermitage at Gougane Barra in west Cork, Fin Barre travelled down the river Lee to found his school and Monastery among the marshes of what is now Cork City. In his lifetime he was honoured as a teacher and described as 'this loving man, Barre of Cork'. He died on this day in the year 623.

A Reading from his *Rule for Monks* by Benedict of Nursia

An abbot who is worthy of the task of governing a monastery must always remember what his title signifies and act accordingly. For an abbot is believed to hold the place of Christ in the monastery, and for that reason holds a name of his, according to the words of the apostle, 'You have received the spirit of adoption of sons, whereby we call you Abba, Father.' Therefore, the abbot should never teach or decree or command anything that would contravene the precepts of God. On the contrary, his teaching should be infused into the minds of his disciples like the leaven of divine justice.

When anyone has been chosen as abbot, he ought to lead his disciples with a twofold teaching, displaying all goodness and holiness by both deeds and words, but preferably by deeds rather than by words. To the receptive in the community, he will communicate the commandments of the Lord best by words; but to the dull and stubborn of heart, he will communicate best by example.

In his teaching the abbot ought always to observe the advice of the apostle Paul when he says, 'Use argument, appeal rebuke.' He must be able to adapt to changing circumstances, now being stern, now using persuasion, displaying both the discipline of a master and the loving gentleness of a father. He will rebuke sternly the ill disciplined and restless, but gently encourage the obedient, docile and patient, to advance in virtue.

Above all, let not the abbot have greater concern for fleeting, earthly, temporal things, so that he ends up overlooking or undervaluing the salvation of the souls committed to him. Let him always reflect on the fact that he has been charged with the government of souls, and that he will have to give an account of his leadership.

25 September

Finnbar of Caithness

Bishop, sixth century

Several saints are commemorated under the names Finnbar and Finian (or Finnian). They include the two Irish abbots, Finian of Clonard and Finian of Movilla, Fin Barre of Cork, and the early sixth-century churchman Vinniau, who corresponded with the Welsh scholar Gildas. One of these may also be identified with Vinnianus who wrote a Penitentiary. A view at present widely accepted identifies Finian of Movilla with the patron saint of Kilwinning in Ayrshire and Kirkunzeon in Kirkcudbrightshire, but this view may have to be revised in favour of Vinniau. The place names preserve a medieval form of Finian (Waning) which is nearer to the Brittonic Vinniau. There are several Irish stories linking a Finian with the diocese of Whithorn before the eighth century. If the stories and the place names belong together, Wynni (to give him his local name) may be one and the same as the correspondent of Gildas, whose dates will have straddled 500. Gildas spent his adult life in Wales, but is traditionally held to come from one of the British kingdoms of the north, usually assumed to be Strathclyde. His correspondent may have been the author of the Penitentiary.

A Reading from the *Conferences* of John Cassian

If you wish to achieve true knowledge of Scripture you must hurry to achieve unshakeable humility of heart. This is what will lead you not to the knowledge which puffs up a man, but to the lore which illuminates through the achievement of love. It is impossible for the unclean of heart to acquire the gift of spiritual knowledge. Therefore be very careful that your zeal for scriptural reading does not, because of empty pretentiousness, prove to be a cause of perdition, instead of being for you the source of knowledge, light, and of the endless glory promised to those enlightened by knowledge.

Having banished all worldly concerns and thoughts, strive in every way to devote yourself constantly to the sacred reading so that continuous meditation will seep into your soul and, as it were, shape it to its image. Somehow it will form that 'ark' of the Scriptures and will contain the two stone tablets, that is, the perpetual strength of the two testaments. There will be the golden urn which is a pure and unstained memory and which will preserve firmly within itself the everlasting manna, that is, the eternal, heavenly sweetness of spiritual meanings and of that bread which belongs to the angels. The branch of Aaron is the saving standard of our exalted and true high priest Jesus Christ. It leafs out forever in the greenness of undying memory. This is the branch which was cut from the root of Jesse and which after death comes more truly alive.

As our mind is increasingly renewed by such study, Scripture begins to take on a new face. A mysteriously deeper sense of it comes to us and somehow the beauty of it stands out more and more as we get farther into it. Scripture shapes itself to human capacity. It will be earthly for those of the flesh, but divine for those of the spirit. Those who once thought of it as somehow wrapped up in thick clouds of obscurity, find themselves unable to grasp either its subtlety or to endure its brilliance.

25 September

Lancelot Andrewes

Bishop of Winchester, Spiritual Writer, 1626

Note: In Wales, Lancelot Andrewes is commemorated on 26 September.

Born in 1555 in Barking, Lancelot Andrewes studied at Merchant Taylors' School and Pembroke Hall (now Pembroke College), Cambridge. After ordination, he held several posts before accepting appointments as Bishop, first of Chichester, then of Ely and finally of Winchester in 1619. Andrewes was present at the Hampton Court Conference in 1604, which furthered the reform of the Church of England, and he was also a translator of much of the Old Testament of what is known as the 'Authorized Version' of the Bible. His preaching and his writings proved highly influential and his holiness of life and gentle nature endeared him to all who met him. He died on this day in the year 1626 and his remains lie in a church which was then in his diocese of Winchester but now is the cathedral for the diocese of Southwark.

A Reading from the *Private Devotions* of Lancelot Andrewes

Let the preacher labour to be heard intelligently, willingly, obediently. And let him not doubt that he will accomplish this rather by the piety of his prayers than by the eloquence of his speech. By praying for himself, and those whom he is to address, let him be their beadsman before he becomes their teacher; and approaching God with devotion, let him first raise to him a thirsting heart before he speaks of him with his tongue; that he may speak what he hath been taught and pour out what hath been poured in.

I cease not therefore to ask from our Lord and Master, that he may, either by the communication of his Scriptures or the conversations of my brethren, or the internal and sweeter doctrine of his own inspiration, deign to teach me things so to be set forth and asserted, that in what is set forth and asserted I may ever hold me fast to the truth; from this very truth I desire to be taught the many things I know not, by him from whom I have received the few I know.

I beseech this truth, that loving kindness preventing and following me, he would teach me the wholesome things that I know not; keep me in the true things I know; correct me wherein I am (which is human) in error, confirm me wherein I waver; preserve me from false and noxious things, and make that to proceed from my mouth which, as it shall be chiefly pleasing to the truth itself, so it may be accepted by all the faithful, through Jesus Christ our Lord. Amen.

alternative reading

A Reading from a biography of Lancelot Andrewes by his pupil and friend Henry Isaacson

The virtues and good parts of this honourable prelate were so many, and those so translucent, that to do him right, a large volume would be but sufficient which I shall leave to some of better abilities to perform, which I shall, by way of epitome, only point a finger at in what follows.

His first and principal virtue was his singular zeal and piety which showed itself not only in his private and secret devotions between God and himself, in which they that were about him well perceived that he daily spent many hours, yea, and the greatest part of his life in holy prayers, and abundant tears; but also in his exemplary public prayers with his family in his chapel wherein he behaved himself so humbly, devoutly, and reverently, that it could not but move others to follow his example. His chapel in which he had monthly communions was so decently and reverently adorned, and God served there with so holy and reverend behaviour of himself and his family, that the souls of many were very much elated.

The whole Christian world took especial notice of his profound and deep learning, yet was he so far from acknowledging it in himself that he would often complain of his defects, even to the extenuating, yea vilifying of his own worth and abilities; professing many times, that he was but a useless servant, nay, a useless lump. Insomuch that being preferred by King James to the Bishopric of Chichester, and pretending his own imperfections and insufficiency to undergo such a charge, as also that he might have not only his clergy, but all others to take notice thereof, he caused to be engraven about the seal of his Bishopric those words of Saint Paul, 'And who is sufficient for these things?'

His indefatigability in study cannot be paralleled, if we consider him from his childhood to his old age. Never any man took such pains, or at least spent so much time in study, as this reverend prelate; from the hour he arose, his private devotions finished, to the time he was called to dinner, which, by his own order, was not till twelve at noon at the soonest, he kept close at his book, and would not be interrupted by any that came to speak with him, or upon any occasion, public prayer excepted. Insomuch that he would be so displeased with scholars that attempted to speak with him in a morning, that he would say 'he doubted they were no true scholars that came to speak with him before noon'.

Of the fruit of this seed-time, the world, especially this land, hath reaped a plentiful harvest in his sermons and writings. Never went any beyond him in the first of these, his preaching, wherein he had such a dexterity, that some would say of him, that he was quick again as soon as delivered; and in this faculty he hath left a pattern unimitable. So that he was truly styled, 'an angel in the pulpit'.

25 September

Sergei of Radonezh

Russian Monastic Reformer, Teacher of the Faith, 1392

Born in Rostov in 1314, Sergei (Sergius) founded, together with his brother Stephen, the famous monastery of the Holy Trinity, near Moscow, which re-established the community life that had been lost in Russia through the Tartar invasion. Sergei had great influence and stopped civil wars between Russian princes and inspired Prince Dimitri to resist another invasion from the Tartars in 1380. Two years before that, he had been elected metropolitan but had refused the office. Altogether, he founded forty monasteries and is regarded as the greatest of the Russian saints and is patron of All Russia. He died on this day in the year 1392.

A Reading from *A Life of Saint Sergius*
compiled by his disciple Epiphanius

One day a Christian from a nearby village, who had never seen the saint, came to visit him. The abbot was digging in the garden. The visitor looked about and asked, 'Where is Sergius? Where is the wonderful and famous man?' A brother replied, 'In the garden, digging; wait a while until he comes in.'

The visitor, growing impatient, peeped through an aperture, and perceived the saint wearing attire shabby, patched, in holes, his face covered with sweat; and he could not believe that this was he of whom he had heard. When the saint came from the garden, the monks informed him, 'This is he whom you wish to see.'

But the visitor turned away from the saint and mocked at him; 'I came to a prophet and you point out to me a needy looking beggar. I see no glory, no majesty and honour about him. He wears no fine and rich apparel; he has no attendants, no trained servants; he is but a needy, indigent beggar.'

The brethren, reporting to the abbot, said, 'This man has been discourteous and disrespectful about you, reproaches us, and will not listen to us.'

The holy man, fixing his eyes on the brethren and seeing their confusion, said to them, 'Do not send him away, brethren, for he did not come to see you. He came to visit me.' He went towards him, humbly bowing low to the ground before him, and blessed and praised him for his right judgement. Then, taking him by the hand, the saint sat him down at his right hand, and bade him partake of food and drink. The visitor expressed his regret at not seeing Sergius, whom he had taken the trouble to come and visit; and his wish had not been fulfilled. The saint remarked, 'Be not sad about it, for such is God's grace that no one ever leaves this place with a heavy heart.'

As he spoke a neighbouring prince arrived at the monastery, with great pomp, accompanied by retinue of boyars, servants and attendants. The prince then advanced and, from a distance, made a low obeisance to Sergius. The saint gave him his blessing and, after bestowing a kiss on him, they both sat down. The visitor thrust his way back through the crowd, and going up to one of those standing by, asked, 'Who is that monk sitting on the prince's right hand, tell me?'

A man turned to him and said, 'Are you then a stranger here? Have you indeed not heard of blessed father Sergius? It is he who is speaking with the prince.' Upon hearing this the visitor was overcome with remorse, and after the prince's departure, came before the abbot and said, 'Father, I am but a sinner and a great offender. Forgive me and help my unbelief.'

The saint readily forgave, and with his blessing and some words of comfort, he took leave of him. From henceforth, and to the end of his days, this man held a true, firm faith in the Holy Trinity and in Saint Sergius. He left his village a few years later, and came to the monastery where he became a monk, and there spent several years in repentance and amendment of life before he passed away to God.

26 September

Wilson Carlile

Founder of the Church Army, 1942

Wilson Carlile was born in 1847 in Brixton. He suffered from a spinal weakness all his life, which hampered his education. After a serious illness, he began to treat his religion more seriously and became confirmed in the Church of England. He acted as organist to Ira D. Sankey during the Moody and Sankey missions and, in 1881, was ordained priest, serving his curacy at St Mary Abbots in Kensington, together with a dozen other curates. The lack of contact between the Church and the working classes was a cause of real concern to him and he began outdoor preaching. In 1882, he resigned his curacy and founded the Church Army, four years after the founding of the Salvation Army. Under his influence it thrived and he continued to take part in its administration until a few weeks before his death on this day in 1942.

A Reading from an address entitled 'The Power of Witness' delivered by Wilson Carlile to a group of bishops attending the Lambeth Conference of 1930

The Church Army regards our bishops, not only as our dear Fathers in God, but as generals of divisions for their dioceses, whilst the vicars are the colonels of the local regiment. *We* are the captains operating under our colonels to enlist and train companies for our holy war.

Church Army evangelists have but little to do with doctrines and ceremonies, theology and philosophy; our first duty is to get each private to fire on the enemy with the love-shots of living witness. We believe that for conversion purposes, a few true testimonies from keen, consistent-living folk are worth hundreds of theological discourses.

As evangelists (men and women) we must be able to speak acceptably ourselves, but our chief business is to call forth sincere persons to confess with their mouth as well as with their life. This they promised to do in their baptism.

We press for attendance at the holy feast for strength to go forth to bring in the 'bad and the good'; note, the *bad* first. We have so to live and labour that when we fall in the fight, platoon leaders are ready to rally round the colonel to carry on the battle.

We want to do the work of an Evangelist and get consecrated communicants enthused with the idea of the early catholic and apostolic days. All must be propagandists or atrophy.

27 September

Vincent de Paul

Founder of the Congregation of the Mission (Lazarists), 1660

Born in 1581 at Ranquine in Gascony, Vincent was educated by the Franciscans and was ordained at the age of nineteen. He was something of a token priest until his conversion in 1609, when he resolved to devote himself and all he owned to works of charity. He founded communities for men and, with Louise de Marillac, helped to begin the Sisters of Charity, the first community of women not to be enclosed and which was devoted to caring for the poor and sick. Vincent worked for the relief of galley slaves, victims of war, convicts and many other groups of needy people. He became a legend in his own lifetime and died on this day in the year 1660.

A Reading from a letter of Vincent de Paul

We should not judge the poor by their clothes and their outward appearance nor by their mental capacity, since they are often ignorant and uncouth. On the contrary, if you consider the poor in the light of faith, then you will see that they take the place of God the Son who chose to be poor. Indeed, in his passion, having lost even his basic human dignity, regarded as foolishness by the Gentiles and a scandal by the Jews, he showed he was to preach the gospel to the poor in these words: 'He has sent me to preach good news to the poor.' Therefore we should be of the same mind and should imitate what Christ did, caring for the poor, consoling them, helping them and guiding them.

Christ chose to be born in poverty and called his disciples from among the ranks of the poor; he himself became the servant of the poor and so shared their condition that whatever good or harm was done to the poor, he said he would consider done to himself. Since God loves the poor, he also loves the lovers of the poor: when you love another person, you also love those who love or serve that person as well. So we too hope that God will love us on account of the poor. We visit them then, we strive to concern ourselves with the weak and needy, we so share their sufferings that with the Apostle Paul we feel we have become all things to all people. Therefore we must strive to be deeply involved in the cares and sorrows of our neighbour and pray to God to inspire us with compassion and pity, filling our hearts and keeping them full.

The service of the poor is to be preferred to all else, and to be performed without delay. If at a time set aside for prayer, medicine or help has to be brought to some poor person, go and do what has to be done with an easy mind, offering it up to God as a prayer. Do not be put out by uneasiness or a sense of sin because of prayers interrupted by the service of the poor: for God is not neglected if prayers are put aside, if the work of God is interrupted, in order that another such work may be completed.

Therefore, when you leave prayer to help some poor remember this – that the work has been done for God. Charity takes precedence over all rules, everything ought to tend to it since it is itself a great lady: what it orders should be carried out. Let us show our service to the poor, then, with renewed ardour in our hearts, seeking out in particular any destitute people, since they are given to us as lords and patrons.

29 September

Michael and all Angels

Michael, Gabriel and Raphael are the three named Biblical angels, depicted as the belovèd messengers of God. Michael, which means 'Who is like God?', is portrayed as protector of Israel and leader of the armies of God, and is perhaps best known as the slayer of the dragon in the Revelation to John. Michael thus came to be regarded as the protector of Christians from the devil, particularly those at the hour of death. Gabriel, which means 'The Strength of God' is the one, according to the Gospel of Luke, who is sent by God to Mary to announce the birth of Christ. Raphael, which means 'The Healing of God', is depicted in the Book of Tobit as the one who restores sight to Tobit's eyes. A basilica near Rome was dedicated in the fifth century in honour of Michael on 30 September, with celebrations beginning on the eve of that day, with the result that 29 September came to be observed as a feast in honour of Michael and all Angels throughout the Western Church.

A Reading from a sermon of Gregory the Great

You should be aware that the word 'angel' denotes a function rather than a nature. Those holy spirits of heaven have indeed always been spirits, but they are only called angels when they deliver some divine message. Moreover, in Scripture those who deliver messages of lesser importance are called angels; whereas those who proclaim messages of supreme importance are called archangels.

Thus it was that not merely an angel but the archangel Gabriel was sent to the Virgin Mary. It was only fitting that the highest angel should come to announce the greatest of all messages.

Some angels are given proper names to denote the service they are empowered to perform. In that holy city, where perfect knowledge flows from the vision of almighty God, those who have no names may easily be known. But personal names are assigned to some, not because they could not be known without them, but rather to denote their ministry when they come among us. Thus, Michael means 'Who is like God?'; Gabriel is 'The Strength of God' and Raphael is 'The Healing of God'.

Whenever some act of wondrous power must be performed, Michael is sent, so that action and name may make it clear that no one can do what God does by his own superior power. So also our ancient foe desired in pride to be like God, saying: 'I will ascend into heaven; I will exalt my throne above the stars of heaven; I will be like the Most High.' Satan will be allowed to remain in power until the end of the world when he will be destroyed in the final punishment. Then, he will fight with the archangel Michael, as we are told by John in the Revelation: 'And there arose war in heaven, and a battle was fought with Michael the archangel.'

So too Gabriel, who is called God's strength, was sent to Mary. Gabriel came to announce the One who appeared in humility to quell the cosmic powers. Thus God's strength announced the coming of the Lord of the heavenly powers, mighty in battle.

Raphael means, as I have said, the healing of God, for when this angel touched Tobit's eyes in order to cure him, Raphael banished the darkness of his blindness. Thus, since this angel is to heal, Raphael is rightly called the healing of God.

alternative reading

A Reading from a sermon of Bernard of Clairvaux

Today we observe the feast of the angels, and you wish me to preach to you a sermon worthy of the occasion. But how can we poor earthworms speak worthily of angelic spirits? Most certainly we believe that they who stand in the presence and sight of God enjoy the good things of the Lord for all eternity. But concerning those good things as Scripture says 'neither has eye seen, nor has ear heard, nor have they entered into the human heart'. So how can a mere mortal speak of them to other mortals given that we have neither knowledge to speak of them nor the ability to understand?

The mouth speaks from the overflowing of the heart; if the tongue is silent, it is from lack of thoughts. But even if the splendour and glory of the holy angels before God is beyond our comprehension, we can at least reflect upon the loving-kindness they show us. For there is in these heavenly spirits a generosity that merits our love, as well as an honour that evokes our wonder. It is only right that we who cannot comprehend their glory should all the more embrace their loving-kindness in which, as we know, the members of the household of God, the citizens of heaven, the heirs of paradise, are so exceedingly rich. As the Apostle says, 'They are all ministering spirits, sent out in the divine service for the sake of those who are to inherit salvation.'

So let nobody think this incredible, given that the creator and King of angels himself came not to be served but to serve, and to give his life for many. It would be strange to reject the idea of the angels' service, when he whom they serve in heaven himself leads the way in serving us! One of the prophets saw them serving God in heaven, and declared: 'Thousands of thousands served him, and ten thousand times a hundred thousand stood before him.' And another prophet when speaking of the Son says: 'You have made him a little lower than the angels.' So indeed it was that the One who surpassed all in majesty, chose to conquer through humility: superior to the angels, he chose to be made inferior to them in their service.

You may ask, why does his coming to serve us make him lower than the angels when they too are sent to serve? The answer is that he is lower in that he not only served us, but allowed us to serve him. Also, the angels render service out of that which is not theirs: presenting to God our works, not their own and bringing to us his grace. That is why when Scripture says 'the smoke of the incense ascended before God out of the angel's hand', it carefully tells us that there was *given* to him much incense. In other words, it is our labours and tears that the angels are offering to God, not their own; and it his gifts and not their own that they are bringing back to us. Thus the Servant who presented himself as a sacrifice of praise, and in offering his life to the Father, still gives us his flesh today, is both lower than all others, but also much higher.

So let us avoid everything that might grieve the holy angels, and instead, if we would enjoy their intimacy, cultivate those things that would please them. There are indeed many things that would please them; for example, being moderate, being chaste, giving up things voluntarily, praying with sighs and tears and with a heart full of loving ardour. But more than these things the angels of peace desire in us unity and peace, for these are things that characterise their own commonwealth, and when they see such things produced in us, they marvel at the birth of the new Jerusalem on earth.

A Reading from an ancient Celtic poem in praise of Michael the Archangel

Thou Michael the victorious,
I make my circuit under thy shield,
Thou Michael of the white steed,
And of the bright brilliant blades,

Conqueror of the dragon,
Be thou at my back,
Thou ranger of the heavens,
Thou warrior of the King of all,
        O Michael the victorious,
        My pride and my guide
        O Michael the victorious,
        The glory of mine eye.

I make my circuit
In the fellowship of my saint,
On the machair, on the meadow,
On the cold heathery hill;
Though I should travel oceans
And the hard globe of the world
No harm can e'er befall me
'Neath the shelter of thy shield;
        O Michael the victorious,
        Jewel of my heart,
        O Michael the victorious,
        God's shepherd thou art.

Be the sacred Three of Glory
Aye at peace with me,
With my horses, with my cattle,
With my woolly sheep in flocks.
With the crops growing in the field
Or ripening in the sheaf,
On the machair, on the moor,
In cole, in heap, or stack.
        Every thing on high or low,
        Every furnishing and flock,
        Belong to the holy Triune of glory,
        And to Michael the victorious.

30 September

Jerome

Translator of the Scriptures, Teacher of the Faith, 420

Jerome was born at Strido near Aquileia on the Adriatic coast of Dalmatia, in about the year 342. He studied at Rome, where he was baptized. He tried the life of a monk for a time, but unsuccessfully. Following a dream in which he stood before the judgement seat of God and was condemned for his faith in classics rather than Christ, he learned Hebrew the better to study the Scriptures. This, with his polished skills in rhetoric and mastery of Greek, enabled him to begin his life's work of translating the newly-canonized Bible into Latin which became the standard version for the Western Church for over a thousand years. He eventually settled at Bethlehem, where he founded a monastery and devoted the rest of his life to study. He died on this day in the year 420.

A Reading from a letter of Jerome to a young priest written in the year 394

Read the Holy Scriptures constantly. Indeed, never let the sacred volume be out of your hand. Learn what you have to teach. As Scripture itself says: 'Have a firm grasp of the word that is trustworthy in accordance with the teaching, so that you may be able both to preach with sound doctrine and to refute those who contradict it.' 'Continue in the things that you have learned and that have been entrusted to you, knowing from whom you learned it'; and be always 'ready to give an answer to anyone who asks you a reason for the hope that is in you'.

Do not let your deeds contradict your words, lest when you speak in church someone may be saying to themselves: 'Why does not this man practise what he preaches? Look at the hypocrite! His stomach is bloated with rich food and he stands here preaching to us about fasting! A thief might just as well accuse others of avarice.' In a Christian priest, mouth, mind and hand should all be in harmony.

When you are teaching in church, try not to seek applause but lamentation. Let the tears of your hearers be your glory. A presbyter's words ought to be seasoned by the reading of Scripture. Do not declaim or rant, gabbling your words without rhyme or reason, but rather show yourself learned in deep things, versed in the mysteries of God. To let forth a stream of words in order to impress an uneducated audience is mark of conceit. The fact that you have a deep conviction will communicate to your hearers, and become authoritative. I learned this from my own teacher, Gregory of Nazianzus. Certainly, there is nothing so cheap as deceiving an uneducated audience by sheer force of words. Such people admire what they are failing to understand.

Many people are building churches nowadays, with walls and pillars of glowing marble, ceilings glittering with gold, and altars encrusted with jewels. Yet little thought is given in the selection of Christ's ministers. Let no one try to contradict me by reference to the ancient temple of the Jews, with its altar, lamps, censers, dishes, cups, spoons, and the rest of its golden vessels. If such things enjoyed the Lord's approval it was because they corresponded to the time when the priests had to offer sacrifices, and when the blood of sheep was redemptive of sins. They were merely figures pointing to a new order. But now our Lord by his own poverty has consecrated the poverty of his house. Let us, therefore, think only of his cross and count worldly riches as refuse.

Finally, would you know what sort of apparel the Lord requires you to wear? Prudence, justice, moderation, courage. These are four virtues which should fill your horizon. Think of them as a four-horse team bearing you, Christ's charioteer, along at full speed to your goal. No necklace can be more precious than these; no gems could create a brighter galaxy. So let them be the decoration you bear and with which you clothe yourself, for they will protect you on every side. They are your defence and your glory; for each of these gems God turns into a shield.

October

1 October

Gregory the Enlightener

Bishop, Apostle of Armenia, *c.*332

Gregory is called 'The Enlightener' or 'The Illuminator' because he brought the light of Christ to the people of Armenia towards the end of the third century. Of royal descent, he seems to have become a Christian while in exile in Cappadocia. Returning to Armenia as a young man, he succeeded in converting King Tiridates to Christianity. With the help of the king, the country was converted and became the first national state to become officially Christian. A cathedral was built in Valarshapat but Gregory centred his work in nearby Echmiadzin, which is still the spiritual centre of the Armenian Orthodox Church. He was consecrated Bishop (Katholikos) in Caesaria in Cappadocia, and was succeeded by his son, Aristages, who attended the Council of Nicæa. Gregory died around the year 332. The writings attributed to him come from about a century after his time but probably preserve the spirit of his teaching.

A Reading from *The Teaching of Saint Gregory*

Behold the sun, the moon and stars. They are so much greater than we mortals, and yet they stand under God's will, constrained by his divine command. The sun does not linger on its course, nor does the moon cease to wax and wane; the stars do not stray from their courses, nor do the mountains move. The winds do not cease to blow; nor does the sea in its deep and furious swells, with its violent raging and huge waves, pass its fixed boundary and destroy the earth; nor does the earth cease to support and sustain its inhabitants. All is ordered by God's command, and his holy and heavenly angels never cease to sing their praises.

The heights of the heavens are his, so are the number of the stars, the waters of the sea and the sand upon the seashore, and the mountains and their valleys. God causes the clouds to form and the winds to blow; he summons the evening, turns the dried up grass green, and gathers the raindrops. Concerning him the spirit of prophecy says, 'Who has measured the waters in the hollow of his hand, and with his span marked off the heavens, and the dust of the earth with his fingers? Who placed the hills in scales and weighed the plains on a balance?' Where is the place that upholds him by whose Word all creatures are suspended? God knows the courses of the planets which circle above and which are neither deflected nor go astray. They appear and stay for a while like hired labourers, and then disappear again. They are rekindled each day and evening, compensating each other, freely returning to their allotted span, changing with the seasons of the year, just as God has ordained.

How do the powers of the stars in the firmament of heaven move, keeping to their courses without diversion? From where do the gusts of violent winds originate? Where do they go and die down, and what are the seasons of each? One wind nourishes the plants with a sweet breeze; another encourages the buds to open; another decorates the earth with flowers of various colours and shades, clothes the naked trees and whispers in leafy branches. From where do the rain-bearing winds originate, born with the sound of thunder and scattered by the lightning storm? Where the Lord commands they go, they descend and water the earth, they make the plants to grow and ripen the fruits that nourish our bodies. From whose womb do the rivers emerge, unceasing in their flow, yet not overflowing in their course to the sea?

Heaven and earth, the sun and moon and the millions of stars, the seas and rivers, the beasts and animals, the reptiles and birds, the fish that swim in the waters, all created things and things yet to be, all reveal their appointed order, following God's command to each. Only the will of man has been left independent of this order to do whatever we will. We are constrained only in being warned not to eat the fruit of that forbidden tree in order that God might make us worthy to receive greater things still; and that by virtue of having grace to accomplish this task, we might receive from our Creator, an abundance of grace.

1 October

Remigius

Bishop of Rheims, Apostle of the Franks, 533

Born in about the year 438, the son of the Count of Laon, Remigius studied at Rheims and was elected bishop and metropolitan of the city when he was only twenty-two years old. In the year 496, he baptized Clovis I, King of the Franks, and about three thousand of his subjects. Under the king's protection, Remigius preached the gospel, created dioceses, built churches and baptized many more Christians. His name is linked to the ampulla of chrism oil used at the coronation of French monarchs, together with the gift of healing. He died on 13 January in the year 533 and his mortal remains were translated to the abbey of St Remi on this day in the year 1049.

A Reading from *The History of the Franks* by Gregory of Tours

Queen Clothild ordered holy Remigius, Bishop of Rheims, to be summoned secretly, begging him to impart the word of salvation to the king. The bishop asked to meet King Clovis in private, and began to urge him to believe in the true God, the maker of heaven and earth, and to forsake all idols which were powerless to help him or his people.

The king replied: 'I have listened to you willingly, holy father; but there remains one obstacle. The people who follow me will never agree to forsake their gods. I will go and reason with them according to what you have said to me.' King Clovis arranged a meeting with his people, but God in his power had gone before him, and before he could say a word all those present shouted with one voice: 'We will give up worshipping our mortal gods, O gracious king, and we are prepared to follow the immortal God whom Remigius preaches.'

News of this was reported to the bishop. He was greatly pleased and he ordered the baptismal font to be made ready. The public squares were draped with coloured hangings, the churches were adorned with white hangings, the baptistery was prepared, the smoke of incense spread in clouds, scented candles gleamed bright, and the holy place of baptism was filled with divine fragrance. God filled the hearts of all present with such grace that they imagined themselves to have been transported to some paradise.

King Clovis asked that he might be baptized first by the bishop. Like some new Constantine he stepped forward to the water, to wash away the sores of his former leprosy and to be cleansed in the flowing water of the sordid stains he had borne so long. As he came forward for baptism, the holy man of God addressed him in these pregnant words: 'Meekly bow your head. Worship what you have burnt; and burn what you have been worshipping.' For holy Remigius was a bishop of immense learning, and above all a great scholar, exemplary in holiness.

Thus it was that King Clovis confessed his belief in God Almighty, three in one, and was baptized in the name of the Father, and of the Son, and of the Holy Spirit, anointed with holy chrism with the sign of the cross of Christ. And more than three thousand of his army were baptized with him that day.

1 October

Anthony Ashley Cooper

7th Earl of Shaftesbury, Social Reformer, 1885

Born in 1801, Ashley Cooper was first elected to the House of Commons in 1826. In 1851, he succeeded his father as the Seventh Earl of Shaftesbury and sat in the House of Lords. His service in Parliament was marked from the beginning by a desire to reform social abuses, an impulse which derived from his strong Evangelical Anglican piety. He campaigned successfully for measures to improve housing and also create schools for the poor. He pioneered legislation on conditions of employment, for example, in mines and factories, particularly with respect to the protection of children. He became the epitome of the Victorian Christian philanthropist, working within the political system to redress social evils. He died on this day in 1885.

A Reading from the life of Anthony Ashley Cooper,
Earl of Shaftesbury by Margaret Cropper

Anthony Ashley Cooper was born in 1801 and his life spanned nearly the entire century. He entered Parliament in 1826 as Conservative member for Woodstock, but his first sessions were marked by a sort of independence which was to become characteristic. He chose to make his first speech in support of a bill to amend the law for the regulation and improvement of lunatic asylums. This was a work that he was never to lay down, and it involved him in his first hand-to-hand struggle against inhuman behaviour.

In 1834 he became chairman of the Parliamentary commissioners overseeing the reform, a post that he kept until his death. The work involved visiting asylums, and when, thirty years later, he gave an account of those early days every horrid detail was still clear in his mind:

> When we began our visitations, one of the first rooms that we went into contained nearly a hundred and fifty patients, in every form of madness, a large proportion of them chained to the wall. The noise and din were such that we positively could not hear each other speak. I never beheld anything so horrible and so miserable.

Something of the misery of his childhood had left him with an inferiority complex which always haunted him, but also gave him a passion for justice. When the Napoleonic War ended, there was a new set of circumstances to be reckoned with in England, and a lack of courage, a sense of fatalism. Also a strange new god had crept into the reckoning of society – the god of economic necessity. In a speech he declared that he had read 'of those who had sacrificed their children to Moloch, but they were a merciful people compared with Englishmen in the nineteenth century'. There were two sets of child workers whom he particularly tried to help during his Parliamentary life: the children working in the mines, and the boys who swept the chimneys of England. In 1842 he succeeded in getting a bill passed ensuring that all women, children and apprentices were taken out of the mines.

Throughout his life, undergirding all his educational and social endeavours was a strong evangelical Christian faith. As a young man he had recorded in his diary some considerations that were to guide him throughout his life. He wrote: 'Now let me consider awhile my future career. The first principle: God's honour; the second: man's happiness; the means: prayer and unremitting diligence. All petty love of excellence must be put aside, the matter must be studied, and one's best done for the remainder.'

Near the end of his life, when he had succeeded to the title of Earl of Shaftesbury, he summed up his views to his biographer:

> My religious views are not popular, but they are the views that have sustained and comforted me all my life. They have never been disguised, nor have I ever sought to disguise them. I think a person's religion, if it is worth anything, should enter into every sphere of life and rule their conduct in every relation. I have always been, and please God always shall be an Evangelical of the Evangelicals, and no biography can represent me that does not fully and emphatically represent my religious views.

Shaftesbury wanted to reform the Church as much as the Tractarians did; what he wanted was a practical, courageous Church, concerned with people's lives. Probably much of his thinking was governed by the fact that he had found the clergy as a body not interested in his work for shorter hours and better conditions. There were some who he knew did care; but he felt that the majority of the clergy were losing their chances of getting into close touch with the working class. He wanted more power for the laity and less for the bishops and clergy. His biography by the Hammonds concludes thus:

> The devil with sad and sober sense on his grey face tells the rulers of the world that the misery which disfigures the life of great societies is beyond the reach of human remedy. A voice is raised from time to time in answer: a challenge in the name of the mercy of God, or the justice of nature, or human dignity. Shaftesbury was such a voice. To the law of indifference and drift taught by philosophers and accepted by politicians, he opposed the simple revelation of his Christian conscience. … When silence falls on such a voice, some everlasting echo still haunts the world, to break its sleep of habit or despair.

1 October

Thérèse of Lisieux

Carmelite nun, 1897

Thérèse was born at Alençon in France in the year 1873. At the age of fifteen she entered the Carmelite Convent at Lisieux in Normandy where two of her sisters were already nuns. Poor health prevented her from following the full rigour of the Rule of her Order, and she died nine years later after much suffering from tuberculosis. Outwardly her life was undistinguished, but she pioneered her 'little way' – fidelity in small things, simple trust and complete self-surrender to God. Her autobiography, a work undertaken at the request of her elder sister Pauline who was Prioress of the convent, was published after her death under the title The Story of a Soul. *Its success was sensational perhaps because it demonstrated to ordinary people that holiness is open to everyone by the faithful doing of small things, the routine duties of daily life performed in the spirit of the love of God.*

A Reading from the autobiography of Thérèse of Lisieux

The retreat before my profession brought no consolation with it, only complete dryness and almost a sense of dereliction. Once more, our Lord was asleep on the boat; how few souls there are that let him have his sleep out! He can't be always doing all the work, responding to all the calls made upon him; so for my own part I am content to have him undisturbed. I dare say he won't make his presence felt till I start out on the great retreat of eternity; I don't complain of that, I want it to happen. It shows, of course, that there's nothing of the saint about me; I suppose I ought to put down this dryness in prayer to my own fault, my own lukewarmness and want of fidelity. What excuse have I, after seven years in religion, for going through all my prayers and my thanksgivings as mechanically as if I too, were asleep?

Anyhow, my profession retreat, like all the retreats I've made since, was a time of great dryness; and yet I felt that all the time, without my knowing it, God was showing me the right way to do his will and to reach a high degree of holiness. You know, I always have the feeling that our Lord doesn't supply me with provisions for my journey, he just gives me food unexpectedly when and as I need it; I find it there without knowing how it got there. It simply comes to this, that our Lord dwells unseen in the depths of my miserable soul, and so works upon me by grace that I can always find out what he wants me to do at this particular moment.

When the great day came, my wedding-day, there was no cloud on my horizon; on the eve of it, my soul had been in such tumult as I had never before experienced. Till then, I'd never known what it was to have a doubt about my vocation, and this was the ordeal I now had to face. That evening, as I made the Stations of the Cross after Matins, my vocation seemed to me a mere dream, a mere illusion; I still saw life at Carmel as a desirable thing, but the devil gave me the clear impression that it wasn't for me; I should only be deceiving my superiors if I tried to persevere in a way of life I wasn't called to. Darkness everywhere; I could see nothing and think of nothing beyond this one fact, that I'd no vocation. I was in an agony of mind; I even feared (so foolishly that I might have known it was a temptation of the devil's) that if told my Novice-mistress about it she'd prevent me taking my vows. And yet I did want to do God's will, even if it meant going back to the world; that would be better than doing my own will by staying at Carmel.

On the morning of my profession I seemed to be carried along on a tide of interior peace; and this sense of peace 'which surpasses all our thinking' accompanied the taking of my vows. This wedding of my soul to our Lord was not heralded by the thunders and lightning of Mount Sinai, rather by that 'whisper of a gentle breeze' which our father Elijah heard there. I offered myself to our Lord, asking him to accomplish his will in me and never let any creature come between us.

3 October

George Bell

Bishop of Chichester, Ecumenist, Peacemaker, 1958

Born in 1881, George Bell was educated at Westminster School and Christ Church, Oxford. After serving a curacy and then spending a short time back at Oxford as a don, Bell was domestic chaplain to the Archbishop of Canterbury and then Dean of Canterbury before being made Bishop of Chichester in 1929. He was interested in all forms of Christian social work and was in the forefront of moves towards Christian Unity, advocating co-operation of all Christian denominations in international and social action. He had many friends in Germany, especially members of the German Confessional Church, and spoke out in their support when they were finding themselves in conflict with the Nazi state. During the Second World War, he spoke in the House of Lords against the indiscriminate bombing of German towns and strongly condemned some of the actions of the Allies; this preparedness to speak the truth as he saw it may have prevented him from attaining the highest office in the Church of England. He died on this day in 1958.

A Reading from a speech of Bishop George Bell
delivered to the House of Lords on 9 February 1944
on the obliteration bombing of the German cities

Mr Attlee, replying to a question in the House of Commons on May 21st, said that the suggestion of a mutual cessation of night bombing, by agreement, was not acceptable to the Government. On being asked why, he replied that it was impossible to trust Hitler to keep his word. In other words, he based his negative attitude, not on military considerations, but on the lack of international trust. An agreement, however, could be put to the test. After all, we could maintain all anti-aircraft defences, weakening nothing, but at the same time refraining from the bombing of Germany by night, having announced that we would refrain. If Germany suddenly broke the agreement, we should not be taken by surprise. The arrangement could, in any event, do us no harm, if we were always prepared. But the fact that our Government had failed would be a great asset to our moral cause. The practical abstention from bombing of any kind, in the form of a tacit mutual bombing truce, was achieved when Athens and Cairo were believed to be in danger of bombing. The British Government then announced that Rome would be bombed if Athens and Cairo were bombed.

I shall be told that it is impossible to make a distinction between military and industrial objectives on the one hand, and non-military and non-industrial objectives on the other hand. My reply is that since the time of Grotius, an attempt has been made to draw a distinction between the combatant and the civilian, and that, although one hears people argue that it is better for the whole community to be in the war, the blurring of the distinction in the present war by air bombing, and particularly night bombing, is, from a moral and humanitarian point of view, a retrograde step.

I would add one final argument which should be weighed at least as fully as that which warns us against the mutual devastation and destruction which will be caused to all Europe if bombing goes on. Little has been said of the effect on the airmen themselves: they know well what spiritual degradation it must be to them to have to fly over territory, dropping bombs, with the certain knowledge that in innumerable cases the bombs must kill the women and children.

At the beginning of the war on September 14th 1939, it was officially announced that 'Whatever be the lengths to which others may go, His Majesty's Government will never resort to the deliberate attack of women and children and other civilians for purposes of mere terrorism.' Granted that there never is deliberate attack by British airmen on German civilians, it is inevitable that civilians should suffer, and suffer far more than can be excused by military necessity, when there is bombing by night.

4 October

Francis of Assisi

Friar, Deacon, Founder of the Friars Minor, 1226

Francis was born in Assisi in central Italy either in 1181 or the following year. He was baptized Giovanni but given the name Francesco by his father, a cloth merchant who traded in France and had married a French wife. There was an expectation that he would eventually take over his father's business but Francis had a rebellious youth and a difficult relationship with his father. After suffering the ignominy of imprisonment following capture whilst at war with the local city of Perugia, he returned a changed man. He took to caring for disused churches and for the poor, particularly those suffering from leprosy. Whilst praying in the semi-derelict church of St Damian, he distinctly heard the words: 'Go and repair my church, which you see is falling down.' Others joined him and he prepared a simple, gospel-based Rule for them all to live by. As the Order grew, it witnessed to Christ through preaching the gospel of repentance, emphasising the poverty of Christ as an example for his followers. Two years before his death, his life being so closely linked with that of his crucified Saviour, Francis received the Stigmata, the marks of the wounds of Christ, on his body. At his death, on the evening of 3 October 1226, his Order had spread throughout Western Christendom.

A Reading from the *Earlier Rule* of 1209 of Francis of Assisi

This is the life of the gospel of Jesus Christ which Brother Francis asked the Lord Pope to be granted and confirmed for him; and he granted and confirmed it for him and his brothers present and to come. Brother Francis and whoever will be the head of this Order promises obedience and reverence to the Lord Pope Innocent and to his successors. And all the other brothers are bound to obey Brother Francis and his successors.

The rule and life of these brothers is this: to live in obedience, in chastity, and without anything of their own, and to follow the teaching and the footprints of our Lord Jesus Christ, who says: 'If you wish to be perfect, go and sell everything you have and give it to the poor, and you will have treasure in heaven; and come, follow me.' And again, 'If any wish to come after me, let them deny themselves and take up their cross and follow me.' And again, 'If anyone wishes to come to me and does not hate father and mother and wife and children and brothers and sisters, and even his own life, he cannot be my disciple.' Or again, 'Everyone who has left father or mother, brothers or sisters, wife or children, houses or lands because of me, shall receive a hundredfold and shall possess eternal life.'

If anyone, desiring by divine inspiration to accept this life, should come to our brothers, let him be received by them with kindness. And if he is determined to accept our life, the brothers should take great care not to become involved in his temporal affairs; but let them present him to their minister as quickly as possible. The minister on his part should receive him with kindness and encourage him and diligently explain to him the tenor of our life. When this has been done, the aforesaid person – if he wishes and is able to do so spiritually and without any impediment – should sell all his possessions and strive to give them all to the poor.

The brothers and the minister of the brothers should take care not to become involved in any way in his temporal affairs; nor should they accept any money either themselves or through an intermediary. However, if they are in need, the brothers can accept instead of money other things needed for the body like other poor people. And when he has returned, let the minister give him the clothes of probation for a whole year, namely, two tunics without a hood, a cord and trousers, and a small cape reaching to the cord. When the year and term of probation has ended, let him be received into obedience. Afterward he will not be allowed to join another Order or to 'wander outside obedience' according to the decree of the Lord Pope and according to the gospel; for no one 'who puts his hand to the plough and looks back is fit for the kingdom of God.'

But if someone should come who cannot give away his possessions without an impediment and yet has the spiritual desire [to do so], let him leave those things behind; and this suffices for him. No one should be accepted contrary to the form and the prescription of the holy Church. The brothers should wear poor clothes, and they can patch them with sackcloth and other pieces with the blessing of God; for the Lord says in the gospel: 'Those who wear costly clothes and live in luxury and who dress in soft garments are in the houses of kings.' And although they may be called hypocrites, nonetheless they should not cease doing good nor should they seek costly clothing in this world, so that they may have a garment in the kingdom of heaven.

alternative reading

A Reading from *The Canticle of Brother Sun*
by Francis of Assisi

Most High, all powerful, good Lord,
to you be praise, glory, honour and all blessing.

To you alone, Most High, do they belong,
and no one is worthy to call upon your name.

Praised be you, my Lord, with all your creatures,
especially by Brother Sun,
who makes the day and through whom you give us light.
He is beautiful and radiant with great splendour,
like you, O Most High.

Praised be you, my Lord,
by Sister Moon and the stars,
who shine clear and precious and beautiful
in the heaven you formed.

Praised be you, my Lord,
by Brother Wind, and by air and clouds,
clear skies and all weathers,
through which you give sustenance to your creatures.

Praised be you, my Lord,
by Sister Water,
who is very useful and humble and precious and chaste.

Praised be you, my Lord,
by Brother Fire, by whom you lighten the night.
He is beautiful and cheerful, powerful and strong.

Praised be you, my Lord,
by our Sister, Mother Earth, who sustains and governs us,
and who produces various fruits, coloured flowers and herbs.

Praised be you, my Lord,
by those who forgive for love of you,
and who bear infirmity and tribulation.
Blessed are those who endure in peace,
for by you, Most High, they shall be crowned.

Praised be you, my Lord,
by our Sister Death, from whom no one living can escape.
Woe to those who die in mortal sin.
Blessed are those whom death finds doing your most holy will,
for the second death shall do them no harm.

Praise and bless my Lord and give him thanks,
and serve him with great humility.

6 October

William Tyndale

Translator of the Scriptures, Reformation Martyr, 1536

Born in Gloucestershire in about the year 1494, William Tyndale studied first at Magdalen Hall (now Magdalen College), Oxford, and then at Cambridge. He became determined to translate the Scriptures from the Greek directly into contemporary English but was thwarted in this by the Bishop of London. So William settled in Hamburg in 1524, never returning to England. When the first copies of his translation arrived in England in 1526, it was bitterly attacked as subversive by the ecclesial authorities. He spent much of the rest of his life making revisions to his work, but also writing many theological works. His life's-work proved good enough to be the basic working text for those who, at the beginning of the following century, were to produce what became known as the Authorized Version of the Bible. He was eventually arrested in 1535 and imprisoned in Brussels on charges of heresy. He was first strangled and then burnt at the stake on this day in 1536. His last words were, 'Lord, open the King of England's eyes.'

A Reading from William Tyndale's *Epistle to the Reader* which he included in his first published version of the New Testament in 1526

Give diligence, reader, I exhort thee, that thou come with a pure mind, and as the scripture saith, with a single eye unto the words of health and of eternal life; by the which, if we repent and believe them, we are born anew, created afresh, and enjoy the fruits of the blood of Christ: which blood crieth not for vengeance, as the blood of Abel, but hath purchased life, love, favour, grace, blessing, and whatsoever is promised in the scriptures to them that believe and obey God; and standeth between us and wrath, vengeance, curse, and whatsoever the Scripture threateneth against the unbelievers and disobedient, which resist and consent not in their hearts to the law of God, that it is right, holy, just, and ought so to be.

Mark the plain and manifest places of the Scriptures, and in doubtful places see thou add no interpretations contrary to them; but (as Paul saith) let all be conformable and agreeing to the faith. Note the difference of the law and of the Gospel. The one asketh and requireth, the other pardoneth and forgiveth. The one threateneth, the other promiseth all good things to them that set their trust in Christ only. The Gospel signifieth glad tidings, and is nothing but the promises of good things. All is not gospel that is written in the gospel-book: for if the law were away, thou couldest not know what the gospel meant; even as thou couldest not see pardon and grace, except the law rebuked thee, and declared unto thee thy sin, misdeed, and trespass. Repent and believe the gospel, as saith Christ in the first of Mark. Apply alway the law to thy deeds, whether thou find lust in thine heart to the law-ward; and so shalt thou no doubt repent, and feel in thyself a certain sorrow, pain, and grief to thine heart, because thou canst not with full lust do the deeds of the law. Apply the gospel, that is to say the promises, unto the deserving of Christ, and to the mercy of God and his truth, and so shalt thou not despair; but shalt feel God as a kind and merciful Father. And his Spirit shall dwell in thee, and shall be strong in thee, and the promises shall be given thee at the last, (though not by and by, lest thou shouldst forget thyself and be negligent) and all threatenings shall be forgiven thee for Christ's blood's sake, to whom commit thyself altogether, without respect either of thy good deeds, or of thy bad.

Them that are learned christianly I beseech, forasmuch as I am sure, and my conscience beareth me record, that of a pure intent, singly and faithfully, I have interpreted it, as far forth as God gave me the gift of knowledge and understanding, that the rudeness of the work now at the first time offend them not; but that they consider how that I had no man to counterfeit, neither was helped with English of any that had interpreted the same or such like thing in the scripture beforetime.

alternative reading

A Reading from *The Obedience of a Christian Man* by William Tyndale, published in 1528

The kings ought to remember that they are in God's stead, and ordained of God, not for themselves, but for the wealth of their subjects. Let them remember that their subjects are their brethren, their flesh and blood, members of their own body, and even their own selves in Christ. Therefore ought they to pity them, and to rid them from such wily tyranny, which increaseth more and more daily. And though that the kings, by the falsehood of the bishops and abbots, be sworn to defend such liberties; yet ought they not to keep their oaths, but to break them; forasmuch as they are upright and clean against God's ordinance, and even but cruel oppression, contrary unto brotherly love and charity.

And let the kings put down some of their tyranny, and turn some unto a common wealth. If the tenth part of such tyranny were given the king yearly, and laid up in the shire-towns, against the realm had need, what would it grow to in certain years? Moreover one king, one law, is God's ordinance in every realm. Therefore ought not the king to suffer them to have a several law by themselves, and to draw his subjects thither. It is not meet, will they say, that a spiritual man should be judged of a worldly or temporal man. O abomination! see how they divide and separate themselves: if the lay-man be of the world, so is he not of God! If he believe in Christ, then is he a member of Christ, Christ's brother, Christ's flesh, Christ's blood, Christ's spouse, co-heir with Christ, and hath his Spirit in earnest, and is also spiritual. Because thou art put in office to preach God's word, art thou therefore no more one of the brethren?

If any question arise about the faith of the Scripture, let them judge by the manifest and open Scriptures, not excluding the laymen: for there are many found among the lay-men which are as wise as the spiritual officers. Or else, when the officer dieth, how could we put another in his room? Wilt thou teach twenty, thirty, forty, or fifty years, that no man shall have knowledge or judgement in God's word save thou only? Is it not a shame that we Christians come so oft to church in vain, when he of fourscore years old knoweth no more than he that was born yesterday?

6 October

Bruno

Founder of the Carthusian Order, 1101

Bruno was born at Cologne in about 1032. He was gifted intellectually and became rector of the cathedral school at Rheims where the quality of his lectures won for him respect and admiration among his pupils, among them the future Pope Urban II. After eighteen years, however, Bruno felt drawn to the monastic life. He and six companions received permission and encouragement from the Bishop of Grenoble to establish themselves at La Chartreuse in 1084. Its ethos was fostered by the ideals of primitive Christian monasticism when, during the third and fourth centuries in the Egyptian desert, solitaries lived in individual houses or cells, but near enough to one another for mutual support. 'Christ's poor men who dwell in the desert of the Chartreuse for the love of the name of Jesus' was how Bruno and his companions described themselves. Silence, austerity, solitude and total renunciation of the world were and are the hallmarks of Carthusian spirituality. Bruno died in the year 1101.

A Reading from a meditation on solitude by Guigo II,
ninth prior of La Chartreuse

'Woe to the lonely one' when you alone, my good Jesus, are not with him or her. How many in a crowd are alone because you are not with them? Be always with me, so that I may never be alone!

I am in no one's company, and yet I am not alone. I myself am a crowd. My wild beasts are with me, those whom I have nourished in my heart from my childhood. There they have made their lairs which they love so much that even in my loneliness they will not leave me. How often have I protested to them: 'Go away from me, wicked ones, so that I may search out the commandments of my God.' It is as though frogs were croaking in my entrails, as if Egypt's plague of flies were blinding my eyes.

Let one sit alone, the Scripture says; and indeed, unless one sits and rests, one will not be alone. So it is good to be humbled, Lord, and to bear your burden. By carrying your burden the proud learn meekness. And you say to those who take up your burden: 'Learn from me, for I am meek and humble of heart.' The one who is mounted on pride does not know how to sit still. But your throne is humility and peace. And now I see that no one can be at peace until they have become humble. Humility and peace: how good it is for a man or woman to be humbled so that they can attain to peace. Then indeed will one sit alone and be silent. The one who is not alone cannot be silent. And the one who is not silent cannot hear you when you speak to him or her.

Scripture says: 'The words of the wise are as a goad' to those who listen to them in silence. Let all my world be silent in your presence, Lord, so that I may hear what the Lord God may say in my heart. Your words are so softly spoken that no one can hear them except in a deep silence. But to hear them lifts the one who sits alone and in silence completely above his or her natural powers, because the one who humbles himself will be lifted up. The one who sits alone and listens will be raised above himself. But where? This surely does not mean a lifting up of the body? No: it means of the heart. But how can one's heart be above one's self ? It can because one forgets one's self, does not love one's self, thinks nothing of one's self. Of what then does one think? Of that which is above one, one's highest good, one's God. And the more one sees and loves God, the more one sees and loves one's self.

8 October

Alexander Penrose Forbes

Bishop of Brechin, 1875

Alexander Penrose Forbes was born in Edinburgh, the son of Lord Medwyn, a judge of the Court of Session. He served with the East India Company for three years but returned to Britain on health grounds and studied at Brasenose College, Oxford. There he was strongly influenced by Pusey, who, after his ordination, appointed him to a slum parish in Leeds in 1847. A few months later, aged thirty, he was elected Bishop of Brechin, a diocese of eleven parishes, one of which (in Dundee) Forbes pastored himself. He exercised a notable ministry among the poor and among the victims of a cholera epidemic. He built the present cathedral for his own congregation, and founded several new congregations in the city. His doctrine of the presence of Christ in the eucharist led to controversy and in 1860 to a trial before his fellow bishops, at which he was supported by John Keble. His Tractarian theology had a growing influence upon the Scottish Episcopal Church for the rest of the century. His writings include doctrinal and devotional works, as well as research into the lives of the saints of Scotland. He died in the year 1875.

A Reading from *Episcopal Scotland in the Nineteenth Century*
by Marion Lochhead

Alexander Penrose Forbes was the first of the great social missionaries in the Scottish Church. The older bishops had known and shared poverty among the fisher-folk and country people, but in Dundee was a poverty degrading and dreadful. 'Poverty is one thing, pauperism is another,' Forbes himself wrote. He went on:

> Poverty is the momentary or even the permanent deprivation of the enjoyment of means; it is the state in which man is condemned to work for the necessities of life; but pauperism is a chronic, normal, even fatal state of misery which hands over a notable portion of living humanity to moral degradation and physical suffering, while a small and privileged class live in the most unexampled luxury. And here is the awful fact that pauperism is measured by the advance of industry, and progress in wealth goes on side by side with progress in misery.

Like Disraeli, Forbes was aware of the two nations in this island with a dreadful gulf between them. He saw the inordinate growth of industrialism, the separation between masters and men, the division and specialization in labour which made people more and more like machines.

This missionary zeal never overwhelmed his other gifts; he was still the scholar and theologian. Indeed, the balance and wholeness of his personality impressed many observers, including Matthew Arnold who noted the blend of worldly wisdom with profound religion.

For Forbes, true belief, right worship, good living were inseparable. He deplored any failure of the sense of worship, of awe, of holiness. Like Keble and Pusey, he taught his people the Catholic doctrine of adoration of Christ in the eucharist, as being inseparable from adoration of the sacred manhood. But it was his Charge to his clergy at his synod of 1857 which led to controversy and to trial. At the heart of it lay the question of Christ's presence in his sacrament. Forbes said:

> Is Christ himself, according to his own word, truly present in the holy sacrament… or has he used a form of speech eminently calculated to deceive men, and are all these blessed words indicating union with him mere figures of language, oriental expressions of exaggerated value to imply that effect upon our souls which a living faith in him proclaims? Is the sacrament of the Lord's Supper the partaking of the Living Christ or merely the memorial of the dead?

While rejecting the doctrine of transubstantiation, Forbes repudiated also the Protestant denial of the real presence, the Protestant assertion of these being 'only a memorial, not a mystery'. For Forbes the teaching of Scripture was plain, that of the Fathers concordant. These made up a strong defence; but the real presence could not be apprehended only by intellectual argument. He wrote:

> If there be one doctrine more than another that touches the heart and subdues the intellect and influences the will, it is that blessed one, that the eternal Son of God, not content with taking upon himself our nature in the mystery of the incarnation, has, by an extension of the same, found a way to communicate himself to us… What a tender delight, mixed with reverence and holy fear, does this truth infuse into Christian hearts.

9 October

Denys and his Companions

Bishop of Paris, Martyrs, *c.*250

Denys, also called Dionysius, was born in Italy at the beginning of the third century and was sent to convert the peoples of Gaul, along with five other bishops. On reaching Paris, he established there a Christian church on an island in the Seine. He and others were martyred in about the year 250 and an abbey was later built over their tombs, dedicated to Denys. The church became the burial place of French monarchs and Denys has long been regarded as patron saint of France.

A Reading from a sermon of Augustine

The Lord Jesus Christ not only instructed his martyrs through his teaching, he strengthened them through his own example. In order that those who would suffer for him might have an example to follow, he first suffered for them. He showed the way and became it.

When we talk of death, we speak in terms of the body and the soul. In one sense, the soul cannot die, but in another it can. It cannot die inasmuch as the awareness of itself endures;

yet it can die if it loses God. For just as the soul is the life of the body, so God is the life of the soul. The body perishes when the soul that is its life departs: the soul perishes when God casts it away. So lest God cast our souls away, let us always live in faith. Only so will we not fear to die for God, and not die abandoned by God.

The death of the body will always remain a fear. And yet Christ the Lord has made his martyrs a counter-balance to our fear. Why worry about the safety of limbs when we have been reassured that the hairs on our head are secure? Does not Scripture say that 'the very hairs on your head are numbered'? Why should our human frailty cause us to be so frightened when the truth has spoken thus?

Blessed indeed then, are the saints whose memory we commemorate on the day of their passion. In surrendering their security in this world, they received an eternal crown and immortality without end. As we gather to remember them in prayer, their example sends us messages of encouragement. When we hear how the martyrs suffered, we rejoice and glorify God in them. We do not grieve because they died. If they had not died, do you think they would still be alive today? Their confession of faith served to consummate what sickness would one day also have brought about.

Therefore, my dear friends, let us rejoice in their commemoration. Let us pray to God that we may follow in the steps of his martyrs. They were mortal like you: their manner of birth no different from yours. They had bodies no different from your own. We are all descended from Adam: we should all seek to return to Christ.

Honour the martyrs; praise, love, preach and honour them. But remember, worship only the God of the martyrs.

9 October

Cynog

Abbot and Martyr, seventh century

Brychan Brycheiniog is said to have raped Banhadlwedd, daughter of Banadl and as a result she gave birth to Cynog. Brychan presented his son with a golden torque, which was preserved as a relic when Giraldus Cambrensis saw it in the year 1188. He apparently became a hermit. The legends linked to Cynog are colourful but confused. A story from the early eighteenth century depicts him as a 'fool for Christ' who deliberately gave up his golden crown for ragged clothes and an iron bolt twisted into a torque. Cynog was believed to have been murdered either by pagan Saxons or by fellow hermits irritated by the special favour that God had showed him. The church of Merthyr Cynog was built over his burial place. Several churches in or near Brycheiniog were dedicated to him.

A Reading from *The Rule of Carthage*,
a Celtic monastic Rule dating from the seventh century,
concerning the duties of an abbot of a community

It is a wonderful distinction if you are the leader of a church, but it would be better by far that you assume in a worthy manner the patrimony of the King.

Sublime is the undertaking you bear if you are the leader of a church; you must protect the rights, whether small or great, of the monastery.

Preach diligently what Christ, the holy one, commands; what you ask of others should be what you yourself do.

You should love the souls of all, just as you love your own. It is your duty to exalt every good and to root out all evil.

Your learning should be visible to all, and not hidden like a candle under a bushel. Your business is to heal all your monks, whether they be strong or weak.

It is your responsibility to judge each one according to his rank and according to his deeds, so that they may present themselves with you at the judgement in the presence of the King.

It is your responsibility to encourage the seniors who are weighed down by sorrow and sickness, that they may frequently invoke the King with floods of tears.

Yours is the duty of instructing the young, that they fall not into sin and the devil not drag them away to his house reeking of death.

You are to return thanks for each and every one who carries out his function in the one pure Church.

Yours is to reprimand the wayward, to correct all, to bring to order the disorderly, the stubborn, the wilful, and the wretched.

Patience, humility, prayers, beloved charity, steadiness, generosity, calmness are to be expected of you.

It is no light task to teach all people in truth, and to foster unity, forgiveness, sincerity, and uprightness in all things.

Be faithful to the constant preaching of the gospel for the instruction of all, and to the offering of the Body of the great Lord on the holy altar.

9 October

Robert Grosseteste

Bishop of Lincoln, Philosopher, Scientist, 1253

Robert Grosseteste (meaning 'large-head') was born at Stradbroke in Suffolk in about 1175. He studied at Oxford and Paris and held various posts until, after a grave illness, he returned to Oxford, where he taught at the Franciscan house of studies. He became Bishop of Lincoln in 1235, then the largest English diocese, which received from him a thorough visitation soon after his arrival. He met opposition in his attempts at vigorous reforms in the shape of his Dean and Chapter in the cathedral at Lincoln, who saw themselves as beyond his jurisdiction. The affair was settled in 1245 when the Pope issued a bull giving the bishop full power over the Chapter. Robert attended the Council of Lyons that year and also travelled to Rome a few years later. His wide-ranging interests covered mathematics, optics and many of the sciences; he translated large numbers of theological works from Greek and wrote his own theological commentaries and philosophical works. He died on this day in the year 1253.

A Reading from the *Memorial* of Bishop Grosseteste addressed and delivered to Pope Innocent IV before the Papal Court at Lyons on 13 May 1250, concerning abuses affecting the life of the Church in England

What is the cause of this hopeless fall of the Church? Unquestionably the diminution in the number of good shepherds of souls, the increase of wicked shepherds, and the circumscription of pastoral authority and power. Bad pastors are everywhere the cause of unbelief, division, heresy and vice. It is they who scatter the flock of Christ, who lay waste the vineyard of the Lord, and desecrate the earth. No wonder, for they preach not the gospel of Christ with that living word which comes forth from living zeal for the salvation of souls, and is confirmed by an example worthy of Jesus Christ.

And what is the cause of this evil? I tremble to speak of it, and yet I dare not keep silence. The cause and source of it is the *Curia* itself! Not only because it fails to put a stop to these evils as it can and should, but still more, because by its dispensations, provisions and collations, it appoints evil shepherds, thinking only of the income it yields for a person, and for the sake of it, handing over many thousands of souls to eternal death. And all this comes from him who is the representative of Christ! He who so sacrifices the pastoral office is a persecutor of Christ in his members. And since the doings of the *Curia* are a lesson to the world, such a manner of appointment to the cure of souls, on its part, teaches and encourages those who exercise the rights of patrons to make pastoral appointments of a similar nature, as a return for services rendered to themselves, or to please those in power, and thus destroy the sheep of Christ.

The cure of souls consists not only in the dispensation of the sacraments, in singing of the hours, and reading of masses, but in the true teaching of the word of life, in rebuking and correcting vice; and besides all this, in feeding the hungry, giving drink to the thirsty, clothing the naked, housing the strangers, visiting the sick and prisoners – especially those who are the parish priest's own parishioners. By such deeds of charity, a priest will instruct his people in the holy exercises of daily life.

The end of the evils of which I speak is not the upbuilding, but the destruction of the Church.

10 October

Paulinus of York

Bishop of York, Missionary, 644

Born in the latter part of the sixth century, probably in Italy, Paulinus was among the second group of monks sent by Pope Gregory to England to assist Augustine in his work. He went with the party that accompanied Ethelburga to Northumbria, where she was to marry the king, Edwin, who subsequently took his wife's Christian faith as his own. Paulinus built the first church in York in about the year 627 and was its first bishop. He travelled much north and south of the Humber, building churches and baptizing new Christians. He had to flee for his life, however, when Edwin was killed in battle by the pagan king, Penda of Mercia, and Paulinus became Bishop of Rochester. He died on this day in the year 644.

A Reading from *The History of the English Church and People* by the Venerable Bede

On learning from Bishop Augustine that the harvest was rich but that the labourers to help him gather it were few, Pope Gregory sent with his envoys several colleagues and ministers of the word, of whom the principal and most outstanding were Mellitus, Justus, Paulinus, and Rufinianus.

Paulinus was a tall man with a slight stoop. He had black hair, an ascetic face, a thin hooked nose, and a venerable and awe-inspiring presence. He was consecrated bishop by Archbishop Justus on 21 July in the year of our Lord 625, and came to King Edwin of Northumbria with Princess Ethelberga, a daughter of King Ethelbert. She had been betrothed to Edwin, and Paulinus was to act as her chaplain and spiritual counsellor. He was determined to bring the nation to which he was sent to the knowledge of the truth. His desire in the words of the apostle was 'to espouse her to one husband, that he might present her as a chaste virgin to Christ'.

Therefore, directly he entered the province he set to work vigorously. His goal was not only, with God's help, to maintain the faith of his companions without them lapsing, but if possible to bring some of the heathen to grace and faith by his teaching. He laboured long, but, as the apostle says, 'the god of this world blinded the minds of those who did not believe, lest the light of the glorious gospel of Christ should shine upon them'.

Although Paulinus found it difficult to bring the king's proud mind to accept the humility of the way of salvation or to accept the mystery of the life-giving cross, he nevertheless continued, by words of exhortation addressed to the people, and by words of supplication addressed to the divine compassion, to strive for the conversion of the king and his nation.

King Edwin hesitated to accept the word of God which Paulinus preached, and used to sit alone for hours at a time, debating within himself what he should do and what religion he should follow. On one of these occasions, the man of God came to him and, laying his right hand on his head, enquired whether he remembered this sign. The king trembled and would have fallen at his feet; but Paulinus raised him and said in a friendly voice: 'God has helped you to escape from the hands of the enemies whom you feared, and it is through his bounty that you have received the kingdom that you desired. Remember now your own promise that you made, and hesitate no longer. Accept the faith and keep the commandments of the God who has delivered you from all your earthly troubles and raised you to the glory of an earthly kingdom. If you will henceforth obey his will, which he reveals to you through me, he will save you likewise from the everlasting doom of the wicked and give you a place in his eternal kingdom in heaven.'

So it was that King Edwin, with all the nobility of his kingdom and a large number of humbler folk, finally accepted the faith and were washed in the cleansing waters of baptism in the eleventh year of his reign, that is in the year of our Lord 627, and about 180 years after the first arrival of the English in Britain. The king's baptism took place in York on Easter Day in the church of St Peter the Apostle which the king had hastily built of wood during the time of his instruction and preparation for baptism; and in this city he established the episcopal see of Paulinus, his teacher and bishop. Soon after his baptism, at Paulinus' suggestion, the king gave orders to build on the same site a larger and more noble basilica of stone which was to enclose the little oratory he had built previously.

Thenceforward for six years, until the close of Edwin's reign, Paulinus preached the word in that province with the king's full consent and approval, and as many as were predestined to eternal life believed and were baptized.

10 October

Thomas Traherne

Poet, Spiritual Writer, 1674

Thomas Traherne was born in Hereford in about 1636. After studying in Oxford and being a parish priest for ten years, he became private chaplain to the Lord Keeper of the Seals of Charles II. Thomas was one of the English Metaphysical poets and yet, in his lifetime, only one of his works was ever printed. It was at the beginning of the twentieth century that his poems, until then in manuscript, were published and he took on the mantle of an Anglican Divine. His poetry is probably the most celebratory among his fellow Metaphysical poets, with little mention of sin and suffering and concentrating more on the glory of creation, to the extent that some regard his writings as on the edge of pantheism. He died on this day in the year 1674.

A Reading from *Centuries of Meditation* by Thomas Traherne

Adam in Paradise had not more sweet and curious apprehensions of the world than I when I was a child. All appeared new and strange at first, inexpressibly rare and delightful and beautiful. I was a little stranger, which at my entrance into the world was saluted and surrounded with innumerable joys. I was entertained like an angel with the works of God in their splendour and glory, I saw all in the peace of Eden; heaven and earth did sing my Creator's praises, and could not make more melody to Adam than to me. All time was eternity and a perpetual Sabbath. Is it not strange, that an infant should be heir of the whole world, and see those mysteries which the books of the learned never unfold?

The corn was orient and immortal wheat which never should be reaped, nor was ever sown. I thought it had stood from everlasting to everlasting. The dust and stones of the street were as precious as gold: the gates were at first the end of the world. The green trees when I saw them first through one of the gates, transported and ravished me, their sweetness and unusual beauty made my heart to leap, and almost mad with ecstasy, they were such strange and wonderful things. The people! O what venerable and reverend creatures did the aged seem! Immortal cherubims! And young men glittering and sparkling angels, and maids strange seraphic pieces of life and beauty! Boys and girls tumbling in the street, and playing, were moving jewels. I knew not that they were born or should die; but all things abided eternally as they were in their proper places.

Eternity was manifest in the light of the day, and something infinite behind everything appeared which talked with my expectation and moved my desire. The city seemed to stand in Eden, or to be built in heaven. The streets were mine, the temple was mine, the people were mine, their clothes and gold and silver were mine, as much as their sparkling eyes, fair skins and ruddy faces. The skies were mine, and so were the sun and moon and stars, and all the world was mine; and I the only spectator and enjoyer of it. I knew no churlish proprieties, nor bounds, nor divisions: but all proprieties and divisions were mine: all treasures and the possessors of them. So that with much ado I was corrupted, and made to learn the dirty devices of this world which now unlearn, and become, as it were, a little child again, that I may enter into the Kingdom of God.

11 October

Philip

Deacon

All that is known of Philip is recorded in the Acts of the Apostles. He was one of the seven Greek-speaking men of good standing, 'full of the Spirit and of wisdom', chosen to distribute food to the Greek-speaking widows, and who are regarded as the first deacons. He is listed second, after Stephen, and following the martyrdom of Stephen it is to Philip that the story turns. Having fled to Samaria, he proclaimed the gospel there to great effect, baptizing many, and preparing the way for Peter and John to come, that the people might receive the gift of the Spirit at their hands. Then he went to Gaza, meeting the Ethiopian official to whom he explained the significance of the prophecy of Isaiah, and baptizing him. The baptism of this African was an important demonstration that the good news is for all people.

A Reading from a treatise *On Baptism* by Tertullian

Those whose responsibility it is, know that baptism is not to be administered rashly. The words of our Lord, 'Give to every one who begs you,' refers particularly to almsgiving. By contrast, the precept: 'Do not give what is holy to the dogs, and cast not your pearls before swine,' is applicable to baptism and should be reflected on carefully, as well as the words: 'Do not lay hands easily on any.'

If Philip 'easily' baptized the Ethiopian official, let us reflect on the clear and conspicuous evidence that the Lord had deemed this man worthy. We learn that the Spirit had guided Philip to proceed to that road; that the eunuch himself was not being idle; that he was not suddenly seized by an eager desire to be baptized; but rather, having been to the temple to pray, was now intently engaged in studying the divine Scriptures. In other words, the man was suitably prepared. Unasked, God had sent his apostle to him, and under the Spirit's direction, Philip ran alongside the official's chariot.

The Scripture the Ethiopian was reading happily related to his search for faith. At his request, Philip joins him in his chariot and sits beside him. The Lord is pointed out to him, by Philip; faith comes to birth; water is at hand; the work is completed, and the apostle is snatched away.

We learn from this incident that those who are about to be baptized should pray constantly, with fasting and prostrations, with prayer-vigils, confessing all their past sins, that they may embody the meaning of the baptism of John: 'They were baptized,' says the Scripture, 'confessing their sins'. To us it is matter for thanksgiving when we publicly confess our sins and failings to one another. By so doing we are not only making satisfaction for our former sins, by mortification of our flesh and spirit, but also laying the foundation of defences against future temptations which will surely follow.

'Watch and pray,'says the Lord, 'lest you fall into temptation.' The reason, I believe, why the disciples were tempted was because they fell asleep: they deserted the Lord when he was arrested. Even the one who initially stood by him, and used his sword to protect him, went on to deny him three times in accordance with the word of prophecy that 'no-one who has not been tempted is fit for the celestial kingdoms'.

The Lord himself, after his own baptism, we read was assailed by temptations when he fasted for forty days in the wilderness. Someone is bound to ask, 'Then should we not fast *after* our baptism too?' The Lord was driven into the desert after his baptism to demonstrate by maintaining a fast of forty days that man lives 'not by bread alone, but by the word of God'.

Therefore, blessed ones, whom the grace of God awaits, when you emerge from that most sacred font of your new birth, and spread out your hands for the first time in the house of your mother, the Church, together with your brothers and sisters, ask from the Father, ask from the Lord, that his own special grace and gifts may be given to you. 'Ask,' says the Lord, 'and you will receive.' Well, you have asked, and have received; you have knocked, and it will be opened to you.

11 October

Canice (Kenneth)

Bishop and Abbot, *c.*600

Born around the year 525, Canice or Cainnech (Kenneth) was a friend and companion of Columba. Adamnán mentions him in his Life of Columcille. The son of a bard from County Derry, he later founded many monasteries in Ireland. His foundation at Aghaboe in Leix became the principal monastery in Ossory diocese. Wales and Scotland cherish their link with him also: there is evidence of his missionary activity in Fife. St Kenneth's Abbey in St Andrews, the earliest established there, is said in the Roman tradition to be of his founding. One of the finest medieval cathedrals to have survived in Ireland, at Kilkenny, is dedicated in his honour. A lonely figure, he copied the Scriptures and became known as the preacher who loved the countryside and animal life. He died in Ireland at Aghaboe around the year 600.

A Reading from *The Irish Saints* by Daphne Pochin Mould

Canice (Cainnech or Kenneth) is one of the most attractive personalities of the early Irish Church. In popularity, he ranks only second to the devotion attaching to Patrick, Brigid, and Columcille (Columba). Founder and/or patron of a large number of churches in Ireland and Scotland, his cult was also known on the continent.

As a friend and contemporary of Columcille, he appears in several incidents in Adamnán's *Life of Columba.* In addition, there are three much later Latin *Lives* of Canice, all stemming from a common original.

The saint seems to have inherited his father's temperament. If he was a cleric, he was also a poet, a quieter, gentler type than his great friend Columcille, with a liking to escape into the solitude of the woods and islands, where the birds cheeped at tide mark or the deer moved softly between the trees to the lake shore to drink. The stories in the *Lives* take us to a number of islands; Inis Ubdain from which he expels the mice for nibbling his shoes, and the Bird Island (probably Hebridean) where the birds make so much noise on a Sunday that the saint orders them to be silent till after Matins on Monday!

Canice was a moving preacher. Comgall who asked him to preach one Sunday, said that often people wept when hearing the word of God, but never as they did at Canice's word. On another occasion in Iona, we learn that Columcille asked who had taught him his interpretation of Scripture. Canice replied, 'When I was on the island at Lough Cree by the mountain Smoir in Ireland, the Son of the Virgin, the Lord Jesus came to me and read the gospel with me and taught me this sense of it.'

In Scotland, Canice visited Iona quite often to judge by the tone of Adamnán's account, and the island has a church dedicated to him and a graveyard. But he also had his own island close to Columcille's, that most beautiful and fertile Inchkenneth in Loch na Keal, a sea inlet off the Island of Mull.

alternative reading

A Reading from an Old Irish poem by an unknown monastic author

Christ's Bounty

I pray you, Christ, to change my heart,
To make it whole;
Once you took on flesh like mine,
Now take my soul.

Ignominy and pain you knew,
The lash, the scourge,
You, the perfect molten metal
Of my darkened forge.

You make the bright sun bless my head,
Put ice beneath my feet,
Send salmon swarming in the tides,
Give crops of wheat.

When Eve's wild children come to you
With prayerful words,
You crowd the rivers with fine fish,
The sky with birds.

You make the small flowers thrive
In wholesome air,
You spread sweetness through the world.
What miracles can compare?

11 October

Ethelburga

Abbess of Barking, 675

Ethelburga was sister of Erkenwald, Bishop of London, and was probably of royal blood. As Bede describes her, it seems she may well have owned, as well as been made abbess of, the joint monastery at Barking. There was a tradition developing of monks and nuns sharing monasteries, often with a woman superior, as for example Hilda at Whitby and Cuthburga at Wimborne. Though they lived quite separate lives, often divided by high walls, they would occasionally celebrate the Daily Office or the Mass together. There was also probably an element of safety involved with the ever-present threat of marauding Danes. Bede relates many miracles occurring around Ethelburga but little else is known of her life. She died on this day in the year 675.

A Reading from *The History of the English Church and People* by the Venerable Bede

Before he became bishop in London for the East Saxons, Earconwald had founded two famous monasteries, one for himself and the other for his sister Ethelburga, and had established an excellent regular discipline in both houses. His own monastery stood by the river Thames at Chertsey in the district of Surrey. The monastery where his sister was to rule as mother and instructress of women devoted to God was at a place called Barking in the province of the East Saxons. Entrusted with the rule of this monastery, she proved herself worthy in all things of her brother the bishop, both by her own holy life and by her sound and constant care of her community; and of this, the heavenly miracles attest.

When Ethelburga, the devoted mother of this God-fearing community, was herself about to be taken from this world, one of the sisters saw a wonderful vision. This nun had lived for many years in the monastery, humbly and sincerely striving to serve God, and had helped the mother to maintain the Rule by instructing and correcting the younger sisters.

In order that her strength might be 'made perfect in weakness' as the apostle Paul says, she was suddenly attacked by a serious disease. Under the good providence of our Redeemer, this caused her great distress for nine years, in order that any traces of sin that remained among her virtues through ignorance or neglect might be burned away in the fires of prolonged suffering. One evening, at dusk, on leaving her cell, this sister saw distinctly what appeared to be a human body wrapped in a shroud and shining more brightly than the sun. This was raised up and carried out of the house where the sisters used to sleep. She observed closely to see how this appearance of a shining body was being raised, and saw what appeared to be cords brighter than gold which drew it upwards until it entered the open heavens and she could see it no longer. When she thought about this vision, there remained no doubt in her mind that some member of the community was shortly to die, and that her soul would be drawn up to heaven by her good deeds as though by golden cords.

And so it came to pass not many days later, that God's beloved Ethelburga, the mother of this congregation, was set free from her bodily prison. And none who knew her holy life can doubt that when she departed this life the gates of her heavenly home opened at her coming.

11 October

James the Deacon

Companion of Paulinus of York, seventh century

The details of the birth and death of James the Deacon are not known, though, since he accompanied Paulinus, he may well have been Italian. James seems to have been very active in assisting Paulinus on his mission in southern Northumbria, but when King Edwin was killed in battle and Paulinus had to flee south, James remained in the north. At some risk to his life, he continued the work of preaching and baptizing around the area which is now North Yorkshire. As an old man, he attended the Synod of Whitby in 664 and, though not a monk and therefore without a community to perpetuate his memory, he seems to have had enough popularity among ordinary Christians to have had a continuing cultus long after his death.

A Reading from *The History of the English Church and People* by the Venerable Bede

Bishop Paulinus was assisted in his ministry by a deacon called James, a man of energy and high reputation in Christ's Church, who lived right up until our own day. So peaceful was it in those parts of Britain under King Edwin's rule that, as the proverb still runs, a woman could carry her new-born child across the island from sea to sea without any fear of harm.

Following the murder of King Edwin, the situation in Northumbria began to deteriorate, and there seemed no safety except in flight. Bishop Paulinus, therefore, returned to Kent by sea with Queen Ethelberga, whom he had previously accompanied to the province. He left behind his deacon James to care for the church of York. He was a true churchman and holy person who remained a long time in that church, teaching and baptizing, and snatching much prey from the clutches of our old enemy the Devil. There is a village near Catterick, where he usually lived, which bears his name to this day. He had a wide knowledge of church music; and when at length peace was restored to the province and the number of believers increased, he began to teach many people to sing the music of the Church after the uses of Rome and Canterbury. At last, old and 'full of days' as the Scripture says, he went the way of his fathers.

12 October

Móibhí

Teacher of Columba, 545

The name of Móibhí has a special association with Glasnevin, Dublin, where he founded a monastery. Among his pupils was Columba. He died in the year 545.

A Reading from the *Conferences* of John Cassian

My sons, when a person wishes to acquire the skills of a particular art he needs to devote all possible care and attention to the activities characteristic of his chosen profession. He must observe the precepts and, indeed, the advice of the most successful practitioners of this work or of this way of knowledge. Otherwise he will be dealing in empty dreams. One does not come to resemble those whose hard work and zeal one declines to imitate.

I have known some people who have come to our monastery in the past from where you live, and who have travelled round countless monasteries, and all for the sake of acquiring knowledge. But it never occurred to them to practise the rules or customs they encountered which were the objective of their travels. Nor would they withdraw into a cell where they could try to practise what they had seen and heard. Instead, they stuck to their old habits and practices, just as they had left their own provinces not for the sake of their own progress, but to avoid the presence of poverty. Not only were they unable to acquire any learning, but they could not even stay here because of the sheer stubbornness of their disposition. They would make no changes in their habits of fasting, in the order in which they recited the psalms, or even in the clothes they wore. What else could we think except that they had come here solely for the purpose of getting fed?

Now I believe that it is for the sake of God that you have come here to our monastery to get to know us. You must, therefore, abandon all those teachings which marked your beginning as monks. You must take to yourselves, completely and humbly, all the practices and teachings of our old masters in the monastic life. It may be that a moment will come when you fail to grasp the deep meaning of a certain statement or mode of conduct. Do not be put off, and do not fail to conform. Those seeking profit only, and struggling to imitate faithfully what they have seen their masters doing and saying, and have not argued endlessly about them, these will receive a knowledge of everything, even while they are still undergoing the experience. But the man who teaches himself by engaging in arguments will never reach the truth.

12 October

Wilfrid of Ripon

Bishop, Missionary, 709

Wilfrid, or Wilfrith, was born in Northumbria in about the year 633. He was educated at the monastery on Lindisfarne, but disapproved of what he judged to be their Celtic insularity. He journeyed to Canterbury and then to Rome. He spent three years at Lyons where he was admitted as a monk. He was appointed Abbot of Ripon and took with him the Roman monastic system and Benedictine Rule, which he immediately introduced. At the Synod of Whitby, his dominance was largely responsible for the victory of the Roman party over the Celts and, when he was elected Bishop of York, he went to Compiègne to be consecrated by twelve Frankish bishops rather than risk any doubt of schism by being ordained by Celtic bishops. There were upsets first with Chad and then with Archbishop Theodore of Canterbury, but the Roman authorities took his side and he was eventually restored to his See. After further disputes, he resigned the See of York and became Bishop of Hexham, spending his remaining years at Ripon. His gift to the English Church was to make it more clearly a part of the Church universal, but his manner and methods were not such as to draw people close to him at a personal level. He died on this day in the year 709, and was buried at Ripon.

A Reading from *The History of the English Church and People* by the Venerable Bede

As a boy, Wilfrid was of a good disposition and behaved well for his age, always bearing himself modestly and thoughtfully, so that he was deservedly loved, admired, and welcomed by his elders as though he were one of themselves. When he reached the age of fourteen, he chose monastic life rather than secular. He informed his father of his desire, for his mother was dead, and he readily consented to his son's godly desires and aspirations, encouraging him to persevere in such a laudable undertaking. Wilfrid therefore went to the island of Lindisfarne and offered himself for the service of the monks, diligently setting himself to learn and practise all that conduces to monastic purity and devotion. Having a quick mind, he very soon learned the psalter by heart and certain other books. Even before he was tonsured, he already exhibited a maturity of monastic outlook in humility and obedience which is more important than any outward tonsure. This naturally endeared him to the older monks as well as to his contemporaries.

When he had served God in that monastery for some years, being a thoughtful youth, he gradually came to realise that the way of life taught by the Irish was by no means perfect; so he decided to visit Rome and see what ecclesiastical and monastic customs were in use at the apostolic see.

On his return to Britain, he was admitted to the friendship of King Alchfrid, who had learned to love and follow the Catholic laws of the Church. When he found Wilfrid to be a Catholic, the king gave him ten hides of land at a place called Stanford, and not long afterwards, a monastery with thirty hides of land at Ripon. It was at this time that the king sent Wilfrid to Gaul, asking that he might be consecrated his bishop, Wilfrid being about thirty years of age.

But Wilfrid remained overseas for some time, as a result of which a holy man named Chad was consecrated Bishop of York at the orders of King Oswy. Chad, having ruled the Church very ably for three years, eventually resigned the see and retired to his monastery at Lastingham, with the result that Wilfrid then became bishop of the whole province of the Northumbrians. Wilfrid died in the year 709 in the district of Oundle after forty-five years as a bishop. The coffin containing his body was later carried back by the brothers to his own monastery at Ripon, where he was buried in the church of the blessed Apostle Peter close to the altar on the south side.

12 October

Elizabeth Fry

Prison Reformer, 1845

Elizabeth Gurney was born at Earlham in Norfolk in 1780. At the age of twenty, she married Joseph Fry, a London merchant and a strict Quaker. She was admitted as a minister in the Society of Friends and became a noted preacher. The appalling state of the prisons came to her notice and she devoted much of her time to the welfare of female prisoners in Newgate. In 1820 she took part in the formation of a nightly shelter for the homeless in London. She travelled all over Europe in the cause of prison reform. She was a woman of a strong Christian and evangelistic impulse and this inspired all her work. She died on this day in the year 1845.

A Reading from *Far Above Rubies* by Richard Symonds

In 1811 Elizabeth Fry was acknowledged as a minister in the Society of Friends. This was to be highly important for it was as a Quaker Minister that she was able to travel without her husband, investigating social problems and organising committees to deal with them.

In 1816, at the age of thirty-six (by which time she had had nine children) she started the work among the female prisoners of Newgate Prison, in the City of London for which she was to become famous. She found over three hundred women, some under sentence of death, some not yet tried, crowded together with their children and infants, cooking, eating, cursing and fighting. With courage and inspiration her first appeal to the prisoners was to co-operate in the organisation of a school for the children. Having obtained their agreement, she was told by the prison governor and sheriffs that her plan was impossible because no room was available. This official resistance caused the prisoners to ally themselves with Mrs Fry and to give up one of their own cells for the school; they were encouraged by her to elect as teacher an educated young woman who was imprisoned for stealing a watch.

Gradually, Elizabeth Fry became a household name, and was transformed from being a prison visitor into a penal reformer. She hated capital punishment, and though it drained her emotions, she would pray with and comfort condemned women in Newgate up to the moment of their execution. Prisoners who were condemned to death, often for thefts of small sums or for forgery, were deliberately seated by her in the front row at her prayer meetings. Politicians and members of the nobility who came to see the spectacle found it harder to take an abstract view of capital punishment when they found themselves facing and praying with women about to be hanged.

In 1818 she was asked to give evidence before a House of Commons Committee on London Prisons, an unprecedented honour for a woman. At the Committee's request she described the methods of her prison work, whose most important features, she explained, were the provision of employment, for which the prisoners were paid, and the supervision of women by female warders instead of men.

Her interests were not confined to prisons. As she travelled the country she also inspected lunatic asylums, set up homes for discharged prisoners and improved the conditions of women who were deported from Newgate to Australia. She was also a pioneer in the training of nurses: several of the 'Fry Sisters' accompanied Florence Nightingale to Scutari.

The forty-four volumes of her journal reveal a complex personality which could be proud, selfish and ruthless for the cause. Nevertheless, there is no doubt that through her personal courage and involvement men and women all over the world have been enabled to recognise in the prisoner behind the bars their own face. Her signal achievement was to acknowledge the humanity of prisoners and to consider their individual needs. She had the gift of touching people's hearts by her own deep religious feeling and her passionate concern for good.

12 October

Edith Cavell

Nurse, 1915

Edith Cavell was born into a clergy family at Swardeston in 1865. After life as a governess, she trained as a nurse, ending up working with the Red Cross in Belgium in 1907. On the outbreak of the First World War, she became involved in caring for the wounded on both sides. She refused repatriation and then began smuggling British soldiers from Belgium into Holland. In 1915 she was arrested and brought to trial. Protecting those who worked with her, she was sentenced to death and executed by firing squad on this day in 1915. She went to her death calmly, forgiving her executioners, convinced she had been doing her duty as a Christian.

A Reading from the last letter of Edith Cavell written to her nurses on the eve of her execution on 12 October 1915

My Dear Nurses
To my sorrow I have not always been able to talk to you each privately. You know that I had my share of burdens. But I hope that you will not forget our evening chats.

I told you that devotion would bring you true happiness and the thought that, before God and in your own eyes, you have done your duty well and with a good heart, will sustain you in trouble and face to face with death. There are two or three of you who will recall the little talks we had together. Do not forget them. As I had already gone so far along life's road, I was perhaps able to see more clearly than you, and show you the straight path.

One word more. Never speak evil. May I tell you, who love your country with all my heart, that this has been the great fault here. During these last eight years I have seen so many sorrows which could have been avoided or lessened if a little word had not been breathed here and there, perhaps without evil intention, and thus destroyed the happiness or even the life of someone. Nurses all need to think of this, and to cultivate a loyalty and team spirit among themselves.

If any of you has a grievance against me, I beg you to forgive me; I have perhaps been unjust sometimes, but I have loved you much more than you think.

I send my good wishes for the happiness of all my girls, as much for those who have left the School as for those who are still there. Thank you for the kindness you have always shown me.

Your matron,
Edith Cavell

13 October

Edward the Confessor

King of England, 1066

Edward was born in 1002, the son of the English King Ethelred and his Norman wife Emma. Living in exile during the Danish supremacy, he was invited back to England in 1042 to become king, and was heartily welcomed as a descendant of the old royal line. Sustained by Edward's diplomacy and determination, his reign was a balancing act between the influences of stronger characters at home and abroad. His reputation for sanctity was built on his personal, more than his political, qualities. He was concerned to maintain peace and justice in his realm, to avoid foreign wars, and to put his faith into practice. He was generous to the poor, hospitable to strangers, but no mere pietist. Having vowed as a young man to go on pilgrimage to Rome should his family fortunes ever be restored, he later felt it irresponsible to leave his kingdom, and was permitted instead to found or endow a monastery dedicated to Saint Peter. Edward chose the abbey on Thorney Island, by the river Thames, thus beginning the royal patronage of Westminster Abbey. He died on 5 January 1066 and his remains were translated to the Abbey on this day in the year 1162.

A Reading from *The Life of King Edward who rests at Westminster*, attributed to a monk of St Bertin

When the one thousand and sixty-fifth year of the Lord's incarnation approached, the zeal of the house of God took possession of King Edward's mind even more warmly, and fired him to the marrow to celebrate the marriage of the heavenly King and his new bride. For it was not the royal sceptre which aroused this love of justice: he found it hidden within him. And so, while the building of the church dedicated to Saint Peter the Prince of the Apostles at Westminster rose into a lofty structure, the glorious king began with duteous zeal to devote himself to the business of this important consecration. He had also become aware of the approaching end of his mortal life and was drawn to the execution of his good purpose before he should reach life's bourn.

At that time the days of the Lord's nativity were approaching, and those men for whom throughout the kingdom the heralds of this great dedication were sounding, had added the joys of the one festival to the other. But on the very night on which the Virgin in childbed gave the light of heavenly glory to those who had been darkened by the shadow of death, and, unstained, brought forth without travail the King of Ages, the glorious King Edward was afflicted with an indisposition, and in the palace the day's rejoicing was checked by a fresh calamity. The holy man disguised his sickness more than his strength warranted, and for three days he was able to produce a serene countenance. He sat at table clad in a festal robe, but had no stomach for the delicacies which were served. He showed a cheerful face to the bystanders, although an unbearable weakness oppressed him. But after the banquet he sought the privacy of his inner bedchamber, and bore with patience a distress which grew severer day by day. The close ranks of his vassals surrounded him, and the queen herself was there, in her mourning foretelling future grief. When that celebrated day, which the blessed passion of the Holy Innocents adorns, had come, the excellent prince ordered them to hasten on with the dedication of the church and no more to put it off to another time.

When he was sick unto death and his men stood and wept bitterly, King Edward said, 'Do not weep, but intercede with God for my soul and give me leave to go to him. For he will not pardon me so that I shall not die who would not pardon himself so that he should not die.' [Then he addressed his last words to Edith, his Queen, who was sitting at his feet, in this wise: 'May God be gracious to this my wife for the zealous solicitude of her service. For she has served me devotedly, and has always stood close by my side like a beloved daughter.' And stretching forth his hand to his governor, her brother, Harold, he said: 'I commend this woman and all the kingdom to your protection. … Let the grave for my burial be prepared in the Minster in the place which shall be assigned. I ask that you do not conceal my death, but announce it promptly in all parts, so that all the faithful can beseech the mercy of Almighty God on me, a sinner.'] Now and then he also comforted the queen, who ceased not from lamenting, to ease her natural grief. 'Fear not,' he said, 'I shall not die now, but by God's mercy regain my strength.' Nor did he mislead the attentive, least of all himself, by these words, for he has not died, but has passed from death to life, to live with Christ.

And so, coming with these and like words to his last hour, he took the viaticum from the table of heavenly life and gave up his spirit to God the creator on the fifth of January. They bore his holy remains from his palace home into the house of God, and offered up prayers and sighs and psalms all that day and the following night. And before the altar of Saint Peter the Apostle, the body, washed by his country's tears, was laid up in the sight of God.

alternative reading

A Reading from a sermon of Ronald Knox

When we venerate Saint Edward, we venerate a failure. We do so advisedly. Not because success in life necessarily falls to the grasping and the unscrupulous, so that success itself should be mistrusted by Christians as a sign of rascality. Not that there have not been great saints who were also great kings, great statesmen, great warriors – Saint Oswald, Saint Dunstan, Saint Joan of Arc. But because we will not let ourselves be blinded by the lure of worldly success so as to forget that the true statesmanship is exercised in the council chamber, and the true warfare fought on the battlefield of the human soul.

Ask yourself which you would rather have been in life, of all those great dead who lie in Westminster Abbey, and you will find it a difficult question to answer: there is so much that dazzles, so much that captivates the imagination. Would you rather have written this, have painted that, have built that, have discovered that, have won this triumph or have carried that enactment? You can hardly say. But ask yourself which of those great dead you would rather be now; your body there, your soul far away – is there any Christian who would not ask to change places with the Confessor? who would not choose his resting-place, there to wait for the opening of the great Doomsday Book, in which nothing is recorded of men and women but whether they meant good or evil, whether they loved or neglected God?

Many of those who sleep in King Edward's Abbey were devoted servants of their kind, who left the world better for their passing. But this is certain, that true satisfaction came to them and true success crowned them only so far as their ambitions were for a cause, not for a party; for others, not for themselves. Our happiness lies in devoting ourselves; success lies in the offering we can make. And our Confessor was a successful man, yes, even in this world, because in his simple piety, in the unaffected generosity of his nature, he set himself to serve his people by easing their burdens, by relieving their necessities, by confirming them in their allegiance to the faith. Great opportunities passed him by, and he never marked them; he might have altered the dynastic history of England, have left us different manners and a different political constitution, if he had been other than he was. Instead, he left all these things to God's providence; and God's providence, using the ambitions of human agents as its puppets, moulded our history beyond expectation. And what do they mean to us now, those human agents? The Conqueror, who diverted the stream of history, went to his grave disappointed and lies there a historical memory. The Confessor, whose ambitions could be satisfied by finding a poor man his dinner, saw no corruption in death, and lives the patron of his fellow countrymen.

One task only he set before himself that had any external magnificence about it, and that was characteristic of him. It was no fortress, no royal palace, no court of justice that he planned: the House of God lay waste, and he must rebuild it. And, as if it were a symbol of the life he lived, built together from little acts of kindness and little sacrifices of self, stone by stone and arch by arch rose the Abbey Church of Westminster, which for all the additions and the restorations that have altered it in the course of the centuries, we still call his church.

14 October

Esther John

Missionary and Martyr, 1960

Esther John was born Qamar Zia on this day in 1929 in British-ruled India. She attended a Christian school, and her Christian faith grew secretly. Fearing marriage to a Muslim, she ran away, took the name Esther John and worked in an orphanage. Her family pressed her to return, but she moved to the Punjab and worked in a mission hospital. She studied in Gujranwala, and became a missionary, bicycling between villages, teaching women to read, and working with them in the cotton fields, but there was still tension with her family. On 2 February 1960 Esther John was found brutally murdered in her bed. She is remembered with devotion by the Christian community with whom she lived and worked.

A Reading from *Mission and Conversion in Pakistan: Esther John (Qamar Zia)* by Patrick Sookhdeo

A study of the life of Esther John requires a consideration of the place of women in Islam. Most historic religions contain strains of ambivalence towards women, and Islam is no exception, with the result that conversion from Islam was often seen to bring greater disgrace on a family if the convert was a woman.

One of seven children, Qamar Zia was born on 14 October 1929. She attended a government school until her father's illness obliged her to leave at about the age of seventeen. After a while she was sent to a Christian school near her home. Later she recalled:

> Just as soon as I set foot in this school I noticed a Christian teacher who was different from anyone I had ever known. I saw her gentle way of speaking, her kindness to all the students and her great faithfulness in her work. Her life made so deep an impression upon

me that I was really puzzled. 'How could any human being be like that?' I wondered over and over again. Later I realized that it was all because God's Spirit was in her.

In this school I began to study the Bible. Two days a week we studied the Old Testament, and two days a week the New Testament. One day in the week we did memory work, learning passages from the Bible and many songs. At first I did not study with zeal, but rather indifferently. I had heard the Christians called blasphemers, and I did not like even to touch their book. One day we were studying the 53rd chapter of Isaiah, memorizing some parts of it, which was very hard for me. It was while studying this chapter that God, by his grace, showed me that there was life and power in this book. Then I began to realize that Jesus is alive for ever. This God put faith in my heart and I believed in Jesus as my Saviour and the forgiver of my sins. Only he could save me from everlasting death. Only then did I begin to realize how great a sinner I was, whereas before I thought that my good life could save me.

After the partition of India in 1947, Qamar moved with her family to Karachi. She wrote to one of the teachers in her school at Madras to tell her the news of her move, and this teacher contacted a missionary in Karachi, Marian Laugesen. Laugesen managed to find Qamar amidst the thousands of newly arrived Muslims from India living in hastily erected barracks-like buildings on the outskirts of the city. Qamar was obviously well aware of the serious implications of her conversion, for she had concealed it from her family.

For the next seven years, Qamar had no contact with any Christians, but continued to read her New Testament secretly. Then her parents began to take steps to arrange a marriage for her; naturally, the chosen man would be a Muslim. On 18 June 1955 she ran away from home and sought out Marian Laugesen. It was arranged that Qamar would stay at the orphanage where Marian was working, and it was at this time that Laugesen gave her the name Esther John.

A culture in which a wife submits absolutely to her husband, and normally lives with her parents-in-law to whom both she and her husband must submit, would have made it quite impossible for her to live as a Christian if she was married to a Muslim. Thus it was that at the end of June she left to travel north several hundred miles to Sahiwal in the Punjab – a safe distance, it was hoped, from her family in Karachi. There, in a mission hospital, she played a full part in its life, and was delighted to be able to do the simplest service for others or to be able to share her faith. Later that year she was baptized.

During the latter months of 1959 she was put under severe pressure by her family to return home. Eventually she agreed to visit them, provided she should be allowed to live as a Christian, and secondly, that she should not be forced into a marriage against her will. No answer came.

On the morning of 2 February 1960 Esther was found dead in her bed, her skull smashed twice with a heavy, sharp instrument so forcefully that it probably killed her instantly. Her murderer was never found or identified, and her death remains mysterious.

If her death seems to human reckoning pointless and useless, her life certainly bore fruit in the example of her courage, commitment, self-sacrifice, faith, gentleness and love, and the joy which she brought to so many who knew her.

15 October

Teresa of Avila

Religious, Teacher of the Faith, 1582

Teresa was born into an aristocratic Spanish family in 1515. Following her mother's death, she was educated by Augustinian nuns and then ran away from home to enter a Carmelite convent when she was twenty-one. After initial difficulties in prayer, her intense mystical experiences attracted many disciples. She was inspired to reform the Carmelite rule and, assisted by Saint John of the Cross, she travelled throughout Spain founding many new religious houses for men as well as women. Her writings about her own spiritual life and progress in prayer towards union with God include The Way of Perfection and The Interior Castle, which are still acclaimed. She knew great physical suffering and died of exhaustion on 4 October 1582. Her feast is observed on 15 October because the very day after her death the reformed calendar was adopted and eleven days were omitted from October that year.

A Reading from *The Way of Perfection* by Teresa of Avila

It seems very easy to say that we will surrender our will to someone, until we try it and realise that it is the hardest thing we can do if we carry it out as we should. The Lord knows what each of us can bear, and, when he sees that one of us is strong, he does not hesitate to fulfil his will in him.

Do not fear that he will give you riches or pleasures or honours or any such earthly things; his love for you is not so poor as that. And he sets a very high value on what you can give him and desires to recompense you for it since he gives you his kingdom while you are still alive. Would you like to see how he treats those who make the prayer 'Your will be done' from their hearts? Ask his glorious Son, who made it thus in the Garden. Think with what resolution and fullness of desire he prayed; and consider if the will of God was not perfectly fulfilled in him through the trials, sufferings, insults and persecutions which he gave him until at last his life ended with death on a cross.

So you see what God gave to his best beloved, and from this you can understand what his will is. These, then, are his gifts in this world. He gives them in proportion to the love which he bears us. He gives more to those whom he loves most, and less to those he loves least; and he gives in accordance with the courage which he sees that each of us has and the love we bear to his majesty. When he sees a soul who loves him greatly, he knows that soul can suffer much for him, whereas one who loves him little will suffer little. For my own part, I believe that love is the measure of our ability to bear crosses, whether great or small. So if you have this love, try not to let the prayers you make to so great a Lord be words of mere politeness, but brace yourselves to suffer what his majesty desires. For if you give him your will in any other way, you are just showing him a jewel, making as if to give it to him and begging him to take it, and then, when he puts out his hand to do so, taking it back and holding on to it tightly.

Such mockery is no fit treatment for One who endured so much for us. If for no other reason than this, it would not be right to mock him so often — and it is by no means seldom that we say these words to him in the 'Our Father'. Let us give him once and for all the jewel which we have so often undertaken to give him. For the truth is that he gives it to us first so that we may give it back to him.

Unless we make a total surrender of our will to the Lord, so that he may do in all things what is best for us in accordance with his will, he will never allow us to drink of the fountain of living water.

alternative reading

A Reading from *Teresa of Avila* by Shirley du Boulay

They say in Spain that to understand Saint Teresa one must look at Castile. Its windswept plains, its granite boulders, its bitter winters and sun-scorched summers were the womb that nourished the 'undaunted daughter of desires' of Richard Crashaw's poem. A gentler landscape would not have produced a woman of such courage and determination.

Teresa entered the Convent of the Incarnation at Avila in 1536 when she was twenty-one years old. Life in the Convent was largely uneventful. Apart from the social life of the parlour, meals and recreational periods, most of the day was spent in church. It was a demanding day and, many would say, a boring routine, though Teresa never complained or even referred to it.

Though Teresa was, for the most part, able to appear calm, even cheerful, beneath the surface she lived in torment. Her writings show clearly that her inner life was deeply troubled and difficult. In fact she describes the first twenty years at the Convent of the Incarnation as a time when she constantly failed God and was buffeted on 'that stormy sea, often falling in this way, each time rising again, but to little purpose, as I would only fall once more'.

She was generous and scrupulously honest in her writing, and it is this first-hand knowledge of her inner life, particularly during this period, which enables us to identify with her as a fellow human being and as a woman. She experienced spiritual apathy, aridity in prayer and a sense of failure common to so many. Had we only known her as the recipient of extraordinary experiences, as a mystic as gifted in prayer as was Rembrandt in art, Beethoven in music or Shakespeare in literature, we would not be able to identify with her so closely, nor would she have touched so many lives.

The stormy sea on which she was tossed was not only the sea of prayer, fraught with problems and highlighting her sense of sin, but also of her richly complex personality. In her, to a rare extent, the opposites met, fought out their various differences and were eventually reconciled. Though part of Teresa's appeal is the extent to which she was in many ways such an ordinary woman, loving and longing to be loved, motherly, practical and skilled in the feminine arts around the house, blessed with down-to-earth common sense, she also had the independence of mind, efficiency and capability in those days normally associated with men.

The contradictions in her nature ranged across all human characteristics; she epitomised the conflicts that tear many apart. Delighting in human relationships she yearned to abandon herself solely to God; commending poverty, she was fastidious; loving and gregarious, she needed solitude; concerned with the things of God, her upbringing would never let her forget worldly etiquette and honour; and wanting nothing more than to be alone with God, she knew she had practical tasks on earth. She knew that virtues have their corresponding vices, and her own moods vacillated between joy and torment. The conflict which obsessed her for twenty years was that she was torn between God and the world.

Anyone who has ever tried to pray will have experienced difficulties; yet there tends to be an unspoken assumption that for saints and mystics prayer is easy. The open and totally honest way in which Teresa admits to her own problems in prayer is one of her most valuable legacies; that she, too, found prayer difficult is not only endearing but also immensely reassuring. She writes of her trials:

> Over a period of several years, I was more occupied in wishing my hour of prayer were over, and in listening whenever the clock struck, than in thinking of things that were good. Again and again I would rather have done any severe penance that might have been given me than practise recollection as a preliminary to prayer. Whenever I entered the oratory I used to feel so depressed that I had to summon up all my courage to make myself pray at all.

She felt imprisoned and alone, unable to believe her confessors, who treated so lightly the shortcomings in her prayer life which she knew, in her heart, were a failure in her obligation to God. But one of the ways in which she is set apart from most people is in the courage and determination with which she persevered; she battled and fought against her problems in prayer as fiercely as any soldier fights his enemy. Through her twenties and thirties she endured boredom, aridity, frustration, disappointment and an acute sense of failure. This period, too often glossed over, was the soil from which the flower of her mysticism was to grow. It should never be forgotten that it lasted from her noviciate until she was about forty years old.

16 October

Gall

Hermit and Missionary, 630

Gall came from Bangor in County Down to be trained in the monastery there by Comgall. He set off for Europe as a missionary with Columbanus and others in 589. Although he did not found the St Gall monastery in Switzerland which bears his name, it stands as a famous reminder of his Christian evangelizing, his gentle life of holiness having made a deep impression both in France and Switzerland. He died on this day in the year 630.

A Reading from *The Life of Saint Gall* by Walahfrid Strabo

The monks were eager to be on their way, so the priest got ready a small vessel and manned it with rowers. Columbanus, the venerable abbot, taking with him Gall and a deacon, embarked after calling upon the name of the Lord in prayer, and steered a straight course for the spot. On landing, they made their way to an oratory which had been dedicated to Saint Aurelia, and was soon restored by Saint Columbanus to its pristine honour.

After engaging in prayer, they surveyed their surroundings and were well pleased with the situation and aspect of the place. In the oratory, however, they found three gilt bronze figures attached to the wall; for the people had forsaken the sacred rites of God's altar and used to worship these images instead, saying, as they offered their sacrifices, 'These are the old gods, the former guardians of this place, and it is by their aid that we and ours have been kept alive to this day.'

Columbanus laid on Gall the duty of preaching to the people and calling them back from the errors of idolatry to the worship of God; for Gall had received this favour from the Lord, that he had no small knowledge of the native idiom as well as of Latin. It was just then time for holding a festival in the temple, and a large crowd of men and women of all ages assembled, desiring not only to celebrate the festival but to see the strangers of whose arrival they had heard. When therefore all were gathered together at the hour of prayer, Gall, in obedience to his abbot's command, began to show to the people the way of truth and to exhort them to turn to the Lord, to cast aside vain superstitions and worship God the Father, the Creator of all things, and his only begotten Son in whom is salvation, life and the resurrection of the dead. And laying hold of the images in the sight of them all, he broke them into pieces with stones and threw them into the lake.

When the people saw this, some of them were converted and confessed their sins, giving glory to God for having enlightened them; others were moved to wrath by the breaking of the images and departed, swelling with rage and resentment. But Columbanus bade water be brought and having blessed it, he sprinkled the area and dedicated it anew as a church, the monks meanwhile going round it in procession and chanting psalms. Then, after calling on the name of the Lord, he anointed the altar, placed within it the relics of Saint Aurelia and laid upon it an altar-cloth, after which he celebrated mass in due order. When all these holy rites had been performed, the people returned to their homes rejoicing.

Saint Columbanus and his fellow-soldiers stayed in this place for three years and built a small monastery there, where some of them laid out a garden and others cultivated fruit trees. Saint Gall used to weave nets and by the mercy of God he caught such quantities of fish that the brethren were never in any want. Indeed, he was able to provide for any strangers who chanced to come and bestowed many a blessing on the people by his toil.

16 October

Nicholas Ridley and Hugh Latimer

Bishop of London, Bishop of Worcester Reformation Martyrs, 1555

Note: In Wales, Nicholas Ridley and Hugh Latimer are commemorated jointly with Thomas Cranmer and Robert Ferrar on 21 March.

Born into a wealthy Northumbrian family in about the year 1500, Nicholas Ridley studied at Cambridge, the Sorbonne and in Louvain. He was Chaplain to Thomas Cranmer and Master of Pembroke Hall in Cambridge before being made Bishop of Rochester in 1547. He had been clearly drawing closer to the Reformers as early as 1535 and, at the accession of King Edward VI, declared himself a Protestant. He assisted Cranmer in preparing the first Book of Common Prayer and was made Bishop of London in 1550. On the death of Edward, he supported the claims of Lady Jane Grey and was thus deprived of his See on the accession of Mary Tudor. He was excommunicated and executed in 1555.

Hugh Latimer was a Leicestershire man, also educated at Cambridge but fifteen years older than Nicholas Ridley. Hugh was articulate and yet homely in his style of preaching, which made him very popular in the university, and he received its commission to preach anywhere in England. He became a close adviser of King Henry VIII after the latter's rift with the papacy and was appointed Bishop of Worcester in 1535. He lost the king's favour in 1540, over his refusal to sign Henry's 'Six Articles', designed to prevent the spread of Reformation doctrines, and resigned his See. He returned to favour on the accession of Edward VI but was imprisoned in the Tower of London when Queen Mary ascended the throne in 1553. He refused to recant any of his avowedly reformist views and was burnt at the stake, together with Nicholas Ridley, on this day in the year 1555.

A Reading from a letter of Nicholas Ridley to John Hooper, Bishop of Gloucester, written from prison on 18 January 1555

My dearly beloved brother and fellow Elder, whom I reverence in the Lord, pardon me, I beseech you, that hitherto, since your captivity and mine, I have not saluted you by my letters; whereas, I do indeed confess, I have received from you (such was your gentleness) two letters at sundry times, but yet at such times as I could not be suffered to write unto you again; or, if I might have written, yet was I greatly in doubt lest my letters should not safely come unto your hands. But now, my dear brother, forasmuch as I understand by your works, which I have yet but superficially seen, that we thoroughly agree and wholly consent together in those things which are the grounds and substantial points of our religion, against the which the world so furiously rageth in these days, howsoever in time past in smaller matters and circumstances of religion your wisdom and my simplicity (I confess) have in some points varied; now, I say, be you assured, that even with my whole heart (God is my witness) in the bowels of Christ, I love you, and in truth, for the truth's sake which abideth in us, and (as I am persuaded) shall by the grace of God abide with us for evermore.

And because the world, as I perceive, brother, ceaseth not to play his pageant, and busily conspireth against Christ our Saviour with all possible force and power, exalting high things against the knowledge of God, let us join hands together in Christ; and if we cannot overthrow, yet to our power, and as much as in us lieth, let us shake those high things, not with carnal, but with spiritual weapons; and withal, brother, let us prepare ourselves to the day of our dissolution; whereby after the short time of this bodily affliction, by the grace of our Lord Jesus Christ, we shall triumph together with him in eternal glory.

alternative reading

A Reading from a sermon of Hugh Latimer, preached at Cambridge in 1529

Evermore bestow the greatest part of your goods in works of mercy, and the less part in voluntary works. Voluntary works be called all manner of offering in the church, except your four offering-days, and your tithes: setting up candles, gilding and painting, building of churches, giving of ornaments, going on pilgrimages, making of highways, and such other, be called voluntary works; which works be of themselves marvellous good, and convenient to be done.

Necessary works, and works of mercy, are called the commandments, the four offering-days, your tithes, and such other that belong to the commandments; and works of mercy consist in relieving and visiting your poor neighbours. Now then, if men be so foolish of themselves, that they will bestow the most part of their goods in voluntary works, which they be not bound to keep, but willingly and by their devotion; and leave the necessary works undone, which they are bound to do; they and all their voluntary works are like to go unto everlasting damnation. And I promise you, if you build a hundred churches, give as much as you can make to gilding of saints, and honouring of the church; and if thou go as many pilgrimages as your body can well suffer, and offer as great candles as oaks; if you leave the works of mercy and the commandments undone, these works shall nothing avail you.

No doubt the voluntary works be good and ought to be done; but yet they must be so done, that by their occasion the necessary works and the works of mercy be not decayed and forgotten. If you will build a glorious church unto God, see first yourselves to be in charity with your neighbours, and suffer not them to be offended by your works. Then, when ye come into your parish church, you bring with you the holy temple of God; as Saint Paul saith, 'You yourselves be the very holy temples of God,' and Christ saith by his prophet, 'In you will I rest, and intend to make my mansion and abiding-place.'

Again, if you list to gild and paint Christ in your churches, and honour him in vestments, see that before your eyes the poor people die not for lack of meat, drink, and clothing. Then do you deck the very true temple of God, and honour him in rich vestures that will never be worn, and so forth use yourselves according unto the commandments: and then, finally, set up candles, and they will report what a glorious light remaineth in your hearts; for it is not fitting to see a dead man light candles. Then, I say, go your pilgrimages, build your material churches, do all your voluntary works; and they will then represent you unto God, and testify with you, that you have provided him a glorious place in your hearts.

16 October

Daniel Rowland

Priest and Preacher, 1790

The son of a Cardiganshire clergyman, Daniel Rowland was born at Nantcwnlle in 1713. He was probably educated at Hereford Grammar School before becoming his brother's curate at Llangeitho. Rowland was profoundly influenced by Griffith Jones. In 1735, after the Welsh Methodist revival began in Llangeitho during a service of the Litany, Rowland started preaching and administering communion outside his parish, often using remote and neglected chapels-of-ease. For a time he and Howell Harris worked closely together. As Rowland's reputation grew, thousands travelled to Llangeitho to hear him and to receive the sacrament from him. In 1763, during a rekindling of the revival, Rowland was deprived of his curacy. He set up a 'New Church' where he held services until his death in 1790. He was buried in Llangeitho Parish Church, of which his son had become rector. Rowland's deprivation by the Church authorities was probably the most disastrous mistake in the history of Welsh Anglicanism.

A Reading from *The Welsh and their Religion* by Glanmor Williams

The letters and diaries of the great Methodist revivalists reveal how much store they set by preaching. Preaching was for them the bellows through which the divine wind of heaven was blown to raise the emotional temperature of their hearers. Only in the volcanic heat created by inspired pulpit oratory could the stubborn heart be melted by those overpowering emotions of guilt, fear, shame, anguish, hope, joy, and certainty, and so surrender itself to the great decision. Only thus could it come to learn that 'heart knowledge' of divine grace, which the Methodists invariably set at the opposite pole to cold and empty 'head knowledge'. The power and efficacy of their preaching were beyond question; there are countless contemporary accounts of the resounding shock it administered to the emotions. One of the most celebrated and succinct of them is Pantycelyn's characterization of the preaching of Daniel Rowland, arguably the most soul-stirring of all the Methodist pulpit orators:

Llais yr udgorn a llef geiriau,
Tarth a thymest', mwg a thân…
Gliniau'n crynu gan y daran,
Fel pe buasai angau ei hun
Wedi cymryd llawn berch'nogaeth
Ar y dyrfa bob yr un.
'Beth a wnawn am safio'n henaid?'
Oedd yr unrhyw *gydsain* lef;
Chwi sy am wybod hanes *Daniel,*
Dyna fel dechreuodd ef.

('Voice of the trumpet and torrent of words, fog and tempest, smoke and fire;… knees trembling at the thunder as though death itself had taken full possession of every one of the congregation. "What shall we do to save our souls?" came the single cry *in unison.* You who wish to know of *Daniel's* history, that is how he began.')

Little wonder that the revivalists pinned so much faith on their preaching, which as often as not was itinerant, open-air evangelism. Faced with large and attentive crowds, freed from the constraints imposed by set services and cramped buildings, uplifted by the divine afflatus that swelled out of the secure assurance of their own salvation, they were able to pull out all the stops in the triumphant *crescendi* of their appeals to their hearers' hopes and fears. We need hardly be surprised at their own certainty that at these moments God sounded his trumpet through them.

17 October

Ignatius of Antioch

Bishop and Martyr, *c.*107

Ignatius was born probably in Syria in about the year 35 and was either the second or third Bishop of Antioch, the third largest city in the Roman Empire. Nothing is known of his life bar his final journey under armed escort to Rome, and where he was martyred in about the year 107. In the course of this journey, he met Polycarp in Smyrna, and wrote a number of letters to various Christian congregations which are among the greatest treasures of the primitive Church. In the face of persecution he appealed to his fellow Christians to maintain unity with their bishop at all costs. His letters reveal his passionate commitment to Christ, and how he longed 'to imitate the passion of my God'.

A Reading from a letter of Ignatius of Antioch to the Church in Rome as he prepared for his forthcoming death

My prayer that I might live to see you all face to face has been granted. In fact, I have been given more than I asked for, since I now hope to greet you in the chains of a prisoner of Christ Jesus, if his will finds me worthy to reach my journey's end.

One thing only I beg of you: allow me to be a libation poured out to God, while there is still an altar ready for me. Then you can form a choir of love around it and sing hymns of praise to the Father in Christ Jesus for allowing Syria's bishop, summoned from the realms of the rising sun, to have reached the land of its setting. How good it is to be sinking down below the world's horizon towards God that I may rise again into the dawn of his presence!

I am writing to all the churches and assuring them that I am truly in earnest about dying for God, provided you put no obstacles in the way. I beg you to do me no such untimely kindness. Let me be a meal for the beasts, for it is they who can provide my way to God. I am God's wheat, to be ground fine by the teeth of lions so that I become the purest bread for Christ. Intercede with him on my behalf, that by their instrumentality I may be made a sacrifice to God.

All the ends of the earth and all the kingdoms of this world would profit me nothing. As far as I am concerned, to die in Christ Jesus is better than to be king of earth's widest bounds. I seek only him who for our sake died; my whole desire is for him who rose again for us. The pangs of birth are upon me. Have patience with me, my brothers and sisters, and do not shut me out from life, do not wish me to be stillborn. Do not make a present to the world again of one who longs only to be God's; do not try to deceive him with material things. Allow me rather to attain to light, light pure and undefiled; for only when I am come to the light shall I become truly human. Allow me to imitate the passion of my God. If any of you have God within you, let them understand my longings and sympathise with me, because they will know the forces by which I am constrained.

It is the hope of the prince of this world to get hold of me and undermine my resolve, set as it is upon God. Let none of you lend him any assistance, but take my part instead, for indeed it is the part of God. Do not have Jesus Christ on your lips, and the world in your heart; do not cherish thoughts of grudging me my fate. Even if I were to come and beg you in person, do not yield to my pleading; keep your mind focused on this written resolve. Here and now, as I write in the fullness of life, I am longing for death with all the passion of a lover. Earthly longings have been crucified; there is no spark of desire for mundane things left within me, but only a murmur of living water that whispers within me, 'Come to the Father.'

18 October

Luke

Evangelist

Luke was a dear friend of the Apostle Paul, and is mentioned by him three times in his Letters. Paul describes him as 'the belovèd physician' and, in his Second Letter to Timothy, as his only companion in prison. He is believed to be the author of the Gospel which bears his name, and that of the Acts of the Apostles. Luke's narrative of the life of Christ has a pictorial quality and shows the sequential pattern from the nativity through to the death and resurrection. The developed sense of theology that comes over in Paul's writings is virtually unknown in those of Luke but, as a Gentile, Luke makes clear that the good news of salvation is for all, regardless of gender, social position or nationality. Traditionally, Luke is said to have written his Gospel in Greece and to have died in Boeotia at the age of eighty-four.

A Reading from a homily of Gregory the Great

Our Lord and Saviour teaches us sometimes through what he says, and sometimes through what he does. For his deeds are teachings in themselves, because when he does something, even without commenting on it, he is showing us what we ought to do. For example, according to Luke, he sent out his disciples to preach in pairs, because the precepts of charity are two-fold: to love God and to love our neighbour. Charity cannot exist except between two persons: love is only possible when we reach out to another.

Our Lord sent out his disciples to preach in pairs, thereby implying that someone who has no love for people should never take on the task of preaching. Very significant too is the statement that he 'sent them ahead of him into every city and place where he himself was to come'. For our Lord follows in the wake of those who preach him. Preaching paves the way, and then our Lord himself comes to make his home in our souls. Initially we hear words to challenge us, and through their agency our minds become receptive to the truth. It was for this reason that through the mouth of Isaiah preachers are commanded to: 'Prepare the way of the Lord; make straight in the desert the paths of our God.'

But now listen to what our Lord has to say after sending out those who are to preach: 'The harvest is plentiful but the labourers are few. Pray therefore the Lord of the harvest to send out labourers into his harvest.' There are only a few labourers for so huge a harvest, something we cannot mention without sadness, because, although there are many who crave to hear the good news, there are few to preach it. The world is full of priests, and yet it is rare that you find one of them at work in God's harvest. We accept the role, but refuse the hard work.

But as for you, my dear brothers and sisters, ponder well the Lord's command. Pray indeed the Lord of the harvest to send out labourers into his harvest. And pray for us that we may be able to serve you as you deserve, that our tongue may never grow tired of exhorting you, lest having undertaken this office of preaching, our silence condemn us in the sight of our just judge.

19 October

Frideswide

Abbess of Oxford, 727

Born in about the year 680, Frideswide was the daughter of a Mercian king who built and endowed a double monastery of which she became the first abbess. She was buried in her monastery, which became the nucleus of the nascent town of Oxford. Her cult was strengthened by her being formally adopted as the patron of Oxford University in the early fifteenth century. However, in the sixteenth century, Cardinal Wolsey suppressed Frideswide's monastery to provide revenues for his Cardinal College (now Christ Church), built on the same site. More recently, part of the shrine has been reconstructed from remains discovered in a well at Christ Church, a reminder of the abbess around whose monastery grew the city and University of Oxford.

A Reading from the *De Gestis Pontificum Anglorum*
by William of Malmesbury

There was of old in the city of Oxford a monastery of nuns, in which rests the most holy virgin Frideswide. The daughter of a king, she spurned the marriage-bed of a king, dedicating her entire person to the Lord Christ. But when her intended had applied himself rigorously to wooing the virgin, having spent his prayers and blandishments in vain, he planned to carry her off by force. When Frideswide heard of this, she decided to flee into the woods. But neither could this hiding place keep her hidden from her suitor, nor could her coldness of heart deter him, for she who fled was pursued.

When the young man's madness became plain, the virgin went further on through secret paths, protected by God, and entered Oxford at dead of night. But by morning her persistent lover had hurried there too, and the girl began to despair of escape; too tired to go any further, she prayed to God to protect her and to punish her persecutor.

When he and his companions entered the city gate, a blow sent from heaven struck him and he became blind. Realising then the sinfulness of his persistence, he sent messengers to beg Frideswide to pray for him, and with the same suddenness with which he had lost his sight he received it again. Hence the kings of England have been afraid to enter that town and stay there because they think it is unfavourable to them and they have all shrunk from putting this to the test.

So there in Oxford, the woman, secure in the victory of her virginity, founded a monastery and ended her days there, obedient to her eternal Bridegroom's call.

19 October

Henry Martyn

Translator of the Scriptures, Missionary in India & Persia, 1812

Born in Truro in 1781, Henry Martyn went up to Cambridge at the age of sixteen. He became an avowed Evangelical and his friendship with Charles Simeon led to his interest in missionary work. In 1805, he left for Calcutta as a chaplain to the East India Company. The expectation was that he would minister to the British expatriate community, not to the indigenous peoples; in fact, there was a constant fear of insurrection and even the recitation of the Magnificat at Evensong was forbidden, lest 'putting down the mighty from their seats' should incite the natives. Henry set about learning the local languages and then supervised the translation of the New Testament first into Hindustani and then into Persian and Arabic, as well as preaching and teaching in mission schools. He went to Persia to continue the work but, suffering from tuberculosis, he died in Armenia on this day in the year 1812.

A Reading from the *Indian Journal* of Henry Martyn

1 January 1807 — Dinapore
Seven years have passed away since I was first called of God. Before the conclusion of another seven years, how probable is it that these hands will have mouldered into dust! But be it so: my soul through grace hath received the assurance of eternal life, and I see the days of my pilgrimage shortening without a wish to add to their number. But oh, may I be stirred up to a faithful discharge of my high and awful work; and laying aside as much as may be, because the Lord has brought me safely to India and permitted me to begin, in one sense, my missionary work.

My trials in it have been very few; everything has turned out better than I expected; loving-kindness and tender-mercies have attended me at every step: therefore here will I sing his praise. I have been an unprofitable servant, but the Lord hath not cut me off: I have been wayward and perverse, yet he has brought me further on the way to Zion. Here, then, with sevenfold gratitude and affection would I stop and devote myself to the blissful service of my adorable Lord. May he continue his patience, his grace, his direction, his spiritual influences, and I shall at last surely come off conqueror! May he speedily open my mouth, to make known the mysteries of the gospel, and in great mercy grant that the heathen may receive it and live.

18 February — Buxar
My birthday – twenty-six. With all the numerous occasions for deep humiliation, I have cause for praise in recollecting the promising openings and important changes which have occurred since my last birthday. The Lord, in love, makes me wax stronger and stronger.

Walked after breakfast to a pagoda within the fort at Buxar where a Brahmin read and expounded. It was a scene, I suppose, descriptive of the ancient times of Hindu glory. The Brahmin sat under the shade of a large banyan tree near the pagoda; his hair and beard were white, and his head most gracefully crowned with a garland of flowers. A servant of the Rajah sat on his right hand, at right angles; and the venerable man then sung the Sanskrit verses of the Huribuns, and explained them to him without turning his head, but only his eyes, which had a very dignified effect. I waited for the first pause to ask some questions, which led to a long conversation; and this ended by my attempting to give them a history of redemption. The Rajah's servant was a very modest, pensive man, but did not seem to understand what I said so well as did the old Brahmin who expressed his surprise and pleasure, as well as the other, at finding a Sahib who cared anything about religion. I afterwards sent a copy of the Nagree Gospels to the servant, desiring that it might be given to the Rajah if he would accept it.

I rose at four and left Buxar, and at nine in the evening reached Dinapore again in safety, blessed be God! May my life, thus preserved by God's unceasing providence, be his willing sacrifice.

23 October

James of Jerusalem

Brother of Our Lord, Bishop and Martyr, *c.*62

James, 'the Lord's brother', was a leader of the Church in Jerusalem from a very early date, and is regarded as its first bishop. Though not one of the Twelve, Paul includes James among those to whom the risen Lord appeared before the ascension, and records that James received him cordially when he visited Jerusalem after his conversion. He was regarded as the leader of the Jewish community when the Church expanded to embrace Gentiles, and was successful in bringing many of his fellow Jews to faith in Christ.

He presided at the Council of Jerusalem. He is understood to have been stoned to death around the year 62.

A Reading from *Antiquities of the Jews* by Josephus

The younger Annas, who, as we have already said, assumed the High Priesthood, was an aggressive man in temperament and very insolent. He was a member of the sect of the Sadducees, who are very rigid when it comes to judging offenders amongst the Jews, as we have already had cause to observe. When therefore Annas came to office he thought he had a good opportunity to exercise his authority. Festus was now dead, and Albinus was still on the road [and yet to arrive in Jerusalem]. So Annas assembled the Sanhedrin of judges, and brought before them the brother of Jesus who was called Christ, whose name was James, together with some others. He accused them of being transgressors of the law, and condemned them to be stoned to death.

But those citizens who were of a more equitable disposition, and scrupulous in legal matters, disliked this action. They appealed to King Agrippa, asking him to order Annas to stop acting in this fashion; for they felt that his actions were not justified. Indeed, some of them went to meet Albinus on the road as he travelled from Alexandria, and informed him that it was not lawful for Annas to assemble the Sanhedrin without his consent. Albinus was persuaded by what they said, and wrote in anger to Annas, threatening to punish him for what he had done. It was on account of this that King Agrippa removed the High Priesthood from Annas when he had ruled barely three months, and appointed Jesus son of Damneus High Priest in his place.

25 October

Crispin and Crispinian

Martyrs at Rome, *c.*287

Crispin and Crispinian were shoemakers and lived in the third century. They are reputed to have preached the Christian faith in Gaul whilst exercising their trade and so, like Saint Paul earning his living as a tent-maker, were no drain on the Christian community. They were put to death for their faith at the beginning of the Diocletian persecution and died in about the year 287 in Rome.

A Reading from an *Exhortation to Martyrdom* by Origen

If we have passed from death to life by our transition from unbelief to faith, we should not be surprised if the world hates us. For no one who has not passed from death to life, but remains in death, can love those who have passed from this dark house of death, as it could be called, to a building flooded by the light of life, built with living stones. Jesus laid down his life for us, and we should lay down ours: I do not say for his sake, but for ourselves; or rather, I suppose, for those who are going to be built up by our martyrdom.

Christians, the time has come for us to boast. For we read in Scripture: 'This is not all we can boast about; we can boast about our sufferings. For sufferings bring patience, as we know, and patience brings perseverance, and perseverance brings hope, and this hope does not deceive us; only let the love of God be poured into our hearts by the Holy Spirit.'

If, [as Scripture elsewhere says] 'just as the sufferings of Christ are abundant for us, so also our consolation through Christ is abundant', then let us accept Christ's sufferings gladly. Indeed, let us share in them abundantly, if we are wanting to receive his abundant consolation. For this is what those who mourn will receive, although perhaps not in equal measure.

God said through his prophet Isaiah: 'In a time of favour I have answered you, on a day of salvation I have helped you.' What could be a more favourable time than the day when for our faith in Christ we are led off under guard, paraded before the world. The triumph is ours rather than theirs! For Christian martyrs in the company of Christ have completely overcome the principalities and powers, and join in his triumph. As they share his sufferings, so they also share in the benefits of his sufferings. They share in the victories he won by his courage in suffering. What other day of salvation is there than the day we depart this world in such a way?

Behold, the Lord is here with his reward in his hand, ready to render to each of us according to our works.

25 October

Lewis Bayley

Bishop and Writer, 1631

Lewis Bayley was born in 1565 and was a native of Carmarthen. Educated at Exeter College, Oxford, he received several church preferments in England and Wales before becoming Treasurer of St Paul's Cathedral and Chaplain to James I. In 1616 Bayley was appointed Bishop of Bangor, remaining there till his death in 1631. His episcopate was marred by his inept handling of Church and State politics, which led to a brief spell in the Fleet Prison in 1621. Bayley's devotional manual, The Practice of Piety *appeared in 1611 and is said to have been based on a series of sermons that he had given while Vicar of Evesham. By 1842 it had gone through eighty English editions, and had been translated into several languages. The Welsh version was published in 1630 and reprinted five times in a hundred years. Among those who were strongly influenced by Bayley's book were John Bunyan and Howell Harris.*

A Reading from *The Practice of Piety* by Lewis Bayley

When prayers begin, lay aside thy own private meditations, and let thy heart join with the minister and the whole Church, as being one body of Christ, and because that God is the God of order, he will have all things done in the Church with one heart and accord, and the exercises of the Church are common and public. It is therefore an ignorant pride, for a man to think his own private prayers more effectual than the public prayers of the whole Church. Solomon therefore advises a man not to be rash to utter a thing in the Church before God. Pray, therefore, when the Church prayeth, sing when they sing; and in the action of kneeling, standing, sitting, and such indifferent ceremonies (for the avoiding of scandal, the continuance of charity, and in testimony of thine obedience), conform thyself to the manner of the Church wherein thou livest.

Whilst the preacher is expounding and applying the word of the Lord, look upon him; for it is a great help to stir up thine attention, and to keep thee from wandering thoughts; so the eyes of all that were in the synagogue are said to have been fastened on Christ whilst he preached, and that all the people hanged upon him when they heard him. Remember that thou art there as one of Christ's disciples, to learn the knowledge of salvation, by the remission of sins, through the tender mercy of God.

Be not, therefore, in the school of Christ, like an idle boy in a grammar school, that often hears, but never learns his lesson; and still goes to school, but profiteth nothing. Thou hatest it in a child, and Christ detesteth it in thee.

26 October

Alfred the Great

King of the West Saxons, Scholar, 899

Born in the year 849, Alfred was the King of the West Saxons who effectively brought to an end the constant threat of Danish dominion in the British Isles. He came to the throne at the age of twenty-two and, after establishing peace, set about bringing stability to both Church and State. He gave half of his income to founding religious houses which themselves acted as Christian centres for education, care of the sick and poor and respite for travellers. He was a daily attender at Mass and himself translated many works into the vernacular, an example of which is offered as a reading here. He evolved a legal code based on common sense and Christian mercy. His whole life was marked by the compassion of Christ. He died on this day in the year 899.

A Reading from the *Prose Preface* from King Alfred's translation of Gregory the Great's Pastoral Care

I would have it known that very often it has come to my mind what men of learning there were formerly throughout England; both in religious and secular orders; and how there were happy times then throughout England; and how the kings, who had authority over this people, obeyed God and his messengers; and how they not only maintained their peace, morality and authority at home but also extended their territory outside; and how they succeeded both in warfare and in wisdom; and also how eager were the religious orders both in teaching and in learning as well as in all the holy services which it was their duty to perform for God; and how people from abroad sought wisdom and instruction in this country; and how nowadays, if we wished to acquire these things, we would have to seek them outside.

Learning had declined so thoroughly in England that there were very few on this side of the Humber who could understand their divine services in English, or even translate a single letter from Latin into English: and I suppose that there were not many beyond the Humber either. There were so few of them that I cannot recollect even a single one south of the Thames when I succeeded to the kingdom. Thanks be to God almighty that we now have any supply of teachers at all! Therefore I beseech you to do as I believe you are willing to do: as often as you can, free yourself from worldly affairs so that you may apply that wisdom which God gave you wherever you can. Remember what punishments befell us in this world when we ourselves did not cherish learning nor transmit it to others. We were Christians in name alone, and very few of us possessed Christian virtues.

When I reflected on all this, I recollected how – before everything was ransacked and burned – the churches throughout England stood filled with treasures and books. Similarly, there was a great multitude of those serving God. And they derived very little benefit from those books, because they could understand nothing of them, since they were not written in their own language. It is as if they had said: 'Our ancestors, who formerly maintained these places, loved wisdom, and through it they obtained wealth and passed it on to us. Here one can still see their track, but we cannot follow it.' Therefore we have now lost the wealth as well as the wisdom, because we did not wish to set our minds to the track.

Therefore it seems better to me that we too should turn into the language that we can all understand certain books which are the most necessary for all to know, and accomplish this, as with God's help we may very easily do provided we have peace enough, so that all the free-born young men now in England who have the means to apply themselves to it, may be set to learning (as long as they are not useful for some other employment) until the time that they can read English writings properly. Thereafter one may instruct in Latin those whom one wishes to teach further and wishes to advance to holy orders.

alternative reading

A Reading from *The Life of King Alfred* by Bishop Asser

In the year of the Lord's Incarnation 849 Alfred, King of the Anglo-Saxons, was born at the royal estate called Wantage, in the district known as Berkshire. In 853 King Ethelwulf sent his son Alfred to Rome in state, accompanied by a great number of both nobles and commoners. At this time the lord Pope Leo was ruling the apostolic see; he anointed the child Alfred as king, ordaining him properly, received him as an adoptive son and confirmed him.

Now Alfred was greatly loved, more than all his brothers, by his father and mother – and indeed by everybody – with a universal and profound love, and he was always brought up in the royal court and nowhere else. In spite of all the demands of the present life, it was the desire for wisdom, more than anything else, together with the nobility of his birth, which characterised the nature of his noble mind; but alas, by the shameful negligence of his parents and tutors, Alfred remained ignorant of letters until his twelfth year, or even longer. However, he was a careful listener, by day and night, to English poems, most frequently hearing them recited by others, and he readily retained them in his memory.

He learnt by heart the 'daily round', that is, the services of the hours, and then certain psalms and prayers; these he collected in a single book, which he kept by him day and night, as I have seen for myself; amid all the affairs of the present life he took it around with him everywhere for the sake of prayer, and was inseparable from it. But alas, he could not satisfy his craving for what he desired the most, namely the liberal arts; for, as he used to say, there were no good scholars in the entire kingdom of the West Saxons at that time.

He used to affirm with repeated complaints and sighing from the depths of his heart, that among all the difficulties and burdens of his present life this had become the greatest: namely, that at the time when he was of the right age and had the leisure and the capacity for learning, he did not have the teachers. For when he was older, and more incessantly preoccupied day and night – or rather harassed – by all kinds illnesses unknown to the physicians of this island, as well as by the cures (both domestic and foreign) of the royal office, and also by the incursions of the Vikings by land and sea, he had the teachers and scribes to some extent, but he was unable to study.

He similarly applied himself attentively to charity and distribution of alms to the native population and to foreign visitors of all races, showing immense and incomparable kindness and generosity to all, as well as to the investigation of things unknown. Wherefore many Franks, Frisians, Gauls, Vikings, Welshmen, Irishmen and Bretons subjected themselves willingly to his lordship, nobles and commoners alike; and, as befitted his royal status, he ruled, loved, honoured and enriched them all with wealth and authority, just as he did his own people.

26 October

Cedd

Abbot of Lastingham, Bishop of the East Saxons, 664

Cedd was born in Northumbria in the late sixth century and joined the monastery of Lindisfarne where he served many years. When King Peada of the Middle Angles became a Christian, Cedd was sent with three other priests to preach the gospel in this new territory. Some time later, King Sigbert of the East Saxons was converted and Cedd, now an experienced missionary, went with another priest to Essex. After travelling through the region they reported back to Lindisfarne where Cedd was consecrated Bishop for the East Saxons. He returned to Essex to continue his work, building churches and two monasteries, and ordaining deacons and priests. While on a visit to Northumbria he founded his third monastery, at Lastingham, where he died of fever in the year 664 after attending the Synod of Whitby.

A Reading from *The History of the English Church and People* by the Venerable Bede

About this time, the East Saxons, who had rejected the faith and expelled Bishop Mellitus, once again accepted it under the influence of King Oswy of the Northumbrians. For Sigbert, their king, was a friend of King Oswy and often used to visit him. Having now become a citizen of the kingdom of heaven, Sigbert returned to London, the capital of his earthly kingdom, after asking Oswy to send him teachers to convert his people to the faith of Christ and to wash them in the fountain of salvation.

Accordingly, Oswy sent to the province of the Middle Angles and summoned the man of God, Cedd, whom he dispatched with another priest as companion to preach the Word to the East Saxons. When these priests had visited the entire province and established a strong Christian community, Cedd returned home to Lindisfarne for consultations with Bishop Finan. When the latter learned the great success of his preaching, he invited to Lindisfarne two other bishops to assist him, and consecrated Cedd bishop of the East Saxons. When Cedd had been raised to the dignity of bishop, he returned to the province and used his increased authority to promote the work he had already begun.

He established churches in several places and ordained priests and deacons to assist in teaching the word of faith and baptizing the people, especially in the city which the Saxons call Orthona and in the place called Tilbury. The former stands on the banks of the River Blackwater, the latter on the banks of the River Thames. Here Cedd established communities of the servants of Christ and taught them to maintain the discipline of a Rule so far as these untutored folk were then capable of doing.

When Cedd had been bishop in the province for many years and had borne the responsibility for the monastery at Lastingham, whose rules he had established according to the usage of Lindisfarne, he contracted the plague during a visit to the monastery, became ill and died. He was buried initially outside the walls of the monastery, but later when a stone church in honour of the blessed Mother of God was built, his body was re-buried in it on the right hand side of the altar. Cedd left the monastery in the care of his brother Chad who was later also to be consecrated a bishop. For there were four brothers, Cedd, Cynebill, Caelin and Chad, all famous priests of the Lord, itself a very rare occurrence, and two of the four became bishops.

27 October

Otteran

Abbot, 563

Otteran, an abbot from Meath, was one of the companions who sailed with Columba from Lough Foyle. Soon after landing on Iona, he died on this day in the year 563. His burial place, the Rèilig Odhrain, later became also the burial place for kings of Dalriada, Scotland and Norway. Scandinavian links with Iona explain the special place Otteran has as patron of the See of Waterford, which was founded by the Danes.

A Reading from part of an *Old Irish* poem concerning the life of prayer of a monk

On the Flightiness of Thought

Shame on my thoughts, how they stray from me!
I fear great danger from this on the Day of Judgement.

During the psalms they wander on a path that is not right:
they run, they distract,
they misbehave before the eyes of the great God.

One moment they follow ways of loveliness,
and the next ways of riotous shame – no lie!

Though one should try to bind them or put shackles on their feet,
they are neither constant nor inclined to rest a while.

Neither the edge of the sword nor the stripe of lash
will subdue them;
as slippery as an eel's tail they elude my grasp.

O beloved, truly chaste Christ,
to whom every eye is clear,
may the grace of the sevenfold Spirit come to keep them,
to hold them in check!

Rule this heart of mine, O swift God of the elements, that you
may be my love, and that I may do your will!

That I may reach Christ with his chosen companions, that we may be together: they are neither fickle nor inconstant: they are not as I am.

28 October

Simon and Jude

Apostles

Simon and Jude were named among the twelve apostles in the Gospels of Matthew, Mark and Luke. Simon is called 'the Zealot', probably because he belonged to a nationalist resistance movement opposing the Roman occupation forces. There is no indication in the Gospels whether Simon moved from the Zealot party to be a follower of Christ or, on the other hand, if after the resurrection he became a supporter of that group, seeing it as a response to God's call to proclaim the kingdom. Luke describes Jude as the son of James, while the Letter of Jude has him as the brother of James, neither of which negates the other. It seems he was the same person as Thaddaeus, which may have been a last name. Owing to the similarity of his name to that of Judas Iscariot, Jude was rarely invoked in prayer and it seems likely that because of this, interceding through him was seen as a final resort when all else failed. He became known, therefore, as the patron saint of lost causes!

The two apostles are joined together on 28 October because a church, which had recently acquired their relics, was dedicated to their memory in Rome on this day in the seventh century.

A Reading from the homilies of Origen on the Book of Joshua

All of us who believe in Christ Jesus are said to be living stones, according to the words of Scripture: 'Like living stones, let yourselves be built into a spiritual house, to be a holy priesthood, to offer spiritual sacrifices acceptable to God through Jesus Christ.'

When we look at the construction of earthly buildings, we can see how the largest and strongest stones are always set in the foundations, so that the weight of the whole building can rest securely on them. In the same way you should understand how some of the living stones referred to by Scripture have become the foundations of a spiritual building. And who are those foundation stones? The apostles and the prophets. This is what Paul himself declares in his teaching: 'You are built upon the foundation of the apostles and prophets, Christ Jesus himself being the cornerstone.'

You should learn that Christ himself is also the foundation of the building we are describing, so that you may more eagerly prepare yourselves for the construction, and be found to be one of those stones strong enough to be laid close to the foundation. For these are the words of Paul the Apostle, 'No other foundation can anyone lay than that which is laid, namely Christ Jesus.' Blessed are those, therefore, who will be found to have constructed sacred and religious buildings upon such a glorious foundation!

But in this building of the Church there must also be an altar. From this I conclude that those of you who are ready and prepared to give up your time to prayer, to offer petitions and sacrifices of supplication to God day and night, such people I say will be the living stones out of which Jesus will build his altar.

Reflect upon the praise that is lavished upon these stones of the altar. 'Moses the lawgiver,' Joshua said, 'ordered that an altar be built out of unhewn stones, untouched by a chisel.' Who now are these unhewn stones? Perhaps these unhewn, undefiled stones could be said to be the holy apostles, who together make one altar by reason of their harmony and unity. For Scripture tells that, as the apostles prayed together with one accord they opened their mouths and said, 'You, Lord, know the hearts of all.'

These then, who were able to pray with one mind, with one voice and in one spirit, are perhaps worthy of being employed together to form an altar upon which Jesus may offer his sacrifice to the Father.

But let us too strive to be of one mind among ourselves, and to speak with one heart and voice. Let us never act out anger or vainglory, but united in belief and purpose, let us hope that God may find us stones fit for his altar.

29 October

James Hannington

Bishop of Eastern Equatorial Africa, Martyr in Uganda, 1885

Note: In Wales, James Hannington is commemorated jointly with Janani Luwum and other martyrs of Uganda, on 3 June.

James Hannington was born in 1847 of a Congregationalist family but he became an Anglican before going up to Oxford. He was ordained and, after serving a curacy for five years, went with the Church Missionary Society to Uganda. He was consecrated bishop for that part of Africa in 1884 and a year later began a safari inland from Mombasa, together with other European and indigenous Christians. He (or his guides) made the mistake of attempting to enter Uganda from the east, through Busoga, the traditional approach of the enemy. The ruler of the Buganda, Mwanga, who despised Christians because they refused to condone his moral turpitude, seized the whole party, tortured them for several days and then had them butchered to death on this day in the year 1885.

A Reading from the Last Journals of James Hannington

Every morning during that hard-fought journey James Hannington greeted the sunrise with his travelling psalm, saying: 'I will lift up mine eyes unto the hills, from whence cometh my help.' He often encouraged his companions in times of doubt and difficulty with the words: 'Never be disappointed, only praise.' His last journals record his anxiety that his travelling companions, in spite of repeated reassurances to the contrary, were in fact uncertain of the path they were taking. On Wednesday 21 October 1885 he and his retainers were taken prisoner by Chief Mwanga's men. The last disjointed entries in his journal read as follows:

Friday 23 October
I woke full of pain and weak, so that with the utmost difficulty I crawled outside and sat in a chair, and yet they guard every move as if I were a giant. My nerves too have received such a shock that, after some loud yells and war cries arising outside the prison fence, I expected to be murdered, and simply turned over and said: 'Let the Lord do as he sees fit; I shall not make the slightest resistance.'

Seeing how bad I am, they have sent for my tent for me to use in the daytime. Going outside I fell to the ground exhausted, and had to be helped back inside in a poor condition to my bed. I don't see how I can stand all this, and yet I don't want to give in, but it almost seems as if Uganda itself is going to be forbidden ground to me.

Wednesday 28 October
A terrible night, first with noisy drunken guards, and secondly with vermin which have found out my tent and swarm. I don't think I got one hour's sound sleep, and woke with fever fast developing. O Lord, do have mercy upon me and release me. I am quite broken down and brought low. Comforted by reading Psalm twenty-seven.

In an hour or two fever has developed quite rapidly. My tent is so stuffy that am obliged to go inside the filthy hut. Delirious.

Thursday 29 October
I hear no news, but was much upheld by Psalm thirty which came to me with great power. A hyena howled near me last night, smelling a sick man, but I hope it is not to have me yet.

These are the last words in his little pocket-diary. According to a boy called Ukutu, one of Bishop Hannington's porters who escaped the general massacre of his party, later that morning the guards came and bound the bishop. As they led him off to the spot where he was to be murdered, he sang hymns nearly all the way. The only English word the African boy recognised in what the Bishop sang was one that recurred frequently: Jesus.

alternative reading

A Reading from *A History of Christian Missions* by Stephen Neill

When the Churches of the West were rich and their countries powerful, when the missionary impulse reawoke after 1790, it was natural for Western Churches to be 'sending' churches and the other countries to be only on the receiving end. It could not have been otherwise. With the existence of a universal Church a new period dawned. The terms 'sending' and 'receiving' lost much of their meaning. Quickly the terms 'older churches' and 'younger churches' grew out of date. At the Second Vatican Council the black bishops of Africa contributed to the debates with mellow wisdom. Christians everywhere had the same work: to present Christian faith and life in the world, Western, Eastern, or Southern, which has its doubts, hostilities, and rival philosophies of life.

The age of missions ended. The age of mission began.

It was still different in different societies. To be a Christian in a half-Christian or post-Christian society, even in an officially anti-Christian but formerly Christian society, is not the same task as to be a Christian in an area which has never heard the gospel before, in a speech which was never used there before, in a society where the organisation was never touched by Christian principles.

A third of the people in the world, perhaps, have not yet heard the name of Jesus Christ, and another third, perhaps, have never heard the gospel presented in such a way as both to be intelligible and to make a claim on their personal lives. There is plenty still to be done.

In this narration we have not tried at any point to conceal the weakness of human endeavour – the sinfulness and pettiness of the agents, the blind selfishness of the Churches, the niggardliness of the support that they have given to the work of the gospel, the mistakes that have been made, the treacheries, the catastrophes, the crimes by which the record is sullied. And yet the Church is there today, the Body of Christ in every land, the great miracle of history, in which the living God himself through his Holy Spirit is pleased to dwell.

31 October

Martin Luther

Reformer, 1546

Note: In Scotland, Martin Luther is commemorated on 19 February.

Martin Luther was born in 1483 at Eisleben in Saxony and educated at the cathedral school in Magdeburg and the university in Erfurt. He joined an order of Augustinian hermits there and was ordained priest in 1507, becoming a lecturer in the University of Wittenberg. He became Vicar of his Order in 1515, having charge of a dozen monasteries. His Christian faith began to take on a new shape, with his increasing dissatisfaction with the worship and order of the Church. He became convinced that the Gospels taught that humanity is saved by faith and not by works, finding support in the writings of Augustine of Hippo. He refuted the teaching of the Letter of James, calling it 'an epistle of straw'. Martin sought to debate the whole matter by posting ninety-five theses or propositions on the door of the Castle church in Wittenberg on this day in the year 1517. The hierarchy chose to see it as a direct attack on the Church, which forced Martin into open rebellion. The Protestant Reformation spread throughout Germany and then Europe, many seeing it as liberation from a Church that held them in fear rather than love. Martin Luther died in the year 1546, having effected a renaissance in the Church, both Protestant and Catholic.

A Reading from Martin Luther's preface to the first volume of Latin writings, published in 1545

Meanwhile in that year [1541] I had already returned to interpret the Psalter anew. I had confidence in the fact that I was more skilful, after I had lectured in the university on Saint Paul's Epistles to the Romans, to the Galatians, and the one to the Hebrews. I had indeed been captivated with an extraordinary ardour for understanding Paul in the Epistle to the Romans. But up till then it was not the cold blood about the heart, but a single word in chapter one, 'In it the righteousness of God is revealed,' that had stood in my way. For I hated that word 'righteousness of God', which, according to the use and custom of all the teachers, I had been taught to understand philosophically regarding the formal or active righteousness, as they called it, with which God is righteous and punishes the unrighteous sinner.

Though I lived as a monk without reproach, I felt that I was a sinner before God with an extremely disturbed conscience. I could not believe that he was placated by my satisfaction. I did not love, yes, I hated the righteous God who punishes sinners, and secretly, if not blasphemously, certainly murmuring greatly, I was angry with God, and said, 'As if it were not enough that miserable sinners should be eternally lost through original sin, crushed by every kind of calamity which the law of the decalogue lays on them, without having God add pain to pain by the gospel threatening us with his righteousness and wrath!' Thus I raged with a fierce and troubled conscience. Nevertheless, I beat importunately upon Paul at that place, most ardently desiring to know what he meant.

At last, by the mercy of God, meditating day and night, I gave heed to the context of the words, namely, 'In it the righteousness of God is revealed, as it is written, "He who through faith is righteous shall live."' There I began to understand that the righteousness of God is that by which the righteous lives by a gift of God, namely by faith. And this is the meaning: the righteousness of God is revealed by the gospel, namely, the passive righteousness with which the merciful God justifies us by faith, as it is written, 'He who through faith is righteous shall live.' Here I felt as if I was altogether born again and had entered paradise itself through open gates. The whole face of scripture appeared to me in a new light. Thereupon I ran through the scriptures from memory. I also found in other terms the same analogy as the 'work of God', (that is, what God does in us), the 'power of God', with which he makes us strong, the 'wisdom of God', with which he makes us wise, the 'strength of God', the 'salvation of God', and the 'glory of God'.

And now, where I had once hated the phrase 'the righteousness of God', so much, I began now to love and extol it as the sweetest of words, so that this passage in Paul became the very gate of paradise for me.

November

1 November

All Saints' Day

From its earliest days, the Church has recognized as its foundation stones those heroes of the faith whose lives have excited others to holiness and have assumed a communion with the Church on earth and the Church in heaven. Celebrating the Feast of All Saints began in the fourth century. At first, it was observed on the Sunday after the Feast of Pentecost; this was to link the disciples who received the gift of the Holy Spirit at Pentecost, the foundation of the Church, with those who were martyrs, giving their lives as witnesses for the faith. In the eighth century, a pope dedicated a chapel to All Saints in Saint Peter's at Rome on 1 November. Within a century this day was being observed in England and Ireland as All Saints' Day.

A Reading from a sermon of Bernard of Clairvaux

Why should our praise and glorification, or even our celebration of this feast day, mean anything to the saint? What do they care about earthly honours when their heavenly Father honours them by fulfilling the faithful promise of his Son? What does our commemoration mean to them? The saints have no need of honour from us; neither does our devotion add the slightest thing to what is already theirs. Clearly, when we venerate their memory, it is serving us, not them. But I tell you, when I think of them, I feel myself inflamed by a tremendous longing to be with them.

Calling the saints to mind inspires, or rather arouses in us, above all else, a longing to enjoy their company which is desirable in itself. We long to share in the citizenship of heaven, to dwell with the spirits of the blessed, to join the assembly of patriarchs,the ranks of the prophets, the council of apostles, the great host of martyrs, the noble company of confessors and the choir of virgins. In short, we long to be united in happiness with all the saints. But our dispositions change. The Church of all the first followers of Christ awaits us, but we do nothing about it. The saints want us to be with them, and we are indifferent. The souls of the just await us, and we ignore them.

Come, let us at length spur ourselves on. We must rise again with Christ, we must seek the world which is above and set our mind on the things of heaven. Let us long for those who are longing for us, hasten to those who are waiting for us, and ask those who look for our coming to intercede for us. We should not only want to be with the saints, we should also hope to possess their happiness. While we desire to be in their company, we must also earnestly seek to share in their glory. Do not imagine that there is anything harmful in such an ambition as this; there is no danger in setting our hearts on such glory.

When we commemorate the saints we are inflamed with another yearning: that Christ our life may also appear to us as he appeared to them and that we may one day share in his glory. Until then we see him, not as he is, but as he became for our sake. He is our head, crowned, not with glory, but with the thorns of our sins. As members of that head, crowned with thorns, we should be ashamed to live in luxury; his purple robes are a mockery rather than an honour. When Christ comes again, his death shall no longer be proclaimed, and we shall know that we also have died, and that our life is hidden with him. The glorious head of the Church will appear and his glorified members will shine in splendour with him, when he transforms this lowly body anew into such glory as belongs to himself, its head.

Therefore, we should aim at attaining this glory with a wholehearted and prudent desire. That we may rightly hope and strive for such blessedness, we must above all seek the prayers of the saints, that what is beyond our own efforts to obtain may be granted through their intercession.

alternative reading

A Reading from a treatise by Hugh Latimer

As touching the saints in heaven, they be not our mediators by way of redemption; for so Christ alone is our mediator and theirs both: so that the blood of martyrs hath nothing to do by way of redemption; the blood of Christ is enough for a thousand worlds. But by way of intercession, so saints in heaven may be mediators, and pray for us: as I think they do when we call not upon them; for they be charitable, and need no spurs.

We have no open bidding of God in Scripture to call upon them, as we have to call upon God, nor yet we may call upon them without any diffidence or mistrust in God; for God is more charitable, more merciful, more able, more ready to help than them all. So that, though we may desire the saints in heaven to pray God for us, yet it is not so necessary to be done, but that we may pray to God ourselves, without making suit first to them, and obtain of him whatsoever we need, if we continue in prayer; so that, whatsoever we ask the Father in the name of Christ his Son, the Father will give it us. For saints can give nothing without him, but he can without them; as he did give to them. Scripture doth set saints that be departed before our eyes for examples; so that the chiefest and most principal worship and honouring of them is to know their holy living, and to follow them, as they followed Christ.

God biddeth us come to him with prayer; and to do his bidding is no presuming. It is rather presuming to leave it undone, to do that which he biddeth us not do. We must have saints in reverent memory; and learn at God's goodness towards them to trust in God; and mark well their faith toward God and his word, their charity toward their neighbour, their patience in all adversity; and pray to God which gave them grace so to do, that we may do likewise, for which like doings we shall have like speedings: they be well honoured when God is well pleased. The saints were not saints by praying to saints, but by believing in him that made them saints; and as they were saints, so may we be saints also.

A Reading from *The Vision of God* by Kenneth Kirk

Although Jesus spoke little about 'seeing God', he brought God more vividly before the spiritual eyes of his contemporaries than any other person has ever done. He gave a vision of God where others could only speak of it. It is worth while to consider for a moment the importance of this factor in his teaching.

There must be both ethics and doctrine in every gospel we present to the world. But the moment ethics predominates over doctrine – the moment, that is, that the thought of man ousts the thought of God from the place of primary honour – the whole purpose of a gospel is undone, whether the gospel be Christian or any other. Ethics, or teaching about man and the conduct proper to him, centres a person's thoughts upon himself; and the end of self-centredness is unethical and unevangelical alike. It is bound to result – as Saint Paul so clearly showed – either in spiritual pride or in spiritual despair: and by neither of these roads can we find our true destiny. The path of purity, humility, and self-sacrifice is only possible to those who can *forget* themselves, can disinfect themselves from egoism; where the mind is centred not upon self, but at least upon one's fellows and their needs, and at most and at best upon God and our neighbours seen through the eyes of God. We cannot by thinking add a cubit to our stature: still less can we, by thinking about ourselves and our conduct, achieve that self-forgetfulness or self-sacrifice which is the hallmark of the saints.

It would be absurd to say that self-criticism and self-examination play no part in the making of saintliness. But the essential fact about religion in its relation to ethics is this – that self-examination and self-criticism are dangerous in the highest degree unless the soul is already reaching out in self-forgetfulness to something higher and better than itself. Self-centredness, even in the morally earnest, is the greatest snare in life: 'Godcentredness' the only true salvation. This throws a flood of light upon the whole of the New Testament. It makes it clear why Jesus spoke first and foremost of God, and only in the second place of man and human conduct. And it gives a reason why the Church fixed upon the single text in the beatitudes – 'Blessed are the pure in heart, for they shall see God' – and elevated it into the summary of all that it had to give to the world.

Where the best Christian thought about the vision of God has differed from non-Christian aspiration is in its emphasis upon the *attitude* rather than upon the *experiences* of worship. What matters is that we should look towards God, rather than that we should here and now receive the vision. But that there is such a vision, and that it is attainable, theology no less than experience affirms. Not only do the saints see God in heaven – not only has the Church seen him in the face of Jesus Christ on earth; for the inspiration and renewal of the individual it has been insisted that the pure in heart shall from time to time have personal experience of God and intercourse with him, both in their prayers and even in the ordinary activities of life.

A Reading from *New Seeds of Contemplation* by Thomas Merton

The forms and individual characters of living and growing things, of inanimate beings, of animals and flowers and all nature, constitute their holiness in the sight of God. Their inscape is their sanctity. It is the imprint of his wisdom and his reality in them.

The special clumsy beauty of this particular colt on this April day in this field under these clouds is a holiness consecrated to God by his own creative wisdom and it declares the glory of God. The pale flowers of the dogwood outside this window are saints. The little yellow flowers that nobody notices on the edge of that road are saints looking up into the face of God. This leaf has its own texture and its own pattern of veins and its own holy shape, and the bass and trout hiding in the deep pools of the river are canonised by their beauty and their strength. The lakes hidden among the hills are saints, and the sea too is a saint who praises God without interruption in her majestic dance. The great, gashed, half-naked mountain is another of God's saints. There is no other like him. He is alone in his own character; nothing else in the world ever did or ever will imitate God in quite the same way. That is his sanctity.

But what about you? What about me? Unlike the animals and the trees, it is not enough to be what our nature intends. It is not enough for us to be individuals. For us, holiness is more than humanity. If we are never anything but people, we will not be saints and we will not be able to offer to God the worship of our imitation, which is sanctity.

It is true to say that for me sanctity consists in being *myself*, and for you sanctity consists in being *yourself* and that, in the last analysis, your sanctity will never be mine and mine will never be yours, except in the communism of charity and grace.

For me to be a saint means to be myself. Therefore the problem of sanctity and salvation is in fact the problem of finding out who I am and of discovering my true self. Trees and animals have no problem. God makes them what they are without consulting them, and they are perfectly satisfied.

With us it is different. God leaves us free to be whatever we like. We can be ourselves or not, as we please. We are at liberty to be real, or to be unreal. We may be true or false, the choice is ours. We may wear now one mask and now another, and never, if we so desire, appear with our own true face. But we cannot make these choices with impunity. Causes have effects, and if we lie to ourselves and to others, then we cannot expect to find truth and reality whenever we happen to want them. If we have chosen the way of falsity we must not be surprised that truth eludes us when we finally come to need it!

Our vocation is not simply to be, but to work together with God in the creation of our own life, our own identity, our own destiny. We are free beings and children of God. This means to say that we should not passively exist, but actively participate in his creative freedom, in our own lives, and in the lives of others, by choosing the truth. To put it better, we are even called to share with God the work of *creating* the truth of our identity.

We do not know clearly beforehand what the result of this work will be. The secret of my full identity is hidden in God. He alone can make me who I am, or rather who I will be when at last I fully begin to be. But unless I desire this identity and work to find it with God and in God, the work will never be done.

2 November

Commemoration of the Faithful Departed (All Souls' Day)

'The believer's pilgrimage of faith is lived out with the mutual support of all the people of God. In Christ all the faithful, both living and departed, are bound together in a communion of prayer.' This simple, agreed statement from the Anglican-Roman Catholic International Commission explains the purpose of the commemoration of all the faithful departed (commonly known as All Souls' Day) on the day following All Saints' Day. The commemoration began as a monastic custom at the great abbey of Cluny, and by the thirteenth century it was universal throughout the Western Church. The medieval rite contained the famous sequence Dies Irae. Although the observance did not survive the liturgical changes of the Reformation, it was restored in the proposed 1928 Book of Common Prayer largely in response to the huge weight of grief following the First World War. In recent years it has become increasingly customary to hold a service (either today or at this season) for the bereaved. In a society which has largely abandoned traditional patterns of mourning, the opportunity to express grief continues to have a valued place in the ministry of the Church. Various readings from the Church's tradition are offered here which acknowledge the hard and painful reality of death in the 'sure and certain hope of the resurrection to eternal life'.

A Reading from an oration of Gregory of Nazianzus

'What are human beings that you should be mindful of us, mere mortals that you should care for us?' What is this new mystery confronting me? I am both small and great, both lowly and exalted, mortal and immortal, earthly and heavenly. I am to be buried with Christ and to rise again with him, to become a co-heir with him, a son of God, and indeed God himself.

This is what the great mystery means for us; this is why God became human and became poor for our sake: it was to raise up our flesh, to recover the divine image in us, to re-create humankind, so that all of us might become one in Christ who perfectly became in us everything that he is himself. So we are no longer to be 'male and female, barbarian and Scythian, slave and free' – distinctions deriving from the flesh – but to bear within ourselves only the seal of God, by whom and for which we were created. We are to be so formed and moulded by him that we are recognised as belonging to his one family.

If only we could be now what we hope to be, by the great kindness of our generous God! He asks so little and gives so much in this life and in the next, to those who love him sincerely. In a spirit of hope and out of love for God, let us then 'bear and endure all things' and give thanks for everything that befalls us, since even reason can often recognise these things as weapons to win salvation. Meanwhile let us commend to God our own souls and the souls of those who, being more ready for it, have reached the place of rest before us although they walked the same road as we do now.

Lord and creator of all, and especially of your human creatures, you are the God and Father and ruler of your children; you are the Lord of life and death; you are the guardian and benefactor of our souls. You fashion and transform all things in their due season through your creative Word, as you know to be best in your deep wisdom and providence. Receive this day those who have gone ahead of us in our journey from this life.

And receive us too at the proper time, when you have guided us in our bodily life as long as may be profitable for us. Receive us prepared indeed by fear of you, but not troubled, not shrinking back on the day of our death or uprooted by force like those who are lovers of the world and the flesh. Instead, may we set out eagerly for that eternal and blessed life which is in Christ Jesus our Lord. To him be the glory for ever and ever.

alternative reading

A Reading from a treatise by Hugh Latimer

The faithful departed have charity in such surety that they cannot lose it, so that they cannot murmur nor grudge against God; cannot be displeased with God; cannot be dissevered from God; cannot die, nor be in peril of death; cannot be damned, nor be in peril of damnation; cannot be but in surety of salvation.

They be members of the mystical body of Christ as we be, and in more surety than we be. They love us charitably. Charity is not idle: if it be, it worketh and sheweth itself: and therefore I say, they wish us well and pray for us. They need not cry loud to God: they be in Christ, and Christ in them. They be in Christ, and Christ with them. They joy in their Lord Christ always, taking thankfully whatsoever God doth with them; ever giving thanks to their Lord God; ever lauding and praising him in all things that he doth; discontent with nothing that he doth.

And forasmuch as they be always in charity, and when they pray for us they pray always in charity, and be always God's friends, God's children, brethren and sisters to our Saviour Christ, even in God's favour, even have Christ with them to offer their prayer to the Father of heaven, to whom they pray in the name of the Son. We many times for lack of charity, having malice and envy, rancour, hatred, one toward another, be the children of the devil, inheritors of hell, adversaries to Christ, hated of God, his angels and all his saints; they in their state may do us more good with their prayers, than we in this state. And they do us alway good, unless the lack and impediment be in us: for prayer said in charity is more faithful to them that it is said for, and more acceptable to God, than that which is said out of [lack of] charity. For God looketh not to the work of praying, but to the heart of the prayer.

Thus we may well pray for the departed, and they much better for us: which they will do of their charity, [even] though we desire them not.

alternative reading

A Reading from the *Holy Sonnets* of John Donne

Death be not proud, though some have called thee
Mighty and dreadful, for, thou art not so,
For, those, whom thou think'st, thou dost overthrow,
Die not, poor death, nor yet canst thou kill me;
From rest and sleep, which but thy pictures be,
Much pleasure, then from thee, much more must flow,
And soonest our best men with thee do go,
Rest of their bones, and soul's delivery.

Thou art slave to fate, chance, kings, and desperate men,
And dost with poison, war, and sickness dwell,
And poppy, or charms can make us sleep as well,
And better than thy stroke; why swell'st thou then?
One short sleep past, we wake eternally,
And death shall be no more: Death thou shalt die.

alternative reading

A Reading from a sermon preached in All Souls College, Oxford, by Austin Farrer

'May they rest in peace, and may light perpetual shine upon them' – those millions among whom our friends are lost, those millions for whom we cannot choose but pray; because prayer is a sharing in the love of the heart of God, and the love of God is earnestly set towards the salvation of his spiritual creatures, by, through and out of the fire that purifies them.

The arithmetic of death perplexes our brains. What can we do but throw ourselves upon the infinity of God? It is only to a finite mind that number is an obstacle, or multiplicity a distraction. Our mind is like a box of limited content, out of which one thing must be emptied before another can find a place. The universe of creatures is queuing for a turn of our attention, and no appreciable part of the queue will ever get a turn. But no queue forms before the throne of everlasting mercy, because the nature of an infinite mind is to be simply aware of everything that is.

Everything is simply present to an infinite mind, because it exists; or rather, exists because it is present to that making mind. And though by some process of averaging and calculation I should compute the grains of sand, it would be like the arithmetic of the departed souls, an empty sum; I could not tell them as they are told in the infinity of God's counsels, each one separately present as what it is, and simply because it is.

The thought God gives to any of his creatures is not measured by the attention he can spare, but by the object for consideration they can supply. God is not divided; it is God, not a part of God, who applies himself to the falling sparrow, and to the crucified Lord. But there is more in the beloved Son than in the sparrow, to be observed and loved and saved by God. So every soul that has passed out of this visible world, as well as every soul remaining within it, is caught and held in the unwavering beam of divine care. And we may comfort ourselves for our own inability to tell the grains of sand, or to reckon the thousands of millions of the departed.

And yet we cannot altogether escape so; for our religion is not a simple relation of every soul separately to God, it is a mystical body in which we are all members one of another. And in this mystical body it does not suffice that every soul should be embraced by the thoughts of God; it has also to be that every soul should, in its thought, embrace the other souls. For apart from this mutual embracing, it would be unintelligible why we should pray at all, either for the living or for the departed. Such prayer is nothing but the exercising of our membership in the body of Christ. God is not content to care for us each severally, unless he can also, by his Holy Spirit in each one of us, care through and in us for all the rest. Every one of us is to be a focus of that divine life of which the attractive power holds the body together in one.

So even in the darkness and blindness of our present existence, our thought ranges abroad and spreads out towards the confines of the mystical Christ, remembering the whole Church of Christ, as well militant on earth as triumphant in heaven; invoking angels, archangels and all the spiritual host.

3 November

Martyrs and Confessors of our Time

In our own time there has been no shortage of people who have given their lives as witnesses to the light of Christ. Christians have been victims of persecution in Europe, of religious prejudice and dictatorial rule in Africa, of fanaticism in the Indian subcontinent; they have been killed in the brutalities of the Second World War in Asia, and the Cultural Revolution in China. Led by their faith and the imperative to work for the kingdom of God, Christians have borne witness against oppression and injustice. They have worked among the poor in the slums, among the diseased and terminally ill, at home and abroad. In these and countless other ways Christians have shown the enduring significance of the good news preached by Jesus Christ.

A Reading from *The Cost of Discipleship* by Dietrich Bonhoeffer

Cheap grace is the deadly enemy of our Church. We are fighting today for costly grace.

Cheap grace means grace sold on the market like 'cheapjack' wares. The sacraments, the forgiveness of sin, and the consolations of religion are thrown away at cut prices. Grace is represented as the Church's inexhaustible treasury, from which she showers blessings with generous hands, without asking questions or fixing limits. Grace without price; grace without cost! The essence of grace, we suppose, is that the account has been paid in advance; and, because it has been paid, everything can be had for nothing. Since the cost was infinite, the possibilities of using and spending it are infinite. What would grace be if it were not cheap?

Cheap grace means grace as a doctrine, a principle, a system. It means forgiveness of sins proclaimed as a general truth, the love of God taught as the Christian 'conception' of God. An intellectual assent to that idea is held to be of itself sufficient to secure remission of sins. The Church which holds the correct doctrine of grace has, it is supposed, a part in that grace. In such a Church the world finds a cheap covering for its sins; no contrition is required, still less any real desire to be delivered from sin.

Cheap grace is the preaching of forgiveness without requiring repentance, baptism without church discipline, communion without confession, absolution without personal confession. Cheap grace is grace without discipleship, grace without the cross, grace without Jesus Christ, living and incarnate.

Costly grace is the treasure hidden in the field; for the sake of it a person will gladly go and sell all that he has. It is the pearl of great price to buy which the merchant will sell all his goods. It is the kingly rule of Christ, for whose sake a man will pluck out the eye which causes him to stumble. It is the call of Jesus Christ at which the disciple leaves his nets and follows him.

3 November

Winifred

Abbess, seventh century

Winifred (Gwenfrewi) is said to have been the daughter of a soldier from Tegeingl (Flintshire) named Tyfid ab Eiludd. Her mother's brother was Saint Beuno. At her father's request, Beuno became Winifred's spiritual director. A nobleman named Caradog tried to force himself on Winifred, who ran to seek sanctuary in Beuno's cell at Sychnant. Caradog caught up with her and cut her head off. A spring gushed forth at the spot where her head landed. Beuno cursed the nobleman (who melted away like wax) and restored Winifred to life. The legend is colourful and curious. That Winifred was the superior of a community of holy women at Gwytherin seems beyond dispute. She was buried there, but in 1138 her relics were moved to Shrewsbury Abbey, and her cult became more widespread. Saint Winifred's well at Holywell was said to be the spring that appeared at her beheading.

A Reading from the *Instructions* of Columbanus on 'Christ the Fount of Life'

Let us follow that vocation by which we are called from life to the fountain of life. Christ is the fountain, not only of living water, but of eternal life. He is the fountain of light and spiritual illumination; for from him come all these things: wisdom, life and eternal light. The author of life is the fountain of life; the creator of light is the fountain of spiritual illumination. Therefore, let us seek the fountain of light and life and the living water by despising what we see, by leaving the world and by dwelling in the highest heavens. Let us seek these things, and like rational and shrewd fish may we drink the living water which 'wells up to eternal life.'

Merciful God, good Lord, I wish that you would unite me to that fountain that there I may drink of the living spring of the water of life with all those who thirst after you. There in that heavenly region may I ever dwell, delighted with abundant sweetness, and say: 'How sweet is the fountain of living water which never fails, the water welling up to eternal life.'

O God, you are yourself that fountain ever and again to be desired, ever and again to be consumed. Lord Christ, give us always this water to be for us the 'source of the living water which wells up to eternal life.' I ask you for your great benefits. Who does not know it? But you, King of Glory, know how to give great gifts, and you have promised great things. There is nothing greater than you, and you bestowed yourself upon us; you gave yourself for us.

Therefore, we ask that we may know what we love, since we ask nothing other than that you give us yourself. For you are our all: our life, our light, our salvation, our food and our drink, our God. Inspire our hearts, I ask you, Jesus, with that breath of your Spirit; wound our souls with your love, so that the soul of each and every one of us may be able to say in truth: 'Show me my soul's desire,' for I am wounded by your love.

These are the wounds I wish for, Lord. Blessed is the soul so wounded by love. Such a soul seeks the fountain of eternal life and drinks from it, although it continues to thirst and its thirst grows ever greater even as it drinks. Therefore, the more the soul loves, the more it desires to love, and the greater its suffering, the greater its healing. In this same way may our

God and Lord Jesus Christ, the good and saving physician, wound the depths of our souls with a healing wound – the same Jesus Christ who reigns in unity with the Father and the Holy Spirit, for ever and ever.

alternative reading

A Reading from *The Holy Wells of Wales* by Francis James

The life of the medieval Welshman was intimately concerned with wells and well-chapels. Pilgrimages to these were made at all times of the year, especially during the *gŵyl mabsant* or wakes. Some of the chapels were elaborate such as that of Gwenfrewi (Winifred) at Holywell, perhaps the most famous well-shrine in medieval Britain.

The well marks the site of the reputed martyrdom and miraculous restoration of Saint Winifred early in the seventh century. The fan vaulting of the undercroft of its chapel shelters a star-shaped pool, the boss over the centre of which is richly carved with details of the saint's life. At the base of the star there is a small rectangular pool with steps down into it for those who came to be healed.

The prestige of Saint Winifred was very high, yet it is a remarkable fact that no other single well or church in Wales was dedicated to her. The well and chapel of Holywell had been granted in 1093 by the Countess of Chester to the monastery of Saint Werberg, and in 1115 her son, Earl Richard, made a pilgrimage to the well. Its possession reverted to the Welsh lords, and in 1240 Dafydd ap Llewelyn granted it to Basingwerk Abbey, which held it until 1537. In 1189 Richard I sheltered in Basingwerk when attacked by the Welsh while he was on a pilgrimage to Saint Winifred's Well. In 1416, 'the King with great reverence went on foot in pilgrimage from Shrewsbury to Saint Winifred's Well in north Wales.' In 1439 the Countess of Warwick presented her russet velvet gown to the chapel, and Edward IV is said to have made a pilgrimage to it. Richard III conferred an annuity of ten marks upon the Abbot of Basingwerk for maintaining a priest at the well. The offerings at Saint Winifred's were worth £10 per annum in 1535. The Lives record many stories of miraculous cures at this well. Bards like Iolo Goch, Ieuan Brydydd Hir, and Tudur Aled, all sang the praises of Winifred and her well.

The Reformation struck heavily at wells and, together with relics and pilgrimages, they were denounced as superstitious. Although not enthusiastically received in Wales, there was no considerable resistance to the Reformation. It was supported by the leading clergy and the great land-owning families, while the majority of the countryfolk whose untutored minds were unversed in the subtleties of theological and political controversy, remained loyal in their hearts to the observances of the medieval Church, and were bewildered when effigies were removed, church wall-paintings obliterated, rood-lofts and shrines destroyed, pilgrimages to wells and sacred sites prohibited. All they knew was that the visible and outward symbols of their faith were removed. They remained bewildered, and afterwards apathetic, until Welsh Nonconformity provided a spiritual leadership such as had not been known in Wales since the Age of the Saints.

3 November

Malachy

Bishop, 1148

To Malachy is due the restoration, re-organization and re-unification of the Church in Ireland after the ravages of the Norsemen. In his time, the dioceses of Ireland were first organized as we know them. Under his leadership the arrival of the Anglo-Normans was less a disaster than it might have been. He co-operated with John de Courcy in the assimilation of the Norman influence in Ulster, including the re-formation of the Abbey of Down under the Benedictine Order. He also undertook the rebuilding of the Cathedral of Armagh and gained the recognition of Armagh as the Primatial See. He died on his way to Rome in the arms of Bernard of Clairvaux on All Souls' Day in the year 1148.

A Reading from *The Life of Malachy* the Irishman
by Bernard of Clairvaux

Malachy was received by us, although he came from the west, like the day star from on high visiting us in its dawning. Ah! How the radiance of that sun filled our house with added glory! How joyful the feast-day that dawned on us at his coming!

Four or five days of this festival of ours had passed when he was seized with a fever and took to his bed, and we too were with him there. When the brothers who had come with him confidently insisted that he ought not to despair of life – since no signs of death appeared in him – he replied, 'This is the year when Malachy must leave the body,' adding, 'See, the day of [All Souls] is drawing near which, as you full well know, I always wished to be the day of my departing. I know whom I have believed, and I am sure that I, who have already a part of my desire, shall not be disappointed of the rest. He who in his mercy has brought me to the place I asked for will not deny me the time that I wanted just as much. As regards this poor body, here is my resting-place; as for the soul, the Lord will provide, who saves all those who put their trust in him. There is no small hope laid up for me on that day on which so many benefits accrue from the living to the dead.'

All Saints' Day was at hand, a universal feast; but as the old saying has it, music in mourning is like a tale out of time. We were there and we sung, but without heart. Weeping we sang, and singing, wept. But Malachy, although he did not sing, did not weep either. What should he weep for, he who was approaching the threshold of joy? To us who were left was left the grief; Malachy alone kept festival.

By nightfall, when we had somehow brought the day's celebrations to their close, Malachy had drawn near, not dusk, but dawn. For surely it was dawn to him, for whom the night was nearly over and the day at hand?

And so it was that with psalms and hymns and spiritual canticles we accompanied our friend on his journey home. In the fifty-fourth year of his life, in the place and at the time he had chosen beforehand and foretold, Malachy, bishop and legate of the holy Apostolic See, taken up as it were by the angels from our hands, fell happily asleep in the Lord.

3 November

Richard Hooker

Priest, Anglican Apologist, Teacher of the Faith, 1600

Note: In Wales, Richard Hooker is commemorated on 30 October.

Born in Heavitree in Exeter in about 1554, Richard Hooker came under the influence of John Jewel, Bishop of Salisbury, in his formative years and through that influence went up to Corpus Christi College, Oxford, where he became a Fellow. He was ordained and then married, becoming a parish priest and, in 1585, Master of the Temple in London. Richard became one of the strongest advocates of the position of the Church of England and defended its 'middle way' between puritanism and papalism. Perhaps his greatest work was Of the Laws of Ecclesiastical Polity which he wrote as the result of engaging in controversial debates. He showed Anglicanism as rooted firmly in Scripture as well as tradition, affirming its continuity with the pre-Reformation Ecclesia Anglicana, but now both catholic and reformed. Richard became a parish priest again near Canterbury and died there on this day in the year 1600.

A Reading from *The Laws of Ecclesiastical Polity* by Richard Hooker

We are in God through Christ eternally according to that intent and purpose whereby we were chosen to be made his in this present world before the world itself was made. We are in God through the knowledge which is had of us, and the love which is borne towards us from everlasting. For his Church he knoweth and loveth, so that they which are in the Church are thereby known to be in him.

For in Christ we are by our actual incorporation into that society which hath him for their head, and doth make together with him one body, he and they in that respect having one name; by virtue of this mystical conjunction, we are of him and in him even as though our very flesh and bones should be made continuate with his. We are in Christ because he knoweth and loveth us even as parts of himself. No man is in him but they in whom he actually is. For he which hath not the Son of God hath not life. 'I am the vine and you are the branches: he which abideth in me and I in him the same bringeth forth much fruit'; but the branch severed from the vine withereth. We are, therefore, adopted sons of God to eternal life by participation of the only-begotten Son of God, whose life is the wellspring and cause of ours.

It is too cold an interpretation, whereby some men expound our being in Christ to import nothing else, but only that the selfsame nature which maketh us to be men, is in him, and maketh him man as we are. For what man in the world is there which hath not so far forth communion with Jesus Christ? It is not this that can sustain the weight of such sentences as speak of the mystery of our coherence with Jesus Christ. The Church is in Christ as Eve was in Adam. Yea by grace we are every of us in Christ and in his Church, as by nature we are in those our first parents. God made Eve of the rib of Adam. And his Church he frameth out of the very flesh, the very wounded and bleeding side of the Son of Man. His body crucified and his blood shed for the life of the world, are the true elements of that heavenly being which maketh us such as himself is of whom we come. For which cause the words of

Adam may be fitly the words of Christ concerning his Church, 'flesh of my flesh, and bone of my bones', a true native extract out of mine own body. So that in him even according to his manhood we according to our heavenly being are as branches in that root out of which they grow.

3 November

Martin de Porres

Friar, 1639

Born in Lima in Peru in 1579, Martin de Porres was the illegitimate son of a Spanish knight and a black, Panamanian freewoman. He joined the Third Order of the Dominicans when he was fifteen years old and was later received as a lay brother into the First Order, mainly because of his reputation for caring for the poor and needy. As the friary almoner, he was responsible for the daily distribution to the poor and he had a particular care for the many African slaves, whose lives were a dreadful indictment of the Christian conquistadores. Martin became sought after for spiritual counsel, unusual for a lay brother at that time. His care for all God's creatures led many to love and revere him and his own brothers chose him as their spiritual leader. He died of a violent fever on this day in the year 1639 and, because of his care for all, regardless of class or colour, is seen as the patron saint of race relations.

A Reading from a homily of Pope John XXIII following the canonization of Martin de Porres on 3 June 1962

Three passions burned in the heart of Brother Martin of Porres: charity, particularly with regard to the poor and the sick, the most rigorous penance, which he regarded as 'the price of love', and the humility which fed these virtues. Allow us to dwell particularly on this last, humility, and to contemplate it in Brother Martin's transparent soul.

Humility brings the vision that one has of oneself within the true limits marked out by human reason. It brings to its perfection the gift of the fear of God, by which the Christian, aware that the sovereign good and its authentic greatness are found only in God, offers him a unique and supreme respect, and avoids sin, the only evil which can separate the soul from him. This is the key to the practical wisdom which governs the life of those who are prudent and discreet. 'The fear of God is the school of wisdom' we are told in the holy book.

Martin de Porres was the angel of Lima. The novices turned to him in their difficulties, the most important of the Fathers sought advice from him. He reconciled households, healed the most refractory diseases, brought enmities to an end, resolved theological disputes and gave his decisive opinion on the most difficult of matters. What an abundance of wisdom, balance and goodness was found in his heart! He was not a learned man, but he possessed that true knowledge which ennobles the spirit, the 'inner light in the heart' which God gives to those who fear him, that 'light of discernment' of which Saint Catherine of Siena speaks. In his soul there reigned the holy fear of God, the foundation of all upbringing, of true spiritual progress, and, in the last analysis, of civilisation itself. 'The fear of God is the beginning of wisdom.'

When we see him raised to the honours of the altar, we admire Martin de Porres with the delight of one who gazes upon a magnificent panorama from the top of a mountain. But it must not be forgotten that humility is the way which leads to these heights: 'Humility goes before glory.' The higher the building, the deeper must be the foundations. As Saint Augustine wrote: 'Before the building is raised, it must go down: before putting on the roof, the foundations must be dug.' Martin teaches us the same lesson.

May the light of his life guide all people on the path of Christian social justice and of universal love without distinction of colour or race.

4 November

Saints and Martyrs of the Anglican Communion

See the readings for 8 November.

5 November

Cybi

Abbot, sixth century

Cybi's medieval hagiographer says that he was a native of Cornwall. He tells us that the saint came to Wales after some years as a pilgrim. Having visited David, Cybi went over to Ireland. He then crossed to Anglesey, eventually establishing his principal monastery at Caergybi (Holyhead). From there an Anglesey folk tradition says that he would visit his 'soul friend' Seiriol at the wells of Clorach halfway between their two monasteries. Another centre associated with Cybi was Llangybi in Caernarfonshire where his holy well drew many pilgrims hoping for healing from a variety of ailments. Many of the places connected with Cybi are on the coast and in a fifteenth-century poem he is described as the captain of a crew of holy men. Like many of the sixth-century saints he seems to have made extensive use of the seaways. He died at Holyhead.

A Reading from *The Saints of Cornwall* by Gilbert Doble

The *Life* of Saint Cybi was written a long time after the saint's time, when the true story of his career had been almost entirely forgotten, and as a result is largely legendary. He is represented in this *Life* as a Cornish saint, who visited Ireland and founded monasteries in Wales. The chief centre of his cult, however, was not Cornwall but Holyhead, and a brief sketch of its history is essential if we are to understand the work done by this great saint and missionary.

The church of Holyhead is one of the finest ancient churches in North Wales. It derived its special importance from being the church of the monastery founded and ruled over by Cybi, from which he evangelized the whole neighbourhood, and also from being the place where he died, and where his body rested. On a stone in the outside wall of the north transept of the church the words *Sancte Kebie, ora pro nobis* (Holy Cybi, pray for us) may still be read. In the churchyard, which is surrounded by an ancient wall (the cemetery of a great Celtic monastery was a very important place, possessing all kinds of rights and privileges) once stood a chapel, now destroyed but remembered by tradition, called *Eglwys y Bedd* (The Church of the Tomb). This represents an ancient Celtic custom, and it may have contained the tomb of Saint Cybi, and perhaps, originally, his body. The relics of Cybi are said to have been carried off, in whole or in part, by pirates. In about 1476 the church was pillaged, and the jewelled shrine containing the bones of Saint Cybi carried off. It was eventually placed on the high altar of Holy Trinity, now Christ Church, Dublin.

The church of Caergybi, as the headquarters of Saint Cybi, the chief saint of Anglesey, held a position of special importance in the ecclesiastical system of North Wales.

6 November

Illtud

Abbot, 530

Born in Brittany in the mid fifth century, Illtud received a good education in all branches of science and art, and seemed destined for academic life in a monastery. However, he chose a military career, leaving Brittany for the court of King Arthur, his cousin, in Somerset. Being spared death on a hunt, Illtud left the royal court for the service of a greater king, Jesus. He settled in a valley near what is now Llantwit Major in the Vale of Glamorgan, being instructed in the monastic life by Dyfrig, ordained priest, and once his monastic school was established, appointed abbot. The school was an important centre of learning, kings and chiefs from the whole country sending their children to be educated by Illtud. Among its pupils were David, Samson and Paulinus. The monks' and pupils' time at the monastery was divided between prayer, study and manual work; the whole valley was cultivated, Illtud inventing a new plough to halve the time taken to prepare the ground. Illtud made a number of visits to Brittany and founded churches there; he later retired to the land of his birth, dying in the monastery at Dol in the year 530.

A Reading from *The Life of Saint Illtud* by an unknown medieval author

Illtud was the most religious hermit, working assiduously with his hands, not trusting in the labours of others. In the middle of the night before Matins, he used to wash himself in cold water, remaining so as long as the Lord's Prayer could be said three times. Then he would visit the church, kneeling and praying to the omnipotence of the supreme creator. So fervent was his religion that he was never observed in any business except in God's service. His whole concentration was on holy Scripture, which he fulfilled in his daily life. Many came to be taught by him; they were trained by him in a thorough knowledge of the seven liberal arts.

Once, in a dream, an angel of God spoke to King Meirchion of Blessed Illtud, saying, 'This Illtud, the most humble servant of God, trusts to conquer by humility so as to remain here and to be secure in his stability. He fights not with visible arms, but strives with invincible virtues. A virtuous man, not afraid of a contest, he drives off his foes with the armour of righteousness. None throughout the whole of Britannia is holier than this blessed man, for he lives according to the monastic rule. Many will come to be taught by him: he will be a refuge and a support to many, like a pillar supporting a house. His protection will be inviolable to you and the princes of this kingdom.'

Thus it was that the venerable abbot Illtud, was hindered by none and remained at peace. He tilled and sowed, and reaped the harvest with his own hands. He trained labourers to cultivate and husband flocks throughout his fields. They increased seed, and performed labours with great profit. He fed the poor, he covered the naked, he visited the sick and those cast into prison. His household eventually numbered a hundred. He was hospitable, never begrudging hospitality to those who needed it. In his bountiful heart there was no hurtful pride, only humility, kindness, and pure and undefiled religion. Very many scholars were attracted to him, of whom we may name four: Samson, Paulinus, Gildas and Dewi (that is, David). These studied with him, and Illtud instructed them in wisdom.

6 November

Leonard

Hermit, sixth century

According to an eleventh-century Life, Leonard was a sixth-century Frankish nobleman who refused a bishopric to become first a monk, then a hermit, at Noblac (now Saint-Léonard) near Limoges. The miracles attributed to him, both during his lifetime and after his death, caused a widespread cultus throughout Europe and, in England alone, over a hundred and seventy churches are dedicated to him. His popularity in England may also be due in part to the enthusiasm of returning crusaders, who looked to him as the patron saint of prisoners.

A Reading from *Pastoral Care* by Gregory the Great

A leader should be exemplary in conduct, so that his manner of life may itself indicate the way of life to his people, and the flock, following the teaching and conduct of its shepherd, will fare better because it is nourished on example and not mere words. For it is clear that by the nature of his role, a leader is bound to set forth the highest ideals, and must therefore live by them himself. His words will permeate the hearts of his hearers more effectively if his way of life commends what he preaches. What he promotes in words, he will enable to be fulfilled by example.

In the prophecy of Isaiah it is written: 'Get you up to a high mountain, O Zion, herald of good tidings.' In other words, those who preach the things of heaven must themselves have abandoned the lower things of earth, and be already scaling the heights. From such a height, a leader will the more readily draw his people, for the integrity of his life will sound forth to all below.

Through active sympathy a leader should seek to be a neighbour to all his people, and through contemplation seek to maintain a clear perspective, so that through his heart of compassion he can transfer to himself the infirmities of others, and through the heights of contemplation transcend the seen in pursuit of what is unseen. This balance is vital otherwise he may so preoccupy himself with lofty aspirations that he despises the infirmities of his neighbours, or else become so enmeshed in their problems that he ceases to seek the things that are above.

Thus it was that the apostle Paul speaks of being led into paradise and being caught up into the third heaven, and yet, though exalted by the contemplation of what is unseen, was able to recall his mind to the needs of daily life. Paul was united by a bond of love with highest and lowest alike, caught up by the power of the Spirit, but content in his compassion for others to share their weakness. That is why he said, 'Who is weak, and I am not weak? Who is hurt, and I do not burn with indignation?' And again, 'To the Jews, I became as a Jew.' He did so, not by abandoning his faith, but by expanding his compassion for others. By transfiguring the person of the unbeliever into himself, he wanted to learn personally how to care for others, giving to them in the same way as he himself would like to receive, were their positions in life to be reversed.

So let not the shepherd of the sheep ever be afraid; for under God, who balances all things, he will be more easily rescued from his own temptations the more he allows himself to feel the temptations that assail others.

6 November

William Temple

Archbishop of Canterbury, Teacher of the Faith, 1944

William Temple was born in 1881 and baptized on this day in Exeter Cathedral. His father was Bishop of Exeter and later Archbishop of Canterbury. William excelled in academic studies and developed into a philosopher and theologian of significance. After ordination, he quickly made a mark in the Church and at forty became a bishop. Within a decade he was Archbishop of York. He is especially remembered for his ecumenical efforts and also for his concern with social issues, contributing notably to the debate which led to the creation of State welfare provision after the Second World War. He died in 1944, only two years after his translation to the See of Canterbury.

A Reading from *Christianity and Social Order* by William Temple

The claim of the Christian Church to make its voice heard in matters of politics and economics is very widely resented, even by those who are Christian in personal belief and in devotional practice. It is commonly assumed that religion is one department of life, like art or science, and that it is playing the part of a busybody when it lays down principles for the guidance of other departments, whether art and science or business and politics.

In an age when it is tacitly assumed that the Church is concerned with another world than this, and in this with nothing but individual conduct as bearing on prospects in that other world, hardly anyone reads the history of the Church in its exercise of political influence. It is assumed that the Church exercises little influence and ought to exercise none; it is further assumed that this assumption is self-evident and has always been made by reasonable people.

A survey of history, however, shows that the claim of the Church today to be heard in relation to political and economic problems is no new usurpation, but a reassertion of a right once universally admitted and widely regarded. But it also shows that this right may be compromised by injudicious exercise, especially when the autonomy of technique in the various departments of life is ignored. Religion may rightly censure the use of artistic talents for making money out of people's baser tastes, but it cannot lay down laws about perspective or the use of a paintbrush. It may insist that scientific inquiry be prompted by a pure love of truth and not distorted (as in Nazi Germany) by political considerations. It may declare the proper relation of the economic to other activities, but it cannot claim to know what will be the purely economic effect of particular proposals. It is, however, entitled to say that some economic gains ought not to be sought because of the injuries involved to interests higher than economic; and this principle of the subordination of the whole economic sphere is not yet generally accepted.

The primary principle of Christian ethics and Christian politics must be respect for every person simply as a person. If each man and woman is a child of God, whom God loves and for whom Christ died, then there is in each a worth absolutely independent of all usefulness to society. The person is primary, not the society; the State existed for the citizen, not the citizen for the State. The first aim of social progress must be to give the fullest possible scope for the exercise of all powers and qualities which are distinctly personal; and of those the most fundamental is deliberate choice. Consequently society must be so arranged as to give to every citizen the maximum opportunity for making deliberate choices and the best possible training for the use of that opportunity. Freedom must be freedom *for* something as well as freedom *from* something. It must be the actual ability to form and carry out a purpose.

Finally, I should give a false impression of my own convictions if I did not state that there is no hope of establishing a more Christian social order except through the labour and sacrifice of those in whom the Spirit of Christ is active, and that the first necessity for progress is more and better Christians taking full responsibility as citizens for the political, social and economic system under which they and their fellows live.

7 November

Willibrord of York

Archbishop of Utrecht, Apostle of Frisia, 739

Willibrord was born in Northumbria and educated at Ripon but the main part of his life was dedicated to his missionary work in Frisia and northern Germany. He built many churches, inaugurated bishoprics and consecrated cathedrals: the Cathedral of Utrecht, with a diocesan organization based on that of Canterbury, is his most well-known foundation. Together with his younger contemporary Boniface, he began a century of English Christian influence on continental Christianity. Alcuin described him as venerable, gracious and full of joy, and his ministry as based on energetic preaching informed by prayer and sacred reading. He died on this day in the year 739 and was buried at Echternach monastery in Luxembourg, which he founded. He is the patron saint of the Netherlands.

A Reading from *The History of the English Church and People* by the Venerable Bede

The venerable servant of Christ, Bishop Egbert, planned to bring blessings to more people by undertaking the apostolic task of carrying the Word of God, through the preaching of the gospel, to some of the nations who had not heard it. He had learned that there were many peoples in Germany, of whose stock came the Angles or Saxons now settled in Britain.

Egbert realised that he was not permitted to go and preach to the heathen himself, being needed of some other purpose for holy Church, so he attempted to send other holy and industrious men for the work of preaching, among whom the outstanding figure by his priestly rank and his merit was one named Willibrord.

When he and his twelve companions arrived, they made a detour to visit Peppin, Duke of the Franks, by whom they were graciously received. Since Peppin had recently conquered Nearer Frisia and driven out King Radbod, he dispatched them to preach there, supporting them with his imperial authority so that no one should interfere with their preaching, and granting many favours to those who wished to embrace the faith. Consequently, aided by God's grace, they converted many folk in a short while from idolatry to faith in Christ.

When those who had come over had taught in Frisia for a number of years, Peppin with their unanimous consent dispatched the venerable Willibrord to Rome, where Sergius was still pope, with the request that he might be consecrated archbishop of the Frisians. His request was carried out in the year of our Lord 696, and Willibrord was consecrated in the church of the holy martyr Cecilia on her feast day, when the pope gave him the name of Clement. He was sent back to his bishopric without delay, fourteen days after his arrival in the city.

Peppin assigned him a place for his see in his own famous fortress, which is known in the ancient language of that people as Wiltaburg, that is, the Town of the Wilti; but it is known in the Gallic tongue as Utrecht. Having built a church here, the most reverend bishop preached the word of faith far and wide, recalling many from their errors and establishing several churches and a number of monasteries in those parts.

7 November

Richard Davies

Bishop and Translator, 1581

Richard Davies, the son of a north Welsh curate, was probably born in 1501. He was a graduate of New Inn Hall, Oxford, where he apparently first came into contact with Protestant ideas. In 1553, on the accession of Queen Mary, Davies was deprived of the English Crown livings to which he had been appointed in the previous reign. He and his family went into exile in Frankfurt. After Mary's death Davies returned and was appointed Bishop of St Asaph. In 1561 he moved to the See of St Davids. Richard Davies was a conscientious bishop and a gifted scholar. He collaborated with William Salesbury in producing the Welsh Prayer Book and New Testament of 1567. His preface to the latter was an Epistol at y Cembru ('Letter to the Welsh') which argued that the reformed Church in Wales had recovered the early Welsh

Christianity of the period before Augustine of Canterbury. Davies also translated some of the Old Testament into English for the 'Bishops' Bible' of 1568. He died in the year 1581.

A Reading from the preface of Richard Davies
to the Welsh Testament of 1567

Take [the book] in your hand, brother, and read: here you may see where you once stood, here you may recognise your own ancient faith, the laudable Christian religion that once was yours. Here you have the faith that once you defended to the point of risking fire and sword the faith in whose cause your co-religionists and learned teachers were martyred. Perhaps it is strange for you to hear that your ancient faith should have been the history of the Testament and the Word of God; for you have never seen a Bible or Testament in Welsh, written or printed. Truth to tell, I have never succeeded in having sight of a Bible in Welsh, except that I remember seeing as a boy a copy of the five books of Moses in Welsh in the house of an uncle who was a learned man. But no one understood the book or valued it. It is doubtful, as far as I know, that you would be able to find in the whole of Wales one ancient Bible in Welsh, since the Welsh lost or destroyed all their books. Yet I have no doubt at all that the Bible was once commonly available enough in Welsh. The perfection of the faith of the martyrs, the clerics and the laity that I have already spoken of above is a strong proof that you once had the holy Scriptures in your own tongue. For nothing is able to secure faith in a man to the point of suffering death in its cause than the Word of God when a man knows it and understands it for himself.

8 November

The Saints and Martyrs of England

or The Saints of Wales

The date when Christianity first came to England is not known, but there were British bishops at the Council of Arles in the year 314, indicating a Church with order and worship. Since those days, Christians from England have shared the message of the good news at home and around the world. As the world-wide fellowship of the Anglican Communion developed, incorporating peoples of many nations and cultures, individual Christian men and women have shone as beacons, heroically bearing witness to their Lord, some through a simple life of holiness, others by giving their lives for the sake of Christ.

A Reading from *The Letter to Diognetus*
by an unknown second-century author

Christians are not distinguishable from other people by nationality or language or the way they dress. They do not live in cities reserved to themselves; they do not speak a special dialect; there is nothing eccentric about their way of life. Their beliefs are not the invention of some sharp, inquisitive mind, nor are they like some, slaves of this or that school of thought. They are distributed among Greek and non-Greek cities alike, according to their human lot. They conform to local usage in their dress, diet, and manner of life. Nevertheless, in their communities they do reveal some extraordinary and undeniably paradoxical attitudes. They live each in his or her own native country, but they are like pilgrims in transit. They play their full part as citizens and are content to submit to every burden as if they were resident aliens. For them, every foreign country is home, and every homeland is foreign territory.

They marry like everyone else. They beget children, but they do not abandon them at birth. They will share their table with you, but not their marriage bed. They are in the world, but they refuse to conform to the ways of the world. They pass their days on earth, but their citizenship is in heaven. They obey the established laws, but in their way of life transcend all laws. They show love to all people, but all persecute them. They are misunderstood and condemned; they are killed and yet gain life. Poor themselves, they make many rich. Materially they possess nothing, and yet they possess everything. They are despised, and yet in this contempt they discover glory; they are slandered, and yet are vindicated. They counter false accusations with blessings, and abuse with courtesy. In spite of the good they do, they are punished as criminals, but in the face of such punishment rejoice like those given a new lease of life. Jews denounce them as heretics, and Greeks harass them with the threat of persecution; and in spite of all this ill-treatment, no one can produce grounds for hostility. In a word, what the soul is to the body, Christians are to the world.

alternative reading

A Reading from a commentary on the Psalms by Jerome

The cross of Christ is the support of humankind. On this foundation column we build our dwelling securely. When I speak of the cross, I am not speaking literally of the wood of the cross, but of the Passion. In this sense, the cross is to be found as much in Britain as in India, and throughout the whole universe. For is not this what Christ means when he says in the Gospel: 'If you do not take up your cross each day and follow in my footsteps, if your soul is not ready to take up the cross as mine was taken up for you, you cannot be my disciple.'

Blessed are those who bear the cross and the resurrection in their hearts, as well as the place of Christ's birth and ascension. Blessed are those who possess Bethlehem in their hearts and in whose hearts Christ is born daily. For what is the meaning of Bethlehem if not 'house of bread'? So let us too be a house of bread, a home for that bread which came down from heaven.

Every day Christ is crucified, for we are crucified to the world, and Christ is crucified in us. Blessed are those in whose hearts Christ rises every day because every day such people are purged of their smallest sins. Blessed are those who every day ascend from the Mount of Olives to the kingdom of heaven, where the olives are large and the light of Christ is born.

alternative reading

A Reading from *The Cost of Discipleship* by Dietrich Bonhoeffer

The body of Christ takes up space on earth. That is a consequence of the incarnation. Christ came into his own. But at his birth they gave him a manger, for 'there was no room in the inn'. At his death they thrust him out, and his body hung between earth and heaven on the gallows. But despite all this, the incarnation does involve a claim to a space of its own on earth. Anything which claims space is visible. Hence the body of Christ can only be a visible body, or else it is not a body at all. The physical body of the man Jesus is visible to all, his divine sonship only to the eye of faith, just as that body as the body of God incarnate is visible only to faith. That Jesus was in the flesh was visible fact, but that he bore our flesh is a matter of faith.

A truth, a doctrine, or a religion need no space for themselves. They are disembodied entities. They are heard, learnt and apprehended, and that is all. But the incarnate Son of God needs not only ears or hearts, but living men and women who will follow him. That is why he called his disciples into a literal, bodily following, and thus made his fellowship with them a visible reality. That fellowship was founded and sustained by Jesus Christ, the incarnate Lord himself. It was the Word made flesh which had called them and created their bodily fellowship with him. Having been called, they could no longer remain in obscurity, for they were the light that must shine, the city set on the hill which must be seen. Their fellowship with him was visibly overshadowed by the cross and passion of Jesus Christ. In order that they might enjoy that fellowship with him, the disciples must leave everything else behind, and submit to suffering and persecution. Yet even in the midst of their persecutions they receive back all they had lost in visible form – brothers, sisters, fields and houses in his fellowship. The Church consisting of Christ's followers manifest to the whole world a visible community. Here were bodies which acted, worked and suffered in fellowship with Jesus.

alternative reading for The Church in Wales

A Reading from a hymn of Bishop Timothy Rees

Arglwydd, trefni mewn doethineb
Ein tymhorau is y rhod;
Daw i ben dy fythol arfaeth
Er pob newid sydd yn bod:
Ti ddewisaist Wlad y Bryniau,
Ddyddiau tywyll a di-wawr,
I egluro dy fwriadau
Er dy glod a'th Enw mawr.

Hyd ein glannau pell a olchir
O'r gorllewin gan y lli
Yr anfonaist ti o'th gariad
Sôn am Groesbren Calfari:
Dros yr Eglwys Lân Gatholig
Collwyd chwys a gwaed dy blant,
A disgleirio'n rhòl dy arwyr
Y mae enw Dewi Sant.

Parchwn, Arglwydd, goffadwriaeth
Pawb o Seintiau Cymru wen,
Yr Esgobion a'r Offeiriaid
A'r Merthyri hwnt i'r llen:

Dewi, Dyfrig, Deiniol, Teilo –
Dewr y safent tros y gwir,
Bu eu pader, bu eu penyd
Yn sancteiddio erwau'n tir.

Mae dy fwriad yn goroesi
Holl ddamweiniau daear lawr;
Mae dy Eglwys Lân yn aros
Byth yn dyst o'th gariad mawr:
Dyro nerth a gweledigaeth,
Arglwydd, yn dy waith o hyd,
A'th ewyllys di a wneler
Yn yr Eglwys a'r holl fyd.

(Lord, who in thy perfect wisdom
Times and seasons dost arrange –
Working out thy ceaseless purpose
In a world of ceaseless change:
Thou didst form our ancient nation
In remote barbaric days,
To unfold in it a purpose
To thy glory and thy praise.

To our shores remote, benighted,
Washed by distant western waves,
Tidings in thy love thou sentest,
Tidings of the cross that saves.
Men of courage strove and suffered
Here thy holy Church to plant;
Glorious in the roll of heroes
Shines the name of Dewi Sant.

Lord, we hold in veneration
All the Saints our land has known,
Bishops, priests, confessors, martyrs
Standing now around thy throne –
Dewi, Dyfrig, Deiniol, Teilo, –
All the gallant saintly band,
Who of old by prayer and labour
Hallowed all our fatherland.

Still thy ancient purpose standeth
Every change and chance above;
Still thy ancient Church remaineth –
Witness to thy changeless love.
Vision grant us, Lord, and courage
To fulfil the work begun;
In the Church and in the nation
Lord of lords, thy will be done.)

9 November

Margery Kempe

Mystic, c.1440

Margery Kempe was born in Lynn in Norfolk in the late fourteenth century, a contemporary of Julian of Norwich. She received many visions, several of them of the Holy Family, one of the most regular being of the crucifixion. She also had conversations with the saints. She was much sought after as a visionary, was endlessly in trouble with the Church, rebuked by the Archbishop of York, and was more than once imprisoned. Following the messages in her visions, she undertook pilgrimages to many holy places, including Walsingham, Canterbury, Compostela, Rome and Jerusalem, often setting out penniless. She was blessed with the gift of tears and seems to have been favoured with singular signs of Christ's love, whereby for long periods she enjoyed consciousness of a close communion with him and developed a strong compassion for the sinful world. Her autobiography, The Book of Margery Kempe, recounts her remarkable life. She died towards the middle of the fifteenth century.

A Reading from *The Book of Margery Kempe*

Note: In this extract Margery Kempe is brought before the court of the Archbishop of York, her outspoken opinions having led her detractors to level the charge of heresy against her.

At last the archbishop came into the chapel with his clerics, and he said to her abruptly, 'Why do you go about in white clothes? Are you a virgin?' She, kneeling before him, said, 'No, sir, I am no virgin; I am a married woman.'

Speaking to her very roughly, the archbishop asked, 'Why do you weep so, woman?' She answering said, 'Sir, you shall wish some day that you had wept as sorely as I.'

And then, after the archbishop had put to her the Articles of our Faith – to which God gave her grace to answer well, truly and readily, without much having to stop and think, so that he could not criticise her – he said to the clerics, 'She knows her faith well enough. What shall I do with her?'

The clerics said, 'We know very well that she knows the Articles of the Faith, but we will not allow her to dwell among us, because the people have great faith in her talk, and perhaps she might lead some of them astray.' Then the archbishop said to her: 'I am told very bad things about you. I hear it said that you are a very wicked woman.' And she replied, 'Sir, I also hear it said that you are a wicked man. And if you are as wicked as people say, you will never get to heaven, unless you amend while you are here.'

Then he said very roughly, 'Why you! What do people say about me?' She answered, 'Other people, sir, can tell you well enough.' Then the archbishop said to her, 'You shall swear that you will not teach people or call them to account in my diocese.'

'No, sir, I will not swear.' she said, 'for I shall speak of God and rebuke those who swear great oaths wherever I go, until such time that the pope and holy Church have ordained that nobody shall be so bold as to speak of God, for God almighty does not forbid, sir, that we should speak of him. And also the gospel mentions that, when the woman had heard our Lord preach, she came before him and said in a loud voice, "Blessed be the womb that bore you, and the teats that gave you suck." Then our Lord replied to her, "In truth, so are they blessed who hear the word of God and keep it." And therefore, sir, I think that the gospel gives me leave to speak of God.'

'Ah, sir,' said the clerics, 'here we know that she has a devil in her, for she speaks of the Gospel.' A great cleric quickly produced a book and quoted Saint Paul for his part against her, that no woman should preach. She, answering to this, said, 'I do not preach, sir; I do not go into any pulpit, I use only conversation and good words, and that I will do while I live.'

When the archbishop heard her defence he commended her for her honesty. And she, kneeling down on her knees, asked his blessing. He, asking her to pray for him, blessed her and let her go.

Then she, going back again to York, was received by many people, and by very worthy clerics who rejoiced in our Lord who had given her – uneducated as she was – the wit and wisdom to answer so many learned men without shame or blame. Thanks be to God.

9 November

George Hay Forbes

Priest, 1875

Brother of Alexander Penrose Forbes, and crippled throughout his life, George Hay Forbes developed an early interest in liturgy and championed the cause of the Scottish Liturgy against those who wished to foster conformity with England by the use of the Book of Common Prayer. He was ordained in 1848 and in that year began a mission in Burntisland, where he worked as a devoted priest for the rest of his life. He set up his own printing press, on which he issued a new Prayer Book in 1850, which met with vigorous opposition. He edited many patristic and liturgical works with meticulous accuracy. A man of deep piety, he died in the year 1875.

A Reading from *Episcopal Scotland in the Nineteenth Century* by Marion Lochhead

Bishop Forbes could truly be described as 'a godly and well learned man', but he was equalled, possibly surpassed in liturgical scholarship by his younger brother, George Hay Forbes. He was born in Edinburgh in 1821. An illness in childhood left him paralysed from the knees down; at the age of thirteen he was sent to France, to be under the care of an orthopaedist, but no cure was effected. By the age of eighteen, however, he was already a scholar, mature in mind, and had begun his special study of Saint Gregory of Nyssa.

This cripple led no crippled or secluded life. He moved about on crutches, helped his father with the administration of church affairs, published a pamphlet on 'The Christian Sacrifice in the Eucharist' and in 1846 went to Venice to examine and collate manuscripts of Saint Gregory. It was a most difficult journey for one who had to be helped to climb stairs and to be lifted into carriages: how he contrived to get in and out of gondolas is not very comfortably imagined! But then and to the end of his life, he forced Brother Body to be obedient to his demands.

That bodily infirmity was given by Bishop Skinner as a reason for refusing to ordain him. An appeal to Bishop Torry was successful and he was appointed deacon in 1848. In 1849 he was priested by his own brother, now Bishop of Brechin, and was given by Bishop Torry the charge of Burntisland, Fife. The congregation was small; there was no church and he held services in the Town Hall. He began a weekly celebration of the Eucharist. An uncompromising High Churchman, he met a good deal of hostility in a very Presbyterian town. This was, in time, to be overcome by his sincerity and devotion. Indeed, local animosity was overcome to such a degree that in 1869 this Episcopal priest was elected Provost of the town.

10 November

Leo the Great

Bishop of Rome, Teacher of the Faith, 461

Leo the Great became Pope in the year 440 and twice proved his bravery in saving the citizens of Rome from the invading barbarians. He was an eloquent and wise preacher, using simple gospel texts to proclaim the Christian faith. His administrative skills were unrivalled and he used the resources of the Church for the good of the people. Rather than further confuse Christians by entering into the controversy over the person of Christ, Leo spoke simply of the humility of Christ who was divine and human in his compassion, uniting Biblical images in prayer rather than dividing in debate. Leo died on this day in the year 461.

A Reading from a letter of Leo the Great, Bishop of Rome,
to Flavian, Bishop of Constantinople, dated 13 June 449;
also known as *The Tome of Leo*

We could not overcome the author of sin and death, unless Christ had taken our nature and made it his own, he whom sin could not defile or death imprison. He was conceived of the Holy Spirit within the womb of his Virgin Mother, whose virginity remained undefiled in his birth as in his conception.

That birth, uniquely marvellous and marvellously unique, should not be understood in such a way as to suggest that the distinctive characteristics of our humanity were excluded by this process of new creation. For whilst it is true that the Holy Spirit made the Virgin fertile, it is equally true that Christ received a real body from her body.

In this way the characteristics of each nature and being were completely preserved in Christ, coming together in his one person. Humility was assumed by majesty, weakness by strength, mortality by eternity; and to pay the debt that we had incurred, an inviolable nature was united to a nature that can suffer. To fulfil the conditions of our inner healing, the man Jesus Christ, one and the same mediator between humankind and God, was able to die in respect of one nature, and unable to die in respect of the other.

Thus in the whole and perfect nature of a human being, true God was born, complete in what pertained to his divine nature, and complete in what pertained to ours.

By 'ours' I mean only what the creator formed in us from the beginning, which Christ assumed in order to repair. In our Saviour there was no trace of those characteristics which the Deceiver introduced to humanity, and which we, being deceived, allowed to enter into our common inheritance. Christ did not participate in sin simply because he entered into fellowship with our human frailty. He assumed the form of a servant without any trace of sin, thereby enhancing our humanity, but without detracting from his divinity. For that 'emptying of himself' whereby the invisible God made himself visible, and the creator and Lord of all willed to become mortal, was a reaching out in compassion, not a failure of power.

Accordingly, he who made humanity, whilst remaining in the form of God, was himself made human in the form of a servant. Each nature preserves its own characteristics without diminution, so that the form a servant does not detract from the form of God.

11 November

Martin

Bishop of Tours, *c.*397

Born in about the year 316 in Pannonia (in modern-day Hungary), Martin was a soldier in the Roman army and a Christian. He found the two rôles conflicted and, under the influence of Hilary, Bishop of Poitiers, he founded a monastery in Hilary's diocese in the year 360, the first such foundation in Gaul. The religious house was a centre for missionary work in the local countryside, setting a new example where, previously, all Christian activity had been centred in cities and undertaken from the cathedral there. In 372, Martin was elected Bishop of Tours by popular acclaim and he continued his monastic lifestyle as a bishop, remaining in that ministry until his death on this day in the year 397.

A Reading from *The Life of Saint Martin*
by Sulpicius Severus

During the three years before his baptism, Martin was a professional soldier, but managed to keep himself free from the vices in which so often soldiers indulge. He was extremely kind towards his fellow-soldiers, and held them in great affection; while his patience and humility surpassed what seemed possible for human nature to sustain. His self-denial needs no praise. It was evident even at this date. In fact, many regarded him not so much a soldier as a monk. By these qualities he so endeared himself to his comrades that they held him not simply in high esteem, but truly loved him.

Although not yet made a new creation in Christ, by his good works Martin was already a candidate for baptism. He regularly came to the help of those in trouble, giving practical help to the destitute, supporting the needy, clothing the naked, and from his military pay would keep back only what he needed for his daily needs. He was already complying with the Gospel precept to 'take no thought for tomorrow'.

One day during a particularly severe winter, a winter so extreme that many of the populace were dying of the cold, Martin was out on duty. He was wearing his soldier's uniform and was armed. He met in the gateway of the city of Amiens a poor man who was destitute of clothing. He was begging for help, but all passed by the poor man without even acknowledging his presence. When Martin, that man full of God, saw the poor man whom no one pitied, he questioned himself about what was best do. He had nothing left save the cloak he was wearing, having already given away the rest of his clothes to the destitute. Unsheathing his sword, he cut his cloak in two, giving one half to the poor man, and wrapping the remaining half round himself.

At this, some of the bystanders started laughing because Martin looked so peculiar. He stood out from the other soldiers, being only partly dressed. Other people of more sensitive understanding, however, were deeply moved by his action, ashamed that they had nothing themselves. They felt this particularly, having more than Martin they could have clothed the poor man without reducing themselves to nakedness if they had wanted to.

The following night, Martin fell into a deep sleep, and as he slept he had a vision of Christ arrayed in part of the cloak with which he had clothed the poor man. He contemplated the sight of the Lord with wonder, and was told to clothe himself with the robe he had given. He heard Jesus speaking to him quite distinctly, 'Martin, you may be still a catechumen, but you have clothed me with this robe.' The Lord, mindful of his own words while on earth, (when he said 'Inasmuch as you have done this to the least of my brothers and sisters, you have done it to me') revealed that he himself had been clothed in that poor man. After this vision the holy man was not puffed up with his own importance, but acknowledging the goodness of God in what had happened, presented himself without further delay for baptism. He was twenty years of age.

[Not long after this the barbarians launched an attack on the two divisions stationed in Gaul. Julian Caesar summoned the army and, in preparation for battle, began to issue each soldier with his pay. Judging this a suitable opportunity for seeking discharge – for he did not think it right to receive pay if he intended to leave the army – Martin addressed Caesar: 'Until now I have served you as a soldier. Give me leave to become a soldier for God. Let the men who are to serve you in the army receive their due pay: I am a soldier of Christ, and it is not right that I should fight.'

The tyrant stormed at Martin on hearing this, declaring that it was from no religious conviction that he was withdrawing from military service, but from fear of the forthcoming battle. But Martin, very courageously and resolute in the face of personal danger, replied: 'If my conduct is ascribed to cowardice, and not to faith, then allow me to take my place in the front-line of battle tomorrow unarmed, and in the name of the Lord Jesus, protected by the sign of the cross rather than by shield or helmet, I will safely penetrate the ranks of the enemy.' Caesar ordered Martin to be put in prison and to put his words to the test the next day.

The following morning, however, the enemy sent ambassadors to Caesar to sue for peace, surrendering both themselves and their possessions. In such circumstances, who can doubt that the victory was due to this saintly man? For Christ has no wish to secure any victory for his soldiers than that an enemy should be subdued without bloodshed, and that no one should be killed.]

alternative reading

A Reading from *The Life of Saint Martin* by Sulpicius Severus

It is beyond my powers to set forth adequately how Martin distinguished himself in the discharge of his duties as Bishop of Tours. He remained just the same as he had been before his ordination. There was the same humility in his heart, and the same unpretentious clothing. He always maintained his role as bishop with true dignity and courtesy, without ever setting aside the life and virtues of a monk.

For a long time he made use of a cell connected to the church, but increasingly this became impracticable with the vast numbers of people visiting him. So he established a monastery two miles outside the city. This exact spot he kept secret and away from people, so that he could enjoy the solitude of a hermit. On one side, his hermitage was bordered by a precipitous rock face of a high mountain, while on the other side, the river Loire cut off the land from the rest of the valley with the result that the place could only be approached one person at a time along a very narrow passage. Here then, Martin constructed for himself a wooden cell.

Many of the other monks also built for themselves hermitages, but most of these were hollowed out caves on the mountainside. Altogether there were eighty disciples who followed the discipline of their saintly master. No one kept anything as his own; everything was held in common. No one bought or sold anything for himself, as is monastic custom. No craft was practised there except that of transcribing texts, and this task was allocated to the younger brothers, leaving the seniors free to devote themselves to prayer. Rarely did one of the brothers go beyond his cell, unless it was to assemble for corporate prayer. They ate communally, once their daily fast was completed; no one drank wine, except in illness; and most of brothers wore simple, rough garments. Softer material was frowned upon which was quite remarkable given that a number of the monks were drawn from the nobility. Although from different backgrounds, all were united in observing a common observance of humility and patient endurance. A number of the monks were subsequently made bishops. For what city or church would not covet as its priests those trained in the monastery of Martin?

12 November

Tysilio

Abbot, seventh century

Tysilio was the son of Brochwel Ysgithrog, prince of Powys. Against his father's will he became a member of the religious community established by Gwyddfarch at Meifod. Tysilio succeeded Gwyddfarch as Abbot of Meifod and under his leadership it became the most important religious centre in Powys. Saint Beuno spent forty days there with Tysilio, after Berriew was overrun by the Saxons. The cluster of churches dedicated to Tysilio in Montgomeryshire and Denbighshire reflect his influence in the area. Three other dedications (in Anglesey, Ceredigion and on the borders of Carmarthenshire and Pembrokeshire) give credence to the tradition that he left Powys for a time in order not to be forced to become its prince. After his death Tysilio became seen as the saintly protector of Powys. He is depicted as such in a famous poem written in the twelfth century by Cynddelw Brydydd Mawr.

A Reading from *Canu Tysilio*, a twelfth-century poem by Cynddelw Brydydd Mawr

'A description of the community at Meifod'

Caraf-i lan a'r llên gan gadredd
Ger y mae Gwyddfarch uch Gwynedd:
Gwyddfidle glywdde glew dachwedd,
Gwydd fynwent, gwyddfa brenhinedd,
Beirdd neuedd, niferawg orsedd,
Breisg adorth, eorth ehofnedd:
Breinawg log, leudir cyfannedd,
Meifod wen, nid meiwyr a'i medd!
Nis medd trais, nis traidd ysgeraint,
Nis daered trefred y trisaint,
Mwy ynddi gwesti gwesteifiaint
Ei balchnawdd nog amrawdd amraint:
A'i balchlan i rhwng ei balchnaint,
A'i balchwyr a'u balchwyr tesaint,
A'i balchlwys eglwys eglurfraint,
A'i balchradd a'i balchrodd tramaint,
A'i balchwawr yn nawr yn newaint
Ai' balchgor heb achor echwraint,
A'i balch offeiriad a'i hoffeiriaint
A'i pharawd offeren hoffaint.

I love a church and its mighty clerics,
By Gwyddfarch's holy place beyond Gwynedd:
A princely wooded place, an honourable churchyard,
A burying place for princes after the bravery of battle,
The desire of poets, a place where many live,
Where there are generous provisions, a place for the courageous,
A privileged monastery on open ground with living space,
Blessed Meifod, no cowardly men possess it!
No violence rules it, no enemies can enter it,
The dwelling place of the three saints
        will never pay such men homage,
The hospitable welcome within its splendid patronage
With no dishonourable intention:
Its fine enclosure between its lovely streams,
Its dignified and zealously devout inhabitants,
Its gorgeous, much-privileged church,
Its beautiful dignity and its immeasurably splendid gifts,
Its lovely dawn after the depths of night,
Its fine chancel a safe sanctuary from violence,
Its dignified priests and their services
And the loveliness of its Mass…'

12 November

Machar

Bishop, *c.*600

Machar was born in Ireland of princely parentage, and was baptized by Colman. He accompanied Columba to Iona, from where he moved to Mull, allegedly because his sanctity aroused the jealousy of some of the other monks. Later he established a mission in the north-east of Scotland, on the site that came to be occupied by the cathedral in Old Aberdeen which is dedicated to him. Saint Machar's Well beside it traditionally provided water for local baptisms.

A Reading from a homily of Gregory the Great

Our Lord in the Gospel says: 'By your patience you will gain possession of your lives.' Patience is the root and guardian of all the virtues. We gain possession of our lives by patience, since when we learn to govern ourselves, we begin to gain possession of the very thing we are.

True patience consists in bearing calmly the evils that others do to us, and in not being consumed by resentment against those who inflict them. On the other hand, those who only appear to bear the evils done them by their neighbours, who suffer them in silence but inwardly are looking for an opportunity for revenge, are not practising patience, but only a charade.

Paul writes that 'love is patient and kind.' It is patient in bearing the evils done to us by others, and it is kind in even loving those it bears with. Our Lord himself commands us: 'Love your enemies, do good to those who hate you; pray for those who persecute you and speak all kind of calumny against you.' Virtue in the sight of our contemporaries is to bear with those who oppose us, but virtue in the sight of God is to love them. This is the only sacrifice acceptable to God.

Often we appear to be patient only because we are unable to repay the evils we suffer from others. As I have said, those who do not pay back evil only because they cannot do so are not truly patient. As Christians, we should not be concerned with the appearance of patience, but with a patience that is rooted in the heart.

13 November

Charles Simeon

Priest, Evangelical Divine, 1836

Born in Reading in 1759, Charles Simeon was educated at Cambridge University and spent the rest of his life in that city. He became a Fellow of King's College in 1782 and was ordained priest the following year, when he became Vicar of Holy Trinity Church nearby. He had Evangelical leanings as a boy but it was whilst preparing for holy communion on his entrance to College that he became aware of the redeeming love of God, an experience he regarded as the turning point in his life. Many of the parishioners of Holy Trinity Church did not welcome him, since he had been appointed through his own family links, but his patent care and love for them all overcame their antipathy and his preaching greatly increased the congregation.Charles had carved on the inside of the pulpit in Holy Trinity Church, where only the preacher could see, the words from John 12:21, when Philip brought the Greeks to our Lord, and they said, 'Sir, we would see Jesus.' These words were a constant reminder to him that people came not to gaze on a great preacher or to admire his eloquence, but to seek Jesus.Charles became a leading Evangelical influence in the Church and was one of the founders of the Church Missionary Society. He also set up the Simeon Trust which made appointments to parishes of fellow Evangelicals. He remained Vicar of Holy Trinity until his death on this day in the year 1836.

A Reading from 'Evangelic and Pharisaic Righteousness Compared', being a sermon delivered by Charles Simeon before the University of Cambridge in November 1809

There is a kind of religion which is held in esteem by mankind at large. An outward reverence for the ordinances of religion, together with habits of temperance, justice, chastity, and benevolence, constitute what the world considers a perfect character. The description which Saint Paul gives of himself previous to his conversion is so congenial with their sentiments of perfection that they would not hesitate to rest the salvation of their souls on his attainments. But what said he of his state when once he came to view it aright? 'What things were gain to me, those I counted loss for Christ. Yea doubtless, and I count all things but loss for the excellency of the knowledge of Christ Jesus my Lord.' He saw that brokenness of heart for sin, a humble affiance in the Lord Jesus Christ, and an unreserved devotedness of heart to his service, were indispensable to the salvation of the soul. He saw that, without these, no attainments would be of any avail. Yea, a man might have all the biblical learning of the scribes, and all the sanctified habits of the Pharisees, and yet never be approved of the Lord in this world, nor ever be accepted of him in the world to come.

Is it not then desirable that those who are in repute for wisdom and piety amongst us should pause and inquire whether their righteousness really exceeds that of the scribes and Pharisees? Would they not do well to study the account which Saint Paul gives of himself previous to his conversion, and to examine wherein they surpass him? Alas! Alas! We are exceedingly averse to being undeceived; but I would entreat every one of my hearers to consider deeply what our blessed Lord has spoken of such characters: 'Ye are they which justify yourselves before men; but God knoweth your hearts: for that which is highly esteemed among men is abomination in the sight of God.'

Lastly, we would suggest some profitable considerations to those who profess to have attained that superior righteousness spoken of in our text. You need not be told that the examples of Christ and his apostles, and indeed of all the primitive Christians, were offensive, rather than pleasing, to the pharisee of old. The same disapprobation of real piety still lurks in the hearts of those who occupy the seat of Moses. You must not wonder, therefore, if your contrition be called gloom; your faith in Christ, presumption; your delight in his ways, enthusiasm; and your devotion to his service, preciseness of hypocrisy. Well, if it must be so, console yourselves with this, that you share the fate of all the saints that have gone before you, and that your state, with all the obloquy that attends it, is infinitely better than that of your revilers and persecutors. You may well be content to be despised by men whilst you are conscious of the favour and approbation of God.

14 November

Dyfrig

Bishop, *c.*532

Born about the year 460 in the area known as Erging (south-west Herefordshire), Dyfrig became the first bishop to have jurisdiction over the area which later became the diocese of Llandaff. He founded a number of monastic schools in Erging, from which his pupils would travel out and themselves begin new communities. They regarded Dyfrig as their spiritual leader – in other words, their bishop. Dyfrig himself would visit the communities his pupils founded, in particular that of Illtud at Llantwit Major. It was his custom to spend Lent on Caldey Island; but it was Bardsey Island, off the Lleyn Peninsula, that became Dyfrig's place of retirement and eventually his death, probably some time between 532 and 550. In 1120 the body of Dyfrig was brought from Bardsey to the new cathedral at Llandaff, and placed on the north side of the altar, becoming a place of pilgrimage.

A Reading from a poem of Meilyr Brydydd in which he reflects upon the inevitability of his own death, the mercy of God, and Bardsey Island where as many as twenty thousand saints were reputed to be buried

The Deathbed Song of Meilyr Brydydd

King of kings, leader easy to praise
I ask this favour of my highest Lord:
Realm-mastering ruler of the sublime and blessed land,
Noble chief, make peace between you and me.
Feeble and empty is my mind, since
I have provoked you, and full of regret.
I have sinned before the Lord my God,
Failing to attend to my due devotion;
But I shall serve my Lord King
Before I am laid in the earth, stripped of life.
A true foretelling (to Adam and his offspring
The prophets had declared
That Jesus would be in the womb of martyrs),
Mary gladly received her burden.
But a burden I have amassed of unclean sin
And have been shaken by its clamour.
Lord of all places, how good you are to praise,
May I praise you and be purified before punishment.
King of all kings, who know me, do not refuse me,

On account of wickedness, for the sake of your mercy.
Many a time I had gold and brocade
From fickle kings for praising them,
And after the gift of song of a superior power,
Poverty-stricken is my tongue on the prospect of its silence.
I am Meilyr the Poet, pilgrim to Peter,
Gate-keeper who measures right virtue.
When the time of our resurrection comes,
All who are in the grave, make me ready.
As I await the call, may my home be
The monastery where the tide rises,
A wilderness of enduring glory,
Around its cemetery the breast of the sea,
Island of fair Mary, sacred isle of the saints,
Awaiting resurrection there is lovely.
Christ of the prophesied cross, who knows me, shall guide me
Past hell, the isolated abode of agony.
The Creator who made me shall receive me
Among the pure parish, the people of Bardsey.

14 November

Laurence O'Toole

Abbot and Archbishop of Dublin, 1180

Laurence was made abbot of the monastery in Glendalough in County Wicklow at the age of twenty-five. Then in 1162 he was chosen by the clergy and laity of Dublin to be their first archbishop. In the days of Strongbow, with whom Laurence worked to restore Christ Church Cathedral in stone, there were many political problems and clashing interests. Laurence has been described as 'self-effacing and self-denying' as he prayed and worked for the settling of differences. He died on this day in the year 1180.

A Reading from *The Irish Saints* by Daphne Pochin Mould

Laurence O'Toole, a contemporary of Thomas Becket, was Archbishop of Dublin during the first Anglo-Norman attack. He stands, therefore, at the end of the development of a purely Irish, with some Scandinavian admixture, culture. He was the sort of man that the reforms (with which the names of Cellach and Mael Maedoc are linked) were producing in the Irish Church before the irruption and disruption caused by the invaders. Like Mael Maedoc, he died on the continent and his biographer was a canon of Eu, with little knowledge of Laurence's Irish background. Native sources on Laurence's activities are few, and thus the would-be biographer is left with hardly any information about what he wants to know, namely the full story of his relations with the invaders. Here was a man who had to negotiate with that same king Henry of England whose actions had led to the murder of Thomas Becket in Canterbury Cathedral.

If Laurence and the other Irish clerics had hoped that the Anglo-Norman invaders could be peacefully integrated into the country and the life of the Church go smoothly forward, it was soon obvious that the very reverse was taking place. Further fighting led in the end to the attempt to stabilise the position by the Treaty of Windsor of 1175. Laurence was a witness to this treaty and we may suppose that he was a leading negotiator. It set out to define the Norman held areas of Ireland and to give a feudal organisation to the kingdoms of Meath and Leinster. By now it was obvious that the incomers could not be dislodged. What is striking about Laurence's position in the tangled affairs of the time is that he seems to have been liked by Irish, Scandinavian and Normans alike in his diocese. There were no national divisions in the petitions for his canonisation.

Following another quarrel between Henry and Ruaidhri Ua Conchobhair, Laurence found himself once again in the role of peacemaker. But he took ill and died at the Augustinian Canons' house of Eu on 14 November 1180, on his way to meet with the king in France. It is possible that if he had gone on, he might have suffered the same fate as Thomas Becket. For there are some brief but significant phrases used of Laurence. Abbot Hughes of Eu in a letter to Pope Innocent II wrote that Laurence had died 'with us an exile and outcast for the liberty of the Church'.

14 November

Samuel Seabury

First Anglican Bishop in North America, 1796

Samuel Seabury was born in Connecticut in 1729 and, after graduating from Yale, was ordained priest in England and assigned by the Society for the Propagation of the Gospel to a church in New Brunswick, New Jersey. During the American War of Independence, he remained faithful to the British Crown, serving as a chaplain in the British army. At a secret meeting of the clergy in Connecticut, Samuel was chosen to seek consecration as bishop but, after a year of fruitless negotiation with the Church of England, he was ordained bishop by the non-juring bishops in the Scottish Episcopal Church on this day in 1784. Returning to America, he held his first Convention in Connecticut the following August and the first General Convention of the American Episcopal Church in 1789. There, they adopted the Scottish eucharistic rite and a similar name to the Church which had proved itself their friend. Samuel died on 25 February in the year 1796.

A Reading from the *Concordat* established between the Scottish bishops and Dr Samuel Seabury, presbyter, in Connecticut, 15 November 1784

The wise and gracious providence of merciful God, having put into the hearts of the Christians of the Episcopal persuasion in Connecticut in North America, to desire that the blessings of a free, valid, and purely ecclesiastical episcopacy might be communicated to them, and a Church regularly formed in that part of the western world upon the most ancient and primitive model:

And application having been made for this purpose by the Reverend Dr Samuel Seabury, presbyter in Connecticut, to the Right Reverend the Bishops of the Church in Scotland:

The said bishops having taken this proposal into their serious consideration, most heartily concurred to promote and encourage the same, so far as lay in their power; and accordingly, began the pious and good work recommended to them by complying with the request of the clergy in Connecticut and advancing the said Dr Samuel Seabury to the high order of the episcopate; at the same time earnestly praying that this work of the Lord, thus happily begun, might prosper in his hands, till it should please the great and glorious head of the Church to increase the number of bishops in America and send forth more labourers into that part of his harvest.

Animated with this pious hope and earnestly desirous to establish a bond of peace and holy communion between the two Churches, the bishops of the Church in Scotland, whose names are underwritten, having had full and free conference with Bishop Seabury after his consecration and advancement as aforesaid, agreed with him on the following articles, which are to serve as a concordat or bond of union, between the Catholic remainder of the ancient Church of Scotland and the now rising Church in the State of Connecticut.

They agree in thankfully receiving and humbly and heartily embracing the whole doctrine of the gospel as revealed and set forth in the holy Scriptures;

They agree in believing this Church to be the mystical body of Christ, of which he alone is the head and supreme governor; and that under him the chief ministers or managers of the affairs of this spiritual society are those called bishops, whose exercise of their sacred office being independent of all lay powers, it follows of consequence that their spiritual authority and jurisdiction cannot be affected by any lay deprivation.

They agree in desiring that there may be as near a conformity in worship and discipline established between the two Churches as is consistent with the different circumstances and customs of nations.

As the celebration of the Holy Eucharist, or administration of the sacrament of the body and blood of Christ, is the principal bond of union among Christians, as well as the most solemn act of worship in the Christian Church, the bishops aforesaid agree in desiring that there be as little variance here as possible. And though the Scottish bishops are very far from prescribing to their brethren in this matter, they cannot help ardently wishing that Bishop Seabury would endeavour all he can, consistently with peace and prudence, to make the celebration of this venerable mystery conformable to the most primitive doctrine and practice in that respect. Which is the pattern the [Episcopal] Church of Scotland has copied after in her Communion Office; and which it has been the wish of some of the most eminent divines of the Church of England, that she also had more closely followed than she seems to have done since she gave up her first reformed liturgy used in the reign of King Edward VI – between which and the form of the [Episcopal] Church of Scotland there is no difference in any point which the primitive Church reckoned essential to the right ministration of the Holy Eucharist.

The bishops aforesaid do hereby jointly declare, in the most solemn manner, that in the whole of this transaction they have nothing else in view but the glory of God and the good of his Church.

15 November

Saints, Martyrs and Missionaries of North America

European settlers first brought Christianity to North America: Spanish, French, British and other settlers colonized the continent bringing their faith with them. In what is now Canada, French immigrants preached among the native Americans, and many, including Jean de Brébeuf and Isaac Jogues, were martyred by the Iraquois between 1642 and 1649. English settlers established various colonies, with different Christian perspectives, and a variety of ministers from the motherland ministered to them: George Fox, Thomas Bray and those sponsored by the SPG and the SPCK which he founded; and John Wesley, who preached his Methodist revival. After the American Revolution, many members of the Church of England fled to Canada, and those who remained organized themselves into dioceses. On 14 November 1784 Samuel Seabury was consecrated in Scotland as the first bishop in North America, and today we remember all who have preached the Christian gospel in that continent and ministered to its people.

A Reading from a speech by Martin Luther King

I am not unmindful that some of you have come here out of excessive trials and tribulation. Some of you have come fresh from narrow jail cells. Some of you have come from areas where your quest for freedom left you battered by the storms of persecution and staggered by the winds of police brutality. You have been the veterans of creative suffering. Continue to work with the faith that unearned suffering is redemptive.

Go back to Mississippi; go back to Alabama; go back to South Carolina; go back to Georgia; go back to Louisiana; go back to the slums and ghettos of the northern cities, knowing that somehow this situation can and will be changed. Let us not wallow in the valley of despair.

So I say to you, my friends, that even though we must face the difficulties of today and tomorrow, I still have a dream. It is a dream deeply rooted in the American dream that one day this nation will rise up and live out the true meaning of its creed – we hold these truths to be self-evident, that all men are created equal.

I have a dream that one day on the red hills of Georgia, sons of former slaves and sons of former slave-owners will be able to sit down together at the table of brotherhood.

I have a dream that one day, even the state of Mississippi, a state sweltering with the heat of injustice, sweltering with the heat of oppression, will be transformed into an oasis of freedom and justice.

I have a dream that my four little children will one day live in a nation where they will not be judged by the colour of their skin but by the content of their character. I have a dream today!

I have a dream that one day, down in Alabama, with its vicious racists, with its governor having his lips dripping with the words of interposition and nullification, that one day, right there in Alabama, little black boys and black girls will be able to join hands with little white boys and white girls as sisters and brothers. I have a dream today!

I have a dream that one day every valley shall be exalted, every hill and mountain shall be made low, the rough places shall be made plain, and the crooked places shall be made straight and the glory of the Lord will be revealed and all flesh shall see it together.

This is our hope. This is the faith that I go back to the South with.

With this faith we will be able to hew out of the mountain of despair a stone of hope. With this faith we will be able to transform the jangling discords of our nation into a beautiful symphony of brotherhood.

With this faith we will be able to work together, to pray together, to struggle together, to go to jail together, to stand up for freedom together, knowing that we will be free one day. This will be the day when all of God's children will be able to sing with new meaning – 'my country 'tis of thee; sweet land of liberty; of thee I sing; land where my fathers died, land of the pilgrim's pride; from every mountain side, let freedom ring' – and if America is to be a great nation, this must become true.

So let freedom ring from the prodigious hilltops of New Hampshire.

Let freedom ring from the mighty mountains of New York.

Let freedom ring from the heightening Alleghenies of Pennsylvania.

Let freedom ring from the snowcapped Rockies of Colorado.

Let freedom ring from the curvaceous slopes of California.

But not only that.

Let freedom ring from Stone Mountain of Georgia.

Let freedom ring from Lookout Mountain of Tennessee.

Let freedom ring from every hill and molehill of Mississippi, from every mountainside, let freedom ring.

When we allow freedom to ring, when we let it ring from every village and hamlet, from every state and city, we will be able to speed up that day when all of God's children – black men and white men, Jews and Gentiles, Catholics and Protestants – will be able to join hands and to sing in the words of the old Negro spiritual – 'Free at last, free at last; thank God Almighty, we are free at last.'

16 November

Margaret of Scotland

Queen of Scotland, Philanthropist, Reformer of the Church, 1093

Born in the year 1046, Margaret was the daughter of the Anglo-Saxon royal house of England but educated in Hungary, where her family lived in exile during the reign of Danish kings in England. After the Norman invasion in 1066, when her royal person was still a threat to the new monarchy, she was welcomed in the royal court of Malcolm III of Scotland and soon afterwards married him in 1069. Theirs was a happy and fruitful union and Margaret proved to be both a civilizing and a holy presence. She instituted many church reforms and founded many monasteries, churches and pilgrim hostels. She was a woman of prayer as well as good works who seemed to influence for good all with whom she came into contact. She died on this day in the year 1093.

A Reading from *The Life of Saint Margaret, Queen of Scotland* by Turgot, Bishop of St Andrews

Many people derive their names from a quality of mind, so that a correspondence is revealed between the sense of their name and the grace they have received. The same is true of this virtuous woman, in whom the fairness indicated by her name was surpassed by the exceeding beauty of her soul. She was called Margaret, that is, 'a pearl', and in the sight of God she was esteemed a lovely pearl by reason of her faith and good works. She was a pearl to her children, to me, to us all, even to Christ; and because she was Christ's, she is all the more ours now that she has left us and is taken to the Lord.

In the Queen's presence no one ventured to do anything wrong, or even utter an unseemly word, for repressing all evil in herself, there was great gravity in her joy and something noble in her anger. Her conversation was seasoned with the salt of wisdom: her silence was filled with good thoughts. She would often call her children to her, and, as far as their age would allow, instruct them concerning Christ and the faith of Christ, and carefully endeavour to admonish them to always fear him.

We need not wonder then, that the Queen ruled herself and her household wisely, since she was always guided by the most wise counsel of the holy Scriptures. What I used frequently to admire in her was that amid the distraction of lawsuits and the countless affairs of the kingdom, she gave herself with wonderful diligence to the reading of the word of God, concerning which she used to ask profound questions of the scholars who were sitting near her.

To the excellent gifts of prayer and fasting, she joined the gifts of mercy. For what could be more compassionate than her heart? Who more gentle to the needy? It was her custom as soon as dawn had broken, to rise from bed, and to continue a long time in prayer and reading the psalms, and as she read she performed this work of mercy. Nine little orphan children who were utterly destitute, she had brought into her at the first hour of the day so that she could feed them. She ordered soft food such as little children delight in, to be prepared for them daily; and when the little ones were brought to her, she did not think it beneath her to pick them up and sit them on her knee, and feed them herself with the spoons from her own table.

Thus Queen Margaret, honoured by all the people, performed for Christ's sake the office of a most devoted servant and mother.

16 November

Edmund Rich of Abingdon

Archbishop of Canterbury, 1240

Edmund was born in Abingdon in about 1175, the son of a rich but pious merchant who himself became a monk later in life. He was educated at Oxford and in Paris. After also teaching in both places, he became Treasurer of Salisbury Cathedral in 1222 and was eventually made Archbishop of Canterbury in 1234. He was a reforming bishop and, as well as bringing gifts of administration to his task, appointed clergy of outstanding talent to senior positions in the Church. He also acted as peacemaker between the king and his barons, many believing that his actions averted civil war. He died on this day in the year 1240.

A Reading from *The Life of Saint Edmund* by Matthew Paris

Blessed Edmund was an outstanding preacher and an eminent teacher at Oxford. The fire of his preaching and the eloquence of his teaching illuminated the minds of his hearers with the knowledge of the truth and kindled in them a love of the good, so that by the effect of his words upon those who heard him, it was clearer than daylight that in him and through him there spoke the One of whom it is written 'It is not you who speak, but the spirit of your Father.' Hence he pleased the clergy, was accepted by the laity, and was to be reverenced even by princes.

When he sat among the elders, he did not cease to console those who mourned. Compassion was brought up with him from infancy: it caused him to embrace the miseries of others and to share as a partner in every affliction. Who was ever gentler in his piety? Who in such a position of eminence thought less of himself, or who, the higher he rose by his merits, was more deflated by his consciousness of sin? We cannot adequately represent the immense charity and charisma by which he converted many hearts, as many people have known and learned by experience.

He was so active in offering hospitality and in other acts of generosity that whatever was within his means seemed to be at the common disposal of everyone. He made the utmost effort to avoid the vice of detraction, a failing that usually creeps into the conversation even of those who watch themselves carefully. So when an occasion occurred or words of detraction were spoken, he either changed the subject or, if the detractor persisted with his words, he would take his leave, not wanting to be polluted by listening. A prebend of the Church of Salisbury was therefore conferred on him, so that he was called and was 'the custodian of the treasure'.

On the vacancy of the See of Canterbury in the year of the Incarnation 1234, by divine inspiration and after the said see had suffered papal and royal vexations unworthy to be told, he was solemnly elected archbishop. For the Convent of Canterbury, to whom, as is well known, the right of election has pertained since ancient times, said, 'Let a man be chosen in whom can be found no just grounds for objection and whose merits will silence all carping detractors.' So, after they had invoked the Holy Spirit and had prayed devoutly, and after they had carefully weighed the merits of many candidates in the balance of reason, the opinion of the electors finally settled and rested upon Master Edmund of Abingdon, the lecturer in theology. And this was undoubtedly according to the will of God.

16 November

Gertrude of Helfta

Mystic, *c.*1302

Gertrude was born in 1256. At the age of five she was given by her parents to be brought up by the Benedictine nuns of Helfta in Thuringia. She was a gifted child and received a good education at their hands. At the age of twenty-five she experienced a profound conversion in consequence of a vision of Christ, and for the rest of her life she led a life of contemplation. Of the so-called Revelations of Gertrude, only The Herald of Divine Love is genuinely hers, written partly from her notes or dictation, and partly by herself. She is sometimes called 'Gertrude the Great' to distinguish her from Gertrude of Hackeborn who was Abbess of Helfta when she was brought there as a child. Gertrude was one of the first exponents of devotion to the Sacred Heart.

A Reading from *The Herald of Divine Love* by Gertrude of Helfta

One day, wearied by the consideration of earthly pleasures, she said to the Lord: 'I can find no pleasure in anything on earth save in yourself alone, my sweetest Lord!' To which the Lord in his turn replied: 'And in the same way, I find nothing in heaven or on earth which could please me without you, because I associate you in love with all that pleases me, and so I always find in love all that gives me pleasure. The greater these pleasures are for me, the greater will be the profit for you.'

That she was assiduous in prayers and vigils is clear from the fact she never neglected to observe any of the canonical hours unless she lay sick in bed with some infirmity or was engaged in some charitable work for the glory of God or the salvation of others. And because the Lord never failed to gladden her prayers with the blissful consolation of his presence, she prolonged her spiritual exercises long after her strength would have been exhausted by any other occupation. She observed so lovingly all the statutes of her Order concerning assistance at Choir, fasting and manual work, that she never omitted any of them without feeling grievous dissatisfaction. Saint Bernard says: 'If you have once been inebriated by the taste of charity, soon every labour and sorrow is made mirthful.'

The freedom of her spirit was so great that she could not tolerate for an instant anything that went against her conscience. The Lord himself bore witness to this, because when someone asked him in devout prayer what it was that pleased him most in his chosen one, he replied: 'Her freedom of heart.' This person, most astonished and, so to speak, considering this an inadequate answer, said: 'I should have thought, Lord, that by your grace she would have attained to a higher knowledge of your mysteries and a greater fervour of love.' To which the Lord answered: 'Yes, indeed, it is as you think. And this is the result of the grace of the freedom of her heart which is so great a good that it leads directly to the highest perfection. I have always found her ready to receive my gifts, for she permits nothing to remain in her heart which might impede my action.'

17 November

Hugh

Bishop of Lincoln, 1200

Hugh was born at Avalon in Burgundy in 1140 and at first made his profession with the Augustinian canons but, when he was twenty-five, he became a monk at Grande Chartreuse. In about 1175, he was invited by the English king, Henry II, to become Prior of his Charterhouse foundation at Witham in Somerset, badly in need of reform even though it had been only recently founded. In 1186, Hugh was persuaded to accept the See of Lincoln, then the largest diocese in the land. He brought huge energy to the diocese and, together with discerning appointments to key posts, he revived the Lincoln schools, repaired and enlarged the cathedral, visited the See extensively, drew together the clergy to meet in synod and generally brought an efficiency and stability to the Church which was to be much emulated. Hugh also showed great compassion for the poor and the oppressed, ensuring that sufferers of leprosy were cared for and that Jews were not persecuted. He both supported his monarch and also held out against any royal measures he felt to be extreme, yet managing not to make an enemy of the king. He died in London on this day in the year 1200.

A Reading from *Magna Vita: The Life of Saint Hugh of Lincoln* by Adam, monk of Eynsham

With the help of many gifted men as his counsellors and members of his household, the new Bishop of Lincoln immediately transformed his diocese. He preached the word of God with vigour, and zealously carried out its commandments following a text of Scripture: 'Where the spirit of the Lord is there is liberty.' He rebuked sinners sternly, with no undue consideration for persons of importance.

The worst abuse in the kingdom, under which countryfolk groaned, was the tyranny of the foresters. For them violence took the place of law, extortion was praiseworthy, justice was an abomination and innocence a crime. When in their usual way the foresters maltreated his people, in defiance of the liberties of the Church, Hugh excommunicated the chief forester. This news aroused the king to great indignation.

It is impossible adequately to record amongst the other marks of his devotion, his great compassion and tenderness towards the sick, and even to those afflicted with leprosy. He used to wash and dry their feet and kiss them affectionately, and having refreshed them with food and drink, gave them alms on a lavish scale. There were hospitals on certain of the episcopal manors, where many men and women afflicted by this disease were maintained. He made a practice of giving gifts of many different kinds to these in addition to the revenue already assigned to them by his predecessors, and frequently visited them himself with a few of his more God-fearing and devout retainers. He would sit in their midst in a small inner room and would comfort their souls by his kindly words, relieving their sorrow by his motherly tenderness, and encouraging those who were so desolate and afflicted in this life to hope for an eternal reward, combining with amazing gentleness words of consolation and exhortations to good conduct. Also if he noticed any tendency to wrong-doing, he would exhort them not to give way to it, and if they had done so to repent, and from henceforth neither to dare nor desire to do wrong. Before his address the women withdrew at his command and he went to kiss the men one by one, bending over each of them and giving a longer and more tender embrace to those whom he saw worse marked by the disease.

Have pity, sweet Jesus, on the unhappy soul of the narrator! I cannot conceal, would that it were concealed from your vengeance, how much I shuddered not merely to touch but even to behold those swollen and livid, diseased and deformed faces with the eyes either distorted or hollowed out and the lips eaten away! To an eye darkened by arrogance the pearl of God did not gleam in the mire. But your servant Hugh, whose eyes you had completely blinded to external superficiality, saw clearly their internal splendour, and therefore those seemed to him the more beautiful who outwardly were the most horribly diseased.

The openly expressed feeling of this saintly man for the divine healer of our wounds, and his words and acts concerning his sick members show plainly how afire Hugh was with love for God and his neighbour. He gave so lavishly to those who were in need that it is estimated that at least a third of his annual income was devoted to almsgiving.

18 November

Fergus

Bishop, *c.*750

There are a number of dedications in the Pictish lands of Caithness, Buchan and Angus recording the missionary work of Fergus in the northeast of Scotland. The three churches he founded in Strathearn are all dedicated to Patrick. He is generally identified with a Pictish bishop who attended a Council at Rome in the year 721. He was the patron saint of the burgh of Wick, and the Aberdeenshire village of St Fergus is probably the site of the small settlement from which his mission radiated.

A Reading from an ancient Celtic Rule concerning the duties of a bishop

If you are a member of the noble order of bishops, take up your service wholeheartedly, be subject in all honesty to the Lord, and let all be obedient to you.

Cure all harmful ailments through the power of the good Lord, establish peace among the people, restrain the noble kings.

In your dealings with clergy and laity alike, act as becomes a pastor. Be assiduous in preaching, be gracious, be pleasant.

The suppression of the wicked who love to do evil, and the exaltation of the truth, are duties that become you.

When accepting holy orders you should be familiar with Scripture, for you will be a stepson of the Church if you are unprepared and ignorant.

It is true indeed that every ignorant person is uncouth, and someone who does not read the testament of the Lord is not a true successor of his.

Truly it belongs to you to condemn all heresy and all evil. Therefore be not yourself guilty of any evil, either in word or in deed.

The wicked will not rise at your approach, nor will they obey you. You yourself will be blameworthy if you are gentle with them.

It is certain that you will be answerable on the great judgement day for the sins of your subjects, as well as for your own faults.

18 November

Elizabeth of Hungary

Princess of Thuringia, Philanthropist, 1231

Elizabeth was born in 1207, the daughter of a king of Hungary, and was given in marriage to Louis IV, Landgrave of Thuringia, with whom she had three children. Theirs was a happy marriage but her husband of four years died of the plague. Elizabeth was driven from the court and she settled in Marburg. There she had a confessor, Conrad of Marburg, whose domineering and almost sadistic ways exemplified one who had himself been a successful inquisitor of heretics. She suffered mental and physical abuse from him, in the name of religious austerity, but bore it all humbly. Elizabeth became a member of the Franciscan Third Order, which reflected her life of caring for the poor, even cooking and cleaning for them. Due to the severe regime under which she lived, her weakened body gave way under the pressure and she died on this day, just twenty-four years old, in the year 1231.

A Reading from the deposition of Isentrude, companion of Elizabeth of Hungary, to the Papal Commission concerning her canonization

While her husband King Ludwig was away on imperial business, there was a general famine, and blessed Elizabeth caused the reserves of corn in the king's granaries to be expended to satisfy the needs of the poor, each day as much as was necessary. Beneath the high castle of the Wartburg there was a large building which she filled with a number of sick people for whom the general almsgiving could not suffice; and despite the long steep hill she visited them several times a day, consoling them and encouraging them to patience, and she sold her own jewels in order to satisfy their needs. She paid no heed to the foetid air and to the stench of corruption made worse by the summer heat and which her attendants only bore with much murmuring.

Once there were in this hospital a number of poor children for whom she provided everything and with much gentleness and kindness kept them near her; and as many as came in all ran to her calling her 'mother'. She paid the most loving care to the worst cases among these children, the deformed, the dirtiest, the weakest, those suffering from the most repulsive illnesses, and would take them tenderly into her arms.

These sick people shared in her general almsgiving, but besides this blessed Elizabeth chose the poorest and weakest and lodged them in a dwelling outside the castle where she could feed them from her own table with her own hands, denying herself and her attendants many things in order to give them to the poor.

A Reading from a homily of John Chrysostom

Do you want to honour the body of Christ? Then do not despise his nakedness. Do not honour him here in church clothed in silk vestments and then ignore him, naked and frozen in the street. Always remember that he who said, 'This is my body', and gave effect to his word, also said, 'I was hungry and you gave me no food', and 'inasmuch as you did not do it to one of these, you did not do it to me'. The body of Christ needs no clothing in the first sense but only the worship of a pure heart. But in the second case it needs clothing and all the care we can lavish upon it.

It is vital, therefore, that we become discerning Christians and learn to honour Christ appropriately in ways of which he approves. When someone is honoured the form of honour bestowed is appropriate to the person receiving it, not the donor. Peter thought he was honouring the Lord when he tried to prevent him from washing his feet, but in reality this was far from the case. In the same way give God the honour he seeks and give your money generously to the poor. God does not need golden cups but he does need golden hearts.

I am not saying that you should not donate golden chalices, but I am insisting that there is no substitute for almsgiving. The Lord will not refuse your gift but he prefers almsgiving; and inevitably so, because in the former case only you, the donor, benefits, whereas in the latter case the poor benefit. The gift of a chalice may be extravagant; the giving of alms is sincere kindness which shows love for our fellow men and women.

What is the point of weighing down Christ's table with golden chalices while he himself is starving? Feed the hungry and then, if you have any money left over, lavish his table. Will you fashion a cup of gold and withhold a cup of water? What use is it to adorn his table with hangings of cloth of gold but refuse Christ a coat for his back? What gain is to be had from such behaviour?

Answer me this question: if you saw someone starving and refused to give them any food but instead spent your money on covering Christ's table with gold, would Christ thank you for it? Would he not rather be furious with you? Or again, if you saw someone in rags and frozen stiff, and then instead of giving them clothing you went and erected golden columns in Christ's honour, would not Christ say that you were mocking and ridiculing him? Imagine that Christ is that tramp, that stranger who comes to you in need of a bed for the night. You turn him away and then start laying carpets on the floor, draping the walls, hanging lamps on silver chains from the capitals of the columns. Meanwhile the tramp is arrested and put in prison, but you never give him a second thought.

Let me repeat, I am not condemning generosity; but I am urging you to care for the poor; indeed, to give the poor priority. No one was ever condemned for not beautifying Christ's house, but those who neglect their neighbour were threatened with hell fire and eternal punishment with devils. Beautify this house if that is what you want to do, but never neglect your brother or sister in need. They are temples of infinitely greater value.

19 November

Hilda

Abbess of Whitby, 680

Note: In Wales, Hilda is commemorated on 18 November.

Hilda was born in the year 614 of the royal house of Northumbria and was baptized in York at the age of twelve by Paulinus. Encouraged by Aidan of Lindisfarne, she become a Religious at the age of thirty-three. She established monasteries first at Hartlepool, and two years later at Whitby. This house became a great centre of learning and was the meeting-place for the important Synod of Whitby in the year 664 at which it was decided to adopt the Roman tradition in preference to Celtic customs. Although herself a Celt in religious formation, Hilda played a crucial rôle in reconciling others of that tradition to the decision of the Synod. She is also remembered as a great educator, exemplified in her nurturing of Caedmon's gift of vernacular song. She died on 17 November in the year 680.

A Reading from *The History of the English Church and People* by the Venerable Bede

In the year of our Lord 680, Hilda, abbess of the monastery of Whitby, a most devoted servant of Christ, after an earthly life given to the work of heaven passed away to receive the rewards of a heavenly life on the seventeenth of November at the age of sixty-six. Her life on earth fell into two equal parts: for she spent thirty-three years most nobly in secular occupations, and dedicated an equal number of years still more nobly to the Lord in the monastic life.

She was of noble birth, being the daughter of Hereric, the nephew of King Edwin. With Edwin she received the faith and sacraments of Christ through the preaching of Paulinus of blessed memory, the first bishop of the Northumbrians, and she preserved this faith inviolate until she was found worthy to see her Master in heaven.

When she decided to abandon the secular life and serve God alone, she went to the province of the East Angles, whose king was her relation, with the intention of going abroad. However, she was recalled home by Bishop Aidan and was granted one hide of land on the north bank of the river Wear, where she observed the monastic rule with a handful of companions for another year.

After this she was made abbess of the monastery at Hartlepool which had been founded not long before, and from there she moved to Tadcaster. When she had ruled this monastery for some years, constantly occupied in establishing a Rule of life, Hilda further undertook to found or organise a monastery at a place known as Whitby, and carried out this appointed task with great energy. She established the same Rule of life as in her former monastery, and taught the observance of righteousness, mercy, purity, and other virtues, but especially of peace and charity. After the example of the primitive Church, no one there was rich, no one was needy, for everything was held in common, and nothing was considered to be anyone's personal property. So great was her prudence that not only ordinary folk, but kings and princes used to come and ask her advice in their difficulties. Those under her direction were required to make a thorough study of the holy Scriptures and occupy themselves in good works, to such good effect that many were found fitted for holy orders and the service of God's altar.

All who knew Abbess Hilda, the handmaid of Christ, called her mother because of her wonderful devotion and grace. She was not only an example of holy life to members of her own community; she also brought about an opportunity for salvation and repentance to many living at a distance, who heard the inspiring story of her industry and goodness.

19 November

Mechtild

Béguine of Magdeburg, Mystic, 1280

Mechtild was born in about the year 1210. The writings for which she is known speak of her experience of the love of God as it was revealed to her. This experience began when she was twelve years old. She responded to it by joining a community of Béguines at the age of about eighteen. After forty years, she moved to the Cistercian convent of Helfta and in about 1270 completed her writings there. Helfta was a remarkable centre of learning at that time with other outstanding personalities in the community. She wrote with poetic sensitivity in direct and simple language of the exchange of love with God. She died on this day in the year 1280.

A Reading from *The Revelations of Mechtild of Magdeburg*,
also known as *The Flowing Light of the Godhead*

I was warned about my book and told by many people
That it should not be preserved
But rather should be thrown in the fire.
Then I did what from childhood I have always done
When trouble overtakes me:
I resorted to prayer.
I bowed myself before my Love and said:
'Lord, I am deeply troubled.
Must I always walk devoid of comfort
For the sake of your glory?
You have tricked me
For you yourself told me to write this book!'

But holding my book in his right hand, the Lord said:
'Beloved, do not be hard on yourself.
No one can burn truth.
Those who wish to rip this book out of my hand
Must be stronger than I!
This book has three parts
And it concerns me alone.

The parchment here before me
Speaks of my pure, righteous and wise humanity
Which suffered death for you.
Your words speak of my glorious godhead
Which flows from hour to hour
Into your receptive soul from my heavenly mouth.
Your words speak with my living Spirit
And embody in themselves the living truth.
So behold in all these words
How graciously they proclaim my holiness
And do not doubt your worth.'

'But, Lord, were I a learned priest,
And had you worked your wonders in a man,
Then you would have derived endless honour
From such writings. But how will any believe me
This unworthy soil
On which you have deigned to raise up a golden dwelling
Wherein dwells your mother
And all creation And all the heavenly host?
Lord, I can find no earthly wisdom in your ways!'

'My daughter, many a wise man has lost precious gold
Through carelessness on the highway of life
Along which he thought he travelled to higher realms;
Leaving others to find the way.
Whenever I have bestowed my special grace
I have always searched
For the poorest, the smallest and most hidden.

The proud mountains cannot receive
The revelations of my grace,
For the flood of my Holy Spirit
By nature flows down into the lowliest valleys.
There are many so-called wise writers
Who, in my eyes, are fools.
And I tell you more, It greatly honours me
And greatly strengthens holy Church
That your unlearned lips should teach
The learned tongues the things of my Holy Spirit.'

20 November

Edmund

King of the East Angles, Martyr, 870

Born in about the year 840, Edmund was nominated as king while still a boy. He became King of Norfolk in 855 and of Suffolk the following year. As king, he won the hearts of his subjects by his care of the poor and his steady suppression of wrong-doing. When attacked by the Danes, he refused to give over his kingdom or to renounce his faith in Christ. He was tied to a tree, shot with arrows and finally beheaded on this day in the year 870. His shrine at the town which became known as Bury St Edmunds was an important centre of pilgrimage throughout the Middle Ages.

A Reading from *The Lives of the Saints* by Aelfric of Eynsham

Blessed Edmund, King of the East Angles, was a wise and honourable man, and by his excellent conduct always gave glory to almighty God. He was humble and devout, and of such steadfast faith that throughout his life he never yielded to any shameful behaviour. He was unswerving in his duties, refusing to compromise his integrity, mindful of the counsel that if you should be made a chief, never exalt yourself, but rather always be among your people as one of them. He was generous to the poor and widows, and like a father gently guided his people towards righteousness, controlling the violent in the land, and allowing people to live securely in the true faith.

Eventually the Danes came with a great fleet of ships, harrying and killing the populace over a wide area. They landed first of all in Northumbria, wasted the land and slew the people. Hingwar, one of their leaders, sent a threatening message to King Edmund, who undismayed turned to the messenger and said, 'Truly you deserve to die, but I will not defile my clean hands with your foul blood, because I follow Christ who has given us an example. Go now quickly, and say to your lord: Edmund the king will never bow in this life to Hingwar the heathen leader, unless he will in faith first bow in this land to Jesus Christ.' The messenger left quickly, and meeting the bloodthirsty Hingwar and his army who were already on their way to confront Edmund, told that wicked man how he had been answered. Hingwar then arrogantly ordered his troops to take the king who despised his command and arrest him.

Edmund stood within his hall and, mindful of the Saviour, threw down his weapons, desiring to imitate the example of Christ who forbade Peter to fight with weapons against the bloodthirsty soldiers. Then those wicked men bound Edmund, insulted him shamefully and beat him with clubs. Then they led the faithful king to a tree, tied him to it with hard ropes, and scourged him, while with true faith he called between the blows on Jesus Christ. The heathen were mad with rage because he called upon Christ to help him, and made him a target for their arrows, shooting at him as if for amusement, until he was covered with arrows as with a porcupine's bristles, as Sebastian was. When Hingwar, the wicked tyrant, saw that the noble king would not deny Christ and with steadfast faith continued to call upon him, he ordered his men to behead him. While he was still calling upon Christ, the heathen drew away the saint and with one blow struck off his head; and so his soul departed joyfully to Christ.

20 November

Priscilla Lydia Sellon

A Restorer of the Religious Life in the Church of England, 1876

Priscilla Lydia Sellon was born probably in 1821. Although never enjoying good health, she responded to an appeal from the Bishop of Exeter in 1848 for workers amongst the destitute in Plymouth. The group of women she gathered around her adopted a conventual lifestyle and, in the face of much opposition, she created the Sisters of Mercy. Her crucial rôle in the revival of Religious Life in the Church of England was enhanced when, in 1856, her sisters joined with the first community founded – The Holy Cross Sisters – thereby establishing The Society of the Holy Trinity. She led her Community in starting schools and orphanages, in addition to sisters nursing the sick in slum districts and soldiers in the Crimea. In her last years, she was an invalid, dying in her mid-fifties on this day in the year 1876.

A Reading from *The Life of Priscilla Lydia Sellon*
by Thomas Jay Williams

The Religious Life for women has, from the time of its revival in the Anglican Communion over a century and a half ago, developed very remarkably. Priscilla Lydia Sellon holds the foremost place in the honoured line of those entirely devoted to this great work of revival and restoration as the foundress and first Superior of the Society of the Most Holy Trinity. During her lifetime Dr Pusey constantly referred to her as 'the restorer after three centuries of the Religious Life in the English Church'.

Writing in 1850 to Miss Augusta Wade, who had expressed a desire to join the newly formed sisterhood, she wrote:

> I am not surprised at the opposition you meet with: the surprise to me is when such a vocation is *not* opposed. It is contrary to every argument of worldly wisdom, and prudence, and excellence. It is, on the very face of it, reckless, mad and enthusiastic. It is counted very mad to 'rise up and forsake all and follow Christ'.
>
> It is said that one can perform domestic duties and the duties of society, and serve our Lord in them. But there are some hearts to whom he has given higher, deeper yearnings which the world knows not of, and which it cannot understand. There are some hearts who cannot live in luxury when our Lord lived in poverty, who cannot be idle when he went about doing good, who cannot but live for his poor when he told us that in ministering to them, we minister to him. There are some hearts who hate wealth and despise 'respectability' which is a very idol in our country, and which word does not bear a Christian interpretation.

21 November

Paulinus of Wales

Abbot, sixth century

Paulinus (Peulin) was the tutor of Saint David. He is connected with the area around Llandovery in north Carmarthenshire and with Llan-gors, east of Brecon, where he may have spent some time as a hermit. It is probable that the monastic school at which he taught David was at Llanddeusant. Rhigyfarch, David's biographer, says that Paulinus had been a pupil of Germanus, and he describes how David cured his teacher of blindness. Paulinus was also said to be the 'aged bishop' who advised the Synod of Llanddewibrefi to send for David to address them. The ancient stone from Caio parish describing Paulinus as a 'guardian of the faith, always a lover of his homeland, most conscientious observer of all that is right' is now generally thought to refer to a godly layman of the same name. It does, however, reflect the ethos of the society of which Paulinus was a part.

A Reading from *The Life of Saint David* by Rhigyfarch the Wise

David was baptized by Ailbhe, a bishop of the Munstermen. The boy was reared in the place that is called the Ancient Blackberry Bush, and he grew up full of grace and of pleasing appearance. There he was taught to read and write and learned the rites of the Church; and his fellow pupils saw a dove teaching him and singing hymns with him.

As time went by, his virtues and merits increased, and keeping his body free from a wife's embraces, he was ordained and raised to the dignity of a priest. He then left that place and went to Paulinus, a disciple of Germanus and a teacher, who led a life pleasing to God on an island in Wincdi-lantquendi.

Now it so happened that this same Paulinus was at that time troubled with his eyes (holy Dewi remained there many years, reading and assimilating what he had read), and it was arranged that the disciples should assemble and, as their master called them, should individually bless his eyes, making the sign of the cross upon them, so that he should be healed by their prayer and blessing. After the other pupils had risen in turn to touch the master's eyes, making the sign of the cross upon them, holy Dewi was asked to touch the master's eyes. But he said in reply, 'I have not yet looked upon my master's face. I have been here reading with him for ten years, but I do not know his face.' Overwhelmed by shyness and modesty, he had avoided looking upon his master's face.

His master then said to him, 'Raise your right hand and touch my eyes without looking, and I shall be healed.' When this was done, the light of day was clearly revealed to Paulinus. The darkness banished from his eyes, the master received the lofty light. They then thanked God, and holy Dewi was indeed praised and blessed by each one of them.

Not long after this an angel appeared to Paulinus and said, 'It is now time that Dewi, who has doubled his talents by putting them to good use, should not bury the talent of wisdom entrusted to him in the earth and become sluggish with the slow torpor of indolence, but should add to the Lord's money which he has received, by a greater increase in profit, so that, established in the joy of his Lord, he may gather in and collect the sheaves of the harvest of souls into the heavenly granaries of eternal bliss.'

22 November

Cecilia

Martyr at Rome, *c.*230

Cecilia was one of the most revered martyrs of the Roman Church, but the only thing known for certain is that, at some point in the second or third century, a woman called Cecilia allowed the Church to meet in her house in Trastevere in the city of Rome and that subsequently the church erected on that site bore her name. She was remembered as a brave woman who risked giving hospitality to the Christian Church when to do so was to court censure and possibly death. According to a tradition that can be dated no earlier than the fifth century, she converted her pagan husband and his brother to the faith, both of whom were martyred before her. She is honoured as the patron saint of musicians.

A Reading from an Exposition of the Psalms by Augustine

'Praise the Lord with the lyre; make melody to him with the harp of ten strings! O sing to God a new song!' My friends, you have learnt the new song: so now forget the old one. We are a new humanity, we have a new covenant with God; so let our song be new; new songs do not emerge from an old humanity. Only a new humanity can learn it, human beings whose old nature has been made new by the grace of God, men and women who enjoy a new covenant which is nothing less than the kingdom of heaven. Our hearts yearn for it. So let us sing our new song not with our lips but with our lives.

'Sing to God a new song. Sing to him with joyful melody.' You ask me in what way each of us is to sing the praises of God. Well, sing to God, but not out of tune. God does not want his ears assaulted by discordant noise: sing in harmony, dear sisters and brothers.

Imagine you are asked to entertain some fine musician with a song. 'Sing a song to please him,' you are asked. There you are, quite untrained in music, anxious and afraid lest you irritate this skilled musician because what might pass unnoticed by an untrained ear will be criticised by a great artist. By the same token, no one is going to rush forward, thinking to please God (even if they think they have a beautiful voice) because God who will listen to that singer, and who will give his verdict on the performance, knows everything in us. Do you think you will command an art so polished that you need never fear singing a jarring note on that discerning listener's ear?

But God himself has provided you with a way of singing. You do not have to bother to search for the right words as if you needed to find a lyric to please God. Simply praise God with 'songs of joy'. It is fine praise of God when you sing with real joy. You ask, how is this done? It means realising that words are not enough to express what we are singing to God in our hearts. At harvest time, both in the fields and the vineyard, the labourers work incredibly hard, and they always begin their day with songs whose words express their joy. But when their joy brims over and words are not enough, they abandon even this coherence and give themselves up to the sheer delight of singing.

What is this joy I speak of, this singing exultantly? It is an inner melody that means our hearts are bursting with feeling that words cannot contain. And to whom does such joy belong if not to the God who is beyond language? When words will not come, and you cannot keep silent, what else can you do but let the melody soar? What else can you do when the rejoicing heart runs out of words and the intensity of your joy will not be imprisoned by language? What else can you do but to sing out to God with 'songs of joy'?

23 November

Clement

Bishop of Rome, Martyr, *c.*100

Clement was active as an elder in the Church in Rome towards the end of the first century and was reputed to have been a disciple of the apostles. He wrote a letter to the Corinthians which focused on ministry in the Church and dealt with controversial issues relating to authority and duty. The letter clearly reveals an exercise of authority on the part of one senior presbyter intervening in a conflict in another Church, and as such it provides valuable information about the history of the developing Church and its ministry at this time. Clement's hierarchical view of Church order set a future pattern for episcopal practice and ministry. He seems to have been president of a council of presbyters which governed the Church in Rome and he appears to be writing on their behalf. A fourth-century document states that Clement was exiled to the Crimea where he was then put to death by being thrown into the sea with an anchor around his neck.

A Reading from a letter of Clement of Rome
to the Church in Corinth

How blessed and wonderful are the gifts of God, my friends! Some of them we can already comprehend – the life that knows no death, the splendour of righteousness, the liberating power of truth, the faith that is perfect assurance, the holiness of living chastely – but what of the things God has prepared for those who wait for him? Only the creator and Father of eternity knows their greatness and their beauty. Let us strive then, to be found among those who wait for him, that we too may share in these promised gifts. And how is this to be done, my friends? By fixing our minds on God; by finding out what would be pleasing and acceptable to him; by doing what is in harmony with his perfect will; and by following the way of truth. Thus injustice, wrongdoing of every kind, greed, covetousness, quarrelling, malice and fraud should all be renounced.

This is the way, dear friends, that we find our salvation, even Jesus Christ, the high priest by whom our gifts are offered, and the defender by whom our weakness is aided. Through him we can gaze into the highest heaven and see the reflection of God's perfect and pure face. Through him the eyes of our hearts are opened, and our dim and darkened understanding unfolds like a flower in the sunlight; for through him the Lord has willed us to taste the wisdom of eternity. As it is written in Scripture: 'He is the splendour of the majesty of God, and is as much greater than the angels as the title he has inherited is more excellent than theirs.'

So my dear friends, let us serve resolutely in the army of the Lord, never swerving from his unerring commands. In the case of our physical bodies, the head is nothing without the feet, and our feet are useless without the head. Even the seemingly insignificant parts of our bodies are necessary and valued for the good working of the whole, each part working co-operatively, all united by a common subordination to maintain the integrity of the body.

In the same way let this corporate body of ours in Christ Jesus be maintained in integrity. Each of us should give precedence to the other according to his or her spiritual gifts. The strong are not to despise the weak, and the weak are to respect the strong. The rich should provide for the poor out of their resources, and the poor for their part should thank God for giving them somebody who can meet their needs. If you are wise, then display your wisdom by good deeds; and if you are modest, let others speak of your modesty instead of proclaiming the fact yourself.

To God we owe everything, and therefore on every count we are under obligation to thank him. Glory be to him for ever and ever. Amen.

23 November

Columbanus

Bishop and Abbot, 615

Note: In Scotland, Columbanus (Columban) is commemorated on 21 November.

Born in Leinster around the year 540, Columbanus became a monk in his youth. In 585 his abbot at Bangor, Comgall, gave him permission to go to Europe, taking several companions including Gall. Three monasteries were established in the Vosges, but his inflexible rule and defiant adherence to the Celtic traditions aroused fierce opposition, and in 610 the Irish monks were expelled from Burgundy. Columbanus crossed the Alps into Lombardy, where he founded the great abbey of Bobbio in 614. His monastic tradition spread widely, until it was superseded by the less stringent Benedictine tradition. Columbanus died at Bobbio on this day in the year 615.

A Reading from a *Rule for Monks* by Columbanus

Monks must everywhere beware of a proud independence and learn true humility as they obey without murmur or hesitation, by which, according to the word of the Lord, the yoke of Christ may be sweet to them and his burden light. Otherwise while they are learning the humility of Christ, they will not feel the sweetness of his yoke or the lightness of his burden. For humility is the response of the soul when wearied with vices and effort, its only refuge from so many evils, and insofar as it is drawn to consideration of this from so many errant and empty things without, to that extent it enjoys repose and recuperation within, so that even bitter things are sweet to it and things which it previously found difficult and demanding it now feels to be plain and easy.

Mortification too, which is intolerable to the proud and hard-hearted, becomes the comfort of those who take pleasure only in what is humble and gentle. But we should realise that no one can perfectly enjoy either this joy of martyrdom or any other benefit that follows unless he has paid particular attention to not being found unready. For if along with this aim, he has wished to pursue or to nourish any of his desires, both entirely preoccupied and thrown into confusion by these intrusions, he will not always be able to follow thankfully where the commandment leads, nor can someone who is stirred up and lacking in gratitude act as he should.

Thus there are three ways of mortification: not to argue back in mind, not to speak with an unbridled tongue, not to go wherever we wish. It demands that we should always say to a senior monk, however unwelcome his instructions, 'Not as I will, but as you will', following the example of our Lord and Saviour, who says, 'I came down from heaven, not to do my will but the will of him who sent me'.

24 November

Colman of Cloyne

Bishop, 601

There are some hundreds of saints called Colman in Ireland. The Colman who built the first church at Cloyne in County Cork was ordained late in life at the age of fifty. He was influenced by Brendan the Navigator as he searched for his vocation. Brendan called him a column or a pillar (columna) of the church and also a dove (columba). He died on this day in the year 601.

A Reading from *The Rule of the Céli dé*
by an unknown monastic author

Any bishop who ordains someone who is unable to instruct people in piety, reading, and spiritual direction, who is ignorant of Scripture and of the laws of the Church, who has not a suitable remedy for every kind of sin – such a bishop is an enemy of both of God and man. That is so because he has insulted both Christ and his Church, and as a consequence he must do penance.

If the sons of Ireland are to be found within the bequest of Patrick, it is because there is a senior bishop in every important territory of the land. The duty of such a bishop is to ordain men to holy orders, to consecrate churches, and to give spiritual direction to rulers, to those in authority, and to those in holy orders. He is to bless and sanctify their families after baptism, he is to care for the infirm of every church, and to order the training of boys and girls in piety and learning. If youth do not devote themselves at all times to study, then not religion, but black paganism will rule the land of Ireland.

Anyone who gives to the Lord the tithes of the fruit of his body, that is, a son, in the cause of learning, will as it were renew the Church in Ireland, and will restore to it the faith which has become extinct. On the other hand, anyone who recalls a son whom he has offered to God and Patrick, withdraws as it were the gifts of the entire world and divides the Church on earth from that in heaven.

It is proper to show respect towards God's ministers and to heed their advice since they are, as it were, God's angels living among men. It is through them that we attain to the kingdom of God by the administration of baptism, by the reception of holy communion, by their prayers, by the offering of the body and blood of Christ, by the preaching of the word of God, by the harmony of law and rule, and in general by doing on earth whatever pleases God.

24 November

Lucy Menzies

Teacher of the Faith, 1954

Lucy Menzies was born in 1882 at the manse of Inchture, Carse of Gowrie, where her father, Allan Menzies, was parish minister, and later Professor of Biblical Criticism at St Andrews University. She became an Episcopalian, but her own life was the epitome of ecumenism. As a scholar and translator, she published many books on the lives of the saints and translated works of medieval and modern spirituality. She is remembered in particular for her work on Columba. She worked closely with Evelyn Underhill, and it was through her that she was made Warden of the Retreat House at Pleshey in Essex for ten years in the 1930s. But it is not only for her spiritual scholarship that she is remembered. Her life of prayer (which she professed always to find difficult) and her deep communion with God shone from her. As she wrote of another, she showed 'the divine charity working through an utterly selfless spirit, absolutely abandoned to God'. She once wrote to a friend, 'God gives us our circumstances and environment to make something of. It is within these circumstances that we are to achieve something – the Lord's way for you is just where you are, and if I may say so, a jolly good way too.' She died in the year 1954.

A Reading from a memoir of Lucy Menzies by Lumsden Barkway

The title of Lucy Menzies' best-known book is an admirable clue to her own character. She was truly a 'Mirror of the Holy'. She reflected that with which her thoughts were constantly occupied, and like a mirror hid herself behind its reflection. The self-renunciation after which others strive is often distorted and unattractive because it is self-conscious and artificial; but her self-abandonment was so complete that it drew no attention to itself. The words on her book-plate represent what she was – a lantern for the divine Light: *Ego sum lux; tu es lucerna.* Her slight and fragile form at times seemed almost luminous. Her name, Lucy, suited her nature.

Her conversion to Anglicanism was certainly assisted if not inspired by the influence of Evelyn Underhill: and she first heard of her through an almost casual remark by the parish minister of Innellan on the Clyde where her family had a holiday house, which led her to borrow *Mysticism.* This, to Lucy's mind, was the turning-point of her life. Correspondence brought them into touch, and everything followed from that.

Through Evelyn Underhill, Lucy was led into the sphere where she had the fullest scope for exercising her special gifts, and which hundreds of persons will always associate with her name. 'Evelyn sent me to Pleshey where I was for ten years, till my eyes made it impossible.' There Lucy left a lasting heritage in the spiritual atmosphere and way of life which she established, and, more obviously, in the lovely chapel which might almost be called her creation. One of her colleagues and most intimate friends recalls how she spent herself unsparingly on the retreat work, unmindful of her physical limitations. 'Lucy was never a conversationalist. Rather she spoke to the heart, and was a Presence. … At Pleshey she burned herself out, as she did to the end for any she could serve; and would wish so to be burnt out. … What she most wanted to do and the people she most wanted to see were always put last.'

25 November

Catherine of Alexandria

Martyr, fourth century

Tradition has it that Catherine was a girl of a noble family who, because of her Christian faith, refused marriage with the emperor as she was already a 'bride of Christ'. She is said to have disputed with fifty philosophers whose job it was to convince her of her error, and she proved superior in argument to them all. She was then tortured by being splayed on a wheel and finally beheaded.

A Reading from a hymn by Ephrem of Syria

In Praise of Virginity

Blessed are you, virgin, with whom
the comely name of virginity grows old.
In your branches chastity built a nest;
may your womb be a nest for her dwelling place.
May the power of mercy preserve your temple.

Blessed are you, heavenly sparrow
whose nest was on the cross of light.
You did not want to build a nest on earth
lest the serpent enter and destroy your offspring.

Blessed are your wings that were able to fly.
May you come with the holy eagles
that took flight and soared from the earth below
to the bridal couch of delights.

Blessed are you, O shoot that Truth cultivated;
He engrafted your medicine into the Tree of Life.
Your fruit exults and rejoices at all times
to drink the drink of the Book of Life.
Blessed are your branches.

Blessed are you, O bride, espoused to the Living One,
you who do not long for a mortal man.
Foolish is the bride who is proud
of the ephemeral crown that will be gone tomorrow.

Blessed is your heart, captivated by love
of a beauty portrayed in your mind.
You have exchanged the transitory bridal couch
for the bridal couch whose blessings are unceasing.

Blessed are you, free woman, who sold yourself
to the Lord who became a servant for your sake!

25 November

Isaac Watts

Hymn Writer, 1748

Born in Southampton in 1674, Isaac Watts was educated at the local grammar school and had the opportunity to go on to university, but declined because he preferred the dissenting academy at Stoke Newington. He received there an education of high academic standard and went on to become pastor to the Independent (or Congregationalist) Church at Mark Lane in London. Because of deteriorating health, he resigned this post in 1712 and retired to Stoke Newington. Seven years later, he opposed the imposition of the doctrine of the Trinity on his fellow dissenting ministers, which led to the belief that he had become a Unitarian. Isaac wrote several collections of hymns many of which are still used in worship. He died at Stoke Newington on this day in 1748.

A Reading from the poetry of Isaac Watts

When I survey the wondrous cross

When I survey the wondrous cross,
On which the Prince of glory died,
My richest gain I count but loss,
And pour contempt on all my pride.

Forbid it, Lord, that I should boast
Save in the death of Christ my God;
All the vain things that charm me most,
I sacrifice them to his blood.

See from his head, his hands, his feet,
Sorrow and love flow mingled down;
Did e'er such love and sorrow meet,
Or thorns compose so rich a crown?

His dying crimson like a robe,
Spreads o'er his body on the tree;
Then am I dead to all the globe,
And all the globe is dead to me.

Were the whole realm of nature mine,
That were a present far too small;
Love so amazing, so divine,
Demands my soul, my life, my all.

The Day of Judgement

When the fierce North-wind with his airy forces
Rears up the Baltic to a foaming fury;
And the red lightning with a storm of hail comes
Rushing amain down;

How the poor sailors stand amazed and tremble,
While the hoarse thunder, like a bloody trumpet,
Roars a loud onset to the gaping waters,
Quick to devour them.

Such shall the noise be, and the wild disorder
(If things eternal may be like these earthly),
Such the dire terror when the great Archangel
Shakes the creation;

Tears the strong pillars of the vault of Heaven,
Breaks up old marble, the repose of princes;
See the graves open, and the bones arising,
Flames all around them.

Hark, the shrill outcries of the guilty wretches!
Lively bright horror and amazing anguish
Stare through their eyelids, while the living worm lies
Gnawing within them.

Thoughts, like old vultures, prey upon their heart-
strings,
And the smart twinges, when their eye beholds the
Lofty Judge frowning, and a flood of vengeance
Rolling afore him.

Hopeless immortals! how they scream and shiver,
While devils push them to the pit wide-yawning,
Hideous and gloomy, to receive them headlong
Down to the centre!

Stop here, my fancy: (all away, ye horrid
Doleful ideas!) come, arise to Jesus,
How he sits God-like! and the saints around him
Throned, yet adoring!

O may I sit there when he comes triumphant,
Dooming the nations! then ascend to glory,
While our Hosannas all along the passage
Shout the Redeemer!

30 November

Andrew the Apostle

Andrew appears to have been one of the first four disciples called by Jesus, and in the Gospels of Matthew, Mark and Luke, is described as a fisherman in partnership with his brother Simon Peter and the brothers James and John. It is in the Gospel according to John, however, that most is learned about him. According to John, all four were disciples of John the Baptist before Jesus summoned them. The two traditions are not irreconcilable. Andrew is honoured as the first 'missionary' because it was he who went off to bring his brother Simon Peter to meet Jesus. Andrew seems to have remained with Jesus until the very end. He was there at the feeding of the five thousand and then later, when some Greeks in Jerusalem wanted to see Jesus, Philip brought them to Andrew who told Jesus of their desire. Tradition has him travelling on several missionary journeys in Scythia, and eventually being martyred by being crucified on an X-shaped cross. He became the patron saint of Scotland because of a legend that his relics had been brought there in the eighth century. The Church in the East also honours him as the founder of the Patriarchal See of Constantinople.

A Reading from *The Cost of Discipleship* by Dietrich Bonhoeffer

The call of Jesus goes forth, and is at once followed by the response of obedience. The response of the disciples is an act of obedience, not a confession of faith in Jesus. How could the call immediately evoke obedience?

The story of the call of the first disciples is a stumbling-block to our natural reason, and it is no wonder that frantic attempts have been made to separate the two events. By hook or by crook a bridge must be found between them. Something must have happened in between, some psychological or historical event. Thus we get the stupid question: Surely the disciples must have known Jesus before, and that previous acquaintance explains their readiness to hear the Master's call. Unfortunately our text is ruthlessly silent on this point, and in fact it regards the immediate sequence of call and response as a matter of crucial importance. It displays not the slightest interest in the psychological reasons for a person's religious decisions. And why? For the simple reason that the cause behind the immediate following of call by response is Jesus Christ himself. It is Jesus who calls, and because it is Jesus, the disciple follows at once.

This encounter is a testimony to the absolute, direct, and unaccountable authority of Jesus. There is no need of any preliminaries, and no other consequence but obedience to the call. Because Jesus is the Christ, he has the authority to call and to demand obedience to his word. Jesus summons us to follow him not as a teacher of a pattern of the good life, but as the Christ, the Son of God. In this short text Jesus Christ and his claim are proclaimed to the world. Not a word of praise is given to the disciple for his decision for Christ. We are not expected to contemplate the disciple, but only him who calls, and his absolute authority. According to our text, there is no road to faith or discipleship, no other road – only obedience to the call of Jesus.

And what does the text inform us about the content of discipleship? Follow me, run along behind me! That is all. To follow in Christ's steps is something which is void of all content. It gives us no intelligible programme for a way of life, no goal or ideal to strive after.

When we are called to follow Christ, we are summoned to an exclusive attachment to his person. The grace of his call bursts all the bonds of legalism. It is a gracious call, a gracious commandment. It transcends the difference between the law and the gospel. Christ calls, the disciple follows; that is grace and commandment in one.

alternative reading

A Reading from a sermon by Mark Frank

Jesus came first and walked by the sea. He looked upon Andrew and Peter and spake to them. And what then? They straightway followed – and who but Jesus?

Let us always think, when we hear Christ calling us to his service, that we cannot make too much haste to follow him. It may be he has called his last, and will call no more; or he will be gone if we make not haste. It is not safe to loiter by the way for fear of temptations that may prevent our good purposes and quite overthrow our holy resolutions. It is an unworthy usage and unmannerly to stand talking to anyone else when God is speaking to us to come to him. Christ would have Andrew and Peter do his business quickly: for in the midst of their work he called them, and in the midst they leave: away with nets, come Christ; fish who will, for them they will follow Christ, not so much as stay to draw up their nets, be what will in them, they care not; let all go, so they may catch him.

And alas what have we, the best, the richest of us as highly as we think of ourselves and ours, more than Andrew and his brother: a few old broken nets? What are all our honours but old nets to catch the breath of the world? What are our estates but nets to entangle us? What are all our ways and devices of thriving but so many several nets to catch a little yellow sand and mud? What are all those fine catching ways of eloquence, knowledge, good parts of mind and body, but so many nets and snares to catch others with? The rational soul itself we too often make but a net to catch flies, petty, buzzing knowledges only; few solid sober thoughts. And our life itself, what is it but a few rotten threads knit together into veins and sinews, its construction so fragile that the least stick or stone can unloose it or break all to pieces?

O blessed saint of this day, that we could but leave these nets as thou didst thine; that nothing might any longer entangle us or keep us from our Master's service! Follow we Saint Andrew as he did Christ; follow him to Christ, cheerfully and without delay, and while it is today, begin our course. Cast off the networks, the catching desires of the flesh and the world, and so you also may be said to have left your nets. And having so weaned your souls from inordinate affection to things below, let Christ be your business, his life your pattern, his commands your law.

Be ye followers of Christ, and let Saint Andrew this day lead you after him into all universal obedience, ready, pure, sincere. You may well throw away your nets, having caught him in whom you have caught glory and immortality and eternal life; and by following him shall undoubtedly come at last out of this sea of toil and misery into the port and haven of everlasting rest, and joys, and happiness.

DECEMBER

1 December

Charles de Foucauld

Hermit in the Sahara, 1916

Charles Eugène de Foucauld was born in 1858 and led a dissipated life as a young officer in the cavalry. In 1883, he went on an expedition to Morocco where he developed a passion for north Africa and its ways. Four years later, he returned to the Catholic faith of his infancy and, after a pilgrimage to the Holy Land, became a Trappist monk in 1890. Desiring an even more austere life, he left in 1897 and became a servant to the Poor Clares in Jerusalem and Nazareth. He was eventually ordained priest in 1901 and went to live as a hermit in Algeria, ending up at Tamanrasset. He became fluent in the local language and his care and concern for the local tribes-people made him accepted and then much loved, though he never sought converts. He composed Rules for brothers and for sisters, though none ever actually joined him. He was assassinated on this day in 1916, a victim of local religious wars. The Little Sisters of the Sacred Heart were founded in 1933, inspired by his Rule for sisters. His writings also inspired René Voillaume and others to adopt a life based on his Rule, eventually becoming The Little Brothers of Jesus in 1945.

A Reading from a letter of Charles de Foucauld to a Trappist monk preparing for his ordination

Your business now is to live alone with God and to be, until your ordination, as though you and God were alone in the universe. You must cross the desert and dwell in it to receive the grace of God. It is here one drives out everything that is not God. The soul needs to enter into this silence, this recollection, this forgetfulness of all created things by which God establishes his rule in it and forms within it the life of the spirit, the life of intimacy with God, the conversation of the soul with God in faith, hope and charity.

Later the soul will bring forth fruit exactly in the measure in which the inner life is developed in it. If there is no inner life, however great may be the zeal, the high intention, the hard work, no fruit will come forth; it is like a spring that would give out sanctity to others but cannot, having none to give; one can only give that which one has. It is in solitude, in that lonely life alone with God, in profound recollection of soul, in forgetfulness of all created things, that God gives himself to the soul that thus gives itself whole and entire to him.

alternative reading

A Reading from *The Go-Between God* by John V. Taylor

A true missionary is one who, like Enoch, walks with God, and derives from constant communion with him a portion of the divine likeness.

This is the real meaning of the approach to mission which has come to be known as 'Christian presence'. It is often confused with that method of approach to people of other faiths which is known as 'dialogue'. Christian presence and dialogue may often go hand in hand, it is true, but they are not the same. One of the purest examples of Christian presence which has ever been demonstrated is that of Charles de Foucauld, and of those who have followed in his steps, the Little Brothers and the Little Sisters of Jesus. Yet they have placed themselves under rule not to preach, nor to offer organised works, such as schools or hospitals, nor to employ any of the usual methods of evangelism. They believe they are simply called to live among the very poor of this world – on a houseboat amid the teeming refugees of Hong Kong, around a tiny courtyard high above the sacred waterfront of Benares, in a workman's shack on one of the sloping streets of Kabul, in an Eskimo hamlet in Alaska, a shanty suburb of Kampala, a labourers' settlement near Port Moresby, built on wooden piles above the sea like any other village of Papua.

Unobtrusively, they keep a routine of communal prayer and silent adoration, but every day they go out in their working clothes to do the same sort of job that their neighbours are doing and to offer them an unstinted friendship in the doing of it. Out of sight, out of mind of the Church as a whole, way below the poverty line, scattered in their twos and threes across the face of the earth, they do not work for their neighbours, they work with them. Their role is that of prayer and of a silent, hidden presence of love.

Such extreme renunciation of all the normal activities of mission would suggest either a lack of concern or a policy of despair, were it not for Charles de Foucauld's ardent passion for evangelism. 'I wish to cry the gospel by my whole life,' he said; and again, 'For the spreading of the gospel I am ready to go to the ends of the earth and I am likewise ready to live until the Day of Judgement.' To live thus totally towards God for the sake of the world is a profoundly missionary and, indeed, redemptive way.

2 December

Saints, Martyrs and Missionaries of Asia

The Christian revelation took place in Asia, and it was there that the first martyrdoms, and the first missionary journeys took place. After the time of the apostles, this continued with early saints such as Ignatius of Antioch and Polycarp. Christian communities have continued to exist in Asia, with many West and East Syrian Orthodox churches. The apostle Thomas is traditionally said to have visited India, and the Syrian Church there claims succession through him. Much later, missionaries from the west came to Asia, such as Francis Xavier whose missionary work extended to India, Japan and elsewhere, and whose feast is celebrated on 3 December. From Cornwall, Henry Martyn went to work in India and Persia. These and other initiatives led to the growth of Christian churches as far apart as

India, China, Japan and Korea. We remember with them on this day the ancient Churches of the Middle East, some persecuted today as on occasion in the past, and pray for their continued witness to the living truth of the gospel.

Note: See also the following individual entries and their readings:

Samuel Azariah Vedanayagam	2 January
Paul Miki	6 February
Pandita Mary Ramaba	30 April
Sundar Singh	19 June
Henry Martyn	19 October
Francis Xavier	3 December

A Reading from *The Go-Between God* by John V. Taylor

The Holy Spirit is *universally* present through the whole fabric of the world, and yet *uniquely* present in Christ and, by extension, in the fellowship of his disciples. The Spirit's witness to the lordship and love of Jesus Christ is a kind of dialogue. In the person of Jesus, and in his body, the Church, the Spirit calls all men and women to respond. It is this which gives us grounds for believing that in any dialogue between the Church and the world, or between Christians and those of other faiths, the Holy Spirit is speaking in both participants.

But the awareness of one another in the Sprit involves awareness of the faith by which each lives. For, as Kenneth Cragg has said, 'Christianity cannot address men and ignore their gods: it may not act in the present and disown the past or wisely hold forth salvation and withhold salutation. In seeking men and women for Christ's sake, it is committed to the significance of all they are in their birth and their tradition, both for good or ill.' That is well said because it emphasizes the dynamically personal quality of any faith that people live by. Debates about inter-faith dialogue usually betray too static an idea of what a religion is. It suggested that what shapes us is the truth *about* God whereas it is the truth *of* God. Consequently a religion is thought to be primarily a body of propositions and regulations, standing over against people who either believe or do not believe, asking for their allegiance and offering a way of fulfilment.

But I believe it is truer to think of a religion as a people's tradition of response to the reality the Holy Spirit has set before their eyes. I am deliberately not saying that any religion is the truth which the Spirit disclosed, nor even that it contains that truth. All we can say without presumption is that this is how people have responded and taught others to respond to what the Spirit made them aware of. It is the history of a particular answer, or series of answers, to the call and claim of him who lies beyond all religions.

3 December

Francis Xavier

Missionary, Apostle of the Indies, 1552

Francis was born at the castle of Xavier in Spanish Navarre in 1506. He was educated in Paris and, with Ignatius of Loyola, became one of the group of seven who took vows as the first members of the Society of Jesus, or Jesuits. Since preaching the gospel overseas was an integral part of the Jesuit vocation, Francis sailed for Goa, on the west coast of India, in 1541. He travelled all over the East Indies, evangelizing and establishing the Church in Ceylon, Malacca, Malaya and notably in Japan, where he left behind two thousand converts. He had just reached China when he died on board ship in December in the year 1552.

A Reading from two letters of Francis Xavier to Ignatius of Loyola, written while working in India between 1542 and 1544

We have visited the villages of the new converts who accepted the Christian religion a few years ago. No Portuguese live here – the country is so utterly barren and poor. The native Christians have no priests. They know only that they are Christians. There is nobody to say Mass for them; nobody to teach them the Creed, the Our Father, the Hail Mary, and the Commandments of God's Law.

I have not stopped since the day I arrived. I have conscientiously made the rounds of the villages. I bathed in the sacred waters [of baptism] all the children who had not yet been baptized. This means that I have purified a very large number of children so young that, as the saying goes, they could not tell their right hand from their left. The older children would not let me say my Office or eat or sleep until I had taught them one prayer or another. Then I began to understand: 'The kingdom of heaven belongs to such as these.'

I could not refuse so devout a request without failing in devotion myself. I taught them first the confession of faith in the Father, the Son, and the Holy Spirit; then the Apostles' Creed, the Our Father, and Hail Mary. I noticed among them persons of great intelligence. If only someone could educate them in the Christian way of life, I have no doubt that they would make excellent Christians.

Many, many people hereabouts are not becoming Christians for one reason only: there is nobody to make them Christians. Again and again I have thought of going round the universities of Europe, especially Paris, and everywhere crying out like a madman, riveting the attention of those with more learning than charity: 'What a tragedy! How many souls are being shut out of heaven and falling into hell, thanks to you!' I wish they would work as hard at this as they do at their books, and so settle their account with God for their learning and the talents entrusted to them.

This thought would certainly stir most of them to meditate on spiritual realities, to listen actively to what God is saying to them. They would forget their own desires, their human affairs, and give themselves over entirely to God's will and his choice. They would cry out with all their heart: 'Lord, I am here! What do you want me to do? Send me anywhere you like – even to India!'

December 4

Clement of Alexandria

Priest, Teacher of the Faith, *c.*215

Clement was born in Athens of pagan parents in about the year 153. The apostles and their immediate successors laid the foundation on which, towards the end of the second century, Clement of Alexandria and others began to create a sophisticated literature in which they sought to explore the relation between Christian thought and the Greek philosophical tradition. Clement is honoured as Christianity's first religious philosopher.

The reasons for his conversion are not known. He had travelled extensively to learn from the best teachers of his day before arriving in Alexandria in 190 where he became the head of the Catechetical School in succession to Pantaenus. He produced an impressive body of writing that drew extensively on both pagan and Christian writings and was centered on the idea of Christ, the Logos, as both the source of all human reason and the unique interpreter of God to humanity. Clement was forced to flee Alexandria by an outbreak of persecution in 202 and is supposed to have died as a martyr in about the year 215.

A Reading from a treatise *On Spiritual Perfection*
by Clement of Alexandria

We are commanded to reverence and honour the One whom we are persuaded is Word, Saviour, and Leader, and to honour the Father through him – not merely on special days, as some do, but continually throughout our lives and in every conceivable way. Such honour is not restricted to certain places or designated shrines, or to certain festivals and appointed days, but is rendered throughout life and in every place by those who are truly spiritual – whether they be living alone or in a community of faith. We are to honour God, returning our gratitude for the knowledge of the way to live.

Accordingly, all of life is a festival. Being persuaded that God is present everywhere on all sides, we praise him as we cultivate the fields; we sing hymns as we sail the sea; in short, we conduct ourselves as citizens of heaven.

The truly spiritual are closely allied to God, being both grave and cheerful in everything they undertake – grave on account of their attention to God, joyful on account of their consideration of the blessings which God has bestowed upon humanity. They always trace up to God their grave enjoyment of all things: food, drink, and pleasing fragrances. They offer the first-fruits of their labours to the One who has given all things, rendering thanks through Jesus who is Gift, Unction, and Word.

In this way the truly spiritual will pray throughout their whole life since for them prayer is the means by which we attain union with God. They will reject all that does not contribute to that end as worthless, because they have already attained that state in which they have received, at least in some measure, the perfection which consists in acting through love. Their whole life is one long sacred liturgy.

4 December

John of Damascus

Monk, Teacher of the Faith, *c.*749

John was born in Damascus in about the year 657. The city by this date was Muslim. John's father, although a Christian, was Chief of the Revenue, and the principal representative of the Christians in the city. In 716, John, by then well-educated in science and theology, became a monk at the monastic settlement of Mar Saba near Jerusalem and later was ordained priest there. He became a prolific writer of theological works and of hymns. His summary of the teachings of the Greek Fathers, called De Fide Orthodoxa, proved an immense influence in the Church in the following centuries, in both East and West. He died on this day in about the year 749.

A Reading from a treatise *On the Incarnation and the Holy Icons* by John of Damascus

In former times God, who is without form or body, could never be depicted. But now that God has appeared in the flesh and dwelt among us, I make an image of God in so far as he has become visible. I do not venerate matter; but I venerate the creator of matter who became matter for my sake, who willed to make his dwelling in matter; who worked out my salvation through matter. I shall never cease, therefore, to venerate the matter which wrought my salvation. Do not insult matter, for it is honourable. Nothing is without honour that God has made.

How could God be born out of material things which have no existence in themselves? God's body is God because he joined it to his person by a union which shall never pass away. The divine nature remains the same; the flesh created in time is henceforth quickened by reason-endowed soul. Because of this I salute all matter with reverence because God has filled it with his grace and power. Through it my salvation has come to me. Was not the thrice-happy and thrice-blessed wood of the cross matter? Was not the holy and exalted mount of Calvary matter? Was not the life-bearing rock, the holy and life-giving tomb, the fountain of our resurrection, was it not matter? Is not the ink in the most holy book of the Gospels matter? Is not the life-giving altar matter? Do we not receive from it the bread of life? Are not gold and silver matter? From them we make crosses, patens, chalices! And over and above all these things, is not the Body and Blood of our Lord matter?

Thus either do away with the honour and veneration all these material things deserve, or accept the tradition of the Church and the veneration of icons. Learn to reverence God and his friends; follow the inspiration of the Holy Spirit. Never despise matter, for matter is not despicable. God has made nothing despicable. Rather, contemplate the glory of the Lord, for his face has been unveiled.

4 December

Nicholas Ferrar

Deacon, Founder of the Little Gidding Community, 1637

Note: In Wales, Nicholas Ferrar is commemorated on 1 December, and in Scotland on 2 December.

Born in London in 1592, Nicholas Ferrar was educated at Clare Hall (now Clare College), Cambridge and elected a Fellow there in 1610. From 1613, he travelled on the Continent for five years, trying his hand as a businessman and then as a parliamentarian on his return. In 1625, he moved to Little Gidding in Huntingdonshire, where he was joined by his brother and sister and their families and by his mother. They established together a community life of prayer, using The Book of Common Prayer, and a life of charitable works in the locality. He was ordained to the diaconate by William Laud the year after they arrived. He wrote to his niece in 1631, 'I purpose and hope by God's grace to be to you not as a master but as a partner and fellow student.' This indicates the depth and feeling of the community life Nicholas and his family strove to maintain. After the death of Nicholas on this day in 1637, the community was broken up in 1646 by the Puritans, who were suspicious of it and referred to it as the Arminian Nunnery. They feared it promoting the return of Romish practices into England, and so all Nicholas's manuscripts were burned.

A Reading from *The Life of Mr George Herbert* by Isaac Walton

Mr Nicholas Ferrar (who got the reputation of being called 'Saint Nicholas' at the age of six years) was born in London. At an early age he was made Fellow of Clare Hall in Cambridge where he continued to be eminent for his piety, temperance, and learning. About the twenty-sixth year of his age, he betook himself to travel, in which he added to his Latin and Greek, a perfect knowledge of all the languages spoken in the western parts of our Christian world; and understood well the principles of their religion and of their manner and the reasons of their worship. In this his travel he met with many persuasions to come into a communion with that Church which calls itself Catholic, but he returned from his travels as he went, eminent for his obedience to his mother, the Church of England.

In his absence from England, Mr Ferrar's father (who was a merchant) allowed him a liberal maintenance; and, not long after his return into England, Mr Ferrar had by the death of his father, or an elder brother, or both, an estate left him that enabled him to purchase land to the value of four or five hundred pounds a year, the greatest part of which land was at Little Gidding, four or six miles from Huntingdon and about eighteen from Cambridge; which place he chose for the privacy of it, and for the hall, which had the parish-church, or chapel, belonging and adjoining near to it. For Mr Ferrar, having seen the manners and vanities of the world and found them to be, as Mr Herbert says, 'a nothing between two dishes', did so condemn it, that he resolved to spend the remainder of his life in mortifications and in devotion and charity, and to be always prepared for death.

He and his family, which were about thirty in number, were like a little college. About the year 1630, he did betake himself to a constant and methodical service of God, and it was in this manner. He, being accompanied with most of his family, did himself use to read the Common Prayers (for he was a deacon) every day at the appointed hours of ten and four in the parish-church, which was very near his house and which he had both repaired and adorned for it was fallen into a great ruin by reason of a depopulation of the village before Mr Ferrar bought the manor.

And he did also constantly read the Matins every morning at the hour of six, either in the church, or in an oratory which was within his own house. And many of the family did there continue with him after the prayers were ended, and there they spent some hours in singing hymns or anthems, sometimes in the church, and often to an organ in the oratory. And there they sometimes betook themselves to meditate, or to pray privately, or to read part of the New Testament to themselves, or to continue praying or reading the psalms. And it is to be noted that in this continued serving of God, the Psalter was in every four and twenty hours sung or read over, from the first to the last verse; and this was done as constantly as the sun runs his circle every day about the world, and then begins again the same instant that it ended.

Thus did Mr Ferrar and his happy family serve God day and night. And this course of piety and great liberality to his poor neighbours, Mr Ferrar maintained till his death, which was in the year 1637.

6 December

Nicholas

Bishop of Myra, *c.*326

Nicholas was a fourth-century bishop of Myra in Asia Minor (southern Turkey). His reputation as a worker of wonders was enhanced by a ninth-century author of his hagiography and he is now best known through these stories. Many of them concern his love and care for children, how he fed the hungry, healed the sick and cared for the oppressed. He saved three girls from a life of prostitution by providing them with dowries and so developed the tradition of bearing gifts to children on his feast day, a practice appropriated by the Christmas celebrations. Nicholas is also one of the patron saints of Russia.

A Reading from a homily of Gregory the Great

Our Lord said to his disciples: 'See, I am sending you out like lambs among wolves.' There are many people, when put in positions of authority, who become hard and severe, relishing the chance to tear their subordinates to pieces, and using their power to terrify and hurt those whom they are called to serve. There is no love in their hearts because they always need to be in control: they forget that they are called to nurture their people as a parent. They exchange humility for pride in the positions they occupy, and though outwardly they may sometimes appear indulgent, inwardly they are full of anger. It is of them that in another place in the Gospels our Lord says: 'They come to you in sheep's clothing, but inwardly they are ravenous wolves.'

My friends, we should remember that we are sent as lambs among wolves, and must therefore guard our innocence lest malice overtake us. Those who undertake any pastoral office should never be the cause of evil, and should actually be prepared to have to endure it.

By gentleness they must soften the anger of the violent: wounded ourselves by ill treatment, we can bring healing to other sinners. If on a particular occasion a zeal for justice requires a display of severity, then let severity have its source in love and not brutality. In this way, authority is demonstrated outwardly, and inwardly we experience a true parental love for those in our care. This is what our blessed Master was teaching us when he himself demonstrated that his was no selfish love, being unconcerned with worldly honour or ambition.

Our Lord continues: 'Take neither purse, nor bag for the journey, nor sandals, and greet no one along the way.' We should have such confidence in God that though we have no material security, we will never lack the necessities of life. Such confidence obviates the necessity of spending time in the pursuit of temporal goods when we should be securing eternal goods for others. We have no leisure for idle conversation in our calling; rather we must hurry along the path of preaching.

7 December

Ambrose

Bishop of Milan, Teacher of the Faith, 397

Born in Trier in 334, Ambrose was of an aristocratic family and was Governor of northern Italy, with his headquarters in Milan. Whilst trying to bring peace to the Christian community, with Arianism and orthodoxy each trying to gain the election of its man as bishop, Ambrose, known and respected by all, though not yet baptized, found himself being urged to accept the rôle of bishop himself, the gathered Christian populace taking up the cry, 'Ambrose for bishop'. He finally accepted and was baptized and consecrated on this day in the year 374. Ambrose proved his worth, becoming a teacher and preacher of great renown, promoting the essential divinity of Christ as being at the centre of Christian faith. He is credited with being the first person to introduce hymns into Western worship, and wrote several hymns himself which gave a clear understanding of orthodox teaching. He came up against the Imperial powers and, with the support of the whole community, stood firm against the interference of the State in Church affairs and matters of faith. He also baptized the future Saint Augustine. Ambrose died on Good Friday, 4 April in the year 397.

A Reading from a treatise *On Penitence* by Ambrose

Show your wound to the Physician so that he may heal it. Though you refuse to expose it to his gaze, Christ still knows it: he is waiting to hear your voice. Wash away the scars of your sins by your tears. That is what the woman in the gospel did. She wiped away the decaying smell of her sin: she washed away her faults when she washed the feet of Jesus with her tears.

Lord Jesus, allow me to wash the stains from your feet which you have contracted since you walked within me. O that you would allow me to wash the steps before you of my faults! But where could I ever obtain the living water with which to wash them? And yet, though I have no living water within me, I can at least offer you my tears, trusting that while I wash your feet with them, I am cleansing myself.

But where do I find the grace of hearing what you said to her: 'Her sins, which are many, are forgiven, for she loved much'? I have to confess, Lord, my debts are greater. The sins that have been forgiven me are more numerous because I have come to the priesthood from the uproar of the law courts and the burden of public life. I am afraid that I may be found ungrateful, if I, to whom more has been forgiven, should be found to have loved less.

And yet if we are unable to equal this woman, the Lord Jesus knows how to help the weak. He himself comes to the tomb to release us. O Lord, I beg you come to my tomb, wash me with your tears for my hardened, dry eyes do not possess tears sufficient to wash me. But if you will weep for me, I shall indeed be saved. As you once called forth your servant Lazarus from the tomb, call forth me. I find myself bound down with the chains of my sins, my feet fettered, my hands tied. I am buried in dead thoughts and works. Yet at your voice I shall walk free, and shall be found worthy to sit at your feast in your house.

Those whom you set free, you also guard. Guard, therefore, your work Lord; guard in me the grace you have given me, in spite of my flight from you. I knew that I was not worthy to be called to the episcopate because I had devoted myself to secular affairs, and yet by your grace I am what I am. Indeed, I am the least of all bishops, the lowest in merit of the bishops. But since you have granted me to work for your Church, guard the fruits of my labour. You called me to the priesthood when I was a lost child. Let me not lose myself in my priesthood.

Above all give me the grace of compassion. Grant me the ability to have compassion on sinners from the depth of my heart: for that is of supreme importance. Give me compassion every time I witness the fall of a sinner. Let me never arrogantly admonish such a person, but let me suffer with him and weep with him. And when I weep for my neighbour, make me weep for myself as well. This is vital, for he who rejoices at the downfall of another is rejoicing at the victory of the devil. Let us rather mourn when we hear that one of us for whom Christ died, has perished, for Christ despises no one.

8 December

The Conception of the Blessed Virgin Mary

This festival in honour of the Conception of the Mother of our Lord is celebrated on this day in both the Eastern and the Western Church. This feast, which dates from the seventh century, marks the dawn of the New Covenant, celebrating the gracious preparation by God of his people to receive their Saviour and Lord, putting 'heaven in ordinary' and showing that mortal flesh can indeed bring Christ to the world.

A Reading from the discourses of Anselm of Canterbury

Sky, stars, earth, rivers, day, night, and all things that are meant to serve us and be for our good rejoice because of you, blessed Lady. Through you they have in a way come back to life, enriched with a new grace that words cannot describe. When they lost the noble purpose of their nature for which they had been made, of serving and helping those who praise God, they were like dead things. They were crushed, disfigured, and abused by idol worshippers for whom they had not been made. They rejoice now as if they had come to life again. Now they are made beautiful because they serve and are used by those who believe in God.

Name	Day	Month	E	I	S	W	M
Hilary	***13***	***Jan***	E			W	
Hilary	14	Jan			S		
Hilda	***19***	***Nov***	E		S		
Hilda	18	Nov				W	
Hildegard	17	Sep	E		S		
Hill, Octavia	13	Aug	E				
Hilton, Walter	24	Mar	E				
Holy Innocents	28	Dec	E	I	S	W	
Hooker, Richard	***3***	***Nov***	E		S		
Hooker, Richard	30	Oct				W	
Howell Harris	1	Jul				W	
Hugh of Cluny	11	May					M
Hugh of Lincoln	17	Nov	E		S	W	
Hugh Latimer	***16***	***Oct***	E				
Hugh Latimer	21	Mar				W	
Ignatius of Antioch	17	Oct	E		S	W	
Ignatius of Loyola	31	Jul	E		S	W	
Illtud	6	Nov				W	
Inglis, Charles	16	Aug		I			
Ini Kopuria	6	Jun	E				
Innocents, The Holy	28	Dec	E	I	S	W	
Irenaeus	28	Jun	E		S	W	
Isaac Watts	25	Nov	E				
Isaac Williams	11	Jan				W	
Isabella, Gilmore	16	Apr	E				
James the Deacon	11	Oct		I			
James the Great	25	Jul	E	I	S	W	
James of Jerusalem	23	Oct		I	S	W	
James the Less (& Philip)	1	May	E	I	S	W	
Janani Luwum	***17***	***Feb***	E				
Janani Luwum	3	Jun			S		
Jarlath of Tuam	6	Jun		I			
Jane Frances de Chantal	12	Dec					M
Jean-Baptiste Vianney	4	Aug	E				
Jebb, Eglantyne	17	Dec	E				
Jeremy Taylor	13	Aug	E	I	S	W	
Jerome	30	Sep	E		S	W	
Joachim	26	Jul	E		S		
Joan of Arc	30	May	E				
John	27	Dec	E	I	S	W	
John of the Cross	14	Dec	E		S	W	
John of Damascus	4	Dec	E				
John of Fiesole	18	Feb				W	
John the Baptist, Beheading of	29	Aug	E		S	W	
John the Baptist, Birth of	24	Jun	E	I	S	W	
John XXIII	4	Jun			S	W	
John Bosco	31	Jan	E				
John, Bunyan	30	Aug	E				
John Calvin	26	May	E				

Name	Day	Month	E	I	S	W
John Chrysostom	***13***	***Sep***	E			
John Chrysostom	27	Jan			S	W
John Comper	27	Jul			S	
John Davies	15	May				W
John Donne	***31***	***Mar***	E			
John Donne	25	Nov				W
John, Esther	14	Oct				W
John Fisher	6	Jul	E			
John Keble	***14***	***Jul***	E			W
John Keble	29	Mar			S	
John Mason Neale	7	Aug	E		S	
John Henry Newman	11	Aug	E			
John Coleridge Patteson	20	Sep	E		S	
John Skinner	12	Jun			S	
John Wesley	***24***	***May***	E			W
John Wesley	3	Mar			S	
John Wyclif	31	Dec	E		S	W
Johnson, Samuel	13	Dec	E			
Joseph of Arimathea	31	Jul				W
Joseph of Nazareth	19	Mar	E	I	S	W
Joseph Butler	16	Jun	E			
Josephine Butler	***30***	***May***	E			
Josephine Butler	29	Jul				W
Josephine Butler	30	Dec			S	
Jolly, Alexander	27	Jun			S	
Jude the Apostle	28	Oct	E	I	S	W
Julian of Norwich	8	May	E		S	W
Julius	20	Jun				W
Justin	1	Jun	E		S	W
Keble, John	***14***	***Jul***	E			W
Keble, John	29	Mar			S	
Kempe, Margery	9	Nov	E			
Ken, Thomas	***8***	***Jun***	E			
Ken, Thomas	22	Mar			S	
Kennedy, Geoffrey Studdert	8	Mar	E			
Kenneth (Cannice)	11	Oct		I	S	
Kentigern (Mungo)	***13***	***Jan***	E		S	
Kentigern (Mungo)	14	Jan				W
Kessog	10	Mar			S	
Kevin of Glendalough	3	Jun		I		
Kieran of Seirkeiran	5	Mar		I		
Kilian	8	Jul		I		
King, Edward	8	Mar	E			
Kivebulaya, Apolo	30	May	E			
Kolbe, Maximilian	14	Aug	E		S	W
Kopuria, Ini	6	Jun	E			
Lancelot, Andrewes	***25***	***Sep***	E			
Lancelot, Andrewes	26	Sep				W
Lanfranc	28	May	E			

Name	Day	Month	E	I	S	W	M
Las Casas, Bartolomé de	20	Jul	E				
Laserian	18	Apr		I			
Latimer, Hugh	***16***	***Oct***	E				
Latimer, Hugh	21	Mar				W	
Laud, William	10	Jan	E				
Laurence	10	Aug	E		S	W	
Laurence O'Toole	14	Nov		I			
Laurie, Albert	26	Apr			S		
Law, William	10	Apr	E		S		
Lazarus	29	Jul	E				
Leighton, Robert	26	Jun			S		
Leo the Great	10	Nov	E		S	W	
Leonard	6	Nov	E				
Lewis Bayley	25	Oct				W	
Lowder, Charles Fuge	9	Sep	E				
Lucy	13	Dec	E			W	
Lucy Menzies	24	Nov			S		
Luke the Evangelist	18	Oct	E	I	S	W	
Luther, Martin	***31***	***Oct***	E				
Luther, Martin	19	Feb			S		
Luwum, Janani	***17***	***Feb***	E				
Luwum, Janani	3	Jun			S		
Lwanga, Charles, and his companions	3	Jun	E		S		
Mac Nisse, Oengus	4	Sep		I			
Macartan	24	Mar		I			
Machar	12	Nov			S		
Mackenzie, Charles	31	Jan			S		
Macrina	19	Jul	E			W	
Maelrubha of Applecross	20	Apr			S		
Magdalene, Mary	22	Jul	E	I	S	W	
Magnus of Orkney	16	Apr			S		
Maieul of Cluny	11	May					M
Malachy	3	Nov		I			
Manche Masemola	4	Feb				W	
Margaret of Antioch	20	Jul	E				
Margaret of Scotland	16	Nov	E		S	W	
Mark the Evangelist	25	Apr	E	I	S	W	
Martha	29	Jul	E		S	W	
Martin de Porres	3	Nov	E				
Martin of Tours	11	Nov	E		S	W	
Martyn, Henry	19	Oct	E		S	W	
Mary, The Blessed Virgin	15	Aug	E		S	W	
- Annunciation to	25	Mar	E	I	S	W	
- Birth	8	Sep	E	I	S	W	
- Conception	8	Dec	E		S		
- Visit to Elizabeth	31	May	E	I	S	W	
Mary Magdalene	22	Jul	E	I	S	W	
Mary, Martha [and Lazarus]	29	Jul	E		S	W	
Mary Ramabai, Pandita	30	Apr	E				
Mary Slessor	11	Jan	E				

Mary Sumner	9	Aug	E				
Maurice, Frederick Denison	1	Apr	E				
Maurus and Placid	15	Jan					M
Maximilian Kolbe	14	Aug	E		S	W	
Mechtild	19	Nov	E				
Mellitus	24	Apr	E				
Menzies, Lucy	24	Nov			S		
Methodius	14	Feb	E		S	W	
Michael & All Angels	29	Sep	E	I	S	W	
Miki, Paul and his companions	6	Feb	E		S		
Mizeki, Bernard	18	Jun	E		S		
Moluag of Lismore	25	Jun		I	S		
Monica	27	Aug	E		S	W	
Moninne of Killeavy	6	Jul		I			
Monsell, Harriet	26	Mar	E				
More, Thomas	6	Jul	E			W	
Morgan, William	10	Sep				W	
Morris Williams	3	Jan				W	
Munchin	2	Jan		I			
Mungo (Kentigern)	***13***	***Jan***	E		S		
Mungo (Kentigern)	14	Jan				W	
Muredach (Murtagh)	12	Aug		I			
Móibhí	12	Oct		I			
Nathi (Crumnathy)	9	Aug		I			
Neale, John Mason	*7*	***Aug***	E				
Neale, John Mason	9	Aug			S		
Neri, Philip	26	May	E				
Newman, John Henry	11	Aug	E				
Nicholas of Myra	6	Dec	E		S	W	
Nicholas Ferrar	***4***	***Dec***	E				
Nicholas Ferrar	1	Dec				W	
Nicholas Ferrar	2	Dec			S		
Nicholas Ridley	***16***	***Oct***	E				
Nicholas Ridley	21	Mar				W	
Nightingale, Florence	13	Aug	E				
Ninian	16	Sep	E		S	W	
Non	5	Mar				W	
Odo	11	May					M
Odillo	11	May					M
Octavia Hill	13	Aug	E				
Oengus Mac Nisse	4	Sep		I			
Olaudah Equiano	30	Jul	E				
Oscar Romero	24	Mar	E			W	
Osmund	16	Jul	E				
Oswald of Northumbria	5	Aug	E		S	W	
Otteran	27	Oct		I			
O'Toole, Laurence	14	Nov		I			
Pachomius	15	May					M

Name	Day	Month	E	I	S	W	M
Padarn	15	Apr				W	
Palladius	6	Jul			S		
Pandita, Mary Ramabai,	30	Apr	E				
Patrick	17	Mar	E	I	S	W	
Patrick Forbes, & the Aberdeen Doctors	28	Mar			S		
Patteson, John Coleridge	20	Sep	E		S		
Paul, Conversion of	25	Jan	E	I	S	W	
Paul, Martyrdom of	29	Jun	E		S	W	
Paul Couturier	24	Mar	E		S	W	
Paul, Vincent de	27	Sep	E		S	W	
Paulinus of York	10	Oct	E				
Paulinus of Wales	21	Nov				W	
Peblig	4	Jul				W	
Perpetua and her companions	7	Mar	E		S	W	
Peter the Apostle	29	Jun	E	I	S	W	
Peter, The Confession of	18	Jan			S	W	
Peter the Venerable	11	May					M
Peter Chanel	28	Apr	E				
Petroc	4	Jun	E				
Philip (and James)	1	May	E	I	S	W	
Philip the Deacon	11	Oct		I			
Philip Neri	26	May	E				
Placid	15	Jan					M
Polycarp	23	Feb	E		S	W	
Porres, Martin de	3	Nov	E				
Prichard, Rhys	11	Jan				W	
Priscilla Lydia Sellon	20	Nov	E				
Prys, Edmwnd	15	May				W	
Pusey, Edward Bouverie	16	Sep	E				
Ramabai, Pandita Mary	30	Apr	E				
Rattray, Thomas	12	May			S		
Remigius	1	Oct	E				
Rhys Prichard	11	Jan				W	
Rich, Edmund of Abingdon	16	Nov	E				
Richard of Chichester	16	Jun	E				
Richard Baxter	14	Jun	E				
Richard Davies	7	Nov				W	
Richard FitzRalph	27	Jun		I			
Richard Hooker	***3***	***Nov***	E		S		
Richard Hooker	30	Oct				W	
Richard Rolle	20	Jan	E				
Ridley, Nicholas	***16***	***Oct***	E				
Ridley, Nicholas	21	Mar				W	
Robert Ferrar	21	Mar				W	
Robert Grosseteste	9	Oct	E				
Robert Leighton	26	Jun			S		
Rolle, Richard	20	Jan	E				
Romero, Oscar	24	Mar	E			W	
Rossetti, Christina	27	Apr	E				
Rowland, Daniel	16	Oct				W	

Rublev, Andrei	18	Feb				W	
Sales, Francis de	***24***	***Jan***	E		S		
Sales, Francis de	23	Jan				W	
Salesbury, William	10	Sep				W	
Samuel Seabury	14	Nov	E				
Samuel and Henrietta Barnett	17	Jun	E				
Scholastica	10	Feb	E		S		
Sellon, Priscilla Lydia	20	Nov	E				
Selwyn, George Augustus	11	Apr	E		S	W	
Seraphim of Sarov	2	Jan	E		S		
Serf	1	Jul			S		
Sergei of Radonezh	25	Sep	E			W	
Shaftesbury, Earl of (Anthony Ashley Cooper)	1	Oct	E				
Sigfrid	15	Feb	E				
Silas, Companion of Paul	30	Jul			S	W	
Simeon, Charles	13	Nov	E				
Simon (and Jude)	28	Oct	E	I	S	W	
Singh, Sundar	19	Jun	E				
Skinner, John	12	Jun			S		
Slessor, Mary	11	Jan	E				
Stephen	26	Dec	E	I	S	W	
Stephen Harding	17	Apr					M
Studdert Kennedy, Geoffrey	8	Mar	E				
Sumner, Mary	9	Aug	E				
Swithun	15	Jul	E				
Tapiedi, Lucian	2	Sep	E			W	
Tassach (Assicus)	27	Apr		I			
Tathan	30	Dec				W	
Taylor, Jeremy	13	Aug	E	I	S	W	
Teilo	9	Feb				W	
Temple, William	6	Nov	E				
Teresa of Avila	15	Oct	E		S	W	
Theodore of Tarsus	19	Sep	E				
Thérèse of Lisieux	1	Oct					M
Thomas the Apostle	3	Jul	E	I	S	W	
Thomas Aquinas	28	Jan	E		S	W	
Thomas Becket	29	Dec	E		S	W	
Thomas Bray	15	Feb	E		S		
Thomas Burgess	19	Feb				W	
Thomas Clarkson	30	Jul	E				
Thomas Cranmer	21	Mar	E		S	W	
Thomas Ken	***8***	***Jun***	E				
Thomas Ken	22	Mar			S		
Thomas More	6	Jul	E			W	
Thomas Rattray	12	May			S		
Thomas Traherne	10	Oct	E				
Timothy	26	Jan	E		S	W	
Titus	26	Jan	E		S	W	
Traherne, Thomas	10	Oct	E				

Name	Day	Month	E	S	W
Tydfil	23	Aug			W
Tyndale, William	6	Oct	E		W
Tysilio	12	Nov			W
Underhill, Evelyn	15	Jun	E		
Valentine	14	Feb	E		
Vaughan, Henry	3	May			W
Vedanayagam, Samuel Azariah	2	Jan	E		
Venn, Henry & John	1	Jul	E		
Vianney, Jean-Baptiste	4	Aug	E		
Vincent de Paul	27	Sep	E	S	W
Vincent of Saragossa	22	Jan	E		
Walter Hilton	24	Mar	E		
Watts, Isaac	25	Nov	E		
Wesley, John & Charles	***24***	***May***	E		W
Wesley, John & Charles	3	Mar		S	
Westcott, Brooke Foss	27	Jul	E		
Wilberforce, William	***30***	***Jul***	E		
Wilberforce, William	21	Jul		S	
Wilberforce, William	29	Jul			W
Wilfrid	12	Oct	E		
William of Ockham	10	Apr	E		
William of Perth (or Rochester)	23	May		S	
William Booth	20	Aug	E		
William Forbes	12	Apr		S	
William Laud	10	Jan	E	S	
William Morgan	10	Sep			W
William Salesbury	10	Sep			W
William Temple	6	Nov	E		
William Tyndale	6	Oct	E		W
William Wilberforce	***30***	***Jul***	E		
William Wilberforce	21	Jul		S	
William Wilberforce	29	Jul			W
William Williams	11	Jan			W
Williams, Isaac	11	Jan	E		
Williams, Morris	3	Jan			W
Willibrord	7	Nov	E	S	
Wilson Carlile	26	Sep	E		
Winifred	3	Nov			W
Woolos	29	Mar			W
Wulfstan	19	Jan	E		
Wyclif, John	31	Dec	E	S	W
Wynfrith (Boniface)	5	Jun	E	S	W
Xavier, Francis	3	Dec	E	S	W

Biographical Notes

The following are biographical sketches of ancient authors *not* listed in the Calendar of Saints whose writings have been used in this anthology.

Aelfric (*c.*955–*c.*1020)
Aelfric, known as 'The Grammarian', entered monastic life at Winchester and became in due course the greatest scholar of the English Benedictine revival, promoting the ideals of St Dunstan. In 1005 he was appointed Abbot of Eynsham in Oxfordshire. Among his many writings was a series of writings on the *Lives of the Saints*, among which was a biography of Edmund, King of East Anglia.

Anastasius of Sinai (d. 599)
Anastasius was a Palestinian monk and later abbot of St Catherine's Monastery, Mount Sinai. He was a strong supporter of orthodoxy, and much of his literary output was directed against all forms of heresy. In 559 he was made Patriarch of Antioch.

Andrew of Crete (*c.*660–740)
Andrew was a native of Damascus. He was a monk of Jerusalem for many years, and in around 692 became Archbishop of Gortyna in Crete. He was a celebrated theologian and hymn writer. He is said to have been the first writer of the compositions called 'canons'. His 'Great Canon', a penitential hymn for Lent, is still sung in the Byzantine liturgy. He was an eloquent preacher and a number of his sermons have survived.

Asser (d. 909)
Asser was a Welshman from St Davids. His name, however, is not Welsh but Hebrew, and was evidently adopted from Asher, the eighth son of Jacob. The custom of adopting Biblical names was common in medieval Wales. He was a scholar and adviser to Alfred the Great. He was made Bishop of Sherborne some time between 892 and 900.

Bernardine of Siena (1380–1444)
Bernardine became a Franciscan Friar at the age of twenty-two. He was responsible for moral reforms in many cities throughout Italy. He was a renowned preacher of great elegance and a promoter of devotion to the Holy Name of Jesus.

Caesarius of Arles (*c.*470–543)
Caesarius was born in France. In 489 he entered monastic life at Lérins. So outstanding was he that he was made Archbishop of Arles. He was deeply influenced by the teaching of Augustine on grace, and was a celebrated preacher.

Cassian, John (*c.*360–435)
As a young man Cassian joined a monastery at Bethlehem, but left it soon after to study monasticism in Egypt. Eventually, he seems to have established himself permanently in the West. He wrote two books on monastic life called the *Institutes* and the *Conferences*, out of the material he had gathered during his sojourn in Egypt, which proved highly influential in disseminating the monastic ideal in the Western Church.

Cogitosus (early sixth century)
Cogitosus was the monastic biographer of Brigid of Kildare.

Eusebius of Caesarea (*c.*260–*c.*340)
Eusebius is sometimes known as the 'Father of Church History'. In 315 he became Bishop of Caesarea. In addition to his many historical writings, Eusebius wrote a number of apologetic works defending Christianity.

Frank, Mark (*c.*1612–64)
Mark Frank was born in Buckinghamshire, and went up to Pembroke Hall (College), Cambridge in 1627, becoming a Fellow in 1634. He was a friend of Nicholas Ferrar at Little Gidding, and possibly, therefore, of Ferrar's other close friend, George Herbert. He was primarily a scholar and preacher who enjoyed the patronage of Charles I. Stylistically, Frank was influenced by Andrewes, but he is more accessible. In his preaching he stands mid-way between the elegant, highly-wrought sermons of Andrewes, and the plain moralistic preaching that came later. His *Course of Sermons* was published in 1642. In 1644, because of his Royalist and Arminian sympathies, he was ejected by the Parliamentary visitors from his fellowship and had to leave Cambridge. On the restoration of the monarchy, he was reinstated, and in 1662 elected Master of Pembroke. He was at the same time Chaplain to Archbishop Sheldon.

Froes, Luis (dates unknown)
Luis Froes was a Jesuit who was in Japan at the time of the martyrdom of Paul Miki and his companions. He was an eye-witness of the events he recorded, and it is from him that we know the names of those who died.

Fulgentius of Ruspe (*c.*462–527)
Fulgentius was a Roman civil servant who became Bishop of Ruspe in North Africa around 502. He was of a scholarly disposition and knew some Greek. He was a strong supporter of the theology of Augustine. Some eighty or so sermons by him have survived.

Gregory of Tours (*c.*540–94)
Gregory was elected Bishop of Tours in 573. In about 576 he began his *History of the Franks* without which the early history of France would be largely unknown. He was a well-informed (if unreflective) historian who had access to original documents.

Guerric of Igny (*c.*1070–1157)
Little is known of Guerric's early life. He seems to have lived a life of prayer and study at or near the cathedral of Tournai. At some point he became a Cistercian novice, and in 1138 was made Abbot of Igny, near Rheims. A number of his sermons have survived.

Guigo II (dates unknown)
Guigo II was the ninth Prior of La Grande Chartreuse.

Hippolytus of Rome (*c.*170–*c.*236)
A leading theologian of the third century, Hippolytus wrote in Greek at a time when Latin was coming to prevail in the Christian community at Rome. His *Apostolic Tradition* was a code of regulations and discipline in the Church which includes eucharistic prayers which are the oldest known in the Roman Church. Theologically and socially, he was very conservative.

Jocelyn of Furness (d. *c.*1185)
Jocelyn was a monk of Furness. Although his *Life of St Kentigern* is late and of limited historical value, the basic shape of the saint's life that emerges is thought to be accurate. In the prologue to his work he claims (like Aelred in his *Life of St Ninian*) to be using an existing narrative, the inference being that these were written in the Celtic tongue.

John of Salerno (dates unknown)
John was a monk of Cluny, and a disciple and eventually biographer of Abbot Odo. During his lifetime the great abbey church of SS Peter and Paul was completed and the influence of Cluny extended.

Josephus (*c.*37–*c.*100)
Flavius Josephus was a native of Palestine and a notable Jewish historian. He was descended from a priestly family. He commanded Jewish forces in Galilee in 66-7; was taken prisoner, and was later befriended by Vespasian and Titus, whom he accompanied to Rome. He wrote his historical works at Rome.

Lactantius (*c.*240–*c.*320)
Before his conversion to Christianity, Lactantius was a teacher of rhetoric. He became a notable Latin Christian apologist, especially remembered for his *Divine Institutes* which were intended to demonstrate the cultural and intellectual credibility of Christianity. The Emperor Constantine made him tutor to his son Crispus.

Matthew Paris (*c.*1199–1259)
Matthew Paris was a monk of St Alban's Abbey, and an expert scribe and illuminator. His chief claim to fame is his *Chronica Maiora*, a history of the world from creation to 1259. He was also the biographer of Edmund of Abingdon.

Origen (*c.*185–*c.*254)
Origen was born in Egypt and became a leading representative of the Alexandrian school of theology. He was the most powerful mind of early Christianity, primarily a Biblical scholar who recognised a three-fold meaning to Scripture: literal, moral and allegorical. He edited the text of the Old Testament in six columns (the *Hexapala*) comparing the Hebrew text with various Greek translations. In his theological treatise *On Principles* he outlines the basic principles of the Christian concept of the world. He was a mystic, and wrote two key ascetical works *On Prayer* and *An Exhortation to Martyrdom*, both of which were read widely. Sadly, the Greek originals of many of his works, including his extensive Biblical commentaries, have been lost. Some are known only now in fragmentary (poor) Latin translation.

Osbert of Clare (*c.*1090–*c.*1155)
Osbert was a monk of Westminster who enjoyed a chequered monastic career. From *c.*1129–33 he was banished from the monastery. In 1136, however, he was elected Prior, and subsequently in 1141 sent to Rome to advocate the canonization of Edward the Confessor. However, he was expelled from the monastery a second time. He wrote the lives of various saints, most notably that of Edward the Confessor, perhaps making use of an earlier anonymous *Life* which some have attributed to a monk of St Bertin.

Peter Chrysologus (*c.*400–50)
Peter Chrysologus was born in Italy, and became Bishop of Ravenna. He was a faithful pastor, many of whose sermons have been preserved. He was named 'Chrysologus' (Greek meaning 'golden-worded') to make him a Western counterpart of John 'Chrysostom' ('golden-mouthed') in the East.

Peter Damian (1007–72)
Peter Damian was born in Ravenna of poor parents. In 1035 he entered the Benedictine hermitage at Fonte Avella, and in 1043 became Prior. He founded many new monasteries and reformed existing ones. He was famous as an uncompromising preacher against the worldliness and corrupt practices of the clergy. He became Cardinal Bishop of Ostia in 1057.

Quodvultdeus (d. *c.*453)
As a young man Quodvultdeus knew and corresponded with Augustine who was bishop in the neighbouring town of Hippo Regis. He was elected Bishop of Carthage, the most important see in North Africa, at the time of the Barbarian invasions. He ended his days in Naples where he had been exiled. A number of his sermons have survived.

Rabanus Maurus (776 or 784–856)
Rabanus Maurus was one of the greatest theologians of his age, and known as the 'Teacher of Germany'. He was educated at the monastery of Fulda and later at Tours under the direction of Alcuin. He was ordained priest in 814, and elected abbot in 822. He resigned the abbacy in 842 to lead a life of prayer and study, but in 847 was made Archbishop of Mainz. He carried forward the evangelization of Germany and wrote many commentaries on Scripture, often with a mystical interpretation.

Rhigyfarch the Wise (eleventh century)
Rhigyfarch was a monk of St David's at the end of the eleventh century. He claims to have based his *Life of David* on earlier manuscripts. In its present form it may well have been written to further the metropolitical claims of the see of St David's.

Rimbert (dates unknown)
Rimbert was a disciple of Anskar and a fellow missionary, who succeeded him as Bishop of Bremen in 865. He wrote his *Life of Anskar* a few years after the saint's death, and it is regarded as one of the best hagiographies of its time.

Socrates Scholasticus (*c.*380–450)
Socrates was a lawyer and lay Christian scholar in Constantinople. He wrote his *Ecclesiastical History* in about 430 in seven books covering the lives of seven emperors. It covers the

period 305–439, and thus picks up where Eusebius left off. His work is highly regarded for its accuracy and objectivity.

Sophronius (*c.*560–638)
Sophronius was born in Damascus. He became a monk first of all in Egypt, later near the Jordan, and finally (from 619) in Jerusalem. In 634 he was elected Patriarch of Jerusalem where he was concerned to promulgate the teaching of the Council of Chalcedon about the two natures in Christ. Some of his sermons and poems have survived, many of which reflect the liturgical customs of the Jerusalem Church. Just before he died he witnessed the capture of Jerusalem by the Saracens under Caliph Omar in 637.

Sulpicius Severus (*c.*360–*c.*420)
Sulpicius Severus trained as a lawyer. Following his wife's death, he became an ascetic and disciple of Martin of Tours. As far as Martin had personal friends, Sulpicius could be numbered among them, and Martin would talk to him freely. As a result of this friendship he wrote his *Life*, portraying Martin as a man of God whose authenticity was attested by God through miracles and visions. His work was highly influential on later hagiography.

Tertullian (*c.*160–*c.*225)
Tertullian was the first major figure in Latin theology. He was born in Carthage of pagan parents, trained as a lawyer, and became a Christian in about 193. It is uncertain whether or not he was ever ordained. He produced a series of significant controversial and apologetic writings. He is particularly noted for his ability to coin new Latin terms to translate the emerging theological vocabulary of the Greek-speaking Eastern Church. He was a man of passionate feeling, full of paradox, with a tendency to extremes. This led him in about 207 to espouse Montanism – a charismatic movement that claimed to be inaugurating the age of the Spirit.

Turgot (*c.*1060–*c.*1120)
Turgot was a Saxon from Lincolnshire who was confessor to Queen Margaret of Scotland. He left her court to become part of the monastic community at Durham, subsequently becoming Prior. In 1109 the last Celtic Bishop of St Andrews died, and King Alexander I appointed Turgot as the first 'Roman' Bishop of St Andrews.

Walton, Isaac (1593–1683)
Isaac Walton was born in Staffordshire, but as a young man travelled to London and became an ironmonger. There he came under the influence of John Donne. He was a strong High Churchman and a Royalist, and after the Battle of Marston Moor in 1644 retired from business. In retirement he wrote not only the *Compleat Angler* (1653) for which he is justly famous, but also his *Lives* of Dr John Donne (1640), Sir Henry Wotton (1651), Mr Richard Hooker (1665), Mr George Herbert (1670) which also contains a pen-portrait of Herbert's friend Nicholas Ferrar, and Dr Robert Sanderson (1678). Based on personal knowledge and remarkable for the beauty of their language, they represent valuable contemporary documents of the period.

William of Malmesbury (*c.*1090–*c.*1143)
William was the chief English historian of his generation. He was a monk of Malmesbury where he was offered, but declined, the abbacy in 1140. His two most important works were the *Annals of the English Kings* (1120) and the *Annals of the English Prelates* (1125) which dealt with respectively secular and ecclesiastical English history. He also wrote a *Life of Dunstan* and a *Life of Wulfstan.*

William of St Thierry (*c.*1085–1148)
William was born at Liége. He entered the Benedictine Abbey of Rheims in 1113, and in 1119 or 1120 was elected Abbot of St Thierry nearby. Before his election as abbot, he had already made the acquaintance of Bernard of Clairvaux, and in 1135 he resigned his abbacy and went to join a group of Cistercian monks from Igny. He wrote a number of influential treatises, including several expositions of the Song of Songs. His last years were devoted to a synthesis of his doctrine and experience, known as *The Golden Epistle*.

Acknowledgements

A. Biographies

The biographical sketches of the saints are largely reproduced from the second edition of *Exciting Holiness*, edited by Br Tristam Holland SSF, Canterbury Press Norwich, 2003, and completed by Simon Kershaw following Tristam's untimely death. The Author is grateful for permission to reproduce material to provide continuity between volumes, as follows:

Br Tristam Holland SSF wrote approximately one hundred and fifty biographies;
The Author of this book wrote the biographies for Augustine of Canterbury, Augustine of Hippo, The Passing of Benedict, Cecilia, The Holy Abbots of Cluny, Cyril of Alexandria, Gertrude the Great, Cyril & Methodius, Gregory of Nyssa & Macrina, Gregory the Great, Ignatius of Antioch, Irenaeus, Jane Frances de Chantal, John Chrysostom, Justin, The Blessed Virgin Mary, Maurus & Placid, Pachomius, Petroc, Thérèse of Lisieux, All Souls' Day and Stephen Harding;

The contributions of other authors are also acknowledged:

Revd Richard Carter for Ini Kopuria;
Sr Catherine OHP for Hilda;
Revd Professor Owen Chadwick for George Augustus Selwyn;
Dr Andrew Chandler for Elizabeth of Russia, Esther John and Manche Masemola;
Revd Dr John Clark for Walter Hilton;
Dr Petà Dunstan for William & Catherine Booth, Josephine Butler, Dietrich Bonhoeffer, John Bosco, Anthony Ashley Cooper, Charles Gore, Octavia Hill, Eglantyne Jebb, John Keble, Edward King, Charles Fuge Lowder, Frederick Denison Maurice, Harriet Monsell, John Mason Neale, John Henry Newman, Florence Nightingale, Edward Bouverie Pusey, Oscar Romero, Christina Rossetti, Priscilla Lydia Sellon, Mary Slessor, Geoffrey Studdert Kennedy, Mary Sumner, William Temple, Evelyn Underhill, Brooke Foss Westcott, and William Wilberforce;
Revd Claire Farley for Hildegard of Bingen;
Sr Gillian Claire OSC for Clare;
Revd Dr Donald Gray for Alcuin;
Revd Dr Gustavo Gutiérrez for Bartolomé de las Casas;
Rt Revd Patrick Harris for Allen Gardiner;
Revd Brenda Hopkins for Jean-Baptiste Vianney;
Revd Dr Ivor Jones for John & Charles Wesley;

Revd Dr Simon Jones for Aidan, Alban, Ephrem and Oswald;
Simon Kershaw for Augustine Baker, Blandina, the Confession of Peter, Fra Angelica and Andrei Rublev, Robert Ferrar, the group commemorations of Africa, Asia, Australasia, Europe, North America, and South America, and of our age, Joseph of Arimathea, the Martyrdom of Paul, Philip the Deacon, and Henry Vaughan.
Revd Stephen Lake for Aldhelm;
Revd Dr Diarmaid MacCulloch for Thomas Cranmer;
Very Revd Michael Perham and the Norwich Diocesan Liturgical Committee, for Edith Cavell, Edmund of East Anglia, Etheldreda, Julian of Norwich and Margery Kempe;
Revd Dr Simon Oliver for Frideswide;
Louise Pirouet for the Martyrs of Uganda;
Br Thomas Quin OSB for Anselm, Bede, Benedict, Birinus, Cedd, Cuthbert, Dunstan, Edward the Confessor, Lanfranc, Scholastica and Thomas Becket;
Revd Bernard Schunemann for Willibrord;
Revd Philip Sheldrake for George Herbert;
Sr Marianne Sodorstrom for Sigfrid and Anskar;
Revd Dr Jo Spreadbury for Bridget of Sweden, Catherine of Siena, John of the Cross, Mary Magdalene, Mary, Martha & Lazarus, and Teresa of Avila;
Revd Sister Teresa CSA for Elizabeth Ferard.

A number of people have contributed specifically to the production of the Irish, Scottish and Welsh biographical material as follows:

Most Revd George Otto Simms, late Archbishop of Armagh, and the **Revd Canon Brian Mayne**, for Ireland;
Revd Canon John Armson, Daphne Brooks, Monica Clough, Revd Stuart Coates, Very Revd Gregor Duncan, Very Revd Malcolm Grant, Canon Brian Hardy, Rt Revd Michael Hare-Duke, for Scotland;
Canon Patrick Thomas and **Venerable Philip Morris,** for Wales.

B. OTHER MATERIAL

Many individuals, societies and friends offered their advice and help in the selection of extracts. The Author is grateful to the following in particular:

Lorraine Blair of Toynbee Hall, for the extracts on Samuel & Henrietta Barnett;
Revd Richard Carter, Chaplain to the Melanesian Brotherhood, for the extract relating to Ini Kopuria;
Sr Tessa Debney SLG for the extracts of and about Teresa of Avila;
Rt Revd Patrick Harris for the extract from the diaries of Allen Gardiner;
Sr Mary Kenchington OSB for the extract relating to William Carlile;
Professor Ann Loades of Durham University, for information and advice on various saints;
Christine Luxton, Secretary to the Papua New Guinea Church Partnership, for information relating to the PNG martyrs;
Revd Phillip McFadyen for the extract relating to Edith Cavell;

Ken Osborne and **Gill Poole** of the Church Mission Society, for help with extracts for Henry Venn and Apolo Kivebulaya;
Revd Margaret Saunders for allowing me to include a poem of hers, hitherto unpublished;
Canon Patrick Thomas for the extract on Tysilio;
Sr Marianne Sodorstrom of Alisike Kloster, Sweden, for selecting and translating the extracts for Bridget of Sweden, Sigrid and Anskar;
Sr Teresa CSA for extracts concerning Elizabeth Ferard;
Janet Vout, for extracts from the writings of Isabella Gilmore.

C. SECOND EDITION

In the production of this second and expanded edition of *Celebrating the Saints* which incorporates the Calendars of The Church of Ireland, The Scottish Episcopal Church and The Church in Wales, the author wishes to acknowledge his debt to *Love's Redeeming Work: The Anglican Quest for Holiness*, compiled by Geoffrey Rowell, Kenneth Stevenson and Rowan Williams, Oxford, 2001, which alerted him to a variety of sources and material. Where this material is copyright, it is acknowledged below. He also acknowledges his debt to Kathleen Jones' recent volume, *Who are the Celtic Saints?*, Canterbury Press, Norwich, 2002, which shed light on some of the more obscure saints in the calendars.

Furthermore, without the support and advice of certain people, this enlarged edition of *Celebrating the Saints*, incorporating the national Calendars of Ireland, Scotland and Wales, would never have emerged:

Simon Kershaw, who following Br Tristam's untimely death, completed the revision of *Exciting Holiness*;
Dr Petà Dunstan, Librarian of the Divinity Faculty, University of Cambridge, for her time, patience and expertise in locating various references and obscure authors;
Revd Alan Moses for his helpful advice on various Scottish commemorations;
Revd William Price for his scholarship and generosity in helping with the Welsh texts and commemorations.

D. COPYRIGHT MATERIAL

The Author and Publishers are grateful for permission to reproduce material under copyright. They are grateful in particular for the cooperation of:

The International Committee for English in the Liturgy Inc., (ICEL), for permission to reproduce the English translation of the non-biblical readings from the *Roman Catholic Liturgy of the Hours*, American Edition; © 1974; all rights reserved; adapted with permission; and
The Church Hymnal Corporation of the Episcopal Church of the United States of America, for permission to adopt the modifications in the ICEL texts employed by J. Robert Wright in *Readings for the Daily Office from the Early Church*, New York, 1991 and *They Still Speak*,

New York, 1993, to accord with Anglican usage (see Wright, *Readings for the Daily Office from the Early Church*, pp.515–23).

Every effort has been made to trace the copyright owners of material included in this book. The Author and Publishers would be grateful if any omissions or inaccuracies in these acknowledgements could be brought to their attention for correction in any future edition. They are grateful to the following copyright holders:

Addison Wesley Longman, for an extract from *The Vision of God*, by Kenneth Kirk, 1931.
R. Brindley Jones, for an extract from *'A Lanterne to their Feete' Remembering Rhys Prichard 1579–1644.*
Bruce Publishing Company (Milwaukee), for an extract from *St Elizabeth of Hungary: A Story of Twenty-four Years*, by Nesta De Robeck, 1954.
Burns & Oates Ltd, for extracts from *Charles de Foucauld: Meditations of a Hermit*, translated by Charlotte Balfour, 1930; *The Complete Works of St John of the Cross*, translated by Allison Peers, 1935; *New Seeds of Contemplation* by Thomas Merton, 1961, used with permission of the Thomas Merton Legacy Trust; *Mary, Mother of God, Mother of the Poor*, by Ivone Gebara & Maria Clara Bingemer, translated by Phillip Berryman, 1989.
Cambridge University Press, for an extract from *Saints and Scholars* by David Knowles OSB, 1963;
The estate of Roy Campbell, for an extract from his translation of *The Poems of St John of the Cross*, 1966.
SCM-Canterbury Press, Norwich, for an extract from *Ponder these things* by Rowan Williams, 2002; and from *In Search of the Lost* by Richard Anthony Carter, 2006.
Catholic Institute for International Relations in association with Orbis Books, for an extract from *The Voice of the Voiceless: The Four Pastoral Letters and Other Statements of Oscar Romero*, translated by Michael J. Walsh, 1985.
Church Army Press, for an extract from *Boanerges and Others*, *c.*1930.
Church House Publishing, for permission to use material translated by the author of this book, first published in *Spiritual Classics from the Early Church*, 1995.
Cistercian Publications Inc., Kalamazoo, Michigan, for extracts from *The Works of Aelred of Rievaulx I*, translated by Penelope Lawson CSMV, 1971; *The Works of William of St Thierry I*, also translated by Penelope Lawson CSMV, 1971; *The Celtic Monk: Rules and Writings of Early Irish Monks*, translated by Uinseann O Maidin OCR, 1996; *The Sayings of the Desert Fathers*, translated by Benedicta Ward SLG, 1975/1983; *The Luminous Eye: The Spiritual World Vision of St Ephrem the Syrian*, translated by Sebastian Brock, 1985.
Clonmore & Reynolds Ltd, Dublin, for extracts from Daphne D. C. Pochin Mould, *The Irish Saints*, 1964.
Community of St John the Baptist, Clewer, for an extract from *A Joyous Service*, by Valerie Bonham, 1989.
Constable & Co., for an extract from *Josephine Butler*, by E. Moberly Bell, 1962.
Darton Longman & Todd Ltd, for an extract from *God and Man*, by Metropolitan Anthony of Sourozh (Anthony Bloom), 1971.
Eagle of Inter-Publishing Service (IPS) Ltd, for an extract from *Worship*, by Evelyn Underhill, 1936.

Faber and Faber Ltd, in association with the estate of T. S. Eliot, for an extract from *Murder in the Cathedral*, by T. S. Eliot, and for the poem 'Journey of the Magi' from *T. S. Eliot: Collected Poems 1909–1962*.
Jean Farrant, for an extract from her book *Mashonaland Martyr: Bernard Mizeki and the Pioneer Church*, 1966.
The Folio Society Ltd, for an extract from *The Trial of Joan of Arc*, translated by W. S. Scott, 1956.
Victor Gollancz, for an extract from *The Theology of Auschwitz* by Ulrich Simon, 1967.
Gracewing/Fowler Wright Books, for extracts from *Far Above Rubies* by Richard Symonds, 1993.
HarperCollins Publishers Ltd, for an extract from *Be Still and Know*, by Michael Ramsey, 1982.
Highway Press, for an extract from *Into the Great Forest: The Story of Apolo Kivebulaya of Central Africa*, by Margaret Sinker, 1950.
Hodder & Stoughton, an imprint of Hodder Headline PLC, for an extract from *Teresa of Avila*, by Shirley du Boulay, 1991.
David Jones in association with the Sussex Record Society, for an extract from Ralf Bocking's *The Life of St Richard*, translated by David Jones, 1995.
Macmillan Publishing Company, a division of Macmillan Inc., for extracts from *Cluniac Monasticism in the Central Middle Ages*, edited by N. Hunt, 1971; *The Protestant Reformation*, edited by Hans J. Hillerbrand, 1968.
Macmillan Press Ltd, for an extract from *Evil and the God of Love*, by John Hick (2nd edition) 1985, altered with permission.
Marshall, Morgan & Scott Ltd, for an extract from *Janani*, by Margaret Ford, 1978.
Constance Millington in association with the Asian Trading Corporation, for an extract from *An Ecumenical Venture: The History of Nandyal Diocese in Andhra Pradesh.*
Mowbray, an imprint of The Continuum International Publishing Group Ltd, (last known copyright holders) for an extract from *The Ladder of Monks and Twelve Meditations*, translated by Edmund Colledge OSA and James Walsh SJ, 1978; and for extracts from *The Terrible Alternative: Christian Martyrdom in the Twentieth Century*, edited by Andrew Chandler, London & New York, 1998.
Orbis Books, Maryknoll, New York, for an extract from Gustavo Gutiérrez, *Las Casas: In Search of the Poor of Jesus Christ*, translated by Robert R. Barr, 1993.
John Murray, for extracts from *Episcopal Scotland in the Nineteenth Century*, by Marion Lochhead, 1966.
Oxford University Press UK, for extracts from *The Book of St Gilbert*, edited and translated by Raymond Foreville & Gillian Keir, 1987; *The Confessions of Saint Augustine*, translated by Henry Chadwick, 1991; *Magna Vita: A Life of Saint Hugh of Lincoln by Adam, Monk of Eynsham Abbey*, translated by D. L. Doule & David Farmer, 1985; *The Life of King Edward who rests at Westminster*, attributed to a monk of St Bertin, edited and translated by Frank Barlow, 2nd edition, 1992; *A Fourteenth Century Scholar and Primate: Richard FitzRalph in Oxford, Avignon and Armagh*, by Katherine Walsh, 1981.
Oxford University Press, New York, for an extract from *The Letters of Hildegard of Bingen*, translated by Joseph L. Baird & Radd K. Ehrman, 1994.
Papua New Guinea Church Partnership, for an extract from *The White-Robed Army of Martyrs*, by Bishop David Hand.

Paulist Press, Mahwah, New Jersey, for extracts from *Athanasius: The Life of Antony*, translated by Robert Gregg, 1980; *Walter Hilton: The Scale of Perfection*, translated by John Clark & Rosemary Dorward, 1991; *Catherine of Siena: Dialogue*, translated by Suzanne Noffke OP, 1980; *Francis and Clare: The Complete Works*, translated by R. J. Armstrong and Ignatius Brady, 1982; *Gertrude of Helfta: Herald of Divine Love*, translated by Margaret Winkworth, 1993; *Ephrem of Syria: Hymns*, translated by Kathleen E. McVey, 1989; *Francis de Sales & Jane de Chantal: Letters of Spiritual Direction*, translated by Peronne Marie Thibert VHM, 1988; *Quaker Spirituality*, edited by Douglas Steere, 1984; *Richard Rolle: The English Writings*, edited by Rosamund Allen, 1989; *Celtic Spirituality*, translated and introduced by Oliver Davies, with the collaboration of Thomas O'Loughlin, 1999; *John Cassian Conferences*, introduced by Owen Chadwick, translated by Colm Luibheid, 1985. In the above, all translations are © their translators.
Penguin Books Ltd., for extracts from *The Lives of the Saints*, translated by J. F. Webb, 1965; *The Prayers and Meditations of St Anselm*, translated by Benedicta Ward SLG, 1973; *Revelations of Divine Love* by Julian of Norwich, translated by Clifton Walters, 1966; *Alfred the Great*, selected and translated by Simon Keynes and Michael Lappidge, 1983; *The Life of St Columba*, by Adomnan, translated by Richard Sharpe, 1995; *Saint Ignatius of Loyola: Personal Writings*, translated by Joseph Munitiz and Philip Endean, 1996; *The Cistercian World: Monastic Writings of the Twelfth Century*, translated and introduced by Pauline Matarasso, 1993; *A History of Christian Missions*, by Stephen Neill, 2nd edition 1986; *The Book of Margery Kempe*, translated by B. A. Windeatt, 1985; Donald Attwater, *The Penguin Dictionary of Saints*, 1965. William Price, for an extract from his study, *Bishop Burgess and Lampeter College*, published by University of Wales Press, 1987.
Routledge, for extracts from *English Historical Documents*, vol. I, edited by Dorothy Whitelock, (2nd edition) 1979; vol. II, edited by David Douglas & George Greenaway, 1968.
SCM Press, for extracts from *Letters and Papers from Prison*, by Dietrich Bonhoeffer, translated by E. Bethge, 2nd enlarged edition, 1971; *The Cost of Discipleship*, by Dietrich Bonhoeffer, translated by R. H. Fuller, 1959; *The Silent Rebellion*, by A. M. Allchin, 1958; *Said or Sung*, by Austin Farrer, 1960; *The Go-Between God*, by John V. Taylor, 1973; John Wyclif, *The Pastoral Office*, in *Advocates of Reform*, The Library of Christian Classics, vol. XIV, edited by Matthew Spinka, 1953.
Sheed & Ward Ltd., for extracts from *The Way of Perfection*, by Teresa of Avila, translated and edited by E. Allison Peers, 1946; *A Treasury of Russian Spirituality*, edited by George P. Fedotov, 1950; *St Odo of Cluny* translated & edited by Gerard Sitwell OSB, 1958.
Wilbert R. Shenk, for an extract from his book *Henry Venn: Missionary and Statesman*, 1983.
SPCK, for extracts from *Their Lord and Ours*, edited by Mark Santer, 1982; *Christianity and Social Order*, by William Temple, 1942 & re-prints; *Priscilla Lydia Sellon*, by Thomas Jay Williams, 1950; *Hildegard of Bingen: An Anthology*, translated by Robert Carver, and edited by Fiona Bowie & Oliver Davies, 1990; Janet Morley, *All Desires Known*, 1992; *The Life and Letters of Charles Inglis*, by Charles Inglis, 1936; and *Celtic Christian Spirituality*, edited and translated by Oliver Davies and Fiona Bowie, London, 1995.
St Vladimir's Press, Crestwood, New York, for a poem by John McGuckin, in *Saint Gregory of Nazianzus: An Intellectual Biography*, by John McGuckin, 2001.
Sutton Publishing in association with St Edmund's Hall, Oxford, for an extract from *The Life of St Edmund*, by Matthew Paris, translated by C. H. Lawrence, 1996.

Tessa Sayle Agency, for the prayer of Evelyn Underhill entitled 'For Wholeness'.
The Liturgical Press, St John's Collegeville, for extracts from the *The Life and Miracles of St Benedict*, translated by O. Zimmermann & B. R. Avery.
Patrick Thomas, for the text and translation of part of a poem by Cynddelw Brydydd Mawr.
The University of Wales, for extracts from Gwaith Cynddelw Brydydd Mawr, volume I, edited by Nerys Ann Jones and Ann Parry Owen, 1991; *Ann Griffiths: The furnace and the Fountain*, by A. M. Allchin, 1987; *The Holy Wells of Wales*, by Francis James, 1954; *Vitae Sanctorum Britanniae et Genealogiae*, edited and translated by A. W. Wade-Evans, 1944; *Wales and the Reformation*, by Glanmor Williams, 1997; and *The Welsh and their Religion*, by Glanmor Williams, 1991.
A. P. Watt Ltd and the Estate of Ronald Knox, for extracts from *Occasional Sermons* by Mgr R. A. Knox, published by Burns & Oates, 1960; and for an extract from *Autobiography of a Saint*, published by Harvill Press, 1958.
The Trustees, Westminster Bank, Cambridge, for an extract from *Mackenzie's Grave*, by Owen Chadwick, 1959.
Rowan Williams, for his translation of the Preface of Richard Davies to the Welsh Testament of 1567.

A new and priceless grace has made them almost leap for joy. They have not merely felt God himself, their creator, ruling them invisibly from above, but they have seen him visibly within themselves using them in his work of sanctification. These immense benefits have come through the blessed fruit of the blessed womb of the blessed Mary.

Through the fullness of your grace, the things in the lower world rejoice in the gift of freedom and the things above the world are gladdened by being renewed. Through the one glorious Son of your glorious virginity all the just who died before his life-giving death rejoice that their captivity has been ended, and the angels delight that their half-ruined city is restored.

O woman, full and more than full of grace, all creation has received of the overflow of your fullness and its youth has been renewed! O blessed and more than blessed Virgin, through your blessing all creation is blessed. Not only is creation blessed by the creator, but creation blesses its creator.

God gave to Mary his Son, the Only-begotten of his heart, equal to himself, whom he loved as himself. From Mary he fashioned himself a Son, not another one but the same, so that by nature there would be one and the same Son both of God and of Mary. Every nature is created by God, and God is born of Mary. God created all things and Mary gave birth to God. God himself, who made all things, made himself from Mary. In this way he remade all that he had made. He who was able to make all things out of nothing, when they had been defaced would not remake them without Mary's help.

God is, then, Father of all created things and Mary is mother of all that has been recreated. God is Father of the institution of all things and Mary is mother of the restitution of all things. God begot him through whom all things were made and Mary gave birth to him through whom all things were saved. God begot him without whom nothing at all exists and Mary gave birth to him without whom nothing that exists is good.

The Lord is indeed with you Mary. For he granted to you that all nature should owe so great a debt to you jointly with himself.

alternative reading

A Reading from *Mary, Mother of God, Mother of the Poor* by Ivone Gebara and Maria Bingemer

Today's feast must be understood in connection with the people of which Mary is both figure and symbol, and in relation to God in whom she believes and who chooses her and gives her a particular vocation and mission within salvation history.

As 'Daughter of Zion' Mary is to be understood as the incarnation of the Jewish people from which she descends and to which she is closely connected. With her the journey of this people on the way toward the Messiah who is the fullness of time comes to its destination. Israel, God's chosen people, is more particularly that people in whose midst God resides and dwells by means of the temple. Jerusalem, the holy city which after the trials of exile once more takes on and represents the community of the chosen people, is the beloved spouse of Yahweh her husband. All her infidelities are redeemed by this God, whose love is more powerful than anything else. Her afflictions are turned into joy by the presence of the husband. Mary personifies and sums up the ancient Zion-Jerusalem. In her the process of renewal and purification of the whole people of God – a process that has as its goal that the people will live the alliance with God more fully – finds a model beginning. Wholly belonging to God, Mary is the prototype of what the people is called to be, chosen 'in him before the world began, to be holy and blameless'.

The full identity of the people, given by God in creation and election, and lost in the people's infidelity and exile, is restored by God in a 'new creation', as it were, with the advent of new heavens and a new earth. In Mary this new creation actually takes place. She is the figure of the re-created people, filled and overflowing with the glory and power of Yahweh, pregnant with the promised Messiah who has now been sent. The time in which God's presence and holiness were restricted to the stone temple in Jerusalem is drawing to a close. Now, in the fullness of time, human flesh is God's temple. It is in the flesh of the woman Mary, full of grace, pregnant with the man Jesus, that the fullness of divine holiness is found in the world. It is in the flesh of every man and every woman who belong to the same race as Jesus and Mary that God must be sought, respected, venerated, and adored.

Today's feast of the conception of Mary rehabilitates woman's bodiliness, which in Genesis is denounced as the cause of original sin, laying on women a blemish and a burden that were difficult to bear. It is this body animated by the divine Spirit that is proclaimed blessed. In it God works the fullness of God's wonders. It is in the flesh and the person of a woman that humankind can see its call and its destiny brought to a happy end.

8 December

Cynidr

Bishop, seventh century

There is some confusion about Cynidr's parentage. Some manuscripts describe him as the son of Ceingar, daughter of Brychan Brycheiniog. Another genealogy claims that he was the son of Gwynllyw and Gwladys and the brother of Cadoc. His most important foundation was at Glasbury, where he was buried. Breconshire was the centre of his activities but he is also linked with Herefordshire. He seems to have spent some time as a hermit on an island in the river Wye at Winforton. It is clear that he was an important ecclesiastical figure in his area, but little else can be said about him with any certainty.

A Reading from a hymn of Bishop Timothy Rees

Arglwydd, trefni mewn doethineb
Ein tymhorau is y rhod;
Daw i ben dy fythol arfaeth
Er pob newid sydd yn bod:
Ti ddewisaist Wlad y Bryniau,
Ddyddiau tywyll a di-wawr,
I egluro dy fwriadau
Er dy glod a'th Enw mawr.

Hyd ein glannau pell a olchir
O'r gorllewin gan y lli
Yr anfonaist ti o'th gariad
Sôn am Groesbren Calfari:
Dros yr Eglwys Lân Gatholig
Collwyd chwys a gwaed dy blant,
A disgleirio'n rhòl dy arwyr
Y mae enw Dewi Sant.

Parchwn, Arglwydd, goffadwriaeth
Pawb o Seintiau Cymru wen,
Yr Esgobion a'r Offeiriaid
A'r Merthyri hwnt i'r llen:
Dewi, Dyfrig, Deiniol, Teilo –
Dewr y safent tros y gwir,
Bu eu pader, bu eu penyd
Yn sancteiddio erwau'n tir.

Mae dy fwriad yn goroesi
Holl ddamweiniau daear lawr;
Mae dy Eglwys Lân yn aros
Byth yn dyst o'th gariad mawr:
Dyro nerth a gweledigaeth,
Arglwydd, yn dy waith o hyd,
A'th ewyllys di a wneler
Yn yr Eglwys a'r holl fyd.

(Lord, who in thy perfect wisdom
Times and seasons dost arrange –
Working out thy ceaseless purpose
In a world of ceaseless change:
Thou didst form our ancient nation
In remote barbaric days,
To unfold in it a purpose
To thy glory and thy praise.

To our shores remote, benighted,
Washed by distant western waves,
Tidings in thy love thou sentest,
Tidings of the cross that saves.
Men of courage strove and suffered
Here thy holy Church to plant;
Glorious in the roll of heroes
Shines the name of Dewi Sant.

Lord, we hold in veneration
All the Saints our land has known,
Bishops, priests, confessors, martyrs
Standing now around thy throne –
Dewi, Dyfrig, Deiniol, Teilo, –
All the gallant saintly band,
Who of old by prayer and labour
Hallowed all our fatherland.

Still thy ancient purpose standeth
Every change and chance above;
Still thy ancient Church remaineth –
Witness to thy changeless love.
Vision grant us, Lord, and courage
To fulfil the work begun;
In the Church and in the nation
Lord of lords, thy will be done.)

12 December

Finnian of Clonard

Abbot, *c.*549

Renowned as one of the greatest teachers and scholars Ireland has ever had, Finnian was responsible for encouraging the growth of monasticism in Ireland. His great foundation was at Clonard close to the centre of political power, but it was as a centre of Biblical study that it was preeminent, and, as a result, Finnian has been called by the title 'Teacher of the Saints'. One of the earliest of the Irish 'Penitentials' (a book suggesting ways in which Christians could seek forgiveness for their sins with programmes of self-discipline) is associated with him, but there may be confusion with Finnian of Movilla. Finnian died on this day in about the year 549.

A Reading from *The Irish Saints* by Daphne Pochin Mould

The second part of the religious history of Ireland begins definitively with the foundation of Clonard in 520. Finnian stands at the very start of the great monastic expansion in Ireland, a man not unjustly named 'Tutor of the Saints of Ireland', a most attractive personality in his own right, as well.

Finnian was born in Leinster, and made his early studies with a certain Forthcern, probably of Cell Fortcheirn in Uí Drona. He is said to have made three monastic foundations of his own in the vicinity. He gained experience of monastic life in Wales, and came back to head its expansion in Ireland. Already it would seem Enda had established a large monastery on Aran, but Clonard, placed in the very heart of Ireland, was an even more influential and vital centre. Three thousand is the number of Finnian's disciples given in the Lives, and quite possibly that is not too extravagant if we take it for the total number of students and monks over the whole period at Clonard.

Tradition, with a liking for the number twelve and for bringing every great saint into contact with every other great saint, has listed the 'Twelve Apostles of Ireland' trained by Finnian at Clonard. Some like Ciaran of Saighir, of course, lived much earlier. The traditional list runs: Ciaran of Saighir, Ciaran of Clonmacnois, Columcille (Columba), Brendan of Birr, Brendan of Clonfert, Colum of Tir da Glas, Molaise of Devenish, Cainnech (Kenneth), Ruadan of Lorrha, Mobi of Glasnevin, Sínell of Cleenish, Ninnid of Inismacsaint. Some of these were really students of Clonard. What the list represents is the formative influence that Clonard had on Irish monasticism.

Finnian appears to have been an attractive teacher, quickly appreciative of his students' abilities. Moreover he seems to have gone out of his way to equip his students when they left. For 'no one of those three thousand went from Finnian without a crozier, or a gospel, or some well-known sign; and round those reliquaries they built their churches and their monasteries afterwards', as the account in the Book of Lismore puts it.

alternative reading

A Reading from *The Penitential of Finnian*

If a cleric is angry or envious or backbiting, gloomy or greedy, great and mortal sins are these, because they slay the soul and cast it down to the depth of hell. But here is a penance for them until these sins are plucked forth and eradicated from our hearts. Through the help of the Lord and through our own zeal and activity, we should seek the mercy of the Lord and victory in these things. We should continue in weeping and tears, day and night, as long as these things disturb our hearts. But by behaving differently, as we have said, and making haste to cure this destructive behaviour, we cleanse away the faults from our hearts and introduce virtues in their places. Patience must supplant anger; kindliness, or the love of God and neighbour, should take the place of envy; for detraction, let us practise restraint of heart and tongue; for dejection, let us seek spiritual joy; for greed, liberality; as Scripture says, 'The anger of man works not the righteousness of God', and envy is judged as if it were leprosy by the law. Ridicule is anathematized in the Scriptures in these words: 'He who ridicules his brother' shall be cast out of the land of the living. Gloom likewise devours or consumes the soul. As the Apostle says, covetousness is 'the root of all evil'.

12 December

Jane Frances de Chantal

Foundress of the Order of the Visitation, 1641

Jane Frances de Chantal was born at Dijon in France in 1572. As a young woman she married happily, and had four children. In 1601, however, her husband was killed in an accident. In her widowhood she resolved to give herself more profoundly to the spiritual life, and took a vow of chastity. In 1604 she met Francis de Sales, and placed herself under his spiritual direction. The correspondence between them which has survived reveals a quite remarkable friendship. In 1610, whilst still maintaining her duties as a mother, she founded the first convent of the Visitation at Annecy in Savoy for women and widows unsuited to the severe ascetic life of many religious congregations. She devoted the remainder of her life to visiting the sick and the poor, and fostering the Order. She had considerable administrative ability, and by the time of her death in 1641 a further sixty-four convents had been founded. Vincent de Paul, who knew her personally and well, said that she was 'one of the holiest people I have ever met on this earth'.

A Reading from a letter of Jane Frances de Chantal to
the Sisters of the Visitation at Annecy,
written from Paris on 30th September 1619

Since our Lord, in his goodness, has gathered our hearts into one, allow me, my dearest sisters, to greet you all, as a community and individually; for this same Lord will not allow me to greet you in any other way. But what a greeting it is! The very one that our great and worthy Father [Francis] taught us: LIVE JESUS! Yes, my beloved sisters and daughters, I say the words with intense delight: LIVE JESUS in our memory, in our will, and in our actions! Have in your thoughts only Jesus, in your will have only the longing for his love, and in your actions have only obedience and submission to his good pleasure by an exact observance of the Rule, not only in externals, but much more, in your interior spirit: a spirit of gentle cordiality toward one another, a spirit of recollection of your whole being before our divine Master, and that true, sincere humility which makes us as simple and gentle as lambs. Finally, strive for that loving union of hearts which brings about a holy peace and the kind of blessing we should desire to have in the house of God and his holy Mother.

All this is what I want from you, my dearest daughters, and I urge you to have great devotion to our Lady to whom I beg you to pray for me. Every day of my life I offer all of you to her maternal care. Good-bye, my very dearest sisters; pray for my needs. Live joyously and serenely with whatever our Lord will do with you and for you. I am yours with all my love.

13 December

Lucy

Martyr at Syracuse, 304

Lucy was a native of Syracuse in Sicily. She lived at the beginning of the fourth century, when the Roman authorities were attempting to reestablish the worship of gods they approved. The emperor himself was the focus of one of the cults. Tradition has it that Lucy, as a young Christian, gave away her goods to the poor and was betrayed to the authorities by her angry betrothed, who felt that they should have become his property. She was put to death for her faith in the year 304. Her name in Latin means Light and, as her feastday fell in December, she became associated with the one true Light who was coming as the redeemer of the world, the Light that would lighten the nations, the Light that would banish darkness and let the eyes of all behold Truth incarnate.

A Reading from *An Exhortation to the Greeks* by Clement of Alexandria

'The commandment of the Lord shines clearly, giving light to the eyes.' Receive Christ, receive power to see, receive light that you may recognise in him both God and man. 'More delightful than gold and precious stones, more desirable than honey from the honeycomb' is the Word that has given us light. How could he not be desirable, he who illumined minds buried in darkness, and endowed with clarity of vision the light-bearing eyes of our souls?

In spite of the countless stars, if it were not for the sun our world would be plunged in darkness. In the same way, were it not for the Word that has given us light, we too would have been no better than poultry, reared in the dark, fattened up for the killing. So let us open ourselves to the light, and thus to God. Let us open ourselves to the light, and become disciples of the Lord. For he promised his Father, saying: 'I will make known your name among the nations, and praise you in the assembly.'

Sing your Father's praises, then, Lord, and make him who is God known to me. Your words will save me; your song will instruct me. Until now I have gone astray in my search for God, but you are light for my path, and in you I find God; in you I receive the Father; in you I become a fellow heir, for you are not ashamed to call me your brother.

Let us all cast off all half-truths; let us cast off the mists of ignorance and the darkness that dims our inner vision, and let us contemplate the true God. Let us raise our hearts in praise to him, singing 'Hail, O Light!' For upon us poor creatures, buried in darkness, imprisoned in the shadow of death, a heavenly light has shone, a light of such clarity that it surpasses the sun's, and of such sweetness that exceeds anything this world can offer us. The light of which I speak is eternal life, and those who receive it will live. The night, by contrast, is terrified of the light, melting away in fear at the approach of the day of the Lord. A light that can never fail has penetrated everywhere: sunset has turned into dawn. This is the meaning of 'new creation'; for the Sun of Righteousness, pursuing his course through the universe, visits all alike, in imitation of his Father who makes his sun rise on all, and rains down his truth upon everyone.

He it is who has transformed sunset into dawn, death into life, and has done so through his crucifixion. He rescued the human race from perdition and exalted us to the skies. He is God's gardener, transplanting what was corruptible to new soil where it would grow incorruptible, transforming earth into heaven. He points out the way of growth, prompting his people to good works, encouraging us to live by the truth, and bestowing upon us a divine inheritance from his Father of which no one can rob us. He makes us divine by his heavenly teaching, instilling into our minds his laws, and writing them on the pages of our hearts. And what are the laws that he prescribes? That all, irrespective of class or status, shall know God.

13 December

Samuel Johnson

Moralist, 1784

Samuel Johnson was born in 1709 and is best known as a writer of dictionaries and a literary editor. In his lifetime he was renowned for his religious beliefs and as a firm supporter of the practice and order of the Church of England. He had been converted to Christianity as young man after reading William Law's A Serious Call to a Devout and Holy Life, and his support of the High Church party was unstinting. Amongst his other writings, his essays entitled The Rambler, which appeared twice weekly between 1750 and 1752, earned him the nickname 'The Great Moralist', then a term of affection and honour. He died on this day in the year 1784.

A Reading from a letter of Samuel Johnson to Mr William Drummond concerning the translation of the Scriptures into Gaelic, dated 13 August 1766

I did not expect to hear that it could be, in an assembly convened for the propagation of Christian knowledge, a question whether any nation uninstructed in religion should receive instruction; or whether that instruction should be imparted to them by a translation of the holy books into their own language. If obedience to the will of God be necessary to happiness, and knowledge of his will be necessary to obedience, I know not how he that withholds this knowledge, or delays it, can be said to love his neighbour as himself. He that voluntarily continues ignorance, is guilty of all the crimes which ignorance produces; as to him that should extinguish the tapers of a lighthouse, might justly be imputed the calamities of shipwrecks.

Christianity is the highest perfection of humanity; and as no man is good but as he wishes the good of others, no man can be good in the highest degree who wishes not to others the largest measures of the greatest good. To omit for a year, or for a day, the most efficacious method of advancing Christianity, in compliance with any purposes that terminate on this side of the grave, is a crime of which I know not that the world has yet had an example.

Let it be remembered that the efficacy of ignorance has been long tried, and has not produced the consequence expected. Let knowledge, therefore, take its turn; and let the patrons of privation stand awhile aside, and admit the operation of positive principles. You will be pleased, Sir, to assure the worthy man who is employed in the new translation, that he has my wishes for his success; and I shall think it more than honour to promote his undertaking.

A Reading from a sermon of Samuel Johnson

'Finally be ye all of one mind, having compassion one of another, love as brethren, be pitiful, be courteous.' For courteous some substitute the word humble; the difference may not be considered as great, for pride is a quality that obstructs courtesy.

That a precept of courtesy is by no means unworthy of the gravity and dignity of an apostolical mandate, may be gathered from the pernicious effects which all must have observed to have arisen from harsh strictness and sour virtue: such as refuses to mingle in harmless gaiety, or give countenance to innocent amusements, or which transacts the business of the day with a gloomy ferociousness that clouds existence.

Goodness of this character, is more formidable than lovely; it may drive away vice from its presence, but will never persuade it to stay to be amended; it may teach, it may remonstrate, but the hearer will seek for more mild instruction. To those, therefore, by whose conversation the heathens were to be drawn away from error and wickedness; it is the apostle Peter's precept, that they be courteous, that they accommodate themselves, as far as innocence allows, to the will of others; that they should practise all the established modes of civility, seize all occasions of cultivating kindness, and live with the rest of the world in an amicable reciprocation of cursory civility, that Christianity might not be accused of making men less cheerful as companions, less sociable as neighbours, or less useful as friends.

14 December

John of the Cross

Poet, Teacher of the Faith, 1591

Born to an impoverished noble family near Avila in Spain in 1542, Juan de Yepes was brought up by his widowed mother and went to a charity school. He worked as a nurse and received further education from the Jesuits before entering the Carmelite Order when he was twenty-one. Having distinguished himself at Salamanca University, he was ordained in 1567 and met Teresa of Avila soon afterwards. Small of stature, he made a great impression on her and she persuaded him to help with her reform of the Carmelite Order. His labours brought him into conflict with the religious authorities, and he was even imprisoned for a period, yet these experiences prompted some of his finest poetry and mystical writing. In particular, he described the 'dark night' of the soul as it is purified in its approach towards God. After ten years as superior to several different houses, he again fell out of favour and was banished to Andalusia in southern Spain, where he died after a severe illness on this day in the year 1591.

A Reading from *The Spiritual Canticle* of John of the Cross

However numerous the mysteries and marvels which holy doctors and saintly souls have understood in this earthly life, there is always more to be said and understood. There are great depths to be fathomed in Christ, for he is like a rich mine with many recesses containing treasures, so that however deep you dig, you never reach their end, but rather in each recess you find new veins with new riches everywhere.

On this account Saint Paul said of Christ: 'In Christ are hidden all the treasures of wisdom and knowledge.' But the soul cannot enter these caverns or reach these treasures if it does not first pass over to the divine wisdom through the thicket of exterior and interior suffering. For even that degree of these mysteries of Christ to which a soul may attain in this life cannot be reached without great suffering, without having received from God the grace of many gifts for the mind and the senses, and without having undergone much spiritual discipline. But note that all such gifts are of a lower order to the wisdom that comes from the mysteries of Christ. They serve merely as preparations for coming to this wisdom.

Oh, if we could fully understand how a soul cannot reach the thicket of the wisdom and riches of God, which are of many kinds, without entering the thicket of many kinds of suffering, finding in this its delight and consolation. A soul with an authentic desire for divine wisdom first desires suffering in order to enter this wisdom by the thicket of the cross.

For this reason Saint Paul exhorted the Ephesians not to grow faint in tribulations, but to be very strong, and rooted in charity, in order to comprehend with all the saints what is the breadth and height and depth, and to know also the surpassing love of the knowledge of Christ, so as to be filled with all the fullness of God. For the gate whereby we may enter into these riches of his wisdom is the cross, which is narrow. Many desire the delights to which that gate leads, but few are prepared to pass through it.

alternative reading

A Reading from a poem entitled
'Song of the Soul that is glad to know God by faith'
by John of the Cross

How well I know that fountain's rushing flow
Although by night

Its deathless spring is hidden. Even so
Full well I guess from whence its sources flow
Though it be night.

Its origin (since it has none) none knows:
But that all origin from it arose
Although by night.

I know there is no other thing so fair
And earth and heaven drink refreshment there
Although by night.

Full well I know its depth no one can sound
And that no ford to cross it can be found
Though it be night.

Its clarity unclouded still shall be:
Out of it comes the light by which we see
Though it be night.

Flush with its banks the stream so proudly swells;
I know it waters nations, heavens, and hells
Though it be night.

The current that is nourished by this source
I know to be omnipotent in force
Although by night.

From source and current a new current swells
Which neither of the other twain excels
Though it be night.

The eternal source hides in the Living Bread
That we with life eternal may be fed
Though it be night.

Here to all creatures it is crying, hark!
That they should drink their fill though in the dark,
For it is night.

This living fount which is to me so dear
Within the bread of life I see it clear
Though it be night.

17 December

Eglantyne Jebb

Social Reformer, Founder of 'Save the Children Fund', 1928

Eglantyne Jebb was born in 1876. After studying at Oxford, she became a teacher for a few years until ill-health led to her resignation. She then devoted her energies to charitable works and in 1913 went to Macedonia to help refugees in the Balkan wars. After the First World War, she and her sister Dorothy Buxton founded the Save the Children Fund, which aimed to help children who were suffering in the post-war famine in Europe, a charity which is now global in its scope. Eglantyne fought for the rights of children to be recognized, the League of Nations passing her 'Children's Charter' in 1924. She inspired many by her personal spirituality and was greatly mourned on her death in Geneva on this day in the year 1928.

A Reading from *Far Above Rubies* by Richard Symonds

Following the Armistice which put an end to hostilities in November 1918, Eglantyne Jebb and her sister Dorothy were shocked that peace brought no relief to Europe. They were aware of the brutal details of the starvation and high mortality in Germany and Austria as a result of the Allied blockade, and of the disinterest of the major statesmen. The sisters responded by setting up a 'Save the Children Fund'.

Early in 1919 Eglantyne appeared in the consulting room of a young London doctor, Hector Munro, who was trying to resume his practice after the war. 'When she spoke,' he recalled, 'everything else seemed to lose its importance', and he found himself on his way to Vienna. His report on this mission described children dying in the streets, and women with spontaneous fractures of the hips whose bones had lost all solidity. Babies were thrown into the Danube or left in hospitals where they were ranged on shelves to die.

Deeply religious herself, Eglantyne on the basis of this report approached the Archbishop of Canterbury who declined however to make an appeal to the Church of England to help. So, snatching Dr Munro from his practice again, she went with him to see the Pope with whom she had a remarkable success. In 1919 Pope Benedict XV was a sad figure, who had been bitterly reviled from all sides for his position during the war. Eglantyne sensed his intense loneliness 'but felt as if I wanted to make him comfortable'. He kept her and Dr Munro for over two hours in a discussion in French. Seizing this opportunity for a constructive initiative, he declared that he would arrange for collections to be made in all Roman Catholic Churches. He followed this up with an Encyclical, which mentioned the Save the Children Fund by name, and insisted that help must go to all needy children and not to Roman Catholics alone.

The Archbishop of Canterbury could now hardly do less, and on Holy Innocents Day in December 1919 collections were made throughout the Roman Catholic and Anglican world, as well as in the Orthodox and Free Churches. The Pope's initiative had internationalised the movement.

Eglantyne's guiding rule throughout her life was to save as many children as possible, irrespective of all considerations of country or creed. But her systematic mind also saw the need for a document which would assert the principle that every child is born with the inalienable right to have the opportunity of full physical, mental and spiritual development. With other social workers in Britain and abroad she elaborated a 'Children's Charter' from which she later distilled what became known as 'The Declaration of Geneva' (text printed below).

The passing of the Declaration, and subsequent adoption by the League of Nations in 1924, marked the high point of Eglantyne's career. The balance of the text reflected her philosophy that not only did the community have the duty to protect and ensure the development of the child, but that the child in return must be brought up to be aware of, and discharge, its duty to the community. Preaching at its ratification in Geneva, she said: 'May God put into our hearts to strive and strive and never cease from striving, until we have clean swept away this appalling blot which disgraces our civilisation, this iniquitous child suffering.'

The Declaration of Geneva

By the present Declaration of the Rights of the Child, commonly known as the 'Declaration of Geneva', men and women of all nations, recognising that humankind owes to the child

the best that it has to give, declare and accept it as their duty, that beyond and above all considerations of race, nationality or creed:
I THE CHILD must be given the means requisite for its normal development, both materially and spiritually.
II THE CHILD that is hungry must be fed; the child that is sick must be nursed; the child that is backward must be helped; the delinquent child must be reclaimed; and the orphan and the waif must be sheltered and succoured.
III THE CHILD must be the first to receive relief in times of distress.
IV THE CHILD must be put in a position to earn a livelihood, and must be protected against every form of exploitation.
V THE CHILD must be brought up in the consciousness that its talents must be devoted to the service of other fellow men and women.

18 December

Flannan

Missionary and Pilgrim, *c.*640

Flannan is one of the many travelling Irish saints who embarked on long journeys, often by water as well as overland, partly as missionaries but also as pilgrims, making a spiritual 'peregrination' to witness on the way for Christ. Flannan succeeded Mo-Lua who founded Killaloe Cathedral in County Clare on the river Shannon. St Flannan's Oratory beside the cathedral is an impressive example of early Irish architecture. Its large size and sound, stone construction have been widely admired. Flannan died on this day in about the year 640.

A Reading from the *Instructions* of Columbanus
on 'Christ the Fount of Life'

Let us follow that vocation by which we are called from life to the fountain of life. Christ is the fountain, not only of living water, but of eternal life. He is the fountain of light and spiritual illumination; for from him come all these things: wisdom, life and eternal light. The author of life is the fountain of life; the creator of light is the fountain of spiritual illumination. Therefore, let us seek the fountain of light and life and the living water by despising what we see, by leaving the world and by dwelling in the highest heavens. Let us seek these things, and like rational and shrewd fish may we drink the living water which 'wells up to eternal life.'

Merciful God, good Lord, I wish that you would unite me to that fountain that there I may drink of the living spring of the water of life with all those who thirst after you. There in that heavenly region may I ever dwell, delighted with abundant sweetness, and say: 'How sweet is the fountain of living water which never fails, the water welling up to eternal life.'

O God, you are yourself that fountain ever and again to be desired, ever and again to be consumed. Lord Christ, give us always this water to be for us the 'source of the living water which wells up to eternal life.' I ask you for your great benefits. Who does not know it? but you, King of Glory, know how to give great gifts, and you have promised great things. There is nothing greater than you, and you bestowed yourself upon us; you gave yourself for us.

Therefore, we ask that we may know what we love, since we ask nothing other than that you give us yourself. For you are our all: our life, our light, our salvation, our food and our drink, our God. Inspire our hearts, I ask you, Jesus, with that breath of your Spirit; wound our souls with your love, so that the soul of each and every one of us may be able to say in truth: 'Show me my soul's desire,' for I am wounded by your love.

These are the wounds I wish for, Lord. Blessed is the soul so wounded by love. Such a soul seeks the fountain of eternal life and drinks from it, although it continues to thirst and its thirst grows ever greater even as it drinks. Therefore, the more the soul loves, the more it desires to love, and the greater its suffering, the greater its healing. In this same way may our God and Lord Jesus Christ, the good and saving physician, wound the depths of our souls with a healing wound – the same Jesus Christ who reigns in unity with the Father and the Holy Spirit, for ever and ever.

26 December

Stephen

Deacon and First Martyr

In the Acts of the Apostles, Stephen is described as one of the seven deacons whose job it is to care for the widows in the early Church in Jerusalem. His eloquent speech before the Sanhedrin, in which he shows the great sweep of Jewish history as leading to the birth of Jesus, the long-expected Messiah, and his impassioned plea that all might hear the good news of Jesus, leads to his inevitable martyrdom by being stoned to death. The description of Stephen in Acts bears direct parallels to that of Christ in Luke's Gospel: for example, the passion; being filled with the Holy Spirit; seeing the Son of God at the right hand of God, as Jesus promised he would be; commending his spirit to Jesus, as Jesus commended his to the Father; kneeling as Jesus did in Gethsemane and asking forgiveness for his persecutors. Witnessing to Jesus by acting like Jesus in every way is thus seen as of the essence of the Christian life.

A Reading from a sermon of Fulgentius, Bishop of Ruspe

Yesterday we celebrated the birth in time of our eternal King. Today we celebrate the triumphant suffering of his soldier. Yesterday our king, clothed in his robe of flesh, left his place in the virgin's womb and graciously visited the world. Today his soldier leaves the tabernacle of his body and goes triumphantly to heaven.

Our king, despite his exalted majesty, came in humility for our sake; yet he did not come empty-handed. He brought his soldiers a great gift that not only enriched them but also made them unconquerable in battle, for it was the gift of love, which was to bring us to share in his divinity. He gave of his bounty, yet without any loss to himself. In a marvellous way he changed into wealth the poverty of his faithful followers while remaining in full possession of his own inexhaustible riches.

And so the love that brought Christ from heaven to earth raised Stephen from earth to heaven; shown first in the king, it later shone forth in his soldier. Love was Stephen's weapon by which he gained every battle, and so won the crown signified by his name. His love of God kept him from yielding to the ferocious mob; his love for his neighbour made him pray for those who were stoning him. Love inspired him to reprove those who erred, to make them amend; love led him to pray for those who stoned him to save them from punishment. Strengthened by the power of his love, he overcame the raging cruelty of Saul and won the persecutor on earth as his companion in heaven. In his holy and tireless love he longed to gain by prayer those whom he could not convert by admonition.

Now at last, Paul rejoices with Stephen, with Stephen he delights in the glory of Christ, with Stephen he exalts, with Stephen he reigns. Stephen went first, slain by the stones thrown by Paul; but Paul followed after, helped by the prayer of Stephen. This, surely, is the true life, beloved, a life in which Paul feels no shame because of Stephen's death, and Stephen delights in Paul's companionship, for love fills them both with joy. It was Stephen's love that prevailed over the cruelty of the mob, and it was Paul's love that covered the multitude of his sins; it was love that won for both of them the kingdom of heaven.

Love, indeed, is the source of all good things; it is an impregnable defence, and the way that leads to heaven. Whoever walks in love can neither go astray nor be afraid: love guides, protects, and brings the one who loves to the journey's end.

Christ made love the stairway that would enable all Christians to climb to heaven. Hold fast to it, therefore, in all sincerity, give one another practical proof of it, and by your progress in it, make your ascent together.

27 December

John

Apostle and Evangelist

Whether or not John the Apostle and John the Evangelist are one and the same, the Church honours on this day the one who proclaims Jesus as 'the Word made flesh' and who is 'the disciple whom Jesus loved'. The Gospel narratives speak of John as one of the sons of Zebedee who followed Jesus. He was present at the transfiguration of Jesus on the holy mountain; he was there with Jesus at the last supper; he was there with Jesus in his agony in the garden; he was there with Jesus and his mother, standing at the foot of the cross; he was there with Jesus as a witness of his resurrection and 'he saw and believed'. According to tradition, John died at Ephesus in advanced old age.

A Reading from the commentary of Augustine on the First Letter of John

'Our message is the Word of life. We announce what existed from the beginning, what we have heard, what we have seen with our own eyes, what we have touched with our own hands.'

Who could touch the Word with his hands unless 'the Word was made flesh and lived among us'? Now this Word, whose flesh was so real that he could be touched by human hands, began to be flesh in the Virgin Mary's womb; but he did not begin to exist at that moment. We know this from what John says: 'What existed from the beginning'. Notice how John's Letter bears witness to his Gospel: 'In the beginning was the Word, and the Word was with God.'

Someone might interpret the phrase 'the Word of life' to mean a word about Christ, rather than Christ's body itself which was touched by human hands. But consider what comes next: 'and life itself was revealed'. Christ, therefore, is himself the Word of life.

And how was this life revealed? It existed from the beginning, but was not revealed to mortals, only to angels, who looked upon it and feasted upon it as their own spiritual bread. But what does Scripture say? 'Humans ate the bread of angels.'

Life itself was therefore revealed in the flesh. In this way what was visible to the heart alone could become visible also to the eye, and so heal human hearts. For the Word is visible to the heart alone, while flesh is visible to bodily eyes as well. We already possessed the means to see the flesh, but we had no means of seeing the Word. The Word was made flesh so that we could see it, to heal the part of us by which we could see the Word.

John continues: 'And we are witnesses and we proclaim to you that eternal life which was with the Father and has been revealed among us' – one might say more simply 'revealed to us'. 'We proclaim to you what we have heard and seen.' Make sure that you grasp the meaning of these words. The disciples saw our Lord in the flesh, face to face; they heard the words he spoke, and in turn they proclaimed the message to us. So we also have heard, although we have not seen.

Are we then less favoured than those who both saw and heard? If that were so, why should John add: 'so that you too may have fellowship with us'? They saw, and we have not seen; yet we have fellowship with them, because we and they share the same faith.

'And our fellowship is with God the Father and Jesus Christ his Son. And we write this to you to make your joy complete' – complete in that fellowship, in that love and in that unity.

28 December

The Holy Innocents

Herod 'the Great' was appointed King of the Jews by the Roman authorities in Palestine and he proved to be ruthlessly efficient in his thirty-three years of dealing with his subjects. In the Gospel according to Matthew, Herod tried to persuade the Magi, to whom he played host on their journey seeking the one 'who has been born king of the Jews', to bring word to him once they had found the child. His desire was to eliminate Jesus and, when he realised that the Magi had tricked him and left the country, Herod killed all the children under the age of two in and around Bethlehem. These were God's 'innocent' ones, paralleling the story of Pharaoh slaughtering the Hebrew children in Egypt.

A Reading from a sermon of Quodvultdeus, Bishop of Carthage

A tiny child is born who is a great king. Wise men are led to him from afar. They come to adore one who lies in a manger and yet reigns in heaven and on earth. When they tell of one who is born a king, Herod is disturbed. To save his kingdom he resolves to kill him, though if he would have faith in the child, he himself would reign in peace in this life and for ever in the life to come.

Why are you afraid, Herod, when you hear of the birth of a king? He does not come to drive you out, but to conquer the devil. But because you do not understand this you are disturbed and in a rage, and to destroy one child whom you seek, you show your cruelty in the death of so many children.

You are not restrained by the love of weeping mothers or fathers mourning the deaths of their little ones, nor by the cries and sobs of the children. You destroy those who are tiny in body because fear is destroying your heart. You imagine that if you accomplish your desire you can prolong your own life, though you are seeking to kill Life himself.

Yet your throne is threatened by the source of grace – so small, and yet so great – who is lying in the manger. He is using you, all unaware of it, to work out his own purposes in freeing souls from captivity to the devil. He has taken up the children of the enemy into the ranks of God's adopted children.

The children die for Christ, though they do not know it. The parents mourn for the death of martyrs. The children make of those as yet unable to speak fit witnesses to themselves. See the kind of kingdom that is his, coming as he did in order to be this kind of king. See how the deliverer is already working deliverance, the Saviour already working salvation.

But you, Herod, do not know this and are disturbed and furious. While you vent your fury against the children, you are already paying them homage, and you do not know it. How great a gift of grace is here! To what merits of their own do the children owe this kind of victory? They cannot speak, yet they bear witness to Christ. They cannot use their little limbs to engage in battle, yet already they bear off the palm of victory.

alternative reading

A Reading from the conclusion to *Evil and the God of Love* by John Hick

The only permissible theodicy is one that sees moral and natural evil as necessary features of the present stage of God's creating of perfected finite persons. Thus the ultimate responsibility for the existence of evil belongs to the creator; and Christianity also believes that, in his total awareness of the history of his creation, God bears with us the pains of the creative process.

What is the greatest difficulty in the way of such a theodicy? It is, I think, the stark question whether all the pain and suffering, cruelty and wickedness of human life can be rendered acceptable by an end-state, however good. Dostoievsky unforgettably presented the negative case in his novel *The Brothers Karamazov* when Ivan engages his brother Alyosha in a long and agonised discussion of the suffering of innocent children. He concludes thus:

> ['It's the defencelessness of children that tempts their torturers, the angelic trustfulness of the child who has nowhere to go and no one to run to for protection – it is this that inflames the evil blood of the torturer. In every man a wild beast is hidden – the wild beast of irascibility, the wild beast of sensuous intoxication from the screams of the tortured victim.
>
> 'People tell me that without such suffering man could not even have existed on earth, for he would not have known good and evil. But why? To me, the whole world's knowledge isn't worth a child's tear to her "dear and kind God"! I'm not talking of the

sufferings of grown-up people, for they have eaten the apple and to hell with them – but these little ones!

'If the sufferings of children go to make up the sum of sufferings which is necessary for the purchase of truth, then I say beforehand that the entire truth is not worth such a price. Too high a price has been placed on harmony.]

'I challenge you – answer. Imagine that you are creating a fabric of human destiny with the object of making people happy in the end, giving them peace and rest at last, but that it was essential and inevitable to torture to death only one tiny creature – a baby beating its breast with its fist, for instance – and to found that edifice on its unavenged tears, would you consent to be architect on those conditions? Tell me the truth.'

'No, I wouldn't consent,' said Alyosha softly.

The implication, of course, is that if there is a God, in the sense of One who is responsible for the world, and ultimately therefore for the existence of evil within it, then that God cannot be good and cannot properly be worshipped as such.

In face of this gravest of all challenges to a Christian faith in God I can well understand and sympathise with the negative response which Dostoievsky has so powerfully articulated. But we believe or disbelieve, ultimately, out of our own experience and must be faithful to the witness of that experience; and together with very many others, I find that the realities of human goodness and human happiness make it a credible possibility that this life with its baffling mixture of good and evil, and including both its dark miseries and its shining joys, including both man's malevolence and his self-forgetting love, is indeed part of a long and slow pilgrim's progress towards the Celestial City. If so, the journey must have many stages beyond the present one; and the end must be good beyond our present imagining – and must be far more positive than the mere 'peace and rest at last' of which Dostoievsky speaks. And in the meantime the fact that the process does not declare its own nature but remains mysteriously ambiguous is a necessary aspect of a soul-making or person-making history.

I therefore end by formulating this ultimate question: can there be a future good so great as to render acceptable, in retrospect, the whole human experience, with all its wickedness and suffering as well as all its sanctity and happiness? I think that perhaps there can, and indeed that perhaps there is.

29 December

Thomas Becket

Archbishop of Canterbury, Martyr, 1170

Note: In England, Thomas Becket may be commemorated on 7 July instead.

Thomas was born in London in 1118, of a family of merchants. After a good education he served as clerk to another burgess then entered the service of Archbishop Theobald of Canterbury. Thomas proved himself an excellent administrator and skilled diplomat. In 1155 he was appointed chancellor by King Henry II. For several years king and chancellor worked harmoniously together in mutual admiration and personal friendship. As a result, the king nominated Thomas as Archbishop of Canterbury to succeed Theobald in 1161.

From the start there was friction, with Thomas insisting on every privilege of the Church. The conflict worsened until 1164 when Thomas fled to France. Encouraged by the Pope he pursued his arguments from exile, sending letters and pronouncing excommunications. Three efforts at mediation failed before an apparent reconciliation brought him back triumphant to Canterbury in 1170. But the nobility still opposed him, and words of anger at court led four knights to journey to Canterbury where they finally chased Thomas into the cathedral, and murdered him on this day in the year 1170. Thomas was undoubtedly a proud and stubborn man, for all his gifts, and his personal austerities as archbishop were probably an attempt at self-discipline after years of ostentatious luxury. His conflict with King Henry stemmed from their equal personal ambitions, exacerbated by the increasingly international claims of the papacy, played out in the inevitable tension between Church and State.

A Reading from a contemporary account of the murder of Thomas Becket, Archbishop of Canterbury, by Edward Grim, an eye-witness

[On the fifth day after the Nativity of Christ, the hour of dinner being over, the saint had already withdrawn with some of his household into an inner chamber to transact some business. The four knights with an attendant forced their way in. They were received with respect as servants of the king and well known to the archbishop's household. For a long time they sat in silence and neither saluted the archbishop nor spoke to him.

William FitzUrse, who seemed to be their leader, breathing fury, broke out in these words: 'We have something to say to you by the king's command: that you depart with all your men from the kingdom and the lands which own his dominion; for from this day forth there can be no peace betwixt him and you or any or yours, for you have broken the peace.'

To this the archbishop answered: 'Cease your threats and still your brawling. I put my trust in the King of Heaven who for his own suffered on the cross; for from this day forth no one shall see the sea between me and my church. I have not come back to England to flee again; here shall he who wants me find me.'

Confounded by these words, the knights sprang to their feet, for they could no longer bear the firmness of his answers. Coming up close to him they said: 'We declare to you that you have spoken in peril of your head.' As they retired amidst tumult and insults, the man of God followed them to the door and cried out after them, 'Here, here will you find me.'

Terrified by the noise and uproar, almost all the clerks and the servants were scattered hither and thither like sheep before wolves. Those who remained cried out to the archbishop to flee to the church; but he, mindful of his former promise that he would not through fear of death flee from those who kill the body, rejected flight. But the monks still pressed him, saying that it was not becoming for him to absent himself from vespers.

The monks hastened to ward off the foe from the slaughter of their shepherd by fastening the bolts of the folding doors giving access to the church. But Christ's doughty champion turned to them and ordered the doors to be thrown open, saying: 'It is not meet to make a fortress of the house of prayer, the Church of Christ, which, even if it be not closed, affords sufficient protection to its children. By suffering rather than by fighting shall we triumph over the enemy; for we are come to suffer, not to resist.']

Straightway those sacrilegious men, with drawn swords, entered the house of peace and reconciliation. In a spirit of mad fury the knights called out: 'Where is Thomas Becket, traitor to the king and the realm?' When he returned no answer, they cried out the more loudly and insistently: 'Where is the archbishop?' At this quite undaunted, the archbishop descended from the steps whither he had been dragged by the monks through their fear of the knights. In a perfectly clear voice he answered: 'Lo! here I am, no traitor to the king, but a priest. What do you seek from me?'

Having said thus, he turned aside to the right, under a pillar. 'Absolve,' they cried, 'and restore to communion those whom you have excommunicated.' But he answered, 'There has been no satisfaction made, and I will not absolve them.' 'Then you shall die this instant,' they cried.

'I am ready to die for my Lord, that in my blood the Church may obtain peace and liberty; but in the name of almighty God I forbid you to harm any of my men, whether clerk or lay.'

Then they made a rush at him and laid sacrilegious hands upon him, pulling him and dragging him roughly and violently across the floor. Then the unconquered martyr understood that his hour had come. Inclining his head as one in prayer and joining his hands together and uplifting them, he commended his cause and that of the Church to God and Saint Mary and the blessed martyr Saint Denys. Scarce had he uttered these words than the wicked knight leapt suddenly upon him and wounded the sacrificial lamb of God in the head, cutting off the top of the crown which the unction of the sacred chrism had dedicated to God, and by the same stroke he almost cut off the arm of him who tells this story.

The archbishop then received a second blow on the head, but still he stood firm and immovable. At the third blow he fell on his knees and elbows, offering himself to God a living sacrifice. The third knight inflicted a terrible wound as he lay prostrate, in such a way that the blood white with the brain, and the brain no less red from the blood, dyed the floor of the cathedral with the white of the lily and the red of the rose, the colours of the Virgin and Mother, and of the life and death of the martyr and confessor.

Neither with hand nor robe, as is the manner of human frailty, did the archbishop oppose the fatal stroke. Bespattered with blood and brains, as though in an attitude of prayer, his body lay prone on the pavement, while his soul rested in Abraham's bosom.

30 December

Tathan

Abbot, sixth or seventh century

Tathan (sometimes known as Tatheus or Meuthi) was the son of an Irish king named Tathalius (Tuathal). He settled in Gwent, where King Caradog gave him a grant of land at Caerwent. Tathan established one of the most famous of the Welsh monastic schools there. Among those whom he taught was Cadoc. It is said that Gwynllyw, Cadoc's father, had stolen Tathan's cow and then tried unsuccessfully to play a practical joke on the holy man when he tried to claim it back. Feeling ashamed, Gwynllyw asked Tathan to baptize the new-born child, who later became his pupil. Another tradition tells how Tathan built a church at Llanvaches, near Caerwent, in memory of the murdered shepherdess Maches or Machuta.

A Reading from a letter of Augustine

At certain times we need consciously to bring our minds back to the business of prayer, and to detach ourselves from other matters and preoccupations which cool our desire for God. We need to remind ourselves by the words we pray to focus on what we really desire. This we do to prevent what may have begun to grow lukewarm in us from becoming cold, or worse still, from being entirely extinguished. The solution is to fan our desire regularly into flame. This is why when the apostle Paul says: ‘Let your requests be made known to God’ his words should not be interpreted as though this is how God becomes aware of human need. God undoubtedly knows our needs before ever we utter them. Paul’s words should be understood in the sense that it is in the presence of God that *we* become aware of our inner desires as we wait patiently upon him in prayer. That is why it is not appropriate that they should be paraded before other folk in ostentatious public prayer.

We should welcome all opportunities for extended periods of prayer when other duties involving good and necessary activity do not prevent us – although even in the midst of activity we can still pray without ceasing by cherishing our deepest desire. And note, praying for long is not the same thing as praying ‘with much speaking’ as some Christians seem to think. To be verbose is one thing; to extend prayer in the warmth of a desire for God is quite another. In the Scriptures we are told that our Lord himself spent a whole night in prayer, and that in his agony in Gethsemane he prayed even more fervently. Is he not giving us an example? In time he is the intercessor we need; in eternity he dwells with the Father and is the hearer of our prayer.

The monks in Egypt are said to offer frequent prayers, but these are very brief and are, so to speak, darted forth like arrows lest the vigilant and alert attention which is vital in prayer be weakened or blunted through being over-extended. In this way even these monastics are demonstrating that mental concentration should not be allowed to become exhausted through excess; and on the other hand, if it is sustained, should not be suddenly broken off. Far be it from us then, to use ‘much speaking’ in our prayer; or if concentration be sustained to curtail our prayer abruptly.

To use a lot of words when we pray is superfluous. But to long for God in prayer, if the desire and concentration persist, is good. It will necessitate beating upon the door of him to whom we are praying by long and deep stirring of the heart. Often prayer consists more in groans than in words, more in tears than in speech. But God collects our tears; our groaning is not hidden from him who created all things by his Word, and who has no need of human words.

31 December

John Wyclif

Reformer, 1384

John was a member of the Wyclif family of Richmond in Yorkshire and was born in about the year 1330. He was a Fellow of Merton College Oxford, and Master of Balliol, but his expulsion from the Wardenship of Canterbury Hall (later incorporated into Christ Church) in favour of a monastic foundation led to a lawsuit and a life-long hatred of things monastic. He was much in favour with members of the royal family and, when disputes arose owing to his attacks on the clergy of the day, he was protected by them from the otherwise inevitable consequence of deprivation of his posts. However, he went on to deny the Church's teaching of the presence of Christ at the Eucharist, the doctrine known as transubstantiation, and it was this that lost him his royal protection. His opinions were formally condemned in 1381 and he was forced out of office by the university the following year. John had already moved to Lutterworth in 1380 and from there he gave his support to such projects as the translation of the Bible into contemporary English. He died on this day in the year 1384, whilst at Mass.

A Reading from The Pastoral Office by John Wyclif

Among all the duties of the pastor after justice of life, holy preaching is most to be praised, for Christ, the primal truth, said to the woman commending the one who bore him in the womb and nourished his body, 'They are blessed who hear the word of God and keep it.' There is no doubt but that preaching the Word of God is as great as hearing it. Moreover, in Christ there were these three things: the highest was the preaching of the Word, then the hearing of it, and finally the keeping of it in deed. Yet in others preaching is more commendable than hearing, just as action is superior to being acted upon. In like manner, Christ, in highest wisdom, commanded his apostles when he ascended into heaven to preach the gospel to every creature; indeed the wisest Master would not have done this unless such preaching were more to be praised in apostle or curate. Hence, among his duties such an activity is more worthy. It is evident that preaching the gospel is the special work of the curate, for Christ advances more in his apostles by preaching to the people than by doing any miracle which in his own person he did in Judea.

Preaching the Gospel exceeds prayer and administration of the sacraments, to an infinite degree. Spreading the gospel has far wider and more evident benefit; it is thus the most precious activity of the Church. Just as the judges of the kings handing down their judgement to the people are especially designated next to the kings in honour, thus those preaching the gospel truly are to be set apart by the authority of the Lord.

alternative reading

A Reading from *The Pastoral Office* by John Wyclif

It seems that the knowledge of God's law should be taught in that language which is best known, because this knowledge is God's Word. When Christ says in the gospel that both heaven and earth shall pass away but his words shall not pass away, he means by his 'words' his knowledge. Thus God's knowledge is holy Scripture that may in no wise be false. Also the Holy Spirit gave to the apostles at Pentecost knowledge to know all manner of languages to teach the people God's law thereby; and so God willed that the people be taught his law in divers tongues. But what man on God's behalf should reverse God's ordinance and his will?

For this reason Saint Jerome laboured and translated the Bible from divers tongues into Latin that it might after be translated into other tongues. Thus Christ and his apostles taught the people in that tongue that was best known to him. Why should men not do so now? And for this reason the authors of the new law who were apostles of Jesus Christ wrote their

Gospels in divers tongues that were better known to the people. Also the worthy kingdom of France, notwithstanding all hindrances, has translated the Bible and the Gospels with other true sentences of doctors out of Latin into French. Why should not Englishmen do so? As the lords of England have the Bible in French, so would it not be against reason that they have it in English; for thus, with unity of knowledge, God's law would be better known and more believed, and there might be more agreement between kingdoms. In England the friars have taught the Lord's Prayer in the English language, as men see in the play of York, and likewise in many other counties. Since the Lord's Prayer is part of Matthew's Gospel, as clerks know, why may not all of the Gospel be turned into English as is this part? This is especially so since all Christian men, learned and ignorant, who should be saved might always follow Christ and know his teaching and his life.

Abbreviations

ACW	Ancient Christian Writers: The Works of the Fathers in Translation; ed. J. Quasten and J. C. Plumpe, New York & Mahwah, New Jersey, 1946– .
BEH	*Ecclesiastical History of the English People* by the Venerable Bede, critical edition by B. Colgrave & R. A. B. Mynors, Oxford, 1969.
CCSL	*Corpus Christianorum: Series Latina*, Turnhout, Belgium, 1953– .
CSEL	*Corpus Scriptorum Ecclesiasticorum Latinorum*, Vienna, 1866–.
CWS	Classics of Western Spirituality, New York & Mahwah, New Jersey, 1978– .
ET	English translation
ICEL	*The Roman Catholic Liturgy of the Hours*, 1974, American edition; ET of non-biblical readings by the International Commission for English in the Liturgy.
LACT	Library of Anglo-Catholic Theology, Oxford, 1841–.
LCC	The Library of Christian Classics, Philadelphia & London, 1953–66.
LRW	*Love's Redeeming Work: The Anglican Quest for Holiness*, compiled by Geoffrey Rowell, Kenneth Stevenson and Rowan Williams, Oxford, 2001.
Loeb	The Loeb Classical Library, Cambridge, Mass., & London, 1923–.
NPNF	The Nicene and Post-Nicene Library of the Fathers, series 1 & 2, general editors Schaff and Wace, New York, 1887–92; Oxford, 1890– 1900; reprinted Grand Rapids, Michigan, 1983–.
PG	*Patrologiae cursus completus: Series Graeca*, 161 vols, ed. J. P. Migne, Paris, 1857–66.
PL	*Patrologiae cursus completus: Series Latina*, 221 vols, ed. J. P. Migne, Paris, 1844–64.
op. cit.	the work previously cited
SC	*Sources Chrétiennes*, Paris, 1940–.

Notes and Sources

The figure in **BOLD** on the left indicates the day in the month, *not* the page number. Where a number of saints are commemorated in the calendar on the same day, the references below are printed in the order of their chronolgy as they appear in the anthology.

Where no source for an English translation is cited, the version is that of the author. If this has been based on an existing (often nineteenth-century translation) it is acknowledged in the notes.

JANUARY

1 a. William of St Thierry, *On Contemplating God*, 9; ET by Penelope Lawson CSMV in *The Works of William of St Thierry I*, Spencer, Massachusetts, 1971, p.38.
b. Mark Frank, sermon 17; *Sermons by Dr Mark Frank*, LACT, Oxford, 1849; vol. 1, pp.258–72 (abridged).

2 a. Basil the Great, *Letter* 2, 1–2; Loeb (4 vols), ed. Roy Deferrari, 1926; ET based on Deferrari, vol. 1, pp.7–11.
b. Gregory of Nazianzus, *Oration 43 'In praise of Basil the Great'*, 15–17, 19–21; PG 36, cols 514–23.
c. 'Saint Gregory Nazianzen', from John McGuckin, *Saint Gregory of Nazianzus: An Intellectual Biography*, Crestwood, New York, 2001; facing p.xvi.

2 'The Duties of an Abbot of a Community', 1–13; *The Rule of Carthage*; ET Uinseann O Maidin, *The Celtic Monk: Rules and Writings of Early Irish Monks*, Kalamazoo, Michigan, 1996, pp.63–4.

2 a. *A Treasury of Russian Spirituality*, vol. 2, ed. & ET by George P. Fedotov, London, 1950, pp.267–9 (abridged).
b. *A Little Russian Philokalia*, vol. 1, ed. & ET Gleb Podmoshensky, Brotherhood of Saint Herman of Alaska, Platina, California, 1978, pp.86, 100–2 (abridged).

2 Constance M. Millington, *An Ecumenical Venture: The History of Nandyal Diocese in Andhra Pradesh (1947–1990)*, Bangalore, 1993, pp.2–20 (abridged).

3 Morris Williams, 'Gyda'r saint anturiais nesu'; ET by William Price.

6 a. Peter Chrysologus, *Sermon* 160; PL 52, cols 620–2; ET by ICEL.
b. Ephrem of Syria, *Hymns 'On the Nativity'*, 23: 1, 3, 10; ET by Kathleen E. McVey, *Ephrem the Syrian*, New York & Mahwah, New Jersey, 1989, pp.187–9.
c. Lancelot Andrewes, *Sermon* 14; *The Works of Bishop Lancelot Andrewes*, Oxford, 1841, vol. 1, pp.238–49 (abridged).
d. 'The Divine Image' by William Blake.
e. 'Journey of the Magi' by T. S. Eliot.

10 William Laud, *Works*, ed. G. W. Scott & James Bliss, 8 vols, LACT, Oxford, 1847–60; vol. IV, pp.430–7 (abridged).

11 Gregory the Great, *Pastoral Care*, II, 8; PL 77, cols 42–3.

11 a. Rhys Prichard, 'The Life and Death of Christ'; R. Brinley Jones, *'A Lanterne to their Feete' Remembering Rhys Prichard 1579–1644*, Swansea, 1994, p.65.

b. William Williams, *'Love for God'*, ET and introduced by Anthony Conran, *The Penguin Book of Welsh Verse*, Harmondsworth, 1967, p.209.

c. Isaac Williams, 'Disposer Supreme'.

11 Richard Symonds, *Far Above Rubies: The Women Uncommemorated by the Church of England*, Leominster, 1993, pp.215, 222–3 (abridged).

12 a. Aelred, *Pastoral Prayer*, 6; ET by Penelope Lawson CSMV in *The Works of Aelred of Rievaulx I*, Spencer, Massachusetts, 1971, pp.112–3.

b. Aelred, *Spiritual Friendship*, II, 11–14; ET by Mary Eugenia Laker SSND, Spencer, Massachusetts, 1977, pp.72–3. Note: The 'Wise Man' Aelred refers to is the author of Sirach 6:16.

12 Bede, *The Lives of the Abbots*, 1; *Baedae Opera Historica*, 2 vols; ET based on C. Plummer, Oxford, 1896.

13 Hilary of Poitiers, *On the Trinity*, I, 1–7, 10–12; CCSL 62A, pp.1–7, 9–12; ET based on NPNF vol. IX, pp.40–3. Note: The text Hilary refers to is Wisdom 13:5.

13 Jocelyn of Furness, *The Life of Saint Kentigern*, 42; ET based on W. M. Metcalfe, *Pinkerton's Lives of the Scottish Saints*, Paisley, 1895 (reprinted 1998), vol. 2, pp.271–2.

13 George Fox, *Journal for 1661*, pp.398–9, 401–2; *Quaker Spirituality*, ed. Douglas Steere, New York & Mahwah, New Jersey, 1984, pp.106–7.

15 Gregory the Great, *Dialogues*, II, 4, 7, ed. U. Moricca, Rome, 1924; ET by O. Zimmermann and Benedict Avery, Collegeville, Minnesota, 1981.

17 Athanasius, *The Life of Antony*, 1–4; ET by Robert Gregg, New York & Mahwah, New Jersey, 1980, pp.30–3. Note: '300 *arourae*' – approximately 207 acres.

17 a. Charles Gore, *Belief in God*, London, 1924, pp.1–3.

b. Charles Gore, *The Holy Spirit and Inspiration*, in *Lux Mundi*, ed. C. Gore, London, 1889, pp.331–2.

18 a. Leo the Great, *Sermon 4*, *'On his Birthday'*; PL 54, cols 148–151.

b. John Chrysostom, *Homily in Ss Petrum et Heliam*; PG 50, cols 727–8.

18 Amy Carmichael, *Things as they are: mission work in Southern India*, London, 1905, chapter 32.

19 William of Malmesbury, *The Life of Saint Wulfstan*, I, 14, III, 20; critical ed. by R. R. Darlington, Camden Society, 3rd series, vol. XL, London, 1928.

Note: William's Latin *Vita Wulstani* is itself a version (made between 1124 and 1143) of an earlier English *Life* by the monk Coleman, Wulfstan's friend and chaplain, who wrote it after Wulfstan's death in 1095. No copy of Coleman's work is known to have survived.

19 D. T. W. Price, *Bishop Burgess and Lampeter College*, University of Wales, 1987, pp.33, 35, 43–9 (abridged).

20 Richard Rolle, *The Form of Living*, 8; ET by Rosamund Allen, *Richard Rolle: The English Writings*, New York & Mahwah, New Jersey, 1989, pp.170–2 (abridged).

21 Ambrose, *On Virginity* I, 2, 5, 7–9; PL 16, cols 197–9.

22 Augustine, *Sermon* 274; PL 38, col. 1254.

24 *The Life of Saint Cadog*, 9; critical ed., and ET by A. W. Wade-Evans, *Vitae Sanctorum Britanniae*, Cardiff, 1944, pp. 45–7.

24 Francis de Sales, *Introduction to Devout Life*, part I, 2–3.

25 a. John Chrysostom, *Homily 2 'In Praise of St Paul'*; PG 50, cols 477–80; ET by ICEL.

b. Augustine, *Sermon* 278, 1–2, 5; PL 38, cols 1268–70.

26 a. John Chrysostom, *Homily* 1 *on the Second Letter to Timothy*, 1–2 (abridged); PG 11, cols. 600–1.

b. Eusebius, *Ecclesiastical History*, 3, 4; PG 20, cols 219–220.

28 Thomas Aquinas, *Summa Theologiae*, foreword, part I, i, 8.

30 *The Letters, Speeches and Proclamations of King Charles I*, ed. Charles Petrie, London, 1935, pp.263–73.

31 Gregory the Great, *Homily 17 'On the Gospels'*, 4–5; PL 76, cols 1140–1.

31 Owen Chadwick, *Mackenzie's Grave*, London, 1959, pp.36–7.

31 John Bosco, *Letter* 4, 201–5; ET based on G. Bonetti, *Saint John Bosco's Early Apostolate*, London, 1934.

FEBRUARY

1 a. Cogitosus, *The Life of Saint Brigid*; PL 72, cols 775, 782–3.
b. 'Ultán's Hymn,' The Brigid Tradition; ET by Oliver Davies, *Celtic Spirituality*, New York & Mahwah, New Jersey, 1999, p.121.
Note: This hymn may be a composition of the seventh century and thus be one of the oldest hymns in the Irish language.

2 a. Sophronius, *Sermon 3 'On the Presentation of Christ in the Temple'*, 6–7; PG 87, 3 cols 3291–3.
b. Ephrem of Syria, *Hymns 'On the Nativity'*, 6: 12–16; ET by Kathleen E. McVey, *Ephrem the Syrian*, New York & Mahwah, New Jersey, 1989, pp.112–3.
c. Guerric of Igny, Sermon 1 'On the Presentation of Christ in the Temple', 2, 3, 5; PL 185, cols 64–7.

3 John Cassian, *Conferences*, I, 18; ET by Colm Luibheid, *John Cassian Conferences*, New York & Mahwah, New Jersey, 1985, p.52.

3 Rimbert, *The Life of Saint Anskar*; text in *Scriptores Rerum Germanicarum*, ed. G. Waitz, Hanover, 1884; ET based on that by Charles H. Robinson, *Anskar: Apostle of the North 801–865*, London, 1921.

3 Cyprian, *On the Unity of the Church*, 5; CCSL 3, p.252.

4 a. *The Book of Saint Gilbert*, 17; ET by Raymond Foreville & Gillian Keir, Oxford, 1987, p.49.
b. *Letter* 13; ET by Foreville & Keir, *op. cit.*, pp.165–7.
Note: This letter is variously dated between 1176–8 and 1186–9.

4 Mandy Goedhals, 'Imperialism, mission and conversion: Manche Masemola of Sekhukhuneland', *The Terrible Alternative: Christian Martyrdom in the Twentieth Century*, ed. Andrew Chandler, London & New York, 1998, pp.28, 41–2.

6 a. Luis Froes, *Historia XXVI Crucifixorum in Japon*, 14; *Acta Sanctorum: Februarium* I, col 769; ET by ICEL
Note: There are several contemporary (or near contemporary) accounts of the martyrs of Japan. The most important (quoted here) is that by Luis Froes, a Jesuit, who witnessed the events he recorded, and supplies us with the names of those who died.
b. Lactantius, *The Epitome of the Divine Institutes*, 54–5; PL 6, cols 1061–2.

9 Rhigyfarch the Wise, *The Life of Saint David*; critical ed. by J. W. James, *Rhigyfarch's Life of Saint David*, Cardiff, 1967; ET Oliver Davies, *Celtic Spirituality*, New York & Mahwah, New Jersey, 1999, pp.205–7.

10 Gregory the Great, *Dialogues*, II, 33 & 34; ed. U. Moricca, Rome, 1924; ET by O. Zimmermann and Benedict Avery, Collegeville, Minnesota, 1981.
Note: In the ancient world, it was commonly believed that at death, a person's soul left their body in the form of a bird. See lso the death of Polycarp (23 February).

14 *The Life of Constantine*, 18; ET by ICEL.
Note: Constantine adopted the name Cyril upon taking monastic vows on his deathbed. He was a deacon; it is uncertain if he was ever ordained priest. Methodius, however, was certainly a monk before he went to Moravia, and probably also a deacon. He was consecrated bishop by Pope Hadrian II in 870. For further background, see J. M. Hussey, *The Orthodox Church in the Byzantine Empire*, Oxford, 1986, pp.90–101.

14 a. Cyprian, *Letter* 58, 8–9, 11; CSEL 3, ii, pp.663–6.
b. George Herbert, 'Love', first published in 1633 in *The Temple: Sacred Poems and Private Ejaculations*.

15 *The Life of Saint Sigfrid*; ET by Sr Marianne Sodorstrom.
Note: This *Life* (also known as the 'Vaxjo Legend' is from the mid-thirteenth century. The official chronicler of the diocese of Hamburg-Bremen, Master Adam, who wrote his account between 1066

and 1075 (*Gesta Hammaburgensis Ecclesiae Pontificium*) states that St Sigfrid came to Scandinavia with King Olav of Norway, and that the first bishop in Sweden was Turgot who had been sent from Hamburg-Bremen; that it was this man and not Sigfrid who baptized King Olof Skotkonung, and that Turgot died of leprosy. These alternative accounts and chronologies reflect a certain rivalry between two jurisdictions: that of the English missionary bishops, and that of Hamburg-Bremen with its Carolingian claims of superiority. What is undisputed is that the English Church sent several missionary bishops to Sweden at this time, notably Saint Eskil (who was martyred) and Saint David.

15 Thomas Bray, *Apostolick Charity, its Nature and Excellence Consider'd in a Discourse upon Daniel 12:3*; London, 1698, pp.19–20, 25–7.
Note: This sermon was preached at the ordination of clergy to be sent to work in the colonies.

17 Bede, *A History of the English Church and People,* III, 17, 25; BEH pp.264, 294.

17 Margaret Ford, *Janani*, London, 1978, p.75.

18 Bede, *A History of the English Church and People*, III, 25–6; IV, 4; BEH pp.294–308, 346.

18 a. John of Damascus, *On the Incarnation and the Holy Icons*, I, 16; PG 94, col. 1245.
b. Rowan Williams, *Ponder these things*, Norwich, 2002, pp.3–4.

20 Homily of Pope Paul VI, 18 October 1964.

23 *The Martyrdom of Polycarp*, 9–10, 13–16, 18–19; *Apostolic Fathers* II, Loeb 25, pp.307–46.
Note: In the ancient world, it was commonly believed that at death, a person's soul left their body in the form of a bird. See also the death of Scholastica (10 February).

27 a. George Herbert, *The Country Parson*, VI; *The Works of George Herbert*, ed. F. E. Hutchinson, Oxford, 1941, p.231; spelling modernized.
b. George Herbert, 'Aaron', first published in 1633 in *The Temple: Sacred Poems and Private Ejaculations*.

MARCH

1 a. Rhigyfarch the Wise, *The Life of Saint David*, 1, 56, 63, 65; critical ed. J. W. James, *Rhigyfarch's Life of Saint David*, Cardiff, 1967; ET Oliver Davies, *Celtic Spirituality*, New York & Mahwah, New Jersey, 1999, pp.191, 210–11.
b. ET by Athelstan Riley, *Saint David in the Liturgy*, ed. Silas M. Harris, Cardiff, 1940, p.76.

2 Bede, *A History of the English Church and People*, III, 28; IV, 2 & 3; BEH pp.316, 334–6.

4 Lactantius, *The Epitome of the Divine Institutes*, 66; PL 6, cols.

5 Rhigyfarch the Wise, *The Life of Saint David*; critical ed. by J. W. James, *Rhigyfarch's Life of Saint David*, Cardiff, 1967; ET Oliver Daviess, *Celtic Spirituality*, New York & Mahwah, New Jersey, 1999, p.193–4.
Note: King Sant, also known as Sanctus; Non, also known as Nonita.

5 'The Duties of a Spiritual Director', 1–9, 21–2; *The Rule of Carthage*; ET Uinseann O Maidin, *The Celtic Monk: Rules and Writings of Early Irish Monks*, Kalamazoo, Michigan, 1996, pp.65–7.

6 *Carmina Gadelica*, I, no:52; ET by Alexander Carmichael, 2nd ed. Edinburgh, 1928.

7 *The Martyrdom of Saint Perpetua and Saint Felicity*, 1, 18–21 (abridged).
Note: The account of the death of the martyrs in the amphitheatre of Carthage consists of an introduction, Perpetua's own narration of their imprisonment and her dreams, and the continuation of the story of their deaths by another writer. Although anonymous, it is possible that this may have been written by Tertullian.

8 Bede, *A History of the English Church and People*, II, 15; BEH, p.190.

8 Caesarius of Arles, *Sermon* 159; CCSL 104, pp.650–2.

8 Edward King, *The Love and Wisdom of God*, ed. B. W. Randolph, London, 1910, pp.277–83 (abridged).
Note: Edward King loved to preach on this text, Psalm 18.35; *cf.* 2 Samuel 22:36; preferring the Authorized Version translation of the text.

8 Geoffrey Studdert Kennedy, *The Hardest Part*, London, 1918, pp.189–201 (abridged).

10 'All alone in my little cell,' Irish Poems, 5; ET by Oliver Davies, *Celtic Spirituality*, New York & Mahwah, New Jersey, 1999, pp.260–1.

16 Gregory the Great, *Pastoral Care*, I, 1–2; II, 1, 3; PL 77, cols 14–15; 25–28.

17 Patrick, *Confession*, 1, 34, 37, 38; critical edition by Bieler, *Libri Epistolarum Sancti Patricii Episcopi*, part 1, Dublin, 1952.

18 Cyril of Jerusalem, *Catechetical Lecture* XVIII, 23–6 (abridged); PG 33, cols 1044–8.

19 Bernadine of Siena, *Second Sermon on Saint Joseph*; *Opera S.Bernardini*, VII, 1627–30.

20 Bede, *The Life of Cuthbert*, 16, 17, 21; ET by J. F. Webb, *Lives of the Saints*, London, 1965, pp.92–4, 105.

21 Gregory the Great, *Dialogues*, II, 35, 37; ed. Moricca, Rome, 1924; ET by O. Zimmermann and Benedict Avery, Collegeville, Minnesota, 1981, pp.71–6.
Note: See also below note under 11 July.

21 a. *The First Prayer Book of King Edward VI*, 1549, Preface.
b. Thomas Cranmer, *A Defence of the True and Catholic Doctrine of the Sacrament of the Body and Blood of our Saviour Christ*, 1551, I, 10, 12; *The Remains of Thomas Cranmer*, Oxford, 1833, vol. 2, pp.300–2.

21 Glanmor Williams, *The Welsh and their Religion*, Cardiff, 1991, pp.132, 135–6.

24 'An Old Irish Homily', dated around the ninth century; ET by Oliver Davies, *Celtic Spirituality*, New York & Mahwah, New Jersey, 1999, p.368.

24 Walter Hilton, *The Scale of Perfection*, II, 40; translated from the Middle English by John Clark & Rosemary Dorward, New York & Mahwah, New Jersey, 1991, pp.280–1.

24 Paul Couturier, *Œcuménisme Spirituel*, ed. M. Villain, Tournai, 1963; ET *Ecumenical Testament.*

24 Oscar Romero, 'The Political Dimension of the Faith from the Perspective of the Option for the Poor', in Oscar Romero, *The Voice of the Voiceless: The Four Pastoral Letters and Other Statements*, ET by Michael J. Walsh, Maryknoll, New York, 1985, p.177.

25 a. Cyril of Alexandria, 'Sermon at the Council of Ephesus 431', *Homily 4*; PG 77, col. 991.
Note: Cyril uses the title *Theotokos* of Mary, literally 'Bearer of God'. In the Latin West this was rendered *Mater Dei*, 'Mother of God'. At the Council this title was formally endorsed as being appropriate for the mother of Jesus Christ, thereby underscoring the reality of the Incarnation.
b. Mark Frank, Sermon 30; LACT, *Sermons by Dr Mark Frank*, Oxford, 1849; vol. 2, pp.34–5, 48–50 (abridged).
c. 'Madonna' by Margaret Saunders – an unpublished poem.

26 Valerie Bonham, *A Joyous Service*, Windsor, 1989, pp.1, 8–10; see also A. M. Allchin, *The Silent Rebellion*, London, 1958, chapter 4.

28 Alexander Scroggie, 'A Funeral Sermon delivered upon the occasion of the death of Dr Patrick Forbes', *The Funeral Sermons, Orations, Epitaphs, and other Pieces on the death of the Right Reverend Patrick Forbes, Bishop of Aberdeen, 1635*; reprinted Edinburgh, 1845, pp.87–9 (abridged).

29 *The Life of Saint Cadog*, preface, 53–4; critical ed., and ET by A. W. Wade–Evans, *Vitae Sanctorum Britanniae*, Cardiff, 1944, pp.123–4.

31 a. *The Sermons of John Donne*, ed. George R. Potter & Evelyn Simpson (10 vols), Berkeley & Cambridge, 1957, vol. 3, sermon 3, pp.110–12.
b. John Donne, *Poems*, 1633.

APRIL

1 Ambrose, *Letter* 2, 1–2, 4–5, 7; PL 16, cols 879, 881.

1 F. D. Maurice, *Sermons 'On the Lord's Prayer'*, I, 2–4; London, 1880, pp.286–92 (abridged).

7 'Glorious Lord', *Celtic Spirituality*, ed. and ET Oliver Davies, New York & Mahwah, New Jersey, 1999, p.267.

8 Griffith Jones, *Selections from Welsh Piety*, ed. W. Moses Williams, Cardiff, 1938, pp.70–1; LRW, p.269.

9 a. Dietrich Bonhoeffer, *Letters and Papers from Prison*, ed. Eberhard Bethge, 2nd ed., London, 1971, p.369.

b. Bonhoeffer, *op. cit.*, p.347–8.

9 Dietrich Bonhoeffer, *The Cost of Discipleship*; ET by R. H. Fuller, London, 1959, p.223.

10 a. William Law, *A Serious Call to a Devout and Holy Life*, 1.

b. William Law, *The Spirit of Love*, I.

10 G. Lecher, *John Wyclif and his English Precursors*, ET by P. Lorimer, London, 1884, pp.43–7 (abridged).

11 George Augustus Selwyn, *Four Sermons on the Work of Christ in the World*, IV; G. H. Curteis, *Bishop Selwyn of New Zealand and Lichfield*, 3rd ed., London, 1889, pp.150–2.

12 William Forbes, '*Considerationes Modestae* (…On Justification)', in *The Works of William Forbes*, ed. G. H. Fsssorbes, Oxford, LACT, vol. I, 1850, p.17.

15 Rhigyfarch the Wise, *The Life of Saint David*; critical ed. by J. W. James, *Rhigyfarch's Life of Saint David*, Cardiff, 1967; ET Oliver Davies, *Celtic Spirituality*, New York & Mahwah, New Jersey, 1999, pp.205–7.

16 a. *The Life of Saint Magnus*, 12, 15; ET based on W. M. Metcalfe, *Pinkerton's Lives of the Scottish Saints*, Paisley, 1895 (reprinted 1998), vol. 2, pp.336–8.

b. *The Life of Saint Magnus*, 25–27; *op. cit.*, pp.347–51.

16 a. Isabella Gilmore, *Reports from the Rochester Deaconess Institution.*

b. Isabella Gilmore, from a letter dated 1894; all extracts compiled by Janet M. Vout.

17 Augustine, *Sermon* 273, 1; PL 38.

17 *Little Exordium*, 17.

Note: The *fistula* was a metal tube through which the laity occasionally received from the chalice at the Eucharist during the Middle Ages.

18 'The Duties of a Monk', 1–19; *The Rule of Carthage*; ET Uinseann O Maidin, *The Celtic Monk: Rules and Writings of Early Irish Monks*, Kalamazoo, Michigan, 1996, pp.679.

19 *Anglo–Saxon Chronicle*, 1011–1012; *English Historical Documents* vol. 1 (*c.*500–1042), ed. Dorothy Whitelock, 2nd ed., London, 1979, pp.244–5.

Note: Alphege's body was translated from London to Canterbury in 1023.

19 *The Life of Saint Beuno*; ET Oliver Davies, *Celtic Spirituality*, New York & Mahwah, New Jersey, 1999, pp.214, 219–20.

Note: *The Life of Saint Beuno* was written in Middle Welsh sometime during the twelfth century, and was probably based on a Latin life of the saint which has not survived.

20 'The path I walk,'Celtic Devotional Texts, 8; ET by Oliver Davies, *Celtic Spirituality*, New York & Mahwah, New Jersey, 1999, pp.300–1.

Note: From the fifteenth century this poem is regularly attributed to Columcille

21 Anselm, *Proslogion*, 14, 16, 26 (abridged); ET by Benedicta Ward SLG, *The Prayers and Meditations of Saint Anselm*, London, 1973, pp.255–8, 266–7.

23 a. Peter Damian, *Sermon 13 'On St George'*; PL 144, cols 567–8.

b. Ambrose, *Exposition of Psalm 118*, 20, 47–50; CSEL 62.

24 a. Bede, *A History of the English Church and People*, II, 3; BEH p.142.

b. Bede, *op. cit.*, I, 30

24 Richard Anthony Carter, *In Search of the Lost: The death and life of seven peacemakers of the Melanesian Brotherhood*, Norwich, 2006, pp.240-1

25 Irenaeus, *Against the Heresies*, I, 10, 1–2; SC 100; ET based on those by John Keble, London 1872, and Dominic Unger, ACW 55, New York & Mahwah, New Jersey, 1992.

26 Albert Laurie, *The Vision of God*, Edinburgh, 1939, p.107.

27 Muirchú, *The Life of Patrick*, 2, 7–8; ET by Thomas O'Loughlin, *Celtic Spirituality*, ed. Oliver Davies, New York & Mahwah, New Jersey, 1999, pp.115–6.

27 *The Complete Poems of Christina Rossetti*, ed. R. W. Crump, Louisiana, 1979.

28 Stephen Neill, *A History of Christian Missions*, London, 2nd ed., 1986, pp.353–4; last two paragraphs, Donald Attwater, *The Penguin Dictionary of Saints*, London, 1965, pp.277–8.

29 Catherine of Siena, *The Dialogue*, 167; ET by Suzanne Noffke OP, New York & Mahwah, New Jersey, 1980, pp.364–5.

30 Richard Symonds, *Far Above Rubies: The Women Uncommemorated by the Church of England*, Leominster, 1993, pp.45–7, 52, 65–7 (abridged).

MAY

1 John Chrysostom, *Homilies on the First Letter to the Corinthians*, 3, 4; PG 61, cols 34–6.

2 Athanasius, *On the Incarnation of the Word*, 8–9; PG 25, cols 80–3.

3 Henry Vaughan, 'The Night' (verses 3–7); 'Peace'.

4 'The Reconciliation of Memories', *Their Lord and Ours: Approaches to Authority, Community and the Unity of the Church*, ed. Mark Santer, London, 1982, pp.149– 60 (abridged).

5 Jocelyn of Furness, *The Life of Saint Kentigern*, 31; ET based on W. M. Metcalfe, *Pinkerton's Lives of the Scottish Saints*, Paisley, 1895 (reprinted 1998), vol. 2, pp.246–7.

8 Julian of Norwich, *Revelations of Divine Love*, 86; ET by Clifton Walters, London, 1966, pp.211–12.

10 *The Rule of Comghall*, 1–10; ET Uinseann O Maidin, *The Celtic Monk: Rules and Writings of Early Irish Monks*, Kalamazoo, Michigan, 1996, pp.31–2.

11 a. John of Salerno, *The Life of Saint Odo of Cluny*, II, 4, 19, 23; ET by Gerard Sitwell, *Saint Odo of Cluny*, London, 1958.

b. Raffaelo Morghen, 'Monastic Reform and Cluniac Spirituality', *Cluniac Monasticism in the Central Middle Ages*, ed. N. Hunt, London, 1971, pp.12– 13, 15.

Note: The narrator refers to Tobit 4:7 ('Turn not your face away from anyone who is poor, and the face of God will not be turned away from you'.)

12 Gregory Dix, *The Shape of the Liturgy*, London, 1945, p.744

13 Thomas Rattray, *The Ancient Liturgy of the Church of Jerusalem*, London, 1744, p. xi. This study was published posthumously, but its influence was profound in shaping the liturgy of the Scottish Episcopal Church of 1764 – see LRW pp.270–1.

14 John Chrysostom, *Homilies on the Acts of the Apostles*, 3, 1–3.

14 'The Saints' Calendar of Adamnán', ET by Oliver Davies; *Celtic Spirituality*, ed. Oliver Davies, New York & Mahwah, New Jersey, 1999, pp.263–4.

Note: 'fosterling' in verse 2 means Christ.

15 David Knowles, *The Sarum Lectures*, 1964.

15 a. Edmwnd Prys's metrical version of Psalm 23, 'Yr Arglwydd yw fy Mugail clau'.

b. Glanmor Williams, *The Welsh and their Religion*, Cardiff, 1991, pp.157–8, 216.

16 *The Voyage of Brendan*, ET by Oliver Davies, *Celtic Spirituality*, ed. Oliver Davies, New York & Mahwah, New Jersey, 1999, pp.155, 157–8, 164–6 (abridged).

Note: This text probably dates from the early tenth century and, along with the *Life of Brendan*, forms an essential source for the tradition about Brendan. The *Voyage* is an account of the saint's journeys across the sea in search of the 'Promised Land of the Saints,' itself a cypher either for the 'Promised Land' of Canaan, or for heaven itself.

16 Richard Symonds, *Far Above Rubies: The Women Uncommemorated by the Church of England*, Leominster, 1993, pp.94, 100, 112–3 (abridged).

19 *The Life of Saint Dunstan*, 11–13, 37; *English Historical Documents* vol. 1 (*c*.500– 1042), ed. Dorothy Whitelock, 2nd ed., London, 1979, pp.898, 902–3.

20 Alcuin, Letter 193; *English Historical Documents* vol. 1 (*c*.500–1042), ed. Dorothy Whitelock, 2nd ed., London, 1979, pp.845–6 (abridged).

21 Socrates Scholasticus, *Ecclesiastical History*, I, 17; ET based on NPNF (2nd series) 2, pp.21–2.

23 Aelred of Rievaulx, *The Mirror of Charity*, I, 7; PL 195, cols 511–12.

24 a. The Journal of John Wesley.

b. Charles Wesley, verses from 'Wrestling Jacob'; full text *The Faber Book of Religious Verse*, ed. Helen Gardner, London, 1972, pp.207–10.

25 a. Bede, *A History of the English Church and People*, conclusion; BEH pp.566, 570.
b. Cuthbert, *Letter on the Death of Bede*; BEH pp.580–6.

25 Bede, *A History of the English Church and People*, V, 18; BEH p.514.

26 Bede, *A History of the English Church and People*, I, 25–7; BEH pp.72–8.

26 John Calvin, *The Institutes of Christian Religion*, 1559; Bk III, 21; ed. John T. McNeill, Philadelphia, 1960, p.920.

27 Philip Neri, Letter to his Niece; A. Capecelatro, *The Life of Saint Philip Neri*, ET by T. A. Pope, London, 1926, pp.345–6 (adapted).

28 *The Life of Saint Melangell*, ET by Oliver Davies, *Celtic Spirituality*, ed. Oliver Davies, New York & Mahwah, New Jersey, 1999, pp.221–2 (abridged).

28 David Knowles, *Saints and Scholars*, Cambridge, 1963, pp.23–7 (abridged).

30 E. Moberly Bell, *Josephine Butler*, London, 1962, pp.70–2, 109, 158.

30 a. The Trial of Joan of Arc; ET of the Orléans manuscript by W. S. Scott, London, 1956; reprinted *The Trial of Joan of Arc*, with introduction by Marina Warner, Evesham, 1996, pp.41, 42, 56, 163.
b. *Occasional Sermons of Ronald A. Knox*, ed. Philip Caraman, London, 1960, pp.58–9.
Note: 'Jeanne la Pucelle' or 'Joan the Maid' seems to have been her nickname. The bishop referred to was Pierre Cauchon, Bishop of Beauvais; the inquisitor was Brother Jean le Maitre.

30 Margaret Sinker, *Into the Great Forest: The Story of Apolo Kivebulaya of Central Africa*, London, 1950, pp.13, 27, 32, 80, 81.

31 a. Bede, *Homily* 1, 4; CCSL 122, pp.25–6, 30; ET by ICEL (adapted).
b. Jeremy Taylor, *The Life of our Blessed Lord and Saviour Jesus Christ*, Part I, sections 1 & 2; *The Works of Bishop Jeremy Taylor*, ed. Charles Eden, London, 847, vol. II, pp.53–9 (abridged).
c. Gerard Manley Hopkins, 'The May Magnificat'.

JUNE

1 Justin, *First Apology*, 2, 6, 11–12; PG 6, cols 329, 336, 337, 341–4.

2 Eusebius, *Ecclesiastical History*, 5, 1; PG 20, cols 416, 425, 432.

3 *The Life of Saint Kevin*; *Vitae Sanctorum Hiberniae*, ed. C. Plummer, 2 vols, Oxford, 1910; ET based on Helen Waddell, *Beasts and Saints*, London, 1934.
Note: Many animal stories, such as this one, are recorded about Saint Kevin. They are probably legendary, but they speak of a close union with nature which is a regular feature in the literature of both the Desert Fathers and Mothers, and early Irish monasticism.

3 Homily of Pope Paul VI, 18 October 1964.

4 *The Life of Saint Petroc*; ET Gilbert H. Doble, *The Saints of Cornwall*, vol. 4, Oxford, 1965, pp.137–8.

4 John XXIII, *Gaudet Mater Ecclesia*; *Acta Apostolicae Sedis* 54, Rome, 1962, pp.814–6; ET *The Pope Speaks*, 8, Rome, 1962, pp.225–7.

5 Boniface, *Letter* 78; *Monumenta Germaniae Historica* III, pp.352–4 (abridged).
Note: The 'wise person' to whom Boniface refers is Julianus Pomerius, *De vita contemplativa*, PL 59, col. 431.

6 'The Duties of a Bishop', 1–9; *The Rule of Carthage*; ET Uinseann O Maidin, *The Celtic Monk: Rules and Writings of Early Irish Monks*, Kalamazoo, Michigan, 1996, p.62

6 Extract from the missionary journal of the Melanesian Mission, written by Dr Charles E. Fox (the only 'white man' to become a Melanesian Brother) six months after Ini Kopuria's death: The Southern Cross Log, January 1946, vol. 52, no:1.

7 *The Penitential of Cummean*, ET by Oliver Davies; *Celtic Spirituality*, ed. Oliver Davies, New York & Mahwah, New Jersey, 1999, p.245.
Note: This is the most comprehensive of the Celtic Penitentials, and makes considerable use of Welsh sources. The conclusion, quoted here, represents a classic statement of the pastoral discretion

that underlines the Celtic Penitential tradition, whereby a confessor or 'soul–friend' is urged to weigh up the individual strengths and weaknesses of a person in spiritual direction.

8 a. *The Prose Works of the Right Reverend Father in God Thomas Ken*, ed. J. T. Round, London, 1938, pp.48–9.
Note: Bishop Ken refers first of all to Francis Turner, Bishop of Ely from 1684; and William Lloyd, Bishop of Norwich from 1690. All three had been deprived of their sees for refusing to swear the oath of allegiance to William and Mary, following the deposition of James II. Turner had just died when Ken wrote the letter.
b. Ken, *op. cit.*, pp.144–6.

9 Adamnán, *The Life of Columba*, Preface II and Book III, 23; ET by Richard Sharpe, *Adamnán's Life of Saint Columba*, London, 1995, pp.105–6, 226–9 (abridged).
Note: *peregrinatio pro Dei amore*– 'choosing to be a pilgrim for Christ'. The language of pilgrimage and exile is Biblical in origin (*cf.* Hebrews 11:13–16), and is a recurrent theme in monastic Celtic literature (e.g. *The Confession of Patrick*). The monk was representative of fallen humanity, a wandering exile for the love of God, seeking his heavenly homeland. *Cf.* also Sharpe, *op. cit.*, p.248.

9 Ephrem of Syria, *Hymns of Faith*, 20:12, 32:1–3; ET by Sebastian Brock, *The Luminous Eye: The Spiritual World Vision of Saint Ephrem the Syrian*, Spencer, Massachusetts, 1985, pp.43–4.

11 Cyril of Alexandria, *Commentary on St John's Gospel*, 12, 1; PG 74, cols 707–10; ET by ICEL.

12 a. John Skinner, *An Exposition of the Song of Solomon*, in *The Theological Works of the late Reverend John Skinner*, vol. II, Aberdeen, 1809, pp.145–6 (abridged).
b. Anthony Mitchell, *Biographical Studies in Scottish Church History*, Milwaukee and London, 1914, pp. 247–50.

14 a. Richard Baxter, *The Reformed Pastor*, 1656, iii; last unabridged edition 1860; abridged edition by Thomas Wood, *Five Pastorals*, London, 1961, pp.240 & 244.
b. Source unknown.

15 a. Evelyn Underhill, *Worship*, London, 1936, pp.3–5 (abridged).
b. Source unknown.

16 Ralf Bocking, *The Life of Saint Richard*, I, 48; ET by Duncan J. Jones, in Sussex Record Society, vol. 79, Lewes, Sussex, 1995, pp.211, 213.
Note: The so-called 'Prayer of Saint Richard of Chichester' goes back at least as far as the thirteenth century, and appears both here in Bocking's *Life* and in a sermon of Odo of Châteauroux. The second part of the prayer was composed in the early twentieth century.

16 Joseph Butler, *The Analogy of Religion*, 1736; conclusion to part 2.

17 a. Quotations drawn from Henrietta Barnett, *Canon Barnett: His Life, Work and Friends*, London, 1919; and Samuel Barnett, *Worship and Work*, Letchworth, 1913.
b. Quotations drawn from above sources, and William Beveridge, *Power and Influence*, London, 1953. The quotation of C. R. Ashbee is used by permission of his daughter Felicity Ashbee. All material was collated and introduced by Lorraine Blair.

18 Jean Farrant, *Mashonaland Martyr: Bernard Mizeki and the Pioneer Church*, Oxford & Johannesburg, 1966, pp.107–20 (abridged).

19 Friedrich Heiler, *The Gospel of Sadhu Sundar Singh*, ET by Olive Wyn, London, 1927, pp.132–3.

20 Bede, *A History of the English Church and People*, I, 6–7; BEH pp.28–34.

20 Columbanus, *Instructions* 1, 3–5; *Sancti Columbani Opera (Scriptores Latin Hiberniae)*, Dublin, 1957, pp.62–6; ET by ICEL.

22 Bede, *A History of the English Church and People*, I, 6–7; BEH pp.28–34.

23 Bede, *A History of the English Church and People*, IV, 19; BEH pp.392, 396.

24 a. Augustine, *Sermon* 293, 1–3; PL 38, cols 1327–28.
b. Rabanus Maurus, *Homilies on Feasts* 26; PL 110, cols 51–2.
c. Metropolitan Anthony of Sourozh (Anthony Bloom), *God and Man*, London, 1971.

25 'An Old Irish Homily', dated around the ninth century; ET by Oliver Davies, *Celtic Spirituality*, New York & Mahwah, New Jersey, 1999, pp.366–7.

26 Robert Leighton, 'Exposition of the Lord's Prayer' in *The Whole Works of Robert Leighton*, vol.V, London, 1870, p.305.

27 Cyril of Alexandria, *Commentary on St John's Gospel*, 5, 2; PG 73, cols 751–4; ET by ICEL.

27 Katherine Walsh, *A Fourteenth Century Scholar and Primate: Richard FitzRalph in Oxford, Avignon and Armagh*, Oxford, 1981, pp.182–4.

27 Alexander Jolly, *The Christian Sacrifice in the Eucharist*, Aberdeen, 1831, p.195; LRW pp.344–5.

28 Irenaeus, *Against the Heresies*, IV, 20, 5–6; SC 100; ET based on those by John Keble, London 1872, and Dominic Unger, ACW 55, New York & Mahwah, New Jersey, 1992.

29 a. Augustine, *Sermon* 295, 1–8 (abridged); PL 38, cols 1348–52.
b. Leo the Great, *Sermon 12 'On the Lord's Passion'*, 2–3, 6–7; PL 54, cols 355–7; ET based on NPNF vol. XII, pp.176–7.

30 a. Eusebius, *Ecclesiastical History*, 2, 25; PG 20, cols 210–11.
b. Lactantius, *The Epitome of the Divine Institutes*, 54–5; PL 6, cols 1061–2.

JULY

1 'The Guardian Angel', translated by Alexander Carmichael, *Carmina Gadelica: Hymns and Incantations*, 2 vols., Edinburgh, 1900.

1 John Cassian, *Conferences*, IX, 1–2; ET by Colm Luibheid, *John Cassian Conferences*, New York & Mahwah, New Jersey, 1985, pp.101–2.

1 a. *Proceedings*, vol. I, p.424; as quoted by Michael Hennell, *John Venn and the Clapham Sect*, London, 1958, p.245.
b. Wilbert R. Shenk, *Henry Venn: Missionary and Statesman*, New York, 1983, pp.30–3 (abridged).

3 Gregory the Great, *Homily 26 'On the Gospels'*, 7–9; PL 76, cols 1201–2.

4 Glanmor Williams, *The Welsh and their Religion*, Cardiff, 1991, pp.1–3.

6 Augustine, *Concerning Heresies*, 88;

6 Sulpicius Severus, *Letter* 2, 1–2; ET based on NPNF (2nd series) 11, Oxford, 1895, p.58.
Note: The authorship of this letter has been questioned.

6 a. Thomas More, Letter 61 'To Mistress Roper'; *Saint Thomas More: Selected Letters*; ed. Elizabeth Frances Rogers, New Haven, 1961, pp.241–2.
b. John Fisher, *The Ways to Perfect Religion*, preface, 6; *The English Works of John Fisher*, ed. John E. B. Mayor, London, 1876, pp.364, 376–7.

8 Augustine, *Sermon* 273, 1; PL 38.

11 Benedict, *Rule*, prologue.
Note: In The Book of Common Prayer The Feast of Saint Benedict is observed on 21 March, the day of his death. This date continues to be observed by monastic communities, but in the wider Church, in part because this date invariably falls in Lent, and in part to honour Benedict as patron of Europe, it has become customary to observe his feast on 11 July.

12 John Cassian, *Conferences*, XVIII, 2–3; ET by Colm Luibheid, *John Cassian Conferences*, New York & Mahwah, New Jersey, 1985, pp.184–5.

14 a. John Keble, *The Assize Sermon* 'On National Apostasy', 14 July 1833, (abridged).
b. John Keble, *Sermons, Occasional and Parochial*, Oxford & London, 1868, pp.262–5 (abridged).

15 Caesarius of Arles, *Sermon* 232; CCSL 104, pp. 919–21.
Note: In the past this has sometimes been listed as a sermon of Augustine ('On the anniversary of Saint Augustine's ordination' *Sermon* 340), but more generally now it is reckoned to be a sermon of Caesarius.

15 Bonaventure, *The Soul's Journey into God*, VII, 1, 2, 4–6; English paraphrase based on ICEL and CWS.

16 Gregory the Great, *Homily 14 'On the Gospels'*, 2–3; PL 76, col. 1128.

18 a. Elizabeth Ferard, *Of the Deaconess Office in General*, 1, 2, 7; from a manuscript notebook written in Elizabeth's best handwriting, and dated 1861.
b. From the manuscript notebook of the Community's chaplain (undated).

Note: The nineteenth–century restoration of the diaconate for women began at Kaiserwerth in Germany in 1831. Founded by Pastor Fliedner and his wife, the institution for training deaconesses trained women for ministry among the sick and poor in the parish, and the teaching and nursing of young children. In 1855, the year before Elizabeth Ferard, Bishop Tait of London had visited Kaiserwerth; and in 1851 Florence Nightingale had trained there for several months. In her diary for 10 November 1858, Elizabeth records how she heard again 'of the continual spreading of the Deaconess work in every direction except in England, and more than ever wished we could have something of the kind in England where the materials for it are so abundant could we but found a Deaconess House on the right principles'.Extracts and background researched by Sr Teresa CSA.

18 Metropolitan Anastassy, *The holy new martyr: Grand Duchess Elizabeth Feodorovna, Orthodox Life*, vol. 31, no. 5, 1981, pp.3–14.

19 a. Gregory of Nyssa, *Homily 6 'On the Beatitudes'*.

b. Gregory of Nyssa, *The Life of Macrina*, 7–10 (abridged); for full text see Virginia Woods Callahan, *Ascetical Works*, Washington DC, 1967, pp.163–91.

Note: Macrina was the oldest of ten children. Gregory tells the story of her life and death (at which he was present). He revered her as the holiest and strongest member of their family. The eight years Gregory refers to is the time he spent in exile having been deposed from his see by the strong Arian faction in the diocese. In 378, following the death of the Emperor Valens, who had supported Arianism, Gregory was allowed to return to Nyssa, and was immediately hailed as a champion of othodoxy.

20 Leo the Great, *Sermon* 97, 2–4; PL 54, cols 458–60.

20 Gustavo Gutiérrez, *Las Casas: In Search of the Poor of Jesus Christ*; ET by Robert R. Barr, Maryknoll, New York, 1993, pp.62–3.

21 a. *A Brief Account of the Life of Howell Harris*, Trefeca, 1791, p.13.

b. Howell Harris, 'Rest not'; *Celtic Christian Spirituality*, ed. Oliver Davies and Fiona Bowie London, 1995, p.86.

22 a. Gregory the Great, *Homily 25 'On the Gospels'*, 1–5; PL 76, cols 1189–93. Note: In his portrayal of Mary Magdalene, Gregory conflates three separate figures: the sinful woman of Luke 7:36–50; the woman who anointed Jesus in Matthew 26:7 & Mark 14:3, who is called 'Mary' in John 12:3; and Mary Magdalene herself.

b. Janet Morley, *All Desires Known*, London, 1992, p.104.

23 Hippolytus (?), *On the Consummation of the World*, 41–3; PG 10, cols 944–5.

23 Bridget of Sweden: *Revelations*, VI, 86; VI, 47; ET by Sr Marianne Sodorstrom.

24 John Chrysostom, *Homilies on St Matthew's Gospel*, 65, 2–4; PG 58, cols 619–22.

26 John of Damascus, *Oration 6 'On the Nativity of the Blessed Virgin Mary'*, 2, 4, 5, 6; PG 96, cols 663, 667, 670; ET by ICEL.

27 B. F. Westcott, *Christus Consummator*, London, 1886, pp.58–9.

27 Ninian Comper, 'Of the atmosphere of a church', Edinburgh, 1936.

28 *The Life of Saint Petroc*; ET Gilbert H. Doble, *The Saints of Cornwall*, vol. 4, Oxford, 1965, pp.139–40.

29 a. Augustine, *Sermon* 103, 1–2; PL 38, cols 613–15.

b. Aelred, *Spiritual Friendship*, I, 45, 69–70; ET by Mary Eugenia Laker SSND, Spencer, Massachusetts, 1977, pp.60–1, 65–6.

30 John Chrysostom, *Homily 20 'On the Acts of the Apostles'*, 3–4; PG 60, cols 162–4.

30 a. William Wilberforce, Speech to the House of Commons, May 1789.

b. Olaudah Equiano, *The Interesting Narrative of the life of Olaudah Equiano, or Gustavus Vassa, the African, Written by Himself*, London, 1789, pp. 146-8, 252-3.

c. Thomas Clarkson, *History of the Rise, Progress and Accomplishment of the Abolition of the African Slave-Trade by the British Parliament*, new ed., London, 1839, p.46.

29 As quoted by Garth Lean, *God's Politician: William Wilberforce's Struggle*, London, 1980, pp.48–50.

31 Basil the Great, *On the Holy Spirit*, 15, 35; PG 32, cols 127–30; ET by ICEL.

31 a. Ignatius of Loyola, *The Spiritual Exercises*, 23; ET by Joseph Munitiz & Philip Endean, London, 1996, p.289.

b. *Reminiscences* or *The Life of Ignatius of Loyola*, I, 4–8; ET by Munitiz & Endean, *op. cit.*, pp.14–15.

AUGUST

3 Bede, *A History of the English Church and People*, I, 17, 21; BEH pp.54–6, 64.

4 Jean–Baptiste Vianney, *Catechetical Instructions*; *Sermons* (4 vols), Lyons, 1883.

5 Bede, *A History of the English Church and People*, III, 2 & 6; BEH pp.214–16, 230.

6 a. Anastasius of Sinai, *Conferences*, 6–10; ET by ICEL.

b. Pseudo–Macarius, *Spiritual Homilies*, Alphabetical Collection 'H', 1, 2; *Coptic Apophthegms*, Paris, 1894.

c. A. M. Ramsey, *Be Still and Know*, London, 1982, pp.64–5, 70.

7 Bede, *A History of the English Church and People*, IV, 27–8; BEH p.432.

7 a. John Mason Neale, *Sermon* 111; J. M. Neale, *Sermons* (3 vols), London, 1875; vol. 2, pp.340–1. Note: No year is given for the date of this sermon.

b. John Mason Neale, 'English Hymnology: Its History and Prospects', in *The Christian Remembrancer*, 18, (July–December 1849), pp.303–4.

8 The reading represents a compilation of testimonies from various followers of Dominic which were submitted during hearings for his canonization process in 1233: *Acta canonisationis Sancti Dominici: Monumenta OP Mist.* 16, Rome, 1935, pp.30, 146–7; ET by ICEL.

9 Adamnán, *The Life of Columba*, Preface II; ET by Richard Sharpe, *Adomnán's Life of Saint Columba*, London, 1995, pp.104–5 (abridged).

9 John Cassian, *Conferences*, I, 2, 4; ET by Colm Luibheid, *John Cassian Conferences*, New York & Mahwah, New Jersey, 1985, pp.37–9.

9 Augustine Baker, *Holy Wisdom*, III, 1, 1–5, 7; ed. 1948, London, pp.341–3.

9 Mary Porter, *Mary Sumner: Her Life and Work*, Winchester, 1921, pp.29–31.

9 a. Hilda C. Graef, *The Scholar and the Cross: The Life and Work of Edith Stein*,London & New York, 1955, pp.227, 229–30.

b. *The Writings of Edith Stein*, London, 1956, p.92.

10 Leo the Great, *Sermon* 85, 1–4; PL 54, cols 435–7; ET based on NPNF (2nd series) 12, Oxford, 1895, pp.197–8.

11 *The Fourth Letter of Clare to Blessed Agnes of Prague*, 4–33; ET by R. J. Armstrong & Ignatius Brady, *Francis and Clare: The Complete Works*, New York & Mahwah, New Jersey, 1982, pp.203–5.

11 John Henry Newman, *Sermons Plain and Parochial*, in 8 vols, London, 1894; vol. 1, sermon 6 'The Spiritual Mind'; pp.72–4, 82.

12 Patrick, *Confession*, 1, 40–1; critical edition by Bieler, *Libri Epistolarum Sancti Patricii Episcopi*, part 1, Dublin, 1952.

12 *The Rule of Comghall*, 1–10; ET Uinseann O Maidin, *The Celtic Monk: Rules and Writings of Early Irish Monks*, Kalamazoo, Michigan, 1996, pp.31–2.

12 Ann Griffiths, verses selected and translated by A. M. Allchin, *Ann Griffiths: The Furnace and the Fountain*, Cardiff, 1987, pp.25–30.

13 Jeremy Taylor, *Holy Living*, 1650, preface.

13 A. M. Allchin, *The Silent Rebellion*, London, 1958, pp.114–5.

13 Octavia Hill, *Homes of the London Poor*, 2nd ed., London, 1883; reprinted 1970; pp.17–19, 89–90, 95 (abridged).

14 Gregory the Great, *Pastoral Care*, IV; PL 77, cols 125–6.

14 a. Pope John Paul II, *Homily for the Canonization of Maximilian Kolbe*, 10 October 1982.

b. Ulrich Simon, *A Theology of Auschwitz*, London, 1967, pp.9–12 (abridged).

15 a. Julian of Norwich, *Revelations of Divine Love*, 25; ET by Clifton Walters, London, 1966, pp.101–2.
b. Hildegard of Bingen, *A Responsory and Alleluia for the Blessed Virgin Mary*; ET by Robert Carver, *Hildegard of Bingen: An Anthology*, edited by Fiona Bowie & Oliver Davies, London, 1990, pp.116–7.
c. Ivone Gebara & Maria Clara Bingemer, *Mary, Mother of God, Mother of the Poor*, ET by Phillip Berryman, London & New York, 1989, pp.119–21 (abridged).
16 John Wolfe Lydekker, *The Life and Letters of Charles Inglis*, London, 1936, pp.240–5.
20 Bernard of Clairvaux, *On the Love of God*, 6–7; PL 182, cols 983–5; ET based on that by 'A Religious CSMV', London & Oxford, 1950.
20 William Booth, *In Darkest England and the Way Out*, London, 1890, pp.277, 280, 285.
23 Augustine, *Commentary on St John's Gospel*, 51, 11–13; CCSL 36, pp.443–445.
25 a. Tertullian, *On Prescription against Heresies*, 20–22, 32; SC 46, pp.112–15, 130.
b. John Henry Newman, *Parochial and Plain Sermons*, II, 27; Oxford, 1873; pp.336–8.
25 Bede, *A History of the English Church and People*, IV, 25; (abridged); BEH p.424.
27 Augustine, *Confessions*, IX, x–xi; ET by Henry Chadwick, Oxford, 1991, pp.170–4.
28 Augustine, *Confessions*, VII, x, xviii; X, xxvii; ET by Henry Chadwick, Oxford, 1991, pp.123–4, 128, 201.
29 Bede, *Homily* 23; CCSL 122, pp.354, 356–7; ET by ICEL.
30 John Bunyan, *The Pilgrim's Progress*, from the concluding pages.
31 Bede, *A History of the English Church and People*, III, 3, 5, 17; BEH pp.218–220, 226–8, 262–4.

SEPTEMBER

1 *The Sayings of the Desert Fathers*, Agathon 26 & 30; ET by Benedicta Ward SLG, Oxford, 1975, pp.20–1.
2 David Hand, 'The White–Robed Army of Martyrs,' *Papua New Guinea Church Partnership* (abridged); an account written for the centenary celebrations of the Church, London, 1991.
Note: Lucian Tapiedi is one of the ten twentieth–century martyrs whose statues were carved for the west front of Westminster Abbey in 1998.
3 Gregory the Great, *Commentary on Ezekiel*, I, 11, 4–6; PL 76, cols 907–8.
4 Augustine, *Sermon* 256, 1, 3; PL 38, cols 1192–3.
4 Bede, *A History of the English Church and People*, III, 7; BEH p.232.
6 From the diaries of Captain Allen Gardiner, paraphrased by Bishop Patrick Harris.
8 a. Andrew of Crete, O*ration 1 'On the Nativity of the Blessed Virgin Mary'*; PG 97, cols 805–9.
b. *The Festal Menaion*; ET by Mother Mary and Archimandrite Kallistos Ware, London, 1969, pp.105, 107, 119, 125.
Note: For use of term Theotokos see above 25 March.
9 *Litany of Confession*, although attributed to Saint Ciaran, must date from a later period. The first line is Latin, otherwise Irish. ET by Oliver Davies and Fiona Bowie, *Celtic Christian Spirituality*, London, 1995, p.45.
9 Charles Lowder, 'A Reply to the Parishioners and Congregation of St Peter's, 22 June 1878', printed in *The Annual Report of the St George's Mission*, vol. 22, pp.11–17.
Note: A letter of complaint with approximately fifty signatures had been presented to the Bishop of London. In support of their vicar, an address signed by 1680 communicants and parishoners of St Peter's was also presented. The extract printed is part of Lowder's letter of thanksgiving to his parishioners. For further details see L. E. Ellsworth, *Charles Lowder and the Ritualist Movement*, London, 1982, pp.154–7.
10 John Cassian, *Conferences*, XIV, 10–11; ET by Colm Luibheid, *John Cassian Conferences*, New York & Mahwah, New Jersey, 1985, pp.164–5.
10 a. Glanmor Williams, *Wales and the Reformation*, Cardiff, 1997, pp.235–6, 240.
b. Glanmor Williams, *op. cit.* pp.352–3.

11 Rhigyfarch the Wise, *The Life of Saint David*; critical ed. by J. W. James, *Rhigyfarch's Life of Saint David*, Cardiff, 1967; ET Oliver Davies, *Celtic Spirituality*, New York & Mahwah, New Jersey, 1999, pp.207–9 (abridged).

12 *The Rule of Ailbhe*, 7–16; ET Uinseann O Maidin, *The Celtic Monk: Rules and Writings of Early Irish Monks*, Kalamazoo, Michigan, 1996, pp.20–1.

13 John Chrysostom, *Homily before his exile*, 1–3; PG 52, cols 427–30.

14 a. Andrew of Crete, *Oration 10 'On the Exaltation of the Holy Cross'*; PG 97, cols 1018–9, 1022–3; ET by ICEL.

b. Anonymous, *The Dream of the Rood*, vv.27–56, 96–100.

15 Cyprian, *Letter 1 'To Donatus'*, 2–4; PL 4, cols 197–202.

16 a. Bede, *A History of the English Church and People*, III, 4; BEH pp.220–2.
Note: Over the centuries 'White House' became Whithorn.

b. Aelred of Rievaulx, *The Life of St Ninian*, 2, 11; ET based on W. M. Metcalfe, *Pinkerton's Lives of the Scottish Saints*, Paisley, 1895 (reprinted 1998), vol. 1, pp.8–10, 24.

16 a. E. B. Pusey, *Parochial and Cathedral Sermons*, Oxford, 1882; sermon 12 entitled 'Saintliness of Christians', pp.167–70.
Note: No year is given for this but it was preached at Hursley on the Feast of the Annunciation (25 March).

b. E. B. Pusey, *University Sermons*, Oxford, 1879; sermon 6, pp.4, 6–8, 42, 60, 61.
Note: The Vincentius Pusey refers to is Vincent of Lérins (d. before 450) who emphasized the rôle of tradition in guarding against innovations in the doctrine of the Church. He is credited with the so-called 'Vincentian canon' or 'rule of faith' that 'we hold that which has been believed everywhere, always, and by all people' (*quod ubique, quod semper, quod ab omnibus creditum est*).

17 a. Hildegard, *The Book of Life's Merits*, IV, 67; ET by Robert Carver, *Hildegard of Bingen: An Anthology*, edited by Fiona Bowie & Oliver Davies, London, 1990, p.87.

b. Hildegard, *Letter* 85r/a; *The Letters of Hildegard of Bingen*, ET by Joseph L. Baird & Radd K. Ehrman, Oxford & New York, 1994, vol. 1, pp.192–3.

19 Bede, *A History of the English Church and People*, IV, 1–2; BEH pp.328–334.

20 Dietrich Bonhoeffer, *The Cost of Discipleship*; ET by R. H. Fuller, London, 1959, pp.219–220.

20 Margaret Cropper, *Shining Lights: Six Anglican Saints of the Nineteenth Century*, London, 1963, pp.50–67 (abridged).

23 Bede, *Homily* 21; CCSL 122, pp.149–51; ET by ICEL.

23 a. Adamnán, *The Life of Columba*, Preface I; ET by Richard Sharpe, *Adamnán's Life of Saint Columba*, London, 1995, p.103.

b. Bede, *A History of the English Church and People*, V, 15.

25 Benedict, *Rule*, 2 (abridged).

25 John Cassian, *Conferences*, XIV, 10–11; ET by Colm Luibheid, *John Cassian Conferences*, New York & Mahwah, New Jersey, 1985, pp.164–5.

25 a. Lancelot Andrewes, 'A Caution before Preaching after the example of Saint Fulgentius', *Preces Privatae*; originally composed in Greek and Latin, and published posthumously in 1648.

b. Henry Isaacson, *The Life of Bishop Andrewes*, London, 1650; LACT, *The Works of Bishop Andrewes*, ed. James Bliss, 1854, pp. xii–xiii, xxiv–xxvi.

25 *A Treasury of Russian Spirituality*, vol. 2, edited & ET by George P. Fedotov, London, 1950, pp.69–70.

26 Wilson Carlile, 'The Power of Witness', *Boanerges and Others*, Oxford, *c.*1930, pp.32–3.

27 Vincent de Paul, *Letter* 2546; ET based on J. Leonard, *St Vincent de Paul: Selected Letters and Addresses*, London, 1925.

29 a. Gregory the Great, *Homily 34 'On the Gospels'*, 8–9; PL 76, cols 1250–51.

b. Bernard of Clairvaux, *Sermon 1 'For the Feast of St Michael'*, 1–3, 5; PL 183, cols 447–50.
Note: Bernard when quoting from Hebrews 1:14 shares the assumption of his contemporaries that the Apostle Paul was the author of the epistle.

c. *Carmina Gadelica*, I, no:77; ET by Alexander Carmichael, 2nd ed. Edinburgh, 1928.
Note: In the Celtic tradition, the Feast of Michaelmas is of special significance. Michael is patron saint of the sea, of coastal regions, boats and horses. This accounts for the numerous dedications to him around the Celtic coast, such as Mont St Michel in Brittany, and St Michael's Mount in Cornwall. On land, he is often portrayed as riding a milk–white steed, an image also associated with St George. Michael the Archangel is also seen as the one whose duty it is to convey the souls of the departed to paradise. These various ideas are reflected in the imagery of the poem quoted here.

30 Jerome, *Letter* 52, 7–8, 10, 13; CSEL 54, pp.426–35; ET based on NPNF (2nd series) vol. 6, Oxford, 1893, pp.92–5.

OCTOBER

1 Gregory the Enlightener (Illuminator), *The Teaching of Saint Gregory*; adapted freely from ET by Robert W. Thomson, *Harvard Armenian Texts and Studies*, Cambridge, Massachusetts, 1970.

1 Gregory of Tours, *The History of the Franks*, II, 31; ET based on O. M. Dalton, Oxford, 1927.

1 Margaret Cropper, *Shining Lights: Six Anglican Saints of the Nineteenth Century*, London, 1963, pp.3–27 (abridged).

1 Thérèse of Lisieux, *The Story of a Soul*; ET by Ronald Knox, *The Autobiography of a Saint*, London, 1958, pp.198–9, 201 (abridged).

3 Hansard HL. Deb., 9 February 1944

4 a. 'The Earlier Rule of 1209', prologue, 1–2; ET by R. J. .Armstrong & Ignatius Brady, *Francis and Clare: The Complete Works*, New York & Mahwah, New Jersey, 1982, pp.109–11.
b. Francis of Assisi, *The Canticle of Brother Sun.*

6 a. William Tyndale, *Epistle to the Reader*, included in his first published version of the New Testament in 1526; *The Doctrinal Treatises of William Tyndale*, Cambridge, 1848, pp.389–90.
b. William Tyndale, 'Of Antichrist', *The Obedience of a Christian Man*, 1528; *op. cit.*, pp.239–40.

6 Guigo II, *The Ladder of Monks and Twelve Meditations*, meditation 1; ET by Edmund Colledge OSA & James Walsh SJ, London, 1978, pp.104–5.

8 Marion Lochhead, *Episcopal Scotland in the Nineteenth Century*, London, 1966, pp.113, 116–7.

9 Augustine, *Sermon* 273, 1; PL 38, col. 1560.

9 'The Duties of an Abbot of a Community', 1–13; *The Rule of Carthage*; ET Uinseann O Maidin, *The Celtic Monk: Rules and Writings of Early Irish Monks*, Kalamazoo, Michigan, 1996, pp.63–4.

9 Robert Grosseteste, *Memorial to Pope Innocent IV*; in G. Lecher, *John Wyclif and his English Precursors*; ET by P. Lorimer, London, 1884, pp.32–3 (abridged).
Note: Not long before his death, Bishop Grosseteste travelled to Lyons to see the Pope and his *curia*, in order personally to deliver his 'memorial' concerning abuses affecting the life and stability of the Church in England, including the impotence of the bishops to remove corrupt clergy, and certain abuses emanating from Rome itself. His petition succeeded, and his personal integrity was vindicated.

10 Bede, *A History of the English Church and People*, I, 29; II, 9, 12, 14, 16; BEH pp.104, 164, 176, 180–2, 186, 192.

10 Thomas Traherne, *Centuries of Meditation*, III, 1–3.

11 Tertullian, *On Baptism*; ET based on NPNF, series 1, vol. 3, pp.677–9.

11 a. Daphne D. C. Pochin Mould, *The Irish Saints*, Dublin and London, 1964, pp.52–4.
b. 'Christ's Bounty', ET by Brendan Kennelly; *The Celtic Monk: Rules and Writings of Early Irish Monks*, ed. Uinseann O Maidin, Kalamazoo, Michigan, 1996, pp.195–6.

11 Bede, *A History of the English Church and People*, IV, 6, 9; BEH pp.354–6, 360.

11 Bede, *A History of the English Church and People*, II, 16, 20; BEH pp.192, 204–6.

12 John Cassian, *Conferences*, XVIII, 2–; ET by Colm Luibheid, *John Cassian Conferences*, New York & Mahwah, New Jersey, 1985, pp.184–5.

12 Bede, *A History of the English Church and People*, V, 19; BEH pp.516–24, 528.

12 Richard Symonds, *Far Above Rubies: The Women Uncommemorated by the Church of England*, Leominster, 1993, pp.228–31, 236 (abridged).

12 The original letter is kept at the *Institut Cavell*, and is read to the nurses each year on the anniversary of her execution. Transcript: Rowland Ryder, *Edith Cavell*, London, 1975, p.218.

13 a. *The Life of King Edward who rests at Westminster*, attributed to a monk of St Bertin, II, 9, 11; edited and ET by Frank Barlow, 2nd ed., Oxford, 1992, pp.111–13, 123–5.
Note: The date when Edward began to be called 'the Confessor' has not been established; but the intention presumably was to distinguish him from his uncle and namesake, Edward, king and martyr, whose feast day is celebrated on 18 March. The anonymous Life quoted here pre-dates that by Osbert of Clare who used and 'improved' it. It was probably written soon after the Conquest (see Barlow). The text, however, is damaged and incomplete, and in parts has had to be reconstructed with interpolations from the later work of Osbert of Clare.
b. *Occasional Sermons of Ronald A. Knox*, ed. Philip Caraman, London, 1960, pp.26, 28.

14 Patrick Sookhdeo, 'Mission and Conversion in Pakistan: Esther John (Qamar Zia)'; *The Terrible Alternative: Christian Martyrdom in the Twentieth Century*, ed. Andrew Chandler, London & New York, 1998, pp.109–11, 114.

15 a. Teresa of Avila, *The Way of Perfection*, 32; ET by E. Allison Peers, London, 1946, pp.136–8 (abridged).
b. Shirley du Boulay, *Teresa of Avila*, London, 1991, pp.1, 29–35 (abridged).

16 Walahfrid Strabo, *The Life of Saint Gall*, 6; ET by M. Joynt, London 1927, pp.70–2.
Note: There are three early lives of Saint Gall: one dating from the end of the eighth century; one by Wettinus (d. 824); and a third by Walahfrid Strabo (d. 849).

16 a. *The Works of Bishop Ridley*, Cambridge, 1843, pp.355–8.
b. 'The Second Sermon on the Card', *Sermons of Bishop Latimer*, Cambridge, 1844, pp.23–4.

16 Glanmor Williams, *The Welsh and their Religion*, Cardiff, 1991, pp.56–8.

17 Ignatius of Antioch, *The Letter to the Romans*, 1, 2, 4, 6–7; Loeb 24, *Apostolic Fathers I*; ET based on Kirsopp Lake, London, 1912, pp.227–35.

18 Gregory the Great, *Homily 17 'On the Gospels'*, 1–3; PL 76, cols 1139–40.

19 William of Malmesbury, *De Gestis Pontificum Anglorum*, ed. Hamilton, *Rolls Series*, London, 1870, p.315; ET by Benedicta Ward SLG, *The Benedictines in Oxford*, London, 1997, pp.5–6.

19 John Sargent, *The Life and Letters of the Reverend Henry Martyn*, London, 1862; 10th ed. 1885, pp.187, 196–7.

23 Josephus, *Antiquities of the Jews*, XX, 9, 1.

25 Origen, *Exhortation to Martyrdom*, 41–2.

25 Lewis Bayley, *The Practice of Piety*, 1611; London edition of 1820, p.197; LRW, p.139.

26 a. Alfred the Great, *Prose Preface to his translation of Gregory the Great's 'Pastoral Care'*; ET by Simon Keynes & Michael Lapidge, *Alfred the Great*, London, 1983, pp.124–6.
Note: This was probably the earliest of the translations undertaken by the king himself, and may date as early as 890. Gregory the Great was concerned principally with ecclesiastical leadership and government, but his language was equally applicable to holders of secular office; hence the appeal to the king. In the prose preface, King Alfred explains why he has translated the work and it is therefore a cardinal document for understanding his mind.
b. Asser, *The Life of King Alfred*, 1, 8, 22, 24, 25, 76; ET by Keynes & Lapidge, *op. cit.*, pp.67–9, 74–6, 90.

26 Bede, *A History of the English Church and People*, III, 22, 23; BEH pp.280–8.

27 'On the flightiness of thoughts,' Irish Poems, 7; ET by Oliver Davies, *Celtic Spirituality*, New York & Mahwah, New Jersey, 1999, pp.262–3.

28 Origen, *Homilies on Joshua*, 9, 1–2; SC 71, pp. 244–6.

29 a. *The Last Journals of James Hannington*, ed. by E. C. Dawson, London, 1888, pp.213–8 (abridged).
b. Stephen Neill, *A History of Christian Missions*, London, 1964; 2nd ed. 1986, pp.477–8.

31 Martin Luther, *Preface to the first volume of Latin Writings*, 1545; critical edition, Weimar, 1938, vol. 54, pp.185–6; ET by Lewis Spitz, *The Protestant Reformation*, ed. Hans J. Hillerbrand, London, 1968, pp.1–3.

NOVEMBER

1 a. Bernard of Clairvaux, *Sermon* 2; *S. Bernardi Opera*, ed. J. Leclercq and H. Rochais, vol. V, 1968, pp.364–8; ET by ICEL (adapted).
b. Hugh Latimer, 'Articles untruly, falsely, uncharitably imputed to me by Dr Powell of Salisbury', *Sermons and Remains of Bishop Hugh Latimer*, Cambridge, 1844, pp.234–5.
c. Kenneth Kirk, *The Vision of God*, Oxford, 1931, abridged ed. 1934, pp.46–7.
d. Thomas Merton, *New Seeds of Contemplation*, London, 1961, pp.24–6.

2 a. Gregory of Nazianzus, *Oration* 7, 23–4; PG 35, cols 786–7; ET by ICEL.
b. Hugh Latimer, 'Articles untruly, falsely, uncharitably imputed to me by Dr Powell of Salisbury', *Sermons and Remains of Bishop Hugh Latimer*, Cambridge, 1844, pp.236–7.
c. John Donne, *Holy Sonnets: Divine Meditations*, 6.
c. Austin Farrer, *Said or Sung*, London, 1960, pp.133–4 (abridged).

3 Dietrich Bonhoeffer, *The Cost of Discipleship*, 1937; ET by R. H. Fuller, London, 1959, pp.35–6.

3 a. Columbanus, *Instructions* 13, *'On Christ the Fount of Life'*, 2–3; *Sancti Columbani Opera (Scriptores Latin Hiberniae)*, Dublin, 1957, pp.118–120; ET by ICEL.
b. Francis James, *The Holy Wells of Wales*, Cardiff, 1954, pp.49–50, 58; second paragraph is a composite description drawn from other sources.

3 Bernard of Clairvaux, *The Life of Malachy the Irishman*; ET by Pauline Matarasso, *The Cistercian World: Monastic Writings of the Twelfth Century*, translated and introduced by Pauline Matarasso, London, 1993, pp.60–3.

3 Richard Hooker, *The Laws of Ecclesiastical Polity*, V, lvi, 7.

3 Pope John XXIII, *Homily following the Canonization of Martin de Porres*, 3 June 1962.

5 Gilbert H. Doble, *The Saints of Cornwall*, vol. 3, Oxford, 1964, pp.106, 128–9.

6 *The Life of Saint Illtud*, 7, 9, 11; critical ed., and ET by A. W. Wade–Evans, *Vitae Sanctorum Britanniae*, Cardiff, 1944, pp.203–9.

6 Gregory the Great, *Pastoral Care*, II, 3, 5; PL 77, cols 28–32; ET based on NPNF (2nd series) 12, Oxford, 1895, pp.10, 13.
Note: It is likely that in this book Gregory intended to provide secular clergy with a spiritual counterpart to the *Rule of St Benedict*. Throughout he uses the term *rector* which is more correctly translated in English as 'ruler' but which has been rendered here by the less hierarchical term 'leader'. Gregory was writing primarily for the episcopate, but the term *rector* could and did include 'secular' as well as ecclesiastical leaders.

6 William Temple, *Christianity and Social Order*, London, 1942; quotation from 1976 reprint, pp.28, 31, 32, 67.

7 Bede, *A History of the English Church and People*, V, 9–11; BEH pp.476, 480, 486.

7 Richard Davies, *Preface to the Welsh Testament*, 1567; ET by Rowan Williams, LRW, p.54.

8 a. *Letter to Diognetus*, 5; SC 33.
b. Jerome, *Treatise on Psalm 95*; CCSL 78, pp.154–5;
c. Dietrich Bonhoeffer, *The Cost of Discipleship*; ET by R. H. Fuller, London, 1959, p.223.
d. Timothy Rees CR; Welsh Version by Enoch Jones (Isylog).

9 *The Book of Margery Kempe*, I, 52; ET by B. A. Windeatt, London, 1985, pp.162–7 (abridged).

9 Marion Lochhead, *Episcopal Scotland in the Nineteenth Century*, London, 1966, pp.154–5.

10 Leo the Great, *Letter 28 'To Flavian'*, 2–3; ET based on NPNF (2nd series) 12, Oxford, 1895, pp.39–40.

11 a. Sulpicius Severus, *The Life of Saint Martin*, 2–4 (abridged); PL 20, cols 160ff. ET based on NPNF (2nd series) 11, Oxford, 1895, pp.5–6.

b. Sulpicius Severus, *The Life of Saint Martin*, 10; PL 20, col. 166; ET based on *op.cit.*, pp.8–9. Note: Martin was the first non–martyr saint to be commemorated in the Western Church. The medieval Office hymn *Iste confessor* ('He who bore witness by a good confession' – *New English Hymnal* 220) was almost certainly written in his honour and later adopted, with much else from the office of this saint, as part of the office of Bishops, and is therefore most appropriately sung today. Modern English translations regrettably omit the original third verse which commemorates Martin's healing miracle.
– see *Hymns of the Roman Liturgy*, ed. J. Connelly, London, 1957, p.151.

12 Cynddelw Brydydd Mawr, extract from 'Canu Tysilio'; *Gwaith Cynddelw Brydydd Mawr*, vol. I, ed. Nerys Ann Jones and Ann Parry Owen, Cardiff, 1991, pp.29–30. ET by Patrick Thomas, *Celtic Earth, Celtic Heaven*, Gomer, 2003.

12 Gregory the Great, *Homily 35 'On the Gospels'*, 4–6; PL 76, cols 1261–3.

13 Charles Simeon, 'Evangelic and Pharisaic Righteousness Compared', *University Sermons*; *Let Wisdom Judge: University Addresses and Sermon Outlines by Charles Simeon*, ed. Arthur Pollard, London, 1959, pp.87–8.

14 'The Deathbed Song of Meilyr Brydydd', *Celtic Christian Spirituality*, selected, translated and introduced by Oliver Davies and Fiona Bowie, London, 1995, pp.49–50.
Note: In Welsh, in the last line of the poem, Bardsey is Enlli.

14 Daphne D. C. Pochin Mould, *The Irish Saints*, Dublin and London, 1964, pp.205– 6, 209–10.

14 E. Edwards Beardsley, *The Life and Correspondence of the Right Reverend Samuel Seabury*, Boston, 1881, pp.150–3.

15 Martin Luther King, Jr., *A Testament of Hope: the Essential Writings of Martin Luther King, Jr.*, ed. James Melvin Washington, San Francisco, 1986, pp.219–20.

16 Turgot, *The Life of Saint Margaret, Queen of Scotland*, 1–3 (abridged); ET based on W. M. Metcalfe, *Pinkerton's Lives of the Scottish Saints*, Paisley, 1895 (reprinted 1998), vol. 2, pp.298–310.

16 Matthew Paris, *The Life of Saint Edmund*; ET by C. H. Lawrence, Stroud, 1996, pp.126–7, 130.

16 Gertrude of Helfta, *The Herald of Divine Love*, I, 11; ET by Margaret Winkworth, New York & Mahwah, New Jersey, 1993, pp.72–3.

17 Adam of Eynsham, *Magna Vita: The Life of Saint Hugh of Lincoln*, III, 9; IV, 3; critical ed. and ET by D. L. Douie and David Farmer, 2nd ed. Oxford, 1985, (2 vols); vol. 1 pp.112–14, vol. 2 pp.12–15.

18 'The Duties of a Bishop', 1–9; *The Rule of Carthage*; ET Uinseann O Maidin, *The Celtic Monk: Rules and Writings of Early Irish Monks*, Kalamazoo, Michigan, 1996, p.62

18 a. Depositions to the Commission of Pope Gregory IX, 1232; ET by Nesta De Robeck, *Saint Elizabeth of Hungary*, Milwaukee, 1954, pp.162–3.
b. John Chrysostom, *Homilies on St Matthew's Gospel*, 50, 4.

19 Bede, *A History of the English Church and People*, IV, 23; BEH pp.404–10.

19 Mechtild of Magdeburg, *Revelations: The Flowing Light of the Godhead*, II, 26; ET based on Lucy Menzies, London, 1953, pp.58–9.
Note: Mechtild's writing is characterized by strong, fresh images, and by dialogues between the soul and God. She was the first mystic to write in her own vernacular (German) rather than Latin.

20 Aelfric of Eynsham, *The Lives of the Saints*; vol. II ed. W. Skeat, London, 1881, pp.315–34.
Note: The 'great Viking fleet' referred to by both Aelfric and Asser (biographer of King Alfred) arrived towards the end of 865 and spent the winter of 865–6 in East Anglia. According to the chronicler Aethelweard, the Viking force was led by 'the tyrant Igwar' (Hingwar), though other sources mention Ubbe. From later Scandinavian tradition 'Hingwar' or 'Igwar' could be Ivar the Boneless. For further discussion see Simon Keynes & Michael Lapidge, *Alfred the Great*, London, 1983, pp.238–9, n.44, & p.241, n.61. See also Dorothy Whitelock, 'Fact and Fiction in the Legend of St Edmund', *Proceedings of the Suffolk Institute of Archaelogy*, 31, 1969, pp.217–33.

20 Thomas Jay Williams, *The Life of Priscilla Lydia Sellon*, London, 1950, p.293.

21 Rhigyfarch the Wise, *The Life of Saint David*, 10; critical ed. J. W. James, *Rhigyfarch's Life of Saint David*, Cardiff, 1967; ET Oliver Davies, *Celtic Spirituality*, New York & Mahwah, New Jersey, 1999, pp.194–5.

22 Augustine, *First Exposition of Psalm 32* (Hebrew: Psalm 33), 7–8; CCSL 38, pp.253–4.

23 Clement of Rome, *Letter to the Corinthians*, 35–8; Loeb 24, *Apostolic Fathers I*; ET based on Kirsopp Lake, London, 1912, pp.67–75.

23 Columbanus, *The Rule for Monks*, 9; ET by Oliver Davies; *Celtic Spirituality*, ed. Oliver Davies, New York & Mahwah, New Jersey, 1999, pp.255–6.

24 *The Rule of Céli dé*; ET Uinseann O Maidin, *The Celtic Monk: Rules and Writings of Early Irish Monks*, Kalamazoo, Michigan, 1996, pp.93–5.
Note: This *Rule* is variously dated between the ninth and twelfth centuries.

24 Lumsden Barkway, 'Lucy Menzies: A Memoir'; in *Evelyn Underhill* by Margaret Cropper, London, New York & Toronto, 1958, pp.xv–xvii.

25 Ephrem of Syria, *Hymns on Virginity*, 24, 1–5, 13; ET by Kathleen E. McVey, *Ephrem the Syrian*, New York & Mahwah, New Jersey, 1989, pp.365–8.

25 Isaac Watts, *Horae Lyricae*, 1706 & 1709.

30 a. Dietrich Bonhoeffer, *The Cost of Discipleship*; ET by R. H. Fuller, London, 1959, pp.48–9.
b. Mark Frank, Sermon 50; LACT, *Sermons by Dr Mark Frank*, Oxford, 1849; vol. 2, pp.382–3 (abridged).

DECEMBER

1 a. *Charles de Foucauld: Meditations of a Hermit*, ET by Charlotte Balfour, London, 1980, p.137.
b. John V. Taylor, *The Go–Between God*, London, 1973, pp.227–8 (abridged).

2 John V. Taylor, *The Go–Between God*, London, 1973, pp.181–2 (abridged).

3 Francis Xavier, *Letter* 4 (1542) and *Letter* 5 (1544); text H. Tursellini, *Vita Francisci Xaverii*, Rome, 1956, Book IV; ET by ICEL.

4 Clement of Alexandria, *On Spiritual Perfection*; *Stromata*, 7, 7, 35–36; PG 9, col. 450–1.

4 John of Damascus, *On the Incarnation and the Holy Icons*, I, 16; PG 94, col. 1245.

4 Isaac Walton, *The Life of Mr George Herbert*; 3rd ed., York, 1817, pp.106–11.
Note: Clare Hall was subsequently raised to collegiate status, and should not be confused with the current institution of that name in Cambridge.

6 Gregory the Great, *Homily 17 'On the Gospels'*, 4–5; PL 76, cols 1140–41.

7 Ambrose, *On Penitence*, II, 66, 67, 70–3, 78; PL 16, col. 431; ET based on NPNF (2nd series) 10, Oxford, 1895, pp.353–5.

8 a. Anselm, *Oration* 52; ET by ICEL.
b. Ivone Gebara & Maria Clara Bingemer, *Mary, Mother of God, Mother of the Poor*, ET by Phillip Berryman, London & New York, 1989, pp.111–13 (abridged).

8 Timothy Rees CR; Welsh Version by Enoch Jones (Isylog).

12 a. Daphne D. C. Pochin Mould, *The Irish Saints*, Dublin and London, 1964, pp.165–8.
b. *The Penitential of Finnian*; ET based on that by John T. McNeill and Helena Gamer in *Medieval Handbooks of Penance*, New York, 1938.

12 Jane de Chantal, *Letter* 178; ET by Peronne Marie Thibert VHM, *Francis de Sales, Jane de Chantal: Letters of Spiritual Direction*, New York & Mahwah, New Jersey, 1988, pp.239–40.
Note: At the head of each of the letters she wrote, and throughout the writings of Francis de Sales, appears the words 'Live Jesus!' '*Vive Jesus!*' became the motto of the Visitation of Holy Mary, the congregation founded by Francis de Sales and Jane de Chantal. It was expressive of the particular vision of the Christian life that they sought to bring to birth in their own persons.

13 Clement of Alexandria, *An Exhortation to the Greeks*, 11; SC 2, pp.181–3.

13 a. *Boswell's Life of Johnson*; Oxford; 1953 ed. pp.373–4.
b. Samuel Johnson, *Sermons*, ed. J. Hagstrum & J. Gray, New Haven, 1978, p.125.

14 a. John of the Cross, *The Spiritual Canticle*, second redaction, stanza 37, 4, stanza 36, 13; ET by E. Allison Peers, *The Complete Works of Saint John of the Cross*, London, 1935, pp.363, 365–6 (from three volumes in one edition).

b. John of the Cross, 'Song of the Soul that is glad to know God by faith', *The Poems of Saint John of the Cross*; ET by Roy Campbell, London, 1966, pp.61–2.

17 Richard Symonds, *Far Above Rubies: The Women Uncommemorated by the Church of England*, Leominster, 1993, pp.78–80, 83–4 (abridged).

18 Columbanus, *Instructions 13, 'On Christ the Fount of Life'*, 2–3; *Sancti Columbani Opera (Scriptores Latin Hiberniae)*, Dublin, 1957, pp.118–120; ET by ICEL.

26 Fulgentius of Ruspe, *Sermon* 3, 1–3, 5–6; CCSL 91A, pp.905–9; ET by ICEL.

27 Augustine, *Commentary on the First Letter of John*, 1, 3; PL 35, cols 1978–80; ET by ICEL.

28 a. Quodvultdeus, *Sermon 2 On the Creed*; PL 40, col. 655; ET by ICEL.

b. John Hick, *Evil and the God of Love*, 2nd ed., London & New York, 1985, pp.385–6.
Note: Hick is quoting from Dostoievsky, *The Brothers Karamazov*, Part II, Bk 5, chapter 4; ET by David Magarshack, London, 1958, p.287. The whole chapter of Dostoievsky, however, is worth reading for background to Hick's argument. The section of the quotation from Dostoievsky (*op. cit.*, pp.282–3) printed in square brackets is additional to that originally quoted by Hick, and is included here, with permission, for its appropriateness to Holy Innocents' Day.

29 Edward Grim, *The Narrative of the Murder of Thomas Becket*; *English Historical Documents* vol. 2 (1042–1189), ed. David Douglas & George Greenaway, London, 1968, pp.761–8 (abridged).
Note: Of the five contemporary biographers of Thomas Becket, each of whom includes an account of the martyrdom, the eye–witness account by Edward Grim is regarded by scholars as the most detached and impartial. His presence was entirely accidental: he was a stranger only lately come to Canterbury for the purpose of seeing the archbishop. The fact that he himself was wounded in the attack is corroborated by nearly all the other biographers and eye–witnesses. It is part of his account, therefore, that is included here (*op. cit.*, pp.761, 767 n.3).

30 Augustine, *Letter* 130, 'To Proba', ix (18); x (19,20); PL 33, col. 501.

31 a. John Wyclif, *The Pastoral Office*, 2; LCC, vol. 14, ed. by Matthew Spinka, Philadelphia & London, 1953, pp.48–9.

b. John Wyclif, *The Pastoral Office*, 2a; *op. cit.*, pp.49–50.

Index of Saints' Days

The saints and their commemorations listed below are those of the Calendars of the Church of England, the Church of Ireland, the Scottish Episcopal Church, and the Church in Wales. These Calendars variously designate saints' days as Festivals, Lesser Festivals or Commemorations according to the degree of solemnity with which they are to be observed. Each of the four Churches of the Anglican Communion in Britain and Ireland has differing, though similar, systems of classification. In addition to these celebrations, a small number of monastic commemorations which are customarily observed by many Anglican Religious Communities in Britain and Ireland have also been included. These additional commemorations are marked in the index by the letter "M".

There are occasional variations of date in the observance of saints' days in the national Calendars, and local usage may dictate further changes. Each saint, however, has only one entry in this anthology and where there is a variation of observance, the date where that entry is located is printed in ***bold italic***. Inclusion in a national Calendar is indicated thus:

E = The Church of England
I = The Church of Ireland
S = The Scottish Episcopal Church
W = The Church of Wales

Feasts of our Lord						
Annunciation	25	Mar				
Birth (Christmas)	25	Dec				
Epiphany	6	Jan				
Holy Cross Day	14	Sep				
Naming & Circumcision	1	Jan				
Presentation in the Temple	2	Feb				
Transfiguration	6	Aug				
Group Commemorations						
All Saints' Day	1	Nov	E	I	S	W
All Souls' Day	2	Nov	E		S	W
Africa, Saints & Martyrs of	20	Feb				W
England, Saints & Martyrs of	8	Nov	E			
Japan, Martyrs of	6	Feb			S	W
Melanesia, The seven martyrs of the Melanesian Brotherhood	24	April	E			
Papua New Guinea, Martyrs of	2	Sep			S	W
Reformation Era, Saints & Martyrs of	4	May	E			

Reformation Era, Saints & Martyrs of	31	Oct				W	
South America, Saints, & Martyrs of	9	Apr				W	
Uganda, Martyrs of	3	Jun	E		S	W	
Wales, Saints of	8	Nov				W	
Saints Days:							
Aaron, Alban, Julius	20	Jun				W	
Aberdeen Doctors, Patrick Forbes & the	28	Mar			S		
Adamnán of Iona (Eunan)	23	Sep		I	S		
Adrian of May Island	4	Mar			S		
Aelred	12	Jan	E				
Agnes	21	Jan	E		S	W	
Aidan	31	Aug	E		S	W	
Ailbhe	12	Sep		I			
Alban	22	Jun	E		S		
Albert Laurie	26	Apr			S		
Alcuin of York	20	May	E				
Aldhelm	25	May					M
Alexander Jolly	27	Jun			S		
Alexander Penrose Forbes	8	Oct			S		
Alfred the Great	26	Oct	E			W	
Allen Gardiner	6	Sep	E				
Alphege	19	Apr	E				
Ambrose	7	Dec	E		S	W	
Andrei Rublev & John of Fiesole	18	Feb				W	
Andrew	30	Nov	E	I	S	W	
Andrewes, Lancelot	***25***	***Sep***	E				
Andrewes, Lancelot	26	Sep				W	
Angelo Giuseppe Roncalli (John XXIII)	4	Jun				W	
Anne	26	Jul	E		S	W	
Anselm	21	Apr	E		S	W	
Anskar	3	Feb	E				
Anthony Ashley Cooper	1	Oct	E				
Antony of Egypt	17	Jan	E		S	W	
Apolo Kivebulaya	30	May	E				
Aquinas, Thomas	28	Jan	E		S	W	
Asaph	5	May				W	
Assicus (Tassach)	27	Apr				W	
Athanasius	2	May	E		S	W	
Augustine of Canterbury	26	May	E		S	W	
Augustine of Hippo	28	Aug	E		S	W	
Azariah, Samuel Vedanayagam	2	Jan	E				
Baker, Augustine	9	Aug				W	
Baldred	6	Mar			S		
Barnabas	11	Jun	E	I	S	W	
Barnett, Samuel & Henrietta	17	Ju	E				
Bartholomew the Apostle	24	Aug	E	I	S	W	
Bartolomé de las Casas	20	Jul	E				
Basil the Great	***2***	***Jan***	E				
Basil the Great	14	Jun			S	W	

Baxter, Richard	14	Jun	E				
Becket, Thomas	29	Dec	E		S	W	
Bede, the Venerable	25	May	E		S	W	
Bell, George	3	Oct	E				
Benedict, The Passing of	21	Mar					M
Benedict, Patron of Europe	11	Jul	E		S	W	
Benedict Biscop	12	Jan	E				
Bernard of Clairvaux	20	Aug	E		S	W	
Bernard Mizeki	18	Jun	E		S		
Beuno	20	Apr				W	
Birinus	4	Sep	E				
Blandina and her Companions	2	Jun				W	
Blane	12	Aug			S		
Boisil of Melrose	7	July			S		
Bonaventure	15	Jul	E				
Bonhoeffer, Dietrich	9	Apr	E		S	W	
Boniface of Crediton (Wynfrith)	5	Jun	E		S	W	
Boniface of Ross	16	Mar			S		
Booth, William & Catherine	20	Aug	E				
Bosco, John	31	Jan	E				
Bray, Thomas	15	Feb	E		S		
Brendan the Navigator	16	May		I			
Bridget of Sweden	23	Jul	E				
Brigid of Kildare (Bride)	1	Feb	E	I	S	W	
Brooke Foss Westcott	27	Jul	E				
Bruno	6	Oct					M
Brynach	7	Apr				W	
Bunyan, John	30	Aug	E				
Burgess, Thomas	19	Feb				W	
Butler, Joseph	16	Jun	E				
Butler, Josephine	***30***	***May***	E				
Butler, Josephine	30	Dec			S		
Butler, Josephine	29	Jul				W	
Cadoc	24	Jan				W	
Calvin, John	26	May	E				
Canice (Kenneth)	11	Oct		I	S		
Carlile, Wilson	26	Sep	E				
Caroline Chisholm	16	May	E				
Carthagh of Lisemore	14	May		I			
Catherine of Alexandria	25	Nov	E				
Catherine of Siena	29	Apr	E		S	W	
Catherine Booth	20	Aug	E				
Cavell, Edith	12	Oct	E				
Cecilia	22	Nov	E		S		
Cedd	26	Oct	E				
Chad	***2***	***Mar***	E		S		
Chad	20	May				W	
Chanel, Peter	28	Apr	E				
Chantal, Jane Frances de	12	Dec					M
Charles	30	Jan	E		S		

Charles de Foucauld	1	Dec	E		S		
Charles Gore	17	Jan	E				
Charles Inglis	16	Aug		I			
Charles Fuge Lowder	9	Sep	E				
Charles Lwanga and his Companions	3	Jun			S		
Charles Simeon	13	Nov	E				
Charles Wesley	***24***	***May***	E			W	
Charles Wesley	3	Mar			S		
Chisholm, Caroline	16	May	E				
Chrysostom, John	***13***	***Sep***	E				
Chrysostom, John	27	Jan			S	W	
Clare	11	Aug	E		S	W	
Clarkson, Thomas	30	Jul	E				
Clement of Rome	23	Nov	E		S	W	
Clement of Alexandria	4	Dec			S		
Cluny, The Holy Abbots of	11	May					M
Colman of Cloyne	24	Nov		I			
Colman of Dromore	7	Jun		I			
Colman of Lindisfarne	18	Feb			S		
Columba (Columcille)	9	Jun			S	W	
Columbanus (Columban)	***23***	***Nov***		I			
Columbanus (Columban)	21	Nov			S		
Comper, John	27	Jul			S		
Confession of Peter	18	Jan			S	W	
Conversion of Paul	25	Jan	E	I	S	W	
Cooper, Anthony Ashley (Earl of Shaftesbury)	1	Oct	E				
Couturier, Paul	24	Mar	E		S	W	
Cranmer, Thomas	21	Mar	E		S	W	
Crispin & Crispinian	25	Oct	E				
(Le) Curé d'Ars (Jean-Baptiste Vianney)	4	Aug	E				
Crumnathy (Nathi)	9	Aug		I			
Cuthbert	***20***	***Mar***	E		S		
Cuthbert	4	Sep				W	
Cybi	5	Nov				W	
Cynidir	8	Dec				W	
Cynog	9	Oct				W	
Cyprian	***15***	***Sep***	E			W	
Cyprian	13	Sep			S		
Cyril of Alexandria	27	Jun	E				
Cyril of Jerusalem	18	Mar	E		S	W	
Cyril & Methodius	14	Feb	E		S	W	
Daniel Rowland	16	Oct				W	
David of Wales	1	Mar	E	I	S	W	
David, King of Scots	11	Jan			S		
Davies, John	15	May				W	
de Foucauld, Charles	1	Dec	E		S		
de Porres, Martin	3	Nov	E				
Declan	23	Jul		I			
Deiniol	11	Sep				W	
Denys	9	Oct	E				

Dietrich Bonhoeffer	9	Apr	E		S	W
Dix, Gregory	12	May	E			
Dominic	8	Aug	E		S	W
Donnan and his companions	17	Apr			S	
Donne, John	31	Mar	E			
Donne, John	25	Nov				W
Drostan (Tristan) of Deer	12	Jul			S	
Dunstan	19	May	E			W
Duthac	8	Mar			S	
Dyfrig	14	Nov				W
Ebba of Coldingham	25	Aug			S	
Edan	31	Jan				W
Edith Cavell	12	Oct	E			
Edith Stein	9	Aug				W
Edmund of East Anglia	20	Nov	E			
Edmund Rich of Abingdon	16	Nov	E			
Edmwnd Prys	15	May				W
Edward the Confessor	13	Oct	E			W
Edward King	8	Mar	E			
Edward Pouverie Pusey	16	Sep	E			
Elizabeth of Hungary	***18***	***Nov***	E			
Elizabeth of Hungary	19	Nov				W
Elizabeth of Russia	18	Jul				W
Ephrem of Syria	***9***	***Jun***	E			
Ephrem of Syria	8	Jun			S	
Ephrem of Syria	10	Jun				W
Equiano, Olaudah	30	Jul	E			
Esther John	14	Oct				W
Ethelburga	11	Oct	E			
Etheldreda	23	Jun	E			
Euddogwy	1	Jul				W
Evelyn Underhill	15	Jun	E			
Fachtna (Fachanan)	14	Aug		I		
Felicity	7	Mar	E		S	W
Felim	9	Aug		I		
Felix	8	Mar	E			
Ferard, Elizabeth	18	Jul	E			
Fergus	18	Nov			S	
Ferrar, Nicholas	***4***	***Dec***	E			
Ferrar, Nicholas	2	Dec			S	
Ferrar, Nicholas	1	Dec				W
Ferrar, Robert	21	Mar				W
Fillan	20	Jun		I	S	
Fin Barre of Cork	25	Sep		I		
Finan of Lindisfarne	17	Feb			S	
Finnbar of Caithness (see also 10 Sep)	25	Sep			S	
Finnian of Clonard	12	Dec		I		
Finnian of Movilla (see also 25 Sep)	10	Sep		I		
Fisher, John	6	Jul	E			

Name	Day	Month	E	I	S	W	M
FitzRalph, Richard	27	Jun		I			
Flannan	18	Dec		I			
Florence Nightingale	13	Aug	E				
Forbes, Alexander Penrose	8	Oct			S		
Forbes, George Hay	9	Nov			S		
Forbes, Patrick, & the Aberdeen Doctors	28	Mar			S		
Forbes, William	12	Apr			S		
Foucauld, Charles de	1	Dec	E		S		
Fox, George	13	Jan	E				
Fra Angelico	18	Feb				W	
Francis of Assisi	4	Oct	E		S	W	
Francis de Sales	24	Jan	E		S	W	
Francis Xavier	3	Dec	E		S	W	
Frederick Denison Maurice	1	Apr	E				
Frideswide	19	Oct					M
Fry, Elizabeth	12	Oct	E		S		
Gall	16	Oct		I			
Gardiner, Allen	6	Sep	E				
Geoffrey Studdert Kennedy	8	Mar	E				
George	23	Apr	E		S		
George Augustus Selwyn	11	Apr	E		S		
George Bell	3	Oct	E				
Gertrude of Helfta	16	Nov					M
Gilbert of Caithness	1	Apr			S		
Gilbert of Sempringham	4	Feb	E				
Giles	1	Sep	E				
Gilmore, Isabella	16	Apr	E				
Gore, Charles	17	Jan	E				
Gregory Dix	12	May	E				
Gregory of Nazianzus	***2***	***Jan***	E				
Gregory of Nazianzus	9	May				W	
Gregory of Nazianzus	14	Jun			S		
Gregory of Nyssa	***19***	***Jul***	E			W	
Gregory of Nyssa	14	Jun			S		
Gregory the Enlightener (Illuminator)	1	Oct			S		
Gregory the Great	3	Sep	E		S	W	
Griffith Jones	8	Apr				W	
Griffiths, Ann	12	Aug				W	
Grosseteste, Robert	9	Oct	E				
Hannington, James	***29***	***Oct***	E		S		
Hannington, James	3	Jun				W	
Harding, Stephen	17	Apr					M
Harriet Monesll	26	Mar	E				
Harris, Howell	21	Jul				W	
Helena	21	May	E		S		
Henrietta Barnett	17	Jun	E				
Henry Martyn	19	Oct	E		S	W	
Henry Venn	1	Jul	E				
Herbert, George	27	Feb	E			W	